WALKING THE WAY

OF THE HORSE

EXPLORING THE POWER OF THE HORSE-HUMAN
RELATIONSHIP

Leif Hallberg

iUniverse, Inc.
New York   Bloomington

Walking the Way of the Horse
Exploring the Power of the Horse-Human Relationship

iUniverse books may be ordered through booksellers or by contacting:

iUniverse
1663 Liberty Drive
Bloomington, IN 47403
www.iuniverse.com
1-800-Authors (1-800-288-4677)

Permission from Linda Kohanov to use excerpts of "Way of the Horse" in "Walking the Way of the Horse"

ISBN: 978-0-595-47908-5 (pbk)
ISBN: 978-1-4401-0491-6 (ebk)

Printed in the United States of America

Praise for Walking the Way of the Horse

"This is a volume to treasure! Leif Hallberg has meticulously crafted a definitive text for the field of Equine Facilitated Mental Health and Education Services. She offers illumination on the various theories and concepts that frame this vast field of working with horses and people for mutual benefit. I learned much from my reading and deeply appreciate the depth of Leif's research. Educators, Mental Health Clinicians, Program Directors, Horse Professionals and certainly students seeking knowledge of the basics will want a copy of this book."
-Barbara K. Rector, MA, CEFIP-ED author of
Adventures in Awareness: Learning With the Help of Horses

"What happens when we get off our 'high horse' and walk beside these powerful yet sensitive beings? A whole new vista of possibilities materializes, seemingly out of thin air, and we realize that horses have more to teach us than we could ever presume to teach them. This ambitious book offers the most comprehensive overview to date of a complex, cutting edge, multi-faceted field, deftly exploring the history, challenges, and as yet untapped potential of the various disciplines that employ horses as educators, therapists, and trainers of advanced human development skills."
-Linda Kohanov, author of *The Tao of Equus, Riding Between the Worlds*, and *The Way of the Horse: Equine Archetypes for Self Discovery*

"The field of equine assisted education and psychotherapy is expanding rapidly throughout the world. What has been needed to assist in this expansion is a well researched text that provides a common language for the new practitioner. This book fits that need perfectly. Ms. Hallberg has reviewed countless books, interviewed the pioneers in the field and compiled an extraordinarily comprehensive text that provides a solid background in one of the most exciting and innovative approaches to mental health of this decade."
-Nancy Waite-O'Brien, PH.D.,
Vice President of Clinical Services at the Betty Ford Clinic,
Board member of CCEFMHEP

"*Walking the Way of the Horse* is the definitive resource in the emerging Equine Facilitated Mental Health and Educational Services Profession. This book is like having your own personal reference guide and consultant in your pocket. I'm really impressed with what I consider to be the most comprehensive text in our profession."
-Stan Maliszewski, PH.D.,
Clinical Associate Professor, University of Arizona
Past Board President of the Center for Credentialing and Education

"This book is a tremendous resource for anyone interested in Equine Facilitated Mental Health and Education. Ms. Hallberg has thoroughly researched this growing field and provided a clear, objective, and concise explanation of the primary categories of EFMH/ES. This book is destined to become a classic."
-Ann C. Alden, MA, CEFIP, NARHA Certified Instructor
EFMHA President 2005-2007

Acknowledgments

This book came to me in dreams and in the waking realization of its necessity. It came to me through the countless horses and people who have guided and directed its process. While writing I found myself calling it "the book," never "my book." This feels indicative of the very process I went through to bring it into the world. It was never mine, and will never be mine. It is ours, the horses' and the wonderful people who have made it what it is. It is a beginning, the start of something far larger than one person.

Unfortunately, it would take another volume simply to thank every animal and every person who had a hand in this book's creation, but I will do my best to acknowledge all those whose contributions immediately impacted the creation of this book.

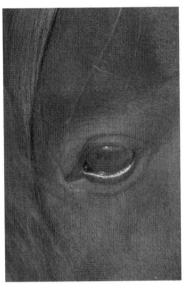

I must start with the horses, because without them this book would have no meaning. I thank my own herd, Suzy Q, Cloudy, Excell, Sunny, and Titan, all of whom are still with me and still providing insight, inspiration, support, and love on a daily basis. I thank Smoky, who is no longer with us but whose kind and gentle soul healed the hearts of many. I thank my San Cristobal Ranch Academy herd - Ally, Rain, Rio, Red, Jackie, Captain, and Bucks. These horses brought me wisdom and offered the gift of kinship, which is no small thing. Many other horses have been in my life who have taught me the valuable lessons that allowed me to get here, but those who I have noted here probably have had the longest lasting impact and given me the most ongoing joy. Thank you my beautiful friends.

"If the only prayer you say in your life is 'thank you,' that would suffice."
-- Meister Eckhart

Next I thank my parents, John and Nancy, because without their undying support, love, encouragement, and inspiration I would not be the person I am today. Your belief in me has never faltered. You are an inspiration to me each and every day, providing me with the hope to never, never give up.

This book could never have come into being without the love and support of Ian, my partner and friend who has been my dearest and most wonderful companion through the years. I love you.

Barbara Rector, my life long mentor, teacher, and friend. Without you… without you where would my life have taken me? You have provided me with direction, hope, inspiration, and guidance. You made this book possible in so many ways. Thank you.

Laura Brinkerhoff, my friend, you have helped me more than words can say. This was our idea, we co-created this dream years ago and without you, would this ever have happened? Your support, challenge, and friendship are invaluable. Thank you.

Without the financial support of Susan and Carl Taylor this book quite simply would never have come into being. Your faith in me and in this process is beyond words. I thank you from the bottom of my heart.

A number of others contributed financially to this endeavor, helping to bring this dream into reality. Thank you Ed and Judith Brown and family, Martha Wagner, Ruth and Larry Rosen, Ray and Judy Brooks, Mary Luther, Marty and Joan Rosen, and Andrea Szekees.

For all those who provided technical or creative help with this book. Liz Harrison, editor, friend, supporter, without you would I have had the faith to create this book? Thank you for all that you have done. Nikki Janson your photographs captured the amazing power of this field. Thank you for all the time you spent making this possible. Shaw Thompson, your front cover art brought to life the nature of this text. Thank you for your beautiful art. Sandee Berry Mills and Kristen Zetzer, thank you for sharing some of your photographs and allowing me to use them. All the ladies of the Fall '07 women's group – you know who you are – thank you for making these photos possible! Nancy Hallberg, Ann Alden, Barbara Rector, Maureen Vidrine, and everyone else who helped read and edit the text, thank you for your tedious work making this book what it is. Ian McNairy, your formatting and work on the cover design was invaluable.

I thank the amazing people without whom there would not only be no book, but no field. These are the people who have dedicated their lives to understanding the connection between horses and humans, and who have been my dearest friends, teachers, and supporters over the years.

Thank you to all those who spent countless hours allowing me to interview them, pick their brains, and who provided all manner of support not just for this project but over the many years and many other projects; Linda Kohonov, Maureen Vidrine, Ann Alden, Dr. Marilyn Sokolof, Chris Irwin, the Dr.'s McCormick, Molly DePrekal, Tanya Walsh, Dr. Nancy O'Brian, Dr. Stan Maliszewski, Paul Smith, Boo McDaniel, and Dr. Suz Brooks. Thank you to Dr. Temple Grandin for the thoughts you shared with me and for your contributions to this field throughout the years.

To those who provided insight and written contributions for this text - Linda Kohanov, Dr. Ellen Gehrke, and Dr. Anne Perkins, your contributions helped me to understand areas of this field that were outside of my professional or personal abilities. Thank you.

To all those who responded to the questionnaires I have sent out over the years. Thank you so much for your time and assistance.

Finally, there have been so many others without whom I could never have created this book: Terry Mullaney, your belief in me and undying friendship, as well as your editing assistance over the years proved invaluable. Robin Wellington, your support and friendship helped me mature to the place where such a book was possible. You "held the high watch" for me, believing that this book was possible. I hope to be able to repay you for all that you have given to me. Andrea Young and family, your personal courage to confront challenges and better your lives and relationships has changed my life. Without you, Esperanza could never have come into being.

To all those at the Salt River Pima Maricopa Indian Community Juvenile Correctional Facility, thank you for your support of me and of Esperanza over the years. I miss you all terribly.

To Joe Ayers, without whom I would never have learned about horses as I did.

Brian Reardon and Lisa Upson, your friendship and loyalty was much needed and greatly appreciated during the last months of the writing of this text.

Denise Helin, Paige Reddan, and Jean Moylan, you have been pillars of support, providing laughter and help with anything and everything. Thank you.

This book is ours. It is a collective effort of many souls and I thank each and every one of you for allowing me to help bring it out into the world in this way. Thank you all.

Contents

Acknowledgments   vii

Forward   xv

Introduction

Section One
Historic to Current: The Evolution of EFMH/ES   1

Chapter One
Co-Evolution: A Brief History of the Horse/Human Relationship   5

Chapter Two
The Ancients: Discovering the Healing Potential of the Horse in
Myth and Story   13

Chapter Three
Transformation: The Birth of EquineFacilitated Mental Health and
Educational Services   27

Chapter Four
Historical and Current Considerations for the Working Horse   71

Section Two
The Healing Nature of Horses   85

Chapter Five
The Horse   91

Chapter Six
Communication   99

Chapter Seven
Relationship   133

Chapter Eight
Development of Self through Horse-Person-Ship   183

Section Three
Overview of Theoretical, Ethical, and
Educational Aspects of Providing an EFMH/ES Method   217

Chapter Nine
Overview of Theoretical Perspectives   221

Chapter Ten
Ethical Considerations for EFMH/ES   241

Chapter Eleven
Cross-Training and Personal Growth   255

Section Four
Equine Facilitated Mental Health and
Educational Services: Methods of Theory and Practice   269

Chapter Twelve
Equine Facilitated Psychotherapy   275

Chapter Thirteen
Equine Facilitated Counseling   305

Chapter Fourteen
Equine Assisted Psychotherapy   329

Chapter Fifteen
Equine Facilitated Brief Intensives   347

Chapter Sixteen
Equine Facilitated Learning   365

Chapter Seventeen
Equine Assisted Education   381

Chapter Eighteen
Equine Facilitated Professional Coaching   393

Chapter Nineteen
Equine Facilitated Human Development   409

Section Five
Conclusion   433

Chapter Twenty
Education, Training and Research   435

Chapter Twenty-One
A Vision for Us All   443

Appendices
Appendix A
Interview Questions for Theoretical Concepts   449

Appendix B
Questionnaire   457

Appendix C
Responses to Terminology Question: Horse as Tool or Horse as Co-
Facilitator?   461

Appendix D
Further Resources   467

Chapter Notes   505
Index   609

Forward

A Horse of a Different Color

When politicians are competing, debating, and vying for our votes during an election, they are often referred to as being in a "horse race". A politician who is "bucking the system" is often described as a "maverick" (a term used to describe a loner horse) and anyone running for office who is not expected to do well is considered to be a "dark horse".

Now why, you might ask, would I be opening the foreword to this awesome book, **Walking the Way of the Horse**, an unprecedented and unbiased overview about the emerging industry of *horse sense for human potential,* with an analogous statement about politicians being in a horse race? Well, to begin with, as this book is being published, the United States is deeply engrossed in one of the most potentially important and wildly contentious presidential elections in recent history. "Time for a change" is the message coming from all of the candidates. **Walking the Way of the Horse** reminds us that horses, who have been with us for time eternal, may hold the key to helping us learn new ways of being that will promote the very change our country (if not our world) is seeking.

In writing this forward, I have come to realize that many facets of the horse industry share communities with the democratic election process. Almost everywhere we look in the horse world we find "politics," many "mavericks," more then a few "dark horses," and also a wide spectrum of debate as to what constitutes "political correctness" when people are working with horses.

However, unlike how often politicians can be tempted to become dirty and divisive during their election process, since the horse whispering revolution of the 1990's there is now an unwritten law that equine professionals should never be critical or outspoken of the training techniques used and taught by other horse trainers, coaches, clinicians or colleagues that we may disagree with. In other words, if we can't say something good about how a trainer works with a horse then we shouldn't say anything at all. The underlying message is that since we all ultimately love our horses then it doesn't really matter "how" we do a specific exercise with a horse as long as we are not abusive and we "get the job done". Unfortunately, that's akin to saying that just because a teacher or a parent isn't "bad" that they are seemingly by default, "good enough."

While it may be politically correct among people to say that there is no one way to train a horse this does not address the issue of how a person should decide which technique is best for building a desirable relationship with their horses. Or in other words, if political correctness prevents us from hearing the candidates openly debate the merits of their opinions then how do we know who to *believe in, trust* and vote for? Of course, the next question that really needs to be asked here is to define what, in fact, a desirable relationship with a horse could, would or should look like? This world of people and horses is all so very, very subjective.

"What a desirable relationship with a horse looks like" is also an appropriate segue into the nature and focus of this incredible book, **Walking The Way of the Horse**, because while the question is so simple to ask, the answer is seldom easy to accept: *We must learn how to listen to our horses and become very aware of their body language because this is their only method for expressing how they feel* about the techniques or methods we use to communicate with them in the name of their "training" or "schooling" or equine guided or facilitated experiences. **Walking the Way of the Horse** bravely defies "politics" and acknowledges the fact that humans must learn how to listen if they are to work successfully with horses. This book is a guide for all those interested in partnering with horses – offering important information about how to safety, respectfully, and successfully include a horse as a part of a treatment or learning team.

While trainers and clinicians often do not agree on how to specifically train horses there is not a horse trainer in the world who will tell you that when a horse lays his or her ears flat back that the horse is anything other then angry. Just the tail of a horse can tell us up to 6 different emotional messages. Ask any horse trainer worth his or her salt what it means when a horse has its tail puckered up tight against his or her hindquarters and the answer will invariably be "fear".

While a swishing tail is annoyance, a wringing tail is communicating escalating irritation. A curled tail is calm and relaxed while a stiff tail pointed on an angle down towards the ground is expressing suspicion or apprehension. A stiff tail sticking straight out or up, or "hightailing it" is screaming out a "yippee, I'm hot stuff and I feel frisky and playful" message. It's not a metaphor but tangibly real to call these body language gestures "tell-tail" emotional signals as to how a horse is thinking and feeling.

My point here is that while there will be no shortage of opinions on how you should work with your horses let's not forget that these experiences between people and horses should first and foremost be focused on safety for both humans and horses. And once safety is a consistent ongoing concern then the next question to ask is whether the well being of the horse has been taken into consideration – how does the horse relate to working, interacting, or playing with us? What are the ethical questions that arise as people come to play with horses? *Does it matter how the horses feel about what we do with them during our "feel-good" equine experiences?*

Walking the Way of the Horse answers that question with a resounding YES. The methods of equine facilitated mental health and education that Leif has defined suggest that the relationship between humans and horses is vital for the safety execution of the service. I believe that horses *are* sentient beings with a mind and emotions of their own so logic says that *how* we choose to back a horse up, or anything else we may ask of a horse, will directly relate to *how* our horse feels about our relationship with them.

If a horse has his or her head up high while the tail is clamped tight or busily swishing then *how* the horse is being asked to do something is not being perceived as very empathetic or user friendly to the horse. However, if *how* you back your horse up creates a level headed, or low headed, or softly well rounded collected frame in a horse with a quiet curled tail, and your horse is licking his or her lips, then *how* you are backing up your horse is working best and most comfortably for your horse according to his or her body language. And, hopefully, what's best for your horse is best for you. Remember, (with all due respect to the late JFK for putting an equestrian spin on his immortal words), "ask not what your horse can do for you, ask what you can do for your horse." Sound like more politics?

Having said all of the above, the debate goes on and on as to whether or not this growing movement of horse sense for human potential is actually about the well being of the horse or is the real focus supposed to be about the growth, healing and learning potential for the human beings? Frankly, I often ask why this question even exists. Why not both? Why would the well being of horses and the health and happiness of people be assumed to be considered mutually exclusive? Why not a truly win-win relationship where horses and people both benefit, change and grow from their experiences together? **Walking the Way of the Horse** helps educate those interested in pursuing a career in equine facilitated mental health or education about how to do exactly this. If we are tuned into our horses, if we are listening, if we are knowledgeable about horses, we will be more likely to create interventions that are in the best interest of both the horse and the participant.

As a writer it is a truism that we should only write what we know about so on this subject I can only speak for myself. I often apply horse training principles to my life – it's what I prefer to call EAPD or "equine assisted personal development" – and I tend to look for real, practical and tangible answers to the questions and challenges that life presents me and that I so often create for myself. I have found that while metaphors may stimulate esoteric thinking in people the horses are far more down to earth and *real* when they are looking for their answers to their issues or questions.

So I ask myself "what have horses shown me that they need from me to not only merely "accept" training as a "dumb" beast of burden but *willingly embrace truly meaningful change as my dedicated partner. And how, if at all, does this apply to my personal growth, healing and development both metaphorically and literally?* Of course, being a horse trainer, as I seriously ask myself that question then I immediately expand my thinking to ask one of the ultimate horsemanship questions of "what does it take for a horse to willingly desire to learn how to perform outstanding *flying lead changes?*" After all, flying lead changes in horses are the epitome of both extreme "change" and "performance ability".

The bittersweet irony here is that 99.9% of the time a horse, being a vulnerable prey animal, tends to "hit the ground running" as soon as it is born and it most often can and will perform beautiful flying changes all on its own before it is even one week old. So our question then evolves into "why do horses that can perform flying changes on their own suddenly end up resisting a human and become stressed and "dysfunctional" when the average person asks for a flying change?"

When we look at this question honestly then the answer should be obvious – the resistance or refusal from a horse when asked to do what it already knows how to do must have something to do with the communication and relationship with the person. Perhaps the human does not know what he or she does not know – meaning in this case - how to ask for the flying change in a language the horse understands. Or perhaps the cue from the person is almost communicated to the horse with body language he or she understands but there is a timing issue and the horse is not prepared or "balanced" well enough to be able to perform the flying change. Perhaps the horse is indeed balanced and has been asked correctly but the horse has a mind of his or her own and the willpower, or dare I say the "ego" of the horse simply and defiantly says "NO." After all, it's true that you can lead a horse to water but you can't make it drink. Just like you can love your horse but you can't make your horse love you.

Is this really so different from us? Just because we love another person doesn't guarantee that they love us in return. Or just because someone loves us doesn't mean that we are able to love ourselves.

If we dare to address this ethical question of how horses feel about how we work with them then perhaps the first concept that arises about how horse sense applies to human potential is whether or not we leaders, coaches, counselors and facilitators in the horse-human relationship are willing to learn to become fully accountable for the fact that *how both our horses and the people we work with feel about us is based entirely on how our behavior affects them while we are working with them.* All of the above statements are not mere metaphors but are very literal transfers when applied to human change.

"How does the leader ask the question of the student?" Is the relationship in question *"balanced"*, meaning is respect balanced with trust? Is focus balanced with awareness? Is work balanced with play and is the decisiveness to lead balanced with an empathy and willing receptivity to listen? What is the most appropriate, correct and beneficial time for the leader, teacher, parent or counselor to ask for "change" to happen?

There are a myriad of reasons why a capable horse will resist and not perform a task when asked but ultimately the responsibility for this comes down to trainer/rider awareness, empathy and competency. In some cases we are finally beginning to realize that when a classroom full of students is performing poorly it makes no "horse sense" to blame the students and crack the whip, pushing them harder to perform better. Instead we have learned to ask "what's up with the teacher and the school administration?"

Change is often difficult, but it is also incredibly rewarding when worked for and achieved. It is also true that knowledge is power – and that according to a couple of infamous quotes by Albert Einstein *"problems can't be solved at the same level they are created"* and that *"to do the same thing over and over again, while expecting a different result, is the definition of insanity".*

Now, after hearing these simple yet profound truths from Einstein consider again the opening statements about "political correctness" among people in the horse industry and ask yourself, for the sake of the horses, when it comes to creating positive change for the better in the horse industry, and in the field of equine assisted experiences, where do you stand when it comes to a philosophy of: "ask not what your horse can do for you – ask what you can do for your horse"?

I believe we all need to ask ourselves these questions because so many of us are not *walking the way of the horse* but are stuck in denial and illusions and instead *are talking the way of politicians,* dancing around the ethical issues that challenge all great moments of change. For some of the louder and more opinionated voices like myself we undoubtedly do need to "*find the serenity to accept what we cannot change*", however, on the other hand, there are also so many wounded healers who are now working with horses that, for the sake of their own balance, healing and growth, most definitely do need to "*find the courage to change what we can*".

Of course, if we truly listen to the meaning found in the Serenity prayer, the words also remind us that meaningful and lasting change will only be possible if we truly develop "*the wisdom to know the difference*". I say this because if we are serenely trying to accept what we boldly need to change about ourselves, or with our horses, or in any relationship, then we are a well meaning "enabler" who is inadvertently perpetuating more of the same old problems and dysfunctions. On the other hand, if we are pushing for change in an area that requires serenity and acceptance then we will most likely be perceived as micro-managing bullies only making an already difficult situation worse instead of better.

The great news that comes with the serendipitous timing of the release of this incredible book by Leif is that the winds of change are blowing and the collective conscious of the horse industry appears to be ready to raise the bar when it comes to horse training ethics and competencies. Having said that, there is a flip side to this new awareness for equine empathy. For instance, take the phrase "natural horsemanship." This can be a dangerous oxymoron. It suggests that horses are fine as they are "naturally", that humans screw them up, and it is the trainer's job to return the animal to its original state of grace in order to learn the secrets of the universe (i.e. make the humans feel better about what they are doing with and to horses). The problem here is the incredible amount of denial that the horse industry suffers from. The fact is there is nothing natural about what we are doing with horses. We are not only trying to convince a prey animal to allow a predator to control its every movement, we are (hopefully) trying to get them to like it. Furthermore, regardless of it we are doing it "naturally" or not, we are controlling their lifestyles, their habits, their diet and exercise routines, the way their feet grow, all so that we can ride them and/or interact with them. Horses are domesticated and have been for thousands of years. Their physiology and psychology has changed. In many cases these changes have resulted in the reality that there is no possible way for them to survive in the wild. They will never be "wild" or "natural" again. Trying to suggest that we can change this often causes confusion and results in real physical consequences for both horse and rider.

Let me reiterate: We are not trying to create something natural here, or allow our horses to behave as they do out in the pasture. I don't want a natural horse; I want a supernatural horse. Horses are "naturally" flight animals—prey victims waiting to happen - who are most often neurotic and can get stressed out at the slightest noise or change in their environment. What I have found we can and believe we should do is tap deeply into and work with to *evolve* the natural psychology, biomechanics and physiology of the herd mind or "prey consciousness". That allows us to pursue our own ends while keeping the horse's best interests in the forefront. That's quite different. That's a horse of a different color altogether!

In the field of equine facilitated or guided work, the horses truly are required to be "supernatural" In some cases they must put aside "natural" tendencies or at the least tone them down so that they can be safe partners for humans to learn and grow from. **Walking the Way of the Horse** helps us better understand the reality of a horse who works in an equine facilitated mental health or education setting and reminds us that horses are evolving and changing – in partnership with humans and the needs of the time.

Of course, the point I'm really trying to make here is that if we hope to develop the kind of integrity that leads to meaningful and lasting change with our horses then *whatever we hope to do for the horse we must first create within ourselves.* In other words, *"healer, heal thyself"*.

Personally, I think the world is desperate for people who can compete with each other without victimizing the loser, for people who can see past their own immediate needs, who can lead with the best interests of the herd at heart. In fact, I think this is the next step in human evolution.

Horses are magnificent creatures that offer us a unique window into our souls and an opportunity to develop them, but we can't ever lose sight of the fact that, ultimately, they are potentially very volatile and dangerous. That means that while we may travel a long way with them on our equine assisted or facilitated journeys, there's one more step the human has to take. If we want to develop the type of empathetic qualities in leadership I've been talking about, there's only one way to convince the horse to willingly give themselves over to us body, mind and spirit. Restraints won't do it, spurs and big, punishing bits won't do it, bribing them with carrots won't do it and trying to communicate with them from the heart on some sort of psychic level won't do it. There's only one pillar this kind of leadership can rest on: the human's own ethics, integrity and competency.

Learning to recognize and expose our denials and illusions about ourselves is the final step we must take before we truly earn the right to tell our horses that we can be and should be their leaders. It's also, I believe, the final and essential step we must take before we can take any kind of reins of leadership with people with confidence and integrity. We need to see clearly, understand accurately, and respond appropriately with our horses (or our children, our students, our staff), but we have to first do so with ourselves.

I don't pretend to understand intellectually how this process works. But I've felt it in myself and seen it in others and I'm convinced it's real. When we work with a horse, we have 1,000 pounds or more of living, breathing archetype prancing around in front of us or underneath us. When we are with the horses, the object of our focused attention in the physical world corresponds symbiotically with a complex series of crucial images and symbolic meanings in our inner world. That correspondence stirs up something inside us, and as our experiences with the horses helps us learn more about ourselves we become better and better at balancing focus with awareness, body language with mind and spirit intentions, male energy with female energy, predator behavior with prey and our past experiences with the present moment and future intentions.

I don't have any scientific way of describing this process. I'm a horseman not a psychotherapist. But it's there, and it's real, and it's growing by leaps and bounds into a mainstream reality. I believe that the "someday" that so many of us have been waiting for has indeed arrived and now this comprehensive and illuminating work by Leif is destined to become a much needed compass for so many of us on our journey down our individual paths as we strive to evolve and learn to walk the way of the horse.

Chris Irwin, 2008
Author of *Horses Don't
Lie* and *Dancing with
your Dark Horse.*

INTRODUCTION

Mitaquye Oyasin, "We are all related" - Lakota

"Spiritualism is the highest form of political consciousness" - Unknown

Welcome

Since the early 1990's, the field of Equine Facilitated Mental Health/ Education Services has experienced explosive growth. Across the United States there are approximately 700 centers that provide at least one of the Equine Facilitated Mental Health or Education methods, and service hundreds of clients. There are three internationally-recognized associations with memberships ranging into the thousands, which are designed specifically to provide support to both practitioners and clients utilizing this work. Approximately 80 therapeutic boarding schools (governed by the National Association of Therapeutic Schools and Programs– NATSAP) utilize Equine Facilitated/Assisted programming to enhance their therapeutic or educational programs. Sierra Tucson, Cottonwood De Tucson, the Betty Ford Clinic, Bermuda Ranch, The Meadows, and other renowned residential treatment centers also utilize Equine Facilitated programming to work with their patients. Corporate training experts are now incorporating the work of Equine Facilitated Mental Health/Education Services to provide team building and professional coaching for their clientele. All of these organizations; non-profit and for profit centers, multimillion dollar corporations, residential treatment centers, and therapeutic boarding schools are hiring professionals to conduct the services offered. The industry of Equine Facilitated Mental Health/Education Services supports close to one thousand professionals across the U.S.[1]

Institutions of higher learning now offer degrees in the field. One can obtain both an undergraduate degree and a master's degree in the field of Equine Facilitated Mental Health/Education Services. [2]

Mental health professionals are billing insurance companies for their work with horses and clients. And most importantly, people from all walks of life are being served through this work and thus far the reported successes seem unparalleled across all socioeconomic and environmental barriers.

The purpose of this book is two-fold. First, I would like to introduce interested individuals to the field of Equine Facilitated Mental Health/ Education Services and to offer those already practicing in the field a resource to help guide their own explorations. This book is deigned to present ideas, concepts, theories, and methods as an overview. It is not meant to be conclusive. The methods presented in this text came from the experiences of many professionals practicing in the field today. These people have dedicated their lives to this work, and many of them have perfected a way of providing a service that they passionately believe in.

The second purpose or hope for this text is that it will be used to help expand our current thinking about the importance of our connection to the natural world. It introduces ways in which horses can help us to reconnect with both our internal and external landscape and offers an introduction to the global implications for "walking the way of the horse."

The process of writing this book has been a journey from its inception to its final creation. As its author, my life has been consumed by the journey. The concept of this book originated in 2001 when Laura Brinkerhoff and I started our Masters program in Counseling/ Psychology with an emphasis in Equine Facilitated Psychotherapy at Prescott College in Arizona. As we progressed through the program we began to see the need for a text that would help define the field of Equine Facilitated Mental Health/Education Services for those desiring to learn about the theoretical and practical applications of the various methods utilized within the field. We proposed a joint thesis project that we envisioned as the initial manuscript for such a book. Unfortunately we learned that we would not be allowed to work together on the creation of a thesis. When this occurred I continued forward with the research Laura and I had already started. Laura went on to write a marvelous thesis that explored the notion of catharsis during an equine facilitated psychotherapy session. My thesis helped me to better understand emerging themes within the field and I began formulating conceptual ideas about the theoretical underpinnings of Equine Facilitated Mental Health/Education Services. But life has an interesting way of altering one's plans, and it was three years before a series of events occurred that made this book possible.

Once I committed to the project the most amazing things started happening. Funding became available that allowed me to research and write this book. I coincidentally met Liz Williams, former Vice President of Publicity and Marketing for a division of Random House Books, who just happened to be living in Bozeman, Montana of all places. Lo and behold it turned out that she had a deep love for horses and a great interest in this work. With her help and support I was able to embark on the journey to create this book as it was truly meant to be written.

I was able to schedule interviews with wonderful people within the field, many of whom I had met in 1997 when I traveled across the United States studying efficacy and program design in emerging Equine Facilitated Mental Health/Education Services programs. These were the same people with whom I had consulted while I wrote my thesis in 2003 and I was able to interview them once again, some ten years from the first time I met them. Watching their progression as professionals, and watching this field expand, grow, and form over a ten-year span has been enlightening and has provided me with invaluable resources. I sent out over 400 questionnaires to professionals practicing within the field and received some 170 responses from all across the United States, England, and Canada. I utilized the information gained from both the in-person interviews that I conducted with individuals considered by many to be "pioneers" of the field and the responses from the questionnaires to help create the theoretical methodology that is presented within the body of this text. I also used quotes taken directly from some of the questionnaires to highlight areas of special interest. For the purpose of understanding the topic at hand as best as possible I read over three hundred books and many articles, theses, and research papers. Furthermore, I utilized my own experience providing Equine Facilitated Mental Health/Education Services to hundreds of clients over a ten-year time span as well as my life-long personal and professional relationship with horses that begin at age three and has continued unhindered for the duration of my childhood, adolescence, and now in my adulthood. Taking all of that into consideration, I nonetheless feel that I have only just begun to scratch the surface of truly comprehending the totality of this field, and its potential to assist our growth and healing.

Once I finally started writing the book it was like my fingers could not keep up with my thoughts. I wrote some five hundred pages in about three months. It was one of the easiest and most rewarding processes I have ever undergone. Writer's block? Never heard of it! I never struggled. It was like I was being inspired by something greater than myself. During the process of writing my own horses started doing things that I had never seen them do before. Private clients who I was seeing during that time reported intense personal growth experiences that were "life-changing" for them. The entire time period during which this book was written seemed soaked in meaning and depth.

In all, this project has been truly wonderful for me, and filled with pure joy. I hope that you enjoy the written journey; meeting horses and people who have made this field what it is today, learning about the historical origins of the horse/human relationship, and exploring the research that helps explain our soul's craving to be near horses.

This book marks a beginning. It is a starting point from which to move forward. It was written to help inspire others to journey forth in the co-creation of a deeper understanding about why the work with horses moves us, empowers us, and heals us. My dream is that the next edition of this text will be edited, not authored, and that those providing methods of Equine Facilitated Mental Health/Education Services will come forward, writing their own unique beliefs about their practice and the theory behind it. I dream of a time when books will be written specifically about Equine Facilitated Psychotherapy, or Equine Facilitated Counseling, or Equine Facilitated Professional Coaching Services, or maybe entirely different methods. Each of the methods presented within this text is filled with enough information in both their theoretical foundations and their practical applications to occupy an entire book in and of themselves!

I firmly believe that horses have a place in our developing consciousness. I want us, as a society and as individuals, to begin exploring the challenging questions about how horses actually do help people so that the gifts horses offer us freely will be valued and used ethically. I hope that we can become better stewards of these amazing creatures, helping to link the information that they provide to other fields like integrative medicine, naturopathic medicine, allopathic medicine, ecopsychology, and many others so that their message can be more clearly heard. I strongly sense that the teachings of the horse can help us reconnect with our instinctive selves, and through this connection, help us to find our way back into the web of life. We are not alone. We are not separate. We are a part of this web, and our hearts and souls long to feel connected. This need for connectedness, recognition of the Divine, belief in the healing power of nature and animals, and most importantly, belief in ourselves, is paramount if we want to bring about lasting change within ourselves or for the environment.

Although this book's primary purpose is to educate others about the theory and practice of Equine Facilitated Mental Health/Education Services, its secondary purpose is to suggest that without interconnection and belief in ourselves, we cannot heal ourselves, and therefore cannot heal our world. The very nature of working with horses as agents of change is rooted in principles of the inner-connected circle of the universe, life in balance.

When a culture believes that all must be in balance in order for health to exist, respect, open-mindedness, diversity, and tolerance tend to exist. In such a culture, animals, nature, and humans all have their distinct and honored places, and it is understood that one cannot survive without the other. We are all connected. As our culture has veered further and further from this perspective, new fields have emerged to help us realize the importance of this interconnection. Biophilia, ecopsychology, and the animal-assisted therapies, with leaders such as Theodore Roszak, Edward Wilson, Michael Cohen, Ralph Metzner, Chellis Glendinning, Allen Schoen, Rupert Sheldrake, and many others, are making important contributions to helping us learn how to re-connect. These teachers suggest that without connection to nature, we may fall more deeply into an evolution that is, in the long term, unsupportable. [3]

Since time eternal horses have been viewed as messengers of the Divine, healers, and spirit guides. The work of Equine Facilitated Mental Health/Education Services is far deeper than merely connecting people and horses; it is about connecting people to themselves, and the inner wisdom that is trying desperately to be heard. Through connection with horses, we find our way. We find the strength and the passion to step forward and bring about change, in our own lives, and in the world.

Walking the way of the horse is not about mystery or veiled mystical, metaphysical complexities. It speaks a truth that has existed since the human race began. It speaks about connectedness and about the terror of being alone, about equality and hierarchical order. It reminds us about gentleness, about harshness and calls for us to listen but be willing to speak out as well. Through the way of the horse we learn about diversity and the reality of existence. We come to understand the potential and beauty of life, and then we are reminded that cruelty may lurk just around the corner. In essence, it speaks about balance and the journey we must all take to trust ourselves and our sense of all things. If we listen carefully we learn about finding our way, our path to the divine. We begin to understand hope and light, and also despair and darkness. The way of the horse is a metaphor for how we could chose to live our lives. It brings us clarity in an otherwise confusing world.

It is important to note that in all of Linda Kohanov's work (*The Tao of Equus, Riding Between the Worlds,* and *The Way of the Horse*) the concept is presented and explored that being with horses can be considered "a way", a spiritual, practical life journey that horses invite us to walk. Initially it might have seemed strange that this book would have a title so closely linked to Ms. Kohanov's. However, after conversations

"The horse represents our lost connection to the natural world and offers a way back home."
~ Deb Marshall, Generation Farms, Nanaimo, BC

between Linda and I, we realized that our orientation and belief system about "the way of the horse" was consistent, and therefore it was appropriate that our books had similar titles. Our overlapping belief systems regarding "the way of the horse" leads me to feel even more strongly that horses have a place in our developing consciousness, and that we have come upon a time where the lessons that they have to teach us will be invaluable.

As with all things, in order to move forward on any quest, be it spiritual, educational, or healing in nature, one must be grounded. One's feet must be firmly planted on this earth with ears and eyes open. Although this book may ask that we spend some time with our heads in the heavens, searching for answers about the healing potential of the horse/human bond, we also must make sure that we are rooted in the physicality of ourselves and of the horses. We all still exist on the physical plane, and in order to move forward on that plane, we must learn how to stay present in our bodies and not rush the process of transcendence. My hope is that this book will remind each of us that it is the simplicity of the horse/human interaction that breeds healing and change, not the complexity.

General Concepts

In this book, we will embark on a journey. Understanding how horses may help humans to evolve consciously means gaining a comprehensive grasp of a multitude of concepts. The book is designed to educate the reader from all walks of life with different interests. Some who read this book may want to learn the tangible theory and practice of this work. Others may read it to gain a deeper understanding of their own personal relationship with horses, and still others may read it to better understand the necessity of our connection to nature and all creatures living therein. We will start our journey by exploring the horse/human relationship throughout time. We will review myth and legend; stories that demonstrate the horse's importance in our long held beliefs about spirituality and connection to the Divine. We'll see how the horse's very nature supports Equine Facilitated Mental Health/Education Services. With all of this as background information, it is my hope that you will move toward an understanding of the theoretical and practical applications of the work. We'll review case studies and stories that help illuminate the theoretical and practical concepts, and we will meet pioneers within the field and read their unique stories, learning the twisting and turnings that have led them here, to find a place within the pages of this book and this growing field.

Wikipedia

Wikipedia is cited as a source for a variety of definitions throughout this text. In most all cases there is another source also used to back up the Wikipedia definitions. However, I found that although not a "recognized source" Wikipedia offered definitions for terms that I could not find elsewhere. Our use of certain words has evolved and changed and in some cases traditional sources are unable to keep up with that shift. Wikipedia seems able to offer non-traditional definitions for concepts that are commonly utilized and discussed within the field of Equine Facilitated Mental Health/Education Services. I found Wikipedia's definitions to be useful in clarifying concepts from another vantage point.

Terms

"Facilitated" and "Assisted"

Within the body of this text the terms "facilitated" and "assisted" will be used at different times to signify different meanings. It is important that the reader understand that neither term is associated with any organization or program, nor is used in this text to denote a specific individual or way of thinking. Rather, "facilitated" and "assisted" are used because of their formal definitions as found in a variety of dictionaries. The word "facilitated" as defined by Merriam-Webster Dictionary means to, "help bring about," whereas the word "assist" or "assisted" means, "to give support or aid" or "to be present as a spectator".[4] It is my belief that horses who work within mental health or educational programs have the ability to both facilitate and assist. I also believe that as a provider of an EFMH/ES method it is appropriate that we understand the differences between the two approaches. Equine facilitated work denotes methods in which the human professional steps back and truly allows the horse to help bring about the work with the client. I believe that in almost every situation, if the horse is given permission to facilitate he or she will do so, and I would like to support that possibility. In my research for this book I found that I was not alone in that belief. Out of thirty-one professionals questioned, only one disagreed with the notion that horses can and generally do facilitate an experience for the client or student.[5] However, there are situations and clients that are better served by an assisted approach. If a provider is using an equine assisted approach the horse will take a less active role in the process, either acting as support staff or just being present during a session. In upcoming chapters the role of the horse and the human is defined for each method based upon whether or not the horse or the human is facilitating.

Equine Facilitated Mental Health/Education Services (EFMH/ES)

In this text I use the umbrella term, Equine Facilitated Mental Health/ Education Services (EFMH/ES) as it is defined, "An umbrella term used to describe both educational and therapeutic services in which humans work in partnership with horses to learn, grow, and change."[6] At the time of publication, under this umbrella term eight methods for working in partnership with horses have been defined; four methods for providing mental health services, two methods for providing an educational or learning service, and two methods which I have currently defined as "other" - methods which combine aspects of both mental health and education/learning services.[7] Although there are many other ways in which people currently provide EFMH/ES in their own individual practices, these seven methods were delineated in a study I conducted. Additionally, these methods were defined by professionals within the field in virtually the same manner by individuals separately interviewed with no prior communication between them regarding the subject matter. The interviewees were asked questions to invoke clarity both regarding the specifics of a method, and the differences between methods.

There are other methods of EFMH/ES outside of the eight I've identified. However, these methods appear less prominent within the field based upon the responses of the interviewees. As in the field of mental health services, many different approaches to providing a therapeutic service have emerged over the years, and text books that deal with theory and practice must be reviewed and new editions come out yearly to include the various theories that have evolved and become mainstream.

Pioneers in this field like Barbara Rector (*Adventures in Awareness: Learning with the Help of Horses*), Adele von Rust and Marlena Deborah McCormick (*Horse Sense and the Human Heart* and *Horses and the Celtic Path*), and Linda Kohonov (*The Tao of Equus* and *Riding Between Worlds*) created much of the theoretical foundation from which the field grew.[8] Later in this book you will meet these women and will learn about their pioneering contributions to this field. Anyone reading this book will benefit from reading all books written by these individuals, as their books help to define and refine their own unique theories and methods of practice. These experts also offer trainings and workshops and for anyone interested in learning more about the theoretical and practical foundations of this work. Attending such trainings or workshops is also highly recommended.

Healing

Throughout the body of this text the word healing may be used. I want to be clear about how I mean this word to be understood. Healing has been viewed by many as a New Age or alternative term, but in the context of this book the Merriam-Webster's dictionary definition will suffice, "to make sound or whole." Healing is derived from the concept of health, which is defined as, "the condition of being sound in body, mind, or spirit."[9] Occasionally I will suggest that horses may "help humans to heal." This generally refers to the potential within the horse/human relationship for the human to find increased physical, mental, emotional, or spiritual health and well being.

Plato once wrote, "The cure of the part should not be attempted without treatment of the whole. No attempt should be made to cure the body without the soul. Let no one persuade you to cure the head until he has first given you his soul to be cured, for this is the great error of our day, that physicians first separate the soul from the body."[10] The idea that humans may find solace, or an integration of the body, mind, and spirit that fosters well being while in the presence of horses is widely utilized and also accepted and included as a definition of healing.

Higher Power, the Divine, or God

At many times throughout this text words will be used to describe a power greater than our individual selves. God, the Divine, Higher Power, and other such terms will be used interchangeably with no intention to offend or otherwise cause discomfort to any reader. Regardless of what it is called, I recognize and honor such a power and realize that throughout the ages each culture or specific religious group has its own unique name for this power and a complex belief system revolving around it. The use of multiple names for such a power is meant only to be inclusive, or to invite the reader to call this power by whatever name he or she so chooses.

The Language of Equus

"The language of Equus" is a term the reader will encounter at various points within this text. This term may have been introduced by Monty Roberts when his book, *The Man Who Listens to Horses* brought national and international recognition to the concept that horses have their own unique language that can be interpreted and understood by humans.[11] Regardless of where the term actually originated, within this text the term will be used to describe a series of non-verbal and verbal communications portrayed repeatedly over time with similar results by a large majority of horses. This "language" can be interpreted, understood, and taught by humans to other humans for the purpose of understanding horses, their communications to both humans and other horses, their motivations, and their responses to external and internal stimuli.[12]

Anthropomorphism

Conflict and emotionality may arise when humans begin assigning human-like characteristics to animals. This concept is called anthropomorphism and is defined by Merriam-Webster's Dictionary as "an interpretation of what is not human or personal in terms of human or personal characteristics."[13] Although there can be negative ramifications manifested by the desire to humanize an animal who is obviously NOT a human being, there is also a positive way in which to view the concept. The Merriam-Webster definition does not suggest that there is anything innately wrong or unhealthy about the act of utilizing our human characteristics to understand or vocalize how or what animals may be feeling, doing, or otherwise responding. It seems that the confusion lies somewhere between the use of human *language* to describe how animals might be feeling or thinking, and the actual belief that we as human beings can *treat* other species as if they were human. The danger appears to come in the second of these options. Treating or responding to an animal as through they were human is both physically dangerous to the human, and emotionally trying for the animal. However, utilizing human language to describe an animal appears to foster a deeper sense of interspecies relationship, and may allow the human to expand his or her thinking to recognize the unique differences between species.

Rebekah Ferran Witter, author of *Living with HorsePower*, says this: "Anthropomorphism is helpful to the degree that it establishes common ground, allowing us to identify with something outside of ourselves, and possibly bond with it."[14] I agree with Ms. Witter's definition. Humanizing animals has the potential to be dangerous and unhealthy, but it is important to recognize the positive ramifications that occur within the human psyche when we connect with other species, in whatever way we can foster that relationship.

There will be parts within this text that will appear to anthropomorphize horses. I hope that you will be able to see the difference between the use of human language, and the recognition that a horse remains a horse, always and forever.

Evolve or Evolution

In many instances when I use either the term "evolve" or "evolution" it indicts a patterned change within the social or emotional state of a species, not the more rigorously defined scientific meaning of these terms. I have tried to use the term "social evolution" to help differentiate between instances, but if occasionally I forgot to do so, please be patient.

Gender Usage/We

Although time consuming and awkward, I have chosen to use "he/she" throughout the book. "We" is used in this text to mutually include those practicing within the field, those reading this book, and the author.

Use of Terms Describing the EFMH/ES Professional

Throughout the text the term "licensed mental health professional" will be used frequently to describe someone who has gained appropriate state licensure to practice a form of mental health services. Occasionally that term will be intermingled with the terms "counselor," or "psychotherapist," generally when this occurs the reader will be educated as to why the change in terminology occurred. Occasionally the term "mental health professional" will also be used. This also indicates someone with appropriate education (Masters Degree in Counseling/Psychology or a related mental health field) and training (specific to EFMH/ES) but who has not obtained licensure. For the purpose of this book all professionals providing a EFMH/ES method are expected to have undergone extensive additional training specific to the field. I do not believe that being a licensed mental health professional or having a Masters Degree in mental health is sufficient training or education to provide an EFMH/ES method.

In regards to those who are offering an Equine Facilitated Education/ Learning Service, the author will use the term "facilitator," "instructor," "educator," "provider" or "professional" to describe the individual providing such a service. It is also expected that anyone providing an EFE/L service has also undergone extensive training and education specific to the field.

SECTION ONE

HISTORIC TO CURRENT: THE EVOLUTION OF EFMH/ES

One   *Co-Evolution: A brief history of the evolution of the horse/human relationship.*

Two   *The Ancients: Discovering the healing potential of the horse throughout time.*

Three   *Transformation: The Modern Introduction of Equine Facilitated Mental Health/ Educational Services*

Four   *Historic and Current Considerations for the Working Horse*

"We are all connected to one another, and by showing us the intricacies of the interwoven threads of life, we understand our part."
- Gandhi

Introduction to Section One

Jesus, Gandhi, and The Cult Stallion of Dereivka all changed the world irreversibly, bringing new dimensions to what future generations would experience daily across the globe.

The journey that horses and humans have taken through the decades tells a story that must not be overlooked. It is a tale veiled in uncertainties, assumptions, and romanticism, but also based in science. It is a tale that eventually leads us to better understand why horses are capable of such acts as healing the human heart. This book does not presume to do this tale justice and it is the advice of the author that anyone reading this book should also read Stephen Budiansky's *The Nature of Horses*, Lawrence Scalen's *Wild about Horses*, and J. Edward Chamberlin's *Horse*,[15] as well as investigate the research of scholars like Marsha Levine, David Anthony, and others whose work manifests the depth of this study. For the purpose of this book, we will sample the research of these equine evolutionary experts that will help the reader understand our intertwined social evolution.

When we think of evolution we tend to think primarily of the human evolutionary life span. We may even consider ourselves "highly evolved" creatures, able to assert control over other species we come into contact with. We may ignore important details like how long other species have been in existence, or what those species might have gained by such a long process of evolution.

The horse is a wonderful example of our species-centric view of the world. It might surprise some that the horse has been evolving for fifty-five million years, the dog for forty million years, and the cat for close to the same, as compared to the paltry one million the human race has accumulated. It is also interesting that although the horse/human relationship is about six thousand years in the making, we are, as Lawrence Scanlan reminds us, just beginning to understand Equus Caballus.[16]

If we examine the impact that horses have had upon the social evolution of the human race, we can begin to appreciate the depth of the relationship between horses and humans. This partnership led to four of the most important and long-lasting sociological developments that the human race has experienced to date; the development of language, warfare, trade, and the creation of a hierarchical society.[17] When we can understand the antiquity of the relationship between horse and human, and the role of horse in the social evolution of the human race, we begin to see their influence everywhere we look, from the names of the cars we drive, to the archetypal symbol of power that the horse represents today.

In this section the reader will be introduced to the horse/human relationship in ancient times and in myth and story, with special emphasis placed upon the manner in which humans perceived the role of the horse as it relates to healing of the mind, body, and soul. The reader will also learn about the fields of Animal Assisted Therapy, therapeutic riding, and hippotherapy as they

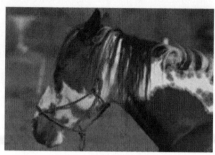

"Look back at our struggle for freedom. Trace our present day's strength to its source; And you'll find that man's pathway to glory is strewn with the bones of a horse."
~ Anonymous

provide foundational underpinnings for the field of EFMH/ES. Pioneers in the field of EFMH/ES will be introduced and the reader can reference Appendix D to learn where these individuals practice today and how to learn more about the services that they offer. Finally it is the horse and always the horse who makes EFMH/ES what it is. It is critical as providers of such services that we have an understanding of both historic and current considerations for the working EFMH/ES horse so we can do this work respectfully and ethically.

CHAPTER ONE

CO-EVOLUTION: A BRIEF HISTORY OF THE HORSE/ HUMAN RELATIONSHIP

Dereivka and David Anthony

Our story begins in a remote corner of the earth in an Eneolithic village named Dereivka. This village sits in the Dneiper Valley of the Ukraine on the west bank of the Dnieper River, and is believed to have been inhabited around 4000 B.C. It was here that David Anthony, Dimitri Telegin, Dorcas Brown, and Natalya Belan-Timchenko made a discovery that would change our view regarding the origins of the horse-human relationship.[18]

Dimitri Telegin and his team discovered a burial site in this region that included a ritualized grouping of horse bones and artifacts surrounding a horse skull belonging to a 7-or 8-year old stallion. Along with the other artifacts were two unique pieces of antler tines with small holes pierced through them. It was believed that these tines were used as a bit, or a steering mechanism to control the horse. This finding led the team to question whether this horse had in fact been ridden. If this were to be the case, the discovery would predate the current belief that horses were first ridden as recently as 1500BC. The team believed that there was no doubt that this burial dated back to the Sredni Stog culture. The use of a pole-mounted head and horse hide, which marked the location of a sacred site is widely documented and appears to correspond with the Sredni Stog culture. The discovery that the grave was found on Copper Age soil buried under Sredni Stog refuse seems to indicate that horse also belonged to this time period.

Although the antler tines sparked curiosity and posed an interesting piece of the puzzle, the tines alone could not provide substantial evidence that horses were actually ridden during that age. Still sure that horses were ridden for the first time by the Sredni Stog peoples, David Anthony, Dorcus Brown, Dimitri Telegin, and Natalya Belan-Timchenko traveled to Kiev to study the teeth of the horses found at the Sredni Stog site. Prior to this trip Brown and Anthony spent considerable time investigating the teeth of both feral horses in North America and modern domesticated horses used for riding. Their findings conclusively demonstrated that horses who have never been ridden have little if any wear patterns on the tongue-side of their teeth. Conversely, horses who have been ridden regularly show on average about 3.56 millimeters of wear on their anterior premolars. Using this information Brown and Anthony were able to compare the teeth of the Dereivka Cult Stallion to those of other horses found at the same site. The team learned that the Cult Stallion's teeth were worn in the same pattern as modern day domesticated horses used for riding. In fact, the beveling on his anterior premolars showed a measurement of 3.5 millimeters, which was almost exactly the same as the wear measurements found on the teeth of modern day horses. This is compared to the 0.82 millimeter measurements found on the teeth of feral horses never before ridden. The strangest part of the team's discovery was that none of the other teeth discovered in the kitchen refuse piles at the Sredni Stog site demonstrated wear marks. The team feels strongly that this discovery clearly points towards the notion that the Cult Stallion of Dereivka was conclusively the first horse ever to be ridden.

Botai and Sandra Olsen

This information caused dissension among many scholars and archaeologists. Most still believed that horseback riding began around 1500BC in central Asia five centuries before the appearance of mounted horses used for battle in the Middle East around 1000 B.C. Anthony's controversial discovery demonstrated that riding pre-dated the invention of the wheel, therefore making the equine/human partnership the first truly notable innovation to impact the spread of culture, language, and transportation.[19]

Archaeologist Sandra Olsen disagrees vehemently with Anthony's interpretation of the wear marks. After new radiocarbon-dating techniques reveled that the skull of the Cult Stallion was actually 2,400 years old she is quoted saying, "It was an iron age horse whose grave had been dug down into a more ancient settlement."[20] It seems unclear if this statement is fact, and there is little reference to Anthony's rebuttal of her claim. Olsen appears to believe that it was the Botai people of Kazakhstan who were the first humans to ride upon the back of a horse. This tribe was in existence approximately 6,000 years ago. She believes that horses were the primary means of sustenance for the Botai people, who used them for meat as well as milk. She does not give an opinion as to what provoked a Botai individual to one day mount a horse, but she muses about the impact of this decision on the Botai tribe. With the taming of the horse came the ability for the Botai people to carry much heavier loads, drag whole carcasses back to the encampment, and travel great distances. The basis of her theory lies in the amount of horse bones she found at the Krasnyi Yar site, both in dwellings and in burial locations near to the site. She also investigated the origins of koumiss, or mare's milk, a local favorite of modern-day Kazakhs. She believes that if the lipids in the mare's milk can be linked to lipids found in Botai pottery she will be able to prove that the Botai did tame the horse, and therefore the logical conclusion would be that they were the first humans to actually mount and ride.[21]

Marsha Levine

Marsha Levine, researcher for the McDonald Institute for Archaeological Research, disagrees with both Olsen and Anthony. She states, "Upon further examination, it is clear that the evidence backing these claims (Dereivka and Botai) is deeply flawed. Careful consideration of the data from both Botai and Dereivka strongly suggests that the vast majority, if not the totality, of the horses from both of those sites were wild."[22]

The debate regarding the evolution of the horse/human relationship does not seem to be a question of whether or not horses were ridden prior to 2000BC, but rather surrounding issues of terminology and direct evidence. It appears that Levine's disagreement with both the

Dereivka and the Botai sites is two fold. First, that domestication of the horses alluded to in either example was highly improbable, and although it might have been possible that humans did mount and ride horses, those horses were wild, not domesticated. Levine defines domestication as the ability for a people to successfully breed the species in captivity. And second, neither Dereivka nor Botai can produce direct evidence that humans did in fact ride horses. She considers direct evidence to be examples of textual, artistic, and funerary objects, evidence that leaves virtually no doubt that the horse was used for riding purposes. Levine states that there is no direct evidence at any site for the origins of horse domestication, and she feels doubtful that there ever will be.

Levine discovered that certain abnormalities of the caudal thoracic vertebrae were associated with the use of a pad for bareback riding. Upon further examination of the vertebrae collected from the Botai site, no such abnormality existed. She cannot comment on the Dereivka bones as the vertebrae were discarded before they could be studied. Rather than try to prove an earlier date for the moment in time when a human mounted and rode a horse for the first time, Levine seems content to use the first Sintashta chariot burials on the south Ural steppe as her origin point for the relationship between horse and human. This burial places horses and chariots in the same grave, therefore demonstrating beyond a shadow of doubt the advanced relationship. These graves are dated circa 2000 BC. However, she acquiesces that there can be no doubt that horses must have been ridden far earlier than that. In fact she states, "They (horses) played an important role in society and, almost certainly had been domesticated for a considerable period of time (prior to their introduction to the chariot)".[23]

Co-Evolution

Levine brings up the concept of co-evolution between human and horse. She discusses the idea that the horse could have been the one to make the first steps towards partnership, rather than the humans instigating the relationship. She hypothesizes that the art of "taming" the horse grew out of an already existing mutual relationship. She goes on to mention the notion that the actual process of domestication probably took many more years and significant cultural advancements. She makes this assumption based on evidence regarding the difficulties of breeding within captivity. The Plains tribes of North America preferred to steal or capture their horses, rather than attempt to breed within captivity. Levine believes that this is further indication to support her notion that domestication occurred much later, after horses had already been ridden. She goes as far as to suggest that due to the extremely difficult task of creating and maintaining an environment where horses felt comfortable, safe, and at ease to the degree that breeding occurred, "domestication (of the horse) could thus, in a sense, have been initiated by the horses themselves." She questions if simply chance (or the decision of the horse) led to genetic changes that would have predisposed some horses to be able to breed in captivity, therefore allowing domestication to occur.

It seems that regardless of all opinions, ideas, theories, and evidence (or lack there of), one truth remains clear. Everyone agrees that someone, sometime, somewhere made the decision to climb on top of a horse and ride, and that this decision brought about profound change in the course humanity has taken since that moment.

Budiansky speaks of Anthony's discovery with awe and respect as he imagines what it must have been like for the human who decided to get onto the back of a non-domesticated animal the size and strength of the "Cult" stallion, who stood at about 14'2 hands tall.[24] We can only imagine what this person must have been feeling and thinking to take this monumental step, but we can appreciate the resounding implications of his or her decision.

Although Levine might disagree, many still believe that humans, through their dominance and power over the horse, forced it into domestication and that it was because humans were more powerful that horses became subservient. The belief in such a model may have led to a way of viewing horses which perpetuated horse abuse and mistreatment throughout the ages. The story of the Cult Stallion of Dereivka allows for a different cosmology if one should choose to believe it.[25]

Imagine

Imagine, a small group of tent-like structures swaying as gusts of strong wind and driving snow push against their sides. Imagine in the distance a small herd of horses grazing on what little forage is left. They are skittish and afraid of humans, but come close as the weather worsens in hopes of finding extra forage near to the encampment. Farther away from the herd stands the head stallion, watching the horizon for danger, ready to alert the herd at the first sign of movement.

"We have almost forgotten how strange a thing it is that so huge and powerful and intelligent an animal as a horse should allow another, and far more feeble animal, to ride upon its back."
~ Peter Gray

Out of the Sredni Stog encampment comes a young woman. She is moving quietly as if she does not want to be seen. She moves closer to the herd and finds a small rock to sit on, gazing in wonder at these majestic creatures. The head stallion raises his head and sniffs the air, sensing her. He moves his herd away, but still she sits. Dusk falls and finally the girl returns slowly to camp.

The next day the herd has moved farther away but they are still within a mile of the camp. Once again the girl walks out across the barren landscape singing gently as she goes. She finds another rock to perch on and continues singing to the horses. Slowly they make their way closer to her.

Over time she comes to love these creatures and even as her tribe moves it seems that the horse herd is always somewhere nearby. The head stallion has grown used to her presence and no longer moves his herd away when she is near. And so we come to the moment where our story moves into uncharted territory.

Is it possible that the young girl and this wild stallion could have formed a bond that made riding seem simply natural? Could it have been that rather than domination and "power over," the horse could have chosen to come into contact with mankind? Is the fact that horses evolved with a gap in their teeth, "diastema," that allows for a bit to sit comfortably in their mouths simply an accident? Can we allow our minds to imagine that horses decided to become domesticated and through this choice, brought profound change to our world? Can we believe in "co-evolution," human and Equus partnering for the purpose of change?

Cultural Evolution and the Horse

Regardless of the distance we allow our minds to stretch, and which theory we choose to believe, one thing is inarguable. Without the Cult Stallion of Dereivka and others like him around the world, the cultural evolution of the human race would have occurred much differently.

Domesticating the horse for travel and weight-bearing purposes caused a myriad of events to occur. Suddenly humans could travel further and faster than they ever thought possible, covering thousands of miles and traveling at distances of up to ninety miles a day. Budiansky reports that the first sizable impact that this had on cultural evolution was the ability to trade exotic items over great distances. The research of David Anthony and his team suggests that with increased trade came social differentiation. He remarks that upon studying graves in the steppes of the Ukraine, a change occurred from communal Mariupol-type graves to individual graves. He suggests that this shift denotes a radical change in the way people perceived themselves and their roles amongst one another. It appears that this was approximately the time when humans began to form hierarchical societies and the corresponding ways of viewing themselves. Suddenly unprecedented quantities and varieties of exotic goods appeared in these individual graves, such as copper ear ornaments, copper spiral bracelets, gold ornaments, and flint knives and axes. Along with this increase of trade came the realization of how large the world was. Tribes began to think in terms of conquest rather than in terms of co-existence.

Out of this change in consciousness came the Huns and later the Mongols. Both the Huns and the Mongols brought terror to the smaller non-horse tribes and with the help of the horse were able to conquer such countries as China, Korea, Poland, parts of Russia, and Hungary. Notions of warfare were changed irreversibly with the introduction of the horse. There seemed to be no end to what devastation the combination of horse and human could bring.[26]

Scholars believe that it was due to the domestication of the horse that our modern languages came into existence as they did. The horse people of the Steppes appeared to have spoken a proto-Indo-European dialogue. Upon reconstruction, that language, now long extinct, seems to have included Sanskrit, Homeric Greek and Latin, as well as such modern languages as English, French, Russian and Persian. Due to the distances that horses could carry humans, the notion of a shared language became a reality, and communication across great distances became possible.[27]

Both Scanlan and Budiansky agree that the domestication of the horse brought a revolution to nearly every aspect of human existence, creating profound and ever-lasting change to the manner in which humans lived their lives. It is reasonable to expect that that relationship continues to evolve.[28]

Summary

Budiansky states, "I would argue that the single invention that has changed human life more than any other is the horse — by which I mean the domestication of the horse as a mount." Although not all-inclusive, this chapter helps to demonstrate the vast impact that horses have had on our cultural evolution. The work of scholars like David Anthony, Marsha Levine, and Sandra Olsen help us to piece together our long history with horses, and how the relationships we formed approximately 6,000 years ago impacts us today. Understanding the possibility of co-evolution provides us with a lens through which to view our continued relationship with horses and offers us new ways to think about the role of horses as healers of the mind, body, and soul.

CHAPTER TWO

THE ANCIENTS: DISCOVERING THE HEALING POTENTIAL OF THE HORSE IN MYTH AND STORY

"The cure of the part should not be attempted without treatment of the whole. No attempt should be made to cure the body without the soul. Let no one persuade you to cure the head until he has first given you his soul to be cured, for this is the great error of our day, that physicians first separate the soul from the body."
-PLATO

Upon domestication, Equus Caballus was an immediate smash hit, but not because of his/her healing abilities, rather because of his/her ability to bring violence to the masses. How then did horses come to be seen as messengers of the Divine, healers and magical beings? It seems that war, death, and dying bring us closer to the Divine. The horse was simultaneously creating devastation and bringing us closer to salvation. In those moments when death is near, man reaches out to find companionship. Is it surprising that horse and God became intertwined? Man sits atop his horse awaiting death and calling to God. When he receives an answer through his steed, what is he to think?

Myth, ancient stories, and teachings from an array of cultures and time periods depict the horse as a link between God and mortals. The horse is commonly seen pulling the sun across the sky, carrying gods and goddesses between heaven and earth, and taking people on journeys between realms of existence. I have chosen only a few examples from countless possibilities to help demonstrate the archetypal nature of thundering hooves through our dreams.

The Druids and the Celts

Both the Druids and the Celts believed that the horse could bring man on a journey between worlds, walking the slender path between life and death. In times of war and terror, when man's closest companion was his steed, each time they went to battle they walked together along that thin line.[29]

From time eternal people have been curious about what may be on the other side of life. Horses exist in a place of in-between. They are both completely grounded, and at the same time, completely connected to the totality of the universe. The research of NASA and the other international joint ventures designed to explore the role of the sun in earth's climactic changes demonstrate that our daily existence is linked to cosmic functioning.[30] Horses, as with any species living closely with the earth, must stay connected to that cosmic functioning in order to survive. The sun's impact on temperature changes we experience here on earth is only one example of how interconnected our survival is with the totality of the universe. Horses seem able to sense earthquakes, storms building, and heavy winters.[31] They make adjustments in their behaviors, habits, and physical appearance in order to survive what is to come. Horses are aware that life and death are intricately connected, and that both exist in every moment of every day.

Life and death form a cyclical and constant pattern; for the earth to stay in balance both must occur. If one can look upon the earth and all of us inhabiting it in evolutionary terms, we may begin to feel at peace with death. The sun is slowly burning itself to oblivion. In a few billion years the sun will be so hot that its rays will cause earth as we know it to wither and die. Scientists believe that by studying the sun and its unique behaviors, we will understand what exists outside of our solar system, and be prepared to evolve as a species well before our sun meets its end.[32] The notion that scientists are already thinking in terms of "billions" of years, and conceptualizing other solar systems beyond our own, tells us that our evolution as a human race is only just beginning, and that there is opportunity for incredible events to occur. Our existence does not begin or end with each of us as individuals; we are only a part of an ever-moving, ever-changing cycle. To know that can offer solace in times of darkness. Larry Dossey, a well respected physician of internal medicine who helped bring to light the theory of a "non-local" mind, a concept that demonstrates just how interconnected we all are, states "if the non-local mind is a reality, the world becomes a place of interaction and connection, not one of isolation and disjunction".[33] Carl Jung, Larry Dossey, Lyall Watson, Rupert Sheldrake, Candace Pert, and Albert Einstein[34] all believed in the power of interconnection, and all realized the enormity that went hand in hand with such a concept. To realize that we are interconnected on a cellular level with all organisms who exist, have existed, or will exist, can bring a certain degree of peace and comfort in times of loneliness or isolation.

Horses help us to ground ourselves and thus be able to witness our existence as a circle, not as linear with finite endings and beginnings. Once we are able to think in these terms, we can begin to explore other realms of our consciousness. If we are able to think about life as a continuum, with no beginnings and no endings, we could allow ourselves the time to explore the deeper and generally undiscovered parts of our human existence. We tend to get so caught up in the time between when we are born and when we die that we trudge along that path without question, simply awaiting the day that we will cease to be. We spend hours, days, and years pondering what happens after we die, and an equal number of hours, days, and years trying hard to avoid death. If we put that much time and energy into living our lives as fully and presently as possible, imagine what realms we could explore. Perhaps the Druids understood that being in the presence of the horse brought humans closer to the present moment, and thus closer to exploring realms of the psyche not yet discovered.

The Celts were deeply spiritual people who found peace in the interconnection of all living beings. They believed that to know God is to know all of his creations, and believed it was important to love and honor them each as individuals. They did not see a separation between religion and nature. They believed that the horse traversed the territory between the living and the dead and was able to carry humans between both realms.[35] People such as Linda Kohanov, EFMH/ES practitioner and author of *Riding between Worlds,*[36] and many others doing the work of EFMH/ES also believe that horses may be able to help people walk "between worlds." We begin to realize that there is not as large of a gap between species as we might have thought, and that communing with, and being open to the natural world somehow helps us to connect with the Divine.

Hindu and Persian Teachings

Hindu mythology tells of the horse as the messenger for the great God Vishnu who will sound the end of evil and wrongdoings on this earth. Vishnu sits astride a white winged horse who holds one hoof aloft, ready to strike the earth with such power that the earth would fall into the sea. All humanity would be destroyed, and the earth would be cleansed. Then all creation would be renovated pure and good, and evil would cease to exist.[37]

It is said in a Persian teaching that the Messiah, Sosiosh, will come on a horse and that his arrival will mark the beginning of Pralaya, or "period of cosmic rest." Both the Hindu and the Persian stories posit that horses have the power to change existence as we know it. In both mythologies, the stories speak to the cycle of death and re-birth, with horses innately tied to the cyclical process that cleanses the soul and brings awaking to goodness.[38]

Greek Mythology

Conversely, Greek mythology recounts the tale of Minerva and Neptune vying to create the most useful object for the services of the human race. Neptune created the horse and Minerva created the olive tree. Interestingly enough, Minerva won, because the Greeks believed that the horse was a projection of war and evil to come, and the olive tree was a sign of peace. It seems that both Neptune and his opposition were correct. Neptune created what could certainly be viewed as the more "useful" of objects, but with his creation the prophecy did come true.[39]

In both of these accounts, we see the horse as bringing both salvation and devastation. The Ying and the Yang, balance incarnate.

Chiron, the centaur of early Greek mythology who has been credited with the invention of medicine and surgery along with numerous

"Being in the presence of horses promotes re-choreographing of neural and biochemical pathways with regards to memory, temporal relations, decision-making, behavioral and motor responses, threat appraisal, imagery, visualization, locus of control, stress responses (including stress hormone regulation), attention, arousal level, breathing patterns, information processing, cognitive and executive functioning. EFP allows clients to 'lay down new tracks' in the brain... e.g. corrective relationship experiences, being successful/mastery, positive self regard/self efficacy, pairing previously stress-provoking thoughts/feelings with relaxing/pleasurable sensations."
~ Maureen Vidrine, M.S., RN, CS
HorseTime, Covington, Georgia

other accomplishments, provides us with our modern-day archetype of the "Wounded Healer." The myth tells us a tale of this majestic centaur who was instructing a young man in the art of the hunt when he was accidentally shot and nearly died of the wound. Chiron cured himself of this deadly wound and in the process, found that he was able to heal and furthermore to educate others in the practice of the healing arts. Chiron lived the rest of his life healing those in need and teaching the heroes and heroines of Greek mythology the art of healing. It is said that both Achilles and Hercules were among his pupils and his name bestowed upon him by the heroes was the Divine Beast. He taught that riding a horse would cure both wounds and diseases. Upon his death Jupiter placed him among the stars. He is known today as Sagittarius, looking down on all humanity from the heavens.[40]

Zechariah and the Horse

The Bible records Zechariah's vision in which the horse is the guardian angel of the world who moves between heaven and earth conveying the Lord's message. It is conceivable to assume that throughout time humans have felt the presence of the Divine when they come into contact with the horse. This feeling may have led to the belief that horses actually are a link between heaven and earth.[41]

In today's rapidly growing field of psycho-spiritual learning, there are many different ways of saying what people have sensed from time eternal: horses help connect people with a sense of a higher power, and through that perceived connection, the world is not quite as lonely. We all desire connection, groundedness, and a sense of our roots. Feeling like one has a direct line of communication between self and the Divine is a powerful way to receive validation that our existence has meaning and purpose, and that we are "here for a reason." Something about being in the presence of horses helps us to realize that there is "a power greater than us," and with this realization comes the ability to accept our powerlessness over many things that occur in our lives. When we have reached that point, we are ready to take in new information and concepts that will help advance us to a different way of thinking and being. Both the McCormicks and Stanislav Grof, author of *The Holotropic Mind* and the co-inventor of "Holotropic Breathwork" speak to the importance of our connection to higher power and both offer suggestions about the vehicles one might take to obtain that sense of connection.[42]

Grof believes that through rhythmical breathing one can induce a trace-state where connection to the totality of the universe is possible. People participating in breathwork sessions have experiences of profound implication. Conversations with long deceased "ancestors," of both the human and animal variety occur regularly, visions from past and future times, and conversations with the Divine all come together to indicate that once in an altered state of consciousness humans can access connection to the totality of time and space, traveling great distances and communing with the Divine.[43]

The McCormicks have found a somewhat different path to the Divine - horses. They believe that in communion with horses human beings are able to feel a sense of connection with the Divine. They follow the "Celtic Way", or spiritual path of the Celtic people and find along that path many indications that the Celtic people believed horses to be the vehicles by which the Divine communicated with humans and visa versa.[44]

Both Grof and the McCormicks seem to fundamentally agree that moving outside of the self and experiencing connection with the Divine has the potential to help us transverse into a world where preconceived boundaries of time and space drop off into meaninglessness and opportunities abound.[45]

Our Bodies and the Divine

Scientific testing reported by Friedmann, Katcher, Lynch, and Thomas link the presence of a companion animal to lowered blood pressure, lowered stress reactions, and fewer doctor visits.[46] People who have reported deep connections to the Divine also tell of feeling less caught up in the day-to-day rush of this existence. Thus they are calmer and probably also have reduced stress reactions and lower blood pressure. There have been accounts of the altered states of consciousness experienced simply by being in the physical presence of someone "holy," or connected to the Divine.[47] Is it possible that due to our belief that horses are somehow connected to the Divine, when we enter into their energy space, we also enter into an altered state of consciousness? Furthermore, does this altered state of consciousness allow human neurochemistry to adjust and change to make room for new thought patterns and ways of being? It seems that if being in the presence of a horse allows us to ground and center, possibly alter pre-existing ways of being, and alter our consciousness, then it seems that we are simply preparing the way for a relationship with our higher power as we perceive it.

Acting Outside of Self

Horses are dynamic and powerful. They exist in a realm far larger than our own, one that has the space to hold polar opposites in the same hand and see how perfectly they meld together. Adele von Rust McCormick, Marlena D. McCormick, and Thomas E. McCormick explore the realms of the horse within the Celtic Way in their new book, *Horses and the Mystical Path*. They comment that the wisdom of horses is not always comfortable for humans to take in and accept. They write, "It (the horse) has highly charged polarities, generated by paradox, that often throw us into a state of tension and chaos. Unlike the dualism of the human mind that separates the world into this-or-that, either-or, horses teach that both ways are true…. We begin to see the underlying unity of all things."[48] Horses do not exist in a world of

19

good and bad or right and wrong. They seem to live in a place of fluid response to "what is" where decisions are made on the basis of what is the *next best thing* to do in that moment, listening to instinct and not questioning whether it is right or wrong. Survival is essential, and the horse does what he/she needs to do in order to insure both his/her own survival and the survival of his/her herd.

Horses appear to have the ability to envision and act upon the "bigger picture" of herd survival, rather than on individual needs, emotions, desires, or wants, and in doing so seem to act "outside of self," an art that we humans may not always recognize or feel comfortable with. To observe a being functioning outside of self can be confusing because we cannot immediately understand why they act in the manner that they do.

An example of such behavior occurs during the young horse's first few years. In the first months after birth he can do no wrong. He can run up to the alpha mare's feed pile and eat happily. He can nip, kick, bite, or otherwise bother any horse in the herd regardless of pecking order. The other horses will tolerate him without discipline. However, once he becomes a yearling, the herd expects him to take his rightful place within the pecking order. Suddenly the youngster finds himself in a strange predicament. He attempts to steal some of the alpha mare's food, and finds himself being chased away. He nips another herd member and gets himself kicked in return. He is confused and unhappy. At this juncture, one of two things will happen. Either the yearling will figure out the societal norms of the herd and conform, or he will persist in his behavior and will be pushed away. If he figures out the rules of herd behavior, and accepts his place in the pecking order, he will be fine and life will continue. If he does not, and continues to challenge the older horses, be a bother to the herd, or otherwise reject the societal norms of the herd, the alpha mare and head stallion will chase him away. At first they will chase him only a short distance and allow him to return. If he adjusts his behaviors he will be allowed to reunite and assume his role. However, if he continues to challenge the herd's system of hierarchy and balance, he will be chased completely away from the herd and left to either die (the most likely possibility), or will join up with other youngsters in his same predicament, a bachelor herd. Life in such a herd is generally short lived and difficult.

The only hope for the yearling's survival is to find a mare or group of mares for the youngster to steal and then begin his own family herd.[49] Either way, the concept of chasing a young being away to his death can be hard for humans to accept. When we hear about this act in the world of horses we can associate it with survival and somehow accept that it was a "normal" thing for the head stallion and alpha mare to do. However, when we come across a similar act between humans, we struggle to accept that there might be a higher purpose behind the action, a purpose that those acting out the behavior may not even understand. It is important to remember that we humans also chase our youngsters away to their death, or at least to a place where struggle is unavoidable.

Many of today's youth find themselves in a similar situation as the young horse. They rebel against their parents, against society, and against the norms that govern our culture. Their parents attempt to discipline and train them, utilizing whatever tools are available to them. In many cases their attempts are in vain and something must be done. The youth may have started using drugs, breaking the law, and violently disrespecting the authority of his parents. Many times once the youth has reached this point, the parents feel as though they have no other options and "chase" the youngster away from the home. The act of "chasing" may look differently dependant upon the resources of the family. The youth may be removed by force from the home and escorted to a therapeutic boarding school or treatment center, or might be violently evicted from the home and forced to remain out on the street by a restraining order filed against him by his parents, or in even more extreme cases might be given away as a ward of the court, his parents deciding that they want nothing else to do with him. In any of these cases the youngster finds himself suddenly expelled from his "herd" and forced to fend for himself out in a world he is little prepared to handle.[50] These scenarios are, unfortunately, becoming increasing common across the United States. Fortune magazine offers this, "On any given night in America, there are approximately 100,000 homeless children. This figure may be seriously understated because a group of San Francisco lawyers known as 'Public Advocates' estimate that in the San Francisco area alone there are 48,000 homeless and that

21

more than 10,000 of that number are children."[51] Stanford University's Michael Wald and Tia Martinez report,

> Ninety percent of the four million fourteen-year-old youths in the United States will make a "minimally successful" transition into early adulthood, five to seven percent which is 200,000-300,000 will reach the age of 25 without having "established positive social support systems" or successfully transiting into early adulthood. They report, "At an age when most young adults are benefiting from fulltime work and close interpersonal relationships, these youth will not have connected to the labor force; most will lack social support systems. About sixty percent will be men; of these, over half will be in prison, while the remaining young men will be mired in protracted spells of long-term unemployment.[52]

Transitioning back to the horse herd, probably the most devastating example of "acting outside of self" involves the killing of a youngster. If a horse is born with a deformity or gets injured or ill early on, the herd stallion may choose to kill the baby in order to protect the rest of his herd. The head stallion would pick the baby up by its neck and swing it, stomp on it, bite it, and finally kill it. Normally, the act of killing within a horse herd is virtually unheard of unless the situation is urgent enough that the stallion must act to save others. The head stallion and lead mare understand that having an injured or deformed baby within their herd is likely to attract predators. To keep the baby alive is to place the rest of the herd in danger. Thus the head stallion and the lead mare hold the larger vision for what must occur in order for the herd to survive and thrive.[53]

The difference between humans and horses isn't our mutual ability to act outside of self for the betterment of society; it is the cultural acceptance of such acts. In other words, once the baby is dead, the mother horse will stand for a time near the body, but will re-join her herd, and appear unfazed by the event within a short period of time. Life goes on, and she continues to trust her herd members, knowing completely that the action had to occur, even though it was painful. In some cases, humans have lost the ability to trust themselves and their innate wisdom of what is right. This has led to a myriad of problems including random acts of violence, and the societal repercussions of our "an eye for an eye" mentality. We prolong the moment until it is no longer a moment, but rather a lifetime of memories, pain, and suffering. Horses remind us to let go and return to the present.

"There are two ways of meeting difficulties: you alter the difficulties, or you alter yourself to meet them."

When an individual is functioning outside of self, he/she has the unique ability to see past, present, and future, and act accordingly, therefore once a decision has been made there is no second guessing, worrying, or continual processing of the event. It is done and over. The notion of functioning "outside of self" is directly related to Larry Dossey's non-local mind[54] and Eckhart Tolle's "presence." In Tolle's book, *The Power of Now,* he discusses the importance of living in the present, and introduces his readers to the notion that once in the present we can move through crisis, pain, and suffering without getting stuck in any of those stages.[55] We have the ability to move forward through our lives, through existence. Horses constantly remind us that "forward" is the way to go, and if we can begin learning from their way, we can radically re-adjust our thinking about moving through trauma.

Life in Balance

There are many other examples of this side of equine nature, and it is important to understand that horses live in balance, walking that line between harshness and gentleness, between exquisite beauty and deep tragedy. Imagine witnessing the head stallion trample a young, unsuspecting, and innocent horse to her death. What feelings arise in your heart? Do you feel confused about his actions, question his reasoning, or think that there is something very wrong with the world? Or do you understand innately why he had to do what he did? The Divine functions in much the same manner. When such a tragedy occurs amongst humans we cannot imagine our God doing something that hurtful. We do not think about the purpose of the action or what possible good it may hold. We assume that God has abandoned us in those moments, and it is only later, if we are willing to open ourselves, that we sometimes can understand the perfection within the action. Some call it hind-sight, the ability to look backwards and view the event with new eyes. It is only in those moments that we can understand the meaning offered to us. Dossey writes about the unity of all things and the interconnection between events, "Within this context of connectedness, evil is mere appearance because it, like everything else, is part of the whole".[56] Humans are capable of functioning completely in the present moment, but knowing innately how that action will impact future events. However, this is a skill lost to many of us. Horses can help remind us that the present moment is all we really have. The ability to witness an act that seems too terrible to have any positive meaning, and, rather than reacting, move with consciousness into a new way of thinking about that act is a practice that is essential to the development of our psyches. We spend precious time thinking about what has passed and how terrible or unfortunate it was, rather than using that same energy to devise ways to move forward with peace and light. Walking the way of the horse helps us all to better understand that journey.

Of Witches and Horses

The prevailing belief in the early history of the horse/human relationship appears to have been that horses were messengers of the Divine, or somehow otherwise connected to the Divine, and that it was through this connection that humans benefited from the horse. Fascinatingly enough this well documented and deeply held belief seems to have met resistance and may have become less prevalent during the 14th century. This change in belief and philosophy seems to have coincided with the Inquisition and the end of paganism in Europe.

Between the 14th century and the 18th century, thousands of women were murdered during the "burning times" when people feared the existence of witches and witchcraft. Today, many believe that the death of these women was not due to a true belief in witchcraft, but rather due to the fear of nature worship and wisdom. Belief in nature worship indicates that any human being can connect directly with the Divine rather than needing the services of a church, preacher, pastor, or other such clergy. This notion may have threatened the Church of England during a time when it needed to be viewed as an all powerful entity. Being pagan simply meant being one of the earth, or someone who lived and worked closely with the earth. However, this term quickly became synonymous with nature worship, and soon anyone who believed in the wisdom of the earth could be called a witch or warlock, and sentenced to death.[57] During this time, M. Oldfield Howey reports that those searching for witches would struggle to find them because the women would transform themselves into horses and gallop away from their pursuers.[58]

Is it possible that the belief in horses as healers was too closely connected to notions of nature worship, witchcraft and other such unsavory ideas, and so was quickly and firmly rejected from common thought?

In its place the realization that horses could be physically healing rose to popularity. This movement was spurred by Liz Hartel of Denmark, who in the 1950's rehabilitated herself from a wheelchair to the back of a horse, and won the silver medal in the Grand Prix dressage competition at the Helsinki Olympics.[59] Her victory brought a change in thinking about the role of horses in relationship to humans. With this awakening came the birth of therapeutic riding as we know it today.

Summary

Throughout recorded history the horse appears as a spirit guide, messenger of the Divine, and healer of the body and soul. In more modern times this belief became a dangerous one, associated with things wild, dark, and uncontrollable. From there forward the horse became a beast of burden, controlled and dominated. Even so, many held fast to the feeling that there was something more to the relationship between horse and human than mere functionality. Understanding the horse's past as it relates to the Divine and to its perceived ability to heal the body and soul helps us as we explore the field of EFMH/ES. With this knowledge we can better understand the metaphorical and archetypal roles clients and students may assign to the horses with whom they work.

CHAPTER THREE

TRANSFORMATION: THE BIRTH OF EQUINE FACILITATED MENTAL HEALTH AND EDUCATIONAL SERVICES

Origins

The originations of EFMH/ES began long ago, when HORSE came into existence. Its birth began on the cave walls of prehistoric man. Throughout time humans have recognized the healing power of horses, viewing them as spirit guides, messages of the Divine, and healers of the psyche.[60] After the 18th century the emphasis appears to have moved away from horses as healers of mind, to horses as healers of the physical body.

Soon after Liz Hartel's Olympic victory, concepts of therapeutic riding and hippotherapy[61] became well known in Norway, Denmark, and England. It was not until 1960 that therapeutic riding and hippotherapy came to North America. Mr. J.J. Bauer and Dr. R.E. Renaud of Toronto created the Community Association for Riding for the Disabled (C.A.R.D.). Closely following C.A.R.D.'s creation the Cheff Center for the Handicapped opened in 1966 in Augusta, Michigan. Both organizations primarily served individuals with physical disabilities and functioned under the belief that horses were helpful to humans with disabilities because of the rhythmic movement of their natural gait.[62] The method proved so popular and appeared so successful that the field of therapeutic riding and hippotherapy blossomed with a speed and velocity unexpected by those providing the service. It was due to this momentum that individuals began realizing the need for guidelines, ethics, and certification within the field in order to keep the clients safe and the service ethical.

In 1969 the North American Riding for the Handicapped Association (NARHA) was created to help oversee therapeutic riding and hippotherapy practices. NARHA limited itself to the work people were doing with horses, and did not branch out to include other animals. Until 1990 NARHA did not publicly recognize the mental health benefits of working with horses, primarily concentrating on populations considered physically handicapped. The notion that horses could be psychologically healing for humans was not clearly defined or addressed in NARHA's literature, nor was it a part of the curriculum for therapeutic riding centers or providers of hippotherapy. Surely many providing therapeutic riding or hippotherapy services observed the mental health benefits of the horse/human relationship, but there was no literature or research, and no professional venue to further explore their observations.[63]

Just as horses have been seen from time eternal as healers of both the psyche and of the physical body, animals of other species have also been viewed as healing or healthful for humans. In ancient Greece and Rome, dogs were kept in temples to promote healing. Individuals who feared for their sanity partnered with dogs and kept them close to ensure their mental health.[64] More recently in the 1700's the York Retreat, founded by the Tuke family, introduced animals as companions to psychiatric patients. This retreat is still in existence today and continues to support the concept of bringing companion animals into psychiatric care.[65] Florence Nightingale stated in 1859, "A small pet is often an excellent companion for the sick, for long chronic cases especially."[66] In the 1950's Konrad Lorenz, a Nobel Prize Laureate, was honored as the "father of the field" for his two books on the subject of companion animals as healers.[67] In the 1960's Boris Levinson, a psychiatrist from New York, began bringing his pet dog into psychotherapy sessions. He observed how children with communication difficulties were able to change behaviors and respond with increasingly more positive affect when in the presence of his dog. His published observations did appear in scientific journals but received both national and international criticism probably because of the innovative nature of his approach and the newness of the method.[68]

Dr. Levinson's ideas eventually took a greater hold on the American public, because in 1977 the Delta Society was created to help provide guidance and structure for those providing animal assisted activities. The term, "animal assisted activities" is defined by the Delta Society as, "AAA provides opportunities for motivational, educational, recreational, and/or therapeutic benefits to enhance quality of life. AAA are delivered in a variety of environments by specially trained professionals, paraprofessionals, and/or volunteers, in association with animals that meet specific criteria". The Delta Society utilized the term animals to describe the broad nature of the work that they supported. However, it was primarily companion animals, or "pets" that their attention was focused upon. Dogs and cats were, and continue to be, the primary animals being worked with under the Delta Society umbrella. The term animal is still being used, although therapeutic and recreational work with horses is not specifically included within the Delta Society definitions.[69]

"Beautiful sisters, come high up to the strongest rocks, we are all fighting women, heroines, horsewomen."
~ Edith Sodergram

In 1979 the Society for Companion Animal Studies (SCAS) was formed in the UK. This group was created to promote and support the study of the human/animal bond.[70] The International Association of Human-Animal Interaction Organization (IAHAIO)[71] was formed in 1990 as an advisor to the United Nations and in 2004 was awarded working partner status with the World Health Organization (WHO) in recognition of the importance of the human/animal bond for human health and well being.[72]

The field of animal assisted activities was born from our innate knowledge of the healing potential of human/animal interactions. The focus of this field was the potential for increased health (both physical and emotional) when a companion animal was introduced into the treatment team. Originally dogs were the companion animal of choice, and "man's best friend" became famed for the powerful interventions provided when a dog was allowed to spend time with patients in a variety of settings. From hospital beds and jail cells to psychotherapy offices, the dog made a name for himself as a valid and competent provider of positive affection, love and joy. Perhaps due to the vast amount of published research on the subject of how companion animals (specifically dogs and cats) impact humans, or perhaps because of other reasons that we will explore later, the field of animal assisted activities became connected in the public's mind primarily with the dog and in some cases cats, but generally not with horses.[73]

NARHA continues to maintain all of the safety standards, accreditation, and to provide instructor training for those individuals and centers providing equine assisted activities. Delta Society has little to do with the development of the equine-oriented fields, and provides similar services to those of NARHA for individuals wishing to pursue the benefits of companion animal activities or therapy.[74]

The birth of EFMH/ES has created a bridge between the beliefs held by both NARHA and the organizations that oversee the safe and ethical facilitation of animal assisted activities. It is within the methods of EFMH/ES that the deeper concepts of our interconnection with all life is addressed, fostered, and brought to light. However, before we can explore that concept, we must understand the roots from which EFMH/ES in modern times grew.

Therapeutic Riding and Hippotherapy

The methods of both therapeutic riding and hippotherapy were based on the premise that the horse's movement is healing for physical ailments. K. Depauw of the Center to Study Human-Animal Relationships and

Environments reminds us that hippotherapy in its original form can be traced back to Europe around the 18th century when doctors used it as a medical intervention for "improving postural control, joint disturbance, coordination, and basic balance".[75] NARHA currently defines therapeutic riding as "mounted activities including traditional riding disciplines or adaptive riding activities conducted by a NARHA certified instructor". NARHA defines equine assisted activities (EAA) as, "An umbrella term inclusive of all the various offerings of NARHA centers and all of the equine activities and therapies designed for people with disabilities or diverse needs. This term is accurately used for making global statements about NARHA center activities."[76]

In 1992 the American Hippotherapy Association (AHA) was formed as a section of NARHA to oversee centers and individuals providing hippotherapy. More recently, AHA was created as its own non-profit 501 (c) 3 organization. AHA remains an affiliate of NARHA, but is independent in all other matters. The AHA defines hippotherapy as, "In the controlled hippotherapy environment, the therapist modifies the horse's movement and carefully grades sensory input. Specific riding skills are not taught (as in therapeutic horseback riding); but rather a foundation is established to improve neurological function and sensory processing. This foundation can be generalized to a wide range of daily activities".[77]

Research
Tissot, Chassaine, and Satter

It appears that the first published acknowledgement that horses could be physiologically healing for humans occurred in 1780 when Tissot of France wrote in his book *Medical and Surgical Gymnastics* that when riding astride a horse, the walk was the most beneficial gait.[78] Then in 1870 Chassaine, a young man studying at the University of Paris, published his thesis about the horse as a treatment modality for patients with neurological disorders.[79] After that it was another hundred years before the healing potential of the horse/human relationship was documented again in the form of a written publication. In 1977 L. Satter reported that hippotherapy had the ability to normalize muscle tone and improve body control, coordination, and orientation in space. He also noted improvement in spasticity and righting reactions including symmetry and head and postural control. Furthermore he also recognized that his patients demonstrated an increase in their motivation to heal.[80]

Tauffkirchen

E. Tauffkirchen reported in 1978 that riding a horse "improved posture, tone, inhibition of pathological movement patterns, and facilitated normal automatic reactions and promotion of sensimotor perceptions". He also suggested that riding helped motivate the study subjects.[81]

Bertoti

D.B. Bertoti's 1988 report helped to move the field of hippotherapy into the mainstream of treatment modalities. In her study on posture in children with cerebral palsy 27 subjects were followed. These children rode twice weekly for a one-hour session. The results of her study showed a decrease in spasticity, an improvement in the ability to weight shift, increased balance and rotational skills, improved postural control, and decreased extensor muscle hypertension. Other outcomes of her study indicated that riding not only benefited the children physiologically, but also psychologically. She notes that the children demonstrated increased self-esteem and self-confidence, and were less afraid of movement and posture change. Her study made it increasingly clear that therapeutic riding or hippotherapy was a valuable treatment modality for individuals suffering from cerebral palsy.[82]

Brock

Also in 1988 B. Brock conducted a study on the effects of therapeutic riding for physically disabled adults. Her findings also concurred that substantial physical gains in posture, balance, decrease of spasticity, coordination, and an increase in back and neck strength occurred from riding astride a moving horse.[83]

Benda, McGibbon, and Grant

Finally in 2003 W. Benda, N.H. McGibbon, and K.L. Grant published a very important study on the improvements in muscle symmetry in children with cerebral palsy after hippotherapy. Their research has greatly helped to change the landscape of therapeutic riding as we know it. They report,

Reduction in spasticity after only eight minutes resulted in an average of more than 60 percent shift towards right/left symmetry in children on the horse compared to those on the barrel, suggesting a most desirable alternative to invasive neurosurgery and injection of botulinum toxin for this condition. (Benda, McGiddon, and Grant, 2003)

They also suggest that the three-dimensional movement of the horse mirrors that of the normal human gait, and therefore someone with a disability can experience an imprinting of his or her nervous and musculoskeletal system while simultaneously experiencing a loosening of certain joints and strengthening of others allowing the person to move more freely.[84]

Needless to say, the study showed no similar results in the children who sat astride a non-moving barrel. They concluded that it was the movement of the horse, not passive stretching that accounted for the measured improvements.

Aetna

Aetna, one of the nation's leading providers of health, dental, group, life, disability and long-term care insurance utilizes a "Clinical Policy Bulletin" to express its determination of whether certain services or supplies are medically necessary. Aetna reaches its conclusions based on a review of current clinical information which includes outcome studies, published medical literature, positions of leading national health professional organizations, and so on. Aetna currently proclaims hippotherapy to be "experimental and investigational because there is insufficient scientific data in peer reviewed medical literature to support the effectiveness of hippotherapy", which essentially means that they will not provide insurance coverage for hippotherapy or therapeutic riding. However, they do introduce D.B. Bertoti's 1988 study and conclude that her study represents the first objective report that demonstrates the positive benefits of hippotherapy. They also record a 2005 study done by Hammer and Associates that validates the notion that hippotherapy is beneficial to humans in a variety of ways.[85]

However, the fact that Aetna considers hippotherapy to be "experimental and investigational" due to a *lack of published literature* speaks volumes to the current state of all forms of equine therapy, from hippotherapy and therapeutic riding to EFMH/ES.[86] More research must be done to provide scientifically what thousands -- if not millions --of people already know: horses are good for humans.

Splinter-Watkins

Kathy Splinter-Watkins of NARHA brings to light the very same issue. She notes in a paper entitled "Research: Past and Future", that although there are hundreds of equine-based therapy centers operating all across the country and the world there is "little documented proof that what we do works, or what about it works best!"[87] It is important to note that there have been a multitude of studies conducted that help validate the healing power of horses, but these studies have been primarily presented at national and international professional conferences or posted on the internet, and not as widely published in either peer reviewed or professional journals. This dearth of scientific research-based literature has caused the field to hover on the edge of acceptance, not yet completely recognized as a valid form of treatment. It is the mission of many within the field to bring recognized research on the benefits of therapeutic riding and hippotherapy into the professional domain. This motivation has led many to invest themselves in the study of the horse/human relationship.

Animal Assisted Therapy

Currently, many organizations exist to help guide and oversee the field of animal assisted therapy/activities (AAT/A). The Delta Foundation, known to most of us as the Delta Society, was established in 1977 in Portland, Oregon, under the leadership of Michael McCulloch, MD. Between 1985 and 1992 the Delta Society funded 20 studies costing approximately $350,000 to discover more about the healing power of animals. The Delta Society's mission is to "improve human health through service and therapy animals".[88] Animal assisted activities (AAA) is another common term used by individuals or organizations who utilize the human/animal bond in their work. Delta Society suggests that, "AAA provides opportunities for motivational, educational, recreational, and/or therapeutic benefits to enhance quality of life. AAA are delivered in a variety of environments by specially trained professionals, paraprofessionals, and/or volunteers, in association with animals that meet specific criteria". They also define animal assisted therapy (AAT) as, "A goal-directed intervention in which an animal that meets specific criteria is an integral part of the treatment process. AAT is directed and/or delivered by a health/ human service professional with specialized expertise, and within the scope of practice of his/her profession. AAT is designed to promote improvement in human physical, social, emotional, and/or cognitive functioning [cognitive functioning refers to thinking and intellectual skills]. AAT is provided in a variety of settings and may be group or individual in nature. This process is documented and evaluated". They offer further clarification about the differences between AAA and AAT in the following quote, "Animal-assisted activities are basically the casual "meet and greet" activities that involve pets visiting people. The same activity can be repeated with many people, unlike a therapy program that is tailored to a particular person or medical condition".

Along with the Delta Society, the International Association of Human-Animal Interaction Organizations (IAHAIO) was founded in 1990 to "gather together national associations and related organizations interested in advancing the understanding and appreciation of the link between animals and humans". IAHAIO's mission is to "promote research, education and sharing of information about human-animal interaction and the unique role that animals play in human well-being and quality of life". Purdue University publishes, in cooperation with IAHAIO, a peer reviewed journal called *Anthrozoos*, which offers professional articles related to the human-animal bond. This publication helps to bring validity to the field and has published hundreds of peer reviewed articles about the human/animal bond.[89]

People, Animals, Nature (PAN) was founded to "facilitate international and multidisciplinary dialogue about the benefits of interacting with nature and other animals and to contribute to the Human Animal Studies body of knowledge through research and education". PAN has been able to help universities across the country develop curriculums based upon the human/animal bond. PAN also believes that humans, other animals, and nature are all interconnected, and that it is within this interconnection that health and healing can occur. They offer a membership through which we can better understand the relationship between people, animals, and nature.[90]

Research

While little comprehensive research has been published in peer review journals that document how the horse is physically and mentally healing for humans, a virtual cornucopia of research exists that documents the healing power of companion animals. Some 52 scientific papers that document research in the field of animal assisted therapy were published between 1988 and 1993. All 52 studies concluded that animals were healing for humans, either physiologically or emotionally depending upon the intent of the research. Since 1993 the research has only magnified, with continuing positive results that demonstrate that the link between animals and humans is beyond a shadow of a doubt, healing.[91]

Levinson, Barker, Campbell, Katcher, and the Rehabilitation Services of Roanke, Virginia

In 1962 Dr. Boris Levinson suggested that his dog provided a "communication link, provided the child with a sense of security in the therapy setting, and quickened the therapy process". Levinson also reported that the new-found treatment method worked well with children suffering from schizophrenia, a withdrawn personality, obsessive-compulsive disorder, and children who were non-verbal, autistic, or culturally disadvantaged.[92]

Sandra Barker, Ph.D. reports that Levinson found his dog particularly beneficial in "helping to strengthen autistic children's contact with reality".[93] It seems that his instincts were well founded as in 1992 Campbell and Katcher conducted a study that helped to support Levinson's ideas. The study demonstrated that indeed animals were able to help autistic children increase their level of social response to both other humans and also to the animal involved in the therapeutic setting.[94] Furthermore, in 2002 a study of autistic children by the Rehabilitation Services of Roanoke, Virginia, revealed that animal assisted therapy is more effective than conventional therapy for those suffering from autism.[95] It seems that Levinson's cutting edge concepts of the 1960's opened the door for future research efforts that would, over time, provide inarguable evidence that animals may help heal humans.

Odendaal

In South Africa in 1981 Johannes Odendaal began publishing his own observations about the healing power of animals. His interesting and informative article entitled "The human-animal interaction movement in South Africa (1981-2004)" helps to bring an international understanding to the development of the field of animal assisted therapy. Odendaal's contributions to the field include articles entitled, "The veterinarian, pets, and psychotherapy" (1981), "The therapeutic value of positive human-animal interaction: The role of phenylethylamine" (1998), "Human-dog interaction: an interspecies evaluation of blood pressure changes as possible indicators of neurochemical changes" (1998), "The role of phenylethylamine during human-dog interaction" (2000), "Animal-assisted interventions of nursing research: Issues and answers" (2002), and "Neurophysiological parameters for affiliation behavior between humans and dogs" (2003). These articles were published in international journals and helped to pave the way for a global exchange of information and ideas about the healing powers of animals.[96]

Odendaal's research tells us that all human beings need attention. He introduces the term, "attentionis egens," a Latin term that describes the need for attention on a "normal, basic emotional level as the prerequisite for all successful social interactions". Odendaal explains that the therapeutic role of a companion animal is most commonly found amongst what he calls the "weaker" people. He defines "weaker" as individuals who are physically or mentally handicapped, the elderly, chronically ill patients, those suffering from long term social deprivation, emotionally disturbed individuals, prisoners, substance abusers, and children, essentially people who cannot compete "on an equal basis for attention among healthy, adult people because of their place in society in relation to the nucleus of activities". He believes that these populations have an increased need for attention due to their conditions and lack of ability to connect with other humans in meaningful and fulfilling ways. He suggests that although the "normal" manner of obtaining attentionis egens is human to human, research has now successfully proven that animals can offer the same companionship and attention as another human, thus fulfilling the same role as a human could within a relationship. He believes that the ability to exchange human for animal is at the root of the therapeutic value of animals.[97]

Benda and Lightmark

William Benda and Rondi Lightmark seem to have similar thoughts about the healing power of animals. They write, "Although we may normally prefer the support of a human being, under duress the quality of the connection becomes more important than the origin of such support". They go on to address the notion that when humans are ill and especially chronically ill they feel isolated, lonely and out of contact with the normal routines of everyday life, furthermore they tend to polarize their experience by adding feelings of guilt for the weight that they add to the lives of their loved ones. This compounds their feelings of isolation and loneliness, thereby making a pet the most logical choice for a supportive, caring individual to attach to during these times of hardship.[98]

Barker and Barker

In 1988 S.B Barker and R.T. Barker engaged in research that led them to discover that "dog owners were as emotionally close to their dogs as to their closest family member". And in fact "one-third of the dog owners [who participated in their study] are actually closer to their dogs than to any human family member."[99] Think about how many people live in self-made or situational isolation, where they feel unable to connect to another human being in a fulfilling manner. Is it possible that Odendaal's notion of the "weaker" populations is broader then he ever imagined? It is conceivable that most of us fall into that category in one way or another, seeking the needed *attentionis egens*, and finding it within our interactions with animals rather than humans.

The other important aspect of Odendaal's work is his study of the physiological impact of the human-animal relationship. Odendaal reminds us that in 1929 it was discovered that when a human strokes a dog the dog's blood pressure will decrease. It took fifty years for research to prove that a simultaneous result occurs within the human stroking the dog! In the 1980's it was discovered that being in the presence of a dog, and stroking that creature produced significant changes in human physiology. Changes in diastolic and systolic blood pressure, plasma cholesterol, plasma triglycerides, and skin conductance responses occurred, and effects were seen on the autonomic nervous system, essentially suggesting that interacting with animals helps to lower stress and anxiety reactions.[100]

Friedmann

Erika Friedmann, a pioneer in cutting edge research that validated the physiological impacts of the human-animal relationship writes, "it has been hypothesized that pets can decrease anxiety and sympathetic nervous system arousal by providing a pleasant external focus for attention, promoting feelings of safety, and providing a source of contact and comfort. They can decrease loneliness and depression by providing companionship, promoting an interesting and varied lifestyle, and providing an impetus for nurturing. The range of benefits that humans might derive from their pets may not pertain only to pet owners; one could speculate that anyone, not just pet owners, could benefit from the presence of friendly animals".[101]

Friedmann conducted a groundbreaking study which compared the survival rates of pet owners and non-pet owners. It was found that only 5.7 percent of pet owners died within one year of discharge from a coronary care unit compared with 28.2 percent of non-pet owners, all other medical and demographic factors being equal. Dog owners in particular were 8.6 times more likely to be alive in one year as compared to those who did not own dogs. This study was later expanded to 369 patients with similar results.[102]

Allen and the State University of New York

In 1991 K.M. Allen and his team of researchers at the State University of New York also conducted an important and timely project looking at the impact of pets on blood pressure. High blood pressure is a major risk factor in several of the leading causes of death in the United States today. Allen was able to determine that owning a pet led to a significant decrease in the rise of blood pressure during stressful situations compared to those who did not own a pet. Intriguingly,

Allen found that this decrease in blood pressure was noted even when the pet owner was not in the same location as the pet, suggesting that the effects of animal assisted therapy is sustainable and long lasting.[103]

The Australian Department of Human Services

On a somewhat more practical note, the Australian Department of Human Services and Health 1995 Statistical Overview conducted an interesting study looking at health costs as they relate to owning a pet. Investigators were able to estimate cost savings of nearly $145 million annually if the population of Australia owned pets. They hypothesized economic savings of $26,244.00 from decreased medical visits, $18.856 million from pharmaceutical savings, and $99,792.00 from decreased hospitalizations.[104] Although the bulk of research has been done to prove that animals bring about physiological and psychological healing to humans, this particular study is of great interest because it opens the door to discussions about the global implications of partnership with animals. If being with animals positively impacts our health, and therefore decreases our medical expenses, think of the ramifications for society and the overall structure of our health care system.

Cole and the American Heart Association

Probably the most notable study that changed the landscape of animal assisted therapy was conducted by The American Heart Association in 2005. The results of their clinical study confirmed for any remaining non-believers that the interaction between humans and animals has measurable positive effects on hospital patients. This study documented that a 12-minute visit with a dog helped heart and lung function by "lowing blood pressure, diminishing release of harmful hormones, and decreasing anxiety". This study, led by Kathie Cole, RN, MN, CCRN, monitored patients' homodynamics, or "the collective system of measurement for blood volume, heart function, and resistance of the blood vessels". Investigators also measured epinephrine and norepinephrine levels before, during, and after the interaction between the patient and the dog. The results from the study concluded that anxiety scores dropped 24 percent with animal interaction verses the 10 percent found in the non-animal interactions. Levels of the epinephrine (the "stress hormone") decreased an average of 17 percent with animal interaction verses the 2 percent drop seen without animal interaction, and actually rose 7 percent in those who had neither human nor animal connection. The pulmonary capillary wedge, a measurement of left arterial pressure, dropped an average of 10 percent with animal interaction verses the 3 percent increase with only human interaction, and the 5 percent increase with no interaction. Finally, systolic pulmonary pressure, a measure of pressure in the lungs, dropped 5 percent during and 5 percent after interactions with animals, whereas it rose during and after interactions with humans or after being alone. Kathie Cole said, "The study demonstrates that even a short-term exposure to dogs has a beneficial physiological and psychological effect of patients who want it." She goes on to say, "This therapy warrants serious considerations as an adjunct to medical therapy in hospitalized heart failure patients. Dogs are a great comfort. They make people happier, calmer, and feel more loved."[105]

The reason that this study was so impactful to the world-wide medical community is that it was sponsored by the internationally known and respected organization. When an organization like the American Heart Association endorses a treatment modality, people come to attention and paradigms shift. This study and the hundreds like it have truly brought change to the traditional medical model of treatment. Entering into a hospital or nursing home is a different experience now, dogs and cats are commonly seen riding elevators, visiting patients, and in general, becoming a part of the treatment team. Few even question their presence -indeed it would be considered archaic for a nursing home *not* to allow their patients the companionship of a dog or cat.

Prothmann and the Clinic of Child Adolescent Psychiatry and Psychotherapy, Leipzig, Germany

Anke Prothmann, et. all, from the Clinic of Child Adolescent Psychiatry and Psychotherapy at the University of Leipzig, Germany, studied the impact of AAT with disturbed children during their study entitled, "Interaction of psychologically disturbed children with a therapy dog". They examined patterns of interaction between patients and pets. They suggested, "Previous observations presume that patients show different behavior patterns during interaction with a therapy dog. The aim of this study is to verify possible specific interactions". They examined the behaviors of ten patients, with a total of forty patients participating between the ages of 6-17 years old. These patients had been diagnosed with the following disorders: anorexia, bulimia, anxiety disorder, and autistic disorder. Their therapy sessions with and without the inclusion of the trained therapy dog were video taped and then were rated by five individuals blinded to hypothesis and diagnosis using a software for interaction analyses. The interaction analyses program separated the results into four categories. The categories were posture, gaze direction, behavior towards the dog, and behavior towards the dog handler. The results showed significant differences in all four of the categories that they tested.[106]

Virginia-Maryland Regional College of Veterinary Medicine

A pilot project conducted by Virginia-Maryland Regional College of Veterinary Medicine and the Department of Psychology from Virginia Tech in 2004 entitled, "Psychological Impact of a Service Dog Training Program on Inmate Trainers" examined the impact of the Prison PUP (Puppies Uniting People) program within a medium-security prison. Employing both qualitative and quantitative methods, investigators discovered that inmates working with dogs demonstrated a reliable decrease in depressive symptoms. Participants of the study presented with mild depression at the beginning of the study (Beck Depression Inventory II scores of 10 and 13) and following the study demonstrated a reliable decrease to below threshold levels. Participants also demonstrated an increase in self-esteem as measured by the Coopersmith Self-Esteem Inventory (scores increased from 88 to 92 and 100), and reliable changes on the Rotter Locus of Control Inventory, demonstrated a marked ability for greater internal focus of control. The success of the pilot project prompted the researchers to suggest that further studies should be done to better understand the psychological and social changes that may occur due to such a program.[107]

Other such studies that examine the psychological implications for AAT abound and can be found through the Delta Society, in *Anthrozoos* publications, and in other professional, peer reviewed journals.

The Modern Introduction of EFMH/ES

What happened to the horse within the context of *animal* assisted therapy? Oddly enough, in the multitudes of books written and research projects conducted in the field of human/animal bonding, the work of horses seems to have gone virtually unaddressed. It almost seems that horses do not fit within the context of "animal", but rather float somewhere outside of that classification.

Could our age old fear and mystification of the horse continue to haunt us even as we move into a new decade of awareness? Dogs, who are most commonly referred to when discussing "animal assisted activities", have been with us from time eternal, ever willing, loyal, and compassionate. Is it possible that dogs have not challenged us at our very core, never co-created cultural or societal evolution, or forced us to look more deeply into our psyches, and so we do not fear them in quite the same manner? Instead they have been content to witness our evolution, going willingly where we go, and supporting our very being-ness. Maybe we can underestimate dogs because of their size and presence, but we cannot do the same with horses. They challenge us constantly and sometimes brutally, and remind us that they are a mystery, an unknown that we cannot quite grasp. Whatever the case may be, the role of equine-specific activities within the larger concept of "animal assisted activities" has not been as developed, as thoroughly researched, nor as commonly utilized by medical professionals.

NARHA came into existence to support the concept that horses could provide a different type of service to clients than dogs could, and that this service was useful and helpful to the clients receiving the said service. NARHA supported the creation of ethical guidelines that would protect first and foremost, the client. NARHA also began to lay the groundwork for standards and practices that would help support the ethical treatment and care of working horses. NARHA's primary focus revolved around the physical and cognitive benefits of therapeutic riding and hippotherapy. However, NARHA also recognized the psychosocial benefits of horse/human interactions. Within the NARHA community, individuals began to foster those benefits, targeting populations who may have needed less of the physical benefits derived from interaction with horses, and more of the psychosocial benefits.[108]

If one were to believe in the notion of a "collective unconscious," one could better understand the birth of EFMH/ES. This work began in dreams, in visions, in feelings, and the people who were experiencing these simply started *doing*. Is it possible that the horse wanted this change so desperately that his message was heard loudly across all barriers? Is it possible that this is what Ms. Barbara Rector first heard when she made the decision to verbally declare that there was more going on between horses and humans than met the eye? Within the NARHA community, the psychosocial benefits of the work between horses and humans was well known to those providing the service, but was not viewed early on as a benefit that would stand alone, one that could be capitalized upon solely with its own unique clientele, methods, and standards of practice. Ms. Rector strongly believed that whatever was going on between horses and humans that was not within the realm of the physical, was equally important and needed to be addressed formally.[109]

Ms. Rector's declaration created a split within the burgeoning field of "horse therapy" but brought needed growth and change to the field. The transformation the field went through over the next sixteen years was truly dynamic, with ideas pouring forth about how horses could be healing in a myriad of different ways.[110]

Within this section of the text individuals and organizations who brought the work of EFMH/ES into the public eye will be spotlighted. There were many people who played invaluable roles within this field, but whose work impacted those on the inside of the work, rather than the masses, people like Ann Alden, Maureen Vidrine, Maureen Fredrickson – MacNamara, Leslie Moreau, Molly DePrekel, Boo McDaniel, Marilyn Sokolof, and countless others, all without whom the field would never be where it is today.

Pioneers of the Field
Barbara Rector and EFMHA

In 1973 Ms. Rector recovered from a serious accident by riding her horse virtually bridle-less and saddle-less through the desert washes of Tucson, Arizona. All those involved in Ms. Rector's recovery process would call it no less than miraculous due to the severity of her injuries. Ms. Rector's prognosis, after the jumping accident that nearly ended her life, was not positive. "We really don't know what will happen," Ms. Rector recalls the doctors saying. With the loving support of her friend and physical therapist, Nancy McGibben, Ms. Rector undertook nearly two years of physical therapy learning how to walk again. During this time Ms. Rector and Ms. McGibbon formed an agreement that would allow Ms. Rector to ride her horse Bintina through the washes of Arizona. The agreement stated that Ms. Rector must be able to fully groom and tack her horse without assistance before she would be allowed to ride. After accomplishing those tasks Ms. Rector, still confined to an upper torso and right arm cast, was able to mount Bintina. Ms. Rector's limited physical abilities decreased her use of conventional aids used to steer or control her horse and so it was primarily her relationship with Bintina that allowed her to return day after day, safe from rides up and down the washes of Tucson.

It was due to this experience that Ms. Rector and Ms. Nancy McGibbon went on to co-found Therapeutic Riding of Tucson (TROT) in the early seventies. Ms. Rector's continued desire to explore the realm of human consciousness led her to leave TROT in 1989 and return to graduate school at the College of the Holy Name in Oakland, California. Here she earned a Masters of the Arts degree with an emphasis in Spiritual Psychology. During her time in California Ms. Rector worked at the Institute of Attitudinal Healing directed by Dr. Jerry Jampolsky, M.D. where she facilitated youth groups and their families through the dying process and worked as an intake counselor. She also started her work with Stanislav Grof to become a certified Holotropic Breathwork therapist. Upon her return to Arizona she assisted Stan and Christina Grof in facilitating a Holotropic Breathwork training for the staff of Sierra Tucson, the premiere treatment center for addictions located in Tucson. The director and owner of Sierra Tucson, Bill O'Donnell, was interested in starting a program to work with adolescents using the work with horses as a treatment method. He had heard about Ms. Rector and was interested in how the work with horses might be of benefit to his clients. Ms. Rector was introduced by Stan Grof to the director of Sierra Tucson and soon a partnership was formed. Ms. Rector was hired by Sierra Tucson to create an equine facilitated psychotherapy program that would become the first of its kind in the country. Ms. Rector was able to design her own facility and gather together a team of horse and human facilitators to provide this new and highly provocative service. By the early 1990's the program was up and running, and Ms. Rector had successfully brought equine facilitated psychotherapy into the treatment spotlight. During her time at Sierra Tucson Ms. Rector hosted workshops for people interested in learning more about this innovative treatment method. Many who started providing this work early on had been in attendance at one of those workshops.[111]

Due to Ms. Rector's involvement in the field of therapeutic riding, she was an active participant in the workings of NARHA, serving on the board of directors and as a member of the medical committee, and it was this very involvement that led to the birth of the Equine Facilitated Mental Health Association (EFMHA). In February of 1996 after a NARHA conference a group of interested individuals came together to discuss the idea of creating a section of NARHA that would oversee and guide the field of Equine Facilitated Mental Health. Present at that initial meeting were Barbara Rector, Boo

"Far back, far back in our dark soul the horse praces... The horse, the horse! The symbol of surging potency and power of movement, of action...."
~ D.H. Lawrence

McDaniel, Beverly Boehm, Annie Shields, Maureen Abbate (now Vidrine), Barbara Abrams, Charlie Koch, Maureen Fredrickson (now MacNamara), Jessie Frazier, Beverly Halpin, Ruth Rahimi, Marge Kittredge, Tate Pearson, Larna Whitson, Michael Kauffman, Betz Haartz, Rebecca Basile (now Bombet), Regina Jackson, Donna Grossman, Health Nelkin, and Norma Lorimer.

It was decided at that first meeting that Barbara Rector and Boo McDaniel would become the first EFMHA co-presidents, a role they would share for the next two years. They lined out the tasks that needed to be accomplished, which included creating standards for the field, creating a code of ethics, creating definitions of EFMHA terminology, and isolating precautions and contraindications for the work. Through her work with TROT and with Sierra Tucson, Ms. Rector had come to view horses as "sentient beings" who could "co-facilitate" experiences for humans. Lodged deeply within the core values of EFMHA this jointly held belief lives on. In fact, it was due to this belief that the word "facilitated" was introduced to the world of equine "assisted" activities.

EFMHA was created as a membership driven organization overseen by a volunteer board of directors who give their time without financial reimbursement.

By March of 1997 EFMHA had published its first newsletter and already had 225 members. This newsletter told of EFMHA's first pre-conference workshop during the NARHA conference held in Orlando in November of 1996. Ms. Rector's Adventures in Awareness pre-conference program hosted by Arabian Nights of Orlando, was well attended by mental health workers, therapeutic riding professionals, and medical professionals all interested in this new method of treatment.[112]

Ms. Rector's contribution to the field of EFMH/ES is notable, and at the 2006 ten- year anniversary of EFMHA, Ms. Rector and Ms. McDaniel were presented with the first Founders Award ever to be given within the field.

By 2006 EFMHA had defined itself further, with the grassroots assistance of all the members and with the guidance and direction of the board of directors.

By 2006 EFMHA has proudly accomplished many of the original tasks it set out to accomplish. It is both a challenge and a benefit that as EFMHA is a section of NARHA, all standards, guidelines, and trainings must be passed not only by the EFMHA board of directors, but also by the NARHA board of trustees. This suggests a lengthy and time consuming process to gain approval, but does guarantee that the product has validity. NARHA is an internationally recognized organization with standards of practice that have been field tested for over thirty years.

Over the past ten years EFMHA successfully developed and field tested its psycho-social safety guidelines, and in 2006 these guidelines were approved by the NARHA board of directors. These psycho-social safety guidelines apply to all NARHA members and centers regardless of whether or not the center provides mental health services to their clientele.

EFMHA has also field tested their standards over the past ten years and these standards of practice have finally been adopted by NARHA in 2005. These standards now apply to all NARHA members and NARHA member centers that provide mental health services.

Furthermore, in 2006 NARHA chose to integrate one of EFMHA's standards which addresses the mental and physical wellbeing of the horses working within the field of equine assisted activities into the overall NARHA standards and center accreditation process. This means that any NARHA member or center accredited by NARHA must adhere to the EFMHA horse care standard regardless of what service they are providing.

EFMHA's Equine Specialist Workshop has now been approved after five years of development and field testing. The first three non-pilot workshops were held in 2006.

EFMHA's Research Committee has created a comprehensive bibliography, which is available to the public on their website, listing a wide array of resources for the interested individual. EFMHA has also helped to foster continued research within the field of EFMH/ES, and during their 10 year anniversary conference the results from five research projects conducted in the year 2006 were presented, marking a major step for the field.

EFMHA offers psycho-social safety guidelines and standards to all who are interested in providing this service regardless of how or where the professional obtained his/her training or experience. EFMHA does not endorse any one specific method of EFMH/ES but requests that individuals practice within the scope of their individual licensure or certification, and follow the EFMHA approved standards and psycho-social guidelines. EFMHA is in the process of creating educational curriculums that will train professionals to these guidelines.

It appears that all working within the field of EFMH/ES believe that EFMH/ES as an educational or therapeutic method was not the creation of any one person or organization. It was a collaborative effort in which many professionals offered ideas, insights, and ways of practice. Ms. Rector and later EFMHA represent the first and most recognized introduction of the field to the general public. However, they certainly do not represent the field as a whole. There are other individuals and other organizations that need to be recognized when speaking to the birth of EFMH/ES.[113]

Greg Kersten, Lynn Thomas, and EAGALA

In the early 1990's a horseman named Greg Kersten began using his work with horses to help humans. Mr. Kersten started working with at-risk youth, prison populations, and within residential treatment facilities in and around Utah and Colorado. He was employed as an addictions counselor, and specialized in working with challenging or violent clients. In 1991 Mr. Kersten developed an equine program at Aspen Ranch, a therapeutic boarding school in Loa, Utah. This program helped to pioneer the use of EFMH/ES in therapeutic boarding schools across the country. Mr. Kersten began bringing into his professional life his own personal love of horses and belief in the power of learning healthful communication skills. Mr. Kersten was invited by NARHA to join forces to promote the therapeutic work that he was doing, but due to differences in opinion about safety protocol that relationship soon deteriorated. Shortly thereafter Mr. Kersten formed a partnership with Lynn Thomas, a licensed mental health professional with whom he had been working closely to provide his own unique brand of EFMH/ES services. Their relationship helped form the basis of their method, Equine Assisted Psychotherapy.

In 1999 Greg Kersten and Lynn Thomas founded the Equine Assisted Growth and Learning Association (EAGALA), an organization dedicated to providing training, education, and support services to people interested in the field of equine assisted psychotherapy.[114] The separation between EFMHA and EAGALA created the first major rift that the field had experienced, and a great deal of misunderstanding and mis-education about the work of EFMH/ES began, and continues into the present. EFMHA and EAGALA share two very separate roles within the field, but a lack of knowledge and clear explanation about their differences has caused both consumers and professionals interested in the field confusion and concern.

The most obvious difference between EAGALA and EFMHA is that EAGALA is primarily a training and member support organization. EAGALA provides workshops and trainings for professionals interested in the method of Equine Assisted Psychotherapy, and provides support for those individuals graduating from their training programs. Individuals attending an EAGALA workshop or training learn an EAGALA sanctioned method that maintains guidelines specific to EAGALA and no other method or organization.

Secondarily, EAGALA is not affiliated with any long standing organization, such as NARHA, and therefore has no secondary board of directors to answer to. EAGALA had been driven primarily by two individuals until the more recent involvement of an active board of directors. There are benefits to EAGALA's model of operation. Within two years they had already created a training manual, a three level national certification program, a code of ethics, a resource manual that details all of the EAGALA certified individuals; what they do and where they are located, a yearly conference where people such as John Lyons and other nationally and internationally known individuals speak, and a network for interested individuals to access so that communication between practitioners is readily available. Although EAGALA has a code of ethics and a procedure for reporting ethical violations, they do not have standards or psycho-social safety guidelines that have been approved over a ten-year course of review, field testing, and revision.[115]

It is important that individuals interested in the field understand the differences between EAGALA and EFMHA, and recognize how to best utilize each organization for the strengths that they both contain.

Over the years EAGALA's safety protocol has been questioned by many practicing within the field of EFMH/ES. Initially EAGALA did not require clients to wear hard hats during mounted activities. Currently, EAGALA no longer sanctions any mounted work, thereby alleviating the concern about hard hat usage. EAGALA's method does not focus on teaching clients, rather their trainings suggest that it is useful to allow clients to make connections for themselves without the direction or intervention of the facilitator or mental health professional. Possibly due to this therapeutic model, EAGALA does not require that facilitators or mental health professionals providing EFMH/ES educate their clients with a safety first orientation to horses prior to horse/human interactions. Lastly, EAGALA sanctioned activities include a number of games which involve bringing together quickly moving loose horses and inexperienced clients in contained spaces without prior equine safety training.

EAGALA provides 3-day Level One trainings which certify people with no prior experience in EFMH/ES methods. Although EAGALA does not state that such certification deems one prepared to provide the said service (in fact EAGALA strongly recommends that individuals continue on to achieve their Advanced training, which is far more extensive and strongly recommended for those interested in the EAGALA model), many who obtain their Level One certification assume that they are prepared to provide an EFMH/ES method with no further education or training. Since during their Level One certification program safety protocol is not taught and the participants engage in games as discussed above, many leave the program assuming that such activities are deemed safe. Their lack of knowledge about equine psychology, physiology, and behavior and their use of these games that have the potential to place clients at great physical risk is the cause of many concerns. I suggest that those interested in learning more about EAGALA attend their Level One program, but should not expect that three-days is enough time to gain all the skills needed to provide an EFMH/ES method. I highly recommended that interested individuals continue through EAGALA's advanced programs or seek other training resources to ensure a well-rounded approach to the field.

Probably one of the most confusing aspects that has arisen out of the rift between EAGALA and EFMHA is the use of terminology. In 2006 the majority of people interviewed believed that the term Equine *Assisted* Psychotherapy was connected directly to EAGALA and their own unique approach to EFMH/ES. Conversely, Equine *Facilitated* Psychotherapy is thought to be directly connected to EFMHA.[116] EFMHA adamantly denies this association, and states that EFMHA as an organization is not tied to any one method of providing EFMH/ES.[117] It is important that the field unites to use whatever term most correctly reflects the work that they do, *not the organization that they are members of.* Within the body of this text readers will gain a deeper understanding of the various methods currently being practiced within the field of EFMH/ES, and will be better equipped to align with whichever method fits the work that they do. At this point in the text, however, it is important to acknowledge that when the terms *assisted* or *facilitated* are used, no direct connections to either EAGALA or EFMHA is intended or implied.

Lynn Thomas remains with EAGALA as the Executive Director, and EAGALA continues to move forward, providing increasing numbers of national and international trainings.

Due to legal issues, in 2006 Mr. Kersten left EAGALA and started his own independent venture called the "O.K. Corral Series". His organization provides training and education for both professionals and non-professionals interested in the work of equine assisted psychotherapy.[118]

Michael Kaufmann, Suz Brooks, and Green Chimneys

Green Chimneys was founded in 1947 by Samuel "Rollo" Ross who remembered the out-of-doors and animals as being the most comforting thing he knew as a child. Dr. Ross continues to reside on the farm in a home he has lived in since he started the farm.

Green Chimneys is a non-profit residential treatment and education center run out of a 166-acre farm in Putnam County, NY. Green Chimneys believes in "restoring possibilities and creating futures for children with emotional, behavioral and learning challenges", Green Chimneys strives to "develop a harmonious relationship between people, animals, plants, nature and the environment through an array of educational, recreational, vocational and mental health services". Green Chimneys utilizes *all* aspects of animal assisted therapy, which includes dogs and other companion animals but reaches farther to create programming around farm animals, horses, and nearly any other animal one could conceive of. Green Chimneys also offers horticultural therapy and nature-based therapies.

Green Chimney's program has attracted national and international recognition, with Senator Hillary Clinton donating two Icelandic horses that children from that country gave to her for the purpose of exposing American children to their nation's prized breed of horse. Paul Newman, Mary Tyler Moore and Sylvester Stallone have all helped to support Green Chimney's mission and through their interest have brought national acclaim to the program.

Although Green Chimneys existed long before EFMHA came into being, both Dr. Suz Brooks, on-site psychologist, and Michael Kaufmann, the director of the farm and wildlife conservation center at Green Chimneys, have implemented EFMHA standards and concepts into their preexisting work. Both Michael Kaufmann and Dr. Suz Brooks maintain active roles in EFMHA as both have been on the board of directors for EFMHA over the years.

Green Chimneys has created a model for bringing together the aspects of animal assisted therapy and EFMH/ES in a nationally recognized and acclaimed manner that lends credibility and validity to the field.[119]

Miraval Resort, Life in Balance and Wyatt Webb

Miraval Resort, ranked as the #1 spa by readers of Conde` Nast and Travel and Leisure, combines "mindfulness" and health in the services it offers. Miraval believes in helping people to find their own unique sense of self and move forward through the world with greater attention and focus. Through its high profile guests, Miraval has been instrumental in moving the notions of mindfulness, yoga, creative expression, and adventure-based activities into the spotlight. Oprah Winfrey stands out as one of those touched by the Miraval experience who is now an international supporter of these less than "mainstream" concepts.

Wyatt Webb, formally of Sierra Tucson, was hired by Miraval Resort in 1997 and created what Mr. Webb now calls, "the Equine Experience." Mr. Webb defines the work that he does by stating, "The Equine Experience simply allows the horse to teach you about yourself. Relationships are our richest arena for learning, if we are able to be honest with ourselves". Mr. Webb also co-authored a book entitled *It's Not About the Horse*, which presents his beliefs about how the work of EFMH/ES could be carried out.[120]

Monty Roberts

In 1996 Monty Roberts published his first book, *The Man Who Listens to Horses*, which attributed his own path to health directly back to his relationship with horses. Within the context of this book Mr. Roberts addressed the notion that working with horses could heal human wounds, and bring about profound changes in functioning. In 2000 he wrote another book entitled *Horse Sense for People*, which took his notions of horse-person-ship to a new level. During this time Mr. Roberts began offering workshops and clinics for people to learn how to improve their communication skills, work through trauma, and find trust. Although Mr. Roberts is rarely thought of as a pioneer within the field of EFMH/ES, he certainly advanced the field in new and unique ways, and introduced the public to the underpinnings of the work. He deserves credit for his role in helping to shift the world view of horses away from a power-over paradigm toward a partnership model.[121]

The McCormicks

In 1997 Adele von Rust McCormick and Marlena Deborah McCormick, a mother/daughter team of psychologists published a book entitled, *Horse Sense and the Human Heart*. This book put into words for the first time the profound ramifications of EFMH/ES.

Horse Sense and the Human Heart explained and defined the work in a clear and concise fashion, giving credence to what was at the time a very new and unusual field. It is written in a fashion which makes it user-friendly to read and to be able to grasp important concepts regarding the work.

The McCormicks had been facilitating this work within their private psychology practices for many years before co-authoring this book. Their experience utilizing this method, and their hands-on practice with a diverse population is demonstrated on each page, suggesting that what they are writing is "tried and true." In 2004 they co-wrote another wonderful book called *Horses and the Mystical Path: The Celtic Way of Expanding the Human Soul,* which demonstrates how Celtic mysticism holds important insights into equestrian-partnered spirituality. The McCormicks operate the Hacienda Tres Aquilas and the Institute for Conscious Awareness in Texas, where they offer retreats, psycho-spiritual analysis certification, and seminars.

The McCormicks have always been a quiet force behind this work, not involved with any of the associations created to support the work, but seemingly content to do what they do best - offer their amazing services and write wonderful books.[122]

Sharon Janus and Rebekah Ferran Witter

Also in 1997 a book called, *The Magic of Horses* was written by Sharon Janus. This book marked an interesting shift within the literature. Mrs. Janus created a book of stories, or anecdotal experiences told by individuals that detailed the profound healing that they experienced while in the presence of horses. This style of writing was capitalized upon over the next nine years and is now common-place within the literature dealing with EFMH/ES. In 1998 Rebekah Ferran Witter also wrote another little known text, *Living with HorsePower: Personally Empowering Life Lessons Learned from the Horse* that provides a wide array of information and stories about working therapeutically with humans and horses. She addressed notions of horse nature vs. human nature, and communication vs. communion, two very important topics that would later be brought to light in many other texts in the upcoming years.[123]

Chris Irwin

Perhaps better known is the work of Chris Irwin, a long time horseman and horse enthusiast. Mr. Irwin wrote his first book, *Horses Don't Lie* in 1998, and his second book, *Dancing with Your Dark Horse* in 2005. Mr. Irwin has become involved in the field of EFMH/ES and now provides trainings and seminars that teach people a method he calls Equine Assisted Personal Development (EAPD).

Mr. Irwin led controversial dialogs spurred by his dislike of and disagreement with the concept of using horses as tools to provide the work of EFMH/ES. Out of this dialog Mr. Irwin's trainings focus on helping people to learn the art of working therapeutically with horses and humans in a manner that is respectful of the horse and focused on the partnership and relationship developed between horses and humans.[124]

Linda Kohanov

In 2001 Linda Kohanov wrote a book entitled, *The Tao of Equus: A Woman's Journey of Healing and Transformation through the Way of the Horse.* Ms. Kohanov took on a project long needed within the field, and obtained the insights and experiences of many within the field who saw the "magic" happen day in and day out, but could not find words or explanations for the experiences that they were witnessing. These were people who were not writers, but rather pioneers of this field, people who were too immersed in their practice to even consider undertaking a project like writing a book. Ms. Kohanov worked closely with many in the field to put into words the ideas, insights, and thoughts that spoke to the work that they had been doing for years without recognition or understanding from the masses.

Ms. Kohanov was able to take all that she learned from these practitioners, and connect that knowledge with her own profound personal experiences with horses and professional experience connecting humans and horses, and write a book that would change the direction of this field irreversibly. Upon Ms. Kohanov's book hitting the shelves, thousands of people all across the country and the world found an answer to that which they had been feeling and thinking, and the field of EFMH/ES gained huge exposure. In 2001 Ms. Kohanov started an apprenticeship program that now draws many people both nationally and internationally who desire to learn about the healing power of horses. Ms. Kohanov's second book, *Riding Between Worlds* was published in 2003.[125]

Ecopsychology, Biophilia, Barn Milieu, and Therapeutic Use of Riding

Ecopsychology and Biophilia

Like the experts at Green Chimneys, there are some within the field who are beginning to sense that the gap between the worlds of therapeutic riding/hippotherapy, animal assisted activities/therapy, and EFMH/ES is closing. Some are beginning to realize that without the human/animal bond we are lost. Principles of ecopsychology and biophilia are beginning to show up in the work that is being done with horses. Ecopsychology is loosely defined as a melding of ecology and psychology which studies the human need for interconnection with nature and the psychological and physiological impact on humans of an unhealthy planet. The work of ecopsychology strives to help humans reconnect with nature and through this connection become more environmentally sensitive and aware. Merriam-Webster Dictionary defines biophilia "a hypothetical human tendency to interact or be closely associated with other forms of life in nature". Traditionally, both ecopsychology and biophilia were theoretical concepts which heightened personal, communal, and governmental awareness regarding the interconnection between humans and the natural world. The principles presented offered a new conceptual framework that voiced the need for humans to reconnect with nature in all its forms. The practical application of the theories thus presented came across initially in "big picture" thinking, like the necessity for policy changes regarding environmental issues, or the need to be more environmentally aware and sensitive to the needs of our planet. Eventually the conceptual framework grew to include such practical applications as wilderness or adventure-based counseling and in the 1990's programs offering wilderness therapy sprang up across the country. These programs capitalized upon the perceived benefits of introducing clients to the natural environment and creating structured challenges that would enable the clients to learn more about themselves and experience the wilderness as they never had before. The theoretical orientation that drove many of these programs was based in principles of ecopsychology - humans need interconnection with nature. "Nature" in the context of wilderness or adventure-based therapy programs was indicative of wild spaces and all that existed therein. Therefore the general belief was that one needed to be in the wilderness to experience the benefits of nature. Furthermore, since wilderness or adventure-based therapy was formulated around an Outward Bound orientation towards group and personal challenge a client would be exposed to such activities as rock climbing, river rafting, kayaking, biking, hiking, camping, skiing, mountaineering, or sailing as a part of their treatment. This model became the generally accepted practical application of ecopsychology. Over the years other ways of providing ecopsychological services have arisen. One of the most prominent being nature-based therapy, which could include such activities as meditation under a tree directly outside of one's home, or a walk in a local park. raising a plant, or breathing deeply anywhere outside. The concepts of nature-based therapy is that a client does not need to be in the wilderness to experience a sense of interconnection (or lack there of) with nature. Nature is all around us, every day, everywhere, from the ants on the sidewalk to the trees surrounding our homes. By learning how to listen, to raise our awareness to the needs of living, breathing non-human organisms all around us, we may begin to feel more connected, and certainly may become more sensitive to the needs of our environment.

Interestingly enough one of the most underdeveloped aspects of ecopsychology is the interconnection between humans and domesticated animals. It seems like ecopsychology focuses on that which is wild more than that which is immediately in front of us, still a part of our ecosystem, still a part of nature. It is my personal belief that through learning interspecies communication skills people can more readily see the larger benefits associated with ecopsychology. It is difficult to learn how to communicate with something as wild as a bear, or something as different from us as a tree or plant. Perhaps in theory we can understand how interconnected we really are with such beings as bears and trees, but in the practical application of that interconnection we may feel somewhat lost. Both dogs and horses offer us the amazing ability to learn how to hone our interspecies communication skills and witness reciprocal communication, affection, and connection. I find horses to be the easiest species to communicate with as their "language" is so clear, organized, consistent, and non-threatening. Furthermore, horses are BIG which makes everything that they "say" that much easier to understand. I feel that learning interspecies communication skills with a horse enables us to begin opening to other possibilities, and allows us to feel deep interconnection with a non-human being. It is through such connection that we begin to experience the benefits of ecopsychology, and from there we can venture forth, looking for other, maybe more subtle ways to bring such theoretical concepts into our daily lives.

EFMH/ES provides a model through which we can further explore interspecies communication. Research has yet to be conducted that examines the benefits of the ecopsychological ramifications of EFMH/ES. However, suffice it to say that some amount of the perceived healing that occurs when humans and horses interact may be the result of being in nature and in relationship with a non-human being.

Barn Milieu

More and more organizations and individuals are beginning to see value in the "barn milieu," a concept that suggests healthful benefits of being outdoors and connected to living things in a more directed and intentional manner. Clients who come to a barn experience nature as they may never have done before. Out at the barn there are spiders, bugs, plants, and sometimes cats, dogs, cows, chickens, sheep, goats, or other farm animals. Clients can begin to experience the interconnection between species, witness interspecies communications and the power of nature at work all around them.

Furthermore, in a barn environment and out of an office new challenges arise that allow clients to demonstrate their normal behaviors without cognitive process. In an office clients may have greater control over their reactions, behaviors, and communication styles. Once out at the barn there are many tangible, hands-on tasks that need to be accomplished, there is new challenge, and there is fear. All three of these elements combined tend to push a client out of his or her comfort zone, thereby encouraging the client to act instinctively. In many cases the manner in which a client responds in an office setting can be challenging for the client to duplicate outside of that setting. Therefore, clients may tend to slip back into old behaviors in the home or work environment. The mental health professional may or may not be completely aware of the changes that the client makes once outside of the office and thus may not be as effective in addressing that shift. At the barn so many of our facades drop away and we become "real", not necessarily intending for others to see all aspects of us. Recently a new client arrived at the Esperanza Center. I ask her how she was feeling about her first session with the horses. She responded, "I feel really nervous. Not about them hurting me or anything like that." I asked her what she was nervous about. She said, "Well, I'm afraid that they are going to see right through me." As we talked about this comment she admitted that she did not like to let others see "all of her" and would always present the most positive front that she could. In her past work with other mental health professionals she felt that she hide the "worst" from them, showing them only her "cheerful" side. She also stated that she had never shared this tendency with anyone before this session. This client's experience demonstrates the power of being out of the office and in the barn milieu. This client had not even met the horses nor engaged in any therapeutic activity prior to making that statement.

In the barn environment the mental health professional or educator generally appears differently to the client. He or she will be wearing casual clothing, may demonstrate affection for the horses and other animals, and may engage with the client on a more human-to-human level. Carl Rogers would probably have enjoyed this approach to counseling! On the other side of the coin, the mental health professional or educator should be aware of the potential for clients to put them up on a pedestal. Work with horses can be seen as very sexy, and for the client, seeing someone that they deeply respect doing something really cool which at times can seem almost magical is a formula for infatuation. As facilitators of EFMH/ES we must be aware of this pre-disposition and work hard to stay grounded. The manner in which I avoid such infatuation is to foster deep relationships between the client and the horse or horses. If the client can begin to see how much the horses really do, and can view me as a guide and safety support person my role decreases and the horses' role increases. Just being out at the barn changes perceptions and opens new therapeutic and educational possibilities.

Therapeutic Use of Riding

The movement of the horse may provide physiological benefit to those presenting with mental health issues. Interestingly enough, virtually the only research we have to date in this field involves the psychological benefits of "therapeutic riding" which indicates mounted work with horses, *not* ground work. The research results show increased self-esteem, self confidence, and self-awareness, and decreased violence or inappropriate social behaviors. They do not, however, help us to understand why when astride a moving horse clients repeatedly report a flooding of emotion and memory, or even the sensation of an altered state of consciousness which in many cases leads the client to make notable behavioral change. Because of the frequency of such events, it comes as no surprise to many facilitators of EFMH/ES that the woman with locked hips attempting to sit the walk comfortably often has been sexually assaulted. Or, that after a short period of time astride a moving horse, clients may experience deep personal reflection, relaxation, excitement, and/or increased focus. In *The Tao of Equus,* Ms. Kohanov quotes this author in a discussion about the perceived benefits of riding for individuals with a history of sexual assault,

> The key was getting these people (those who move into a dissociative state) to move whenever they lapsed into a freeze mode, using the energy of the horse to jump-start muscle groups associated with running. I eventually came across another equine therapist whose intuitive response to an abuse survivor coincided with these insights. Leif Hallberg, founder of the Esperanza Equine Learning Center near Phoenix, Arizona, worked with a woman who experienced flashbacks of sexual assault while taking a riding lesson. As her client slipped into a dissociative state, Leif felt the instinctual urge to 'shake the woman out of it' by compelling her student to trot the horse. The effect of this faster gait tossed the woman gently up and down while simultaneously moving the muscle

groups associated with jogging. Like a prey animal trembling and running off after coming out of freeze mode, the pent-up energy in the student's pelvic area was released, and she ended the session in a state of relief and empowerment, despite the sudden emergence of this long-suppressed memory.[126]

The woman had never told another human being about her history of sexual abuse, and it was only through the movement of the horse that her memories surfaced and were allowed to come forth.

Over and over stories like these are told within the field of EFMH/ES. According to practitioners, there seems to be something about the rhythmical movement of the horse's gait that can be cathartic for people who struggle with psychological and mental health issues, and can sometimes stimulate feelings and memories long forgotten. In order to understand these types of experiences, research must be conducted to help us better understand what actually does happen to both the human body and the human mind when astride a horse, and how that physiological experience has a psychological impact upon the client.

With all of the research that has been done demonstrating the psychological effects of riding on issues such as self-esteem, self-confidence, and self-awareness, and the dearth of research conducted on the effects of ground work or ground-based activities on the psychological wellbeing of clients, one would think that mounted work would be a normal inclusion into the work of EFMH/ES. Fascinatingly enough, that is not the case. Many individuals providing an EFMH/ES do so only utilizing ground-based activities and no actual mounted work. From what the research we have available to us is showing, and from the anecdotal evidence is telling us, it would seem that mounted work should be considered a useful therapeutic intervention, and should be included as needed within a client's treatment plan.

As we explore the responses that people have to interactions with horses, it becomes increasingly clear that horses may help to connect nature, our physical selves, and our mental health. While practicing EFMH/ES methods we may see examples of this interconnection.

To be responsive and responsible practitioners we must be highly educated, trained, and experienced. We must know the lines between disciplines, and be trained and educated to make decisions about when and how to cross them. We must understand when it is appropriate to introduce certain concepts or methods, and when it is not useful or ethical. We must be trained in the facilitation of many differing skills, and must be aware and educated about an array of information not normally utilized by educators or counselors.

It is here that our field must grow. Many desire to do this work because it is so profound, and because it brings each of us closer to that which we all desire - clarity and connection. However, we must also recognize that without proper training, education and research regarding the ramifications of bringing humans and horses together, we cannot help to guide this field towards longevity and future successes.

Recent Research

By 2006 several research projects had been conducted within the field of EFMH/ES, but only a few of these projects resulted in publication in any major scientific journal. In this section, a selection of research projects, some published in peer reviewed journals and others presented as pilot projects with results not yet published in any major journal, will be offered as samples of the types of projects individuals are interested in and attempting to undertake. These projects help pave the way for future research and provide professionals within the field with data that may be used to help garner funding for EFMH/ES programs.

Burgon

In 2003 *Anthrozoos* published the results of a study conducted by Hannah Burgon, Department of Social Work at the University of Exeter in the United Kingdom, entitled, "Case studies of adults receiving horse-riding therapy." The purpose of this study was to "examine the psychotherapeutic effect of riding therapy on a group of adult users of a social services mental health team in South Devon". The objectives were multifaceted, generally revolving around the notion that although research had been conducted to examine the physiological benefits of hippotherapy, little has been done to look at the psychotherapeutic benefits of horseback riding. Burgon was curious about the role of confidence, self-esteem, and social/interaction skills. She was also interested in discovering if these skills were actually able to be transferred back into the daily lives of the participants. Using a case study, participant observational methodology, Burgon found that the participants did in fact benefit psychologically from a relationship with the horse. Her findings suggest that working with horses increases confidence and self concept, and aided social stimulation. She also found that transferable skills were acquired. This study was particularly interesting as it appears to be one of the first that focused on the psychological benefits of working with horses to be published in a recognized peer reviewed journal.[127]

Bizub, Joy, and Davidson

Also in 2003 Anne L. Bizub a post-doctoral research fellow from Yale University's School of Medicine partnered with Ann Joy, a supervisor for the Connecticut Mental Health Center's Ambulatory Rehabilitation Services, and Dr. Larry Davidson, an Associate Professor of Psychiatry at Yale University's School of Medicine to conduct a research project that would address how working with horses might help individuals suffering from severe mental illness learn life skills and promote individual expression. The results of this research project were published

"Being on top of a horse provides a change in perspective, as with going different speeds, sitting in different positions, i.e. backwards, forwards, sideways, etc. All provide this sense of changed perspective. In the process of riding, body awareness improves via somatosensory input/stimulation/integration. Opportunities arise for skills development in motor planning, visual-spatial analyses, visual motor skills, fine and gross motor coordination, auditory discrimination, as well as verbal and non-verbal language decoding, comprehension, and response, sequencing, balance, tone normalization, experiencing 'good touch', mutual rhythm, and gravitational challenge."
~ Maureen Vidrine, M.S., RN, CS
HorseTime, Covington, Georgia

in the *Psychiatric Rehabilitation Journal* in 2003.

The researchers discovered that after ten weeks of therapeutic riding services offered once a week for two hours to five individuals suffering from psychiatric illness, notable changes emerged in their sense of self-awareness, self-identity, self-efficacy, and self-esteem. Furthermore, the researchers observed that the clients participating in the service gained a deeper sense of interpersonal relationships, and demonstrated a higher level of connection with others. The researchers stated, "Another participant who had been very withdrawn has become an active member at Fellowship Place (the residential facility that the participants came from), occupying an important post in the clubhouse's governing body." Further results include a participant who "credits her participation in the program with elevating her self-esteem so dramatically that she is pursuing both residential and financial independence". Another participant who previously had "limited interactions with others" started working in the on-site store at Fellowship Place. All five of the participants had notable and observable positive reactions to their time spent with horses. The researchers determined at the end of the ten week project that, "the results of the study demonstrate that there are numerous benefits to horseback riding for people with psychiatric disabilities".[128]

Kaiser, Spence, Lavergne, and Bosch

In 2004 Lana Kaiser, Linda J. Spence, Annique G. Lavergne and Kerrie L. Vanden Bosch from Michigan State University's Human–Animal Bond Initiative within the College of Nursing conducted a pilot study to determine the effect of a five-day therapeutic riding camp on issues of anger, self-competence, and quality of life in children with no known physical or psychological disability, and no known history of psychotropic medications. The researchers used the Children's Anger Inventory, Peds Quality of Life, and Self Perception Profile for Children as instruments to measure the success of the project. These inventories were administered on the first day of the project prior to riding, and on the last day after riding. The team determined from analyzing the data gathered that horseback riding in a therapeutic setting did in fact help decrease anger levels and increase feelings of self-competency. The team states, "Data analysis suggests that five days of therapeutic riding day camp can significantly impact on anger. These changes may be related to the child's relationship with the horse, the social environment of camp, the horse and riding, increased contact with nature, or a combination of these factors." The results of this study were published in a 2004 publication of *Anthrozoos*.[129]

Roberts, Bradberry, and Williams

The Journal for Holistic Nurse Practitioners published the results of another 2004 research project conducted by F. Roberts, J. Bradberry, and C. Williams that examined the effect of therapeutic riding on nursing students. They determined that the service was of as much benefit to the nursing students as it was to the children who normally participated in the service. Their hope was that "by identifying beneficial educational outcomes of this nontraditional learning assignment, the authors hope readers will explore similar possibilities for nurses at various stages of their professional development".[130]

Gatty

Carolyn M. Gatty, an assistant professor in the Master's of Occupational Therapy program at Chatham College in Pittsburgh, conducted a pilot study designed to examine the impact of therapeutic riding on self-esteem. The participants were children with physical disabilities, unlike the above mentioned study that examined the impact of therapeutic riding on people with no psychological or physiological impairments. Ms. Gatty utilized the Rosenburg Self-Esteem scale for children. This instrument was utilized pre and post every session that the children attended, prior to riding the horse. Ms. Gatty and her team discovered significant gains in self-esteem. They report, "These findings were consistent with past studies; although, this was the first to yield a statistically significant increase." However, Ms. Gatty does suggest that without a control group, it is difficult to determine precisely what brought about the change in self concept:

> This pilot study did not include a control group, therefore a treatment effect can not be conclusively drawn, as there are many extraneous factors that may have affected the subjects' self-esteem. Furthermore, due to sampling methods, these results cannot be generalized to all disabled children and adolescents participating in therapeutic riding.[131]

They hypothesize that, "Positive influences on self-esteem may have resulted through the development of unconditional bonds with the horses, confidence gained by 'controlling' an animal 10-20 times their size, and a sense of physical improvement." The results of this study have not been published in a scientific journal to date.

Gehrke

Probably one of the most unique studies conducted to date was a pilot study created by Dr. Ellen Gehrke in collaboration with the HeartMath Institute.[132] Dr. Gehrke, a professor of international business and management at Alliant International University in San Diego, began working with horses in 1997. Over the years Dr. Gehrke came to realize that her work with horses transferred directly to her work in organizational management, coaching, and leadership training.

Dr. Gehrke's first pilot study, "Horses and Humans Energetics: The study of Heart Rate Variability (HRV) between Horses and Humans," tested heart variability in both the human and horse subjects as they interacted. The study used electrocardiograph (ECG) recorders to track heart variability when horses were resting, moving, interacting with each other, and interacting with humans. The ECG recorders projected increased coherent heart rate variability (HRV) patterns for both the horses and the humans during times of close, calm contact between them and the human participant. HeartMath suggests that coherent HRV patterns are the result of positive emotions and facilitate brain function. These results could be interpreted to suggest that when in the presence of horses, some humans, in specific situations or interactions, may experience a sense of increased brain function and an influx of positive emotional states.

The other fascinating piece of data gathered indicated that horses have diverse emotional states that can be stimulated by interactions with other horses and humans. It was discovered that when horses who were close were separated for even short periods of time, their heart rate variability adjusted to demonstrate stress or "incoherence." Conversely, when the horse was stroked and spoken to with love and kindness, the horse's heart rate variability adjusted into what the data analysts considered to be "coherent," or demonstrating a positive emotional state. Dr. Gehrke suggests, "If I learned one thing from this study, it's to spend more time stroking and petting your horse!" One could hypothesize from the initial results of Dr. Gehrke's research that the manner in which one cares for and treats horses may have a direct impact on their physical, and thus mental, wellbeing. The assumption could be made that horses who live in high stress, or "incoherent" situations may be more apt to develop stress related illnesses, and therefore live less fulfilling lives.

Furthermore, Dr. Gehrke's initial research suggests that when two horses who are close friends are together, their heart rates can move into a state of "entrainment" or, "a state in which two or more of the body's oscillatory systems, such as respiration and heart rhythm patterns, become synchronous and operate at the same frequency". The results from her study demonstrate periods of time when two individual horse's heart rates were synchronized to beat in the same rhythm. HeartMath suggests that the benefit of entrainment is that, "In this mode, the body's systems function with a high degree of efficiency and harmony, and natural regenerative processes are facilitated". This might indicate the benefits of pairing horses together who enjoy each others company, verses pairing horses who are obviously unhappy with each other. In Dr. Gehrke's study, data was gathered on two horses who were not close, but who were not clear adversaries. They discovered that during the 24 hour data collection, the horses never entered into an "entrained" state of being, and yet the two horses who were best friends existed for the majority of the 24 hour period in virtual entrainment.

This pilot study marks the beginning of a new kind of research within the field of EFMH/ES. Although there is great validity in testing instruments such as Rosenburg's Scale for Self-Esteem, the Beck Inventory, the Children's Anger Inventory, Peds Quality of Life, and Self Perception Profile for Children, along with the other assessment tools used to test the psychosocial benefits that may be derived from the horse/human relationship, Dr. Gehrke's research helps move the field into a new era. If we can begin to discover how the human body and the human mind are linked, we may be better able to design more effective treatment methods. Furthermore, if we can isolate markers within the human body that indicate positive or negative emotional states, or psychological well-being, we may be more adapt at understanding the interconnection between physiology and psychology.

Horses and Humans Foundation

In an effort to help support and guide the creation of research projects like Dr. Gehrke's, a non-profit organization called the Horses and Humans Foundation was created. The vision for this organization was that of Molly Sweeney and in 2002 a group of interested individuals met in Prescott, Arizona to begin making her dream a reality. By 2004 that dream had been realized and the Horses and Humans Foundation was officially brought to life. The organization's purpose is to fund research in equine assisted activities (EAA).[133]

The introduction of such an organization is an exciting step for the field of EFMH/ES, and the hope is that many other organizations will be developed to fund diverse research projects that support ethical and efficacy-based practices within EFMH/ES.

Summary

The growth of EFMH/ES has been dynamic and fraught with all of the complexities a new field must experience in order to mature. The field of psychology existed for approximately one hundred years before anyone created a national exam that would test the competency of individuals wishing to do the work professionally. EFMH/ES is young, but has certainly learned from the challenges of other fields which have gone before. We can look objectively at the fields of art therapy, of play therapy, or of psychology as a whole and learn from the journeys they each took to get where they are today.

Ann Alden, 2005-2207 EFMHA president, and Marilyn Sokolof, past EFMHA president, both acknowledge that we are playing catch up to a field that has "taken flight without a flight plan".[134] If this field is to find a sustainable and long-term mode of operation that will firmly lodge the methods of EFMH/ES into the realms of treatment and education, we must slow down and become educated about what it is that we are doing. We must get into the driver's seat and take steps to control the direction of this field. If we allow momentum to carry us, we may find ourselves without a field within the next few years.

Although passionate, interested, and willing, an influx of individuals providing an EFMH/ES method without training specific to the methods, theories, ethical considerations, and legal ramifications of EFMH/ES may be the reason for the increase in accident rates and the corresponding raise in insurance rates for those providing EFMH/ES. If accidents continue to occur, and non-EFMH/ES trained, educated, experienced and supervised people continue to practice, the field may lose validity and come to a crashing halt. We must be willing to obtain proper education and training, even if we already have college degrees or life-long experience with horses. We sit teetering upon the brink of something amazing or devastating; it is up to us to make a decision about which way the scales will tip.

In further sections of this text the reader will come to better understand the field and also be exposed to recommendations in regard to the education and training needed to do this work safely and professionally. There is much for us to do, but excitement and enthusiasm, coupled with ethical decision making and increased education can help to move us successfully into a new decade.

CHAPTER FOUR

HISTORICAL AND CURRENT CONSIDERATIONS FOR THE WORKING HORSE

Within the field of EFMH/ES many speak about the horse and about the "magic" that happens when horses and humans connect. As we learn about the many ways in which horses can be helpful for humans, we must simultaneously question how we can be helpful for horses. With the introduction of EFMH/ES, we have moved into a new paradigm of working with horses. Our notions about the general aspects of horse-person-ship must shift to include the horse as "sentient being".[135] If we are willing to accept that the horse is a sentient being capable of assisting humans move through life with increased awareness, sensitivity, and clarity, we must also be willing to realize that the manner in which horses are treated directly impacts their ability to be present within this work.

Horses who work in EFMH/ES programs are different from horses who work in other disciplines. As facilitators of an EFMH/ES method, our perception of their care, training, and lifestyles must alter to meet the requirements of a new job. No one would question that a roping horse may need to hone talents, skills, and develop musculature different from that of a show jumper. It is much the same with horses working in EFMH/ES programs. As we grow in our understanding of this new and blossoming field, we begin to see our responsibly as stewards of the very horses employed by those within the field. We recognize that working with horses in an EFMH/ES program will look very different than working with horses in a more traditional riding program. We must learn and understand those differences to be able to professionally and ethically provide any of the EFMH/ES methods.

The EFMH/ES Horse

The EFMH/ES horse can be any horse interested and willing in pursuing the career with intention, compassion, love, and clarity. It is important that EFMH/ES professionals learn to put aside the old paradigm of horse training that does not foster the horse's own unique gifts and voice. This may challenge some of the concepts that we as horse people have come to hold as truth.

In order for EFMH/ES horses to do their work, they must feel heard. They need to feel that they are listened to and that the information that they give is taken seriously and utilized. Many horse people will be familiar with the term "shut down", which, when applied to a horse, means that he/she has been trying desperately to communicate his/her thoughts, feelings, emotions, and desires and that no one has listened. When a horse tries this over and over again with the same results, he/she will generally go one of two ways. The horse will either begin to "scream," which will result in violence - kicking, biting, bucking, rearing, or other such "acting out" behaviors, or he/she will shut down. When this happens, he/she will tolerate whatever the human decides to do, and his/her life will slide by with little joy or passion. The EFMH/ES horse must never come to the point where he/she needs to make a decision between those two options. Therefore the EFMH/ES horse person must be well-versed at understanding, as Monty Roberts calls it, "the language of Equus", and must be able to interpret what the horse has to say, therefore validating that the horse's opinions are worthwhile and important. Cherry Hill, in her 2006 book *How to Think Like a Horse,* provides clear and concise information about how humans can begin to interpret a horse's behaviors and actions. She writes,

> You can tell what a horse is thinking by looking at his overall stance, the position of his head and neck, the use of his ears, and the action of his tail and legs. In general you will be able to tell if the horse is fearful, passive, assertive, or aggressive. You will know whether he is welcoming you or telling you to stay out of his space. Once you know the larger, more graphic signals, you will become aware of the subtler precursors to those movements.[136]

She continues, "As you learn to read horses and become a keen observer of their body language, you'll find that often before a big movement, there are lots of little signals." Her book is a must read for any person new to the field desiring to learn more about equine behavior. Her book also helps support the horse in his or her attempts to communicate feelings, attitudes, desires, and emotions.[137]

The EFMH/ES horse must also be a horse who is willing and interested in doing the work of EFMH/ES. Many horses do not fit this mould yet. They are the horses who want to compete, to jump higher, ride the next level of dressage test, chase the cow, or perform other challenging physical feats. They want to race, feel the wind on their faces, hear the crowds roar as they sail across the finish line, complete the course in the shortest amount of time, or bring their rider to some other form of victory. We must be aware of each horse's unique talents and honor them. He or she will show us what it is that they love, we only have to pay attention. An EFMH/ES horse is one who is ready to do the victorious work of helping people, quietly and without applause. This is a horse who may have suffered his or her own trauma, or lived out that dream of competition and is now ready to share his/her gifts in a different way. Sometimes age does factor into the suitability of an EFMH/ES horse, and sometimes it does not. Some young horses are ready for the highs of visible competition, ready to challenge themselves intellectually and physically and others are born with the gift of healing. We must not make judgments about age until we meet and work with the horse. Sometimes the stiff old gelding with cancer is the one who loves the work more than anyone and who brings the most intense healing to his clients. We must be open minded. They will guide us and help us to find what it is that they each desire.

Probably the most important aspect of an EFMH/ES horse is that he/she is one who can transform the energy he/she takes on from his human client and let it go. There does not yet appear to be any scientific reason why some horses are able to do this and others are not. Sometimes it is an issue of overload. The horse is being asked to work with truly ill people and has just taken on too much and needs a break. But other times it is simply that the horse is not capable of transforming the energy which is given to him/her and that horse takes it on and allows it to impact him/her. It is our job as horse caretakers to ensure that we are not asking a horse such as this to do therapeutic work. Sometimes it is only one client or type of client that the horse cannot handle. If this is the case we can be wary of this contradiction and help steer and guide the client away from working closely with that particular horse. Some horses may do wonderfully well in an Equine Facilitated Learning session, but cannot work in an Equine Facilitated Psychotherapy session.[138] Other times the horse's difficulty with a client is due to poor herd management or horse care. The horse is simply overwhelmed by trying to take care of himself/herself and simply does not have the energy to help take care of someone else. These are all important factors that must be taken into consideration when working therapeutically or educationally with horses.

Finally, the EFMH/ES horse must be one who is willing to communicate. He/she must be willing to put himself/herself out there regardless of his/her past successes or failures with human/horse communication. Many times it takes re-training and conditioning before a horse who has been "shut down" will open up. From the experience of this author, one of the most amazing accomplishments of an EFMH/ES facility is to rehabilitate these types of horses. The work of EFMH/ES, done well, appears to be healing for the horses as well as for the humans. We can utilize EFMH/ES to help horses regain the use of their "voice" and learn how to come forward as healthful communicators. However, we need to be careful as to how we integrate such horses into our work. We need to be aware that they might not always be safe for clients, but also recognize at the same time that in many ways it is the bond between the client and the horse that ends up healing them both. We need to have a well-balanced herd with horses who are healthful communicators and who can work with the clients who need that sort of relationship. Having a few horses who are challenged tends to provide a more diverse atmosphere and one that more closely models the lives of our clients. Allow the horses to take the lead -they will always tell the truth and go where they are comfortable going. If we listen, they will guide their own healing process.

Although all of this might look relatively simple on paper - being able to foster a herd of horses who are not shut down, who are receptive to the work, who can clearly and effectively communicate their feelings and thoughts, and who are safe - it is not! Every aspect of the horse's life adds up either to create a healthful and happy EFMH/ES horse, or not. This means that the notion of an EFMH/ES horse is really less important than the notion of the EFMH/ES horse person. It is up to us to create a space and a way of being with horses that fosters the development of the aspects we desire in an EFMH/ES horse. If we humans do not do our jobs properly, the horse will not be as effective as he/she might be. In many ways the creation of such a system is a form of science. There is a way to attain such a space, through proper handling, care, training, and communication and it is reproducible with the same sort of results each time.[139]

We in the field of EFMH/ES need to evolve to better understand the needs of our equine partners. It is they who make the work what it is. Without their equal participation we are not doing EFMH/ES. It is the horse who makes EFMH/ES what it is.

Historical Ramifications of Care, Lifestyle and Horsemanship

Caring for horses is an art, and one that has been in the process of development since humans and horses first came together. In order to gain perspective about horse care we must reach back to learn about its roots.

The first people to ride horses rode bareback with nothing between them and their mounts. Over time the stirrup was invented and was attached to a strap that went around the horse's belly and over a fleece pad that helped prevent chafing of the rider's body against the horse's hair. The stirrup was extremely useful in battle and for ease of mounting and dismounting. From there leather was used to create a saddle-like adornment that was somewhat sturdier than the fleece covering. The saddle was developed as a small and lightweight object to help the rider stay atop his mount, and to give him more power in his legs during warfare. Saddle designs evolved over time and across cultures, but similarities exist in all forms of saddles except for the newly developed Western saddle. All saddles were made so that communication between horse and rider was possible at subtle and minute levels. This was a reality birthed out of need, just as the

Western saddle was also birthed from the need of the humans using it. For time eternal humans counted on their ability to communicate instantaneously with their horses as a means of keeping themselves safe. During warfare it was only the subtlest shift of weight that could mean the difference between life and death. Therefore saddles had to be created to make communications between human and horse as precise as possible.[140] Xenophon's method of horsemanship introduces notions of interconnection between horse and rider, and the vast importance of refined forms of riding. From his treatise on horsemanship comes the fundamentals for all forms of refined contemporary riding as we see it today.[141]

The McCormicks reflect that those offshoots include Latin Dressage, German Dressage, Centered Riding, Hunter-Jumper, and Three Day Eventing. They also comment that some of the same classical principles are used in the western tradition as well.[142] In modern day English riding, the need to be able to communicate directly and instantaneously with one's horse is essential, and is the foundation for any good English rider. Subtlety is highly valued and it is believed that if an observer cannot see the commands that a rider is using to move his or her horse through a series of gaits then perfection has been attained.

The western riding movement originated around the late 1700's out of necessity due to the harsh conditions and lifestyle of the old west.[143] The western tack or equipment as we know it today was inspired largely by the Spanish vaqueros who also spent large periods of time in the saddle. Western riding and tack met the needs of hard-working men and women who spent hours if not days in the saddle chasing cattle, roping cattle, and covering vast amounts of land to do so. The western saddle was developed to be strong

"We are each other's reference point at our turning points."
~Elizabeth Fisbel

76

enough to rope and dally from (use of the horn to secure a rope to for the purpose of gaining increased friction). The tree of the saddle had to be strong enough to support such action, as well as sturdy enough for hours and hours of non-stop riding. The practice of "neck reining" (which is guiding the horse using only one hand) also came from necessity. The cowboy needed the other hand to rope with, and so the horse had to be trained to respond to only one hand. In an article posted by EquestrianMag.com entitled "Horseback Riding: A History of Style" the author stated, "There is little time (in working western riding) for communication between the rider and horse while working in the field. The horse must know what to do without being told. This is one of the major differences between the Western and English riding style."[144]

The care of ranch horses has gone through a transformative journey since the 1700's. In the early days of the old west the horse was honored and respected and treated much like a family member. It was the horse who made life possible. It was the partnership between the horse and the human that allowed for such feats as moving a thousand head of cattle across hundreds of thousands of acres in all weather conditions. Without the horse the west could never have been won. Horses were invited into homes during cold spells. Horses were companions and sometimes the only being a cowboy had to speak to for days or weeks on end. Horses were cared for and given whatever comfort that the owner could afford as he understood that without his horse he would be nowhere. Over time, and specifically with the introduction of the motorized vehicle, this reality dwindled and soon horses became either a tool, a machine to serve a utilitarian purpose, or a conquest – something to master and control. With this shift in thinking came new horrors and abuses. Training processes became vulgar and crude. Violence became an acceptable way of working with horses. Horses lost their role as companions for many and became expendable. Cowboys began using up horses, offering them little in return for the horse's gift of labor and dedication. But even during those dark times there were many who believed in a different way of working with horses. It was that message that people like Tom Dorrance, Monty Roberts, Buck Branaman, Ray Hunt, Linda Tellington-Jones, and Sally Swift took to heart as they brought the wisdom of 400 century B.C. Greek cavalry officer, Xenophon into the modern light.[145]

Lawrence Scanlan in his book *Wild about Horses* introduces his readers to Xenophon and helps demonstrate how this amazing horseman's teachings continue to be useful in today's horse world. Xenophon urged his students never to be aggressive or harsh with their horses. He told them that being clear and firm was most useful and to, "reward him with kindness when he has done what you wish and admonish him when he disobeys". He also reminds us that when our horses are afraid we should lead them slowly and patiently to the object of their fear and, "Show that there is nothing fearful in it, least of all to a courageous horse like him; but if this fails, touch the object yourself that seems so dreadful to him, and lead him up to it with gentleness". He was extremely clear about his feelings regarding the use of a whip. He writes, "Riders who force their horses by use of the whip only increase their fear, for they then associate the pain with the thing that frightens them."[146] The roots of true horsemanship grow from Xenophon's words. Unfortunately some who work with horses have un-learning to do, as that period in time when horses were viewed as machines to do a job with no feelings or emotions left its finger print on many modern-day horse people. Furthermore, many believe that the mechanistic way of dealing with horses is the "cowboy" way, or the "western" way, and try to live up to a past that might not be wholly understood.

When we begin to explore the origins of riding we begin to see that each discipline has a purpose and a use. It is useful as an EFMH/ES practitioner to pair the proper discipline with the proper clientele. For instance, knowing that the Western saddle was developed to handle sturdy use, but not originally designed to foster feel, timing, or subtle communications between horse and rider helps to guide the EFMH/ES professional in a direction when choosing tack for certain types of sessions or clients. Furthermore, we can help to dispel myths around the western riding tradition and the "cowboy way" of horse care. We can begin educating our clients about the history of horsemanship, about the trends that humans have gone through to get to where we are today, and probably most importantly, we can help our clients begin to see the interconnected nature of things. We can use Xenophon and Monty Roberts as perfect examples of two people living in two completely different times who had similar notions about the same thing. We might even begin to believe that horses have been teaching us (those who are willing to listen) how to train them, care for them, work with them, and form relationship with them. No one human has ever created anything completely original. Monty Roberts, Tom Dorrance and other pioneers of "natural horsemanship" did not create something new. They merely listened and brought back a way of doing things that is centuries old, since the beginning of the horse/human relationship.[147]

We as practitioners can help other horse people and in some cases our clients as well, to broaden their perspectives about listening to their horse, and maybe break down some of the barriers between English and western riding. If we can realize that all good riding is based upon one similar set of beliefs that includes healthful care and treatment of horses, balanced riding, patience, kindness, and a non-violent approach to every aspect of horsemanship, we might be better able to lessen tension between disciplines. The horses are trying to tell us a way to be with them. If we can become still enough within ourselves to listen, we may soon be riding and working with them in much the same manner regardless of discipline or style.

Horse care is one of the things still tainted by the unfortunate mechanistic era in the horse/human relationship. Many people's ideas about horse care are either self- serving, meeting the needs of the human rather than the horse, or neglectful, demonstrating that a horse is disposable and can be replaced relatively easily. It is imperative that the EFMH/ES horse receives unbiased care that is the best that it can be. If this means putting aside practices that make the human feel good inside, or on the other hand, putting the needs of the horse before the humans, it must be done. We must move into a new way of being with horses, one that helps us develop our listening skills so that we can hear what the horses want from us.

The Care, Lifestyle, and Training of the EFMH/ES Horse

The basic necessities of horse care refer to how we treat and work with our horses, and our ability to keep them happy, healthy, and comfortable. The horse is a prey species who as Ms. Rector always says, "wakes up in the morning thinking he will be someone's breakfast".[148] In order for a horse to be able to provide the clear, compassionate, and safe communication that we desire of him or her, we must be able to provide a safe and comfortable space for him/her to exist within.

The way in which a horse lives is very important to his/her ability to hold a safe container for the client. If a horse is coming out of a herd environment where he or she is bottom of the pecking order, struggling with food stress, and is physically uncomfortable because he/she did not sleep all night, he/she is probably not going to be able to be present for his/her client. He/she will generally either be short tempered and on edge, and therefore potentially dangerous, or shut down because he/she is sleepy, thinking about food, and not happy.

As we determine what needs to occur for the clients to obtain the maximum benefit from the service, we must deal with issues of safety first and foremost. If the horse who is working in the session is not safe, the experience will change dramatically. Some might say that part of the benefit of working therapeutically with horses is the very fact that they are dangerous.[149] That may be true, but horses are big and have the ability to hurt us even when they are fully aware and present. We do not need the added risk of an unhappy, hungry, and sleepy horse. Our job as facilitators is to keep the clients physically and emotionally safe. Our job as horse people is to do the very same for our horses, therefore decreasing the risk of unneeded accidents. In doing this work, we can step into dangerous and uncharted territory. We need all the help we can get. Having present horses can make the difference between a healthful and beneficial session, and a dangerous one. Even if the horse is not creating a dangerous situation, without the help of the human facilitator the horse may experience burn out. Horses who are invested in this work but who are being placed by their human care-givers in potentially dangerous situations tend to work overtime to ensure that the human client is kept safe. This creates stress and burnout for such horses. They need the help of their human counterparts to create and maintain a safe container for the work to occur within.

This belief system must trickle down into all aspects of horse care. Because we are asking something very different of our EFMH/ES horses, their general care will be different. We are asking that they help to keep other less present and aware beings safe, and we are asking that they communicate an on-going stream of thoughts, feelings, and beliefs to us for the duration of their session. In essence we are asking them to be part of the treatment team, having equal or sometimes even more responsibility then the human counter-parts. However, at the present time, there are no mandatory requirements that state how an EFMH/ES horse should be cared for, treated, or trained. EFMHA has created a set of psycho-social guidelines which are invaluable for any who might be interested in providing this service.[150] Within the content of these psycho-social guidelines, the horse's well being is addressed. However, these guidelines only act as navigational aids, not as laws that govern working horse care. Perhaps some day we will be able to create and enforce a work and living standard for horses employed within an EFMH/ES environment. Until that time arrives all those providing an EFMH/ES service can utilize EFMHA's guidelines and should create their own deeper understanding of how horse care impacts the success of EFMH/ES services. Their horse's training, care, and living standards should be adjusted to match the information thus gained.[151]

Within the field of Animal Assisted Therapy, therapy dogs must go through an extensive training process which qualifies them to work within therapeutic settings. They must past tests that demonstrate their ability to be therapeutic and safe for the clients who work with them.[152] In the field of EFMH/ES there is no field-wide, standardized training or test that trains and certifies horses who work within a mental health or educational environment. Both NARHA and EFMHA have specific guidelines, screening procedures, and schooling recommendations that all NARHA/EFMHA members and accredited centers are responsible for upholding. However, not all providing an EFMH/ES method are NARHA/EFMHA members or work out of a NARHA accredited center. Furthermore, a majority of the recommendations, training and exercise protocol, and screening procedures are orientated more towards therapeutic riding or hippotherapy requirements. The responsibilities of EFMH/ES horses can be vastly different than those of therapeutic riding or hippotherapy horses, and thus they need a different exercise and training regime, and different standards by which assessment is conducted.

Without requirements that go beyond an individual membership organization, virtually any person with a horse could potentially hang up a shingle and begin to provide this service. Clients have only their trust in the facilitator and their own research of the field as a whole to rely upon for their safety. Of course they sign a waiver before they come into contact with the horse stating that they understand horses can be unpredictable and potentially dangerous, that they are willingly engaging in the process. But what does that really mean to a large majority of our clientele? Do they actually understand just how dangerous this work can be if they are paired with an unsafe or non-therapeutic horse or placed in unsafe scenarios by untrained or inexperienced facilitators?

If this field is to gain national and international credibility within the medical and scientific fields, the physical safety of the client must be highly valued and measures must be taken to decrease the potential for physical harm. Without training programs for both the human facilitators of this work, and the horses employed within the field we cannot ethically justify the question many ask: "why horses?" This question relates to the notion that if horses are so "unpredictable" and "potentially dangerous" why are we suggesting that they can be helpful, or healing for humans? How can licensed mental health professionals and doctors who assume the ethical responsibility of protecting their clients from unnecessary harm suggest that an EFMH/ES method be employed as a part of treatment? Many doctors and licensed mental health professionals have determined that the good outweighs the bad, but it is conceivable that with a nationally or internationally recognized training and certification program for horses doing the work of EFMH/ES (and of course the humans as well), a larger majority of medical and mental health professionals might become more comfortable referring their patients to an EFMH/ES program for treatment.

If we look at models offered by seeing eye dog training and certification programs, or Delta's therapy dog training and certification program we could begin crafting something comparable. Of course work with horses is very different than work with dogs, and that the type of training and the expectations of the horses would be very different. However, the horses are the most important aspect of any EFMH/ES method, and therefore should be respected and honored as such.

By suggesting that not just any horse can do this work, we add value and honor to those who can. We also help promote the importance of listening to our horses rather than forcing them into careers that they may not like or be suited for.

"Horses are not like bulls - once a bull has you off his back he will turn and come after you. It seems like he almost enjoys it. A horse is just scared - and wants nothing more to do with you once you are off. He just wants to be as far away from you as possible."
~ Bronc Rider, Livingston, MT

Summary

Our ability to deeply understand our horse counterparts, and their ability to provide a helpful or healing service for clients is what separates EFMH/ES from any other sort of mental health or educational service. It is the horse who makes this EFMH/ES. Without the horse's unique contribution and the facilitator's ability to understand and utilize the information provided EFMH/ES does not exist. It becomes, as Ann Alden, M.A. and 2005-2007 president of EFMHA called it, "equine present" education, learning, or mental health services.[153] It is essential to this work that we understand our horses and that we are capable of evaluating and training such horses to determine which are suited for this work and which would rather be doing something else. To be open and willing to adjust our past notions of horses, horse care, and horse training is also essential if we are to value our horse counterparts and therefore fully gain the gifts that they are offering.

SECTION TWO

THE HEALING NATURE OF HORSES

Five   *The Horse*

Six   *Communication*

Seven   *Relationship*

Eight   *Development of Self through Horse-Person-Ship*

"A horse is a horse of course."- Unknown

Introduction to Section Two

The horse draws us in, evoking archetypal images that harmonize with our very souls. We feel the pull and find ourselves wanting a deeper connection with these majestic creatures. As facilitators of an EFMH/ES method we have three options. We can mystify the process, suggesting that what happens between horses and humans is "magical". We can become such highly attuned and skilled horse-people that

we can understand and explain the actions and behaviors of the horse, thereby making the experience tangible. Or, we can accept both. This means that we are both highly skilled and trained to understand and relay information provided to us by the horse that is grounded in

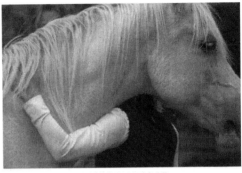

"The horse is God's gift to mankind."
~ Arabian Proverb

simple functionality and physicality of a horse being a horse, but simultaneously we can honor the truly beautiful and magical aspect of the horse's willingness to be in relationship with us. That, in and of itself, is a blessing, a gift given to us by the Divine, by evolution, or by whatever greater source one believes in. That is the magic. That is the mystery.

This section suggests that through understanding the nature of horses we will be able to provide services to clients and students that both de-mystify the horse and offer insight and awareness into the greater mysteries of life. To be respectful of another being generally suggests trying hard to "walk in their shoes," or at the least learn about them enough to understand their cultural origins, maybe speak their language, and show them that you are open to learning. In the field of EFMH/ES we often speak about respect and about honoring the horse. In order to do that fully it is important to do all that we can to understand them- how they function, how they communicate, what they like and do not like, how their bodies work, what feels good, what scares them, and what brings them joy. Through learning the things that are known, the things that can be easily learned and taught, and the things that are not mysteries, it seems like a door is opened into another place, a place where mystery and awe of the workings of our universe emerge.

It is the author's hope that through reading this section individuals will come to recognize why horses do some of the wonderful and amazing things that they do, and will be able to use that information in their work with clients and students of EFMH/ES and through that gain entrance into that place where mystery does exist. Furthermore, the author hopes that the readers will become inspired to learn more, to truly throw themselves into the process of learning HORSES. The very process of getting to know horses deeply is exciting, challenging, and quite possibly healing for the mind, the body, and the soul.

Books abound that detail the quality of the horse's nature as healing or helpful to humans. Monty Roberts, Chris Irwin, the McCormicks, Linda Kohanov, Barbara Rector, Mary Midkiff, Ingrid Soren, and Rebekah F. Witter all have written

"Animals were once, for all of us, teachers. They instructed us in ways of being and perceiving that extended our imaginations, that were models for additional possibilities."
~ Joan McIntyre

compellingly on this subject. Many theses have also been written that help to validate the nature of horses as it is helpful for humans desiring learning, growth, and change. Laura Brinkerhoff, Susan Taylor, Marla G. Kuhn, and this author all have self-published theses that are on file at their respective institutes of higher education, and are available to the public.[154] Hundreds of articles have been written and published in local, national, and international magazines, newspapers, and scholarly journals that portray the nature of horses as being of help to humans in the process of healing, growth, and change. People like Lawence Scanlan, Cherry Hill, Stephan Budiansky, Klaus Ferdinand Hempfling, Mark Rashid, Tom Ainslie and Bonnie Ledbetter, Monty Roberts and many others have further contributed to this field by offering behavioral perspectives about how horses think and communicate.[155]

People can quickly see and accept how the process of learning safe and compassionate horse-person-ship skills could be healthy or healing for humans. The majority of the anecdotal evidence speaks to the reality of this idea, and most of the research current in the field of EFMH/ES addresses the ways in which horse nature can provide healthful experiences for humans.[156]

Through the research of this author, which includes an extensive literature review of books, theses, articles, information collected from interviews, and the personal and professional experience and observations of the author, three overarching themes have emerged that define how the nature of horses may help humans.. These themes are; communication skills development, relational skills, and the development of self through horse-person-ship.[157]

Before we can begin this investigation, we must come to understand a few basic concepts about horses and how they function in order to conceptualize how and why they do what they appear to do for humans. The information about horses provided in the next chapter is limited and rudimentary - however, the purpose of this text is not to detail the physiological, psychological, and behavioral nature of horses. Many other accomplished authors have already laid the groundwork for such knowledge. I suggest that readers explore as many books cited in this text as possible, and seek out training and workshop experiences from experts in the field to better understand the depth and breadth of the concepts introduced here.

CHAPTER FIVE

THE HORSE

Herd Nature

Horses are herd-oriented animals who live closely together in highly organized, and relatively sophisticated family groups. The Merriam-Webster Dictionary defines "herd" as, "a congregation of gregarious wild animals." It defines "gregarious" as, "tending to associate with others of one's kind" or "marked by or indicating a liking for companionship."[158] Horse herds seem to have evolved this way to ensure the survival of their species. They prefer close physical proximity to one another, have created a social hierarchy that mandates protection by one member to another or others, have day-time sleep patterns with watchers set to alert the sleeper to danger, utilize constant movement to keep themselves safe, and have a skeletal system and the musculature that allows them to flee at high speeds for long distances - all to keep themselves alive. These are powerful instincts, honed over thousands of decades. To know and understand these survival skills is to gain a deeper understanding of horse behavior.

Pecking Order

Herd structure necessitates a well-organized and rarely challenged hierarchy called a "pecking order." The herd is run primary by an lead mare and head stallion whose roles are distinctly different and therefore do not promote confusion or conflict between the two in leadership positions. The lead mare guides the herd to food and water and manages any other area of general herd maintenance and health. The head stallion provides protection and patrols the exterior of the herd, keeping the horses moving. Dependant upon the size of the herd he also is responsible for breeding appropriate mares to ensure the reproductive health of the herd. Under the lead mare and head stallion all the other members of the herd fall into order based upon their general nature, temperament, and physiology. The more passive

Horses value close relationships and seem able to sustain them over long periods of time with only a minimum of strife and difficulty.

the horse the lower he or she falls in the pecking order. Young horses and old horses either fall at the very bottom, or have little role within the workings of the herd or the pecking order. The safety and success of the herd depends upon how well the pecking order remains intact and how little actual violence or physical altercations occur between horses vying for shifting positions within the herd.

Bonding

Not only does the instinctual behavior of horses promote group cohesion, but it also promotes interpersonal relationship development. Horses enjoy company and tend to bond fiercely not only with their overall herd, but with one other individual horse in particular. This phenomenon has been called "pair bonding" by many authors of equine behavior and herd dynamics books. Pair bonding describes a close relationship that is formed between two horses. These horses will seek each other out to graze with, stand by, mutually groom, play, or sleep by, one standing guard while the other naps. These pairs tend to feel a deep sense of security and confidence when they are together and appear to completely enjoy each others company. They also seem prone to arguments and occasional disagreements which can lead to a few hours of separation with angry looks exchanged and a general showing of unusual attention paid to a different horse. However, most of the time these disputes are solved within a few hours or a day and soon the two are happily back together once again.

Horse Nature

The very nature of horses seems indicative of their role within our evolving consciousness. They enjoy companionship and relationship, strive to get along rather than fight, are affectionate and enjoy play, and are curious, willing, adaptable, and communicative. They learn from past experiences and remember their past, learning how to do things differently in the future. Horses developed these characteristics because it is these very attributes that allowed them to survive for thousands of years. Although these attributes tend to make them enjoyable animals to spend time with and potentially to learn from, their reasoning is much simpler, it has kept them alive.

Curiosity

As Cherry Hill reminds us, it is curiosity that leads a foal to find his first drink of milk and thus survive.[159] Curiosity allows horses to discover new forage, new sources of water, and better grazing areas. Without curiosity horses might live in perpetual fear of the world, but instead if they are allowed to foster their curiosity, they become interested and inventive. They learn to understand what is *actually* dangerous versus what might just appear scary. This distinction provides a constant source of interest and excitement in life and allows horses to push past unreasonable fear towards a greater likelihood for survival. Horses, if given the chance, will investigate everything and will do so thoroughly and thoughtfully until they feel they understand it. It is through curiosity that horses come to understand their world without the immobilizing fear of what might be.

Stability and Adaptability

Horses desire stability and routine but are willing to adapt to situations as they unfold. Horses have routines that they tend to abide by unless an unusual situation evolves. If this happens they are generally able to adapt and move forward with the new plan. Their ability to adapt provides horses with a greater likelihood for ongoing survival.

Horses eat, sleep, drink, groom, defecate and urinate with some semblance of order and routine. Ms. Hill provides a useful graph that helps us better understand just how adaptable horses are. She explains that in the wild horses eat about 16 hours per day, spend about 5 hours standing at rest, spend 1 hour lying down, and two hours playing or socializing. In a non-wild herd environment she records that horses spend about 12 hours eating, 8 hours standing, 2 hours lying down, and 2 hours playing or socializing. In a stall situation with no herd turn out and three feedings a day a horse may spend 18 hours standing, three hours eating, and 3 hours lying down.[160] Although horses are adaptable, the stalled horse without proper turn out, socialization, or interesting exercise that challenges him/her tends to develop more neurotic habits and bad behaviors, and is less able to exhibit flexibility and adaptability in other situations such as trail riding, pasture turn out, or herd interactions.

Horses survive because of their close interpersonal relationships and the ability to maintain a system of communication and relationship building that promotes relative inter-herd peace vs. interspecies violence.

Communicative

Horses are extremely communicative. Clear communication and role setting that is conducted in a non-violent manner is highly valued, whereas violence, dominance, and aggression are considered dangerous to the overall survival of the herd. There are many ways in which horses communicate. More in depth information regarding equine communication will be presented within the next few chapters. For this section, suffice it to say that it is well within the scope of horse nature to communicate with each other and with other species. The herd structure relies heavily on communication, without which its survival would be unlikely. Horses must develop highly attuned communication skills in order to preserve the pecking order and to retain the success of the herd relationship. Furthermore, without communication skills horses would not be able to develop multi-faceted relationships with one another that can exist over many years. Horses choose a non-violent and communicative approach to problem solving whenever possible and viable.

Mutual Grooming, Play, and Leisure

Horses enjoy spending time with each other in play, in grooming, or in simply being close to one another. They seek out the horse with whom they are pair bonded and offer nibbles along the withers, neck, and back. The other horse will generally reciprocate, nibbling and scratching back. When finished with that activity they will tend to stand nose to tail with one another so that each can swish the flies away from the other's face. Horses enjoy touch and tend to seek it out whenever possible. However, they are also opinionated about the type of touch they receive, and will not be interested or engaged if the human attempts to touch them in an uncomfortable way such as slapping at them or tickling them.

If the mood inspires them they will engage in "horse play," frolicking about the pasture or field, nipping at each others faces and flanks or play kicking, bucking, or rearing. They will run around, one chasing the other, stopping occasionally to nip at each other until one of them runs off again. This activity can go on for an hour or more until the horses get tired of the game and go back to grazing or napping. Sometimes pairs will play multiple times a day, engaging each other in rousting activity to be followed by rest and eating. It is clear to see in observing pair bonding that they are not attempting to hurt each other and will go to great lengths to avoid causing the other pain or physical injury.

Learners

Horses tend to learn by association which is the natural ability to link a stimulus to a response. The horse is able to make connections or associations between a diverse and complex array of information. This allows horses to learn a great number of tasks, verbal commands, and body delivered commands. The second way in which horses generally learn is through habituation, or a repeated exposure to stimulus. Stephan Budiansky reminds us, however, that horses who survive in the wild are those who can recognize the difference between the "crashing noise heard in the underbrush" versus "the leaf rustling in the wind" and make decisions about which to spook away from and which to ignore.[161]

Since horses are naturally sensitive, they can respond almost immediately to the cues that their rider provides for them. They are also naturally cooperative and willing (unless soured by another human) and are interested in obtaining positive validation for their actions. They like touch, as we learned earlier, and will work for positive touch, verbally comforting exchanges, or other forms of affection. Since they are also naturally curious, they tend to be engaged and interested in the process of new learning. It has been said that a horse's memory is "second only to an elephant." thereby suggesting that horses may be able to remember information received from years ago. This can be both a blessing and a curse, as a horse with a bad learning experience may be less inclined to attempt a similar task for fear of a similar reaction. However, memory also encourages relationship development and allows for horses to retain information gained from horse to horse interactions as well as from human to horse interactions.

Horse Physiology

Smell

Horses are extremely sensitive to odors and react strongly to unusual, frightening, or pleasant odors. Horses commonly utilize the vomeronasal organ, also called Jacobson's organ, which is a chemoreceptor, or sense organ that responds to chemical stimuli such as that of certain pheromones. This organ is located in the in the roof of the mouth close to the vomer and nasal bones. Horses utilize their Jacobson's organ regularly to identify the physiological state of other animals, how long ago the animal passed by, or if a mare is in estrus. Fascinatingly enough, Lyall Watson speaks of the human use of the Jacobson's organ in his book, *Jacobson's Organ*. He suggests that humans and other animals can smell the physiological changes that occur within the body when powerful emotions are present, when physical aliment exists, or when mental illness is present.[162] In the work of EFMH/ES, horses will many times peel back their upper lip in the common "Flehman

Response" when they come into contact with an individual who smells differently because of strong emotion or physical or mental illness.)

Hearing

Horses have thirteen muscles in each of their ears, allowing their ears to pivot nearly 180 degrees around in both directions. Horses can hear better than humans can in numerous ways. They are able to hear at higher frequencies and are able to hear sounds from greater distances than humans can. The very survival of a horse (in the wild) depends upon his or her ability to hear at great lengths and react accordingly. Therefore, their ability and desire to listen is deeply rooted in their very survival. Through their natural ability to hear and their interest in listening, horses help humans learn to hone their own abilities in both of these areas. Horses also enjoy lower and more soothing tones of voice rather than yelling or harsh tones. They respond more favorably to such tones and therefore help encourage the people working with them to speak more softly, kindly, and gently. The soft spoken but rough and ready cowboy comes to mind. Those who work with horses for their vocation learn quickly what works and what does not. Ms. Hill reminds us, "The soothing tones calm the horse. Hence the term 'horse whisper'".[163]

Vision

Horses see with monocular vision. This sort of vision increases the field of view, but decreases the depth perception. Animals with monocular vision can see two objects at once, but have limited forward or binocular vision. Thus, the horse must lower or raise his head or turn it to one side or the other in order to see an object in front of him clearly. Due to the horse's vision patterns, he has blind spots that must always be considered. Both directly in front of him and directly behind him the horse cannot see the approaching human or animal. Therefore he may shy away or become uncomfortable with someone or something in that area. The eye of the horse is designed to see and perceive things at great distances and to provide information regarding things that might lurk in the shadows off to the sides. The way in which a horse sees helps to remind the humans who interact and work around horses to stay focused and present in their bodies. If a human becomes unfocused or distracted and moves suddenly into and out of a horse's blind spot, the horse may react unfavorably. Anyone working around horses soon realizes that in order to be safe, the horse must know where the human is at all times, and therefore, the human must be aware of where he or she is in time and space.

Touch

Horses enjoy touch and seek it out in many different ways. Within herd life, horses engage in physical contact which can include rubbing or scratching against other horses or objects and rolling repeatedly to help remove unneeded hair or scratch itchy areas of their bodies. Due to their tactile nature, horses provide humans with potentially more healthful models for how touch can be pleasant, useful, and enjoyable without being too intimate or personal. Many horses actively seek physical contact with their human counterparts, and show obvious signs of enjoyment when touched appropriately. Horses are also very sensitive to how touch is administered, and dislike certain types of touch. Horses tend to communicate clearly when touch is uncomfortable or done incorrectly, such as if people try to pat, slap, or tickle them. Touch can be a powerful way to connect or bond with horses - just as it is with humans.

Summary

Understanding the concepts presented in this chapter is necessary for those interested in pursuing the work of EFMH/ES. We need to understand both how the horse reacts to humans, and how he/she perceives the world around him/her. Without this knowledge is it virtually impossible to determine what occurs between humans and horses and it is difficult to respectfully partner with a horse if one does not understand their basic functioning principles. It is the hope of this author that anyone reading this text will choose to read many other books written on the subject of equine physiology, psychology, and behavior, and seek to personally experience horses in a hands-on and tangible manner. Only through personal connection with horses does deep awareness and understanding occur.

CHAPTER SIX

COMMUNICATION

"That we know so little about this potentially complex system of communication in horses is testimony to our own sensory ineptness." - Stephan Budiansky

Introduction and Overview of Equine Communication

It is important to understand a few critical aspects of equine communication before we delve into how that communication style can be of help to humans. We need to know the way in which each of our horses think, what their "baseline" behaviors are, and how they normally respond in a variety of situations. We must know how to read their body language, their subtle cues, and be willing to interpret those signs and signals for our clients. We should be able to bring the lessons learned from interacting with horses into our modern world in a way other humans can understand and appreciate. If we do not understand equine communication, we cannot do this. We can only guess or make up things based on what we think the horse might be saying, or allow the client to interpret without intervention, guidance, or a conceptual framework.

One of the best ways to learn equine communication is to spend long hours with horses. Both observation and education offer us tools to decipher their language. Reading horse books, learning from horse people who know and intuitively understand horses, and being willing to listen to our horses without preconceived ideas about outcome are additional ways to gain needed information about how horses communicate.

Communication is defined by Merriam-Webster's Dictionary as, "a process by which information is exchanged between individuals through a common system of symbols, signs, or behavior."[164] Horses have their own unique process through which they impart information. They utilize the same process or method of communication regardless of whether they are attempting to communicate within their species or outside of their species. Equine communication appears to move through a series of four distinct levels.[165]

The first level involves the horse's ability to perceive or set a clear intention that will be followed by physical action. In the second level of communication, minimal sensory information is received by the thalamus region of the horse's brain. This information passes through the thalamus and is processed, thereby resulting in a visible action or reaction. The third level of communication is the demonstration of that visible action or reaction. It is at this level that the average human will begin to perceive the communication. The forth and final level of equine communication generally results in violent physical action or reaction. It is at this level that the average human will react or respond to the horse's communication attempts.

Understanding these levels and being able to respond appropriately is not only essential for keeping humans safe, but also for the successful and masterful facilitation of EFMH/ES.

Equine Vocal Communication

During any of the four stages of equine communication horses may utilize their "voice" to communicate information and feelings vocally.[166] The majority of a horse's communication is non-vocal in nature, but they still have a voice and do use it. The various intonations of their voice have different meanings, and as with their ears, can have vastly different meanings between horses and instances. The area of vocal communication between species is fascinating in and of itself. Alan Beck and Aaron Katcher report in their book *Between Pets and People* that dogs can understand approximately 130 human words and respond accordingly.[167] No such study has been done with horses, but suffice to say that horses also have the capability to understand some amount of human language. If it is possible for animals to understand us, then it must be possible for us to understand them, and furthermore, for communication to exist between us. Horses use their voices both to other horses and to us. They nicker when we come near and when they are feeling affectionate. They nicker to each other, seemingly questioning how the other is doing. They call loudly across the pasture when we drive into the stable. They call to each other. They scream when hurt, unhappy, or in the midst of battle. Male horses use a throaty nicker when trying to impress the mares and the mares may respond back with a squeal. They snort when they see something that frightens them, or just when the weather cools and they feel the excitement of change. Their voices are multi-faceted and differ from horse to horse and situation to situation.

Many humans are the most fascinated by the horse's vocal communications and wish to understand what they are trying to say. Those of us who are verbal learners can relate the best to verbal or vocal expressions even in other species. Therefore, as an EFMH/ES facilitator it is important to know and understand each horse's unique vocal communications, and be able to help clients understand and decipher what it is that the horses might be saying.

This basic overview of equine communication will be of benefit as the reader continues on to learn more specifically how equine communication may be of help to humans.

Level One – Intention
The first level of equine communication occurs when a horse either sets an intention, or perceives another horse's intention. Merriam-Webster defines intention as, "a determination to act in a certain way".[168] While the manner in which horses seem able to set or perceive intentions or "think in pictures" to communicate is not clearly defined scientifically, it may be that the presence of mirror neurons in the equine brain could explain the phenomenon. Imagine what it would be like to have cognition without the spoken language. Imagine being able to understand each other through the subtlest of non-vocal communications

"Smell remembers and tells the future... Smell is home or loneliness. Confidence or betrayal.
– Charrie Morage

and send complex messages to each other without the spoken language.

Dr. Temple Grandin, author of *Thinking in Pictures,* believes that animals do "think in pictures", a way of perceiving or sending intentions which relies heavily on the animals predisposed ability to sense images or create images within their minds. Dr. Grandin proposed this concept in 1995 when she compared her own visual process as a woman with autism, to that of the cattle she worked with. She states, "My experience suggests that these animals think in discrete visual images".[169] In 1997 Dr. Grandin wrote an article entitled "Thinking the Way Animals Do" for Western Horseman magazine. In this article she suggests that her form of thinking, which relies almost solely on visual imagery, mimics the way in which animals think. She writes, "I have found that really good animal trainers will see more detailed pictures. It is clear to me that visual thinking skills are essential to horse training." She goes on to write that "People with autism and animals both think by making visual associations". Her work suggests that horses function better when they are able to sense or perceive the humans intentions, and that the manner in which they best perceive such information is aided by visual imagery on the part of the human.[170]

Willis and Sharon Lamm of KBR Horse Training explain the art of communicating to one's horse. According to the Lamms', communicating with horses also involves an interactive process. Mr. Lamm writes that "horses think in pictures (images). Thus when I am trying to work through a problem I break it down into mental pictures and I have much better success." He goes on to suggest that setting an intention that includes a tangible image, created within the mind, appears to help horses and humans during the training process. He says,

> In summation, I'm not here to suggest that this is telepathy at work. Maybe it's just that through imaging we get better perspective as to how our horses view things and it generates some subtle but important changes in our approaches and mannerisms. Perhaps we feel (or appear) less tense and more thoughtful and that makes our horses more comfortable.

Maybe it's a little bit of all of the above. All that really matters to the horses and to those of us who try imagining is that it works.[171]

Although there is no scientific evidence that proves that horses have the mental capacity to create intentions or utilize visual imagery to project or receive intentions, many who have been with horses long enough have altered their training techniques to include setting intention through visualization. Monty Roberts and Buck Brannaman are two well known examples of horseman who believe that sending images to your horse creates an outcome.[172]

Monty Roberts brings up the notion of the horse's predisposition to think in images in *Horse Sense for People*, "the autistic, like the horse, thinks spatially, or in pictures". During his Join-Up clinics Mr. Roberts utilizes imaging to help guide the horse through a series of movements that eventually demonstrate that Mr. Roberts is in fact speaking the language of Equus.[173]

Barbara Rector teaches people through her Adventures in Awareness program to create an image of what they want the horse to do, not what they *do not* want the horse to do. She suggests, "horses do not think in the negative." She believes in the power of setting an intention of what you would like to see occur, and then creating a mental image of that event.[174]

During an adjudicated youth group facilitated by The Esperanza Center, a young Native American man shared his experience.

> One day I was working with Suzy Q [the horse]. I had her tied up and was brushing her. I went to pick out her foot and she stepped on me. I wanted to knock the shit out of her, but I didn't. Leif came up and asked me what was wrong. I told her that her horse just broke my toes. (Authors note: Esperanza staff examined his foot and determined that his toes were not broken or otherwise injured.) She asked me what I had been thinking. I said that I was thinking real hard about not wanting my foot to get stepped on. I told her I was thinking about how my foot was so close to Suzy's and that she could

just pull her foot out of my hand and set it down right on my foot. Then Leif made me clean the other foot, but she told me to think only about what I wanted to happen. I did. I thought about Suzy Q just picking up her foot like I wanted her to. She did and I felt more safe. I never got stepped on again.[175]

This experience demonstrates Ms. Rector's belief that when we think in pictures out of fear or anticipation, we may be sending an image or intention to our horses that we did not mean to communicate. Take for example the young man in the example above. He pictured Suzy Q stepping on his foot. Suzy, although confused as to why he might want such a thing to occur, obliged. However, when he changed the image in his mind to match his actual intention, Suzy Q held her foot up and allowed him to clean out the manure and dirt without incident.

For humans, the benefit of learning how to set an intention and support that intention with a mental image not only allows us to further our relationship development with horses and other animals, but it also helps us to create intention and congruent messages that will increase our ability to be assertive in a healthful manner.

Level Two – Minimal Sensory Information
The second level of communication that horses appear to utilize involves sensory information that is decoded and processed by the thalamus region of a horse's brain.[176] Interestingly, humans may find it difficult to process sensory information that occurs below the level of the cerebral cortex - however, horses appear able to process and utilize such information. Therefore, when humans witness either other humans or other species who can process and react to minimal sensory information, misconceptions may occur. One such common misconception is demonstrated by the story of Clever Hans.[177]

Clever Hans was a horse owned and trained by Wilhelm von Osten, a schoolmaster from Berlin. Von Osten believed that Hans was able to read minds and use that unusual talent to answer questions asked by Von Osten correctly. He touted his horse's unique abilities and eventually the Prussian Academy of Science created a commission to research the story. The commission from the Prussian Academy of Science determined that Hans' unique ability had nothing to do with mind reading, as Von Osten had believed, but instead they were able to prove something even more amazing and although they probably had no idea at the time, far more impactful. The commission proved that in fact Hans perceived the slightest change in Von Osten's body posture and anxiety level that cued Hans to recognize what the correct answer was. Von Osten would tense as the horse began to respond and relax when he got to the correct answer. Hans used this miniscule communication upon which to base his own actions. The communication between Von Osten and Hans was totally imperceptible to the outward eye of the observers, and was only discovered through testing and research.

Although the commission was able to prove that Hans was not performing a feat of supernatural ability, they effectively proved something far more interesting. This discovery clearly demonstrated that "mind reading" is as simple and as commonplace as being able to read subtle non-verbal or vocal cues and be perceptive enough to gauge human emotions as a communication tool. It also provided a link between species. If Hans is able to understand the non-verbal/vocal cues of Von Osten, what is to say that Von Osten could not also understand the cues of Hans, therefore making interspecies communication a reality? If we can reclaim that which our mammalian brains have buried deep, if we can recognize that minimal sensory information does in fact provide us with recognizable and decipherable material, we may hold one of the secrets to human evolution.

Biologist and author Dr. Lyall Watson speaks to this notion in his book *Dreams of Dragons*.[178] He introduces a race of early humans known to science as Boskopoids. These were a curious people with a cranial capacity 30 times larger than ours. Watson calls these interesting little creatures Strandloopers, Afrikaans for "beach walkers." He proposes that their childlike qualities and lack of interest in a mechanized society proved to be their downfall. They were unable to succeed by biological standards. Success in biological terms indicates continued survival, and the Strandloopers were unable or unwilling to live by those terms. Watson proposes that they were a people who lived almost entirely within the context of their huge brains. He suggests that they probably utilized the majority of their brain capacity, developing unknown (to us) talents and skills. However, due to the time spent in the far reaches of the brain and intellect, they did not fall into the creation of a material culture. He suggests that we of the American culture place more value on technology than we do on intellect, and therefore only develop portions of our brains that help in this advancement. Due to this tendency, we also frequently look down on other species or cultures who do not place value on the same things as we do. Take for example the recent research done with whales and dolphins that demonstrates our underestimation of their brain function and intellect. Research suggests that both of these creatures could meet or even exceed our own intellectual capabilities. When a species does not spend the majority of its time, energy, and brain power concentrating upon manipulation and technical advancement, what other characteristics could evolve? Watson asks that we bring this question into our consciousness. He furthermore suggests that if we were to change our perspective we could utilize our talents to develop sensitivity, awareness, and raise our consciousness in profound ways that would better our world for all beings living within it.

We have come to a time in our world where people like Edward O. Wilson cry out for sanity, for help.[179] Biodiversity on the planet is suffering so greatly that by the end of this decade Wilson predicts that we will have lost one half of the species that once existed on the earth. He reminds us that because of our human impact, the balance of the natural world has been disrupted. Before humans the rate of species extinction almost exactly mirrored the rate that new species came into existence, therefore the world continued to function in balance. However, now with human impact we are destroying the very habitat where these new species are able to come into being, causing the world to slip into a state of disequilibrium, life out-of-balance. Wilson reminds us that placing our emphasis upon the material acquisition of "things" may indeed be our downfall as a race. We must stop and remember the Strandloopers. Our evolution as a species may not be one of technological advances beyond our current imagination. Rather, it may be in our decision to explore the realms of our intellect, to push the boundaries of our minds, or to heighten our awareness so that we can hear the call of the universe, pleading with us to stop the devastation.

Horses, dolphins, and whales could be modern "Strandloopers," beings who explore the reaches of the mind each day through their very existence. However, horses, dolphins and whales live in harmony with the changing times. They adapt and adjust in ways that the Strandloopers might not have been able or willing to do. Horses may be in a unique position to help humans evolve. They helped humans move into the mechanized world though their willingness to become domesticated, and they certainly seem to have the ability to help us hone our non-verbal communication skills, our sense of awareness, and re-kindle our sensitivity. They help us realize that interspecies communication is possible, and therefore may help us to listen to the voice of the natural world calling out for stewardship and protection.

Through the subtlest of non-verbal/vocal communications horses speak to each other and to us. If we are observant we can become aware of minimal sensory information, and respond accordingly, therefore validating for the horses that we can understand them.

Horses can sense through the smallest of actions, body posture, smells, and tones of voice how the approaching human is doing emotionally and physically. They respond accordingly, either inviting the human into their space, or using cues to suggest that they are uncomfortable with that human in their space in the current mood or state that he or she might be in at the time. When riding a horse, the smallest movement of the head can cue the horse to turn directions or stop. Locked hips will change a horse's pace and sometimes influence their gait. Tension or anxiety within the rider will produce a physical response within the horse. Whether the human realizes it or not every single moment he or she is in the presence of horses, communications abound. Everything that the human does and thinks, and every emotion that the human comes to the session with is taken in by the horse, assessed, and utilized. Although many people might think this level of sensitivity is a form of "magic," thanks to Hans, Von Osten, and the Prussian Academy of Science we now know better. We realize that in fact it is the horse's innate ability to understand, perceive, and respond to the subtlest forms of non-verbal/vocal communication that occurs both within and between species. We are quite literally having a conversation with our horses, but currently it is generally only the horse who realizes this.

Level Three – Observable Non-Vocal Communications

The third level of equine communication is more observable and is generally the first level that humans notice when working with horses. This is the level where non-vocal communication becomes visible to the outward eye. This level deals with the twitch of an ear, the swish of a tail, or the crinkle of a nose. Horses will do everything in their power to avoid physical displays of violence. Budiansky reports that horses are not violent by nature, and do not enjoy or seek to engage in physical violence; rather they use elaborate techniques such as "bluffing," and establishing pecking order to avoid using violence. Budiansky writes that "although it may not seem obvious to anyone who has watched horses shoving, biting, kicking, and squealing at one another, the establishment of a dominance pecking order among horses is actually a way to avoid violence".[180] Although actual fighting may occur when a new horse is introduced to a herd, once the pecking order has been re-established, acts of violence are rare. The head stallion and alpha mare utilize non-vocal communication skills to keep the pecking order intact and to ensure that no one vies for their position. Budiansky describes the various ways in which horses use non-verbal signs and acts to communicate their intentions, such as the lowering of the ears, the stretching of the neck and head, or the swishing of the tail. He suggests that these actions are actually the manifestations of bluffing and are used to help avoid physical confrontation. He also notes that "bluffing" will only work for a certain period of time before the horse has to actually engage in a physical altercation to back up his or her bluff.[181]

For humans, this type of communication can seem almost imperceptible and it is often hard to discern what act means what. It is only after careful and continual observation of a herd that meaning can be derived from these actions. In other words, when is the swish of a tail a warning to another horse or human, and when is it brushing off flies? It is important that an EFMH/ES facilitator knows his or her herd well enough to recognize these subtle differences. That knowledge can keep a client safe or can be used to invoke deeper meaning within a session.

The swish of a tail can provide needed assessment of a client's case, and if the EFMH/ES facilitator does not know the difference between a fly and an emotion, the client's physical safety may be jeopardized.[182]

Ears

The twitch of an ear has multiple meanings all of which can provide valuable feedback for clients and for facilitators. A horse's ear is home to thirteen different muscles and is a virtual cornucopia of information. There are four basic positions that horses place their ears in depending upon the message they are trying to convey. Of course besides those four positions there are literally hundreds of variations for each of those positions depending upon the individual horse. However, understanding the four basic positions will help clients to better understand the way in which they are impacting their horse partners.

Attentive: Both Ears Forward

When the horse moves both ears forward this indicates attentiveness, excitement, or wariness. When the horse's ears are in the forward position it is time for the human to pay attention as well. What is the horse seeing or looking towards? Is there something in the bushes that the rider or person working with the horse needs to attend to? Or, is it the active imagination of the horse that is at work? If this is the case perhaps the rider simply needs to help ground and calm the horse, encouraging him or her to explore the object further. Maybe the horse is just looking at the human as he/she moves across the field, approaching with a halter. Whatever the case may be, when the horse's ears go forward, the underlying message to the human is "pay attention."

Listening: Ears Cocked

When horses listen they tend to cock one ear backwards and one ear forwards. When the ears are in this position the horse is generally attending to what the rider or person working with them is doing, saying, thinking, or acting like. This ear position is a good sign; one to bring to the attention of the client and one that can open interesting conversations. Ask what it is that the horse is listening to within the client and see what answers are received. In a horse training or schooling session the cocked ear indicates that the rider and the horse are connecting, and that the horse is listening to what is being asked of him/her.

At Rest: Floppy

When both ears are "floppy" or off to the sides it generally indicates a horse at rest. Notice when horses are napping, their ears hang sideways; the most restful position for the equine ear to be in. However, this is the easiest position to confuse because many horses use "floppy" in different ways. They can use "floppy" to convey listening to something behind them. Floppy can also be a precursor to both ears flat back, and it can even sometimes precede a spook, or jumping away from something behind them. However, if the human knows his or her horses well enough, he/she will be able to discern the many meanings of floppy.

Upset: Ears Pinned Back

Finally when both ears are pinned flat back against the horse's head, it mean WATCH OUT! This ear position indicates anger, unhappiness, or general dis-pleasure. This is a very important position to be highly aware of. If the client is working hands on with a horse and the horse's ears go back, it is important to teach the client self-preservation methods and ask that she step away from the horse. At this point in time, from a safe distance and vantage point the EFMH/ES professional can ask the client to survey the situation. What made the horse's ears go back? Was it another horse bothering her over the fence? Was it something the client did physically to the horse that evoked the reaction? If so, what was it? Is there an injury or wound in that area that the horse might have been reacting to? Or is it something that the client was thinking, feeling, or otherwise communicating to the horse that met with her dis-pleasure? If so, what was that thought, feeling, or other form of communication and how can it be more healthfully worked through? Whichever way the facilitator goes with this clear equine communication, it is important that clients know how to protect themselves in that moment. Make sure that the client moves to a safe distance before processing the experience and figuring out what might have happened.

Hooves

The cocking of a hoof is another clear communication device that if properly understood can keep humans safer around horses. Full-grown adult horses weigh on average between 900-1200 pounds. They carry that weight on four relatively spindly legs, and sometimes those legs need a bit of a rest. Horses will rest their weight on three feet (two fronts and a hind) and switch the hind regularly while at rest. Horses will also lift their hind legs and extend them into a stretch to relieve tension or constrictions in their legs. Neither of these motions should concern the client. However, the actual cocking of a hind leg as a warning sign should be of concern to the client. When a horse cocks his/her leg as a warning, his/her ears will be pinned back and his/her tail will be swishing, therefore informing those nearby that something is wrong. If the client can understand the difference between resting and cocking, he/she will be able to notice the warning cock and remove himself/herself to a safe location well out of harms way. Horses may also stomp their feet. This action generally indicates that they have flies on their legs which are bothering them. It is useful to inform clients of this potential and also utilize fly spray prior to a session to help alleviate the need to stomp. Finally, horses can use their front legs and hooves to strike at other horses. This might occur when two horses meet for the first time or when a male and female horse see each other when the female is in "heat." It is important to be aware of this tendency, and either intervene before the client is placed in a situation when such action may occur, or teach the client how to stand well out of the way if the horse were to be placed in a situation where striking was likely.

Tail

The tail swish is another important non-vocal communication device horses use in a number of ways. A clenched tail can demonstrate nervousness or anxiety. A tail held high can indicate excitement. A tail swishing coupled with a cocked hoof and pinned ears is a fairly reliable sign of an upset or angry horse. A tail swishing with ears at rest, forward, or listening on a warm day generally indicates that the horse wishes to dissuade flies from landing on his/her body. Finally, a tail hanging comfortably can indicate a relaxed horse.

Level Four – The Scream

Finally, if all of the other forms of communication at a horse's disposal do not work, or do not convey the message that they are trying to get across, they may resort to actual violence. Once a horse has reached that level, the humans around him should take notice. This is not a normal act, and one that came into being because of a lack of listening skills from those around him. It is as if equine communication begins with an intention, moves to the faintest whisper, and then ascends to a clearly spoken voice, and if those three levels do not get the message across, ends in a scream. Horses who bite, kick, buck, rear, or otherwise engage in violent acts are horses who have to scream to be heard. The humans in those horses' lives need to evaluate their listening skills and hone in on the message that the horse is trying to communicate. Within a horse herd, the horses who revert to these behaviors with other horses are probably somewhat mal-adapted creatures who were not raised in a herd environment or around other horses who could help them develop their communication skills. Many times these are horses who wish to challenge the horses higher on the pecking order, but are not skilled enough in the subtleties of equine communication to get the desired response.

It is within the horse/human relationship where "screaming" becomes a problem, and one that should be heard and immediately responded to. If a horse has to go to that level to make his point clear, there is a problem. Subtlety has ceased to work, and the horse has decided not to give up and settle into quite dissatisfaction. Within the field of EFMH/ES the desire to be heard is, in fact, an admirable trait for a horse and one that is indicative of an amazing therapy horse, if he or she is given the right treatment by humans who are willing to listen.

When a horse has reached the fourth level of communication, accidents happen. People get hurt. Other horses get hurt. It is an unsafe and un-supportive environment to be in, and one that is wholly un-therapeutic. All functioning needs to cease until the problem is sorted out and the horses feel heard and respected.

As Budiansky states, equine communication is complex and truly amazing. To learn how to communicate with horses is healing in and of itself. They guide us on a journey of non-violence, cooperation, honesty, and truth. They ask that we become congruent and whole in our thoughts, and that we bring to the forefront that which is real and true.[183]

Violence

In many cases behaviors which could be referred to as "violent" in nature will be aimed at another horse. It important to note that the word "violent" is used within the context of this text as it is defined by Merriam-Webster's Dictionary as "marked by extreme force or sudden intense activity",[184] and does not reflect a value-laden meaning. Possibly the warning was meant for another horse who was tied too closely or who was passing by too closely. The ears go back but the other horse does not respond, either because he or she cannot due to human restrictions, or because of a dominance battle brewing. If the other horse does not move away with the simple twitch of an ear or swish of a tail, the cocked hoof and possible warning kick normally does the job. These are again non-violent acts used as bluffing techniques to maintain or establish dominance. However, if the client does not understand these communications, he/she might end up a casualty of a non-violent act. For instance, if he/she happens to be moving behind the horse just at the moment that the horse gives the warning kick, he/she could end up getting kicked himself/herself. Generally such an injury would be minor, but for a client who might have fear issues that experience could be counter productive to the educational or therapeutic session. Furthermore, it could have been avoided by facilitation and education. Horses usually do not do anything violent without multiple warnings of a non-violent nature.

Instinctual Communications

All animals other than industrialized humans function primarily from instinct. Merriam-Webster's Dictionary defines instinct as "a largely inheritable and unalterable tendency by an organism to make a complex and specific response to environmental stimuli without involving reason and for the purpose of removing somatic tension". It also offers as a definition of instinctual, "behavior that is mediated by reactions below the consciousness level".[185] We are hard-wired to behave and react in certain ways germane to our species, and adapted to circumstances. Therefore, our ability for cognition during moments of instinctual response is fairly limited. We act because the very physicality of our being is instructing us to do so. Horses, like all other animals rely upon instinct to guide their actions, behaviors, and decisions. They live by a well-ordered code of conduct that incorporates all aspects of their instinctive nature.

Instinct and the Spoken Language

As we humans have evolved and grown farther away from our animalistic selves we now live in a world so filled with choices that must be made using our cognitive abilities that many of us find ourselves in a constant state of confusion. This confusion may atrophy our ability to decide anything. We become trapped within our freedom. We must think before each action we take, and generally there is someone there asking us why we made the decisions that we made, questioning our "reasoning," and wondering if we "thought it through." They want us to explain our behaviors and our actions using words that they too can understand. Simply knowing that we might have to explain ourselves sometimes stops us from ever doing the very thing that we want to do the most.

Albert Einstein once said, "The words or language, as they are written or spoken, do not seem to play any role in my mechanism of thought."[186] Arthur Koestler stated, "Language can become a screen which stands between the thinker and reality. This is the reason why true creativity often starts where language ends."[187] To put feelings, desires, dreams, and sometimes even simply actions into words can be paralyzing and can make the speaker think that he or she cannot convey the message in a way that anyone else will understand or accept. When working with horses, we do not have to put these feelings, decisions, actions or thoughts into words. We can simply allow our instinct to lead us and the horses will accept our decision without question. To be free from having to explain ourselves even if it is just for a few hours each week can be liberating and can remind us that there are other ways to be. Barbara Rector reminds us, "Such freedom to be in the moment evokes intuition - internal guidance allowing for the expression of a High Self."[188]

Instinct and Safety

Many times we want to act or behave in a certain way with no particular reason for that desire. We might meet someone who seems perfectly nice, but we feel anxious, tense or even afraid when in his/her presence. If we listen to that feeling, we may decide not to spend more time in the presence of that individual. When asked why we behaved the way we did, coming up with an answer can be very difficult because, if the truth be known, we acted on instinct and there is no language for our reason.

We are still animals, and we still have instincts and as Barbara Rector reminds us, "horses facilitate awareness of our own instinctual nature and its influence on our thoughts, behaviors, and feelings".[189] If we can learn to listen to our instinctual urges, we may be able to keep ourselves healthier and safer. Our human instinct tells us when others are dangerous, what we need to eat and when we need to eat it. We may be able to pick up on storm patterns and know when to leave a place that might be in danger of earthquake or other natural disaster.[190] However, many of us are so disconnected that it is challenging to recognize and respond to our instinctual, or intuitive promptings.

Instinct and Evolution

Biologists have suggested that as we evolve so do our instincts. Rupert Sheldrake's work on morphic fields would support this notion.

> Morphic fields, like the known fields of physics, are non-material regions of influence extending in space and continuing in time. They are localized within and around the systems they organize. When any particular organized system ceases to exist as when an atom splits, a snowflake melts, an animal dies, its organizing field disappears from that place. But in another sense, morphic fields do not disappear: they are potential organizing patterns of influence, and can appear again physically in other times and places, wherever and whenever the physical conditions are appropriate. When they do so they contain within themselves a memory of their previous physical existences.[191]

He continues, "Like the organisms they shape, these fields evolve. They have a history and contain an inherent memory." He states,

"It should be possible to observe the progressive establishment of new habits as they spread within a species."[192] For our purposes, this validates the notion that new habits or instincts can come into being over time. Therefore, can we as humans become aware of our own evolutionary process? Do we know what changes have occurred within our very "hard-wiring" to make us act and react in an instinctual manner? It is possible that through being quiet and getting in touch with our instinctual urges we can begin to understand the answers to these questions. Is it possible that working with horses can help us understand the direction evolution may be leading us in? And when we become conscious of this direction, are we more open to the possibilities and power of choice?

Instinct and Present Moment Awareness

In working with horses we can begin to retrace our instinctual nature, We may learn both where we have been and quite possibility, where we are going. We can begin to honor our instinctual urges while in the presence of horses, and we can begin allowing those instincts to come out through our non-verbal communication with horses. We can accept that which Albert Einstein and Arthur Koestler felt and believed - the spoken language may have no place in the interior thought process.[193] We can recognize that our instinctual urges also have no cognitive process attached to them, and thus they are extremely difficult to put into words. In the work of EFMH/ES we are not asked to put them into words, but rather to allow them to simply be. In the process of being silent and honoring our instincts we are guided deeper into our true selves. Following instinct and allowing the use of non-verbal communication to express that drive we find ourselves completely and totally in the present. It is here that spiritual connection is found. It is here that the truest sense of healing and peace is found.

Since horses rely upon instinctual urges and act upon those urges without verbal communication of that reality, they find us doing the same thing to be normal and understandable, unlike many other humans we might come into contact with. Therefore we can begin to feel safe and supported trying out the new skill of listening to instinct and communicating through non-verbal cues our decisions and motivations.

Intentional Communication

Merriam-Webster's Dictionary defines intention as "the determination to act in a certain way" or intent as "the state of mind with which an act is done."[194] In the work of EFMH/ES, the word "intention" is used to describe our energetic focus regarding an action or decision. Intention appears to be useful in nearly everything that we do when in the presence of horses. We use intention when we create our congruent message and project that intention to the horse in the form of a clear mental image. Without intention the horse will not receive the message we are attempting to send him. Many times our intention is not what we verbally state that it is, rather it is something deeper, something secret that we are uncomfortable to say. Sometimes keeping our intentions hidden is a part of our manipulative communication. Sometimes it is because we are ashamed or embarrassed of our intentions. Sometimes it is because we are unclear as to what our intentions are, and sometimes it is because we do not feel safe within the conversation to actually share our intentions. For example, it can take weeks or even years before our friends or partners learn what we truly want out of the relationship. We let others guess what it might be that we want, and then feel upset or hurt when they are unable to meet our needs. Horses do not appear to engage in this sort of behavior. They have a clear intention from the moment they want something, and they utilize congruent message sending to get their communication across clearly to the other party. We have a great deal to learn from horses about the power of intention.

"One Mind" or "The Collective Unconscious"

Our minds are very powerful, so powerful in fact that even with our profound scientific advances we still barely understand their workings. The notion that we can think a thought and have that thought come into being or influence someone else across time or space would have been called un-scientific at best or crazy at worst. The notion that we are all connected by one universal mind, and therefore might be able to exchange and share information over time and space *without verbal dialog* would seem even more impossible.

Larry Dossey, Rupert Sheldrake, and Lyall Watson[195] are three individuals who are advancing modern understanding of the power of the mind. Larry Dossey believes in the concept of "One Mind", as did Carl Jung, the Swiss psychologist, when he proposed his "collective unconscious."[196] The idea of One Mind is essentially that we are all connected through a central mind, consciousness, or Divine power, whichever way one chooses to define it and that we are all interconnected through that entity. Henry Margenau, a prominent scientist suggests that "if my conclusions are correct, each individual is part of God, or part of the Universal Mind. I use the phrase 'part of' with hesitation, recalling its looseness and inapplicability even in recent physics. Perhaps a better way to put the matter is to say that each of us is the Universal Mind but inflicted with limitations that obscure all but a tiny fraction of its aspects and properties".[197]

Dossey's belief in the power of the mind and the interconnection between all living beings helps to explain how we can utilize our minds to create events, or heal illness. He has researched and written extensively about the power of prayer and our ability to help heal people over great distances simply by praying for them. He also suggests that we have the ability to cure our own bodies of serious illnesses by the act of sending an intentional picture or message of what we want to see differently.[198] These are not poorly thought out ideas presented by a lay person or para-psychologist. This is the work of many years of scholarly research by an eminent physician of internal medicine. He collaborates with Watson's belief that it is through communing with nature that we find a way to connect with the One Mind or Universal Mind. He takes Watson's thoughts one step further, and suggests that, "if we wish to preserve our world, we must first find our Mind by recovering our connection with the Earth".[199]

Morphic Fields

Rupert Sheldrake's research regarding morphic resonance helps to provide scientifically valid evidence that such concepts actually exist and are provable. Sheldrake writes in his book *The Presence of the Past*, "The process by which the past becomes present within morphic fields is called morphic resonance. Morphic resonance involves the transmission of formative causal influences through both space and time. The memory within the morphic fields is cumulative, and this is why all sorts of things become increasingly habitual through repetition."[200] He also suggests that "all humans draw upon a collective memory, to which all in turn contribute".

In another one of his books, *Why Dogs Know When Their Owners Are Coming Home*, Sheldrake proposes that through his morphic resonance theory mental telepathy is possible, and that it is the intention of an action that can be sent across time and space therefore impacting the recipient before the human ever engages in the action. He shares stories of people across the world who have thought some sort of thought only to have another human being perceive their thought and act upon it. One such story he shares in the book involves a husband and wife. The husband had arranged to meet the wife at a store. He then decided to pick her up at her office, but never called her to tell her that change in plan, figuring he would meet her before she ever left the building. However, he got stuck in traffic and so decided to return to his original plan of meeting her at the store as intended. He waited and waited at the store but she never arrived. Once they both returned home they compared stories. She was confused and told him that she had waited and waited for him at her office, since that was where he was going to pick her up. He was further confused because he had never told her his change in plan. Somehow he had sent that thought to her, she had picked it up, and acted upon it. Sheldrake also proposes that this sort of telepathy is not only valid within species, but across all species, therefore allowing communication to occur on an interspecies level.[201]

Other Species and Intentional Communication

Many people might not consider plants as species between which this notion of "telepathy" or intentional communication might occur, but Lyall Watson in his book *Dreams of Dragons*, helps us to think differently.[202] He recounts a tale told by Cleve Backster, an ex-intelligence agent and expert on the use of lie-detecting equipment, which will be paraphrased here. Upon retirement, Mr. Backster began a series of experiments using his polygraph equipment on plants. He started by trying to measure a response from watering his plants. This action proved useless and the plants did not respond. Mr. Backster then decided to utilize "the threat-to-well-being principle." Essentially he planned to torture his plant by burning its leaves. Mr. Watson reports

Mr. Backster's comments on this attempt, "at the very instant of this decision (to burn its leaves), there was a dramatic change in the tracing pattern in the form of an abrupt and prolonged upward sweep of the recording pen. I had not moved, or touched the plant, so the timing of the response suggested to me that the tracing might have been triggered by the mere thought of the harm I was intending to inflict." Mr. Backster's work was discovered by an electronics engineer named Pierre Paul Sauvin who designed a silicon chip potentiometer that was significantly more sensitive than the polygraph machine and was able to register finer shades of plant responses. Both he and Mr. Backster were able to prove that the intentions, behaviors, and affections (or lack thereof) of humans towards plants drastically altered their life span, health, and wellbeing.

Further studies have been done that examine the responses of trees in forests that are being cut down, or are about to be cut down, and the interesting responses of trees being attacked by parasites or bugs. A study of alders and willows in the forest surrounding Seattle, Washington, showed that these trees were producing a chemical that made their bark and leaves unpalatable to the tent caterpillars and webworms who were endangering them. Watson reports, "they do this (release chemicals) in direct response to actual attack, but like the poplars and maples on the other side of the continent, trees that have not yet been infested show evidence of taking preemptive precautions as well." The trees were actually able to send a clear message so that other trees could protect themselves from attack. Probably the most amazing part of this is that the trees' responses are measurable and provable, making it possible that if we humans were more sensitive, we too have the possibility to pick up on communications from plants. All of this information lends credibility to the hypothesis that by sending a clear and intentional message we can impact others in a profound manner.[203]

The power of the mind and the power of our thoughts and intentions is not something to handle lightly, or to push away as some sort of strange and "non-scientific" idea. Rather, we must learn to embrace our ability to use our individual intentions to guide and direct our lives in a healthy way and through doing so, help promote the health of other species whose voices are harder to hear.

Intention and Horse-Person-Ship

In working with horses the use of intention becomes an everyday part of good horse-person-ship. Phoebe Robinson, a Prescott College graduate discussed her experiences while taking a leadership course based out of Esperanza, An Experiential Learning Center in her article entitled, "The Equine Experience: The role of horses in adventure education."

> We found that we needed to be confident and intentional in everything we did or the horses would just ignore us, yet if something was overly directive or dictatorial the horse would resist or show their dislike of that method. This was done through their response in body language – usually of annoyance; ears laid back, tail swishing, and nose crinkling.[204]

If we want the horse to understand us, we must use intention to send a clear and precise picture of what we want. Therefore, we must first know what it is we want, and then be willing to ask for it. Just those two notions bring up life-long issues for many people. How often are we allowed to truly express what it is we want in our lives, and furthermore, how often are we in a safe enough environment to practice the art of asking? Unfortunately until things shift within our world this sort of congruent, honest, and straightforward communication is not taught nor fostered widely enough to bring about large scale change. Working with horses provides us the space and ability to begin practicing this important skill. Once we begin to find comfort within the arena of horse work, we can begin to take this skill back into our daily lives and begin using it to change the way we move through the world.

Assertive Communication

Horses will always remind us to live in balance. In their presence we can never go too far in any one direction without being brought back to center. We might think that living an "enlightened" life means being filled with light, love, beauty, and gentleness. If our thoughts veer too far in that direction one only has to think of God, or horses, to be reminded that true enlightenment may be the ability to live all along the spectrum from polar opposite to polar opposite, therefore living in complete harmony and balance. Words and concepts of good and evil, right and wrong, good and bad cease to exist and we begin to recognize that all of these things occur within any given moment, any decision we make, or any action we take. Therefore, in an "enlightened" state of being we begin to understand when to use silence and when to use assertion, when to be gentle and when to be firm.

Assertion Vs. Aggression

To be assertive does not mean being aggressive. Merriam-Webster's Dictionary defines assertion as the ability "to state or declare positively,"[205] a definition that does not give us much to work with when trying to learn the art of assertiveness. However, many leadership coaches, life coaches, and communication skills trainers utilize the term "assertive" to help teach their clients how to find healthful ways to get their needs met within communication. Many of us struggle to walk the thin line between aggression and assertion within daily communications. Either we are too gentle and thus allow others to "walk all over us" or we are too harsh and send a message that we later regret.

"Horses naturally and primarily use their bodies to 'know' the world, and training methods that respond to their socio-sensual way of being are the most effective. Although human beings at this time in history rely heavily on language, we are still wired up, as our ancestors were, to learn things through our bodies that can only be described in language after the fact. Some examples are: sensing danger, reading the wind before a storm comes, and responding to the look on a child's face."
~ Ann Romberg and Lynn Baskfield, Wisdom Horse Coaching, Minneapolis, Minnesota

In their world, horses will do almost anything to avoid true conflict. They use Stephan Budiansky's concept of bluffing to hold their ground and rarely have to remind others of their role within the herd.[206] They use assertiveness techniques if they need to remind a newer horse, or if another horse within the herd desires to challenge their position. They have developed a way of being that promotes ongoing health and well being within the herd. Chris Irwin describes this quality in his book, *Horses Don't Lie,*

Horses have worked out how to compete without causing the fear, pain, and distrust that we go through because in a herd, the horse who loses the battle is not regarded as a victim. In fact in prey consciousness the loser is actually empowered because it now acknowledges a stronger horse that will look after it. Horses know that after any contest of wills, they must still all live together in the herd.[207]

Horses present many teachable moments for people struggling with their assertion skills. Pairing the non-assertive human with the non-alpha horse tends to be very healing for both parties, if facilitated properly. The non-assertive human generally struggles greatly to get the horse to focus, pay attention, or do what is asked of him/her. Finally the human will ask for help, or the facilitator will step in and help the human reflect upon what he or she is doing, and what they might be able to do differently. Within a few sessions the human may learn to find his/her assertive voice, and is able to make forward progress and the horse becomes notably more comfortable and focused while in his/her presence.

If the client who could benefit from adjusting his/her aggressive nature to one of a more assertive and "partnership" model of communication is paired with the alpha horse successful results may also be produced. Asking the client to meet the alpha horse where he/she is, rather than asserting himself/herself in a power-over manner helps the client to recognize these tendencies in his/her place of work, or relational life.

Assertion and Respect
Learning assertive communication techniques shows us how we can "earn our rightful places in society while strengthening its fabric instead of ripping it" as Chris Irwin suggests.[208] We can begin to address issues of power and control, issues we all seem to struggle with from time to time, and learn how to move through our communications with grace and agility. We begin to learn how to get our needs met within the context of healthful and mutual relationships. We learn how to set and maintain verbal and non-verbal boundaries. We are able to

express ourselves in a way that actually gets heard by those we wish to impact.

Non-Verbal Communications

Earlier we learned about the horse's use of non-vocal communication. We saw that communication between horses is usually non-vocal. How can existing in a non-verbal word help humans? Eckhart Tolle, author of *The Power of Now* states, "so, the single most vital step on your journey towards enlightenment is this: learn to disidentify from your mind. Every time you create a gap in the stream of mind, the light of your consciousness grows stronger."[209] In order to speak we must think. We must use our minds to come up with the way to formulate a sentence that is "logical" and "makes sense" to the listener. Furthermore, speaking indicates that we expect someone outside of ourselves to listen, and therefore we must think about that being, what he or she might expect, want, or feel comfortable hearing. We place value judgments on our words, worry about how they might have impacted those that heard them, and analyze the intended "meaning" behind their usage.

The Power of Silence

When we enter into the non-verbal realm the landscape changes, the rules are different, and we find ourselves walking in a strange and unknown land. In that moment we have created the "gap" that Tolle refers to. We tap into an internal dialog that we cannot hear when we are speaking. During silence we become more present and more aware of ourselves in time and space. We have the chance to ground ourselves and recognize where we are and what we are doing. It is through this quiet grounding that we begin to listen to our instincts, to our "gut" feelings, to our sense of intuition, and to the horses' subtle messages. We begin to know ourselves more fully, and find the core of our beings. We begin to trust our sense of things and to feel safe within our bodies.

Satori

Tolle writes, "Zen masters use the term 'satori' to describe a flash of insight, a moment of no-mind and total presence."[210] When working with horses we sink into the world of quiet presence. Once in

"We have a hunger of the mind which asks for knowledge of all around us, and the more we gain, the more is our desire, the more we see, the more we are capable of seeing."
~Maria Mitchell

that state we are open to experiencing "satori" and those flashes of insight provide increasingly clear and poignant messages.

Although nearly all spiritual practices accept that silence can lead to enlightened thought, working with horses is different. Horses are large and "scary" to many. They have the ability to hurt or even kill human beings. Within their presence we may feel small and sometimes powerless. Although they are a prey species and we are technically the predator, when in the presence of horses we tend to feel like the prey. Our roles become reversed. For many humans the experience of feeling like prey, and being in a hyper-alert state of awareness for an extended period of time is unusual. It is *not* the experience one gets from going to a Buddhist monastery, sitting in prayer in a church, or any of the more traditional forms of attaining an "enlightened" state through silence and reflection. When working with horses every aspect of our being tingles with energy caused from the fear of possible physical injury and a sense of heightened awareness but we are not allowed to leave our bodies in search of escape. Rather, we are forced to remain present and aware of the current moment. Therefore, when in silence with horses we may be both experiencing "satori," and actually putting the very information we receive from our state of present awareness and hyper attention to use to change patterns and behaviors exhibited in our daily lives. This profound melding between being forced into an alert and heightened state of awareness, and actually using the information we gain from that state may cause sometimes instantaneous change that would otherwise take many years to come into being.

It is the essence of silence that allows us to find a "satori"-like state, and therefore experience these profound gifts that the horses offer us. The other beautiful aspect about work with horses is that we can begin this work simply, with learning how to listen to the non-verbal/vocal communications between horses and between horses and humans. In work with horses, done right, moments of "satori" may come, simply and gracefully.

Congruent Communication

What does it mean to send a "congruent message"? Merriam-Webster's Dictionary defines congruence as "the quality or state of agreeing or coinciding" and congruous as "to come together, agree: being in agreement, harmony, or correspondence".[211] In EFMH/ES practice I define congruent message sending as:

> A congruent message is one that embodies internal and external consistency, which includes harmonious alignment of voice, body language, mental image, thought, and feeling.[212]

Using this as a working definition of congruent message sending, we can examine what others within the field of EFMH/ES believe about horses and their ability to teach us how to be congruent.

Horse Nature and Congruency

Chris Irwin writes, "Horses don't lie", and he is right.[213] It is simply not in the make up of a horse to engage in such behaviors common to human beings. Roberts, Rees, Budiansky, Witter, and Irwin all agree that horses never lie, cheat, steal, or delude, and furthermore, that they are honest, truthful, and congruent.[214] Budiansky, Rees, Roberts, and Scanlan also agree that it is the horse's instinctual nature that makes horses function from this vantage point.[215] In order to survive the horse must react immediately with all faculties to achieve whatever it is that he or she needs or wants. If there is hesitation or second guessing, death is possible. Humans, on the other hand, have forgotten that we too have similar survival instincts, and instead have been taught how to think through things in a logical manner, and furthermore suggest that this way of being is more evolved.

Horses are able to model a way of communicating that is completely congruent, honest, sensitive, aware, and non-manipulative. Their language is understood across continents; the language of Equus is an international language which demands that the speaker is honest, open, congruent, and clear.[216] Imagine if we all spoke a language such as this. Would we still have war? Would we still continue to devastate the natural world? If we could understand each other in our totality without games, manipulations, or lies, what would our world look like?

Barbara Rector and Congruent Message Sending

Barbara Rector coined the term "congruent message sending" in the 1990's.[217] She views congruency within horses as the ability to ask for what they want or need with all of their being. She suggests that the horse's use of voice, body language, heart, and spirit are all aligned and thus they project a "congruent" message. Ms. Rector created an activity she calls Round Pen Reasoning. In this activity she teaches her students how to communicate congruently. She models the use of congruent message sending by moving a horse around the inside of a round pen using body language, voice, image, and heart. The students observe Ms. Rector moving the horse, and once she has demonstrated the hands-on application of congruency, she invites into the round pen anyone who would like to try the activity. Once the student gets into the pen and attempts to move the horse in the same manner Ms. Rector did, it becomes quickly clear that the skill of congruent communication is one that is under-used and somewhat uncommon in the average American. Ms. Rector is then able to assist the student in learning a new skill and practicing that skill in an experiential and supportive fashion.

The horse helps Ms. Rector in the teaching process as he/she will only respond when the student has asked correctly. Therefore the student is constantly made aware of when he/she is being congruent and when he/she is not. The activity may produce profound results, and the connection between the work with the horse in the round pen and the way the student communicates in his/her daily life comes into focus in a way not many people have a chance to experience. The horse continues to be a horse, and is merely requiring that the human speak the language of Equus correctly. "Correctly" in this context means being able to use the proper body language, the proper voice commands, send a clear and consistent picture to the horse of what it is that is desired, and ensure that the heart, the mind, and the spirit desire the same thing. Once all of these aspects are aligned, the horse easily moves through the series of gaits asked for by the human. Irwin, Roberts and Rees agree that in order to reciprocate equine communication in a way that the horse can understand and accept, the human must also be congruent in his communications.[218] This essentially means that the human must change past communication styles that do not foster congruency. Ms. Rector's Round Pen Reasoning provides a format to make those changes.

Round Pen Reasoning

To the observer of this activity, it becomes clear when the human is in alignment and speaking a language that the horse can understand, and when he/she is not. Issues of passivity, aggressive communication styles, or confusion in regards to what the student wants or does not want come to the forefront. The student is able to clearly see patterns, make decisions about changing those patterns, and then get the opportunity to try out a new way of being.

Monty Roberts, one of the first people to teach the way of the horse on a national and international level introduces the round pen in a way that helps bring to light the healing power of learning congruency. He writes, "The round pen is a place where two entities come together; at first they are disconnected, but then with proper discourse they become harmonious and synchronized."[219] Mr. Roberts has been able to work successfully with troubled horses using congruent communication, gentleness, compassion, and listening skills. Through this process it appears that humans also become healthier. People who watch him work a horse in the round pen report that they have a profound experience just from observing the process.

The Power of Congruency

When we witness congruent communication it seems to touch something deep inside and appears to release feelings and emotions. It makes us able to connect more deeply with our own sense of self. We feel listened to, heard, and accepted. We can be whoever we have become, and still know that there is possibility for change. Only by acknowledging who we are can we change into who we want to become. Congruent communication brings us into ourselves and asks that we become honest not just with others in our lives, but with our internal sense of self. It seems that much of the reason we are not congruent and honest on the exterior is that we are unable to do so on the interior. We must start inside and work outwards.

Chris Irwin's books cry out for humans to listen, to begin paying attention to the way of the horse, and to begin using the lessons learned from that observation in their own lives. He discusses congruency at many points in both of his books. He reminds us that horses are always clear and honest, "You see, horses don't lie. They don't separate how they feel and how they act. The expression 'what you see is what you get' could have been coined for them. Whether they are feeling scared, confused, submissive, bold, or just relaxed and confident – they tell you exactly where they're at and what they want from you and mean it to the bone." He requests that humans open their minds and allow the horse to teach them how to "communicate with the same depth and transparency it has."[220]

Implications of Congruency

Mr. Irwin suggests that there is much to be gained from communicating in the same fashion that horses do and goes as far as to state, "I believe that what we can learn from horses is becoming a necessary stage of human evolution".[221] This statement, although bold, is possibly the most useful and impactful concept presented in any book thus far written on this subject. We must begin looking at the global ramifications for walking the way of the horse. The ramifications of congruent communication are as far reaching as ending global disputes and opening our hearts and minds to notions of interspecies communications. If we were to alter our sense of consciousness about the environment and all that exists within it to one of inclusion, acceptance, and harmony we could put behind us the paradigm of devastation, segregation, and manipulation.

The McCormicks also speak to the notion of congruency in their book *Horse Sense and the Human Heart*.

> In relating to animals, most of the communication patterns we
> maintain in relationships with other people are inappropriate
> and futile. Because they are blissfully free of ego and all the

psychological machinations it gives rise to, animals respond to what's beneath the surface. We can't disguise our feelings from animals because we give off telling cues, including movement and smell, that convey our true state. Feelings bring about chemical changes, some of which result in release of pheromones. Animals smell our fear, anger, contentment, etc. To establish trust with animals, we have to base our interactions on honesty, mutual respect and compassion. If we don't they'll know it and respond accordingly.[222]

This statement again reminds us of a way of being in which we treat ourselves and those around us with honesty, compassion and respect. If we took that message outwards to our governments, leaders of corporations, teachers, prison guards, and all those who have a profound impact on humanity and the environment, imagine what our world would be like. We might ask ourselves why we have become a nation and a world so focused on obtaining material possessions and accumulation of wealth. Could it be that we are desperately trying to fill a void created by a lack of true intimacy and warmth? Is it possible that through our consumerist lifestyle we have cut all ties to interconnection between not only ourselves and the natural world, but also simply between each other as human beings?

Rupert Sheldrake comments about our loss of sensitivity towards congruency.

> Perhaps this decline in sensitivity is not a feature of our being human or using language, but a more recent phenomenon, a result of civilization, literacy, mechanistic attitudes, and dependence on technology. There seems little doubt that people in traditional non-industrial communities were often more perceptive than educated people in industrial societies.[223]

It seems that without congruent communication skills the very act of communication can be used for manipulation or can be overly confusing and filled with cultural nuances that must be understood before the actual message behind the words becomes clear.

In the movie "The Interpreter" Nicole Kidman's character suggests that it is through misinterpreted words war begins. The character feels that her role as an interpreter is a peace advocate, helping to keep peace by correctly interpreting the nuances and meanings of the spoken language.[224] We have become somewhat deviant about our use of the spoken word. Our large brains allow us to concoct tricks and manipulations that we can use over other humans, thereby enforcing our intellectual prowess and functioning from a "power over" vantage point. If we were able to accept Sheldrake's notion that there is something to be gained from communicating out of a place of sensitivity, humility, and heart we might end a great deal of the strife and confusion that the spoken language brings about.

The act of congruent communication unites us, brings us close, and gives us the experience of true intimacy we crave so deeply. The deeper we dig into the earth to find oil, gold, diamonds, and other resources that we think will bring us wealth and power, the less connected to true intimacy we become, and more hungry we get. And so we dig deeper. The cycle must end or we will kill ourselves in the pursuit of "happiness." The horses offer, through teaching us a way of communicating that is real, a way to feel. Once we begin feeling we can begin engaging in meaningful relationships that fulfill us. We can stop digging.

Summary

When we enter into the space of a horse or herd of horses it is as if we are crossing a border into a foreign country. This country has its own language and unique culture. We are merely visitors in this country, desiring the chance to learn from and be a part of something new, something different. As a conscientious traveler we try hard to learn the language of those whose country we are visiting. We study their culture, do our best to not offend, and try to fit in as best as we can for the time that we are there. We are respectful and open to learning. If we approach our work with horses from this vantage point it is likely that we will learn a great deal from their species. Through the process we may even choose to integrate such components as feel useful to us or our situations. We may find ourselves looking at the world differently.

Our other option is to demand that horses adapt and adjust to our culture, and learn to understand our language. In some cases it is forgotten that the ways in which horses communicate are based on a complex and highly structured system that can be taught just like any other foreign language. People may feel threatened or afraid of horses because they simply do not understand them. If we do not assume that it is our right or our need to control horses within the context of our

"*Silences make the real conversations between friends.*"
~Margaret Lee Runbeck

cultural norms, but rather open ourselves to learning how horses manage each other, do behavior modification, and generally communicate, we tend to be far more successful in our work with horses and far less fearful.

Since the goal and desired outcome of any EFMH/ES service is to learn from the way in which horses interact with humans and visa versa, it would seem logical that we must invest ourselves in learning the language of Equus, understanding the unique components that make up the equine culture, and open ourselves to the lessons learned from stepping into another culture.

CHAPTER SEVEN

RELATIONSHIP

Implications for Interspecies Connections

Dr. Allen Schoen writes in his beautiful book, *Kindred Spirits,* "Co-species connections can be mystical. They can be illuminating. They can be magical."[225] There can be no doubt that our need for connection goes far deeper and reaches further than simply human-to-human connections. We desire beyond all else to feel heard, seen, appreciated, and validated for *who we truly are*, not for our roles within society, not for our achievements. We want to know that someone or something really understands us down to the very marrow of our beings. With the introduction of ecopsychology and biophilia our cries are being acknowledged, and a solution offered. If we can re-connect with nature and all living things, we may find our path to inner peace. All other animals live within the harmonious web of life. They are innately connected, almost whether they like it or not. They are a part of the food chain. They live and die cyclically, returning to the very earth that birthed and fed them. They are irrevocably interconnected. There is a single pulse that runs through every one of them, keeping them tied like an umbilical cord to the earth and to each other. Humans are the only species that have tried, and in many ways succeeded, to sever that cord. It is no wonder that we feel disconnected. We are. We have separated ourselves as far as possible from the web of life. In fact now we attempt to control and manipulate that web, as if we were on the outside looking in. The conundrum that individuals like Edward O. Wilson[226] like to point out is that we are actually still within the web, which means that our decisions not only impact the other beings within the web, but also impact us and our very ability to survive and evolve. Somehow we forget this and see ourselves as separate, removed from the fate of this planet. Then we wonder why we feel so lonely, so isolated. We were not meant to be separated from the other beings on this planet. We are a part of the natural world, and our split from that has brought about serious repercussions.

Jerome Bernstein, a prominent Jungian analyst in Santa Fe, New Mexico has written a book called *Living in the Borderland* which helps to identify the profound ramifications that exist within the psyche due to our disconnection from nature. He writes,

> An ego cut off from a relationship with nature tends to be left with its own reflections on itself, unmediated by the transpersonal dimension, and readily trapped it its own mentalisms. Thus it is more prone to power inflations. It tends to be addicted to power and materialism, and thus has spawned modern warfare with the capability to eliminate life as we know it: Overpopulation; runaway greed; a century (20th) that despite its 'advances' has seen the worst carnage in human history; human and cultural genocide without precedent; a violent assault on the ecology

"The horse mirrors our internal state, being in or out of congruence."
~ Deb Marshall, Generation Farms, Nanaimo, BC

that the species may not survive; and a fear/panic of the realm of magic, and the rich and complex spirituality associated with it.[227]

He suggests our mental health may be connected to our environment's state of wellbeing (or lack thereof), and if this were to be the case, it would prove just how interconnected we still are to the web of life. However, the trouble is that regardless of how connected we actually are, we have chosen to view ourselves as disconnected, and it is through that very incongruent act that our struggles have arisen.

Bernstein quotes Carl Jung from *Man and his Symbols,*

> Man feels isolated in the cosmos because he is no longer
> involved in nature. Natural phenomena have lost their
> symbolic implications. Thunder is no longer the voice of an
> angry god, nor is lightening his avenging missile. No river
> contains a spirit, no trees is the life principle of man... no
> voices now speak to man from stones, plants and animals,
> nature is gone, and with it the profound emotional energy this
> symbolic connection supplied.[228]

Without connection to nature we are cut off. We are alone. We live
in incongruence, not wholly a part of nature, yet still completely
connected through our very psyches. We cannot understand our
confusions, our longings, or the seeking of our soul to feel seen and
heard. To live in such an incongruent state produces its own kind of
illness; stress. We can never be completely at peace. We are always
left wanting, left wondering, unfulfilled even when we think we have
everything that we could ever want. The increase of stress-related health
issues is so monumental that it has brought about a shift in our medical
model. The integration of the mind and body has not been commonly
addressed within the medical model until this recent emergence of
stress- related ailments. This change indicates the predominance of
stress-related ailments within the medical community and the impact
that stress has had on our country. The notion of integrative health care
is becoming an increasingly valid model because it helps to address the
multi-faceted aspects of stress related health issues. One can no longer
easily separate out the physical from the emotional. Stress crosses all
barriers and attacks whatever is available, whether it resides within the
physical or emotional dominion.

If we are to find a way back to health; physically, emotionally, and
spiritually we must come to realize that we can no longer disregard our
roots. We cannot put aside that we are *a part of nature*, and we must
change our view of the world to embrace this reality.[229]

The field of ecopsychology, the Bioneers movement, and scientists like
Edward O. Wilson[230] all help to raise our awareness about these issues,
and help put into perspective some of our unanswered questions,

longings, and unfulfilled desires. They provide theories and help change governmental policy. They help people to understand the dire importance of changing one's lifestyle. However, they do not provide a way to learn how to go forward and back simultaneously, bringing us into the web. The work of EFMH/ES offers this to us. It gives us the practical application of how to put these theories into our daily lives. To *think* about such theories only moves us back into our mechanized brain, back into the very thing that separates us from other animals. Changing our lifestyles to respect the environment is necessary, practical and important, but again, it does not bring us back to our animal roots, nor teach us the skills we must learn to regain the lost art of interspecies communications. Going into nature is amazing, and is a wonderful way to connect with the natural world, but some may find it hard, at least in the beginning, to connect with plants, trees, rocks, and water. Seeing wildlife raises our heart rate, brings us lofty joy, and reminds us that we are truly still a part of the food chain. But, again it is hard to practice our interspecies communication skills without receiving feedback that is understandable.

Pets provide yet another avenue to explore interspecies connection. The trouble with pets is that many times they are too domesticated, and therefore do not hold the space for wildness and reminding us that we are a part of their world, rather than them being a part of ours. Horses, however, are able to hold that wild space. They are able to remind us that we are entering into their world, and that in order to stay safe, we must learn to speak their language. Furthermore, horses actually teach us how to communicate in a manner that seems to be understandable for many different species. We can practice our new skills while in the presence of horses and actually receive feedback. We can make mistakes and try again. And through it all, we form life-long passionate relationships that transcend all boundaries that normally exist between species.

It is through work with horses that we can begin to re-connect with the natural world in a practical and tangible sense. It is through learning the way of the horse that we begin to realize that we are not alone. When in the presence of horses we can begin to learn how to evolve our relationship with the web of life. We cannot go back. We cannot become cavemen once again. We must honor our evolutionary development and hone our new talents and skills. But we must find a way to do this that keeps us tied to the cord of the earth. We must begin making this journey practical and understandable. We must de mystify the process and bring it to people in a palatable manner that they can accept. By working with horses, and through the relationships that are created, profound change is possible, and the creation of a new paradigm becomes a "logical" next step. It is less scary, less "weird," and more natural if one can experience the practical application before becoming inundated with the theory.

In upcoming chapters we will explore how horses teach people a new way of relating to one another, through their very being-ness. Remembering the implications of forming interspecies relationships, we can conceptualize how using these skills might help bring about a paradigm shift.

Empathy and Compassion

In researching the impact that horse nature has on human relationships, empathy and compassion continually appear. However, it seems that when trying to write about the role of empathy and compassion within the horse/human relationship the end resort is case studies and stories about clients who self report having profoundly benefited from such relationships. There is no viable research that suggests horses are innately empathic or compassionate towards one another; rather it seems that when in the presence of horses humans are able to connect with their "greatest self," and find the place inside where compassion and empathy reside.

It may be that because horses do not appear to make judgments in the same manner that humans do, we consider them to be "non-judgmental," and feel safe from ridicule while in their presence. It may be this very characteristic that leads humans to assume that horses are compassionate and empathic.

Growing up in the Salt River Pima Maricopa Indian Community life is different. Gang culture has infiltrated nearly every generation. Children grow up without parents or grandparents due to gang wars. Alcoholism and diabetes run rampant alongside animal abuse and child abuse. The threat of violence never leaves and families sit on the ground in their living rooms, devoid of furniture, to avoid being shot during the regular drive by shootings that occur in many neighborhoods. There is no time for appreciation of beauty, and the reservation land has been devastated by litter, gun fire, dead dogs, and burned homes, making beauty hard to see. Kindness and gentleness are luxuries not afforded to the residents of the Salt River Pima-Maricopa Indian Community. The jail is the closest place to a home most of the youngsters know, and they come back frequently, many times for no other reason than to be safe, fed, and cared for. The people working in the jail understand the plight of the juveniles and therefore provide as much nurturing, empathy, and kindness as they can within the context of their jobs.

The inmates of the jail are mixed together in cells, divided by gang rather than by age or by crime. This allows the small facility to keep some semblance of peace between inmates and avoids some of the more major gang related incidents. These young people are incarcerated for all kinds of crimes - from murder, drive by shootings, and rape to petty theft and running away from home. By the time they get to jail, they have seen it all; from watching loved ones killed to taking part in severe animal abuse as a game. Their appreciation and respect for beauty and nature has been buried deep beneath layers of hate, anger, fear, and loneliness.

These young men were introduced to Taja, Shawnee, Suzy Q, Sunny, Excell, and Smokey, a treatment team of horses ranging in age, experience, breed and color, as different from one another as their human counter-parts were from the young clients they were serving. It was quickly realized however, that differences somehow ceased to exist once the men stepped off from the van and had their shackles removed.

The Esperanza staff worked with the SRP-MIC Juvenile Correctional Facility inmates for four years. The changes that occurred for the inmates are almost beyond words. Their resilience and greatness of spirit became apparent within moments of meeting them. It seems that all they needed was a vehicle to help them connect to what was already inside of them, buried deep beneath layers of pain. They were able to put aside generations of hatred, mistreatment, and cruelty and become loving, compassionate, and gentle.

The Story of Taja

A notable memory was of two young men who were in opposing gangs and hatred each other. They had vowed to kill each other if ever given the chance. The strange thing about the two was that they were actually related, and looked so much alike that most of the jail staff called them by the others' name regularly. In the beginning of their time with horses we kept them separated, because we were aware of their hatred and felt that it was be unsafe to try and bring them together. During their separate weekly sessions each young man chose the horse he was most drawn to. Both of these men choose a small gray Arab mare named Taja. Word slowly got around the jail that both of these men were working with the same horse on different days. Finally after the staff had been working with these two young men separately for many months, we made the decision to try and integrate the them into one group. At first things were touch and go; it looked like a fight might be eminent, but suddenly it became apparent that the cause of the argument had veered away from their gang differences and was centered around who would get Taja. They had realized that both of them normally worked with Taja when they came to Esperanza, and now that they were both there together, who would work with Taja? At this point Esperanza staff intervened and it was suggested that because Taja was extremely muddy that day (just luck, or was it?) she needed both young men to work together to brush her. Next thing the guards knew the men were walking off together with a clearly defined plan of how they would brush Taja without getting too close to one another. For the first few weeks they would not talk nor make eye contact. They each stayed on one side of her, thereby keeping Taja's body between them at all times. They had a strange agreement regarding the use of the shared grooming box. Once one of the men would finish with the curry comb or hard brush he would gently toss it under Taja to the other man so that they never had to ask each other for anything. Somehow they were so observant of the other that this method worked for a number of weeks without the use of the spoken language. They would ride, one leading Taja with the other on top. Never did they do anything that might scare or bother Taja in an effort to frighten the rider, not because they cared for the other human, but because they cared too much about Taja and how that action might impact her.

They both were extremely athletic and learned to ride quickly and well. Soon they were progressing to a saddle, learning two-point, and finally learning how to trot. The first day that they trotted they were so excited that after the riding component of the session we heard all of this noise and commotion coming from their grooming area. We dashed over, ready to break up a fight, and instead found them rolling on the ground in laughter. Apparently trotting had bounced them around enough to loosen their hearts and allow them to laugh together. Over time they learned to canter and even to jump small cross bars. Regardless of their past history, they were always together during the horse component of the session, providing safety support on the ground for the other who was riding. They were constantly competing to show up the other one, and gain more praise from the staff, but they were always careful and respectful of Taja. Within a few months they were housed together in a jail cell, and made a "public" announcement (to their respective gangs) that because they were blood (relations, not to be confused with Bloods, the gang) they needed to stick together. They declared a truce and both gangs allowed them to communicate due to their blood relations. Both of them became less active in their gangs, although neither of them left the gangs entirely.

The Safety of Connection

It was through their complete compassion, love, and respect for Taja that this relationship was made possible. Many other stories exist of individual gang members who made major changes due to their connections with the horses at Esperanza. Young men were able to become consistent and passionate fathers to children they had long neglected. Some made decisions about their use of violence and changed their actions to become more peaceful. A few were able to get completely out of the gang that they had been in. Many of them developed an unspoken truce that did not end at Esperanza, but followed them out onto the streets. Young men would tell of how they ended up in a neighboring gang's area at night, and got passed by a car full of opposing gang members. Normally this would end very badly for the single misplaced youth out of his "hood," but, in the car was another "horse therapy" kid, and suddenly the car was passing by, no guns, no stopping, no violence. It happened enough that many of the youngsters joked that they wanted Esperanza sweatshirts that they could wear out at night, because if someone from "horse therapy" recognized them it was safer, and there was less likelihood of violence. As profound as that was, probably the most moving change involved the treatment of animals. *All* of our students reported a complete cease in their acceptance or tolerance of animal abuse, even going as far as to get into fights to protect an animal that someone else was about to abuse. They reported that since working with the horses they realized that animals had feelings, thoughts, and emotions, and that they did not want to hurt animals any longer.[231]

It is through stories like these that we begin to see how horses allow people to experience true empathy and compassion for each other. Taja did not like one of those young men more than the other; she cared deeply for both of them. This modeled a way of being never before conceived of by these young people, and it was through walking Taja's way that the men were able to move forward in peace.

Both Schoen and Sheldrake[232] document similar examples of individuals responding to this sensitivity. Horses take people to new levels in relationship. They, as with other animals, illuminate the healing power of love. Horses seem to allow people to practice new-found skills and due to the horse's ability to communicate, the individual is able to see the different reactions between a relationship that is healthy and loving, and one that is based on domination and mistreatment. Through connection with horses the SRP-MIC juvenile corrections inmates learned how to "walk in the shoes of the other," or discover true empathy. Empathy is not the act of feeling sorry for someone else. It is truly the ability to see yourself within the other. When gang members are able to connect with each other, acts of violence towards self and others become more difficult.

Implications of Compassion and Empathy
Imagine if we took the lessons learned from the gang members on the Salt River Pima-Maricopa Indian Community out into the world at large. Imagine the change in our global relationships. Imagine the

impact that true empathic understanding would have on war. Our reality would shift completely. Empathy in its truest form is possibly one of the most powerful tools we possess if we want to bring about personal and global change. The young men at the SRP-MIC juvenile correctional facility show us the power of that change. They also show us that even when violence is multi-generational and ingrained into the very marrow of their bones, that it is possible to move beyond that reality and co-create something different. These were young, uneducated, inexperienced men, not world leaders with degrees from Ivy League schools, who possess experience, intellect, knowledge, and the endless resources to learn anything that they already do not know. Our SRP-MIC clients model that which our world leaders should look more closely at, empathic understanding and its impact on societal change.

Expanding Our Potential

Psychologists Carl Rogers and Irvin Yalom both note that empathy or as Roger's calls it, "accurate empathy" is an essential component in the healing relationship between client and therapist.[233] Yalom furthermore suggests that not only does the therapist need to understand and be able to exhibit this trait, but that the client must also learn empathy. He notes, "Keep in mind that our patients generally come to see us because of their lack of success in developing and maintaining gratifying interpersonal relationships."[234] He suggests that in order to develop and maintain relationships one must be able to be empathic towards others, and demonstrate that empathy in a healthful manner. While working with horses, humans seem able to connect on a deeper level with themselves and their true feelings. It may be that through this connection the ability to understand others stems. If we can understand ourselves; our motivations, behaviors, and actions, we probably will have a better empathic understanding of those around us, and be better prepared to engage in meaningful and healthful relationship development.

The McCormick's write,

> By following where the horse leads us emotionally and spiritually, we begin to expand our view of life. Horses give humans a broader perspective on life in general. They give us

a keener appreciation of how intelligent and sensitive other creatures are, and this helps develop our own humility and compassion.[235]

The McCormicks touch on the notion that through expanding our conscious understanding of other species we are able to recognize our interconnection with all beings, and thus gain compassion and humility. When we come to realize that we can communicate with other beings, and that those other beings have thoughts, feelings, and a consciousness similar to our own, we begin to change our behaviors and actions. We become more compassionate and more careful about the way we move through the world. If we adjust our own thinking to be more compassionate towards other life forms, we in turn benefit. Through our experience with horses we are reminded that we are only a small part of the whole, and that we must remember how to live with compassion.

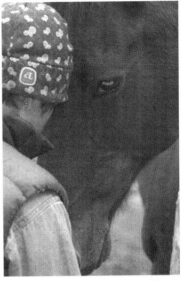

"It is so fascinating (but totally understandable) that elements which 100 years ago were a part of everyday life - music, dance, art, and animals - are now being (re)introduced to our information-rich but experience-poor society as 'therapy.'"
– Maureen Vidrine, HorseTime, Covington, Georgia

It almost seems that the reason compassion and empathy are not found readily within non-human animals is that they have no need for either value. Imagine if we lived in harmony with the earth and all beings existing therein. If we truly understood the web of life we would move through our days recognizing how we each impact the other, and being aware of our "weight" upon the earth. Is that not the truest form of both empathy and compassion? We are so disconnected from ourselves and our world that it is no surprise that we need to "learn" concepts such as empathy and compassion, and that these concepts are viewed as "higher order functioning." Could it not be that both of these concepts are human inventions that try desperately to bring back our lost sense of interconnectedness to all beings? It seems that going back to our animalistic selves is in fact getting us closer to what we consider an "enlightened" way of being. If this theory is correct, horses help us to become more animal-like by teaching us the way in which they move through the world, and it is through that very way that we re-connect with skills lost to us.

Respect

The very fabric of the horse herd is based upon mutual respect; respect for each other, for a hierarchical order, and for the laws of nature and instinct. Without deeply ingrained respect the horse herd would not survive. Monty Roberts, Chris Irwin and Stephan Budiansky[236] all concur that horse herds are comprised of a hierarchical system called by many a "pecking order." Essentially this refers to the flow chart of leadership within the herd. A horse herd is run by a lead mare and head stallion. The mare guides the herd to food and water, controls the daily routine and movement of the herd, and ensures the general wellbeing of the herd. Mary Midkiff quotes horsewoman and author Susan Boucher as she discusses the role of the alpha mare,

> She may not be the biggest or the strongest but she is the wisest, with a self-assurance that inspires confidence. If the lead mare is relaxed and grazing, the others eat, and if she startles and bolts, the others follow. In the landscape of horses, spookiness is in fact a virtue. The mares, among themselves, determine hierarchy – not only their own, but that of their offspring.[237]

Herd Dynamics and Respect

The head stallion controls the perimeter of the herd, standing watch to ensure that no predators disturb the herd. He alerts them to far off danger, and is willing to fight to keep the mares and babies safe. He and the lead mare work in equal partnership to run the herd. The members of the herd offer the ultimate respect to the lead mare and head stallion by placing their fate in the hands (or hooves as the case may be) of their leaders.

As a lead mare or head stallion begins to get older, younger members of the herd will step up to challenge their role. In the case of the lead mare this will generally be observed by subtle attempts to move her around or push her away from choice food or the water source. If the

younger mare is able to do this in times of hardship and food/water shortage, and other horses follow the younger mare, it is likely that a role change will occur soon. If the lead is ready to relinquish leadership, the younger mare will step into her role without violence or physical altercations. The older mare will step down and assume a "crone" role within the herd. With head stallions the conflict is generally more physical and sometimes could result in the death of one of the horses. However, in either case once the leadership has been established, all members of the herd will follow that horse, again demonstrating the quality we humans attribute to respect.[238]

Leadership, Respect and Horses

A plethora of books have been written about the importance of the human assuming a leadership role over the horse, and thousands of horse trainers will tell their students how important it is for the horse to feel that his rider is in control. With many horses this notion holds true. Having someone more powerful than him/her who guides the direction he/she goes in and makes the decisions for him/her is actually extremely relieving for many horses. The human learns how to guide the horse as the alpha within his/her herd would guide

him/her. Mark Rashid, in his book *Horses Never Lie: The Art of Passive Leadership*, disagrees with the concept that horses must be controlled by an "alpha-like" leadership style. He suggests instead that we need not lead through challenge and aggression, but rather by developing a long standing, positive, and mutually respectful relationship with horses.[239]

To learn how to be with horses in this manner takes time, patience, and observation of the behaviors of horses. Once we spend the time to really get to know our herds, we find that some horses, generally the alphas of the herd, do not want to be submissive to just any human. In fact they find that position extremely uncomfortable and foreign. They live the bulk of their lives directing other horses, leading the herd, and managing many aspects of the herd's existence. To step down from that role and be submissive to a human who has not gained their respect and trust is asking a great deal. This means that a different approach should be taken with the alpha horses of the herd. Practicing the art of balancing assertion with respect, listening, and being open to doing things differently is a wonderful lesson for any of us. The alphas of the herd request that we do that dance. In order to be respected by a horse we must set clear boundaries and hold them, but on the other hand be completely respectful of the power, greatness, and nobility of the alpha horse's role. We must show the alpha that we will meet her in the middle, and acknowledge that she is powerful and has her own strongly held beliefs about the way things should be. Once we have demonstrated that we are willing to learn from her, and listen to her, and respect her, we can begin making equal requests of her.

When working with other horses within the herd who are not alphas the rules change once again, and we must be sensitive enough to understand that subtle shift. With these horses, consistent assertion of your role as leader creates comfort and a safe working relationship between horse and human. With the non-alpha horses, being the leader allows them to relax into themselves and their natural role. With people who are new around horses the whole experience is generally filled with caution, hesitation, and sometimes fear. Therefore when they are paired with a non-alpha horse, that horse is able to perceive the human's hesitations and feels immediately like someone has to take control of the situation, and since it isn't the human, the horse decides that he had better do it, even if he is uncomfortable doing so. Once the non-alpha horse takes over things tend to go from bad to worse. The horse is not used to being in a leadership position and so will react in a number of ways. He/she might become overly sensitive to anything that might be "scary" in the surrounding area and start spooking, therefore scaring the human and possibly frightening them further. He/she might decide that he/she does not want to do whatever it is that the human is asking, and since the human is not using assertion to get the message clearly across, may take matters into his/her own hands and refuse to do whatever it is that the human wishes. Or, he/she may be distracted from the human and spend the session calling to his/her herd mates, telling them about the terrifying human who does not know what they are doing, asking the other horses to get over there and help him/her.

What it Takes to Earn Respect

Chris Irwin suggests that respect is earned between horses by not only demonstrating intelligence, strength and foresight, but more importantly by the demonstration of consistency. He writes, "You may be strong enough to establish leadership, but you also have to be consistent enough to keep it."[240]

He also believes that horses need to ultimately respect their riders or human partners in order to feel safe. Children want to feel respect towards the people "controlling" their lives, and want to be treated respectfully in return. This is very similar to the way in which clients experience those working therapeutically with them, or students experience while learning from educational professionals. Many times we take for granted that children, clients, students, and animals innately respect us as professionals, parents, or owners without our having to earn their respect. Within the horse herd the lead mare and head stallion are not just assigned these roles, they have to earn them. If the lead mare proves incapable of leading her herd to water and a good source of food, or the head stallion cannot protect his herd from predators, these horses would be challenged by other members of the herd and if found lacking, would step down. Within our human culture, we have a tendency to "force" our authority upon others less powerful than ourselves. Animals, children and others compromised in some way by societal standards seem to suffer the most from our less than respectful behaviors.

If we are asking our children or clients to make changes that we ourselves have not made, how can we hope to instill respect and act as a useful guide for them? If we are not treating our animals in a way that encourages respect, but instead demand through violence, fear, or other forms of cruelty that they respect us, our relationships will suffer and the very results we hope to achieve will go unmet.

Confidence and Competence

Chris Irwin also suggests that horses need to feel respect for us, respect however, that is earned through a demonstration of competency and confidence in our abilities.[241] Confidence in its truest form is a result of education, knowledge, and training. Many times we portray a "fake" version of confidence, one that is not based in actual knowledge, but rather in our own belief in ourselves and our abilities of the past. Horses can sense this difference and recognize the "cheaters" from those who have spent many long years learning the art of horse-person-ship. We can, however, be confident within ourselves and honest about our lack of knowledge as it relates to horses. If we take this path, and open ourselves to learning from the horses, we will be respected by them in a different way, not as leaders, but as willing students. Within the hierarchical organization of the horse herd there is a place for these types of horses, the ones who are willing to watch and learn from their elders or superiors, but not assert themselves as leaders. Many humans who come to the work of horses become confused between the two types of confidence. They try to take the leadership role before they have earned that right. Horses will happily relinquish the leadership role only when and if they have found someone else who is more qualified then themselves. Unfortunately people are taught that they need to be the "leaders" of their horses, even when sometimes they are untrained, uneducated, and unprepared to do so. If this is the case the horse will nearly always rebel. This will be demonstrated through horse and rider conflicts and the rider will traditionally vocalize these conflicts by saying something like, "my horse will not ... (do this or that)." Generally a fight will then occur between the horse and the human. This fight will either lead to the horse becoming more "shut down" and growing increasingly less interested in horse/human partnership, demonstrating this by finally giving in to the human even through he does not want to, and does not respect the human's desires or wishes. The other avenue left to the horse is to continue to fight. This generally ends sadly with the horse being sold or gotten rid of because he was "uncooperative," "dangerous" or otherwise unsuited for human/horse partnership.

These ideas connect directly to the work of EFMH/ES and our personal development. If we can learn to first recognize what areas we are confident and competent in, and in which areas we need further training, education, and experience, we can delve deeper into our own psyches. We learn how to challenge ourselves by going back to school, taking additional trainings, or spending more time doing our own personal growth work. If we can learn to listen to the horses in a respectful manner we will have the information we need to proceed forward. Coming into awareness about our own competencies also gives us personal strength and the motivation to realize how unique our skills are, and how able we are to learn new things and grow as human beings.

Equality and Partnership

Many times we seek to "be equals," and live in "partnership" with each other. Horses help to dispel the idealistic nature of these words, and help us to recognize that it is not about being equal. They help us to learn that partnership is about the melding of many people's unique talents and strengths, and the willingness of each of those individuals to "stand in their own power" and assert themselves as leaders in whichever aspect they have confidence and competence. Horses remind us that we are definitely not all "equals," and that there is value in a hierarchal system that respects competence and confidence. However, without partnership the hierarchal system breaks down, leading to a common theme that we see within our very governmental and large corporate structure. Every horse within the herd has his or her own unique role and is valued and respected for that role. Without each and every one of them, the herd could not function. As Marianne Williamson reminds us, our greatest fear is not that we are inadequate, but rather that we are stronger and greater then we can imagine.[242] It is our very strength that terrifies us, and because we have a poorly defined model of how to exhibit our strengths, we are left either touting these strengths in a manner that is offensive to others, or staying small in order to not offend others. Horses teach us that it is ok to be great, that it is ok to be different, and that we are not all equal.

I don't think that we know how to be "not all equal" very well without being disrespectful. In order to do what horses do, we must learn how to be respectful *for the right reasons*. Frequently in our culture we are respectful of others because of their wealth, power, or prestige. Those who truly earn respect by "leading the herd to good food and water sources" are many times discounted and disregarded. For instance, those who have been attempting to lead our government away from unsustainable sources of energy towards the investigation of renewable resources such as solar power have rarely earned the "respect" of the masses. It seems like the time is coming to evaluate our alphas and head stallions. Where are they leading us, and is that where we want to go? Why are we not actively confronting our leaders, as the younger generation of horses do to their elders when the elder's ability to lead in a healthful way is in question?

Walking the way of the horse is about learning how to more clearly understand the concepts of respect and leadership. It is about learning what our roles are within the "herd," and about being willing to confront and move forward if old paradigms of leadership are no longer working. It is also about learning what we do and do not know, and being willing to get the education, training, and experience to deepen our human existence.

Companionship, Intimacy, Coherence, Bonding, and Nurturing
Companionship
Barbara Rector recollects a study conducted by the University of Michigan Agricultural Science Department asking 7th -10th graders in schools all across the country what they wanted to do or experience most. The most common response was "go hang out with a friend," obviously an easy and uncreative response used by those unsure of or uncomfortable with their thoughts. The second most common response across all socioeconomic boundaries, and not limited to a particular gender was "to ride a horse."[243]

Horses are powerful imaginal figures for nearly all young children. Horses appear as an icon of power and prestige throughout the world. An old Spanish proverb states, "A horse is worth more than riches."[244] In 1998 Lawrence Scanlan reminded us that the number of horses in America had grown from 6.6 million to 6.9 million just in that year.[245] Robert Miller, DVM suggests "the horse is a common fetish in human culture, often deified for augmenting man's speed and strength."[246] Horses are ever-present in award winning and popular films, television programming, and music. Everywhere we look we can find the ramification of our love and devotion for the horse, from the abundance of "horse-isms" we utilize on a daily basis without even realizing their origins, to the toys that young children cherish. We are surrounded by the horse, and his/her beauty and magnificence never ceases to amaze and enthrall us.[247]

Young boys dream of becoming cowboys, young girls take English riding lessons and dream of the Olympics one day. Women, as they mature, look back to their past, and find the horse, ever present, ever waiting. They seek out new ways to bring back that relationship so long ago left by the wayside of life, by career, marriage, and children. They may learn how to speak up, find their sense of self, or learn to live within their power. Men may become gentler and more open while in the presence of horses, learning how to listen, touch gently, and bring compassionate respectfulness back into their careers and relationships.[248]

Many children appear to find solace in the presence of the horse, and may engage in life-changing relationships that can move them through the trying and difficult times of growing up. Horses become dearly loved companions and friends, who challenge their human partners to be the best that they can be. Within our relationships with horses we can learn how to form attachments, how to show love and affection, what it means to nurture something, and how to experience true intimacy. Horses draw us in, prancing and dancing through our dreams, glistening, beautiful creatures who inspire poetry, art, and romance. We are caught, helpless within their presence, wishing and desiring connection and relationship with them. Waiting desperately to understand their language, be privy to their secrets, and share

"If a client is struggling with trust issues from past experiences, she may eventually discover that her horse provides a non-judgmental listening ear, a warm huggable neck and soft eyes to gaze into. As she interacts with her horse and comes to the realization that the horse likewise is learning to trust her, she begins to form a bond with him. She learns to trust him as she spends time grooming, bathing, braiding or perhaps just scratching his neck. As caring staff members come alongside, the hope is that, through their kindness, encouragement and consistency a human relationship will form and the patient will learn to trust people as she has learned to trust the horse."
~ Cheryl E. Musick, Remuda Ranch, Wickenburg, Arizona

in communion with them. Horses become a source for connection to the Divine to many, and the barn becomes their church.[249]

Interestingly, people seem to be divided into two camps; either those who are "horse-crazy," or those who are terrified of horses, disliking them because of a past event, or deep personal aversion to their very nature. Very few people are neutral about horses. Horse people are strongly opinionated and passionate, so much so that the ongoing joke in the field is "what's the only thing that two horse people can agree upon? That the third horse person is wrong." This joke, although humorous is generally true and therefore the field of any horse related service is filled with confusions, contradictions, egos, and the desire to be right. One would think that a field based upon undying love and dedication to a creature like the horse would be filled with compassionate, loving, gentle, and patient people all working together for a common good. However, passionate dedication has its own set of strengths, and relationships with horses seem to make us unusual and unique human beings, willing to fight for what we believe in and the relationships we cherish.[250]

We can find many case studies about young women and their relationships with horses. It seems that the notion of horses helping humans to learn what positive relationships can be, and reminding us in times of struggle that we do have a loving ear to tell our woes to is well documented. However, to take this topic to a somewhat different level, we need to investigate the notion of true intimacy, a concept many of us may struggle to understand or implement in our daily lives.[251]

Intimacy, Coherence, and Bonding

As the Esperanza client shares with us in the adjacent quote, it seems like all of us long to feel *seen*. The quality of "feeling seen" is something few of us ever get to experience. Many of us wear masks of protection and form layer upon layer between our "true" selves and the selves we portray to the world on a daily basis. We may feel lonely, disconnected from not only nature, but our own species. Some of us live in boxes surrounded by possessions, and have interactions with people on superficial levels, but in our hearts we long to feel connected. We desire that moment when a beloved horse looks over his shoulder and *sees* us, sees all of our idiosyncrasies, our strengths, our weaknesses, our passions, and our pain. Linda Kohanov explains her thoughts regarding intimacy in her book, *The Tao of Equus,* and gives us a beginning from which to further our explorations of what true intimacy might be.

> Over the years I have come to realize that horses are not a substitute for sex. Rather, sex is often a substitute for the kind of multi-sensory connection that horses, unlike many people in our society, are able to provide without reservation. Sex as portrayed in the media, and played out in many short - and long – term relationships, is a quick-fix high that briefly and just barely, quenches our thirst for true intimacy.[252]

Humans may quite literally experience "oneness" in moments of healthy sex, and since they may have rarely recognized that experience anywhere else, look to sex as a way to feel such a connection. However, as we move forward through this section, it will become clear that intimacy can occur outside of sex, and we will learn how one may be able to obtain such a state of being through work with horses.

One could say that true intimacy is sharing the experience of being seen with another being. It may be the feeling of total submersion within another, to the point of feeling a merging of two souls, or energies. Science has given us a language to use to describe this experience, it is called entrainment.

The Institute of HeartMath, a nonprofit 501(c)(3) organization, is a "recognized global leader in researching the critical link among emotions, heart-brain communication and cognitive function." HeartMath endorses recent biomedical research that demonstrates that the heart is not just a simple pump, but a "highly complex, self-organized information processing center with its own functional 'brain' that transfers information via the nervous system, hormonal system, bioelectromagnetic interactions, and other pathways." HeartMath believes that "the messages the heart sends the brain not only affect physiological regulation, but can also profoundly influence perception, emotions, behaviors, performance, and health." HeartMath has taken this research and developed a system of scientifically validated tools and technology that can help people "engage their hearts to reduce stress and improve health, learning, performance, and quality of life."[253]

Their research covers areas of emotional physiology, heart–brain interactions, heart rate variability and autonomic function, music research, and emotional energetics, intuition, and epigenetics research. It is through deeper understanding of our hearts that we begin to learn that by utilizing techniques that help adjust our heart variability into a state of coherence, we can reduce stress and become more present and engaged in our lives.

There are many ways in which the work of HeartMath is important to this text; however for this particular chapter, it is important to understand the two ways that this research impacts our ability to find intimacy.[254] First, when one learns how to live a life in a present and engaged manner, the chance of recognizing and fully experiencing moments of true intimacy becomes greater. Moments of intimacy are found tucked between commonplace occurrences, found hidden behind casual words, and lodged firmly within pre-existing relationships. We move so quickly that we miss much of what makes life worth living. By learning how to move into a state of increased awareness and harmony, we can open ourselves to deeper and more meaningful experiences of each other and the natural world. HeartMath offers the concept of "coherence," which provides a physiological explanation for the benefits of a more aware, conscious, and harmonious way of being,

This mode is associated with a sine wave-like pattern in the heart rhythms, a shift in autonomic balance towards increased parasympathetic activity, increased heart-brain synchronization and entrainment between diverse physiological systems. In this mode, the body's systems function with a high degree of efficiency and harmony, and natural regenerative processes are facilitated.[255]

HeartMath continues on to explain that sustained periods of coherence are rare and although "specific rhythmic breathing methods may induce coherence and entrainment for brief periods, our research indicates that individuals can maintain extended periods of physiological coherence through actively self-generating positive emotions."[256] Essentially this means that the suggestion to "think positively" is not simply a meaningless aphorism, but actually allows us to move into a state of coherence. HeartMath also suggests,

When the physiological coherence mode is driven by a positive emotional state, we call it psycho-physiological coherence. This state is associated with sustained positive emotion and a high degree of mental and emotional stability. In states of psycho-physiological coherence, there is increased synchronization and harony between the cognitive, emotional and physiological systems, resulting in efficient and harmonious functioning of the whole.[257]

Imagine our ability to experience intimacy if we were functioning from a place of synchronization and harmony, where we could feel the differences in experiences, and recognize an intimate moment when we experience it?

The second way in which the work of HeartMath can help us learn about and possibly experience intimacy is through the concept of "entrainment." Wikipedia defines entrainment as "the process whereby two connected oscillating systems, having similar periods, fall into synchrony."[258] Christian Huygens, a notable physicist, created the term in 1666 upon his observation of two pendulum clocks that self adjusted to create the same swinging rhythm.[259] The human heart is able to go into entrainment with another human heart when two people are both in a coherent state of being. "Coherent" has positive connotations as suggested by HeartMath's research relating to feelings of love or appreciation, whereas incoherence indicates a negative state with feelings relating to anger, anxiety or frustration. When two people are incoherent, entrainment is unlikely. To enter into entrainment with another being is a powerful experience. It means that your two hearts have adjusted their own unique rhythms to beat as one. This is intimacy, in its purest form. We long for it, seek it out, but have little if any awareness about what is actually happening within our bodies that makes us crave such a connection.

Dr. Ellen Gehrke[260] partnered with HeartMath to research what occurs when humans come into the presence of horses. In 2006 Dr. Gehrke finished her first pilot study which concluded that when utilizing what HeartMath calls a "heart lock in," which is essentially deep breathing, and the projection of positive thoughts and feelings towards the horse, she was able to demonstrate that the human heart *and* the horse heart go into a coherent state. We will discuss those results in other areas of the text, but for the purpose of discussing intimacy, her results regarding the horse/horse relationship are very revealing.

Gehrke found that horses who were deeply fond of each other and who were pair bonded with one another, live in a state of nearly constant entrainment. Imagine what it must be like to feel so completely bonded and connected to another being. Imagine sharing the same heart beat as another human being. One might wonder if other creatures living closer to the natural world also live in nearly constant state of entrainment with one or more of their fellow species. Think of the impact this notion must have on their actions and behaviors. If they are interconnected on this energetic and physiological level might they be less likely to engage in acts of destruction towards each other and the environment that sustains them? Could a deeper understanding of our hearts and their function be the thing that links us back into the ever-connected web of life?

It seems that if it is possible for two horses, or two clocks for that matter, to exist in a state of entrainment, then we humans should certainly be able to do the same.

We are reminded by HeartMath that without a positive emotional state, coherence cannot occur, and therefore neither can entrainment. Think of the profound ramifications if our race was able to move quickly and easily into a coherent and entrained state of being. We would no longer be lonely. Could it be possible that our addictions to food, drugs, alcohol, and sex would cease to exist? Could we feel *seen* on a regular basis? What would this do for our self-esteem, our sense of self worth, and the negative actions we engage in when we do not feel good about ourselves?

The McCormicks have put into words the quality of entrainment in their book *Horse Sense and the Human Heart,*

> Intimacy must always have true friendship as its foundation. With this basis, the relationship is lasting because it emanates from the heart. Participants in this kind of intimacy appear to be connected by an invisible thread that has the potential to bind them together even after death.[261]

Dr. Gehrke's research[262] tells us that coherence, if not actual entrainment, is possible between horses and humans. Her initial research also explained to us that horses live in a coherent state nearly all of the time. This could indicate that we humans, who live in a highly incoherent state most of the time might find it hard to feel entrainment or true intimacy with other humans, and due to our current social constructs around intimacy, it could be hard to "practice" getting coherent with another human. If we could learn how to adjust our hearts and move into a state of coherence while in the presence of horses, we might be better able to open ourselves to experiencing connection, if not actual entrainment,

"Cloudy turned his head around to look at me, and it was like I was seen, seen for the first time in the most intimate way I could ever imagine."
~ EFMH/ES Client

with another being. We can practice within the context of our horse/human relationship, and slowly, at our own pace, begin taking these lessons out into our human to human interactions. Therefore, it seems that working with horses could have a profound impact on our ability to become intimate, and could decrease the "loneliness epidemic" that seems to be sweeping our nation.

Nurturing

We live in a world filled with hurry, rush, and stress. Many of us have little opportunity to nurture ourselves even in the most basic of ways. Recently a medical doctor who is a client at Esperanza working on body awareness and career re-structuring said this,

> Wow, I actually realize now when I have to go pee, and I stop and take the time to go. Before (her work with the horses) I was so stressed and rushed so much of the time that I never even noticed when I had to go pee, and would realize by the end of the day that I had not gone to the bathroom all day long, nor had I drunk any water.[263]

This extreme example probably resonates for many people in high stress, fast-paced careers. These most basic elements of caring for ourselves have gone by the wayside as we struggle to maintain our pace and not fall behind.

In order to keep food on the table, gas in the car, a place to live, and our other bills paid, most Americans must work well over forty hours a week. Many cannot even make enough money to live from one job, and must have two. *This is without putting money towards savings or retirement.* Our wages stay the same as our expenses climb higher and higher. Our debt to income ratio hangs over our heads, and the fear of being homeless becomes terrifyingly real for many lower to middle class Americans. Millions of people live without health insurance, and cannot afford to take care of their bodies. The notion of *nurturing* ourselves is for many about as far off as the moon. However, without nurturing our stress levels increase and we may develop stress-related health issues.[264]

We want to take the time for a long walk in the park with our children and dogs. We long to eat a home cooked and healthful meal. We want to laugh, to play, to feel free from the stresses of our jobs. We want to go outdoors and breath deeply, allowing ourselves the time and space to become quiet. We want more than a week off a year, we want *time* to be ourselves outside of our jobs.

The process of changing ones life is filled with the fear of the unknown. We desperately seek to be another way, but struggle to make the leap to get there. Working with horses has interesting ramifications for manifesting change. Mary Midkiff in *She Flies Without Wings* discusses how the very nature of horses is nurturing:

> Horses possess an instinct to nurture themselves. A grazing horse is a horse taking care of herself in the most primal of ways... Horses instinctively enact all the nuances contained in the word 'nurture.' As a matter of habit they feed, protect, sustain, support, train, and condition themselves every single day. Over thousands of years of neglect, we humans have been losing our instinct to nurture ourselves in the innate, self-satisfying way the grazing horse does.[265]

Interestingly enough, at Esperanza we have found that people, once in the presence of horses for long enough, struggle with living an unfulfilling, stressful, and un-nurturing life. They observe and spend time with the horses and watch Ms. Midkiff's beliefs in action. They see that the horses place high value on self care and self nurturing. They see them lazing around the field, taking naps in the warm fall sunshine, and waking up to nibble here or there. The clients become surrounded by the slow pace of life at the barn.[266]

Laura Brinkerhoff, founder of Leap of Faith Equestrian Services in Tucson, Arizona, commented that when clients arrive at her facility, they tend to take a huge sigh and tell Ms. Brinkerhoff how calm and at peace they feel just stepping out of the car onto her property.[267] It is this quality that a well run EFMH/ES program should strive for. The sense of wellbeing and happiness exudes from the horses and from the very land that the facility rests upon. It is the feeling of supporting a life of nurturing, of well-being. Clients who work in high stress environments, or have stressful home lives where nurturing does not occur, may not recognize what it is that they are experiencing, but generally over time they come to desire this feeling within their own lives. Once they have reached this decision, life change is possible.

Many times the horses react negativity to people who come from high stress lives and bring that energy with them to the barn.[268] The horses might walk away from these clients, and make a clear point of involving themselves in a particular nice clump of grass. It is almost as if the horses just do not want that incoherent energy in their space, and remembering the work of HeartMath, it is no wonder. For beings who exist a great deal of their lives in a coherent state, having someone who disrupts that is annoying at the very least. For these clients, it generally takes a re-evaluation of their energetic presence before the horse is willing to work with them. Once they have experienced a coherent way of being, it is hard to leave that behind and go back to incoherence. Therefore, life changes become necessary.

As a people, and as a society, we must learn how to nurture ourselves. Again, we must ask ourselves, is our alpha leading us in the right direction? Is there a way to bring about change in our own lives, and what would that take? Are we going to continue to support the direction that our alpha is taking us in, or are we going to confront and challenge, listening to what our body's needs are?

Therapeutic Presence

Presence is defined by the American Heritage Dictionary as, "1. the state or fact of being present; current existence or occurrence, 2. immediate proximity in time or space, and 3. the area immediately surrounding a great personage, especially a sovereign."[269] Within the mental health field, both Irvin Yalom and Carl Rogers[270] used the concept of "therapeutic presence" in their work. Rogers suggested that having a therapeutic presence encompassed "attentiveness, bodily and sensory openness, enhanced awareness, connection, integration, and focus." He felt that it was the sense of simultaneously being there with and for the client, an awareness that helped to shape the client's feelings of safety and openness.

The notion of the therapeutic presence is also found commonly within the medical field, in particular with nurses. Phyllis MacDonald du Mont Ph.D., R.N., professor at the University of Tennessee, in a paper entitled, "The concept of therapeutic presence in nursing" quotes Paterson & Zderad as they define therapeutic presence as "A fully present understanding of the other without a concurrent loss of the concrete self."[271]

Suzanne Scurlock-Durana writes about therapeutic presence in *Complementary Therapies and Wellness: Practice Essentials for Holistic Healthcare*

> In this chapter therapeutic presence, which is the unspoken, unseen connection between therapist and client that occurs in every therapeutic intervention, will be addressed. This means knowing how to remain connected to one's resources, grounded, attuned (i. e., not feeling numb), and fully present in the face of challenging, sometimes emotional, therapy situations. It means being empathetic and feeling connected to clients without taking on their frustration, anxiety, pain, or grief. It means facilitating a healing therapy session while honoring one's own boundaries and the boundaries of the client. To accomplish this means learning how to be in touch with and nurturing of oneself, so that the therapist's therapeutic presence can catalyze and nurture the healing process for clients. This can create a challenge, because many people have been taught that it is somehow bad to focus on their own bodies and emotions--that they should choose to ignore pains and suppress feelings.[272]

Body Awareness, Congruency, and Therapeutic Presence

When working with horses if we do not learn how to stay connected and aware of our own bodies, and learn how to express the feelings and thoughts that arise within our bodies, we may be placing ourselves in jeopardy of getting injured. Horses generally chose not to tolerate incongruence, and therefore, learning how to put a voice to our body's innate wisdom becomes a therapeutic tool rather than an unethical use of self disclosure. Many mental health professionals are not taught about authentic sharing of personal experience within the moment.

In fact in some schools of thought such sharing could be viewed as unethical. Horses can teach us about the benefits of such sharing. For some clients, working with horses and with the human facilitators who are authentically themselves can be a very powerful experience. Human beings tend to learn from modeling, and if they witness both the horse and the human facilitator modeling authentic expression, it may become easier for the client to recognize when and how to use the same tools.

Interestingly enough, it appears that some lawyers are also being trained in the principles of therapeutic presence. At the City University of New York, School of Law, professors Victor Goode and Jeanne Anselmo offer as a part of their teaching, education about the use of a therapeutic presence. They suggest that having a therapeutic presence, "sustains ones centered presences in challenging circumstances." Their vision is to use the concepts surrounding therapeutic presence to "assist students and attorneys to bring a centered, grounded, open, aware, active and concerned connection to their interactions with clients." They offer a check list of what the student or lawyer needs to develop in order to have a therapeutic presence.[273]

1. Inner connectedness and trust in ones own inner purpose and process.
2. Self care and self reflective practices.
3. Creating a safe and supportive environment through deep listening practice.

Furthermore, they offer steps towards attaining a therapeutic presence.

Center: Connect to ones intention for the interaction and ones deeper commitment

Breathe: evaluate ones personal and professional resources in that moment

Ground: Place ones feet on the ground, drop breath and center of gravity to lower abdomen.

Practice Deep Listening: Compassionate listening to understand the person without judgment.

Horses can help teach mental health professionals, nurses, or others interested in learning how to create and sustain a therapeutic presence. The concepts laid out by Victor Goode and Jeanne Anselmo are the very principles people must learn how to attain when working safely with horses. For clients, the experience of being in the presence of a creature who emulates these very characteristics can be innately healing, simply due to the welcome and much needed sense of feeling heard and seen for who we truly are, not for the masks or stories we use to hide behind.

The Science Behind Therapeutic Presence

J. Watson in *Nursing: Human Science and Human Care* describes transpersonal caring as entering into "the experience (the phenomenal field) of another and the other person enters into the nurse's experience. This shared experience creates its own phenomenal field and becomes part of a larger, deeper, complex pattern of life."[274] This is a highly provocative statement, reminiscent of the words of Jesus when he said, "For where two or three gather together because they are mine, I am there among them."[275] Some call it the "holy third," which defines the experience of two beings connecting without losing their unique sense of self, and through that connection something greater than the both of them arises.

From Larry Dossey's non-local mind, Rupert Sheldrake's morphic fields,[276] to the concepts of quantum physics, we are taught that on a molecular level, relationships exist within an energetic field, and in fact relationships in and of themselves can create their own energetic fields, or morphic fields. Scientists like Capra, Gribbin, Murchie, Pert, and Zukav all support the notion that each person is an integral part of that energy field, affecting and being affected by everything around them, simply by their very presence.[277] HeartMath suggests,

> Human energetics research conducted at the HeartMath Research Center demonstrates that the electromagnetic fields generated by the heart, which extend a number of feet external to the body, contain information that is modulated by one's emotional state. Further, this research reveals that an individual's cardiac field can be detected by other people in proximity. This is among the first scientific research to show

that energetic interactions between people can be measured and that these interactions can produce physiological effects.[278]

One could hypothesize that if a mental health professional or individual within the medical field were coherent, the client being attended to by that individual might enter into a state of entrainment with that human being, and therefore feel true intimacy and connection. Furthermore, it is possible that when deep connection occurs, humans feel seen and that through the very act of feeling *seen*, healing occurs. If we feel truly seen, we might drop barriers that have long stood in our way of getting the help that we need to make positive changes in our lives. We might trust in a way that we have never done before, and through opening our hearts and allowing new ideas and knowledge to enter, we might come away with new tools.

As we learned in the past section, the potential for horses and humans to enter into a coherent state may be possible, if both the horse and the human are able to become present and positive. Therefore, it seems further possible that the horse himself/herself actually provides a therapeutic presence and it is through this presence that change can occur. Barbara Rector in her book, *Adventures in Awareness: Learning with the help of horses*, speaks to the notion of "spontaneous healing," a concept presented by Andrew Weil, MD Director of Integrated Medicine at the University of Arizona. Weil suggests that there may be a connection between expanded awareness, developing our consciousness, and those events that many call "miracles," incidences of healing that occur without a clear path of origin.[279]

The question then begs to be asked, could it be that the principle of the "holy third" or the morphic field created by two individuals completely present, aware, focused, open and coherent presents opportunities for healing, both emotionally and physically? Regardless of the answer, we certainly can speculate on the healthful experiences that humans experience when they come into the presence of horses, and we can surmise that this reaction on the part of the human could be directly tied to the concept of a therapeutic presence that the horse naturally exudes.

Mirroring or Reflective Feedback

Encarta Dictionary defines a mirror as "something that accurately reproduces, describes, or conveys something else" and reflective as, "characterized by deep careful thought" or "able to reflect light, sound, or other forms of energy".[280] In the work of EFMH/ES people speak commonly of a phenomenon generally called "mirroring," or the perceived ability of the horse to accurately reflect back to the his/her human client a key piece of information regarding the client's functioning that is needed in order to bring about change. During this section we use the term "reflective feedback" rather than "mirroring" to describe the concept.

The McCormicks, in their book *Horse Ssense and the Human Heart* write,

> Our work taught us that the horses were skillful guides, divine messengers in a sense, who can show us who we are and point us in a direction we need to go. They act as larger-than-life sized mirrors, reflecting back to us the totality of who we are, complete with light and shadow.[281]

Ingrid Soren writes in *Zen and Horses*, "the world is only a mirror of ourselves, and I was finding that horseback riding held up that mirror more clearly than anything I had experienced before."[282] Both of these perspectives suggest that while in relationship with horses, humans

"It seems that the heart connection between horse and person is a regulator in itself, and it often provides the deepest experience of safety and love the person has ever had."
~ Deb Marshall,
Generation Farms,
Nanaimo, BC

can learn to see themselves differently and possibly more completely.

As we learned from the research of Dr. Gehrke, horses live in a congruent and coherent state most of the time. Therefore when people enter into their space and act or function in ways that are not congruent or coherent, the horse may react, reflecting to the human how the horse perceives them. Truly good horse people throughout time have come to understand this concept and have taken the information from their horses to heart. From Olympic riders to natural horsemanship "gurus," it is generally believed that nearly always it is the horse who is right, and that we must learn how to listen to the feedback given to us by the horses in order to stay safe and have successful interactions with our horses. We must learn how to change our behaviors, mindsets, and attitudes if our horses reflect back to us that we are unsuccessful in our attempts to communicate with them. We have to learn how to read and respond to our horse's view of us. Without this awareness, horse people can burn their horses out, have unsuccessful rides, or can never quite achieve the level to which they aspire. It is only with open and ongoing communication *between* the horse and the rider that partnership occurs.

Many of us will identify with the experience of coming to ride and finding our horse in a terrible mood – unwilling to do anything that we request. At this juncture we have two options; either we can attempt to force the horse to do the task at hand or we can stop and reflect upon own mood, perhaps giving the horse a long rein, walking around the arena and taking some deep breaths to center ourselves. After a time or two around, we generally discover that we are also feeling grumpy, unwilling, and out of sorts. Once we realize this, we can change our approach to the riding session. This shift generally results in a more successful ride for both of us. After an experience like this, we start to realize that the horse is simply reflecting our state of being, and once we change our perspective and attitude, the horse follows. This concept can be directly applied to the work of EFMH/ES, and it can be taken to far greater depths; sometimes bearing clean the very souls of those engaging in the process.

Why Horses?

Stephan Budiansky in *The Nature of Horses* suggests that the very nature of horses provides the reason why horses are capable of this type of behavior:

> The keen ability of horses, as of all social animals, to 'read' and correctly interpret symbolic social signals is perhaps the most

important key to their surprisingly peaceful subordination to humans in the domestic relationship... The well known ability of horses to 'mind read' is neither so extraordinary nor so mystical as it is often made out to be; it is hardly surprising that an animal whose entire socioecology is based on an ability to read subtle social cues can pick up on the hesitations, uncertainty, and lack of self-assurance of one rider, and the confidence and resolution of another.[283]

Recognizing that horses are not magical, although many of us perceive their actions as such, is important, because as Budiansky reminds us, the horse continues to simply do what it does best - be a horse. Things do not have to be magical to be truly amazing.

In many cases people do not have the language to de-mystify the deeper nature of horses, and for many who seek meaning and a connection to a more spiritual path, the gifts of Equus can provide that experience. Without a deep understanding of the language of Equus or the nature of horses as a species, it is understandable how their actions appear to be mystical and hardly within the capacity of words. That being said, it seems that horses do exist in two worlds, as Linda Kohanov suggests in her book *Riding Between Worlds*. One can be a horseperson, understand the language of Equus, and be educated in the area of horse nature, and still be awed by the keen ability that the horse demonstrates to clearly and precisely provide for clients just the experience that they needed to bring about profound change.[284]

Larry Dossey, M.D. speaks to this ability in his forward to the McCormicks' book, *Horse Sense and the Human Heart*,

> Horses are especially effective in helping people understand and overcome fear and aggression, bringing harmony and alignment between the unconscious and the conscious mind, and developing conscience and an awareness of the effects of one's behavior on others. Through their uncanny ability to 'mirror,' horses spark a deeper understanding of our behavior, and inspire us to a more spiritual, mystical, and philosophical orientation to life.[285]

Barbara Rector who has been an avid supporter of the concept, and possibly even coined the term "mirroring," has this to say,

> Work with horses provides a clear precise mirror of our inner thoughts, feelings, attitudes, and beliefs. The Adventures in Awareness process works with horse as a reflective mirror of our interpersonal relationship dynamic, and provides an interesting awakening to our personal capacity for empowerment.[286]

She believes that it is an innate ability of the horse to mirror our thoughts, feelings, actions, behaviors, and unspoken desires. It is through this mirroring process that the clients come to more fully understand who they are and how they impact the world around them. She believes that "authentically empowered individuals make healthy behavior choices, thus reducing societal violence."[287] We will discuss this issue in further depth in chapters to come. However, it is important to recognize that once people begin waking up and becoming more self aware, their ability to make choices about their behaviors and actions increases. Through work with horses our understanding of how we impact the world around us begins to come clear, and we are faced with the challenge of making new and different decisions.

Often we utilize relationships to define our sense of self. However, the trouble with this approach to self discovery and awareness is that the other humans with whom we interact generally bring with them their own issues, histories, and motivations. It seems more difficult to understand ourselves through the looking glass of another human. Horses, on the other hand, appear to be clearer about who they are and more straightforward in their motivations, both as a species and as individuals. Perhaps due to this sense of clarity they do not become emotionally "bought into" our human experience, and instead can provide reflective feedback about how our actions, behaviors, and communication styles truly and instantly impact them.

Our Souls Bared Clean
Many times we do not realize the defenses we put up against the world around us, and we may not even know exactly why we have created these barriers. However, many mental health professionals come to realize after years of working with wounded human beings that the ego

tries to do its best to protect the human being it resides within. Even when we might not be able to recognize the reason, we must honor the ego's attempts to protect us, and not undo all of its hard work until we have a different way to address the wounds that caused us to need defenses in the first place. We cannot expose ourselves naked to the light of day without preparation and planning. We must help the ego to see that its complex defense mechanisms are not needed anymore because a new coping strategy has been put into place.

While many of us exist behind our defenses, animals know better. They can sense, through smell particularly, what is true. Lyall Watson speaks to the profound impact of smell in his book, *Jacobson's Organ.*[288] In this book, Watson suggests that animals are fully able to recognize and understand a large variety of odors, and will adjust their behaviors to reflect the "truth" the odor reveals. Imagine what it would be like to have your unconscious or unaware feelings, thoughts, and even sometimes personality, bared clean before virtual strangers who you have only just met! The McCormicks help us to understand just how profound and potentially invasive the nature of reflective feedback from the horse can be:

"Horses enjoy taking time to stand in the shade relaxing, unlike people who rush about in our fast paced world. Often our patients feel guilty and unproductive if they are not busy.) Horses take time to play, nipping, rearing, kicking and galloping with their peers. Our horses teach the patients how to enjoy child-like play, relaxation and enjoyment."
~ Cheryl E. Musick, Remuda Ranch, Wickenburg, Arizona

In relating to animals, most of the communication patterns we maintain in relationships with other people are inappropriate and futile. Because they are blissfully free of ego and all the psychological machinations it gives rise to, animals respond to what's beneath the surface. We can't disguise our feelings from animals because we give off telling cues, including movement and smell that covey our true state. Feelings bring about chemical changes, some of which result in release of pheromones. Animals smell our fear, anger, contentment, etc. To establish trust with animals, we have to base our interactions on honesty, mutual respect, and compassion. If we don't they'll know it and act accordingly.[289]

Facilitated properly, reflective feedback can provide what clients report as "life changing" realizations. However, facilitated poorly, the same qualities may have the potential to bring an unstable ego to the breaking point. If a human being has had the need to hide for many years, and has built their entire lives around a façade created to mask deep feelings, memories, or history of trauma, having that mask ripped off with little or no warning has the potential to awaken its last vestiges of survival, creating a fight or flight reaction, or a dissociative state first, which if the body is not allowed to engage in such action, will recede to a complete psychotic break from reality.

The Reality of Reflective Feedback

Reflective feedback is probably the most provocative and easily misused of all benefits that working with horses offer in an educational or therapeutic setting. We must understand the scope of our individual practices and make ethical and professional decisions before delving into the area of reflective feedback. It may be that the psyche is the most fragile of our faculties, and within the process of reflective feedback, all defenses that were created, generally for good reason, can be stripped away within moments of being in the presence of the horse.[290] Only one with extensive training, education, and practice should attempt to utilize reflective feedback as a therapeutic or educational tool.

Since anecdotal evidence suggests that reflective feedback may be of educational and therapeutic value, a large majority of the work done with horses and humans utilizes the principles of reflective feedback.[291] Done well utilizing reflective feedback in an educational setting is generally the simplest and safest way of working with the information that the horse provides to us. As facilitators we may see far more than that which we share with our clients in an educational setting. However, we must recognize the scope of our practice, and practice ethically within those parameters.

Reflective Feedback in an Educational or Learning Environment

The process of receiving reflective feedback from a horse can include learning how to observe our own communication style in action. Many practicing in the field of EFMH/ES use Barbara Rector's model of "round pen reasoning," or a similar concept to help students learn about communication skills.[292] Principles of equine communication can teach us ways of round penning a horse that taps into his/her ability to perceive minimal sensory information, and that through learning the way in which horses move each other around the pasture, we can essentially learn to speak the language of Equus.[293] While the student is in the process of learning this new language, his/her own unique struggles with communication may arise, and the facilitator learns where the challenges lie. Through teaching the student the language of Equus and setting the goal of being able to communicate successfully with the horse to move him or her around the round pen at specified gaits, the student can learn how to more effectively communicate in his own life. Within this kind of work, the horse provides continuous reflective feedback about how the human is communicating.

Example

A client struggles to assertively instruct the horse to walk forward. The horse patiently awaits the correct command, but the woman struggles to ask for what she truly wants. The facilitator continues to work with her, providing her tangible skills that she can utilize both in the round pen, and back out in her daily life. Once the woman has

found her voice, and asks the horse using congruent communication, the horse immediately moves forward at the walk. The woman experiences success, and is able to practice her new communication skill in a safe and non-threatening environment. Therefore she has learned a new and extremely viable tool that is hers to take away from that

"The horse tells us things that no one else would dare, and we are more likely to accept it."
~ Deb Marshall,
Generation Farms, Nanaimo, B.C.

session. In an educational setting the debrief process would veer away from the implications of her non-assertive communication style from the past, and instead stay in the present, focused on the skill itself. The facilitator would not ask leading questions that could move the session into a therapeutic one, but rather stay grounded and focused on the act of teaching a skill.

Reflective Feedback in a Therapeutic Environment

Horses appear able to reflect feedback to the clients in an EFMH/ES session that could be viewed as a deeply psychotherapeutic process of making the unconscious conscious, a goal of Freud, Jung, and other renowned psychoanalytic practitioners. They believed that learning about the inside of one's self was the final frontier and marked the birth of enlightenment in psychological terms.[294] Furthermore, issues of transference and projection appear to occur regularly within the reflective feedback process. People may project deeply felt issues upon the feedback offered to them by the horses. Facilitators must be highly skilled and trained to understand both transference and projection, and to differentiate it from the horse authentically reflecting unconscious thoughts, feeling, or behaviors.[295] Facilitators engaging in this work must know the therapeutic horse staff intimately, and therefore be able to notice subtle nuances and shifts in behavior and body language in order to make these distinctions. It becomes clear that the concept of receiving reflective feedback can easily move from educational, such as learning a communication technique, to deep psychotherapy within seconds, based upon the ability of the facilitator to either keep the session educational, or to allow it to deepen and extend into psychotherapeutic realms.

Example

A man who was in jail for rape, attempted murder, and gang activity was a participant at Esperanza's Equine Facilitated Psychotherapy program. Titan, a 15'2 hand half draft-half mustang gelding who is very large and very masculine was this particular client's choice of a horse to work with. The client chose Titan out of the herd due to Titan's aggressive nature, chasing all of the other horses, threatening them, and generally acting tough and "bad ass" as the client called him. After a few moments of such behavior, the other horses, fully aware of

Titan's role within the herd, moved away from him, leaving him alone in the far corner of the arena. The other horses then proceeded to frolic and play with each other, completely ignoring Titan. Every so often, if they got too close, Titan would make a dash towards them chasing them back and then retreating into his corner. The mental health professional was standing back, observing the clients as they watched the horses interacting. The client who had chosen Titan started the activity talking loudly, ignoring the request to remain silent, and reflecting to anyone who would listen how "bad ass" "his" horse was. As the activity continued the mental health professional observed the client becoming increasingly quiet, finally standing alone watching Titan's behavior. The activity came to a close and all clients circled up for a processing group. The client who chose Titan remained silent during the entire group. Finally at the very end of the group he spoke. "I am Titan."

Over the next few months the client worked with Titan twice a week. Every session he had new realizations about his own motivations for past behaviors and actions. Titan reflected back to him a scared man, someone who lived his life in fear of ever letting anyone in., someone who put up walls created by violence to keep others out. During his time at Esperanza the client was able to address and begin working through a long history of child abuse and post traumatic stress disorder created by witnessing extreme acts of violence perpetrated by his father towards his mother, himself, and his siblings. By the conclusion of his treatment both he and Titan were able to co-exist within their respective communities, using new skills to relate and connect with others. Upon his release from jail the client was able to write a letter to the woman he raped,

"Horses are much better at regulating their systems than we are, as long as we don't interfere too much. The mirror they offer can give better information about what is happening in a client's body than anything else I know of. When the client makes a shift, it is immediately recognized by the horse. These experiences are easily embodied and become lasting."
~ Deb Marshall, Generation Farms, Nanaimo, BC

explaining the kind of person he was then and how he had changed. He continued to stay connected to Esperanza, even following his release, and continued working with Titan. In the four years Esperanza worked within the jail setting he was not arrested again for rape or acts of violence

The Potential Dangers of Reflective Feedback

Currently in the field there is a plethora of short-term workshops being offered by inadequately trained/educated individuals to an unscreened clientele coming to "experience the method," "learn about EFMH/ES" or attend a "personal growth workshop." New facilitators of EFMH/ES may have personally experienced the magic of receiving reflective feedback from horses, and have capitalized upon the allure of such powerful information. Unfortunately, without lengthy training, education, and practice specific to the field of EFMH/ES, the facilitator could share information gained through the reflective feedback process with a client or participant who is unstable emotionally, and unprepared to hear the information relayed. Due to a lack of training, education and expertise, the facilitator may not be aware that this is occurring and thus take no steps to process with or stabilize the participant.

Another disadvantage of short term workshops is that the facilitators rarely know what happens to the clients upon leaving the workshop. There is little if any mechanism for tracking the clients' mental health status prior or post, and wrap around services are generally not in place to monitor a client's care upon leaving. Furthermore, many of the individuals attending the workshops may be unaware of their own personal issues, issues that have been stuffed down for many years. One weekend with the horses can bring things into the light that have never seen day. If the participant is not in individual counseling outside of the workshop, or has not done his/her own work, the intensity of the experience can push him/her into further masking of his/her deeper issues, therefore making the door that much harder to open the next time.

During an interview with Linda Kohanov, we joked that the toughest job of the EFMH/ES facilitator is to try and slow catharsis, prolonging the process so that the clients can leave with a clear understanding

regarding the process of making the unconscious conscious. Although a part of our conversation was in jest, there is a very serious component to this as well. As facilitators of this work we must learn how to slow down the process and make it palatable. Ms. Kohanov and I both recognized the unfortunate trend within the field to provide an instant "awakening" within those coming to experience the work on a short term basis.

Ms. Kohanov shared a story during her interview that became her own personal impetus for learning the act of "slowing it down." She told of her father, who was a survivor of physical and ritual abuse. Over the years he had been heavily medicated just to make it from day to day. However, due to health problems, he would find himself in the hospital on a multitude of occasions and it was here that Ms. Kohanov learned how to help him modulate his experiences:

The worst situation would be, anytime he went in to get some kind of surgery the psychiatrist who had him on these drugs and the physician treating his medical condition would not communicate and so they would take him off of his medications. When that happened I would sit with him as he was having drug withdrawals and a psychotic break at the same time that he was recovering from open heart surgery. I would sit with him and talk with him and all the material that had been suppressed from the drugs would come out, like the flood gates would open and it would all start coming at once. And so one of the techniques I teach people about going into the body literally came from sitting with my father in these states. When he would get overwhelmed I would say 'where is the fear rising in your body, pick the place where the fear is rising from,' and he would respond, 'my chest is ripping apart,' and I would say 'so make a deal with your body, you haven't listened to it, the drugs have been suppressing it, tell your body that you'll make a deal, that you'll listen to it from now on. But only if it releases the information a little bit at a time.' I would hold his hand and say 'ask your body to send you one piece of information now, one thought or one memory.' He would then tell me only one simple memory - not the most extreme, but very symbolic of a lot of stuff, and his whole body would relax and he would calm down. I use this concept when I teach people how to do body scans. I suggest to them that they go to the one sensation that has the most to offer and make a deal with it, you'll listen to it from now on but only if it releases the information one piece at a time. Therefore they learn how to modulate the intensity of the information being released.[296]

When humans first experience the reflective feedback process, they may feel somewhat like Ms. Kohanov's father did - flooded with information, feelings, thoughts, and memories that have been stored or suppressed within the body for years. This can be completely overwhelming and counter productive to the therapeutic work. Facilitators must learn how to help clients process the information that they receive in a healthful manner, without inducing further overload. The horses do not think like this, and they do not monitor how much or what kind of information they reflect back to the human. It is therefore the job of the human facilitator to help modulate that information.

There is a vein of thinking that suggests that the human psyche has the ability to take in only what it can handle. This concept may be true for fully functioning human beings, but for those suffering from a past history of trauma, mental illness, or a world view or paradigm that does not allow for free expression of thoughts and feelings, the psyche can become overwhelmed quite easily. Individuals may not experience a psychotic break, but certainly may experience fight or flight, or dissociative states. This can lead to clients misunderstanding what a facilitator has said, or what the basic premise of the work might be. A common phenomenon in this field occurs when a person who goes to a workshop or training, becomes triggered by the work, and leaves "bad mouthing" the facilitator or their method. Through the grapevine the facilitator hears what the participant is saying, and wonders how on earth he or she managed to get *that* from the workshop. Once the participant goes into a dissociative or fight or flight state, information does not get clearly integrated and can become blurry and open to the mis-translation of the participant.

It is up to the facilitators of this work to learn what the warning signs are of dissociation, fight or flight, or the onset of a mental break, and to do everything in their power to avoid such situations, or healthfully work through them should they arise. It takes a great deal of formal education and hands on training to understand these warning signs. It also takes an understanding and awareness of issues revolving around scope of practice, and the knowledge of how to direct a session either towards a therapeutic focus, or towards an educational focus, depending upon the training and education of the practitioner, the needs of the client, and the agreement rendered between client and practitioner.

Boundaries

Encarta Dictionary defines "boundary" as "the point at which something ends, or beyond which it becomes something else."[297] We often are confused by boundaries; what they are, how to set them, how to maintain them, what our motivations are behind creating boundaries, and most importantly, which boundaries that we set are for healthful reasons, and which are not. Boundaries within the human psyche are not clearly defined or mapped out, like the boundaries between countries, neighborhoods, or those that surround sports fields. We are taught rules that help us understand and comply with the exterior boundaries we move through on a daily basis. We learn societal boundaries that define us as a gender, as a race, as a culture, or define our individual role within the larger paradigm. However, we are rarely taught about our internal landscape, and how to navigate that terrain in a healthful manner.

The Human Struggle

Personal boundaries continue to flummox some of us, providing a constant source of confusion and mixed messages within relationships.

"*The body has a cellular memory which, when activated through somatic learning, can reveal patterns and beliefs that are antithesis to what we say we want. Energy patterns also play in to somatic awareness, e.g., where the person blocks energy, where energy moves, how to ground it and direct it consciously. When these patterns come to light, participants are able to take effective action immediately.*"
~ Ann Romberg and Lynn Baskfield,
Wisdom Horse Coaching
Minneapolis, Minnesota

We tell people to come close and then push them away. We deeply desire contact, but create such forceful boundaries that no one can get close or we set no personal boundaries but feel taken advantage of or wounded when people respond accordingly. We lock ourselves off from the world behind thick walls created out of fear and loneliness. We become exhausted because we continue to allow people to "walk all over us," taking advantage of our giving natures.

Essentially we have limited guidelines for learning how to set and maintain healthful, balanced boundaries. It may be that the more we become disconnected from each other as a species, and from our natural world, the harder it becomes to practice boundary setting, and thus the more inept we become. In the past, when we relied upon our human and environmental connection to survive, we had to learn how to set and maintain more healthful boundaries. Even then it was a system of trial and error, some getting it better than others.

Horses and Boundaries

As Chris Irwin, Monty Roberts, and most experienced horse person would tell us, horses live in a world of clearly defined boundaries.[298] They are unafraid to communicate their spatial, emotional, and physical needs to those around them. They set clear expectations for behaviors and do not tolerate disrespect of their personal boundaries. If they are lower down on the pecking order, they will remove themselves from areas or situations where their personal boundaries might be crossed. If they are higher up on the pecking order they will assert their needs clearly to all around them, setting the limits of their boundaries for all to witness. Mixed or incongruent messages are almost unheard of within the horse herd, and rarely, if ever would you find a horse allowing someone to violate his boundaries.

In working with horses we are given the opportunity to learn about boundary setting, and discover what our personal boundaries are. Furthermore, we can practice setting boundaries, feel what it is like when another being disrespects our boundaries, or recognize our own motivations behind the very boundaries that we set, all of this within the emotionally safe environment of working with horses.

Levels of Boundary Setting

At Esperanza we help clients to recognize the various levels and types of boundaries that exist within our internal landscape. We help clients develop their use of boundary setting on a multitude of levels, from the energetic to the physical. We help them to gain an awareness of their energetic presence and how this presence can impact those around them. We examine the phenomenon that Carl Jung called the "collective unconscious"[299] or what Larry Dossey more recently termed "the non-local mind."[300] We begin to recognize that our experiences of the world are not just created inside of our own individual vacuums, but rather that we are capable of picking up on an entire sea of interconnected information, thoughts, feelings, and energies. Therefore, we must learn how to set boundaries at this invisible level, protecting ourselves from a bombardment of stimuli that does not belong to us, or even to those close to us, stimuli that can in fact be connected to a different time and a different place altogether. When we learn how to create these sorts of healthful boundaries, we can become more open to our sensitive and perceptive sides, and learn how to listen and differentiate between what is ours, and what is other.

Jerome Bernstein[301] has identified a personality concept he termed "Borderlanders," which describes people who are extremely sensitive and aware of the natural world and its ability to communicate with those who are able to listen. At Esperanza we recognize that many of our clients are borderlanders, or people with heightened sensitivity who are drawn to the work because of this innate sense. The work with horses helps them to integrate their sensitivities in a healthful manner, learning how to set clear boundaries about how information enters into their psyche, therefore becoming able to understand and process the information they are receiving in a different and more healthful manner.

Bernstein reminds us that depression is quickly becoming a large scale issue in the United States. Without proper training, education, and practice we are becoming consumed by an existential angst that can be felt reverberating around us all. The use of healthful boundary setting, taught through the way of the horse, may have the potential to help us move past taking personal ownership over the feelings and sensations we are experiencing, thereby becoming incapacitated by illness, and incapable of taking action-oriented steps to solve the deeper problems of our world. Learning how to separate out what is ours, and what is "other" can allow us the space, time, and emotional strength to take action to protect our environment, make personal life changes that support the nurturing of the natural world and its inhabitants, and move into a place of strength and power vs. weakness, illness, and helplessness.[302]

Learned Helplessness and Boundaries
Without the learned experience of setting and maintaining healthful boundaries we have a tendency to move towards a state of "learned helplessness."[303] We may feel manipulated by the world around us, by others in our lives, and by our own psyches. We seem to feel out of control and powerless to do anything about our state of being. We may even give away our right to choice, and allow others to dictate our direction in life. We take to complaining and commiserating about our fate, and continue trudging down the same path we have unknowingly and unconsciously created for ourselves. The notions of mindful choice, taking a proactive stance in the direction that our lives are going, and taking ownership over the choices that we do make on a daily basis that change the course of our destinies is essential if we want to live fulfilling and healthful lives. We must move out of blame and into self-awareness and self-responsibility. Within the context of relationships, we must learn how to set and maintain healthful boundaries, and how to understand the subtle energetic influences

that change our experience of the world and ourselves on a moment to moment basis.

In the work with horses we are almost forced into experiencing this new and proactive approach to life. If one wants to have successful interactions with horses, one must set clear boundaries, take an active and positive role in co-creating relationship, and become mindful of our energetic beings.

Summary

Horses live in a constant state of relationship with one another. To survive is to be in relationship. To be alone is to face death. Horses understand that deep into the very marrow of their bones. Humans can learn a great deal about relationship from interactions with and observations of horses. It is through relationships that we define our sense of self. Horses provide us with moment by moment information about how we impact those around us and how we move through this world, and thus how well or how poorly we do relationship. The work of EFMH/ES takes the information provided by the horses and helps the client or student to find ways of integrating that information back into his/her daily life.

Horses seem to evoke feelings of comfort, of safety, and of love in clients or students who form relationships with them. In many cases the horse becomes the one being that a student or client feels safe to share deep personal reflections with. Through connection with a horse, humans may learn how to form deeper, more meaningful, and more healthful relationships with those of their own species.

For those interested in EFMH/ES, understanding the reasons behind equine behavior is essential in helping co-create metaphor transfer. In most cases, it is the relationship that forms between the horse and the client or student that is unique to this field, and it is this aspect that seems to evoke the most positive results within treatment or education. We long to feel connected. We desire above all else to be seen for who we truly are. Horses, through their very nature, provide this for us.

CHAPTER EIGHT

DEVELOPMENT OF SELF THROUGH HORSE-PERSON-SHIP

Becoming Yourself

"It appears that the goal the individual most wishes to achieve, the end which he knowingly and unknowingly pursues, is to become himself." - Carl Rogers

Carl Rogers wrote a book in 1961 that was heralded as "the classic work on the human potential for growth and creativity." This book, *On Becoming a Person*[304] helps the reader gain an understanding of the concepts, theories, and skills needed to help an individual move into and through the stages of human development and self-awareness. Fascinatingly enough, the very material Rogers lays out within his ground breaking book has direct correlations to the work between horses and humans. Rogers presents a process he calls "being a person," and within the outline of this process concepts such as "getting behind the mask," experiencing feelings, and discovery of self within experiences are addressed. Already in prior areas of this text the reader has learned how horses help humans to see themselves more clearly and learn how to move beyond the masks that they wear. We have discussed how in working with horses the very experience of feelings becomes a tactile and provocative element of treatment or education, and in this chapter we will learn how we experience ourselves both within the context of our internal and external landscapes. It would appear that if we utilize Carl Rogers' model for "becoming a person," we can validate that when humans come into constructive contact with horses, the potential for self growth and development may occur.

In the following chapter we will learn about how horses may help to co-facilitate the experience of learning about and developing oneself through the art of horse-person-ship. We will explore the steps necessary to facilitate the process of growth and change, and we will examine the potential for heightened awareness, sensitivity and responsibility.

As Charles Tart writes in *Waking Up*, "Ideas about awakening, enlightenment, and spiritual growth are absolutely vital to us. They are also dangerous ideas. They are dangerous to the comfort and stability of our ordinary lives."[305] If we are willing to engage with ourselves on a level of deep personal reflection and growth, we must also be prepared for the changes this journey will bring to our daily lives. Patterns that we have co-created over the years will fall by the wayside as we recognize their limitations and replace them with new skills. Relationships will change because we will no longer have the ability to move through the world unaware of pain, suffering, and struggle, or joy, excitement, and connection. We find ourselves taking new and proactive steps to bring about healthfulness in our own lives, and therefore come to realize that there are certain ways of being, actions, or activities that we can no longer support. The people around us may become confused and surprised by our changes, and may attempt to pull us back into old and more comfortable patterns. Change is struggle, and certainly the process challenges us on nearly every level.

Accepting the lessons gained from walking the way of the horse can be difficult. Many come to this work for a "quick fix," or to "feel good," and instead find that the work with horses opens Pandora's Box, leaving the client with a very different experience than he or she might have expected. As facilitators of this work, those interested in it, or clients who might consider pursuing this as a treatment method, be warned that there are very few "short term" treatment methods that are ethical, successful, or appropriate. This work, if done in a therapeutic manner, may, quite literally, change your life, and if one is not willing or ready to put the time, energy and hard work into the process, the outcome can be overwhelming.[306] This chapter speaks to concepts that can be utilized in either an educational or therapeutic setting.

The Now: Grounding, Focus, Awareness, and Presence

*So for the first time in my life I went into a gallop around the field,
clutching Jade's thick brush of a mane. I had to stay totally focused
both on every part of her movement and on my own position. The
concentration was intense, and probably an intrinsic part of the enjoyment.
The mindfulness that arises from this degree of concentration is single-
pointed, the mind is not divided between one thing or another. I had
to be there in the present moment: Any thought, whether of fear or of
judgment or self-consciousness, would have unbalanced both of us.*
- Ingrid Soren, Zen and Horses[307]

For millennia, spiritual teachings have emphasized that without focus and awareness of the present moment, enlightenment cannot occur.[308] Whether we are seeking spiritual enlightenment or personal enlightenment gained through self-growth and development, it seems that the concept of being fully grounded within one's physical body, and oriented in time and space to the present moment is necessary. Without such an orientation it is difficult to understand ourselves, or to learn and grow. For it is only by becoming fully aware of the body and grounded in the Now that memories which have become trapped, leading to rote enactment of maladaptive patterns can be re-patterned and possibly changed.

Eckhart Tolle writes in *The Power of Now,*

> The whole essence of Zen consists in walking along the razor's edge of Now – to be so utterly, so completely present that no problem, no suffering, nothing that is not who you are in your essence, can survive in you. In the Now, in the absence of time, all your problems dissolve. Suffering needs time; it cannot survive in the Now.[309]

When humans come into contact with horses it is common to hear them say, "I forgot all my worries while I was with the horse."[310] This experience echo's Tolle's description of the essence of Zen, and can remind us that within these pure moments of timelessness, we learn who and what we truly are. However, working with horses requires a somewhat more pragmatic approach. Becoming present, grounded, aware and focused offers a way to begin, and a practice for how to re-connect with our true selves. It offers the experience of fully *knowing* oneself, but in some cases, may not offer the solution of how to work through and deal healthfully with maladaptive patterns, or unsatisfying relationships or careers, and other such real life struggles. As we continue we will learn how horses help to not only bring us into the present and into an awareness of self, but also how they can help us to learn the skills for making tangible change within our lives.

In working with horses we must exist in the present moment completely otherwise accidents are possible, and even likely. Horses live constantly in the present moment, totally aware of themselves and their surroundings, and relentlessly focused.[311] Their very survival depends upon how successfully they can achieve this state of being. When in the presence of horses we are drawn into their unique way of being, and may find ourselves relieved of our worries, stresses, anxieties, and other issues. During traditional riding lessons students are taught how to "leave their stuff at the gate" prior to coming into the arena for a ride. Good riding instructors know the importance of getting their students focused, present, and aware before beginning the potentially dangerous undertaking of learning to ride, or challenging their already existing skills.[312]

Within the work of EFMH/ES concepts of present moment focus, grounding, and body awareness are crucial in helping people better understand who they are, what they are feeling, and what they think. Some humans have a tendency to be unsure or unaware when it comes to these core issues, and generally move through the world in a fog, attempting to understand themselves but never really knowing how well they have succeeded. In order to bring about change, be it behavioral or communication style change, or larger issues of functional change, knowing oneself is a prerequisite. The present moment has a huge amount to offer the human who is willing to listen and pay attention to the subtle (and not so subtle) signs that are being given by the horse on a moment to moment basis.

We may lose much of the richness of life by living outside of the present. Eckhart Tolle asks, "Have you ever experienced, done, thought, or felt anything outside of the Now?" He answers his own question, "Nothing ever happened in the past; it happened in the Now. Nothing will ever happen in the future; it happened in the Now."[313] Conceptualize for a moment the notion that living outside of the Now decreases our interaction with life, and decreases the richness found in every interaction we have. Boredom appears to be a fairly common state of being for many residing within the United States.[314] It is no wonder, for if we are living in the past or in the future, we cannot experience anything. We can only use our memories or the projections of past memories to create the future. We are not living the experience. When we come fully into the present it is almost as if the world changes color. Everything looks differently, brighter, clearer, and richer in tone and texture. We find ourselves lost in the call of a bird, the smell of warm pine needles in the late summer sun shine, or the feeling of a wet horse nose on our cheek. We feel consumed by a multitude of sensations, overwhelmed by the realness of life.

It is here, in the present, that change can take place. One cannot change the past, nor change the future, rather we can only change our own perception of the events that did take place or will take place. And that realization generally occurs within the present moment.[315] People engage in both therapeutic and educational programs in order to change - either to learn something new that will help guide and direct the course of their lives, or to change their felt connection to the past, and therefore hopefully change how they live life. In school we are constantly taught to look ahead to our future, and the entire purpose of higher education is to prepare for that ever looming notion of the future. In many cases mental health services are also based around both the past and the future, with the goal being to help individuals come to

terms with and accept their pasts, therefore ensuring that they will not carry out the same patterns in their future. When using the concept of the present and the importance of present moment awareness we should be thoughtful of how unusual and possibly even unorthodox this approach might feel to some. Thus, when individuals come to experience the work of EFMH/ES, and find themselves brought (by the horse and sometimes with the help of the human facilitator) immediately and fully into the present, their reaction can be somewhat unexpected.

By being brought fully into the present we may encounter a "felt" experience of everything co-existing around us. We may be inundated with "Technicolor" sensations, feelings of ourselves and our bodies that we may never have had before, and experiences of other beings and how they connect and relate to us. Suddenly the world feels filled with interconnection and the web of life becomes something felt vs. something intellectualized. This experience can be intoxicating, leaving the "feeler" with an overwhelming sense of connection to the place, people, and animals who were around when the experience took place. Although this is innately a wonderful and healing experience, the potential hazard is that we may have no clear idea or picture of how to attain this same sense without the factors being the same. In other words, how does the client attain a sense of the present moment in every interaction that he/she has, and how does he/she implement the self reflection that he/she had while in the present moment back into his/her "normal" life? It is here that the facilitation skills of the human educator or mental health professional comes into play.[316] The horse is fully capable of bringing humans into a felt experience of themselves, the natural world, and all beings co-existing therein, but it falls upon the human facilitator to help the client or student both retain the lessons learned while in the presence of horses, and also create a new behavioral paradigm that brings the notion of present awareness into their daily existence.

Forward Movement

Once the human has become grounded, focused, and aware of his or her body within the present moment, it is time for the work to move forward. Chris Irwin writes, "Everything about staying alive for a horse involves forward movement. I can hardly stress this enough: Horses

feel the need to go forward at all times."[317] Herein lies the metaphor. Once a human being has come into the present moment, the job of the human facilitator is to help guide the student or client towards a life lived in the present moment. In order to move forward one must be firmly lodged within his/her experience of the present. Getting stuck generally means that one's mind is still circling around events of the past, or envisioning what the future could hold, and therefore becoming impotent in the present.

"I am _____. I am responsible for myself today, my perceptions and my experiences, thus I contribute to the safety of the group."
Barbara Rector's
Adventures in Awareness
Safety Contract

A lack of forward movement may mean that the individual is in a holding pattern. There are certainly cases where such a holding pattern is healthful and necessary prior to making decisions and implementing changes. However, change cannot happen within either stagnation or contemplation. Many times people come to either an educational or therapeutic setting desiring change, but are unable or unwilling to get out of the revolving cycles of the past and the future. Until they are willing and able to move forward, change may be impossible.

In the work of EFMH/ES the clients are allowed the experience of being around creatures who not only live completely in the present, but who also engage in forward movement as a healthful self protection device, therefore modeling for clients a new and different approach to living life. By the human facilitators use of education about the way in which horses think and function, and by the teaching of new skills that would help the client better or more successfully interact with the horse, the client is allowed to practice these new skills within the context of the horse/human relationship.

Irwin states, "Too often when we want to control a horse, we attempt to stop it from moving. This violates the horse's deepest nature."[318] A well known dressage riding instructor in northern California did not believe in teaching her students to back up their horses, as her feeling was that within this very action existed an ultimate demonstration of our "power over" domination of the horse. She believed that backing up a horse went against all of his natural tendencies, and that it was only when horses submitted to dominance did backing up occur in the wild. Due to the nature of a dressage test, her students and their horses did have to learn how to back up at least a few steps, but her method for inviting that learning process, and her nearly non-existent use of the exercise allowed her horses to back up without feeling a loss of control, and without feeling a sense of fear.[319] To ask a horse to back up is asking him to move blindly into a space that could hold all manner of dangers. It is asking him to trust you as his rider implicitly. If the rider has gained that respect, the horse will engage in the activity with little fear, but unfortunately many people use the very act of backing up as punishment for their horses, thereby tapping into the instinctual and fear based reality that creates dis-trust.

Imagine the power in using this as a metaphor while working with a woman who has been "pushed into a corner" all her life by her father, mother, and husband. Imagine how well she can relate to the feeling of being backed up without being able to see where she is going, or what danger lies behind her. Imagine being told that it is within the process of backing up that something positive will occur. Every fiber of her being resists this notion, but society tells her that she must go backwards to discover the future. Then imagine being told that it is through moving forward that change is possible. The feelings of freedom, of possibility, and of power and control over her own destiny arise, and hope becomes real.

Horses want to move forward. Everything within their very being calls them towards forward motion. If we as facilitators can help our clients learn the same skills and practice those skills within the context of working with horses, the possibility for deep and long lasting change exists.

Self-Awareness and Self-Image

When human beings are able to become present in the moment, connect to their body, and ground their thoughts into the here and now, they may be able to access information about who they are, how they feel, what they think, and what drives them. Furthermore, they may be better able to make conscious decisions about their actions rather than reacting. They experience what it is like to be in the driver's seat of their destiny. It is in these moments of centered, focused awareness that they are able to define themselves. As Carl Rogers reminded us, it is the desire of all humankind to become truly themselves. Many times this process is called gaining self-awareness.[320]

The Impact of Self-Awareness

The societal connotations of a population who functions from a place of self-awareness and conscious decision making are fairly profound. As Ms. Rector has already alluded to, clinical studies demonstrate that societal violence is linked to a lack of self-awareness.[321] In 2002 the World Health Organization released the World Report on Violence and Health. This report took three years to compile and benefited from the contributions of 160 experts worldwide. The report was peer reviewed by scientists and holds within it the comments and contributions from representatives from all of the worlds regions. This report clearly links issues of self-esteem and self-awareness to a propensity for violence worldwide. The impact of self-aware individuals upon all levels of society is massive. The World Report on Violence and Health helps bring perspective to the vastness of the problem:

> Each year, over 1.6 million people worldwide lose their lives to violence. Violence is among the   leading causes of death for people aged 15–44 years worldwide, accounting for 14% of deaths among males and 7% of deaths among females. For every person who dies as a result of violence, many more are injured and suffer from a range of physical, sexual, reproductive and mental health problems. Moreover, violence places a massive burden on national economies, costing countries billions of US dollars each year in health care, law enforcement and lost productivity.[322]

Imagine a treatment method that was effective in targeting key areas of violence prevention by bringing human beings into a self-aware state of being that allowed them to begin making conscious choices.

The work of EFMH/ES has accumulated a large amount of anecdotal evidence that suggests that this method may in fact be a viable and sustainable way to drastically reduce violence through the introduction of self-awareness building.[323]

In 2000 Four Mile Correctional Center in Canon City, Colorado, was having immense success introducing prison inmates to wild mustangs and teaching the inmates how to gentle the horses and prepare them for successful adoption. The director of that program stated, "The program teaches the inmates communication skills and responsibility, and gives them goals and skills."[324]

In 2003 the Nevada Bureau of Land Management published an article about the Warm Springs Correctional Facilities wild horse training program. The director of that program says this about the inmate wild horse training program, "Most important to me is that the guys get along with each other and that they respect the program, the horses and each other. They have to watch out for each other with these animals. They're wild when we get them. It can be dangerous if you don't pay attention." He goes on to suggest that the men in the wild horse program learn values like self respect, self-esteem, and honesty.[325]

At the Marion County Correctional Institute in Ocala, Florida, where injured or retired racehorses come to be rehabilitated with the help of prison inmates, one of the participants of the program comments, "Everyone in this program relates to these horses. They feel the pain they are going through and that helps an inmate. It changes them. They get connected to the horses. You and the horse become one and that makes you a better person". The Thoroughbred Retirement Foundation, this country's oldest and largest Thoroughbred horse rescue group is helping to make programs like the one existing at the Marion Country Correctional Institute a reality. Monique Koehler, founder of the Thoroughbred Retirement Foundation believes that working with horses helps rehabilitate prisoners and provides them with career skills useful upon their release. She believes the hundreds of success stories involving inmates over the years have proven her right.[326]

The examples continue with success stories from both the United States and countries outside of the U.S. It appears, through anecdotal evidence, that something profound is occurring between humans who have already committed violent crimes or have a predisposition to commit such crimes and the work with horses. The next step is to research precisely which factors are co-occurring to make the work of EFMH/ES successful with such a population. The anecdotal information indicates that such research would be useful, and also indicates that with or without formal research horses are helping humans come into a deeper awareness of themselves and their impact upon the world.

Self-awareness may lead to living a life more fully, and more presently. Self-awareness also may allow people to understand their motivations, learn what help and assistance they might need to become more healthful, and take proactive steps in their lives towards healthier relationships, careers, and child raising practices.[327]

The Story of "T"

At Esperanza our Native American inmates benefited on many levels from the work with horses. However, one story calls out, wishing to be told. Many of the inmates had already had children by the time they were 12 or 13. One particular inmate who worked with us for a number of years had a daughter who he had fathered at age 12. During her early life this young man was heavily involved with the gang culture - running drugs, stealing cars, and becoming involved in drive by shootings and other violent acts. Both he and the mother of the child used alcohol and drugs both during the pregnancy and following the birth of their daughter. By the time this young man came to us he was disconnected from both his child and from the mother, who by that time had righted her life and was raising the child alone.

At Esperanza T, as we will call him, chose a horse named Sunny, a young Arabian mare who believed herself to be the baby of the herd. Sunny was prone to spooking and seemed at times afraid of her own shadow. In the beginning T and Sunny worked solely on becoming comfortable with each other on the ground. The focus of the sessions were primarily on T, and his issues regarding choices and behaviors within the jail setting. After a time T approached the Esperanza staff, suggesting that it might be time for him and Sunny to start working on Sunny's issues. This was an interesting request for a non-horse person to voice, but we felt it was appropriate to hear him out.

T suggested that what Sunny needed was someone to help her better understand boundaries, and also better understand the world around her so that she would not be so afraid of everything. He suggested that she needed someone strong and confident to show her that people and things were not always as bad as they seemed. He wanted to help her "grow up," and felt that he was the person to be in that role. Over the course of a year T was able to do everything he had suggested, and Sunny grew into a confident, independent, and strong horse. Towards the end of his work with Sunny T approached the staff, and informed them that he was going to take the step to be "jumped out" of his gang. He told the staff that it was time for him to become a father to his daughter. He explained that before his work with Sunny he was afraid that he was not capable of being a father to his daughter, and therefore made decisions to stay as far away as possible. After working with Sunny and undertaking the project to "help her grow up," he realized that he was actually capable of providing his daughter with the love, dedication, and direction that was needed.

Upon his release from jail T approached his gang and informed them that he wanted out. That night T ended up in the local hospital, recovering from a gun shot wound in the stomach. He had been shot and nearly killed in the pursuit of getting "jumped" out of the gang, but luckily, he survived that night, and three years later was still out of the gang and living with his daughter and her mother, being a supportive and loving father.

I will never forget that night. T had called me after being shot, and told me where the ambulance was taking him. I arrived at the hospital just as the ambulance got there. I went with him through all of the emergency room procedures, sat outside of the operating room while they removed the bullet, and sat in his room until he awoke. He shared many things with me, one of which stands out beyond all else to this day. He told me that it was Sunny who gave him the strength to stand up and fight for his life. It was Sunny who taught him that he was a good person and thus allowed him to realize that he could be a good father. It was Sunny who gave him permission to find and reclaim his soul.[328]

Parenting and Self-Awareness/Self-Identity

The story of T helps to demonstrate how powerful the work with horses can be for individuals desiring to learn healthful parenting skills and engage in new self-awareness practices.

Starting as early as the prenatal stages of development, Lloyd de Mause of the City University of New York, reminds us in his presentation, "Restaging Fetal Traumas in War and Social Violence,"[329] that it is in childhood where the building blocks of life are created. It is here that we become predisposed towards violence, or towards health. Until we, as a culture, can understand just how deep the importance of parenting goes, and what the ramifications of negative parenting are on society and the environment, violence and environmental devastation are likely to continue. It is our responsibility to recognize that self-awareness and conscious decision making play a vast role in the development of healthful parenting skills. It does not matter how many books a prospective parent might read, nor how many parent education courses they might attend, until they are self-aware human beings with the ability to make conscious choices, and take responsibility for their own actions, thoughts, beliefs, and behaviors, children may be parented unconsciously.

The work of EFMH/ES teaches real-life parenting skills by introducing notions of responsibility, compassion, love, and commitment and by aiding and guiding parents towards greater self-awareness. The effects of violence are more costly, both on a societal level and on an environmental level, than they were in the past. The level of violence is no longer limited to fist fights in schools, but instead has the capacity to impact large numbers of the populous, and is financially draining on our economy. In most cases we tend to utilize more resources dealing with the aftermath of violence than we do attempting to prevent violence. This allocation of funds impacts our ability to bring large scale societal change and locks us into a holding pattern of increasing violence. By introducing services like EFMH/ES to children at early stages of their development, we may be able to help prevent violence before it ever occurs. Many provides of EFMH/ES dream of a time when all school children could experience the gifts horses have to offer, and feel that through introducing EFMH/ES to schools the level of violence within the school systems would decrease.

As T experienced, his self-image changed as his self-awareness grew. He came to identify himself as a parent, rather than as a gang member. With his new found self-awareness, T reached out to learn what exactly his new self-image meant. Through his work with Sunny, his ability to recognize, define, and refine his self-image was made possible, and through that work he made the decision to change the path that he was on, letting go of his identity as a gang member and embracing his role as a father.

At KILDEN, the Norwegian Information and Documentation Centre for Women's Studies and Gender Research they pose an interesting question that links a lack of self-awareness to violence:

> Is it possible that gender equality and the 'empowerment' of women lead to less violence? And can it be possible that the percentage of women who are still exposed to abuse actually remain in the violent relationship because they do not have access to the resources and the self-awareness that is required to confront a man or partner who uses violence?

They also comment on emotionality and self-awareness:

> Among the writers referred to in this report it is particularly Per Isdal (2000) who emphasizes the importance of and the need for change in the upbringing of boys. Isdal writes that boys are largely exposed to a gender role that deprives them of the opportunity to develop a rich emotional life. He points to the necessity of breaking down the emotional prison that the traditional male role has constituted.[330]

In work with horses, humans may be brought into direct contact with their emotions. While in the presence of horses some people report experiencing intense feelings of fear, love, sadness, frustration and anger, and joy. Possibly because we are in the present moment more fully when close to horses, we are more capable of having a felt experience of our emotions.[331] Horses appear to evoke such an experience because of their own authentic expression of emotion. Therefore we are given permission to respond, and since horses are so large, so potentially scary, and so filled with animation, we have a hard time ignoring their responses. The invitation to authentically feel and experience emotions can be quite powerful for many clients experiencing EFMH/ES.

Of Horses and Men

In work with horses the values of being compassionate, loving, gentle, respectful, and sensitive may be fostered on a daily basis. Men coming into contact with horses tend to find themselves hugging, kissing, and otherwise acting "thoroughly unmanly" when they are in the presence of the horse with whom they have connected. From hardened

"Breathe, center, connect to the earth that you stand upon. Find your body, find your heart - Open"
~ Group Opening

criminals and youth gang members, to struggling fathers and leaders within their communities, men find the opportunity to develop a rich emotional life without being criticized or ridiculed. Within the work of EFMH/ES men may learn how to redefine their self-image, therefore making it possible to break free of social constructs that tell them who they are supposed to be.[332]

Work with horses demands that we are present-moment focused, and because of this the horses invite us to become more self-aware and recognize our desired self-image. We are allowed to be deeply who we are while in the presence of horses. We discover hidden qualities about ourselves that we never knew existed, and we learn how to capitalize upon those qualities in healthful and productive ways. We learn how to understand ourselves and we feel what it is like to make conscious choices about our lives.

Self-Esteem and Self-Confidence

F. Rodewalt and M.W. Tragakis write in their article, *Self-Esteem and Self-Regulation: Toward Optimal Studies of Self-Esteem* that "self-esteem is the third most frequently occurring theme in psychological literature and has already resulted in over 25,000 articles, chapters, and books refer to the topic".[333] The concept of self-esteem is, according to Wikipedia, one of the "oldest concepts in psychology".[334] It appears that the concept was first coined by the American psychologist and philosopher, William James, in 1890 and currently has three distinct types of definitions within the field of modern psychology, each of which has generated its own method of research, findings, and practical

"Horses move through this world in a way that people of our time desperately need to emulate. Horse nature helps us to connect with our own essential selves, our own tru nature."
~Robin Wellington

applications. William James presented the notion that self-esteem is found by dividing one's "success/pretensions."[335] In the mid 1960's Maurice Rosenberg and others of the social learning theory suggested that self-esteem was the "stable sense of personal worth or worthiness that can be measured by self-report testing". Finally in 1969 Nathaniel Branden defined self-esteem as, "a relationship between one's competence and one's worthiness". More recently in 2003 C. Sedikides and A.P. Gregg wrote, "Self-esteem or self-worth includes a person's subjective appraisal of himself or herself as intrinsically positive or negative to some degree."[336]

Research

Experiencing an increase in self-esteem and self-confidence are considered common benefits from the work of EFMH/ES. These two factors have also been some of the most researched within the field, probably due to the relative ease of utilizing a pre-and post assessment tool to determine improvement.

From the early work of Carlson in 1983, Dismuke in 1984, Brock in 1988, Mason in 1988, Stuler in 1993, and Crawley, Crawley, & Retter in 1994, to the more modern pilot studies of Carolyn M. Gatty, Krista Meinersmann, Florence Roberts, and Judy Bradberrry, and Patricia Cody the concept of clients gaining in self-esteem and self-confidence while working with horses is well documented.[337]

The large amount of anecdotal evidence also supports the theory that if properly facilitated, the work of EFMH/ES may be able to help individuals gain self-confidence and self-esteem. The McCormicks, Linda Kohanov, Barbara Rector, Mary Midkiff, and many others all concur that working with horses can help individuals come to a more healthful place in their recognition of personal skills and talents, and opens the door to further development of human potential.[338]

How Horses Instill Self-Esteem and Self-Confidence

Working with horses seems to naturally instill a sense of self-confidence and self-esteem. Learning how to be in the presence of a creature so massive, so potentially dangerous, and so unpredictable (to a newcomer to the work with horses), is truly an amazing process. Humans who lack self-esteem and self-confidence may question their ability to succeed at anything, and when faced with the task of getting to know and safely work around such a huge beast, they may seriously question their potential for success. However, since the horse is by nature a prey animal, and generally a gentle soul, once the human has been taught the proper handling skills and techniques, and set up in a success-oriented scenario, the likelihood for failure is very slim. Therefore, the individual is able to face an obstacle that might otherwise have stopped them in their very tracks, and overcome their fear, discomfort and self doubt to have a successful and deeply meaningful exchange.

Learning to ride well is a challenge, and it takes skill, dedication, and perseverance. When students learn how to master the challenges involved in the art of good horse-person-ship, they begin to recognize their own unique strengths, talents and gifts. Many who come to EFMH/ES programs have no concept of what they do well, or what their strengths and talents might be. Rather, they have been inundated with all of the things that they do wrong, and how they negatively impact the world around them. They might be in relationships that do not foster or allow for their own exploration of passions and gifts, and over time they may have come to doubt their ability to grow. When they come into contact with the horse and begin gaining skills, their sense of self, their self-image, and their level of self-esteem may begin to change. They realize other talents and skills that they did not know they had, and they begin to take a more active role in their lives, feeling better equipped to do so.

Reality Check

Countless are the stories of EFMH/ES clients who have benefited from an increase in self-esteem and self-confidence while in the presence of horses. However, unfortunately there have also been failures. These failures are generally not spoken of, nor can you find them in current texts about the field. However, they exist and occur more than we would like to think. In an interview with Linda Kohanov, when asked the question, "what are the failures of the field to the clients we serve," she said:

> I would have to say that failures do occur in this field. I think that sometimes clients get shamed during this work. Some facilitators demonstrate how to do something with horses and then without providing any information about how to achieve a similar result, ask the client to attempt the skill. The client tries to do what the facilitator did with little or no success. Their "failure" to accomplish the task is then the fodder for the processing session. I think that this is an unfair and inappropriate use of an EFEL (Equine Facilitated Experiential Learning) method. The client ends the session recognizing an area that he or she needs to address, but also experiencing a blow to his/her self-esteem or feeling shamed into the insight.[339]

Ann Alden, president of EFMHA, also shared a story about a mental health professional who had limited training in the work of EFMH/ES. This individual set up an activity where the outcome, if facilitated properly, might lead to a bonding experience many call "imaginary lead line," which is essentially the art of connection between horse and human which allows the human to walk the horse around the arena without the use of a halter or lead rope. This occurs only when the human and the horse have bonded or connected, and the horse feels invested in the relationship and trusting enough to follow the human. The mental health professional attempted to use this activity to demonstrate for the client that she *was* someone who others cared for, loved, or wanted near to them. However, due to poor facilitation and a lack of understanding about the language of Equus on the part of the mental health professional, the client instead experienced a failure.

The client attempted to get the horse to move around the pen with her, but the horse was uninterested due to a poorly managed herd situation, and a lack of time and relationship building between the horse and the client. The mental health professional had frontloaded the situation, expecting that it would be successful, and so when it proved otherwise, she had no opportunity to allow the client to take a different, but still healthful, lesson away with her. Rather, the client viewed the situation as yet another failure on her part to be lovable.[340]

In hearing this story many people might think that this is an uncommon incident, however, each person interviewed for this text contributed a different story that essentially stated the same thing. There are failures occurring within this field, and they range from unsafe use of the horse/human relationship, to a lack of education and training in the art of EFMH/ES facilitation. Being in the presence of a horse brings many humans pure joy, and a sense of uninhibited love. They feel better about themselves and their lives just by coming to the barn, breathing in fresh air, and seeing these majestic creatures. *All of this occurs without the intervention of the human facilitator.* Therefore, clients appear more prone to "buy into" the work of EFMH/ES even with poor facilitation, unsafe conditions, or even unethical use of the method. Simply being around horses is enough for many people. However, for others being in the presence of horses can be terrifying, or can lead to an unsuccessful and unfulfilling attempt at connection. Without skilled facilitation, the potential for clients to experience personal failure or become afraid increases. We must begin raising the bar and training people in the true *ART* of EFMH/ES facilitation.

Traditional therapeutic training does not generally include experiential facilitation skills, as was demonstrated in the case of Ms. Alden's story. Furthermore, the knowledge of an activity does not equate the experience and deep understanding of the methodology behind the creation of

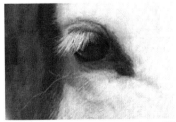

"The horse is an intrigal link to the client's authentic self."
~ Karen Head, Equinection,
Asheville, NC

that very activity. For instance, traditionally trained psychodynamic psychotherapists would not expect a lay person to understand the nuances and depth of a Gestalt activity or interaction, nor would they expect an untrained and uneducated individual to engage a client in a psychotherapeutic session. The field of EFMH/ES is very similar. It is in understanding the deep nuances, theory, and concepts of the work *specific* to EFMH/ES that makes it possible to facilitate experiences that are ethical and helpful for clients.

People can have experiences around horses that raise their self-esteem and self-confidence, research has helped to make this notion valid. However, who is actually facilitating? And what is the role of the human facilitator in the process of self-esteem and self-confidence building? Through interviewing, observation, and time spent in the field it has become painfully clear that not all EFMH/ES facilitators are helping to co-create healthful situations that raise self-confidence and self-esteem. We would be foolish to assume that the blanket statement, "EFMH/ES helps people develop higher self-esteem and self-confidence" is accurate. It would be more accurate to suggest that, "If properly facilitated by someone with training, education, and expertise, EFMH/ES may have the potential to help people develop higher self-esteem and self-confidence".

Intuition

Merriam – Webster Dictionary defines intuition as "the power or faculty of attaining to direct knowledge or cognition without evident rational thought and inference".[341] Webster's Unabridged Dictionary defines intuition as "the immediate knowing or learning of something without the conscious use of reasoning; instantaneous apperception".[342] Transcendentalist, inventor, architect, engineer, mathematician, poet and cosmologist, Buckminster Fuller, believed that intuition is a core skill for human evolution, being central to major breakthroughs in science, art, industry, and all human endeavors.[343]

It would seem that Carl Jung's collective unconscious, Rubert Sheldrake's morphic fields, and Larry Dossey's non-local mind[344] all help to explain the phenomenon of intuition. If we can accept that there exists a body of knowledge that includes all things ever taught or learned that is within our grasp, then it seems only logical that one could immediately gain access to any information desired without needing to learn it. The question is, how? How does one tap into this body of knowledge? How do people simply know things without ever having to be taught? How is it possible for people to intuitively sense an event before it happens? These are questions that many scientists have

"Today I know that I cannot control the ocean tides, I can only go with the flow... When I struggle and try to organize the Atlantic to my specifications, I sink. If I flail and thrash and growl and grumble, I go under. But if I let go and float, I am borne aloft."
~ Marie Stilkind

been pondering for centuries. They are also some of the questions that have actually been answered by the works of those mentioned above and by other scientists working within the realm of quantum physics. For the purpose of this section, the question we need to concentrate on is how do horses help people tap into their own sense of intuition? And, what are the benefits of such a practice?

Quite simply, life is easier, less stressful, and more enjoyable when you begin to trust your intuition. It is almost like having an internal Global Positioning System (GPS) that helps you navigate the streets of life. Choices become simpler. We know what we want and thus we spend far less time agonizing over what we should or should not do. We have fewer relational conflicts and are better able to protect ourselves from the emotional drain of unhealthy, unproductive relationships. In essence, when we listen to our intuition, we have more energy to devote to all the other aspects of our lives. In much the same way that instinctual communication assists us in our decision making process, our ability to listen to our intuition allows us clarity and gives us a sense of personal empowerment. Horses and the work of EFMH/ES help us to better understand our sense of intuition, and provide us with tangible tools to learn how to foster our intuitive skills.

Finding our Bodies
In order to be able to learn how to hear our intuition, we must first be securely lodged within our physical bodies. We must be grounded in the present, and aware of ourselves in time and space. Therefore, all of the qualities that make horses helpful in the aspects of present moment

awareness and grounding also become useful in learning the skill of listening to our intuitions. Briefly stated, when we are in the presence of something so large, so potentially dangerous, and so magnificent as a horse, we are pulled firmly back into our bodies. If simply being in the presence of a horse does not do that for a client, proper facilitation by the human counterpart, and well designed activities will generally ensure that the client learns how to connect with his/her body, become centered, and able to move into present state awareness quickly and easily. Once we are in our bodies we are able to learn how to listen to our bodies. Listening to our bodies suggests that our bodies hold a body of knowledge, and that they are able to communicate in a manner we can understand. For instance, obesity is a growing issue in the United States.[345] People eat food that their bodies do not want. They eat more than their bodies desire. It is quite possible that no one has ever taught the people struggling with such issues how to listen to their body's unique and specific communications about what to eat, when to eat it, and when to stop eating. Many who are taught the skill of learning how to listen to their bodies self-report profound awakenings in regards to their body awareness and diet control. Many report that they come to realize that their bodies have been communicating all along, and that by listening to the urges of the body, proper weight can be maintained.

Listening to our Bodies
Once we have learned how to listen to what our bodies have to say, we are ready to begin delving into the deeper and sometimes confusing sense of intuition. Our bodies seem to act as a transmitter through which information is passed. It seems that it is harder for our minds to open up and grasp information coming from non-ordinary sources and easier for such information to be passed through our bodies. Therefore, we must learn how to listen to our bodies. Once we have become comfortable with this avenue for accessing information, our brains seem more willing to accept and believe the validly of these non-ordinary sources.

Possibly because the lines between instinct and intuition are so blurred, we generally do not recognize what is an instinctual urge and what is our intuition. We can think of instinct as our animalistic selves becoming activated and reacting to information pre-programmed within our very DNA, whereas intuition appears to be our ability to tap into some other information source outside of our physical beings. A challenging but useful practice is to begin separating out our sense of instinct from our sense of intuition. It helps us understand what to do with the information we receive if we understand its origins.[346]

Modeling

Horses model for humans that even a creature as driven by their instincts as they appear to be, can still make apparently rational decisions about how to control, understand, and adjust behavior to fit circumstances. When humans come into contact with horses and observe their behaviors, humans make certain judgments about the differences between instinctual action and intuitive information. The human is able to perceive the differences between the instinctual and intuitive processes *because of what they observe in the horses.*

Connection to Non-Ordinary Source

Throughout time the literature suggests that people believed horses connected them to the Divine.[347] Even in current times, people report feeling that horses connect them to a source (Higher Power, the Divine, or the Collective Unconscious) that provides insight and information gained in a non-ordinary fashion. In my 2003 study, I found that 53% of all participants strongly believed that there is a connection between horses and whatever they might call the Divine. The majority of participants described the benefit of such a connection with a Divine source in the following ways: feeling the presence of the Divine makes people feel less alone, connecting to a Divine source provides us with intuitive information, the Divine is a source of energy greater than oneself which instills wonder and awe, and having a connection with the Divine allows us to listen to a source of guidance outside of ourselves. Making a leap, it would almost seem that these participants are speaking both about a Divine source, and Jung's notion of a collective unconscious which suggests that outside of the realm of our normal consciousness exists information that anyone can access. This information can help people learn, discover, or perceive things instantaneously without study, practice, or prior knowledge. Perhaps when in the presence of horses, if a human is grounded, aware, and open, he or she has a different level of clarity about how to access such information. It may appear to be "intuition" that brought about that clarity, but who is to say exactly where such information arrived from?

Implications of Intuition
To intuit something indicates a sudden change in perception, a shift in ones consciousness that allows something completely new and un-thought of to enter *without the hard work and lengthy process* that one normally attributes to change. Imagine what this could mean to the fields of mental health, of education, and certainly of human growth and development. Imagine if humans could intuit information that they needed to make huge personal strides towards health without having to spend years gaining the skills, personal enlightenment, and self-realization that it generally takes. Think of how our potential both as individuals and as a people could expand if within a life time we could move beyond the issues that currently bind us to dis-health. It is nearly inconceivable. Imagine a world where *health* was normal, and whatever personal growth work we did was only to expand our wellness and further investigate our human potential.

Many facilitating the work of EFMH/ES are already moving in this direction. They are concentrating upon a strengths-based, health and wellness model of treatment and education verses a model of dis-health and disease. It seems that this work lends itself easily to investigating human potential and helping humans discover and capitalize upon their strengths. If humans can learn to use their sense of intuition more fully, it may have the potential to enable us to move more quickly through the process of gaining self-awareness and thus healing ourselves.

A Thought To Ponder
Is it possible that horses have the capacity to receive and respond to both instinctual *and* intuitive information? The basis for this notion is observation and antidotal evidence, not scientific data recovery. However, the concept itself is compelling. It is fairly obvious to the knowledgeable horse person when a horse is reacting from an instinctual urge. A great deal of study and testing has been done to isolate what instinct is within animals, and how each species differs

in their instinctual posturing, behaviors, and thought-processes. For a very long time the majority of equine behaviors could be directly linked to instinct. However, with the introduction of EFMH/ES, it is anecdotally suggested that horses may be engaging in behaviors that appear to go against our commonly held understanding of instinct. In fact, in many cases it seems that horses may be resisting instinctual urges, and choosing other behaviors that would appear un-horse-like. In many cases horses appear to act in this manner during a reflective feedback process. Could it be that horses are using their intuition and, through tapping into, observing, or sensing the human's energetic or physical body, are able to gain useful information about the human? And furthermore, is it possible that through their behaviors and actions, the horses are attempting to share that information with the human in question?

Within the field of EFMH/ES people have tried to explain this phenomenon by suggesting that horses are simply acting upon their instinctual urges, and that everything they do can be explained through their instinctual prey and fight or flight nature. After enough years observing horses, learning about the instinctual actions of horses, reading a majority of the literature available in the field currently, interviewing others doing this work, and watching horses working within EFMH/ES circumstances it has become very clear that there is something else occurring when horses begin to truly "facilitate" this work. What is this "something else" that occurs, and how can we scientifically test the phenomenon to better understand its origins? What is happening when Cloudy (a horse) chooses to lie down and Excell, Suzy, and Sunny (his herd mates) cease all movement for exactly eleven minutes at exactly the same time a woman whose son was murdered enters into their space. Is it strange that the horses stayed completely immobile, frozen in time and space until I reflected back to the client that with her arrival into the pasture the energy felt stagnate and stuck, as though to move would be terrifying? Why did the horses stop what they had been doing mere moments before and freeze all movement? Why did Cloudy, who had been munching peacefully prior to the client entering into the pasture, suddenly drop to the ground, not rolling, nor relaxed, but tense and still as death itself?

Tears poured down the client's face as she said, "no one has ever been able to *see* how I really feel. I feel completely frozen in that moment, when it happened. I just cope. Everyday I wonder if there is something wrong with me because I don't show anything, not sadness, not anger. I am just there, stuck. There is no movement in my life." We stood still in the pasture and suddenly she took a deep breath. At the very moment that she exhaled, Cloudy got back to his feet, swished his tail and starting walking over to Excell. Suzy and Sunny went back to fighting over scraps of breakfast hay, and Excell and Cloudy started "face-playing," engaging each other in movement, life, and energy. What made the horses able to enact exactly what the client had not been able to vocalize since the tragedy of her son's death?

Regardless of what may or may not be scientifically provable regarding the horse's use (or lack there of) of intuition, we can be relatively certain that intuition and instinct within the human race are two different processes, and we can recognize the benefits of understanding and becoming responsive to both. As we have learned, horses can innately help us to become grounded and in our bodies, the first step of understanding both our instinctual and intuitive abilities.

Power

People throughout time have recognized the unsurpassed physical power of the horse. It is the very thing that has drawn humans to horses from as far back as the days of the Cult Stallion of Dereivka. Seeing something so free, so beautiful, so graceful, so filled with unbridled passion and potency reminds us of that which we all crave to experience. People feel the pull towards horses regardless of their desire or ability to ever mount one. However, once someone has sat atop of a horse, their perspective of the world fundamentally alters. To be astride a creature so powerful, so large, and so beautiful opens the heart, engages the soul, and lifts the spirit.

Horses represent the ability to live fully within their power. As humans some of us tend to dismiss our personal powers, be unaware of what those powers might be, or discount our abilities. We may be terrified of our greatness, and instead exist within mediocrity. Our gifted children tend to be marginalized within our public school systems, and as our human intelligence grows, our schools do little to challenge the growing minds of our children. At the San Cristobal Ranch Academy and many other therapeutic boarding schools it is all too common for the IQ levels of the students to range up into the 140's, virtual geniuses hidden behind dysfunctional social behaviors. Many of the students attending such programs are extremely intelligent, but due to our public school systems and other educational intuitions, lackluster parenting skills, and a cultural tendency towards the "dumbing of society," these young men have become bored. They may be smarter then their parents, smarter then their school teachers, and smarter than most of the adults with whom they come into contact. Therefore they experience little if any personal challenge, and have to invent challenges to keep themselves busy. They become involved in counter-productive activities that lead to potential violence, and the subsequent financial burden on American society.[348]

Dr. Normal D. Livergood, who holds his Ph.D from Yale University uses the results from the National Assessment of Adult Literacy (NAAL) to highlight his beliefs about American education. The results from the 2003 NAAL research suggest that 14% of the American population are below basic comprehension, 29% maintain a basic comprehension, 44% have an intermediate comprehension and only 13% are considered to have a proficient literacy. He suggests that "Some thirty million adults in the U.S. do not have the skills to perform even the most basic tasks such as adding numbers on a bank slip, identifying a place on a map, or reading directions for taking a medication. Eleven million Americans are totally illiterate in English."[349]

His point is that we are a highly uneducated and non-intellectual country with a majority of our populous incapable of understanding the complexities of our governmental system, unable to engage in dialogue that compares and contrasts complex systems or concepts, or understand literature written above the sixth to eighth grade level. We exist within a state of mediocrity, as the statistics he presents indicates. 44% of the American public, or 95 million people, have an intermediate comprehension which he suggests allows them to undertake and comprehend "moderately difficult activities such as finding information in reference materials". Only 13% or 28 million people have a proficient comprehension which allows them to undertake "complex activities such as comparing viewpoints in two different editorials".[350]

In 1992 the National Center for Education Statistics stated that 50% of the Americans surveyed could not read well enough to find a single piece of information in a short publication, nor can they make low level inferences based on what they read.[351]

Someone once said, "Knowledge is power," and it would seem that in our culture of rapidly growing illiteracy, humans are beginning to feel as though they have no power; no power over their own lives, over the relationships that they engage in, or over who they become. We feel that we have become powerless to impact our own lives.[352] Therefore we allow decisions

"Riding turns 'I wish' into 'I can'."
~ Pam Brown

to be made, from an individual level, to a community level, to a governmental level, that are not necessarily of our choosing. However, we feel that nothing we can do will help to change the world around us. So we do nothing. Of course we know in our hearts that all it takes is breaking out of the trance. We are powerful, powerful beyond measure, and we have the ability to bring about profound change on all levels of our existence. We must remember how to stand up and live within our own personal power. We must stop disempowering ourselves, and move forward, not complaining about what isn't, but instead taking action to make what is.

A culture with humans living comfortably within their own personal power is one driven by active engagement and choice. It is one where its members feel able to impact the whole, as well as able to live their own lives in a manner that feels right and good to them. Horses can teach us how to become more ourselves, and expose us to power as a healthy and vital component of self. They remind us what it would be like to live within our power, and they demand that we become self-confident enough to experience our greatness. Both from an archetypal and a practical viewpoint, horses reflect power; theirs and our own. They continue to act as our very measurement for power. Even in a world of machines, we still call the energy that flows through their metal and synthetic veins *horsepower*. We still find our breath taken away when we watch horses gallop through a field, their hooves pounding the earth, beating a rhythm never to be forgotten in our hearts.

The work of EFMH/ES can help people discover their power. It can teach them new ways to learn, and expose them to concepts that challenge their intelligence. Horses are rarely, if ever, boring, and thus stimulate even the most morose and jaded brain, bringing hope, interest, curiosity, and life to those who have become caught in the dark. When one feels more powerful and capable, one is more willing to take on new tasks and learn new skills. In many cases adults who have been referred to the work of EFMH/ES who are nearly illiterate and very afraid to change this, will seek adult learning classes and engage in pursuing knowledge after or during their work with the horses.[353] After learning

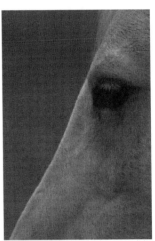

"The conscious and unconscious inner process is tapped into when in the presence of the horse."
~ Susan Taylor

about horses and how to safely and productively be around them, other things that may have seemed daunting or even terrifying may change form and become possible.

Horses can teach us how to find our power, and the work of EFMH/ES can guide people to find a direction once this power has been uncovered. Learning how to make personal choices and how to healthfully impact others, community, and society is a skill, not necessarily an innate behavior. EFMH/ES can teach people, through learning the way of the horse, how to make these types of choices. Once people begin realizing the extent to which their power and control actually goes, they come to realize that they have a choice in nearly everything that occurs with them, for them, or around them.

They begin to become actively engaged in their own lives and reach out to help others do the same.

We as a culture must become empowered. We must learn how to take a proactive role in our own lives, in our communities, and in our governmental process. We must learn to find our sense of power.

Responsibility, Integrity, and Commitment

Once we have learned how able we are to make choices about our lives, we realize that we have a huge responsibility to ourselves, our loved ones, and the world. We can no longer act as the ostrich in the sand, hiding his head to avoid life. We suddenly become active inventors along life's journey. We learn that to act with integrity and commitment is to guide with light in dark places.

It seems that in our society today we have few national role models from whom we can learn responsibility, integrity, and commitment. We watch the news and learn that someone's word means little if anything in this new age of deception, dishonesty, and fly by night actions. Our children's role models are music stars who sing of death, violence, and rage, and the movies they watch are filled with senseless acts of the same. Their parents are forced, due to our descending economy, to spend more time at their jobs, and therefore the children are more likely to learn a majority of their moral, ethical, and practical behaviors from sources other than their parents. With the increase in non-farming or ranching communities, the notion of children having responsibilities that actually mean something at an early age has virtually disappeared. Parents try to instill work ethic, responsibility, and commitment, but without something that is real, such as caring for animals, tending to crops that produce the very food that they consume, or working side by side with their parents to earn a livelihood, children find ways to manipulate, get out of, or completely disregard the tasks or chores that the parents assign in the hopes of teaching them these valuable lessons.[354]

Many children, and especially adolescents, report feeling useless, disempowered by a lack of responsibility. They desire to find something meaningful, something that will challenge them. Children want desperately to be seen as individuals, and by the time they have reached adolescence are willing to fight to the death (sometimes literally) to obtain a sense of power and freedom. Parents cling to them, rightly terrified of the world that exists beyond the home, afraid to let them experience a true sense of success or failure for fear of the consequences.

The work of EFMH/ES can be incredibly useful for today's youth. Working with horses can instill responsibility, integrity, and commitment in a safe but real setting. Children learn how to care for something authentically, and can be given responsibility that is, without a shadow of a doubt, real. They learn what it means to commit to another living, breathing creature, and learn what it feels like to act with integrity even when it is the hardest thing to do. They generally feel a sense of pride and power when they are able to prove to the adults around them that they have accomplished an assignment or task that helped a horse in some fashion. They glow when they master a challenge that has the potential to be dangerous. To feel that an adult trusts them to undertake a task that is complex, physically challenging, and has a twinge of danger associated with it, can change a child's entire perspective of themselves and their abilities. Horses represent to children that it does not matter how big you are, how strong, or how old, as long as you do what is right. The children come to realize that their unique contribution is not only accepted, but valued for the success of the whole. They report feeling wanted and needed, and thus begin recognizing their own skills and talents, as well as realize how huge of an impact they can have on others around them.[355]

Our country would be a very different place if all children had the opportunity to learn how to care for, ride, and be in the presence of horses. The work of EFMH/ES helps to introduce a new intervention for the parenting struggles that are all too common in today's world. Of course the work with horses can also help adults who have struggled to learn the lessons of responsibility, integrity, and commitment, and either using an educational approach, or a therapeutic one, adults also can learn how to acknowledge their behavior patterns, and begin making steps towards life change.

Normalization

The very concepts discussed within this chapter may not be considered "normal" to many. Through the work of EFMH/ES we may have an opportunity to make concepts such as integrity, compassion, self-awareness, respect, love, and sensitivity normal within this society. Imagine a world filled with people who believed that normal is being self-aware, self-empowered, forward moving, responsible, and integral!

EFMH/ES is an alluring and potentially powerful way to introduce our population to a new way of perceiving normal. Horses urge us to be more ourselves; more comfortable and secure in our personal power and our sense of ownership over our lives. Learning to be around horses safely and productively teaches us vital lessons about responsibility, integrity, and commitment. We learn how to ground ourselves in the present moment, and how to listen to our intuition. We feel heard and seen when we are with horses, and are able to practice the art of being authentically ourselves. Within the work of EFMH/ ES we are allowed to "become a person," as Carl Rogers believed all humans desired to do. We are given the skills and the strength to step forward, within our personal lives, and as members of this earth, to defend what is right and what is healthful. We are empowered to make proactive choices and we learn how to accept our greatness without shying away. We are offered the gift of companionship and we learn how to co-exist with another species. Through this very act, we come to realize that we are all interconnected, a vast web of life expanding around the globe, linking us to everything that exists. We are no longer alone.

"I think horses help access the Divine because of their awareness of the present moment. When present, a new realm of experiences become available as a person is able to access parts of himself/herself that are outside the normal ego structure. These experiences are very powerful and therefore have tremendous healing potential. Horses help people access this realm as it is the one they live in all the time"
~ Jacey Tramutt

Summary

To become "one's self" is not as easily attained as we might imagine. In many cases the very process of transitioning through the stages of life are filled with such trauma that it seems nearly impossible to let go of. We are all struggling to understand our potential, as individuals and as a species. The daily routine of survival is fraught with challenges that make it difficult to delve into the advancement of self. Therefore, we tend to remain firmly lodged somewhere on our path towards true understanding. Through work with horses people have been able to find new ways of viewing the course of their lives, and have been able to make alterations that lead them closer to a deeper understanding of human potential. All of the information that we need is accessible to us, we just have to know where to look. Horses help us find parts of ourselves we had forgotten or forsaken long ago, and through their very horsey-ness, they help us to travel "there and back again," walking paths that have long been overgrown with the weeds of our daily existence. We learn to see ourselves through their eyes, and in doing so, are able to recognize our powerful strengths as well as understand more clearly the stumbling blocks we place in our own paths. We learn how to listen to our bodies and through doing so find a sense of trust in the universe. We feel our power and instead of running, we stay.

SECTION THREE

OVERVIEW OF THEORETICAL, ETHICAL, AND EDUCATIONAL ASPECTS OF PROVIDING AN EFMH/ES METHOD

Nine   *Overview of Theoretical Perspectives*

Ten   *Ethical Considerations of Equine Facilitated Mental Health and Educational Services*

Eleven *Cross Training and Personal Growth*

Introduction to Section Three

In this section we will explore the theoretical, ethical, and educational aspects of providing an EFMH/ES method. In order to understand this complex and multi-faceted field it is necessary to start with a basic understanding of the conceptual framework that the methods originated from. This knowledge and information allows us to gain a sense of the scope and depth of the field, and helps us to understand the considerations that are associated with the use of an EMFH/ES method.

With the introduction of a horse into the treatment or educational team, new ethical and legal considerations arise. In order to safely and appropriately provide an EFMH/ES method it is our responsibility as facilitators to understand how to keep our clients, our horses, and ourselves emotionally and physically safe. This entails understanding our responsibilities as providers of an EFMH/ES method, and being trained, educated, and supervised adequately to provide the service we advertise.

For those who have seen an EFMH/ES method change a life, we can appreciate the importance of keeping this field alive and well. We do not want to lose the gift given to us by the horses because of the unethical use of a method. It is our responsibility as stewards of this work to respect the depth and breadth of this field, and honor it by becoming appropriately trained and educated in all of its unique nuances. It is up to us to help move this field towards national and international recognition as a valid and viable treatment or educational

"The sight of [that pony] did something to me I've never quite been able to explain. He was more than tremendous strength and speed and beauty of motion. He set me dreaming."
—Walt Morey

method. We must demonstrate competency, and demonstrate to those who are not yet sure that this work can be done safely and ethically. To become a "mainstream" treatment or educational method we must focus on providing services that are professionally facilitated by specifically educated and trained individuals and demonstrate that there is consistency between providers. In other words, if two professionals suggest that they provide "Equine Facilitated Psychotherapy," but one is actually providing a learning or educational service while the other is providing a psychotherapeutic service we confuse our clients and devalue our ability to demonstrate professional competency and understanding of the field as a whole. Consistency and standardization regarding the manner in which we provide services and how we are trained, educated, and certified will move this field from being viewed as "alternative" or "fringe" towards a broader scope of professional acceptance of this field as a valuable treatment or educational service.

CHAPTER NINE

OVERVIEW OF THEORETICAL PERSPECTIVES

Overview and Introduction of Psychology, Counseling, and Psychotherapy

Historical Overview

Psychology, as a way of perceiving self, owes its original roots to the masters of philosophy. Beginning with Simonedes (500 b.c.) who believed in the importance of organization and memory, thinkers like Socrates (460-399 b.c.) who commanded, "know thyself," Hippocrates (460 b.c.) known as the father of medicine but who used dream analysis to understand emotional disorders, Plato (427-437 b.c.) who believed that individuals had innate knowledge and thought that the brain was the seat of perception, and Aristotle (384-322 b.c.) the progenitor of the idea "Tabula Rasa," or the mind as a blank writing tablet ready to be scribed upon, all believed in the concept of psychology. It was Descartes (1596-1650), however, who made the distinction between the mind and the body and developed the concept of consciousness. Descartes defined psychology as a science that studied consciousness. Philosophy gave us a way to view both ourselves and the world around us, and offered us the ability to analyze and evaluate the mind and all that it entails.[356]

In more recent times Sigmund Freud and Carl Jung popularized the idea of psychology. Although they came to disagree on many aspects of the field, they both believed in the importance of making the unconscious conscious.

In the early development of psychology, those who helped patients with psychological issues were physicians, trained in medicine but who specialized in the workings of the human psyche. They engaged in the clinical practice of psychology. The word "clinical" is derived from the Greek, "kline," which means bed, (and is also found in the root of the word "recline"). Clinical practice traditionally referred to care provided at the bedside of an ill patient, or in the case of Freud, at the side of a patient reclining upon a couch.[357]

Analysis of the patient utilizing the concepts of transference and projection was considered the method for helping to bring the unconscious into the conscious. The role of the treating physician was to be a "blank screen" and offer little if any personal disclosure, therefore encouraging the patient to engage in personal reflection using the physician as a mirror onto which he/she could project and transfer feelings and thoughts. The physician rarely shared his/her personal reactions but rather analyzed and reflected the various projections offered by the patient. Through this process the patient was brought to an awareness of his/her unconscious thoughts and behaviors and given the freedom to change. Advice was rarely if ever given by the treating doctor, and issues that did not reside in the deeply psychological were not commonly addressed.[358]

Psychologists

It is from this orientation towards psychology that "psychologists" were born. In order to legally use the term psychologist an individual must have obtained a doctorate in psychology, literally becoming doctors of the psyche. An

"I am my own heroine."
~Marie Bashkirtseff

individual without a Ph.D. cannot legally be considered a psychologist in any state in the United States except for Minnesota where Masters level professionals may call themselves psychologists. Psychologists can either be research and educationally trained, or they can opt for the clinical track. A clinical psychologist is someone who has been trained and educated to provide psychological services to those in need. Classically, psychologists are educated, trained, and prepared to deal with the deep inner workings of an "ill" psyche, one that needs the expertise of a doctor.[359]

Masters Level Practitioners

At a Masters level of education every state has different definitions for the type of service that the professional can provide, and corresponding licensure requirements (although many states are moving towards reciprocity between states). "Licensed Professional Counselor" (LPC) appears to be the most widely used of all terms. Some states call the practitioners "Licensed Mental Health Counselors" (LMHC), or "Licensed Clinical Mental Health Counselor" (LCMHC), or "Licensed Professional Clinical Counselor" (LPCC). Many states offer a level system by which an individual can begin clinical practice as soon as they graduate from a Masters program with supervision, and can work towards earning (through supervision hours) decreased mandatory supervision and increased flexibility. Individuals who wish to practice mental health care as a Masters Level professional can be licensed in every state in the United States except California and Nevada.[360]

Mental health professionals are licensed as a "counselor" in all states who currently provide licensure, however, there is an array of titles individuals providing a mental health service may call themselves including but not limited to; "therapist," "psychotherapist," or "mental health services provider." The use of the term "therapist" can be misleading or confusing to some, as there are many different types of therapists within the medical profession, the most common of those being physical therapists, occupational therapists, and massage therapists. To avoid confusion, this author will use the term, "licensed mental health professional" as an umbrella term to describe all individuals with appropriate education, training, state licensure, and national certification needed to provide a mental health service.

Each different state and different licensing title indicates either subtle or vast differences between the scope of practice permissible for that individual. However, as a general statement, the American Counseling Association suggests that licensed counselors can provide any service fitting this description:

> The application of mental health, psychological, or human development principles, through cognitive, affective, behavioral or systematic intervention strategies, that address

wellness, personal growth, or career development, as well as pathology.[361]

Therefore, a Masters level licensed mental health professional, regardless of the title they use can utilize principles of psychology to address conditions as severe as pathology, or could also utilize a cognitive/behavioral approach to address issues of life skills, career skills, or personal development and wellness.

It is the ethical responsibility of the licensed mental health professional to understand the scope of practice for his/her specific education, training, and licensure. The licensed mental health professional is

also responsible for ensuring that the client receives appropriate services for their issues, conditions, or diagnosis. If the licensed mental health professional is unable to provide the needed service due to a lack of training, experience, or education, or if the service falls outside of the scope of the professional, that individual is ethically bound to refer the client to a more appropriate professional.[362]

"A horse is the projection of peoples' dreams about themselves- strong, powerful, beautiful - and it has the capability of giving us escape from our mundane existence"
~ Pam Brown

Drug and Alcohol Counselors

Individuals both with and without a Masters degree can become a Certified Substance Abuse Counselor (CSAC) as it is called in many states, or a Certified Drug and Alcohol Counselor (CDAC), or a Licensed Alcohol and Drug Counselor (LADC) as it is called by other states. Those without a Masters degree can achieve this licensure by meeting requirements such as having a GED or high school diploma, taking a training course, and acquiring a total of three (3) years of supervised experienced within the field, and sitting for and passing the national exams. These requirements may change by state, but remain similar in nature. An individual receiving such certification or licensure is allowed to treat only within their scope of practice, which generally includes any and all issues directly related to addictions and recovery.[363]

Social Workers

Individuals who graduate with their Masters degree in social work (MSW) are also eligible for state licensure (Licensed Social Worker – LSW, Licensed Masters Social Worker – LMSW, Licensed Clinical Social Worker – LCSW). Each of these categories indicate an increase in supervised practicum hours and an adjustment in regards to the scope of practice the professional may engage in. In many states a licensed social worker with appropriate supervised practicum hours may engage in the process of providing a mental health service to a wide range of clientele, similar to that of a licensed mental health professional.[364] Individuals may also obtain a Ph.D in Clinical Social Work, which provides them with the same scope of practice as a psychologist, although their theoretical orientation may differ somewhat.

"Psychotherapy" and EFMH/ES

Utilizing self-administered questionnaires, a Likert-type scale, and personal interviews this author collected data from approximately 140 professionals within the field of EFMH/ES over a span of five years. The information collected has been utilized in a number of ways. For the purpose of this section that information will be used to better understand the terms "Equine Facilitated Psychotherapy (EFP), and Equine Assisted Psychotherapy (EAP) which are commonly used to describe mental health oriented work with horses. From the data gathered, it appears that some within the field feel concerned by the use of the term "psychotherapy" to describe all aspects of the mental health services that can be provided in conjunction with horses.[365]

In order to explain the concerns that some EFMH/ES professionals have with the use of the term "psychotherapy" a few key points must be presented.

1. In most states any licensed mental health professional with appropriate education, training, licensure, or certification can provide psychotherapy as long as it falls within the scope of practice within their individual state.

2. Within that framework, each individual professional can define psychotherapy as he/she sees fit, based upon their own theoretical orientation.

3. Therefore, psychotherapy can include such aspects as experientially-based methods, life-skills orientation, or a wellness model of treatment.

4. Psychotherapy that is not labeled brief psychotherapy or brief intensives should include a long term approach to therapy and should not be called a "brief" intervention.[366]

5. Psychotherapy must include mutually agreed upon goals co-created at the onset of the service and revised accordingly throughout the treatment.

6. Psychotherapy should include a mutually agreed upon commitment between Licensed Mental Health Professional and client that indicates scope of practice, length of time, and other details of the service (confidentially and legal issues, relationship between client and professional, etc.).

7. Psychotherapy should be indicated as an appropriate treatment method based upon mental health diagnoses.

8. Psychotherapy can only be provided by licensed mental health professionals who are educated, trained, experienced, and are working within the scope of practice outlined by their individual licensure

The observations gained from the data indicate that some professionals currently practicing within the field of EFMH/ES feel that the term "psychotherapy" is being misused as it relates to EFMH/ES because a number of the suggested requirements (as listed above) are not being met by all EFP and EAP professionals. These individuals report that EFP and EAP is, on occasion, being practiced without mutually agreed upon goals, without a commitment to treatment by either the professional or the client, and in some cases, is provided outside of the scope of the provider's licensure.[367] Furthermore, those responding to the questionnaires, surveys, and interviews agree that there are professionals providing EFP and EAP without proper training, education, and supervision in the method, thereby violating ethical boundaries imposed by national certifying boards, state licensure boards, and membership organizations such as the ACA that state any licensed mental health professional providing a method or service must have prior education, training, and supervised practicum experience.[368]

Beyond the more ethically-based issues, individuals commented upon the theoretical orientation from which they view psychotherapy. It seems that many feel that psychotherapy denotes a more insight-based approach to counseling that stems from a medical model approach. This suggests that psychotherapy may deal more predominately with a disease model of diagnosis and treatment rather than a wellness model. Further distinctions have been made that suggest some individuals practicing within the mental health field believe that when providing a counseling service the counselor deals more specifically with life skills or vocational skills issues where a psychotherapist may deal exclusively with a dysfunctional psyche and the deeper issues that may arise from such conditions.

Others within the field suggest that psychotherapy is open to any interpretation the individual mental health professional uses, as long as it falls within the ethical and legal guidelines of each individual professional's licensure.

The author has chosen to utilize the criteria suggested above to define psychotherapy." For the purpose of clarification, the term psychotherapy will denote a more insight-based approach to mental health, and will adhere to the concept that unless specified, psychotherapy mandates long term treatment and consent, and must adhere to ethical and legal requirements for providing such a service.

Counseling vs. Psychotherapy

Merriam-Webster's Dictionary defines "psychotherapy" as the "treatment of mental or emotional disorder or of related bodily ills by psychological means", and "counseling" as, "professional guidance of the individual by utilizing psychological methods especially in collecting case history data, using various techniques of the personal interview, and testing interests and aptitudes."[369] Utilizing this definition as well as information compiled from the surveys, questionnaires, and interviews, the author has determined that some of the Equine Facilitated Mental Health methods are more clearly "psychotherapy" while others utilize a "counseling" approach. The reader will observe these differences as the various methods are presented and defined.

Equine Facilitated Mental Health Services

After compiling the results from all questionnaires, surveys, and interviews it appears that within the field of EFMH/ES as it currently exists, a number of different approaches to providing a mental health service in conjunction with horses *do* exist. Therefore, the author has deemed it useful to consider all activities in which horses and humans come together for mental health purposes "Equine Facilitated Mental Health Services" (EFMHS). This broad umbrella term covers all aspects of mental health treatment in which horses are included regardless of whether they are an assisted or facilitated method.

Overview and Introduction of Education and Learning

"The traditional learning model emphasizes language and the rational thought process as the main access to learning. Indeed, language is what western education is based on. We study and we learn, we study and we learn, and eventually we might take a written or oral test to show what we learned. All this is done through the medium of language. Our emotions, may come into play in response to what we are learning and, in the traditional learning model, the most acceptable way to respond to emotions is to express them in language, usually in critiques or analysis of presented material. The other option is to suppress them. As for body involvement, most often we sit in a chair while learning in the traditional way, perhaps actively using our bodies only to take notes."
-Ann Romberg and Lynn Baskfield, Wisdom Horse
Coaching, Minneapolis, Minnesota

Confusions

The words "learning" and "education" can be confusing, opaque, and lack clarity. For the purpose of this text, we must be able to differentiate between education or learning, and therapeutic services. Without such clarity, individuals who believe themselves to be providing an educational or learning service can move into territory that is traditionally considered mental health. In some cases this is natural and may even be healthful and useful within the context of the setting, the consent of the participant, and the experience of the facilitator. In other cases this occurrence ends badly for all involved, creating unethical and unhealthful situations that may wound the participants, horses, or even facilitators.

As a result, we must begin creating our own deeper sense of what that difference means within an EFMH/ES setting.

In the past there was no need to clarify the differences between education and mental health services. Education existed within the formal setting of an educational institution, such as a school, college, or university. The purpose of education was to acquire a skill or body of knowledge about certain predetermined topics. Educators taught students these skills or knowledge base. Generally it was assumed that students did not learn through experience or self-teach concepts offered in educational settings. Rather they learned pre-determined information directly from the educator. Furthermore, it was assumed that individuals within an educational setting were generally well human beings, coming to the educational institution for the purpose of gaining knowledge and skills, not for the purpose of self discovery, growth, or change.[370]

However, as our educational system has adjusted to include alternative forms of education and learning, the notion of learning through experiences and allowing education to become a form of life process has become more prevalent. With this new way of viewing education or learning, we begin to realize that in order for our education to become useful we must personalize and internalize it. In order to do this, we must activate or open components of our psyche that within more traditional education would not need to be exposed. We must be willing to take in the information we are presented, and find a way of connecting that experience to our past, present, and our future. Through this process memories, feelings, and thoughts may become exposed. The outcome of this process is that the student may experience a deeper level of self-awareness and thus may internalize and personalize each piece of knowledge more aptly. Furthermore, behaviors, attitudes, self concepts, and even maladaptive patterns may be adjusted or may fundamentally change during this process.

To further confuse matters, the process of internalizing and personalizing information tends to look very much like group or even individual counseling or psychotherapy. Therefore, individuals who engage in a non-traditional or alternative learning process may find themselves undergoing a form of counseling or psychotherapy without consent or even knowledge.[371]

Dr. Perkins presents a concept that was once commonly found when defining the differences between education and mental health, "If there is a problem with thoughts or with behavior then therapy attempts to 'change' the bad behavior and replace it with a more constructive or helpful behavior. It also implies that a 'client' has a 'disorder or a disordered behavior' that needs to be fixed. Therapy attempts to utilize 'learning' for a specific purpose. So, it could be considered a 'subset of learning'".[372]

In the past psychotherapy or counseling was considered part of a possible treatment model for disease, not a path followed by well people desiring to expand their human potential and engage in conscious awareness pursuits.[373] Dr. Perkins reflects, "Using the term 'learning' or 'education' removes the 'disorder stigma' which is attached to the term 'therapy'. In that way, healthy people are allowed to experience 'improvements in thoughts or behaviors' as a result of experience but are not considered disordered in doing so."[374]

The interesting piece of this dilemma is that many licensed mental health professionals utilize wellness models that remove disorder or disease stigma.[375] These licensed mental health professionals do not view their clients through the lens of DSM-IV diagnosis codes, but rather see them based upon their strength as individuals, and their interest in pursuing self-learning, growth and change.[376] Therefore, the commonly held belief that psychotherapy or counseling can be defined by its orientation towards disease or disorder is no longer a valid definition that can clear the confusion between education and learning or mental health services.

Dr. Stan Maliszewski, Ph.D, past board president of the National Board for Certified Counselors, and professor at the University of Arizona in the Department of Educational Psychology, suggests that because of the confusion caused by the interface between education and counseling or psychotherapy, the work of EFMH/ES should only be provided if there is a trained and educated licensed mental health professional on site. Dr. Maliszewski states in reference to an interview question, "You have done an excellent job of pointing out the dangers associated with those who say they are practicing EAL (Equine Assisted Learning) and it inevitably can easily cross over to EAP (Equine Assisted Psychotherapy). This is why I generally recommend that a licensed therapist always be present. It just appears too potentially risky without one."[377] He does go on to suggest that there can be a difference between education or learning and mental health services, "Education/learning is information giving. Counseling is helping others to help themselves." However, the line generally becomes so blurred in the facilitation of an educational or learning service that he feels concerned with the notion of non-therapeutically-trained and educated individuals providing an EFMH/ES service.[378]

It seems that we may be approaching a time where we must re-define both mental health services and education.[379] Clients appear to be benefiting from a non-disease and diagnosis form of mental health services that include aspects of experiential education or learning-based practices and in many cases students participating in experiential learning or educational programs may get needs met that might go unsuccessfully addressed in traditional psychotherapy.[380] Cross-training for professionals who work within either an educational or learning realm, or a therapeutic realm may be necessary in the future. Certainly within the field of EFMH/ES cross-training should be mandatory, as any EFMH/ES method will invariably include aspects of both mental health and education/learning.

Why it Matters

People may be confused as to why differentiating the two experiences actually matters, especially considering the possible benefits of interface. It seems that the manner in which this question can be answered is by addressing the two most prevalent ethical violations possible if professionals are unable or unwilling to distinguish through practical application, the differences between the two services.

Scope of Practice

Ethically it is the responsibility of the licensed mental health professional or educator to provide a service that is within their scope of practice. This mandates that the professional must only provide a service that they are educated, trained, experienced, and licensed or credentialed to provide.[381] In traditional education, an educator is not usually specifically trained to deal with issues of the psyche and a licensed mental health professional is generally not trained to provide an educational experience for clients. If the lines are blurred between mental health and education/learning, either professional may find themselves acting outside of their scope of practice, and thus potentially engage in an unethical use of authority or power, misuse an intervention, or trigger a client into an emotional state that the facilitator is not trained to handle.

Consent to Treatment or Permission to Treat

The second way in which misuse of an educational or therapeutic approach can become an ethical violation is   due to "informed consent" or permission to treat. When a client arrives at a mental health service, he/she is asked to sign a waiver giving the professional "permission to treat."[382] This indicates that the client understands the role of the mental health professional, understands the method(s) that will be utilized within treatment, comprehends the type of topics that may be addressed, and is willing to participate in a process of deep psychological reflection, growth, and change.[383] Within an educational or learning service, the student or participant generally does not expect to experience deep personal revelations, nor do they give permission for the educator or facilitator to probe into their psychological functioning. They do not consent to a process of deep psychological reflection, growth, and change. Therefore, if an educator or facilitator pushes the boundaries between mental health services and education or learning, he or she is doing so without the student's or participant's willing or consensual comprehension of the process.

The Importance of Knowing the Difference

For both of these reasons it is ethically important that providers of an EFMH/ES service are able to recognize the difference between mental health services and education or learning services. If a professional chooses to use a method that includes within its title education or learning, it is their responsibility to understand how that method is distinctly different from one that uses any term that denotes a mental health service. The professional is ethically responsible for ensuring that their facilitation does not cross lines they have not been given permission to cross, or that merges into territory that they are not trained, educated, or licensed/certified to provide.[384]

If a licensed mental health professional is trained in educational or learning models, he/she can ethically state that he/she provides an educational or learning-based experience for his/her clients.[385] If the licensed mental health professional desires to utilize principles of learning or education service interfaced with a mental health service, this information regarding his/her unique therapeutic approach should be clearly stated within the Consent to Treatment form. If, on the other hand, the licensed mental health professional wishes to differentiate between an educational or learning service and a therapeutic one, either based upon the needs of specific populations or if he/she is providing training or educational workshops for other professionals, then the licensed mental health professional must ensure that his/her explanation of the service and facilitation style makes the difference clear and tangible for those participating. The client should be educated, knowledgeable, and consensual in regards to participating in either type of service. However, if the licensed mental health professional is not trained in educational or learning methods, he/she should not state that he/she provides such a service.

Currently EFMH/ES services are commonly distinguished from one another by suggesting that an educational or learning service indicates that life skills, relational skills, or communication skills are the focus of the service and that the service is based upon a wellness model rather than a disease model. Although this may be accurate and not a misrepresentation of an educational or learning service, to suggest that the only difference between a mental health service and educational one resides within content or philosophy is inadequate. Today's growing focus on a wellness model of treatment rather than on a disease or diagnosis model of care has shifted our definitions for what counseling or psychotherapy can include. Individuals desiring to provide an EFMH/ES method are recommended to utilize the ethical guidelines to determine which type of service they provide, rather than utilizing a philosophical orientation to make that decision.

This leaves us with the complex, albeit extremely important job of defining what is meant by the terms educational or learning in regard to the work of EFMH/ES. For our purposes, I am going to suggest the following definitions.[386]

Education and Learning Services Defined for the Purpose of EFMH/ES

Educational Services

These services take place within institutions of education, as in traditional or alternative learning environments such as schools, colleges, or universities. The purpose and goal of these services is to teach students new skills, or new ways of viewing and integrating old skills. They are based on the premise of the educator giving or imparting information to the student(s), or creating educational scenarios from which the student can derive information regarding a topic which the student may then choose to use this in any manner he or she deems appropriate. The desired outcome is that the student finishes the program with an increased knowledge base that is demonstrated through the tangible application of information (i.e. written or practical exams, or other forms of competency testing). Within an educational setting, evaluations are not based upon a value judgment of how the information is utilized, or even if it is utilized outside of the educational institution. Rather evaluations are based upon the student's ability to demonstrate competency within a subject. These institutions do not provide tangible life skills, and are not responsible for the functionality of the students during his/her educational experience.

Learning Services

These services take place at alternative learning centers such as therapeutic boarding schools, wilderness programs, retreat centers, institutes designed to provide learning-based experiences, and training or educational centers. The purpose and goal of these services is to facilitate the process of learning new concepts, thoughts, ideas, or notions that lead to enhanced personal success and functionality. The content of the material taught is skills-based and has immediate practical applications. The primary goal of these services is to provide information that promotes, encourages, or embraces behavioral change. These services have a higher degree of internal support and an increased attachment to the outcome. The desired outcome of these services is that the individual or group leaves not only having accomplished the process of learning a new skill or task, but also demonstrating a tangible improvement in functioning life skills. Competency testing is self-evaluated based upon the student's perception of success.

Mental Health and Experiential Education – An Intermingling

Due to the complexities of EFMH/ES and the potential for possible intermingling between the educational and therapeutic methods of EFMH/ES, it seems essential that all professionals utilizing an EFMH/ES method be trained in basic counseling skills, counseling ethics, and experiential education methods, models, and facilitation skills.

Significant changes in both the mental health field and educational field have occurred over the past few decades that are extremely important to the growth of humanity, but have caused confusion between the two fields. This confusion appears clearly demonstrated within the work of EFMH/ES.

Horses do not differentiate between an educational setting and a therapeutic setting, and will engage in the reflective feedback process[387] with no regard for the goals of the individual client or the session. Furthermore, clients do not generally understand or differentiate between the two approaches either, and may be unaware of the boundaries that can be crossed during an EFMH/ES session. It seems to be solely the responsibility of the facilitator to understand the differences and be highly trained and skilled in guiding the experience towards whichever approach is most appropriate for the client, and that is within the professional scope of the facilitator. Even with a highly trained and skilled facilitator, the potential for an educational method to merge into a therapeutic one is high, and is, in fact, commonplace within the work of EFMH/ES.[388] Even trainings designed to teach the work of EFMH/ES to mental health or educational professionals may tend to merge into the realm of the therapeutic, without the consent or prior knowledge of the participants.

Experiential Education

> *"Experiential learning is holistic, placing the emphasis not so much on the rational mind as on other parts of the self. As members of a culture that emphasizes language and the rational mind, we forget that much of our learning comes through our senses and emotions. Our bodies are our great allies in learning, but we forget to acknowledge the part they play as receptors and containers of our learning."*

- Ann Romberg and Lynn Baskfield, Wisdom Horse Coaching,
Minneapolis, Minnesota

With the introduction of experiential education, the field of education has adjusted to include factors that never before would have existed within an educational domain. The Association for Experiential Educators defines experiential education as "A philosophy and methodology in which educators purposefully engage with learners in direct experience and focused reflection in order to increase knowledge, develop skills and clarify values". The use of the words *"focused reflection"* and *"clarify values"* seems to interconnect education and mental health in an unusual and potentially impactful manner. They suggest that "learners are engaged intellectually, emotionally, socially, soulfully and/or physically." And that this involvement produces a "perception that the learning task is authentic." They also state "Relationships are developed and nurtured: learner to self, learner to others and learner to the world at large." These statements are indicative of what normally would be perceived of as therapeutic concepts and goals rather than traditional educational goals.[389]

Mental Health

The field of mental health has also begun to lean towards a more psycho-educational approach. As an outcome of therapy clients are often urged to become more proactive in their lives, and learn to take initiative, make decisions, and become personally responsible for their actions.[390] The Association for Experiential Educators appears to also agree with this concept: "Experiences are structured to require the learner to take initiative, make decisions and be accountable for results. Throughout the experiential learning process, the learner is actively engaged in posing questions, investigating, experimenting, being curious, solving problems, assuming responsibility, being creative, and constructing meaning".[391]

Licensed mental health professionals are taught how to facilitate and support authentic personal reflection by creating an emotionally and physically safe space, setting clear boundaries, utilizing healthful confrontation, and being empathic, respectful supports of the process.[392] The Association for Experiential Educators defines the educator's primary roles as "setting suitable experiences, posing problems, setting boundaries, supporting learners, insuring physical and emotional safety, and facilitating the learning process".[393]

An Intermingling

It seems that experiential education as it currently exists, operates as a melding of both education and mental health. Although the positive connotations of this method are clear, the negatives are also clear. When does education end and mental health services begin? Are educators qualified and trained to provide a mental health service? What about "permission to treat?" Students do not consent to psychological treatment when they decide to engage in an educational activity or program. Therefore it is not ethical for an educator to attempt to provide a mental health service.[394] On the other side of the coin, are mental health professionals trained and educated to facilitate experiential learning activities? Are they trained and educated to understand learning styles and learning processes? Are their facilitation skills proficient? Do they understand group process within an educational setting?[395]

To add a further complication, educators who are properly trained in experiential education have been able to demonstrate that they are fully capable of providing a healthful therapeutic experience, and are able to move their students through intense emotional states safely, achieving goals that have been traditionally considered to be psycho-therapeutic.[396] Does this mean that they are acting in that moment as mental health professionals, and thus, where are the ethical lines between education and mental health drawn? It seems that some experiential educators feel that their field is being encroached upon by mental health professionals attempting to provide an experiential learning service without proper training and education, which is unethical in its own right.[397]

Foundations of EFMH/ES

Regardless of which "creation" story we believe, Barbara Rector's contributions to the field of EFMH/ES have provided a theoretical basis from which much of the work originates. Ms. Rector has influenced a great many of the people both originally in the field and those new to the field through her educational programs, philosophy, and practical application of the work. Ms. Rector strongly believes that much of EFMH/ES is based theoretically in experiential education, and thus has trained and educated many to understand and practice EFMH/ES methods using experiential education as a theoretical underpinning. She utilizes experiential education activities, facilitation styles, and learning concepts in her work with horses, and therefore even when providing "therapy," continues to use her experiential education approach. Due to this, many others in the field today utilize a similar approach to providing any of the methods of EFMH/ES, be they therapeutic or educational.[398]

Since the work of EFMH/ES is based in the theories of experiential education, but also seems provocative enough to move people into a psycho-therapeutic state, regardless of which method we use, practitioners need to be dually trained in both experiential education and mental health concepts to conduct this work from a well rounded and competent vantage point.

Summary

As professionals providing an EFMH/ES method it is imperative that we understand the differences between both the theoretical underpinnings of a method and its practical applications. We must provide the service that we say we do. We also must understand the differences between services and which service is applicable for which clientele. If we understand such nuances, we will be better able to ethically, safely, and productively serve the clients that we are trained and educated to serve. Furthermore, we will better understand when to refer and what type of service might be best suited for the clientele. It is our responsibility as professionals to delve deeply into the work that we do, fully understanding its subtle nuances and always being open to learning.

CHAPTER TEN

ETHICAL CONSIDERATIONS FOR EFMH/ES

Competence

Currently in the field of EFMH/ES the largest ethical concerns stated by the EFMH/ES professionals interviewed are a lack of competence regarding the practical applications of EFMH/ES, a lack of equine knowledge and awareness, and a lack of general safety awareness. [399] In 2006 The Commission for Certified Equine Facilitated Mental Health and Education Professionals (CCEFMHEP) [400] came into being. Forefront in their mission is the creation of competency standards for professionals interested in providing an EFMH/ES method. CCEFMHEP's mission is, "To promote excellence in the equine facilitated mental health & education profession through a credentialing process defining a foundation of knowledge and experience to support safe, humane and ethical practice." Their vision is, "A world where equine facilitated mental health & education is valued as a recognized partner in the healing and learning process."

The CCEFMHEP has created two exams; one for the professional educator, and one for the professional counselor or psychotherapist. Taking the CCEFMHEP exam helps promote standards of practice for the field as a whole. The CCEFMHEP state:

> The development of the new credential further supports the goal of mental health and education professionals who incorporate equines in their scope of practice to have these interventions recognized as valid and effective. The new credential will validate the expanded education, skills, and experience needed to be successful as an Equine Facilitated Interaction Professional. Today's mental health and education

professionals face increasingly complex regulatory and outcome requirements. CCEFMHEP assumes the responsibility to raise its professional and educational standards to meet the current and future demands of professionals who include equines as an integral part of their delivery of services. Currently there is no organization providing certification based on theoretical grounding in broad competencies that meet national credentialing standards. The CCEFMHEP certification tests professionals for a body of knowledge required in order to effectively partner with animals in mental health and educational settings.

Until individual states decide to adopt either the national certification exam, or develop their own state specific licensure exam and requirements for practice, the CCEFMHEP may not be mandatory in order to legally practice an EFMH/ES method in this country.[401]

The equivalent in the field of mental health is the National Board for Certified Counselors, Inc. and Affiliates (NBCC) which is "an independent not-for-profit credentialing body for counselors, designed to establish and monitor a national certification system, to identify those counselors who have voluntarily sought and obtained certification, and to maintain a register of those counselors." The counselors who have met the predetermined standards in their training, education, and experience, and who have successfully passed the National Counselor Examination for Licensure and Certification become Nationally Certified Counselors. This certification is voluntary but has gained a great deal of merit and recognition within the field of mental health and therefore can provide credibility for the individual who has passed the test.[402]

In some states the NBCC's national exam is used as the state equivalent for licensure. In others different exams are used to better measure the specific needs of that state's demographics.

Prior to the Commission, there was no non-biased organization that set competency standards for the field of EFMH/ES. Each membership organization or independent training organization could determine what "competent" might mean based upon their own criteria. However, since the inception of the CCERMHEP, the field of EFMH/ES has clear guidelines for professional competency. This marks an important and timely leap forward for the field, but does not come without argument and disagreement.

Many in the field still feel that EFMH/ES professionals need NOT be knowledgeable on a general and practical level about horses and do not need to have horse experience and training to be able to provide the said service for paying clients as long as the partner with a "horse professional". One model that has been introduced suggests that a licensed mental health professional can pair with a horse professional to provide an Equine Facilitated Mental Health Service, and thus the licensed mental health professional does not need to understand horses or have a basic knowledge of horse psychology, physiology, behaviors, or safety protocol. The horse professional could be anyone with horse experience as there are no competencies set for such an individual.

Lynn Baskfield and Ann Romberg of Wisdom Horse Coaching in Minneapolis, Minnesota feel differently, "Ethically, the [EFMH/ES] facilitator must honor the integrity of the horse, i.e. not be abusive due to lack of knowledge, or ignore, due to lack of understanding, what the horse has to tell us, for the sake of accomplishing some task with the horse."

Regardless of how much we love horses, recognize their helpful/healing abilities, and see the impact that any equine facilitated or assisted approach has on clients/students, we must also see that horses are horses. And as the Equine Inherent Risk Law reminds us, equines are dangerous, unpredictable, and may cause serious bodily harm or death. The manner in which we conduct our services determines how much "safer" we can make our programs. It is up to us as facilitators of equine experiences to ensure our clients/students safety to be best of our ability. This means that it is our responsibly to provide our clients/students with the information and skills needed to maintain their physical safety. Any challenge course program, adventure based program, or wilderness program requires that all students/clients undergo an intensive safety and equipment presentation and training prior to engaging in a high risk activity. Participants are never subjected to an experience without first clearly understanding the risks and having appropriate training to decrease the risk factor. If humans come into partnership with horses and do not have adequate safety training, the risk for serious accidents increases.

Not only is it critical to provide every student/client with a general safety training and education that includes a basic overview of equine psychology, behavior, physiology and communication, but we must also evaluate how safe our activities are. If we are placing horses in situations/activities that increase their natural fight/flight/freeze response we may be placing our clients in greater danger. When a horse goes into a fight/flight/freeze response their primary concern in for their own safety. In such a state horses will trample people, knock into them, kick, bite, or whatever it takes to get away – to get safe. They are not thinking relationally. In general they are not thinking about the good or well being of their human partner. If we are inviting unknowing clients into an arena with loose horses and providing instructions to those clients that engages the horse's flight/flight/freeze response, we may be endangering our clients.

For those of us who are mental health professionals, we must consider the ethical requirements we are bound to. As mental health professionals we are required by law to keep our clients as physically and emotionally safe as possible. If you are working with clients that you obtained or who were referred to you, consider this statement. If you are not a horse person, how can you guarantee that you are "keeping your client as physically and emotionally safe as possible"? You are entrusting your clients to a horse professional to keep them safe. This may be a person who you trust explicitly but legally and ethically, it is you who will in jeopardy if the client gets injured. And the question will be asked, were you providing a service that you have been educated, trained, and supervised to provide?

The practice of medicine, law, science, psychology, and any other professional discipline requires years of extensive training, education, and experience. If we want equine facilitated mental health services to take its place as a viable, ethical, and respected professional disciple, it would seem that those interested in pursuing a career in this field need to get the additional training, education, and experience to be considered competent. Even those of us who are already mental health professionals, this concept remains the same. The concept is similar to medical doctors, we have our general information to be able to practice within the methods we have been trained, educated, and supervised to provide. But, if we want to become specialists, we have to do more training, education, and supervision to ensure that we are truly competent to provide the specialty. Just to become a credentialed "play therapist" a licensed and experienced mental health professional must obtain an **additional** 150 hours of education/training from an institute of higher learning, have completed 500 hours of supervised play therapy facilitation, and obtained 50 hours of play therapy supervision. This is to include PLAY into therapy – not a 1000 pound live animal who is considered by nearly every state in the country to be "dangerous and unpredictable, and who may cause bodily harm or death."

Imagine an art therapist trying to provide art therapy with little if any understanding about art, about the unique process of art as therapy, or about the theoretical underpinnings of art therapy. Imagine trying to interpret a client's relationship to the art he/she just created with little or no understanding of art as therapy.[403] Or, imagine trying to facilitate a challenge course experience for a group of students without prior training in experiential learning methods, facilitation skills, and without a deep and comprehensive knowledge of the challenge course and all the safety regulations that are inherent to the method.[404] It is nearly inconceivable and sounds not only unethical but certainly dangerous.

Now imagine trying to use the horse/human relationship as a learning or therapeutic tool with no formal training, expertise, or knowledge of horses. At least for the most part, art experiences and challenge courses are unlikely to severely physically injure or kill the client or student participating in the service. Horses, on the other hand, are huge, potentially dangerous creatures who have the ability to harm or kill human beings.

It would seem only logical to assume that it is dangerous to attempt to provide an EFMH/ES method without prior knowledge, experience, education, and training in equine psychology, physiology, behavior, and general horsemanship skills.

Before the field of art therapy was recognized by state licensing boards and had its own national certification process, the same confusions and lack of competencies existed. However, due to state licensure and national certification, educational programs at colleges and universities, and a deeper understanding of the theory behind the work, art therapy has changed into what is considered by many to be a professionally valid treatment method. It would be inconceivable for an art therapist or art educator to know little or nothing about art and provide art therapy services for charge to clients or students.

Even if a licensed mental health professional does not agree with the CCEFMHEP standards for competency, they are still bound by the ethical codes of their respective membership associations and licensing or certification organizations.

The National Board for Certified Counselors (NBCC), the American Psychological Association (APA), and the American Counseling Association (ACA) all concur that the use of a method or treatment intervention without proper training, education, and supervision is unethical (See Tables 2, 2.1, 2.2).

Table 2: The National Board for Certified Counselors Code of EthicsA.6.

Certified counselors offer only professional services for which they are trained or have supervised experience. No diagnosis, assessment, or treatment should be performed without prior training or supervision. Certified counselors are responsible for correcting any misrepresentations of their qualifications by others.[405]

Table 2.1: The American Psychological Association Code of Ethics 2.01 (a)

Psychologists provide services, teach, and conduct research with populations and in areas only within the boundaries of their competence, based on their education, training, supervised experience, consultation, study, or professional experience.[406]

Table 2.2: The American Counseling Association Code of Ethics C.2.a.

Counselors practice only within the boundaries of their competence, based on their education, training, supervised experience, state and national professional credentials, and appropriate professional experience.[407]

Furthermore, any licensed mental health professional who is certified by the NBCC or is a member of APA or ACA can be subject to review and possibly lose their license to practice if they violate this code of ethics (see Table 3).

Table 3: The National Board for Certified Counselors, Preamble to Code of Ethics.

This code provides an expectation of and assurance for the ethical practice for all who use the professional services of an NBCC certificant. In addition, it serves the purpose of having an enforceable standard for all NBCC certificants and assures those served of some resource in case of a perceived ethical violation.[408]

Even the Equine Facilitated Mental Health Association (EFMHA) and the Equine Assisted Growth and Learning Association (EAGALA) state that EFMH/ES providers who are members of their respective organizations must practice within their scope of training, education, and licensure and can be reported if they violate that code (See Tables 4, 4.1).

Table 4: EFMHA Code of Ethics, 2.2

The Member offers services within the scope of their practice, competence, education, training, and expertise.[409]

Table 4.1: EAGALA Code of Ethics, 7.

The EAGALA associate will regularly evaluate his/her own professional strengths and limitations and will seek to improve self and profession through ongoing education and training.[410]

For those who are not licensed mental health professionals and who provide an Equine Experiential Learning or Education service the Association for Adventure Educations (AAE) clearly states that individuals providing experiential education must provide services within their scope of education and knowledge (See Table 5).

Table 5 Association for Adventures Educators Standards,

Staff also recognize the boundaries of their competence and do not provide services outside of those boundaries. Staff provide services only after undertaking appropriate education; participating in ongoing training; and seeking appropriate supervision, consultation, or advice where necessary.[411]

Competency within EFMH/ES

The CCEFMHEP has set the following competency standards for professionals desiring to pursue a career in EFMH/ES.

1. Copy of current license to practice counseling or psychotherapy in the state in which you provide services (for Mental Health examination)

   OR

   Copy of certificate, current education qualifications to provide services in your state (i.e. teaching license or coaching certificate), or MS/MA in education related field (for Education examination).

2. Three (3) years full time equivalent (6,000 hours) experience in the field of counseling, psychotherapy, or education, at least 1,000 hours of which is in equine facilitated mental health or education.

3. At least 60 hours of education/training in the field of equine facilitated mental health or education in the last three years.

Although this may seem like a sizable undertaking, it is this author's personal belief that EFMH/ES done poorly and without proper training and education, is a dangerous and unethical use of a treatment or educational intervention, method, or treatment. If the fields of play therapy and art therapy require stringent demonstrations of competency, shouldn't a field which pairs individuals struggling with self-awareness issues, personal safety issues, mental illness, violence and aggression, and other such instabilities, with a large creature who is known for its sudden movements, fight or flight responses, and who is considered "unpredictable" and "potentially dangerous" by insurance companies and state laws, have even more stringent requirements for competency?

Informed Consent

The Informed Consent or Consent for Treatment form provides information about the method of treatment utilized by the provider, the ethical considerations inherent to the method, polices and procedures specific to the method, and should include information about the method which clarifies the differences between an in-office session and an at-the-barn session. The signing of this form by the client indicates that he or she understands the implications of their decision to participate in a service and has agreed to such participation.[412] Kim Shook of Bella Terra in Mattawan, MI says this about informed consent, "Clearly understand the context in which a client has come to you for service (professional development, personal growth, or counseling) and ensure that you stay within the respective ethical and legal boundaries." If a professional does not utilize an Informed Consent form, confusion may offer between the needs of the client and the professional services offered by the facilitator.

Confidentiality

Many licensed mental health professionals who offer an EFMHS method have stated that EFMHS provides unique challenges for the professional, especially in the realm of confidentiality.[413] Karen Head of Equinection in Ashville, N.C. shares her feelings about confidentiality, "Absolute confidentiality is a must. This work asks people to feel at a core level within themselves and I believe that a protected and safe environment must be established and maintained. This privacy can be difficult to insure at a public stable". By its nature, all of the EFMHS methods are provided in a setting where complete confidentially is virtually impossible to guarantee. In the barn milieu situations may arise that would never occur within a traditional office setting. An emergency ailment affecting one of the horses at the barn might occur, and the vet would have to come to the site immediately. A hay delivery, scheduled for the next day might arrive unplanned for, or the shoer might mix his days and come to the facility without prior contact with the barn manager. People are not used to the notion that at a horse barn confidentially might be needed or desired. It is suggested that the mental health professional work closely with the barn manager and other staff at the facility to secure privacy during sessions. Furthermore, it is recommended that EFMHS be provided at a facility with a locking gate that can be closed and locked during session times. The EFMHS mental health professional should alert his or her clientele to the notion that if an emergency does occur, confidentially may have to be broken.

In some cases the EFMHS mental health professional may need other support staff. If this should be the case, the licensed mental health professional should ensure that such individuals are trained in the method, and the client has been given a choice prior to the session whether such an inclusion is acceptable. All licensed mental health professionals, clients in a group setting, or any assistants, helpers, or other support staff participating in a session should adhere to general principles of confidentially. However, prior to deciding to participate in an EFMH service, the client should fully understand that it is possible that they will be seen by individuals who are not a part of their therapeutic experience at some point during their treatment. It is important that EFMHS professional provide clarification for the client, using written documentation that describes the differences between confidentially in an EFMH session and confidentiality in an office-based mental health session.

Touch

Another issue that can arise during EFMH/ES sessions is the ethical consideration regarding touch during a mental health service. Licensed mental health professionals generally do not touch their clients while in an office setting. However, in the work of EFMH/ES touch may become necessary for safety reasons and the client should be made aware of this difference. Clients should be carefully screened to ensure that the use of touch for safety reasons will not be counterproductive to their treatment, or compromise their emotional safety in any way. If there is concern that the client is in an emotionally or physically vulnerable space where touch, even for emergency purposes, would be upsetting or inappropriate, the licensed mental health professional should not utilize an EFMHS method. If touch is necessary, it is recommended that the licensed mental health professional or anyone assisting ask permission of the client prior to touching them. Many licensed mental health professionals include within their general Consent for Treatment form information about the use of touch and provide further information about how and when touch might be used during an EFMHS session.

Dual Relationships

At The Esperanza Center we have found that it is extremely difficult if not impossible to ensure that we will not engage in dual relationships with our clients. We believe firmly that our clients should be able to move through services as it is best for them. This means that a client could enter into Esperanza services as a therapeutic client and when or if they are ready, they may transfer into our regular riding program, and over time may even come back to volunteer. The client understands that each phase of the program is considered a part of their treatment and that we are bound by the same confidentiality requirements regardless of what area they are working within. Furthermore, we also recognize that we are operate in a small town, where we will inevitably see each other out at stores, restaurants or social engagements. We make sure that our clients understand the complexities of our service, and such complexities are addressed within our informed consent agreement. Each mental health professional or EFMH/ES center must determine their own policies regarding dual relationships. We have found a way that makes sense for us and for our clients. However, this way may not be right for everyone or for every center. It is vital that whatever adjustments the individual or program decides to make, the client is informed and understands the parameters from which the program/individual operates.

Issues Specific to the EFMH/ES Professional

"This work can transform people – facilitators have an obligation to know themselves and their abilities – recognizing their limitations, only working with populations that they are competent to help, staying within the context of the question that they are able to facilitate. Additionally, they should be cognizant of referring and helping people beyond the program, if necessary."
-Dr. Tracy Weber, Kaleidoscope Learning Circle, Birch Run, MI

The Mental Health Professional

The licensed mental health professional who utilizes an EFMHS method may develop a more personal relationship with the client in an EFMHS session than in a traditional talk therapy session. This may be due, in part, to the client witnessing the licensed mental health professional in an environment that necessitates hands on application of life skills. The client may witness the mental health professional dealing with frustrations, peer relationships, decision making, conflict, and organizational skills. The client may also witness authentic sharing of love and care between the licensed mental health professional and a specific horse or horses, and thus may begin to feel safer and more closely connected to the licensed mental health professional.[414]

The licensed mental health professional may also demonstrate care about the horses' living environment and general daily upkeep, and thus model for the client that the environment he/she is in is both physically and emotionally safe. Clients tend to base their assumptions of safety around how animals, children, the elderly, or other disadvantaged populations are cared for. If the licensed mental health professional demonstrates care and concern for the horses and their general maintenance, and the facility that the client comes to is well kept with obvious appreciation and love for the animals who reside there, the client is more likely to assume that he/she will also be treated in the same manner, and thus feels instantaneously safe. When this occurs the client may be more prone to open and honest dialog about his/her feelings in the presence of a licensed mental health professional whom he/she trusts will keep him/her safe and well cared for.[415]

Many providing an EFMH/ES method do so from their own homes. Clients arriving at the facility may witness the licensed mental health professional engaging with family members, with other pets, or dealing with functional issues of the facility. The client might see the licensed mental health professional dealing with frustrations or challenges within this environment. Furthermore, regardless of whether the clients come to the licensed mental health professional's home, or to another facility, the licensed mental health professional may look differently out at the barn then he/she does while at the office. His/her clothing, demeanor, or other outwardly observable features may give the client deeper insight into the licensed mental health professionals personal life, likes, dislikes, and personality.

Regardless of what the situation or factors may be, EFMHS certainly seems to present the licensed mental health professional with a number of interesting interpersonal and ethically oriented challenges.

The Educator, Coach, or Other EFE/L Professional
Probably of the utmost importance for the professional who provides an EFE/L service is ensuring that the participants clearly understand the parameters of the service and recognize and understand that it is NOT a mental health-based service. Furthermore, the EFE/L professional should clarify his/her training and education so that the participants can make informed decisions about the applicability of the service for their needs. Without such clarification, the EFE/L professional may find himself or herself in situations where a participant assumes that the professional is therapeutically trained, and may share information that the professional is unprepared and untrained to handle. Deb Marshall of Generation Farms in Nanaimo, BC agrees, "The practitioner (of EFMH/ES) must stay within their level of expertise and seek consultation or refer when appropriate."

Regardless of the EFE/L professionals ability to clarify and define his or her role and the service provided, many participants appear to experience emotions and feelings that would normally be considered as an outcome of a psychotherapeutic intervention. Within the context of the session, the EFE/L professional must be trained and capable of handling such experiences healthfully. Therefore, the upcoming chapter regarding cross-training for professionals is vastly important for the EFE/L professional.

Leif Hallberg

Summary

As the field of EFMH/ES grows and blossoms, professionals wishing to integrate the methods of this work into their own practices, or open new businesses which offer methods of EFMH/ES should be aware of the ethical implications involved. It is the hope of this author that those wishing to pursue a career in this field will obtain cross training, education, and supervision that helps prepare them for the unique intermingling of experiential education and mental health. Furthermore, clients who are interested in pursuing EFMH/ES as a treatment or education method have the right to understand what the service entails, and if the professional facilitating the experience is appropriately educated, trained, supervised, and/or credentialed to provide the service.

CHAPTER ELEVEN

CROSS-TRAINING AND PERSONAL GROWTH

Cross-Training for EFMH/ES Professionals

In order to demonstrate competency within the field of EFMH/S there are necessary skills and a knowledge base that *anyone* (either mental health professional or educator) considering a career in this field, or considering providing an EFMH/ES method for payment is recommended to obtain. Those who are already mental health professionals will have knowledge in some of these areas, and those who are already experiential educators will have knowledge in other areas. Cross-training is necessary so that both mental health professionals and experiential education facilitators have the same basic knowledge and education. The author chose these particular skills and theoretical perspectives as core competencies based upon responses from those interviewed and also from personal experience, training, and education.

Basic Counseling Skills or Communication Skills

The individual practicing any method of EFMH/ES must understand and be able to put into practice concepts of empathy, respect, authenticity, and confrontation, as well as demonstrate an understanding of conflict resolution, effective listening skills, open ended questions and reflective feedback. The individual must be prepared to sit with a student or client's discomfort, healthfully manage intense emotional states, and understand how to de-escalate situations.

Counseling Ethics

The EFMH/ES facilitator must have a working knowledge of basic counseling ethics which include having an understanding of state and federal laws that apply to anyone providing a therapeutic service.

Although the method that an individual facilitator is using might be purely educational in theory, an individual attending such a service may decompensate or enter into an intensive emotional state so quickly that the educator does not have the ability to get a licensed mental health professional immediately at the site to assist. Furthermore, due to the lack of clarity in the field currently, a participant might not be aware of the differences between an educational experience and a therapeutic one, or may be unable to control their emotions during a session and so present with therapeutic issues. Knowing the ethical boundaries of such a service can keep the facilitator aware and out of legal or ethical trouble. It can also help to protect the very people who we are serving, as many times they are unable to emotionally, spiritually, and even sometimes physically protect themselves. Understanding the National Board of Certified Counselors ethical code, the American Counseling Associations ethical code, and both EFMHA and EAGALA's ethical codes are critically important for an EFMH/ES facilitator. Furthermore, understanding the legally binding issues such as duty to warn, the right of informed consent, confidentiality, mandatory reporting, the civil commitment law, and the right to refuse treatment are all necessary for anyone providing the work of EFMH/ES.[416]

Basic Introduction to Psychopathology

As many EFMH/ES providers who state that they provide equine facilitated learning services do not engage in extensive historical data collection, intakes, speak with past mental health professional or psychiatrists, or review the results from past psychological testing they accept clients virtually blind. Therefore, for educational providers it is profoundly important to have a basic understanding and knowledge of psychopathology. A student or participant might arrive at an educationally-based workshop, session, or other service and present with characteristics of severe mental illness, possibly responding to internal stimuli and be completely unsuited for the method and unsafe to be on the premises under those conditions. If the EFMH/ES provider does not have a basic understanding of a condition such as this, he/she might be unaware of the safety risk and not take active steps to rectify the situation. In no way does having a basic understanding of psychopathological characteristics suggest that the educator should engage in treatment of the individual, or attempt to diagnosis what might be occurring. It simply gives them an understanding from which to get further help, remove the client from the premises, or take other such action, thereby keeping the other students and horses safe.

Introduction to Experiential Education

As stated in the above section, experiential education serves as an underlying theory from which the work of EFMH/ES is based. Therefore, anyone who states that they provide the said service must also demonstrate a certain level of understanding and competency in both the theoretical concepts of experiential education and the practical applications of such concepts. Probably in its most simplified form, experiential education is learning through doing. The premise being that without hands-on experience of a concept, change, growth, and learning do not occur as easily or as naturally. The Association for Experiential Educators offers this guideline as to who are experiential educators:

> Experiential Educators include teachers, camp counselors, corporate team builders, therapists, challenge course practitioners, environmental educators, guides, instructors, coaches, mental health professionals.. . . . and the list goes on. An Experiential Educator is anyone who teaches through direct experience.[417]

Even though many mental health professionals would never consider what they do as "teaching," when the horse is introduced and they use any sort of activity that helps the client come to a different way of viewing themselves or the world around them, experiential learning is occurring. Therefore, the work of EFMH/ES even when utilizing a mental health method is still rooted in experiential education.

Introduction to Experiential Education Facilitation and Group Process

Probably one of the most important aspects of experiential education is facilitation and more specifically, group facilitation. Many who provide an EFMH/ES method work with groups, be they educational groups, team building groups, corporate groups, or mental health groups. Wendy Wood of The Red Road in Northern California feels strongly about the need for individuals to be trained as *facilitators,* not just counselors or educators, "I believe it is unethical – no matter which 'model' you use – to have facilitators who are not trained, professional, competent facilitators of human interactions."

Facilitating EFMH/ES in a group setting is not like facilitating group therapy as it is generally taught in traditional mental health or social work programs. Nor is it like teaching in a regular classroom group. Dependent upon state licensing requirements, many traditionally educated mental health professionals only take one required course in their Masters education regarding group facilitation, and therefore graduate with limited if any hands-on experience with group process and group dynamics. Facilitating experiential groups is very different from facilitating a talk therapy group or individual session. In fact, the very use of the word, facilitate, is contraindicated for many traditional mental health professionals, and so they may have little understanding or knowledge about any type of active facilitation style.

Many who come to this work from backgrounds other than mental health are also in the same situation. Facilitation is an art form, something that is learned through much hands-on practice, and with the guidance and supervision of a skilled professional who oversees the learning process. It is certainly not something that everyone is innately good at, and sometimes it is not even something that one can learn and then become good at. Certain people have a knack for facilitation, and others do not. It is important that those coming to the work of EFMH/ES gain supervision and hands-on guidance to better understand their own unique styles, and make decisions about whether or not this work is right for them *prior* to charging for their service as a competent professional.

EFMH/ES is truly its own unique entity, but one that is strongly based in the principles of experiential education group facilitation. Therefore, to healthfully, competently, and successfully facilitate an EFMH/ES experience, facilitators need to understand group dynamics, facilitation styles for both group and individual sessions, and be trained in experiential education or learning methods of facilitation. They must also have gone through extensive hands-on practice with the supervision of a professional skilled in facilitation of EFMH/ES prior to conducting this work for payment.

Introduction to Myth and Metaphor

Unless individuals have studied Jungian psychology, the notions of myth and metaphor tend not to exist within traditional mental health training or education programs. The field of experiential education utilizes metaphor fairly regularly, but tends to lack the deeper psychological ramifications of the metaphors that they use. The work of EMFH/ES has roots deeply imbedded in both myth and metaphor. Much of the time clients or students are drawn to EFMH/ES simply because of the mythical and metaphoric connotations of the horse/ human relationship. It is important to understand the motivation that causes people to chose a certain path, be that towards treatment or education, as it helps to tell the story of how they are, or who they wish to become. Horses have flown through our dreams on the gilded wings of myth and metaphor. They have existed across the globe as the metaphoric bearers of God's will, or messengers of the Divine. They bring light and power, and people are drawn to them not only for their actual representation of power, but also to their metaphoric connection to that power. To understand the use of myth and metaphor helps clients find a voice for the unique experiences that they have when in the presence of horses.

A goal of mental health services is to meet the client where he/she is, and help lead or guide them to where they desire to be. The word counselor means to give advice or to advise another human being about a direction or concept. If we do not understand our psyches deep connection to both myth and metaphor we may struggle to meet our clients where they are, and thus have a difficult time helping them towards the discovery of their next steps on the path of life.

For educators or other types of facilitators who use basic concepts of myth or metaphor within sessions it is important to have an understanding of how those avenues can trigger a deeper psychological truth or memory that has been held inside of the psyche and that becomes accessible through the use of myth or metaphor. Without understanding the deeper ramifications of using both of these aspects, an educator or other non-mental health facilitator can quickly find themselves in uncharted waters, in danger of crossing an ethical boundary that they did not even know existed. We must be highly skilled when dealing with matters of the psyche, and we must not use lightly activities that can trigger deep places within the mind.

Equine Psychology, Physiology, and Behavior

Without the horses, EFMH/ES as a therapeutic or educational method does not exist. As the reader will learn in the upcoming sections, EFMH/ES has its own unique theory base. The main reason for this is the role of the horse within treatment or education. Therefore, anyone desiring to provide an EFMH/ES service must be well trained in equine psychology, physiology, and behavior. Without a working knowledge of how horses communicate, how they think, what certain behaviors mean within both a herd dynamic situation and a horse-to-human situation, and an understanding of basic physiological aspects of the horse, the human EFMH/ES facilitator is unequipped to competently provide this service. In all but one EFMH/ES method, the relationship between the client and the horse is understood to be the primary catalyst for change, growth, or heightened personal awareness and therefore it is necessary for the human facilitator to understand that relationship from both perspectives. Deb Marshall of Generation Farms in Nanamimo, BC agrees, "Excellent skills with horses and an exposure to numerous disciplines and approaches are necessary, such that they (anyone providing an EFMH/ES method) have a solid basis of horsemanship and the flexibility to honor the horse and encourage its natural responses."

Horses behave in ways that may be impossible to understand without a deep knowledge and understanding of their psychology and physiology, and their behaviors can appear quite terrifying or at the least confusing to the lay-person attempting to work with them. Sadly enough the majority of mistreatment or abuse of horses comes from a lack of knowledge and understanding about their psychology and physiology. Even when human beings are attempting to be "kind," "gentle," and "respectful," but have limited understanding of horses, their behavior toward the horse can in fact be abusive and emotionally harmful. Horses are extremely complex beings with their own unique language, culture, and consciousness. To assume that one can understand their complexities, interpret their behaviors, or work safely around them without training, education, supervision, and time is a dangerous assumption.

Equine Safety Skills

As discussed before, horses can be dangerous and can cause harm or even death to inexperienced, uneducated, and untrained individuals. It is simply unethical for people to provide an EFMH/ES method to clients or students without training, education, and knowledge of horse safety protocol. The National Board for Certified Counselors, the American Counseling Association, and the American Psychological Association, EFMHA, and EAGALA all state in their code of ethics that individuals providing a mental health service are ethically bound to ensure to the best of their ability the safety (physical and emotional) of the client being served.[418] To be untrained, uneducated, and inexperienced in equine safety protocol directly places the client or student is jeopardy. Regardless whether the facilitator or mental health professional has an assistant who is considered a horse professional, it is still the ethical responsibility of the mental health professional to ensure the client's safety. It is the mental health professional who will be liable if the client is injured and may be in jeopardy of losing his/her license, not the unlicensed horse person. The horse professional cannot be everywhere at every moment, and a situation could arise where the mental health professional or facilitator is placed in a position where a lack of horse safety knowledge could put their client in danger.

Facilitators who are not mental health professionals do not have an ethical code to which they are bound. However, if they are EAGALA members or EFMHA members, they are bound to both of these organization's codes of ethics. In both EAGALA's code and EFMHA's code it specifies that it is the responsibility of the facilitator to ensure that the student or participant is emotionally and physically safe. EFMHA furthermore states that it is the responsibility of the EFMHA member providing the EFMH/ES service to maintain the physical and emotionally safety of the *horse* partner as well. EFMHA has a principle that is dedicated entirely to outlining the necessity for the EFMHA member to be well-versed in horse-person-ship skills and knowledge prior to providing an EFMH/ES service.

Therefore, utilizing all of the sources available, it is clear that to be incompetent regarding horse safety protocol is unethical for either a mental health professional or an education facilitator providing an EFMH/ES service.

Human/Animal Bonding and Basic Concepts of Ecopsychology

In order to remain ethically aligned we must demonstrate competency within the method we chose to utilize. Understanding the foundations of the method is essential to being able to demonstrate that competency.

The work of EFMH/ES is based largely on the more complex concepts of our human interconnectedness with nature and the natural world. In order to successfully facilitate the work of EFMH/ES we need to be educated and knowledgeable about how this interconnectedness impacts our clients and their desire to attend such a service. It is also useful to understand what the ecopsychological factors are that play into the success of a session verses what the equine-specific factors are. If we do not know how to make this distinction we cannot isolate what factors are helping our clients, and which are more beneficial for what type of population. If we do not begin to understand these differences, we will struggle to create valid research projects that demonstrate efficacy within the field.

We also need to understand the field of companion animal activities so that we can compare and contrast the work of EFMH/ES with knowledge and authority. We cannot simply piggyback onto the already existing research done on companion animals and humans. We need to understand the similarities and differences so that we can design research that targets the work of EFMH/ES specifically.[419]

Foundations of EFMH/ES

Until this text book little has been written that actually clarifies the notion that the work of EFMH/ES stands alone as either an educational method or a therapeutic method. Rather, mental health professionals and educators have been bringing already developed concepts and theories with them to the work of EFMH/ES and simply adding the horse. There is a unique theory and a multitude of practices that professionals interested in providing an EFMH/ES method must be aware of and trained in. On an introductory level, having a working understanding of the theories and practices will allow professionals and clients alike to choose which method is the most suited for them, and as professionals, allow them to obtain further training in the areas they are most drawn to.

Inevitably educational programs through universities or colleges will begin teaching a Foundations of EFMH/ES course, as well as a Theory and Practice of EFMH/ES course on an introductory level. Hopefully any organizations that provide lengthy and professional training for interested individuals will also include these aspects so that all people practicing within this field have a common theory base from which to understand the work. Just as in the field of mental health, people must be taught the foundational underpinnings before moving on to develop their own unique concepts and approaches.

Basic Non-Profit and For-Profit Business Management Models
Many individuals who are interested in providing an EFMH/ES method start their own businesses which provide only EFMH/ES. In this situation they have to opportunity to decide if they wish to pursue the work from a for-profit or non-profit orientation. It is useful for individuals newly developing EFMH/ES programs to learn basic business management skills and explore both non-profit and for-profit models. Considerations like volunteer management, barn and herd management, client or participant services, employment responsibilities, taxes, payroll, and other such management issues specific to the work of EFMH/ES are important to understand prior to considering a career in this field. Clients, potential funders, insurance companies, or outside providers interested in referring clients to an EFMH/ES service, need to know if those managing the program have adequate business knowledge and skills. If they do not, the quality of the service might be compromised, and therefore the success of the program could also suffer.

For mental health professionals who already have a thriving practice, the addition of an EFMH/ES component still necessitates some changes in the management of the service. If the mental health professional intends to utilize volunteers, concepts of volunteer management are necessary. If the mental health professional decides to employ others to assist with the facilitation of EFMH/ES then it is recommended that he/she obtain training and education in staff management and program management.

For everyone intending to provide an EFMH/ES service specific insurance is necessary, and the corresponding forms are therefore also necessary. Forms and correct documentation specific to the work of EFMH/ES must be developed and staff and volunteers trained in how to utilize these forms.[420]

Initial Practicum or Supervised Facilitation

Individuals interested in pursuing a potential career in EFMH/ES are recommended to have hands on experience observing, assisting, and facilitating within an EFMH/ES pre-existing program or programs. It is extremely important for someone interested in EFMH/ES to witness a variety of methods and the facilitation styles that are utilized for those methods. Interested individuals should have the opportunity to facilitate and co-facilitate sessions utilizing a variety of EFMH/ES methods (within their professional capabilities) with a variety of clients. These sessions should be supervised by a professional within the field. This supervision should include assistance creating activities according to population, goals, and method, and following the session the supervisor should debrief the success of the session and the facilitation style of the individual.

The interested individual should be exposed to all operational aspects of an EFMH/ES program and gain a basic understanding of the entirety of the process from intake and treatment planning (or educational planning) to facilitation, and finally debriefing skills with volunteers or staff. They should have an understanding of the barn management and horse training and exercising techniques used by the facility as well as have exposure to facility policies and procedures.

Personal Growth

All licensed mental health professionals are required to seek professional supervision, and are generally either highly encouraged or required to attend personal counseling or psychotherapy while they are in professional practice. This requirement is in place to help ensure that issues of counter-transference or triggering do not interfere with the mental health professional's ability to work healthfully with a client. In regard to the work of EFMH/ES it is very important for both those interested in providing the service, and those already providing the service to seek supervision by someone working within the field, and also to experience for themselves the work of EFMH/ES.

It is always useful for a mental health professional to personally experience whatever it is they are going to ask a client to experience. In the experiential education field most facilitators have personally experienced the activities that they facilitate for their student. Therefore, they have a personal connection to the activities, and a deeper understanding of the manner in which the activities could impact and affect people. Furthermore, the work of EFMH/ES can bring up in both mental health professionals and other facilitators deeply buried issues, just as it does with clients. If the facilitator has not experienced first hand the work of EFMH/ES then he or she may not realize core issues that could potentially become triggered by the EFMH/ES work. Cindy Wright-Jones of Moriah Mounts in LaPorte, Colorado feels similarly, "I think both professionals (licensed mental health professionals and education professionals) should be willing to undergo equine therapy to understand what it is like to be in the clients shoes."

There are many situations in which the horse cannot differentiate between the client and the facilitator due to the facilitators own personal issues. The horse may engage in a reflective feedback process with the facilitator *instead* of the client. When this occurs there can be unusual role reversals which have the potential to be unethical. Barbara Rector believes that all who are present at an EFMH/ES session are participants, including the facilitators. She prepares all of her clients and staff for this reality and therefore when the horse offers reflective feedback to a non-client, the stage is already set for this to be a healthful transition. However, if she did not set up her sessions as such, and a facilitator was triggered without a safety container like Ms. Rector creates, the possibility for an EFMH/ES session to become unethical and unhealthy exists.[421]

A facilitator might also become personally triggered by the information that the horse is offering to a client, and thus be unable to facilitate a healthful interaction. Many mental health professionals believe in the work of EFMH/ES because it appears to induce profound change far more quickly and dramatically then traditional talk therapy methods.[422] However, the very concept that draws mental health professionals to this work is also the very factor that can cause unethical misuse of the method. Mental health professionals who have only experienced talk therapy as their own personal treatment method may be exposed to the same responses that their clients feel when they participate in an EFMH/ES session. The likelihood for deep issues to surface quickly and without warning is fairly high, and mental health professional may experience issues rising to the surface that they thought had been worked through.

Educators or other types of facilitators are as much at risk for the type of triggering that the work of EFMH/ES can bring. Educators are not required to do any personal growth or therapeutic work to be eligible to provide a service such as this and thus may have a personally therapeutic encounter when they are least expecting it. It is highly recommended by the author that educators also seek supervision while providing an EFMH/ES method, and also experience the methods for themselves prior to charging for such services.

Any way you chose to view it, it is important for any type of EFMH/ES facilitator to engage in their own personal process utilizing EFMH/ES as a treatment method. Dr. Tracy Weber of Kaleidoscope Learning Circle in Birch Run, MI, adds this, "I am passionate about facilitators walking their talk and being authentic, as well as being competent and knowing their limitations."

It is highly recommended that this personal growth process be long term, and not in a three-day workshop or retreat. It should include ongoing weekly sessions for a long enough period to ensure that personal issues have time and space to arise, and there should be the opportunity to return to that professional for follow- up sessions as needed. Another model that also works well is an intensive retreat venue which lasts at least a full week with space for both individual and group processing. This should not be considered educational or used as a training, but rather it should be a personal growth intensive designed to help individuals work through personal issues that are brought up by work with horses. Upon completion of this service the facilitator should obtain a supervisor within the field whom he or she can meet with on a regularly scheduled basis to discuss client or student issues and any personal issues that may have arisen.

Summary

In order to provide an ethical and safe EFMH/ES method, professionals should undergo rigorous educational exploration into areas that tend to arise during an EFMH/ES session, or are necessary for the safe facilitation of such services. As professionals new to the field, or as clients seeking services it is useful to gain an understanding of the type of education and training necessary to provide such services. For clients seeking EFMH/ES services it is advisable to question the provider about his/her education, experience, and supervision within the field of EFMH/ES. Facilitators who offer an EFMH/ES method without training and education specific to the field may be functioning from a limited vantage point, and therefore may compromise the physical and emotional safety of their clients, their horses, and themselves. It is the recommendation of the author that all those interested in providing an EFMH/ES method obtain adequate training, education, and supervision prior to accepting clients or charging full market cost for services offered.

SECTION FOUR

EQUINE FACILITATED MENTAL HEALTH AND EDUCATIONAL SERVICES: METHODS OF THEORY AND PRACTICE

Twelve   *Mental Health Methods: Equine Facilitated Psychotherapy*

Thirteen   *Mental Health Methods: Equine Facilitated Counseling*

Fourteen   *Mental Health Methods: Equine Assisted Psychotherapy*

Fifteen   *Mental Health Methods: Equine Facilitated Brief Intensives*

Sixteen   *Educational/Learning Methods: Equine Facilitated Learning*

Seventeen *Educational/Learning Methods: Equine Assisted Education*

Eighteen   *Other Methods: Equine Facilitated Professional Coaching*

Nineteen   *Other Methods: Equine Facilitated Human Development*

Introduction to Section Four

In the seventeen years that the field of EFMH/ES has been developing in the United States many volumes have been written about the healing potential of horses. As a developing field the first books were created to honor the experiences that individuals were having with horses. These books told stories of profound impact, awakening our minds and hearts to the possibilities that existed. Pioneers like Barbara Rector and the McCormicks wrote books that provided insight into their own unique methods and belief systems, books that helped shape the field as we know it today.

Then in 2001 Linda Kohanov did something no one had done before. She began to define what might be happening between horses and humans. She put into words the feelings that many were experiencing but could not find the language to describe. Her first book, *The Tao of Equus*, changed the field of EFMH/ES fundamentally, moving the notion of horses as healers of the mind and soul into new realms of public exposure.

The struggle for those interested in the field of EFMH/ES has been trying to make sense of the resources and information available from differing sources, each with their own unique approach and belief system in regards to the field. Due to this, it has been difficult for those interested to gain a broad understanding of the field as a whole. This book was designed to provide an overview of the field, giving the reader an understanding of some of the ways in which horses are currently facilitating or assisting the human learning and growth process.

This section introduces only the EFMH/ES methods that were defined by a majority of professionals interviewed or surveyed within the field. Since 1997 I have been conducting surveys, questionnaires, and interviews with professionals practicing within the field of EFMH/ES. Through this process of data collection a variety of different methods have surfaced. The information used to create the methods presented in this section came directly from a consensus of systematic evaluation of the information obtained from responses to interviews, questionnaires, and surveys, not from any one individual's personal beliefs regarding this field or the methods utilized.

The purpose of this section is to define the EFMH/ES methods most prominently utilized by those interviewed, surveyed, or otherwise questioned. These methods have been identified by professionals who have been practicing in the field for over ten years, and who are considered "pioneers" of these methods. The methods have been separated into two broad categories: those which employ educational or learning strategies and those which are mental health services.

It may be confusing to some why I have chosen to continue to proliferation of acronyms used to define the field of EFMH/ES. Many feel that we already have too many titles and names for what we do. I agree the there is confusion about what we do, what it is called, and how it is provided. But, after all of my research I have found that there are distinctly different approaches that have been presented consistently by numerous professionals providing an EFMH/ES method. Therefore, I feel it is appropriate for us as a field to understand these differences and learn from the uniqueness of each method. That being said, those of us who have been doing this work for a long time recognize that most of the time we intermingle methods, providing what I like to call an eclectic approach to EFMH/ES. That being said, I have also learned that in order to truly understand something we must first break it apart and understand all the parts of the whole. Then we can begin reconstructing it in a way that makes sense for our particular use based upon clientele, setting, and specific needs. In the field of counseling/psychology we learn about the various methods created by our forefathers. We learn to understand what populations may be best served by which method. We learn different approaches and techniques. And finally we learn how to intermingle techniques and methods to provide the best service for our client's unique needs. My intention for this section of the book is to help facilitate that process.

The first four methods presented are considered Equine Facilitated Mental Health Services (EFMHS) and for the purpose of these chapters we will assume that the methods presented are facilitated by a mental health professional who is licensed within their state of residence or eligible for licensure, and who has been specifically trained and educated, and has gone through a supervised practicum which qualifies them to provide EFMHS services. In reading these chapters it is advisable to reference

Section Three for further clarification of terms and ethics related to providing such a service. Any professional providing an EFMHS method should be able to clearly differentiate between a mental health service and an education or learning service and utilize referral sources when necessary. An EFMHS professional should not provide a learning or educational service unless they are specifically trained to do so.

The next four chapters will present the Equine Facilitated Education and Learning Services (EFE/LS) as defined by the EFMH/ES professionals interviewed, surveyed, or otherwise questioned. Once again it is highly recommended that the reader reference Section Three, as the definitions provided there will help clear up potential confusions that may arise regarding terminology. It is also important to state that within an EFMH/ES context, any educational or learning service should be offered only by those with extensive education, training, and experience within the method that they offer. The facilitator of these services should work closely with a licensed mental health professional who is available on-call to assist with consultation or supervision. Furthermore, the facilitator of any EFE/L service should be in contact with referral sources for mental health methods of EFMH/ES and should be trained and educated to recognize the need for referral to a therapeutic method of EFMH/ES when and if the need arises.

EFE/L providers must understand and be able to differentiate their service from a mental health service, and be trained to facilitate only within their scope of practice. Ideally, anyone providing an EFE/L service is a dually trained professional with a Masters degree in either education or counseling, and who has been specifically trained and educated, and is experienced in providing an EFE/L method. If the individual does not have a Masters degree, he or she should be able to demonstrate at least five years of supervised experience within an EFE/L method, and be educated in experiential education principles, methods, and facilitation techniques.

Although EFE/L is not a mental health service, the methods can easily become confused and quickly merge with one another. This can happen to the best of facilitators and when it does, the facilitator must be prepared, trained, and educated to safely guide the session back in a healthful and safe direction.

The following chapters outline methods of EFMH/ES that resulted from the questionnaires, surveys, and interviews, but in no way are representative of the field as a whole. There are many different ways to ethically and safely provide an equine facilitated or assisted service. The methods presented in this text are representative of the individual options, thoughts, and ideas of those who participated in any of the surveys, questionnaires, or interviews, and are subject to the interpretation of the author. In the years to come new editions of this text will include emerging methods, or methods that are currently in use but were not defined by those interviewed or surveyed.

Those already in practice within the field of EFMH/ES will appreciate the concept that it is extremely difficult if not impossible to stick completely within the boundaries of only one of these methods. Every provider has his or her own unique style and way in which the service is provided. That being said, there is also a benefit in understanding the unique differences between methods, and learning how to make conscious choices when moving between methods. The model closely resembles what is called an eclectic approach to counseling or psychotherapy. The professionals who utilize such an approach have been classically trained in a multitude of theories or methods, and after time spent in the field, begin choosing and picking which components of the various models, methods, or theoretical orientation best fits them, the situation, or the client. However, they would not be able to create their eclectic approach without a solid understanding, education, and background in these fundamental approaches.

In the upcoming section the reader will be introduced to four EFMHS methods: Equine Facilitated Psychotherapy-EFP, Equine Facilitated Counseling-EFC, and Equine Assisted Psychotherapy-EAP, two EFE/L methods: Equine Facilitated Learning-EFL and Equine Assisted Education-EAE, and two "other" methods: Equine Facilitated Professional Coaching-EFPC and Equine Facilitated Human Development – EFHD.

All throughout this section it is highly recommended that the reader revisit Section Two, as many of the practical applications of the methods are based on information that is retrievable in those chapters.

CHAPTER TWELVE

EQUINE FACILITATED PSYCHOTHERAPY

Introduction

Equine facilitated psychotherapy (EFP) is the cornerstone from which the field of EFMHS grew in the United States. Without the formal introduction of this work as a mental health method the field would not have come to be as it currently exists today. The notion that horses could help facilitate psychological awareness and growth processes was validated first by those doing the work of psychotherapy.[423]

Although services closely related to EFP were practiced years before in Europe, EFP as treatment method was brought closer to "mainstream" with Barbara Rector's introduction in the early 1990's of the method at Sierra Tucson, the prestigious treatment center in Tucson, Arizona.[424]

Most involved in the field of EFMH/ES agree that there was no one "founding" individual, but rather that those providing EFP services emerged more predominately following Sierra Tucson's outward support of the method. Many individuals helped to form the method - notably the McCormicks, a mother-daughter team of psychologists who began using EFP as their primary treatment method in private practice in Calistoga, California, Maureen Vidrine, director of HorseTime in Covington, Georgia, one of the early programs to begin providing EFP, and whose programs and services could be considered as "best practices" for new comers to the field and Marilyn Sokolof of Horsepower, in Florida, a psychologist who helped pioneer the method.

EFP as a term covers a broad range of psychotherapeutic services in which the horse is viewed as a "co-facilitator." EFMHA defines EFP as:

Equine Facilitated Psychotherapy (EFP) is experiential psychotherapy that includes equine(s). It may include, but is not limited to, a number of mutually respectful equine activities such as handling, grooming, longeing, riding, driving, and vaulting. EFP is facilitated by a licensed, credentialed mental health professional working with an appropriately credentialed equine professional. EFP may be facilitated by a mental health professional who is dually credentialed as an equine professional.[425]

Due to the broad scope of EFP, individual consensus of how such a service is implemented is difficult to obtain. However, through questionnaires, surveys and interviews the author was able to gather a variety of sources who agreed upon one method of psychotherapy in which horses were seen as co-facilitators, and that met with the consensus study done by the author regarding the definition for "psychotherapy." This is not the only method used to provide a psychotherapeutic equine experience for clients, but it is the method that showed consistency between interviewees and therefore was chosen to be represented within the initial edition of this text.[426]

A defining feature of this method is that the client must present with the cognitive processing abilities to make insight-based work possible. Although there may be other forms of psychotherapy where insight is not necessary, within this model, the capacity for insight is essential. American Heritage Stedman's Medical Dictionary definition of "psychotherapy" was used in the creation of this method. "The treatment of mental and emotional disorders through the use of psychological techniques designed to encourage communication of conflicts and insight into problems, with the goal being personality growth and behavior modification."[427] As this definition suggests, "psychotherapy" is utilized within this chapter as a means of treatment for psychological or pathological disorders and indicates that insight is a desired or needed component of the treatment.

Key Concepts

Reflective Feedback

Reflective Feedback[428] provided by the horse to the client can act as a mirror through which the client and the licensed mental health professional can view the client's projections and transferences. This may allow the client to perceive, from an external perspective, his/her own psyche and its unique functioning. The process of Reflective Feedback allows the client to engage with the horse in a nearly biofeedback-like process during which the client has the ability to witness how his/her own behaviors impacts others near to him/her, and also demonstrates the ability, or lack thereof, to change behaviors and patterns. Reflective Feedback is a clear, non-judgmental process by which the client can begin to make unconscious actions, behaviors, thoughts, feelings, and attitudes conscious. Therefore, clients are able to perceive themselves more fully as unique and individual human beings, separated yet completely connected to their pasts and to the world around them. Once this realization has been formed, clients may recognize their ability to make choices about behaviors, attitudes, thoughts, and feelings and may begin to establish an internal locus of control.[429]

Psychodramatization and Reflective Feedback

Psychodrama is generally considered a form of drama therapy, and was created by Jacob Moreno[430] in the nineteen-seventies. Merriam-Webster dictionary defines psychodrama as, "an extemporized dramatization designed to afford catharsis and social relearning for one or more of the participants from whose life history the plot is abstracted."[431] Wikipedia defines psychodrama as, "a form of drama therapy which explores, through action, the problems of people. It is a group working method, in which each person becomes a therapeutic agent for others in the psychodrama group." It continues:

> Psychodrama attempts to create an internal restructuring of dysfunctional mindsets with other people, and it challenges the participants to discover new answers to some situations and become more spontaneous and independent. Although a primary application of psychodrama has traditionally been as a form of group psychotherapy, and psychodrama often

gets defined as 'a method of group psychotherapy,' this does a disservice to the many other uses or functions of the method. More accurately psychodrama is defined as 'a method of communication in which the communicator[s] expresses him/her/themselves in action.'[432]

In the work of EFP, horses assume the role of "group members" either singly, or intermixed with human participants. The client is able to observe the actions and behaviors of the horse group, with or without other humans involved, and project their own "internal restructuring" onto the dynamic.

EFP operates under the principle that horses may be able to clearly enact and reflect both current and past events specific to a client's life in such a manner that the client is able to re-experience a past event and make decisions about how they would like to alter that event in the here and now. The client may gain a deeper understanding of both their childlike response to the event, but is then able to assess the event utilizing new skills and beliefs about who they are currently. They are given the ability to step in and make changes to a past event, therefore enforcing the ability for change in the future. They are able to practice new ways of being within old scenarios and thus feel more capable of handling potentially triggering situations in the future.

Analysis of Reflective Feedback Process
Psychoanalysis investigates mental processes which are, according to Freudian thought, almost inaccessible in any other way, except through the analysis of inner experiences such as thoughts, feelings, emotions, fantasies and dreams.[433] The manner in which the client interacts with the horse and the resistance and/or transference that arises from that interaction can provide the licensed mental health professional with a "window into the soul" of the client. Essentially, the horse reflects, through behaviors and actions, the deep mental processes of the client that are generally unconscious ways of being. The horse is able to do so probably because of their ability to perceive the minimal sensory information that the client projects without his/her conscious awareness. The licensed mental health professional is then able to visually and tactually experience the client's unconscious, and can analyze the information demonstrated by the horse.

Furthermore, through the process of Reflective Feedback, the client is also able, with the assistance of the licensed mental health professional, to witness his/her own unconscious, therefore helping to make the unconscious conscious. The client is then able to explore repressed or unconscious impulses, anxieties, and internal conflicts, and through this process may be able to free psychic energy for mature love and work.

Investigation of Life Story through the process of Reflective Feedback and Psychodrama

> *"Many times the horses appear to act out issues that the clients present while the client is presenting their story."*
> *-Pam Roberts, Equine Partners, Florissant, CO.*

When asked to verbally convey their life story, clients tend to fall into rote memorization of the telling. This means that the client will not experience the telling of the story from any other part of the body except the mind. This can leave out vital information that is stored in muscle memory, the senses, or other realms of the unconscious that are not made easily accessible through the spoken language. The story itself becomes part of the body's system that carries information from one point to another and the more the story is told in the same manner, the deeper the track becomes and the harder change is to manifest.[434] In EFP the client is afforded a new way to tell his/her story. Words may not be necessary. The horse reflects the story via his/her actions back to the licensed mental health professional and to the client. The horse senses all aspects of the story, from the subtle tensing of the stomach muscle to the change in biochemistry as experienced through odor and therefore is able to reflect a more complete version of the story.[435] This version generally contains information that the client and the licensed mental health professional may not have known before, at least on a conscious level, and therefore the client experiences the "telling" of his/her story from a very different vantage point. We could hypothesize that this new way of experiencing one's life story could help to create new neuropathways in the brain that allow for change in the behaviors, feelings, actions, and thoughts of the client, therefore repatterning maladaptive processes.

Relational Needs

The process of EFP assumes that humans are relational creatures who benefit from one-on-one, group, and communal relationships with other living beings.[436] EFP also assumes that humans need to interact with all beings, human and non-human alike and that it is through this interconnection with other beings that a client is able to form a clear definition of self.[437] EFP assumes that self is created, defined, refined, and re-sculpted through relationship. EFP believes that horses provide humans with the ability to reconnect with relational skills, foster new skills that assist in the development of the self through relationship and help humans to gain self-awareness and self-esteem necessary to pursue needed relationships with other beings.[438] Other methods of EFMH/ES view relational needs as equally important, however, in EFP relational needs are directly linked to maladaptive patterns and behaviors from childhood or other pivotal experiences or times in development that need to be brought to consciousness by the reflective feedback of the horse so that the client can make conscious decisions to change.

Reclaiming Power and Control

In order to operate from an internal locus of control, the client must experience and be able to reconnect to a personal sense of power and control. The concept of an "internal locus of control" is attributed to Julian Rotter's work that suggested two types of people, those with an internal controlling mechanism who viewed the world around them and the events that occurred as within their control, or those with an external controlling mechanism who viewed themselves as controlled by the world around them or events that they had no power over. Therefore, those with an internal locus of control tend to be more likely to succeed vocationally, personally, and within a therapeutic setting. A goal of psychotherapy would be to help a client find their own internal controlling mechanism and utilize it for future growth.[439]

EFP suggests that through working with the horse, clients gain the ability to achieve feelings of personal power and control, and thus are able to shift the locus of control from external to internal. A historical understanding of the client's past power and control issues are necessary to better understand the client's point of reference in regards to these topics. In EFP the client is exposed to a visual manifestation of their locus of control. The concrete demonstration of how they move through the world as either controlled by external forces or in control through their internal strength is a powerful treatment tool. Clients will tend to struggle with the notion of an internal or external locus of control and may misinterpret notions of power and control, therefore creating new issues within their relationships, or sense of self. EFP allows the client the opportunity to visually experience how personal power and control impacts another living being, and affords both the client and the mental health professional the ability to process the various attempts made by the client to transfer their locus of control from exterior to interior.

Integrative Approach Connecting Mind, Body, and Spirit
EFP is, according to a number of the EFMH/ES professionals interviewed, an integration of a number of major psychotherapeutic methods, bringing them together simultaneously. Marilyn Sokolof, psychotherapist and past EFMHA president suggests that EFP integrates aspects of cognitive-behavioral therapy, Gestalt therapy, psychodynamic psychotherapy, experiential therapy, somatic psychotherapy, and can include aspects of addictions and recovery treatment.[440] This concept, in and of itself, can be profound, and may help to explain why the work of EFP can be so powerful for many clients. However, EFP also offers two other aspects that some traditional psychotherapeutic methods do not, the addition of physical movement and action, and an emphasis regarding personal connection to spirit.

In EFP the client experiences his/her body in a way that may draw out deeply unconscious feelings, thoughts, and memories. Through decades of research and anecdotal information that has come from the therapeutic riding field, it is clear that the process of riding astride a horse reduces tension and decreases spasticity, provides balance and coordination which is bilateral, and stimulates the brain in a multitude of ways. The horse's rhythmical, three dimensional gaits appears to relax hyper-tense muscles which can release memories held within parts of the human body.[441] While astride a horse, the EFP client may experience a flooding of memories which are felt, not thought. The client may begin crying, laughing or otherwise spontaneously releasing tension without conscious awareness of what is occurring within their minds, bodies, and spirits. Through facilitation by the licensed mental health professional, the client may be able to make the unconscious experience conscious with a recollection of deeply buried memories, thoughts, or feelings. Until experiencing the rhythmical motion of the horse's gait, this information can remain locked within the body.

The movement of the horse, in a safe and controlled environment, also appears to provide relaxation which seems to promote easy dialog.[442] EFP clients who may be uncomfortable within traditional talk therapy, and find it difficult to speak openly and honestly about their experiences may find talking easier while astride a horse.[443] Furthermore, speaking is not always a necessity within the work of EFP, rather the client may internalize new information and make personal changes without ever having to verbally declare their personal insights or realizations.[444]

Notions of Spirit and especially a connection to something greater than one's self are commonly found within the work of EFP.[445] Clients who have felt desperately alone with no faith that there is anything or anyone who can understand them may experience a deep sense of connection to the horse, and through that experience feel that there is a power greater than themselves available to them. Due to the metaphoric and mythical connotations of the horse throughout time, clients may experience the feeling that they are in the presence of a higher power, simply by being near to a horse. This sensation sometimes helps them to alleviate psychic longings and the loneliness of the soul.

The Therapeutic Process

Therapeutic Goals
The most prevailing goal of EFP is to help the client make unconscious feelings, thoughts, behaviors, and actions conscious.[446] This necessitates the reconstruction of the client's life story, as told through the process of reflective feedback and Psychodramatization. The secondary goal is for the client to realize their own power of choice, and thus begin changing maladaptive patterns that negatively impact their lives. EFP is designed to help reduce psychological dysfunction and to promote deeper psychological healing. The EFP method suggests that the client

benefits from an integrative approach to treatment that is designed to bring about significant change. A goal of EFP is to help the client connect with his or her body and therefore potentially gain new depth and understanding of past events that shaped their psyche. The EFP method proposes that at the end of treatment, the client will have:[447]

- Shifted their locus of control from external to internal.

- Recognized their responsibility within the process of change.

- Come to a deeper awareness of unconscious motivations.

- Learned to co-create more healthful and fulfilling relationships.

- Discovered a sense of a power greater than themselves.

- Begun the process of learning to listen to their bodies.

- Re-constructed their life story to include the information held within their physical bodies.

- Gained insight that is not only an intellectual understanding of the material, but also a felt experience of the information which includes deeply buried feelings and memories.

- Experienced a decrease in psychological dysfunction and moved towards a more healthful and fulfilling psychological existence.

Horse's Role, Function, and Relationship to the Client

The horse assumes the more traditional psychotherapist relationship with the client, with a few notable exceptions. The horse provides the "blank screen" approach normally utilized by the licensed mental health professional in traditional psychotherapy.[448] In EFP the client may project and transfer unconscious thoughts, feelings, behaviors, and actions onto the horse, as well as onto the licensed mental health professional.[449] The horse also helps open the doors of the psyche by providing unconditional love and affection, which a licensed mental health professional may be ethically uncomfortable doing within a psychotherapeutic relationship. Humans are more inclined to share honestly and openly with a being that they feel loved and cared for by.450 The horse provides both reflective feedback and the Psychodramatization of the client's life story which is based upon the projection and transference from client to horse, but also helps to ground the client in the here and now by the mere physicality of his/ her presence. In an EFP session the horse should be considered an equal facilitator, providing the clients with felt experiences of a visual nature. The horse should be allowed the ability to freely engage the client in the reflective feedback process and the Psychodramatization of the client's life story. The manner in which the session is designed should encourage the client and the horse to interact in this free-form process.

The work of EFP is relational in nature, which means that it is based upon the relationship that is developed between the horse and the human. Judith V. Jordan in her book *Women's Growth and Connection: Writings from the Stone Center*, and in her later book *The Complexity of Connection*,451 discusses the notion of a relational approach to counseling and psychotherapy. She and her co-authors propose that women develop differently than the generally male-oriented concepts of human development normally seen in developmental psychology texts. Jordan writes that women are relational in nature, meaning that everything within the context of their daily lives is in some way interconnected with other living beings and thus they engage with the world around them differently than men might. Although the concept is based around a "feminine" model of relating to the world, this model is geared towards a humanitarian approach to living life, which certainly includes men and fosters their own unique growth and development.

Since the work of EFP is also relational in nature, the horse and the human need the time and space to connect, interact, and form relationships with each other. This necessitates that the client become familiar with concepts that promote the development of such a relationship. The horse should be allowed the freedom to mutually choose the individual he or she wishes to develop relationship with. This means that although a great deal of reflective feedback and Psychodramatization can be done between a client and unknown horses, or horses who do not connect with a certain client, once the treatment has moved on to the development of relationship between horse and human, the horse should be included in the decision making process.

Licensed Mental Health Professional's Role, Function, and Relationship to the Client

The licensed mental health professional's primary role is to interpret and analyze the client's experience of the horse, and the horse's experience of the client.[452] This necessitates a deep understanding of the language of Equus, and an understanding of the personality and normal behaviors of each horse who engages with clients. The licensed mental health professional offers a literal translation of the client's experience utilizing as purely as possible the seen communications from the horse to the client.[453] The licensed mental health professional will need to clearly define his/her role within an EFP session to the client prior to providing such a service, as the role of the licensed mental health professional within the EFP method may look differently than it would in a more traditional setting.[454]

The EFP licensed professional will engage with the client occasionally on an educational or skills-based level. As the client begins recognizing maladaptive behaviors as seen through the lens of the horse/human relationship, and makes decisions to begin the process of change, the licensed mental health professional will be required to work with the client to learn tangible new skills for how to work with the horse in a different and potentially more healthful manner.[455] As the client experiences successes within the horse/human relationship, the licensed mental health professional helps the client to transfer that information back into daily life without horses.

The licensed mental health professional must also utilize safety training and transfer a basic understanding of safety protocol to the client. Ethically, it is the licensed mental health professional's responsibility to maintain the safety of the therapeutic relationship, not that of an assistant who is hired to provide the equine specialization and safety support.[456] Therefore it is the responsibility of the licensed mental health professional to engage on a therapeutic level with the client about concepts of personal safety. This educational lesson can quickly become a therapeutic intervention used to create metaphor for the client. If the client can have a felt experience of learning how to keep himself/herself physically safe around a huge creature like the horse, he/she may access unconscious memories, thoughts, or feelings about other times in his/her life when he/she was unable to do this for himself/herself or others in his/her life. The use of metaphor within the EFP session is the responsibility of the licensed mental health professional, and finding how tangible horse activities or skills provide metaphoric connections back to the client's daily life can be a powerful intervention and treatment tool.[457]

The EFP licensed professional does a great deal of observation and interpretation, and asks probing questions. The relationship between the client and the licensed mental health professional may be conceived of as less important to the experiential process in EFP than the role of the relationship between the client and the horse. The EFP licensed professional may assume a lesser role so that the client can derive a bulk of his/her knowledge and understanding from the experiences he/she has with the horse rather than the licensed mental health professional. However, the role of the EFP licensed professional is vital as the interpreter of the experience, the translator between the horse/human relationship and human/human relationships, and as the holder of the safe container.

Generally in an EFP session the horse facilitates the experience, and the licensed mental health professional analyzes, interprets, and translates the outcome. Therefore, the licensed mental health professional generally does not spend a great deal of time in planning activities, or facilitating activities except for basic safety skills or skills needed for the client to reach a new desired level in her relationship with the horse. Rather, the horse and the client are encouraged to determine and direct the interactions without a large degree of structure or input from the licensed mental health professional. Pam Roberts of Equine Partners in Florissant, CO agrees, "I may dream up activities, but the horses change them around as we go."

Table of EFMH/ES Methods *

Method	Category	Facilitator Qualifications	EFMH/ES Trainings/Memberships Recommended	Key Concepts
Equine Facilitated Psychotherapy (EFP)	EFMHS	Psychotherapist Counselor Psychologist Social Worker Other mental health professional w/appropriate education/licensure/training/supervision	EFMHA Member Epona/AIA/Esperanza/Three Eagles Ranch Trainings Prescott College -Masters Program Carroll College – Continuing Education Courses	Insight-Based Psychotherapy Reflective Feedback Psychodrama Holistic Approach Horse as Co-Facilitator or Facilitator
Equine Facilitated Counseling (EFC)	EFMHS	Psychotherapist Counselor Psychologist Social Worker Other mental health professional w/appropriate education/licensure/training/supervision	EFMHA and EAGALA Member Esperanza Training Prescott College- Masters Program Carroll College – Continuing Education Courses	Present and Future Focused Counseling Life Skills Focused Health and Wellness Orientation Horse as Co-facilitator or Employee
Equine Assisted Psychotherapy (EAP)	EFMHS	Psychotherapist Counselor Psychologist Social Worker Other mental health professional w/appropriate education/licensure/training/supervision	EAGALA Member EAGALA Level Two or Three Certification Prescott College – Masters Program	Experiential Therapy Activities Based Challenge By Choice Group Oriented Horse as Tool or Employee
Equine Facilitated Brief Intensives (EFBI)	EFMHS	Psychotherapist Counselor Psychologist Social Worker Other mental health professional w/appropriate education/licensure/training/supervision	EFMHA and EAGALA Member Epona/AIA/Esperanza/EAGALA Three Eagles Ranch Trainings Prescott College- Masters Program Carroll College – Continuing Education Courses	Brief Psychotherapy Collaborative Services Integrative Approach

* Please note that these are the recommendations of this author solely based upon her own experiences with the below mentioned organizations.
There may be other appropriate training/educational/membership/etc. recommendations that the author is not aware of.

Table of EFMH/ES Methods

Method	Category	Facilitator Qualifications	EFMH/ES Trainings/Memberships Recommended	Key Concepts
Equine Facilitated Learning (EFL)	EFE/L	Masters Degree in Education Experiential Educator Special Education Teacher Counselor or other Mental Health Professional w/Additional Training/Experience in Experiential Education	EFMHA Member Horse Power Training Program AIA Training Program Carroll College – Human/Animal Bonding Program Prescott College – Experiential Education Program	Serves Special Needs Populations Life Skills, Social Skills, and Communication Skills Based Work Ethic Training Experiential Learning
Equine Assisted Experiential Education (EAEE)	EFE/L	Masters Degree in Education Counselor or other Mental Health Professional w/Additional Training/Experience in Experiential Education Teacher or College Professor w/Additional Training/Experience in Experiential Education	EAGALA, EFMHA, and EGEA Member Prescott College- Experiential Education Program Prescott College – Centaur Leadership Courses Carroll College – Continuing Education Courses AIA Training Program	Experiential Education Serving Fully Functional School, College, and University Populations Teamwork and Cohesion Building Facilitation Skills Training Leadership Skills Training Therapeutic Skills Training
Equine Facilitated Professional Coaching (EFPC)	Other	Masters Degree in any of the following: Counseling/Psychology Human Development Organizational Management Business Management Training and Certification from the IAC or other nationally-recognized coaching organizations.	Equine Guided Education Association (EGEA) Member Leadership Outfitters Training Rolling Horse Ranch Training	Professional Coaching Services Leadership Development Personal Development Team Development
Equine Facilitated Human Development	Other	Masters or Advanced Degree in any of the following: Counseling/Psychology Human Development Spirituality Integrative Medicine Training in a number of additional areas (see method)	EFMHA Member EGEA Member Epona/AIA/ Three Eagles Ranch Trainings Holotropic Breathwork Training Expressive Arts Training See additional recommendations within chapter.	Leadership Skills Relationship Development Increased Sensitivity, Intuition, and Awareness Creativity Advanced Communication Skills

If the EFP session is one-on-one, it is recommended that the licensed mental health professional employ an additional assistant who is trained and educated in the method, who is available on site if the licensed mental health professional needs a horse handler or other safety back-up during the session. This individual would not participate in the session and would not be within ear shot of the session unless the licensed mental health professional needed them present.

If it is an EFP group session, the licensed mental health provider should co-facilitate with another EFP trained and educated licensed mental health provider. In other forms of EFMHS that are not as deeply probing or insight based, it is not as important to have the EFMHS group service co-facilitated by two licensed mental health providers, but due to the intensity, duration, and potentially deeply revealing process of EFP, ethically it appears more appropriate to avoid co-facilitation with someone who is not a licensed mental health professional.

Dependant upon the ratio of participants to horses, and the level of engagement between clients and horses, other horse handlers who have been trained in the EFP method, theory, and practices should be available to assist during specific activities of an EFP session which do not include deeply probing or insight-based reflections.

Client's Experience in Therapy

It is important that clients interested in EFP understand that they are engaging in a long term treatment method and must be willing and able to commit to the duration of treatment.[458] Typically EFP would be offered on a weekly or bi-weekly basis in the barn or stable milieu, and the client would expect to experience both hands-on horse time and one-on-one psychotherapy time.

The client would be made aware of the differences between traditional psychotherapy in an office, and EFP. They would understand the confidentiality issues that exist within the barn milieu and would generally be asked to sign a confidentiality waiver which states that the licensed mental health provider cannot predict or control complete confidentiality within that environment.[459] Furthermore, discussion of touch would occur, and an additional waiver may be included that helps define and explain how touch may come into play during an EFP session. The client would be informed of the possibility of assistants or co-facilitators and would be introduced to these individuals and given the right to refuse (privately) their presence if they were uncomfortable with them *prior to their inclusion in a session.* The client and the licensed mental health professional would discuss the role of the professional within EFP and the professional would ensure that the client understood the differences and was comfortable with the method.

The client would also be informed of the potential risk involved with EFP and be asked to sign a waiver stating that he or she understands the potential and inherent risks associated with this treatment method.

EFP clients are generally asked to make a commitment to the licensed mental health provider that they will actively engage in the therapeutic process which includes interacting with the horses, processing their experiences with the horses, and sharing components of their past, as appropriate. EFP clients will generally not be encouraged to make major life changes while engaging in EFP, but rather will be encouraged to remain vested in the process of acquiring insight and self-awareness.

EFP clients are considered ready to terminate services when the treatment goals created between them and their licensed mental health professional have been met to the satisfaction of both the client and the professional, and when the horse reflects consistent change. EFP sessions should be terminated by the licensed mental health professional if the client is demonstrating an on-going lack of interest or engagement with the service, or if the client is unwilling to participate in the horse-oriented aspects of treatment.

At the completion of EFP treatment, an EFP client may be referred to an Equine Facilitated Counseling service provider to begin the process of tangible life change.[460]

Practice: Therapeutic Techniques, Processes, and Procedures

Overview

EFP utilizes techniques that are directed towards fostering self-awareness, developing a deeper understanding of symptomology, repatterning maladaptive behaviors, and bringing unconscious behaviors, thoughts, feelings, and actions into consciousness. The techniques facilitate relationship-building, care and compassion, and affectionate positive regard. The therapeutic method proceeds from unconscious actions, to a recognition of actions, to interpretation of the actions, and finally to the integration of insight thus gained into daily life. Through this process it is hoped that the client will be successful in changing maladaptive behavioral patterns, thereby decreasing psychological dysfunctional.[461]

Populations who are best served by this treatment method are individuals diagnosed with psychological disorders such as bi-polar, schizophrenia, borderline personality disorder and other personality disorders, major depression, anxiety, post traumatic stress disorder, eating disorders, and individuals dealing with the long lasting effects of trauma: sexual, physical, and emotional. On occasion, depending upon the individual client, EFP is also useful for those recovering from substance abuse, or other forms of addiction. These clients however, must be cognitively functional enough to process information and engage in self-examination.[462]

The five significant techniques of EFP are (1) Body grounding and awareness activities, (2) Fluid Psychodrama Process and Interpretation, (3) Reflective Feedback Interpretation, (4) Use of expressive arts as processing tools, and (5) Deep contemplative and process work.[463]

Body grounding and awareness activities

For EFP to be safely conducted, clients need to be trained in body grounding and body awareness practices.[464] Although there are many deeper ramifications of body awareness and grounding techniques, the first and most important emphasis should be placed purely on creating safety. When a client enters into the space of a horse, if they have not been taught how to ground and how, at least on a rudimentary level, to become aware of where they are in time and space, accidents are more likely to occur. Many clients who engage in EFP work are disconnected from their physical bodies, and may be unaware of where their bodies are at any given moment. Therefore they are prone to minor accidents such as tripping, stumbling, stubbing toes, smashing figures, hitting their heads, or other such small injuries.[465] They tend to place their bodies in harm's way, such as standing directly in the blind spot of a horse, or placing their foot exactly where the horse is able to place his. It is highly recommended that the licensed mental health professional utilize body grounding and awareness techniques to help the client initially become aware of his or her body in time and space, therefore becoming safe enough to begin interacting with the horses. Such techniques include the use of body scans, guided imagery, breathing methods, and other such concepts.[466]

Once the client has practiced these methods, and is ready to be exposed to horses, the constant reminders of body awareness and grounding become commonplace within any given session. In order to access deeply unconscious material, the body must become an actively engaged participant. Material is stored within muscle memory, and in EFP, especially the movement of the horse while astride, but even the movement of the human body while grooming, walking, or otherwise physically engaging the body, may unlock secrets hidden in the body.[467] Therefore, it is important that the licensed mental health professional be skilled in body awareness and grounding techniques, and is able to utilize them when necessary to either keep the client physically safe, or help the client move towards a deeper understanding of their psyche.

Fluid Psychodrama and Interpretation
Psychodrama[468] in an EFP setting denotes a complex exchange between the client and the horse. The client will engage with the horse in a safe and secure setting, like a round pen, and arena, or a fenced pasture. There is no expectation placed upon the interaction other than for the client to experience interaction with the horse. However, this technique might be utilized after a conversation regarding family history, history of relationships, or other poignant material.[469] The technique can be used to help shed new light upon an old story or way of telling a story, or it can be used to break through mental and emotional blocks that

are holding back the treatment process. Therefore, the interactions that occur between the horse(s) and the client might have specific information even though no expectations were placed upon the actual activity. Occasionally a licensed mental health professional will use the activity to gain specific information, and thus will frontload the activity by suggesting a train of thought indicative of that information prior to entering into the horse(s) space.

Regardless of which approach the licensed mental health professional uses, prior to this or any interaction between horses and clients, the professional has spoken with the client about safety, and has provided a level of education about equine safety skills for the client. The client is therefore aware and trained in how to keep herself or himself safe when engaging with the horse. In many cases the licensed mental health professional will give the client the option to either go into the space with the horse(s), or remain outside of that space.

If the client decides to enter into the horse(s) space, the licensed mental health professional and potentially a safety support person will enter with them. The role of the professional in this technique is to remain at a distance and observe the interactions between the horse(s) and the client. The role of the safety support person is to stay completely neutral and distant, but be willing and able to engage with the client if his or her physical safety is in jeopardy.

Once the client has made the decision to either enter or not enter into the horse(s) space, the client is asked to remain in silence until he or she feels "complete" with the experience. The client is told that he or she can interact with the horse(s) in any manner that she/he likes, as long as it is safe for both her/him and the horse.

At this point the licensed mental health professional simply steps back and begins observing the interactions as they play out. The horse or horses may begin acting out a series of complex behaviors that appear non-horse-like in nature, or at the least not indicative of normal horse or specific herd behavior. Sometimes the client will step in and actually engage in the psychodrama process as one of the actors, and other times he or she will simply observe the horses acting out a dramatization. Within the process of psycho-dramatization between horse and client, the horse and/or horses and the client engage in a process that is unstructured and fluid, allowing the horse(s) a full range of expression towards or with the client.

Once the client is "complete" the licensed mental health professional and the client may choose to sit to discuss what occurred between the horse(s) and the client. The client might project feelings and thoughts onto the actual interaction between horses or between themselves and the horses, and other times the client may transfer complex ideologies, histories, roles, or relationships onto the horse or horses.[470] The licensed mental health professional might engage the client in an interpretation of the observations that he or she witnessed, using both a deep working knowledge of the horse(s), herd dynamics, equine communication, and a deep understanding of the workings of the human psyche. This material generally opens new doors and allows for changes in perception about the past, the present, or the future. The licensed mental health professional can then engage with the client to discover new ideas for how to approach old behaviors or patterns, and ask the client to enter back into the horse(s) space to utilize a new and different paradigm or belief set.

Reflective Feedback Interpretation
Reflective Feedback can be utilized in other EFMH/ES services, the difference is that within an EFP session the licensed mental health professional analyzes and interprets the exchange.

Reflective Feedback, also called mirroring by many in the field, is a process by which the horse's behaviors and actions may accurately reflect the functionality of the client.[471] This generally relates to communication, relational, or behavioral styles. Reflective feedback appears to be most successfully utilized when the client is given a specific task to accomplish with the horse. For instance, the client is taught how to move the horse around the round pen at one or two specific gaits, or the client is asked to lead the horse somewhere, groom the horse, or otherwise engage in a task with the horse. It is important when utilizing this technique to actually *teach* the client how to successfully accomplish the stated task, otherwise the potential for failure is high, and this leads to a very different intervention than what is generally desired with reflective feedback. This technique is not designed to trick the client into demonstrating maladaptive behaviors due to the frustration that arises because of a lack of understanding and knowledge about how the horse is trained.

Once the client has been taught how to achieve the skill that is desired they are allowed to experiment with that skill, using their current behaviors, attitude, and personal styles. The horse may then react to the particular style the client uses, reflecting back to the client how successful or unsuccessful that approach is. Once the client and the licensed mental health professional witness how the horse reacts to the client's style, interpretation and analysis can occur, and possibly a shift in behavior will ensue.

In EFP, reflective feedback is not used as a technique to teach new skills, but rather as a process by which clients can come to a deeper understanding of their outward styles and functionality as perceived by others around them. They can chose to make decisions based upon the information gained, but the focus of the psychotherapeutic session is not to invoke intensive practice of a new skill, but rather to foster deep process and conversation about unconscious behaviors.

Use of Expressive Arts as Processing Tools

"The client is allowed to experience and interpret whatever he understands that the horse has offered. Creative arts encourage personal expression and introspection. I believe that the bridge between the horse experience and the client's personal insight could be through the arts."- Karen Head, Equinection, Asheville, NC

EFP sessions often trigger deeply unconscious patterns which may be less accessible through the use of other treatment methods. Many of these unconscious patterns are held in a place inside the soul where the spoken word is nearly useless in the retrieval process.[472] Through Psychodramatization and reflective feedback, the horses may bring into the light those deeply held feelings, beliefs, thoughts, behaviors, and actions. Once the client witnesses his or her own unconscious process made conscious, it can be difficult to assimilate the information gained. It can be especially hard to put the felt experience into spoken language in the moment. If the client is allowed too long to process and intellectualize their experience, the free flowing stream of consciousness that accesses the deeper and generally unconscious regions of the brain may cease. Therefore, it is important that following an experience with a horse, the client is offered a way of expressing stream of consciousness thoughts and feelings without having to form a complete or analytical thought processes. The transfer between the felt experience and the spoken word is complex and filled with opportunities to lose the deeper meaning within the language used.[473]

There exist a multitude of ways in which the client can remain connected to his or her unconscious felt experience while still beginning to process the experience.

Art

If the licensed mental health professional is specially trained in the use of art as therapy, utilizing a creative arts process following an EFP session can be an extremely impactful way of allowing thoughts and feelings to come forth without the use of the spoken word. Clients can be asked to stay in silence following their work with the horses, and can be brought to a safe area where art supplies, paper, magazines, clay or other such resources are set up. The client is then invited to utilize whatever medium he or she is drawn to for the creation of a reflection about their internal process.

Free Flowing Stream of Consciousness

This can either be done astride a horse, if the client is safe utilizing that intervention, or next to the horse if that is more appropriate. If the client is mounted, side walkers and a horse handler may need to be involved, which means that the client will have had to agree to them as a part of his or her session. If mounted, the client will be asked to simply move into free association as the horse moves at the walk around the pen. The client will generally be encouraged to close his or her eyes, again only if he/she feels safe and comfortable in doing so, and then will be asked to begin speaking anything and everything that is going through his/her mind/body/soul at the moment. The safety support team will ensure the client's safety on top of the horse, and the horse handler will control to direction and speed of the horse. This frees the licensed mental health professional to stand back and observe the client's body language, the horse's behaviors and body language, and listen to what the client is expressing. If the client is unsafe or uncomfortable astride a horse, the client can do free association[474] while standing next to the horse stroking it, or laying his/her head into the horse's mid-section. Again, the licensed mental health professional can encourage the client to close his/her eyes and engage in free association with no limits, judgments, or analysis of thought patterns. Once again, a horse handler will need to be present to ensure the safety of the activity, while the licensed mental health professional observes the horse and the client during their interaction.

Drumming or other Musical Expression

The licensed mental health professional can offer the client the ability to utilize sound and music as a form of expression.[475] Drums, other musical instruments, or use of voice can be suggested or made available to the client. This method would generally occur somewhere safe where neither the client nor the licensed mental health professional have to be concerned with potential dangers, and therefore there is no need for a safety support team.

Journaling

The client can utilize a journaling exercise to express free association, thoughts, and feelings following an EFP session.[476] In this case they should be allowed to choose a place around the facility where they feel comfortable and safe and engage in either free flowing stream of consciousness writing, or specific techniques suggested by the licensed mental health professional, such as non-dominant handwriting, or scribble-into-words.

Spirit Horse Painting

To utilize this technique the licensed mental health professional should have an understanding of art therapy methods and practices. This activity necessitates the use of a safety support team which generally includes a horse handler and in some cases an additional support person who helps organize and facilitate the actual use of the materials. The licensed mental health professional should be free to observe, and interact with the process only when necessary. The client is offered the ability to engage in mutually choosing a horse who is also willing to participate in the activity. Generally this would be a horse with whom the client has formed a deep relationship, and who is a part of the treatment team. The client is offered a full selection of vegetable-based and non-harmful water color paints and an array of tools such as sponges, soft brushes, and so forth that can be used to paint upon the body of the horse. There are many ways in which this technique can be utilized. The licensed mental health professional can set up a free association art expression activity where the client simply paints their stream of consciousness onto the body of the horse, or it can be more directed depending upon the needs of the client. Either way, the client is then allowed to apply paint onto the horse in a manner symbolic of their internal processes. The licensed mental health professional should be attuned to the behaviors of the horse, and recognize if the material that the client is placing upon the horse's body is negatively impacting the horse. If this becomes the case, it is advisable for the licensed mental health professional to reflect this back to the client, and/or recommend that the activity be finished using paper or other materials.

Following the use of this technique, the horse will need to be washed. This activity can either become a part of the therapeutic process, with the client choosing to "wash away" memories or thoughts that are no longer useful to them, or they can be given the option to take a photograph (it is recommended that the licensed mental health professional have a digital camera or Polaroid available on-site for this purpose) to solidify the process. If the client is not going to wash the horse himself/herself, the horse handler should engage in this activity while the client and the licensed mental health professional move to another location. This activity should only be done in the summer, or warm months when bathing is healthful for the horse.[477]

Whichever technique the licensed mental health professional utilizes, the professional is constantly engaged in analysis of the process. The professional should be equally observing the horse and the client, and the relationship that exists between them. It is through this observation that analysis and interpretation can occur.

Deep Contemplative Process Work
Following the use of an expressive, free association activity, the licensed mental health professional and the client generally retire to somewhere

private where deep contemplative process work can occur. This space might be inside of an office, next to the pasture where the horses are, or under a tree in the shade somewhere. It is here that the client can share personal reflections about the entire session, and is able to put voice to thoughts, felt experiences, or other concepts if he/she chooses to do so. It is also here that the licensed mental health professional may be able to help the client make translations from the work that they did with the horses or the expressive process, back to their history or life story, or to their present state of being.

Method Example

This method example was retrieved from the archives of Esperanza, An Experiential Healing Center. It was dated January, 2003. "I" refers to this author.

"Is this Esperanza?" "Yes, how may I help you?" "I'm driving, I'm lost. I saw your ad and I thought I would come over, but I can't find the street. I love horses. As a girl I dreamed about owning a horse. A horse of my own. But you know- life. I got married. Now I can't even cook dinner. What street are you on? How do I get there from here?" "Where is here?" I ask. "You know, my husband might divorce me. I can't even shop anymore. I get lost in the market. Sometimes I don't even get there. I just drive around. And then he has to come and find me." "I'm sorry, I didn't quite catch your name." "Oh, oh, I'm Mary." "Ok Mary, could you pull over the car, is there somewhere safe to pull over?" "Yes. Yes that's a good idea."

Mary pulls the car over and we brainstorm where she might be. I finally figure out what the cross streets are and give her detailed directions to our facility, luckily only a few blocks away. Moments later a car pulls up. I meet her in the driveway. She looks as if she has not showered in weeks. Her hair is graying, laying flat against her head. Her clothes are covered in food stains and I notice that her hands are shaking. I lead her into the office, get her a glass of water, and we sit down. Already it has become clear that she is struggling through a manic/depressive cycle. Her words come out faster and faster pouring over each other, tumbling into the world without reason or order. Her thoughts bounce from one idea to the next, racing, changing tone and content about every three minutes. First she is joyous that she might be able to take "riding lessons" again, a childhood dream. Then she is crying, telling me about her husband and their deteriorating marriage. Then about how excited she is for his company party, an event she is hosting at their home, and the elaborate meal she intends to cook.

We get through the paperwork somehow and walk outside to the barn. The horses are turned out in the arena. I instruct her to stand along the outside of the fence. We attempt to do a grounding activity, which is relatively unsuccessful. I ask that she search the herd for the horse whom she is most drawn to. She walks the fence line, suddenly quiet. Quiet for the first time since she arrived. The horses begin to move, restless and uncomfortable. Nine of them move off to the farthest corner of the arena, away from her. One remains. He meets her gaze and walks directly over to her. Cloudy. Shy, aloof Cloudy. Cloudy who has only just learned how to express himself. Cloudy, just discovering who he is without his Grand Prix career. Cloudy who does not work with clients. I hold my breath. Cloudy moves directly up to Mary and extends his head over the fence to smell her. She reaches up to touch his face. He's head shy. Normally he does not let anyone touch his face but he lets her. She strokes his cheeks, his forehead, runs her hand across his nose. Cloudy stands, looking at her.

After our first meeting Mary started coming to Esperanza twice a week for individual sessions. In the beginning it was nearly useless to converse with Mary. Instead she worked with Cloudy. I stayed back, watching and ensuring their safety, offering observations about how Cloudy responded to her. Each time she came her mood swings lengthened, from three minutes to five minutes, then from five minutes to 1/2 an hour. Cloudy reflected for her each transition between depressive and manic. When she was manic he was uncomfortable, easily irritated, and fast paced. When she was depressive he was withdrawn, quiet, and aloof. However, he never left her and never did anything to jeopardize her safety and every day that she came, the other horses removed themselves and he came over to greet her. Our sessions consisted of an array of activities, from quiet grooming and touching, to walking with Cloudy, to discussions in the shade of a large pine tree with Cloudy eating grass near us. We utilized a number of art activities to help Mary process information she gained from Cloudy. This method allowed Mary to express herself without having to find the words for her internal struggle. At first art was the only way for Mary to convey her feelings, thoughts, and experiences. With each visit Mary's ability for cognitive processing increased, and as her mood swings became further apart she began to discover her own "baseline" or place of normalcy. We were able to converse from that place more frequently with and without the use of art. Finally one day Mary declared that she was ready to ride Cloudy. Cloudy is large, 16'3 hands tall and well muscled. His movement is fluid, graceful and BIG. I was not sure, but I trusted Cloudy explicitly. He had taken over the equine aspect of Mary's treatment. I never set up an activity, nor did I facilitate anything during the entirety of her treatment. Cloudy and Mary would begin interacting, moving through stages, from simple touch with Cloudy loose in the arena, to formal grooming, Cloudy staying by her. Other times he wanted to move, and they would walk always together. Some days when her manic behaviors were intense Cloudy would run, moving rhythmically, free longeing around Mary, demonstrating the need for release, for movement of something stuck. Other days they would just be near each other, Mary in a chair, Cloudy standing by. Mary spoke with Cloudy at length, sharing secrets too dark for the human ear. Cloudy leaning down towards her, sometimes touching her chest or stomach as she spoke. I stood away, watching. When we would come back together I would share any observations I had about Cloudy's behavior, and she would share any insights she felt ready to share.

So the day she wanted to ride I decided to trust the process. She stepped up onto the mounting block and smoothly came to rest on Cloudy's back. He shifted and then stood still. She wanted him to walk, and so off we went. But something was wrong. Cloudy's beautiful big gait was transformed into small uncomfortable steps, lurching around the arena. I looked up at Mary and saw that her hips were locked, completely unmoving. We came to a halt. We began to talk about her hips, and what they represented. She did not know. I asked her to begin slowing focusing on relaxing her hips and allowing them to move rhythmically with Cloudy's movement. Music was softly playing in the background, Native drum beats mirroring Cloudy's steps on the earth. Around we went, slow, lurching, but moving. All of a sudden Cloudy's neck dropped, his back stretched, and his steps lengthened. We were floating, moving cleanly across the earth. I looked up. Mary's face was covered in dirty tears. Tears pouring down her cheeks, landing on Cloudy's withers, spilling down onto the earth. We walked. Her hips moving with Cloudy's gait, telling him the tale she had so long buried. The music continued, but it sounded lighter, quicker. Cloudy came to a smooth halt on his own accord, licking and chewing he stood there. Mary bent down and hugged him around his neck. The she sat up tall and stretched her arms above her head, taking a deep breath and letting it out loudly. She looked down at me, eyes clear. "I know now what happened to me. Everyday I felt like I was going crazy. It was like something inside was clawing its way through me, wanting to get out. But I could not find it. Everyone said it was just my mental illness (Bi-polar). No one believed that there was something else. But I knew. I could not remember it though, could not make anyone else believe me. Now I remember."

Mary's recollection freed her in many ways. From that day forward our treatment was on a fast track towards recovery. At six months her medications had been cut in half. At eight months she had enrolled in college, finishing the degree she never had been able to complete and was medication free. Her marriage was on the mend and she was successfully shopping and cooking (and driving!).

I will never forget the day that Mary pulled into the driveway eight months from the first day I had met her. She gets out of the car, calling to Cloudy over the fence. I watch her walking confidently across the parking area towards me. Smiling, relaxed, beautiful. Her hair glowing, short and blond, styled to perfection, riding breeches and a white polo shirt, also gleamingly clean. She reports struggling with subtle shifts in her moods every few weeks, but observably these shifts are normal, what any of us would experience. Responses to stimuli that we all deal with. A few days later I received a phone call from her psychiatrist. "What did you do to Mary?" He asks. "I just have never seen anything like it." "I did nothing to Mary." I respond. "Cloudy and Mary did that to Mary."

Mary stayed with Esperanza transitioning first to a horse exerciser, and then began helping with our groups of severely mentally ill patients who we saw on a weekly basis. She worked with us for another year following her nine-month treatment. Mary's bi-polar symptoms did not return in the year we spent with her following the closure of her treatment.

Summary and Evaluation

To provide EFP, the licensed mental health professional must be highly skilled, trained, and educated in a multitude of disciplines, which include intensive training in EFP, expressive arts training, and an understanding of body awareness and grounding techniques along with traditional psychotherapeutic training. EFP deals with complex psychological disorders in an attempt to help re-pattern maladaptive behaviors and decrease psychological dysfunction. This method is based upon concepts of psychoanalysis, using the horse/human relationship as the "blank slate" onto which the client's projections and transferences are presented. The licensed mental health professional remains the observer, interpreter, and translator, helping the client to witness his or her own internal process through the relationship that is formed with the horse. The treatment method is fluid and unobstructed in its application, and the licensed mental health professional generally does not engage in facilitation of pre-planned activities. The horse is most apt to facilitate whatever activities occur, while the licensed mental health professional observes. Clients who engage in EFP generally must be functional enough to process deep unconscious thoughts, feelings, behaviors, and actions, and to engage fully in the process of insight-based therapy.

There are significant differences between traditional talk psychotherapy and EFP. One of the most fundamental differences arises within the concept of confidentiality. The EFP licensed mental health professional cannot guarantee complete confidentiality, and in many cases will need to introduce the use of a horse handler and even occasionally a safety support team, who will witness a part of the client's deep psychological process.

Furthermore, due to the unpredictable nature of a horse barn, issues can arise with individuals coming into and out of the barn setting. Clients need to understand the unique issues that result from the barn milieu, and the licensed mental health professional must assess whether or not such an environment is appropriate and manageable for their clients.

Another fundamental difference between traditional insight-based psychotherapy and EFP is that the role of the licensed mental health professional is significantly altered. In an EFP session the client may witness emotions, feelings, thoughts, and personal sharing arise from a licensed mental health professional. Due to this authentic sharing, a deeper and more personable relationship may form between the client and the professional. Furthermore, the licensed mental health professional may find herself or himself in the unique position of educating the client about specific safety-related topics, and may be seen by the client as a guide more than a "blank slate." Finally, it is the relationship between the client and the horse that is most importantly fostered. The licensed mental health professional remains as inactive within the treatment method as possible, providing the safety support, structure, and interpretation and translation, but not acting as the primary source for insight.

EFP is an integrative approach to treatment, which means that the client will be exposed to techniques that engage the body, the mind, and the spirit. Furthermore, EFP contains elements of many traditional psychotherapeutic methods. Between the integrative approach, and the use of a multitude of psychotherapeutic concepts, EFP tends to have fast-acting, and fairly profound treatment outcomes. However, EFP should not be mistaken for a "short term" form of treatment, as it still constitutes a long term, deeply psychological process that necessitates a lengthy commitment between client and licensed mental health professional.

CHAPTER THIRTEEN

EQUINE FACILITATED COUNSELING

Introduction

Equine Facilitated Counseling (EFC) offers clients the ability to learn critical life skills, address their communication and relational skills issues, and find the support and guidance of caring, compassionate mentorship.

The definition of the term "counseling" as it is used here is taken from its more traditional, or dictionary, usage. Merriam-Webster suggests that to provide "counseling" is to provide "professional guidance of the individual by utilizing psychological methods especially in collecting case history data, using various techniques of the personal interview, and testing interests and aptitudes." The ACA define "counseling" as "the application of mental health, psychological or human development principles, through cognitive, affective, behavioral or systemic intervention strategies, that address wellness, personal growth, or career development, as well as pathology." The intention behind utilizing the word "counseling" to define what occurs during an EFC session is to suggest that not all individuals seeking "counsel" do so for psychological or pathological reasons. That may be the case with some clients, but the inclusion of "human development," "wellness," and "career development," opens other doorways for clients who have no prior diagnoses and whose issues are not psychological or pathological in nature.

This method of counseling is considered to be "integrative" in nature. Merriam-Webster's dictionary defines to "integrate" as "to form, coordinate, or blend into a functioning or unified whole."[478] This definition describes EFC well, as professionals within the field suggest that this approach takes a multitude of tangible practices and integrates or combines them into what is reported as a powerful therapeutic tool.

In this method the concept of integrative is utilized to help clarify the wrap-around service approach outlined later in this chapter which suggests that professionals may work together to integrate their strengths and areas of expertise to help one client or one family become healthier or more functional.

The licensed mental health professional within this method will be called a counselor, also based upon the Merriam-Webster's definition that such an individual provides advice and gives counsel to those seeking direction or assistance. It is assumed that the counselor within this method is a licensed mental health professional who may choose to call himself or herself a counselor rather than any of the other terms available.

EFC offers clients the ability to remain in the here and now and practice the tangible skills that they learn through their relationship with the horse. They can experience successes and learn how to work productively with failures. EFC does not necessitate that clients investigate their pasts, nor engage in deep, long term psychotherapy to experience an increase in health. The focus is on increasing human potential through a health and wellness orientation. It is through relationship between the horse and the human, and learning tangible skills within this relationship that growth and healing can occur.

EFC works well for clients who are seeking a tangible, result-oriented counseling method and who present with life, relational, vocational, or communication skills issues that are in some way impeding their ability to move their lives forward towards attaining greater human potential. Many EFC clients have no prior diagnosis, or if they do, the diagnosis tends to be oriented towards depression, low level anxiety, or a stress-related ailment. Youth populations are also commonly served by an EFC approach.

Key Concepts

Wrap-Around Services

Due to the nature of EFC, a wrap-around[479] approach tends to work well. The EFC method attempts to help clients change the manner in which they live their lives. In order to help solidify this goal, the counselor and the client may need to include other services, other professionals, or family members into the treatment milieu. EFC generally utilizes a treatment team approach, pulling in as many professionals or other outside influences as deemed necessary or healthful for the individual client's needs. Wrap-around services help the counselor to better understand the depth and scope of the client's issues, and thus create a more dynamic and effective treatment plan. EFC clients experience the sensation of being cared for by a supportive community of people who are all there to guide, assist, support, and foster healthful growth.

Present and Future Focused

EFC is present and future focused. It brings clients into the here and now, and helps them to find a grounded and aware vantage point from which to look into the future. EFC does not engage in the intensive collection of past histories or life stories; rather it views clients as they present in the here and now. The horses provide a useful model for how life can be lived in the here and now, and the EFC counselor will utilize metaphor and story telling to help the clients visualize how the lessons learned from being with horses could be transferred back into their daily lives.[480]

The EFC counselor will engage with the client, teaching them tangible aspects of the horse's psychology and herd dynamics, therefore allowing the client to make metaphoric connections and practice the skill of being in the present while with the horses. The EFC counselor will help guide and direct the client to remain in the present, rather than drifting back into past reminiscence or looking forward into the future too early in treatment. The EFC counselor believes that it is only within the present moment that change is possible, and therefore conducts all activities, conversations, and interventions with that notion in mind.

In EFC, present moment awareness and focus is gained through hands-on activities with the horses. These activities help the client to recognize the feeling of being completely in the present moment. Body awareness and grounding activities may also be used, but will be taught as personal techniques to use outside of treatment.[481]

The use of future planning will come into play once the client has learned how to become grounded within the present moment. Until that time, the future is rarely discussed and the client is reminded by the counselor to remain in the here and now.[482]

Changing Behaviors and the Power of Choice

Unlike the work of EFP, EFC concentrates on helping the client to first recognize behaviors, and then change those behaviors in the here-and-now setting of the EFC program. The EFC counselor utilizes mentoring, problem solving, brainstorming, and tangible, hands-on activities as vehicles to help the client make changes.[483] EFC is an action-oriented form of treatment, and focuses on the engagement between the counselor, the client, and the horse.

EFC is based on the premise that individuals have the power of choice. EFC clients are encouraged to assess their own personal choices and how those choices impact themselves and the world around them. They are encouraged to do self-inventories that lead to decisions about personal choice, and tend to foster the desire for personal change and growth.[484]

Kay Kelly Anderson, M.Ed. shares her thoughts, "In traditional talk therapy--the best it gets is that the client comes in and tells me how they handled it (in the past) and we can discuss ways to cope differently next time (in the future) In equine facilitated therapy you observe the clients coping with the events unfolding (right now) and can coach them to try again with different coping responses in a relatively low risk environment. The client gets to experience the success of trying a new coping skill in the here and now. It is the most powerful intervention I have ever used in 18 years as a therapist."

Life Skills Orientation

Clients are taught a multitude of life skills for the purpose of increasing human potential, learning more functional ways of living, and changing patterns that are not currently serving them. It is through hands-on practice, activities, and processing that the client comes to acknowledge what skills he or she needs to improve upon.[485] The EFC counselor does not engage in psychoanalysis, interpretation, or translation of the client's behaviors, and therefore it is the client who motivates the treatment. The counselor sets up activities that will help the client come to a heightened awareness of functionality issues, but the client must initiate the decision to address and work through these issues. Once the client has come to this point, the counselor, the horse, and the activities that engage the client and the horse will be used in conjunction to provide mentoring, guidance, and support. Common life skills issues that arise within EFC involve communication skills, relational skills, vocational awareness, and functional living skills. As an outcome of working through basic life skills issues, personal change tends to occur.

Communication Skills

We are not generally taught how to communicate congruently or authentically, and this may raise fundamental issues surrounding our ability to understand one another. EFC clients may report problems with co-workers, family members, children, spouses, or others in their lives that they seem to be unable to communicate successfully with. These issues lead to psychological discomfort and a sense of disheartening failure within interpersonal relationships. EFC employs the horse to help the client learn new skills and practice those skills in the safe environment of the EFC program, with the less intimidating task of communicating with a horse rather than another human being. The horse provides tangible and immediate feedback that the client can understand. The counselor acts as the guide and mentor while the horse and the client engage in activities designed to promote communication skills development.[486]

Relational Skills

An operating premise of EFC is that a great deal of personal discomfort presented by clients attending EFC sessions comes from a disconnect between self and others, including the natural world. EFC uses the relationship that develops between the horse and the client as a metaphor for what may be lacking in the person's daily life. Clients are given tangible assignments that will help them to foster relationship between themselves and the horse. The relationship that ensues is used to help clients recognize what they might desire in their other relationships outside of the EFC environment. Discussion and processing occur and the counselor helps the client to problem solve new ways of approaching relationship. Clients are then given the opportunity to practice these new skills with the horse before trying them with other human beings. The horse offers feedback which helps the client decipher how successful or unsuccessful he/she has been in the attempt to adjust or change behaviors.[487]

Functional Skills

Many clients come to EFC because of functional life skills issues. They are unable or unwilling to deal with daily living concepts such as personal hygiene, nutrition, money and/or time management, cooking, cleaning, and personal life organization. EFC utilizes metaphor to help clients learn functional living skills. Through work with horses clients may come to better understanding how to both care for themselves and for others in their lives. They learn tangible skills such as the importance of nutrition, the value of organization, and the necessity of hygiene. EFC counselors help clients to make connections from the work that they do with horses back to their daily lives, and assist them in creating plans and strategies that foster increased responsibility and support more healthful lifestyle choices.

Vocational Awareness

Once an EFC client has experienced successes in areas such as communication skills, relational skills, and functional living skills, they tend to begin questioning their chosen vocation. As they realize their power to choose the direction that their life goes in, and recognize that they also now have the tangible skills to make changes possible, they generally begin examining their vocational choices. They realize that the pre-conceived paradigms or patterns they *think* control their lives are in fact controllable by them. With this new awareness, they generally look towards the areas in their lives where their greatest struggles lie.

In most cases vocational issues arise almost immediately when an EFC client reaches this stage in treatment. The EFC counselor is responsible for helping the client realistically address the feelings that arise, and working in partnership with the horse, strategize a plan to help the client recognize his or her passions, dreams, desires, and skills.

Health and Wellness Orientation

EFC counselors believe that their clients are innately healthy human beings who may lack the necessary skills, motivation, and education to bring that healthful way of being into their daily lives.[488] EFC functions from a wellness model, not a disease model, and therefore the manner in which treatment occurs demonstrates this orientation. EFC counselors believe that through working with the horse, humans are able to access greater human potential, and work towards a fuller, healthful, and nourishing life. EFC employs the horse to help teach the client new ways of addressing old patterns and behaviors that are counter productive to achieving a healthful existence. EFC utilizes metaphor to help the clients understand the areas in which they self-sabotage their own potential and decrease the options to explore their unique abilities. Once EFC clients realize their patterns, activities are utilized that help the clients re-orientate their lives.

EFC counselors believe in a strengths-based method of treatment, and focus equally on the client's strengths and how to capitalize on those strengths.

Self-Esteem and Self-Awareness

Some clients who are appropriate for an EFC intervention as those struggling with long term issues of self-esteem and self-awareness. Clients generally enter into treatment with little faith in their ability to listen to their feelings and thoughts. They also tend to feel demoralized by the past decisions, actions, or life choices that they have made, and have lost confidence in their ability to take healthful action.[489] In many cases they have been spending a great deal of their time in either the past or the future, and little time in the present. This may lead to a state of inactivity and passive and/or aggressive self-hatred. EFC employs the horse to help the client learn both self-awareness skills, and through working with the horse, the client tends to gain self-confidence and self-esteem.[490] He or she feels the ability to make positive and sometimes dramatic change within his/her life, and learns to listen to intuition and instinct. Through practice with horses, the EFC client may be able to recognize new skills and talents, and self-loathing or self-hatred may decrease, and self-confidence and self-awareness may increase.

The Therapeutic Process

Therapeutic Goals

The primary goals of EFC are designed to help the client increase their human potential[491] and adjust their thinking from a disease or dis-health model to one of health and wellness. EFC utilizes practical applications of activities that are designed to help the client experience, in the here and now, their ability to change behaviors, thoughts, feelings, and attitudes.[492] EFC counselors encourage change during the course of treatment, and believe in the client's ability to undergo such change. EFC treatment would be considered omplete when the following goals were met:

- The EFC client demonstrates continued ability to exist in the here and now, and understands that if he/she desire change, it will only be possible if he/she is utilizing present moment awareness.

- The EFC client has learned new life skills, especially regarding communication skills, relational skills, and functional life skills, and is able to demonstrate the ongoing application of these skills within all aspects of his or her life.

- The EFC client has addressed vocational issues, if any exist, and has started the process of change in order to bring health and wellness into his/her vocational life.

- The EFC client demonstrates an increase of self-esteem and self-confidence.

- The EFC client demonstrates a higher level of self-awareness and the ability for personal reflection as it relates to change.

- The EFC client demonstrates increased health and wellness, and is able to sustain lifestyle changes between counseling sessions.

Horse's Role, Function, and Relationship to Client

In EFC the horse becomes a co-facilitator and an employee, helping to teach, model, and reflect specific tools, lessons, or skills to the client. Within EFC, the horse participates in activities designed by the counselor with specific goals and objectives in mind. In this context, the horse acts as an employee, helping the counselor by teaching, modeling, or reflecting. At other times, the horse acts as a co-facilitator, bringing to light different information that the client or the counselor may have missed.

It is critical that the feelings and needs of the horse are taken into consideration prior to a session. As an employee, there may be times when the horse needs to work due to staffing shortages or other logistical details. However, even in those cases the counselor, horse handler, or other assistants need to be completely aware of the horse's mental state, abilities, and desires as this will change the horse's level of participation and safety. If it is possible to allow the horse to choose whether to work or not, the participation level of the horse will increase greatly, therefore making the session more successful and safer in all areas.[493]

An EFC counselor should be knowledgeable and aware of which capacity the horse is working within during an EFC session, and should not confuse the horse's role. There are times in an EFC session where the horse is an employee, doing as the counselor, horse handler, assistant, or client asks, and there will be other times when the horse takes over the facilitation of the session. Regardless of which role the horse assumes, all horses within an EFC program should be treated with respect and kindness, and should be offered benefits according to his or her duties. Horses working within an EFC session may need to be trained differently than those working within an EFP session, and different horses may fit better for the role of employee vs. the role of co-facilitator in an EFC session. Some horses appear more comfortable with expression and assistance in the role of co-facilitator, while others seem happy to assist in the role of employee, with less need to express or facilitate.

In general the horse within an EFC session is, ideally, willing to engage with the client in a relationship that helps the client learn life skills, come into present awareness, and recognize his or her own human potential. However, unlike EFP there are times when the horse is asked to work even if he or she does not feel drawn to a particular client, but instead is a willing participant in an activity simply so that the client can practice a skill.

An EFC horse may have feedback for the client at any given time during an EFC session, when and if this occurs, the EFC counselor should listen to the horse, and be aware of subtle communications that may be reflect feedback offered to the client. The EFC horse should be allowed to communicate in this fashion at any time during a session *regardless of the activity that is going on, or the intention of that activity.*

An EFC client is likely to form close personal relationships with the horse(s) with whom they work. The horse will help the client to learn new skills and gain a deeper understanding of his/her abilities. The horse's relationship with the client is rather like that of a teacher to a student, and the counselor can help to foster this type of relationship in the manner by which the role of the horse is described to the client.

Counselor's Role, Function, and Relationship to Client
An EFC counselor is an active facilitator and creates activities based upon the needs of the client in any given moment. The EFC counselor must be trained and highly skilled in the art of facilitation and able to create activities on the spot without prior planning or preparation. The EFC counselor helps facilitate a relationship between the horse and the client by creating skills-based activities that teach important life skills, increase self-esteem, self-confidence, and self-awareness, and foster human potential.[494] The EFC counselor may also, at times, act as a case manager or lead counselor in a treatment team approach, and thus should be trained and educated in this style of treatment.[495] Furthermore, the EFC counselor may engage the client and his or her family or significant other in family and/or marriage counseling, and

thus it is critical that the EFC counselor be trained, educated, and practiced in marriage and family counseling.[496]

When the horse engages the client in a reflective feedback process, the EFC counselor can bring the attention of the client to the horse and ask the client for ideas about what the horse is trying to communicate. The EFC counselor is not advised to translate or interpret the horse's communications on a deep psychological level. Rather the EFC counselor can focus on the life skill that the client is addressing in the present moment, and utilize the reflective feedback from the horse to help the client more clearly see his or her own unique style or process in regards to the skill.[497]

The EFC counselor generally will not engage the client on a deeply psychological level, nor does he or she attempt to investigate the client's past history at any depth unless the topic arises during a session and is important to the development of the client's skills. The EFC counselor will keep the session present moment focused, and guide the client towards the ability to stay within the present moment.[498]

The EFC counselor will help the horse to better understand the intentions for the activity, and provide clear instruction for both the horse(s) and human(s) working within a given session.

The EFC counselor tends to form a close, mentor-like relationship with the client, and may engage in personal sharing when and if appropriate. The counselor role-models the goals of an EFC session for the client by "walking the talk" of the work. It is suggested that the EFC counselor be an individual who is living his or her own personal life by the goals outlined in an EFC program, and is open and willing to demonstrate how a life lived in such a way looks.[499] The EFC counselor will also engage the client in an educational manner, and therefore should be trained and skilled in the use of experiential education or learning methods and techniques.[500]

The EFC counselor tends to be strengths-focused, and thus will use techniques such as asking the client what is going right within their lives, vs. what is going wrong. The EFC counselor believes that the client has strengths and talents that can be capitalized upon and recognized. The counselor helps the client to come to a similar recognition by reflecting back to the client the various strengths and skills that he or she possesses.[501]

It is more likely during an EFC session that multiple staff members will be needed because of the focus on skills-based activities. If the EFC session is a group session, the counselor should co-facilitate with another counselor trained and educated in EFC. Horse handlers or other assistants also trained and educated in EFC methods and techniques may also be employed depending upon the number of clients and activities conducted. Due to the likelihood that activities in which an assistant is needed will occur in an EFC session, it is important that the client be forewarned about this difference from the onset of treatment. It is also important that the counselor discuss with the client the notion of a treatment team approach, suggesting that wrap around services will probably be recommended at some point during the treatment, and that in the context of EFC, marriage and/or family counseling may be conducted.

EFC counselors tend to brief their staff prior to an EFC session, explaining possible activities that may be facilitated, the staff's roles within the activities, and the general goals for the session. Using this technique, the EFC staff are aware of the general issues that the client or clients are working with. Following an EFC session the counselor can hold a debrief session with staff to discuss the successes or issues that arose during the session. The staff should be given the opportunity to ask questions, bring up their own issues or struggles relevant to the case, and offer suggestions for the next session.

Due to the wrap-around nature of the service, EFC counselors also act as case managers, learning and understanding the scope and depth of the client's issues and helping to facilitate dialog between all members of the treatment team.

Client's Experience in Equine Facilitated Counseling
An EFC client should be prepared for the action-oriented and solution-focused nature of EFC, and ready to actively engage in the process of change. An EFC client who is not able or willing to engage in that process during treatment may be referred to an EFP service. An

EFC client is given needed information so that he or she can clearly understand the goals of an EFC treatment approach, and recognize that the length of treatment is based upon their ability to meet both those goals, and their own personal goals.

EFC is focused on the process of gaining life skills, and engaging in the process of life planning. Therefore, the EFC client should be aware of the hands-on, and activity based method of treatment.

The EFC client should also be made aware of the role of the counselor within the treatment method, recognizing the difference between an EFC counselor and other, more traditional mental health professionals.

As with all of the EFMHS methods, the EFC client should be made aware of safety and confidentiality issues inherent to the method.

An EFC client is considered ready to terminate services once their treatment goals have been met, and they are able to demonstrate the ongoing ability to sustain change. At any point in the treatment if the counselor determines that the clients issues are rooted in deep pathology or otherwise contraindicated for this treatment method, the services will be discontinued and the client will be referred to an EFP psychotherapist, or if none are available in their area, a traditional psychotherapist or psychologist, or referred to another appropriate service.

Practice: Therapeutic Techniques, Processes, and Procedures

Overview

The techniques of EFC are designed to help clients gain an awareness of their own human potential, and create change within their daily lives to foster an increase in that potential.[502] EFC utilizes techniques that help guide and move clients towards a place of healthful functioning and a wellness model from which to live their lives. EFC is designed to promote personal growth and awareness, and raise self-confidence and self-esteem. EFC does not support a disease model of treatment, and believes that all clients have the ability to change, grow, and develop beyond functional to exceptional.

Populations best served by EFC are those without serious psychological issues.[503] EFC clients might present with diagnoses of minor depression, low level anxiety, stress symptoms, low self-esteem and self-confidence issues, ADD/ADHD, marital issues, or family systems issues. Youth at-risk populations are also well served by the work of EFC, as well as other youth populations who are in need of directional assistance. With these commonly treated conditions individuals report successful outcomes in many cases. EFC clients should be able to engage fully in the process of life change, and be willing to equally participate in a mentoring and educational relationship between themselves and the counselor, the horse, or others involved in the process.

There are five significant techniques utilized by EFC counselors: (1) Pre-planned or sporadic activities, (2) Skills acquisition, (3) Present awareness practices, (4) Use of metaphor and story telling, and (5) Life planning.[504]

Pre-Planned or Spontaneous Activities

EFC is a hands-on, experientially based method of treatment, and thus clients are encouraged to experience or witness their own processes in order to recognize the need for change. Once they have identified those areas they would like to change, they need a way to practice new ways of being. EFC activities offer such a vehicle. Even in the assessment process, the EFC counselor may choose to utilize an activity so that he or she can witness the client's processes first hand, vs. listening to the client explain his or her feelings or intellectualized thoughts about behaviors, actions, skills, etc.[505]

Furthermore, EFC is relationally based, and therefore the method bases its successes upon the lessons learned by the client from the horse/human interaction.[506] In order for this relationship to develop fully, the client and the horse need to go through a series of activities or tasks together, challenging both themselves and their relationship. From this experience, the client will learn which skills he or she needs to foster, and where his/her unique strengths and talents lie.

EFC sessions can include both pre-planned activities and spontaneous activities. Generally an EFC counselor will utilize a mixture of the two, starting a session with a pre-planned activity, and then allowing the horse to co-facilitate a different direction or orientation based upon the first activity. A typical EFC activity may include a skill to be learned as well as a metaphor from which insight can be gained. Horse skills activities are commonly found in EFC sessions; grooming, leading, round penning, as well as mounting and riding, can be useful for EFC clients. Non-horse skills-based activities can also be utilized in an EFC session, as well as games that promote team building or trust. These could include blind riding, trust walks, ground games played with people and horses, trail rides either on the ground or mounted, or other such interventions.

EFC activities are generally set up with little or no front loading regarding the desired outcome, but the client is taught the proper skills to have a successful interaction with the horse. The activity is then allowed to unfold as the horse and client dictate. However, the EFC counselor is on hand and ready to intervene for the purpose of stopping potential abuses to the horse, or to address safety-related concerns. The EFC counselor facilitates based upon the premise that the client needs to learn new and more healthfully-based practices, not to support old patterns or behaviors. The focus of the treatment is forward oriented, and thus the counselor may intervene to point out old habits, actions, or behaviors as they emerge rather than allowing the client to continue engaging with the horse in an unhealthful manner. The emphasis of the treatment is for the client to witness his or her unhealthful processes, and then quickly move forward to learning and practicing new styles. Therefore, the majority of the treatment is based upon learning the new skills and practicing those, rather than on experiencing past behaviors that are no longer useful.[507]

In any given activity, the client should be educated first in a healthful way to engage with the horse, then given the opportunity to try out the new skill. Generally during this first attempt the client will recognize old patterns emerging, and with the help of the counselor, will stop and acknowledge those behaviors or patterns, and re-start with the support of the horse and counselor.

At the completion of the activity, or anywhere during the activity that seems appropriate or needed, the counselor will facilitate a de-brief or processing session during which the client is given the opportunity to share or express reflections, thoughts, ideas, or process what is going well and what is not. During this time the counselor facilitates, guides, asks leading questions, and brings the client's attention back to the horse and what information the horse is offering.

Skills Acquisition

The EFC client is taught tangible horse-person-ship skills as a part of his/her treatment. These skills are used to help create metaphor, increase the healthfulness of the horse/client relationship, and support wellness. Through learning these skills the client generally gains self-esteem and self-confidence, as well as a deeper self-awareness. The skills act as a metaphor for daily living skills used by the client and through learning a new way to approach and practice these skills, the client is allowed the time and space in a safe environment to practice a new way of being.

EFC counselors may or may not decide to utilize riding as a part of this skills acquisition. This decision should be made based upon the needs of the client, not upon the counselor's ability (or lack thereof) to facilitate this skill. This means that all EFC counselors should have the training, education, and ability to provide mounted work as a part of their practice, if and only if, the needs of the client dictate using such a technique.[508] Furthermore, counselors should be trained in how to utilize riding as a therapeutic tool vs. an educational tool, and make adjustments in their style dependant upon the needs of the client.

All EFC horse-person-ship skills should be taught with professionalism, dedication to the care and well-being of the horse, and a deep understanding of equine psychology, physiology, and behavior. Proper equipment should be provided at all times, and the clients should experience a professional approach to learning the said skills. EFC should not be conducted if the provider does not have adequate professional equipment, education, training, and experience.

Present Awareness Practices

EFC concentrates on bringing the client into the present moment in order for them to make needed change. In order for the client to enter into this state, he/she must be able to recognize and differentiate between past, present, and future thinking and awareness. All three aspects of awareness and cognition have their place and their use in treatment.[509] A client attending EFC will generally be taught techniques to move gracefully between these three states of awareness so that when it is time for change, they will be prepared to move into present awareness focus and make the needed changes.

Present awareness practices take on many forms in EFC. However there are three broad categories that generally exist within the work of EFC: (1) Physical interactions, (2) Energetic boundary setting, and (3) Meditation, breathing, and conscious movement. Within any of these categories many activities are utilized by EFC counselors to help create the successful integration of new skills.[510]

Physical Interactions
The first and most simple form of moving into present moment awareness is the physical implications of being in the presence of a horse. While using skills-based instruction, the counselor teaches the client how to approach, meet, greet, and interact with the horses in a safe and aware manner. The client learns that in order to keep herself/ himself safe within the horse/human interaction, he/she must stay within the present moment at all times. The counselor teaches the client a number of skills that encourage the client to remain within the present moment, and become more highly attuned to their physical bodies. Nearly any simple horse-person-ship activity will do for this process; grooming, cleaning hooves, leading, meeting and greeting, herd dynamics, or most any other form of interaction where the client is in close proximity to the horse, and actually physically engaging with the horse or horses.[511]

Energetic Boundary Setting
The second and somewhat more complex activity that can be used to help clients move into a present moment awareness is energetic boundary work. While observing the herd dynamics and learning the language of Equus, the client generally begins to recognize how horses set and maintain their boundaries. This realization tends to grow into conversation and discussion about boundary setting and the issues that arise within our culture around how we set (or do not set) healthy and productive boundaries. The counselor is then given the opportunity to offer the client the experience of utilizing what he or she learned from

watching the horses to begin investigating their own unique energetic boundaries and how to clearly convey those boundaries for others to observe.

While utilizing this technique, the client generally recognizes that in order to set clear boundaries that are healthful and authentic, one must be functioning from a place of present moment awareness. Therefore, in order to successfully complete any of the boundary setting activities, the client must learn the art of setting aside past and future thinking, and remain grounded in the present. Furthermore, the client is asked to listen to his or her body, and utilize the information thus gained to help create the boundaries that feel the most authentic and real for them *in that moment*. Through this technique, the client becomes aware that boundaries are not like brick walls, but rather fluid and ever changing, like water, adapting to situations as they arise without preconceived structure. They realize that it is only within the present moment that they can successfully create an authentic boundary that is appropriate for the given situation, and that this boundary is only created by listening to the call of the body.[512]

Meditation, Breathing, and Conscious Movement
The third way that present moment awareness can be presented to EFC clients is through quiet mediation, breathing, and conscious movement. Many clients spend the bulk of their time moving quickly and unconsciously through their days, rushing from one experience to the next without time to process both where they just were, and where they are going. Living in such a way, we become out of touch with our physical bodies and find ourselves hitting our heads, elbows, or running into large objects that we should have noticed and avoided. Our minds are moving faster than our bodies can keep up with. We are unaware of our breathing and how our breathing impacts our heart rate and our emotional state of being. Within the work of EFC, the counselor can utilize meditation, breathing, and conscious movement activities to help the client learn how to become present moment focused and aware of how the world looks when one stops to "smell the roses." In EFC, the horse helps to facilitate these activities by offering themselves as examples of present moment awareness. Horses move consciously nearly all of the time. It is rare to see a horse stumble

or fall, hit his head on something, or run into a large and obvious object. Their breathing is easy to observe, to feel, to connect with, and clients are able to experience a sense of awareness about breath through this connection. Most horses seem to exist much of the time in a semi-meditative state, munching on grass or hay, gazing out into the far distance, or enjoying a good brush. They also demonstrate the ability to transition between such a meditative state and immediate action and movement. This ability helps clients to recognize that, as with boundary setting, nothing is constant. Rather, they must learn how to be flexible and how to move between states of consciousness as the need arises.

EFC uses breathing, meditation, and conscious movement activities which help teach clients the need to slow down, become aware, and retain flexibility in all that they do. Through this practice, EFC clients learn how to connect and respond to the present moment, *precisely as they find it*, not how they remembered it, or how they thought it would or should be.[513]

Use of Metaphor and Story Telling

The EFC counselor can use story telling as a way to help the client think in a new or different way about an old paradigm that is no longer serving them, and to recognize metaphors as they arise. The EFC counselor will utilize individual horse's stories, and the stories arising out of herd dynamics to offer the client the permission to create metaphor. It is through this metaphoric process that the client is able to take the lessons learned at the barn home and apply them to everyday life.[514]

Metaphor

Once the story has been told the EFC counselor can invite comments, thoughts, or feelings from the client. Generally it is here that the client will begin to make connections between the story told and his or her life. From there the counselor can offer the chance for the client to begin the process of readjusting the paradigm. Through healthful interactions with the horse or horses the client begins to practice a new and/or different way of being and experiencing life.

Story Telling

The EFC counselor understands the language of Equus and herd dynamics well enough to tell the client authentic stories about how horses interact and live within a domestic or feral herd. The EFC counselor is advised to understand the differences and similarities that exist between the behaviors of a domestic herd vs. that of a feral herd. These stories could be about one particular horse and his or her unusual behaviors. Sometimes it is the life story of a horse. Other times it is more general, discussing the behaviors of the very herd that the client is working with. The story could even be about the herd behaviors of feral horses with no real connection to the actual herd that the client knows. It is the role of the EFC counselor to know and understand the appropriate usage of these stories, and the timing in regards to when they should be told.

It is advisable to tell these stories in the presence of horses or in the presence of the one horse whom the story is about. Ensuring that the client is physically and emotionally comfortable during the story telling tends to lead to better results as well. The EFC counselor should be able to both witness how the client is reacting to the story, and also how the horse herd or individual horse is reacting to the telling of the story.

Example of Metaphor and Story Telling

San Cristobal Ranch Academy - Family Reunification Session

During an EFC session the counselor tells the family members about how horses form a hierarchical power structure, with the alpha mare and head stallion on the top, and all the other horses falling into line under them. The counselor asks the family members to pick out who they think the head "stallion", alpha mare, and "low man on the totem pole" are. During this observational process, the family members began making connections between themes occurring in their lives and the role that a specific horse plays within the herd hierarchy. In this session the father, who assumes a leadership position both professionally and personally, but who has been struggling with undisclosed issues of depression, loneliness, and self doubt, notices how the head "stallion" must stay removed from the herd, observing and maintaining the safety of the herd at all times. He also notices that the other horses respect the head stallion but seem to have limited personal relationships with him. The father states that he thinks the head stallion is lonely all by himself out there on the fringes of the herd and that he probably wishes he wasn't a leader. The father continued on to say that he understood the plight of this horse due to his own role within the family unit. This metaphoric connection opened the door for the family to communicate for the first time about their familial roles and voice authentic feelings regarding those roles.

Life Planning

A large component of EFC is the co-creation of the client's "life plan." This plan is developed and reworked over and over again throughout the EFC process, thereby teaching the client the need for flexibility, forward movement, and the consistency of change. However, the plan is also continually being executed, tried, and experimented with throughout the process, allowing the client the ability to experience successes, failures, and any other emotions that arise. Through this process the client comes to determine what aspects of the plan are working, which are not, and what needs to be added. The client may come into treatment with one set of life goals, but after being in treatment for a number of weeks or months, may recognize different goals that are more profound. The purpose of the plan is to help the client move towards achieving a sense of greater human potential through experiencing feelings of success, health, and wellness vocationally and personally.[515]

Through work with horses the EFC client is afforded the ability to practice new skills, recognize areas in which their actions or behaviors are counter-productive, and gain a present moment awareness that allows change to occur. The EFC counselor acts as a guide and supporter along the journey, helping to facilitate the client's process of learning, growth, and change.[516]

At the completion of treatment, an EFC client ideally would have achieved a generally stable and significantly more healthful way of life. The client may then demonstrate comfort with the process of continuing the creation of his or her life plan as the need arises, and should demonstrate a level of comfort with transition, creative thinking, and problem solving.

Method Example

This Method Example was provided by Laura Anthony of Horse Sense of the Carolina's.

Suzie is a 10-year-old little girl living in a foster home. She is at her 9th placement since being taken from her family of origin. At her last placement, her foster parents at that time decided to adopt her biological brother but chose not to keep her because of her behavior problems. Suzie's history includes neglect, physical, emotional, and sexual abuse. She has been diagnosed with Reactive Attachment Disorder (RAD). Suzie has had repeated changes of primary caregivers which has prevented formation of stable attachments. As a result, she now responds to her caregivers with a mixture of approach, avoidance and resistance to comforting.

Suzie's foster parents came to Horse Sense of the Carolinas Inc., as the last chance before sending Suzie on to another foster home. Thus far, Suzie has caused $2000 worth of damage to their home. She has been physically abusive especially towards the foster mother and has made accusations toward the foster father about sexual abuse. The foster parents report that whenever they start to feel any emotional closeness with Suzie, her behavior suddenly becomes aggressive and at times violent. For Suzie, being vulnerable to her caregiver feels terrifying since in the past she has been taken away from anyone she has grown close to.

At her third equine session Suzie was introduced to Gus, a retired police horse. She was asked to participate in an activity called "Catch and Halter." Whenever Suzie reached out to touch Gus, he flinched and pulled away from her. We asked Suzie what Gus needed from her in order for him to let her put the halter on. She replied, "He needs to trust me." We then asked how she could help Gus to trust her. She put down the halter and lead rope and stood face to face with Gus and studied him for a while in silence. After a long pause we told her that Gus is very lonely. We think he wants to trust her but is afraid. Suzie admitted that she knows how that feels. She wants to trust her foster parents but pulls away every time they reach out to her.

Suzie stood with Gus for several more minutes before she slowly reached out to pet him. This time Gus did not flinch or pull away from her. Suzie noticed that Gus's body language became very relaxed; he lowered his head and his eyes softened. When she was sure that Gus was calm she slowly reached down, picked up the halter and lead rope and put it on. Gus did not resist this time. We asked Suzie what changed. She replied, "I was very patient and gave Gus plenty of time to get used to me. I waited until he was relaxed and calm before I tried to put the halter on. I think he trusts me now." Suzie left the session thinking about Gus and her relationship with her foster parents.

Two weeks later, Suzie's foster parents reported that Suzie had been very well behaved with no instances of aggression or violence since prior to her equine session.

Summary and Evaluation

EFC is an integration of a number of approaches which are generally strengths, competency, and skills-based forms of treatment. The outcome of the treatment is significant life change demonstrated by continued stability within daily routine. Due to its integrative nature, EFC treatment utilizes a wrap around, or team approach, pulling in as many professionals as are deemed necessary or useful by the EFC counselor. The EFC counselor acts as a case manager or lead therapist to ensure that all members of the team are in communication and are working towards the same general goal or set of goals.

EFC strives to increase human potential through focus and attention on the health and wellness of the client rather than on disease. EFC clients are those who desire profound and long-lasting life change and are able and willing to work to bring about this sort of change in their lives. An EFC counselor believes that all clients come with the ability for profound change and that they are all innately healthy human beings. EFC focuses on a strengths-based method of treatment, and the EFC counselor will work to increase the clients already existing strengths rather than focusing on their aliments or problems.

This method is actively facilitated by the counselor who acts as a mentor, educator, and role model for the client. The EFC counselor must be educated, trained, and practiced in the art of facilitation and must have a deep knowledge and understanding of horses; their communications, actions, behaviors, and herd dynamics. The EFC counselor must also be highly proficient in the area of equine skills building and safety, and able to facilitate activities that necessitate human/horse contact.

The horse in an EFC session is considered an employee or sometimes a co-facilitator, depending upon the set up of the activity. The horse may either follow the lead of the counselor, simply participating in the pre-organized activity created by the counselor (employee), or will chose to change the nature of the activity based upon the need to reflect something incongruent occurring within the activity or for the client (co-facilitator). It is important that the EFC counselor be willing and flexible enough in their facilitation style to listen to the horse(s) if they choose to adjust the direction of the session.

Although EFC could be considered somewhat more "short term" than EFP, EFC's treatment goals necessitate profound change. For some clients this change can come rapidly and they will be able to demonstrate sustainability within a few months. For others this form of treatment will be longer term, and they may need to take time off from treatment to practice new skills, knowing that they can return when and if they find themselves unable to maintain the changes that they have made. EFC does not have to happen consecutively, as EFP necessitates. EFC clients can come in and out of treatment, dependant upon what they and the treatment team determine is most useful.

EFC is present and future orientated, and an EFC counselor is not inclined to do extensive historical data gathering, and will not engage in analysis of past memories, thoughts, or feelings. The EFC counselor will facilitate the client's forward progression and will help the client understand that change can only occur within the present moment. Therefore, EFC as a treatment method is generally based in present moment awareness versus a past or future orientation.

CHAPTER FOURTEEN

EQUINE ASSISTED PSYCHOTHERAPY

Introduction

Equine Assisted Psychotherapy (EAP) is a method of EFMHS based almost solely on the model of experiential and/or adventure-based therapy.[517] Likened to the challenge course, EAP utilizes the horse as a tool that provides an experience for clients to learn about themselves and how they impact the world around them.[518] This method was created by EAGALA and is practiced predominately by those certified through EAGALA's training program.

In general, EAP is utilized as a group therapy method, but can in some cases be used for individual clients.[519] EAP is not usually facilitated in such a manner that the horse/human relationship becomes the primary focus, but rather the treatment capitalizes upon the experience that clients have when attempting to achieve a set goal or series of goals that involve horses. Activities and games are created that challenge the group and through this challenge the participants recognize their own process and may learn how to take responsibility for themselves and for others within the group. EAP helps to illuminate various roles and personality styles that the participants may not be aware of, and offers the ability for the group to witness personal insights gained through the activities.[520]

Because EAP utilizes many aspects of adventure-based or experiential therapy, EAP as a theory is somewhat redundant, but as a method it is commonly used within the field, and therefore should be presented. The reader may observe many similarities between EAP and challenge course facilitation, or other adventure or experiential methods, and the EAP licensed mental health professional should be educated, trained, and practiced in all forms of experiential counseling including the use of the challenge course. There are fundamental differences between challenge courses and the work of EAP as well, and it is important that licensed mental health professionals understand these core differences and provide the safest and most ethically driven service possible.

EAP is different than any of the other types of EFMH services because of the potentially provocative and intense nature of the activities, and because of the use of the horse as a tool rather than the use of the *relationship* between the horse and the client. When the work of EFMHS is relational in nature, and is not based primarily on activities, the likelihood for accident may be less as the activities move at the pace of the client and the horse rather than being driven by the energy of the group and the activity that is occurring.[521] In many cases EAP licensed mental health professionals will utilize games that target the predator/prey dynamic between horses and humans, and thus may spark an instinctual response from the horse that could lead to a potentially dangerous situation.[522] All of that being said, EAP, done well, appears to have the potential to be impactful and positive in nature and may have the ability to move groups into different states of being and functioning. There is a huge amount of power within inherent physical risk, and this factor can lead to personal and group insight and change.[523] It is important, however, to recognize that due to its unique differences from any of the other forms of EFMHS, EAP may be more dangerous and thus EAP licensed mental health professionals should be well trained and educated in providing this form of treatment. Due to these considerations, three-day workshops that introduce the method do not provide sufficient training to begin offering this or any other EFMHS method to clients for payment. EAGALA's advanced training program and requirements should be considered mandatory for those new to the field who are interested in providing EAP.

EAP can be successful on a short term basis depending upon the level of functionality of the clientele, and the goals of the group. In some cases, such as if used for family counseling, or if working with defiant clients, or other forms of extremely challenged clients, EAP should be considered a long term approach to treatment.

EAP is still considered a mental health service, rather than an educational service due to the provocative nature of the method. Regardless of how the method is facilitated, deep personal issues may arise during the facilitation of EAP, and therefore a trained licensed mental health professional must be on site assisting or lead facilitating in order for EAP to be considered ethical.

Key Concepts

Inherent Risk

Probably the most important distinction between a challenge course and a horse lies within perceived danger versus real danger. A challenge course is created to simulate danger without placing the client in actual physical danger. The profoundness of the challenge course is that the clients can perceive that they are in danger, and then with the support and help of the team, can come to recognize that they are physically safe. Challenge courses are inspected by nationally recognized organizations that certify the safety of the course. Each course is designed to meet specific safety codes, and any participant, should they be so inclined, can ask to see the paperwork that certifies that the course was built to meet all standards, that it has been inspected on a regular basis, and has passed all inspections. The client can furthermore ask to see the equipment log, which notes the history of every piece of equipment used on the course at any given time. Ropes or any other equipment that have sustained a fall will be taken out of rotation and new equipment will replace them. The client can see the stability and safety of the equipment, and is taught before ever engaging in a challenge course session how to safely utilize the needed equipment. Rigorous safety orientation is conducted with clients before they ever step foot onto any of the elements of a challenge course, high or low.

Challenge course instructors also are mandated to go through extensive training and education to ensure that they are capable of keeping clients safe at all times on any and all of the elements commonly utilized in a challenge course. They are trained at length in the use of the equipment and must pass a practical and written test to demonstrate their ability and understanding. A client can request to see the challenge course instructor's certification of completion of a recognized challenge course training program and can research the validity of such a training program.[524]

On the other hand, horses are considered "inherently physically dangerous and unpredictable" by the majority of insurance carriers and state laws. Not including riding lesson or summer camp programs for fully functioning students, The North American Riding for the Handicapped Association (NARHA) is the only organization that inspects facilities and equipment to ensure that they are "safe" for therapeutic work. NARHA has guidelines that require mandatory reporting of equipment flaws, horse incidences, and other safety risks. However, NARHA's site accreditation is only applicable for centers that are NARHA accredited.[525] It is not required by state or national law that programs providing an EFMH/ES service become accredited by NARHA. Neither the Equine Facilitated Mental Health Association (EFMHA), a section of NARHA, or the Equine Assisted Growth and Learning Association (EAGALA) require that EFMH/ES programs obtain or retain NARHA site accreditation.[526] Licensed mental health professionals who currently provide EAP or any form of EFMH/ES are not required by their state licensing boards or national certifying boards to go through any additional formal training or education, and could be inexperienced in this method of treatment and still offer the service to clients.[527]

Furthermore, EAP is facilitated in some cases without providing a safety lesson prior to conducting the treatment method.[528] In any other form of experiential or adventure-based counseling if safety is an issue (rock climbing, challenge course, river rafting, kayaking, hiking, backpacking, etc.), the licensed mental health professional and/or facilitator will teach the client the necessary skills to stay safe while engaging in the activity.[529] If the facilitator or licensed mental health professional did not provide the client or clients with a safety skills orientation, they would be considered negligent and may be liable for legal action against them in the case of an accident. As already stated, working with horses is inherently dangerous, but there are tangible safety skills that can be taught to help clients remain as physically safe as possible during an EAP activity. If an EAP licensed mental health professional or facilitator does not teach safety skills specific to horses and horse behavior prior to an EAP session, he or she is may be placing himself/herself in jeopardy legally and ethically, and is possibly placing the client or clients at greater risk for physical injury. Clients and others participating in the service should be aware of this, and would be advised to discontinue services if the licensed mental health professional or facilitator does not provide safety training prior to the activity. Dr. Tracy Weber of Kaleidoscope Learning Circle in Birch Run, MI, agrees, "We feel that it is vastly important to begin each program with a horse safety talk in order to prepare the client and help them understand horse behavior. We employ a 'challenge by choice' philosophy where it is up to the participants whether or not they want to be near the horses."

In some cases licensed mental health professionals facilitate EAP like they would facilitate a low element on a challenge course or a series of initiatives (essentially games) that have almost no perceived or inherent risk. In these types of activities the licensed mental health professional can allow the client to make choices and witness how those choices play out within the group dynamic because there is little if any actual danger associated with the activity. The licensed mental health professional can ask questions and help the group process their own unique experiences with little if any direction or safety instructions.[530] However, as the inherent risk level rises, the level of safety instruction grows and the client must practice skills in order to demonstrate that he or she truly understands the safety protocol and mechanisms.[531] EAP is not *perceived* risk; there is a real physical danger, equivalent to a rock climbing experience, a mountaineering experience, or a river rafting experience. The method's power is magnified *because* there is real-time risk involved. Due to this risk, there are skills that the client must have in order to safely engage in the process. For ethical and legal reasons, it is essential that EAP licensed mental health professionals begin teaching the safety skills necessary to keep their clients as safe as possible while engaging in this treatment method.

The differences between an EAP activity and a challenge course activity must be clearly stated and clients receiving the service should understand the risks involved and be allowed to make educated decisions about whether this is a treatment method they feel comfortable engaging in.

Furthermore, clients seeking or participating in an EAP service should find out the training and education of an EAP licensed mental health professional to ensure that they are truly knowledgeable and prepared to conduct this sort of experiential treatment approach.[532]

Challenge by Choice

Challenge by Choice is a phase coined first by Karl Rohnke, an Outward Bound instructor who was one of the founders of Project Adventure, a non-profit organization started in 1971 to "provide leadership in the expansion of Adventure-based experiential programming". Project Adventure was designed to help bring Outward Bound's "impelling into challenge" philosophy into the urban education system. Rohnke discovered that urban youth were resistant to participating in mandatory adventure-based activities within a school setting and he felt uncomfortable forcing students to participate against their will.[533]

In the wilderness youths were able to witness the natural consequences of their decisions and actions, and thus made increasingly healthful choices over the time that they were exposed to wilderness travel and the adventures that naturally occurred in that environment. However, back in the urban landscape, natural consequences were not as easy to come by, and youth resisted adults telling them how to engage in adventure-type activities. Rohnke's decision to allow participants to choose whether or not to participate brought about a shift within the field of adventure-based activities, and led to the creation of Rohnke's hundreds of creative group games and initiatives.[534]

Challenge by Choice indicates the highest level of personal choice afforded to individuals within an adventure-based setting. In many adventure or experiential treatment facilities clients arrive at the facility with no personal choice in regards to the treatment method.[535] This is the case for juvenile or adult offenders, youth of any sort sent to treatment without consent, or any other population who were not given the right to refuse or accept treatment. These populations tend to assume that they will not be given a choice in anything that they engage in, and thus have given up on authority figures, the system that they exist within, or their own sense of personal power. They view the world as a place where their voice does not matter, and thus their actions also do not matter.[536] In the work of EAP, the licensed mental health professional can help to instill a sense of personal empowerment within each of the clients participating. Even if the clients arrived without consent, the EAP licensed mental health professional has the ability to give each client the choice of whether or not to participate, and regardless of their choice, can help facilitate their decision in a non-shaming or guilting manner.

The Challenge by Choice approach helps clients realize that they have the power and control to choose their own destiny. If this concept is facilitated properly, over time the client may come to realize that they are in the driver's seat of their own lives. When this realization occurs, even over something as simple as whether or not to participate in an experiential activity, the client may begin to see how his/her actions and behaviors actually contribute to the world, and impact those around him/her. The client may realize that he/she has the power to make decisions, and is in control over those decisions, be they positive or negative. Once this happens, the client may start to think about his/her decisions and possibly begin to bring conscious thought and awareness to how he/she moves through the world.[537]

In an EAP session, clients should always be allowed the power to choose, especially because of the inherent risk involved in working around or with horses. Barn rules can be instilled so that clients who choose not to participate understand what is expected of them in order to help maintain the safety of the rest of the group. This could include rules like asking the client to remain in a designated area, or asking that he/she refrain from speaking to the other clients during the activity, or any number of requests that the facilitator feels important for the safety of the clients.

Another less commonly found component of the Challenge by Choice principle as seen in an EAP session is the role of the horse. If the clients are allowed to choose whether or not to participate in any given activity, shouldn't the horse be allowed to choose as well? Some providing EAP believe that this is important to the success of the session, others do not. In order to answer this question, we must return to the ethical responsibilities of the licensed mental health professional to the client. It is the responsibility of that individual to keep the client safe at all times. Therefore, if the horse is not mutually willing to engage in the

EAP process and the licensed mental health professional forces him or her to do so, it may prove unsafe for the clients, and can become an ethical violation. If the EAP licensed mental health professional recognizes that the horse is unhappy and unwilling to participate, it is his/her ethical responsibility to remove or otherwise attend to that horse.[538]

One of the desired outcomes of EAP is for the client to come away with a deeper understanding of his or her impact on the group, and potentially on the world around them. Utilizing a Challenge by Choice orientation offers the client a powerful opportunity to see that they are in control of their actions, decisions, and behaviors. It is through this realization that the client can begin the process of growth and change.

Activity Based
EAP is activity based, which necessitates planning and preparation, and well-honed facilitation skills on the part of the licensed mental health professional.[539] Activities are the primary focus of an EAP session, and the licensed mental health professional will generally have an understanding of the needs and goals of the group prior to their arrival so that each activity that it used targets issues relevant to the group.

Initial EAP activities can be used to create fun experiences that promote laughter, reducing inhibitions and breaking down barriers.[540] These sorts of activities help groups to move more smoothly through the first awkward stages of group process and prepare them for the next level of challenge. Following the use of these "ice breakers," EAP licensed mental health professionals can then introduce a series of activities that move the group through increasingly difficult tasks, challenging their cohesion, their level of trust, and their overall functionality. Groups are challenged to pool their resources and work together to find solutions and accomplish tasks. As the series continues, each member of the group may be given the opportunity to demonstrate their trust (or lack there of) in other members of the group through a series of sequenced actions which draw upon emotional issues such as the fear of falling (if using mounted work), the fear of physical injury, the fear of failure, or the fear of losing control.[541]

Programs using EAP are most often designed to explore group interaction, problem solving, and leadership. In some cases EAP activities are used to help families come together and work through issues that are impeding their ability to function. In other cases EAP activities are used for corporate groups, youth at risk populations, or counseling groups such as individuals dealing with terminal illness, diabetes, eating disorders, addictions, or other issues. Some of the commonly perceived outcomes of EAP activities include enhancement of cooperation, decision making, self confidence, positive risk taking, cohesion, self-esteem, self-awareness, trust, leadership, communication, goal setting, and teamwork.[542] EAP activities are not generally recommended for survivors of sexual assault and domestic violence, or offenders of either group due to the non-relational and fight or flight-based nature of the horse/human interactions utilized in this method.[543]

Processing the Experience

After and sometimes during each activity, the licensed mental health professional will bring the group together to process the experience. Processing entails verbal dialog regarding the client's feelings, thoughts, and behaviors as they occurred during the activity. The licensed mental health professional may ask questions specific to a certain member, or more general regarding the functionality of the group as a whole. Each member of the group will be given an opportunity to speak and share their process.[544] Generally the licensed mental health professional will have set up safety protocol for the group to follow regarding concepts such as using "I" statements and respectful language. During the group process members might make observations about how they functioned as a group which can open up dialogue, either leading to agreement or disagreement between members. Clients may come to deep personal realizations during the group process, coming to better understand themselves and their actions.[545]

The licensed mental health professional will generally request that the clients reflect about how certain horses acted or responded to them or to the group during the course of the activity. In some cases the licensed mental health professional might even stop the activity to suggest that the client or group observe the horse or horses in the moment and make comments about what the horses are doing. Other times the licensed mental health professional might allow the entire activity to pass without interruption, allowing the group to have their own process regardless of how challenging, frustrating, or upsetting that might be for individual members or the group as a whole.[546] Generally every group goes through sections of the activities where they are experiencing challenge or frustration, and it is by working through these experiences as a team that success occurs. During the processing component of the session the licensed mental health professional might ask open-ended questions about how that segment of the activity was for the group, helping them to put into words the experience and how they worked through it. During processing the licensed mental health professional might also ask questions about what each member gained from the activity and what the group as a whole gained that can be transferred back to their daily lives, work environments, or other group interactions.

Group Oriented

EAP is generally a group-oriented method of treatment. It is not specifically designed to treat individuals.[547] Utilizing a group counseling approach, individuals may be able to see themselves and their roles within society, community, or family more clearly. In this method, the group provides the reflective feedback[548] and occasionally the horse or horses are included in that reflective process. However, the horse's feedback may or may not be used within the EAP process. The focus of the counseling is on how the group functions and how each member engages with each other during the activities. The licensed mental health professional observes and focuses on the clients and how they interact with each other more than on the horse(s) reactions to the clients.[549]

The group is expected to go through the normal stages of group development while in EAP treatment. If the group is short term the stages are more closely related to those proposed by the experiential educational field and can occur within a one day or one half-day EAP experience.[550] If the group is long term and consistent in nature, the stages of group development may more closely resemble Yalom's notions of group development.[551]

The Therapeutic Process

Therapeutic Goals

The primary goal of EAP is to utilize the group's experience of the activities conducted to bring about awareness, growth, and change. Through participating in pre-planned activities individual members of the group and the group as a whole may develop a new sense of awareness and insight about their behaviors and actions.[552] Although EAP can be short term in nature, goals are generally created by the group prior to their arrival and shared with the licensed mental health professional at that time. The professional then designs activities that will target those goals. If EAP is provided as a long term and ongoing group process, goals are still set by the group members, but may be adjusted as the group moves through various stages of development.[553] Common goals that may be met by groups and individuals are as follows:

- Group cohesion
- Improved teamwork
- Trust building between members
- Heightened awareness of self and others
- Increased self-esteem and self-confidence
- Discovering how behaviors and actions impact others.
- Increased healthful communication skills
- Increased leadership skills
- Increased ability to problem solve as a group and individually

Horse's Role, Function, and Relationship to Client

In EAP the horse is considered a living, breathing "tool" who can be used in the creation of adventure or experientially-based activities.[554] The role of the horse within EAP is to participate in activities that are created by the licensed mental health professional. The amount and quality of interaction and participation by the horse in any given activity is the choice of the horse. No expectations are set on the horse in regards to behaviors or actions. The horse generally reverts back to an instinctual or fight or flight response when placed in a non-relational environment with humans who are attempting to move or otherwise direct the horse around an enclosed space. This reaction on the part of the horse is fully accepted and in some cases encouraged by the licensed mental health professional.[555]

The horse is not usually the main focus of the therapeutic method, and the relationship between the client and the horse tends to be limited to the questions asked of the client or group by the licensed mental health professional regarding how the horse's behavior might be useful in reflecting upon the success of the group in any given activity. The licensed mental health professional is generally not as focused on the horse as in other EFMHS methods, and generally does not interpret the communications from the horse to the group.[556] Therefore, if the horse is interested in providing reflective feedback, he or she must provide it in such a way that the group cannot miss the desired meaning. The licensed mental health professional generally does not engage in any form of analysis regarding the client's reaction to the horse or the horse's reaction to the client or group.

The horse is not generally encouraged to develop an on-going relationship with the clients or group and in some cases the licensed mental health professional may not have a closely linked relationship with individual horses or horse herd.[557]

Licensed Mental Health Professional's Role, Function, and Relationship to Client

The licensed mental health professional within the EAP method generally does not become involved or engaged with the clients or group on a deep or personal level. Many EAP professionals choose to remain more aloof and distant, providing open-ended or redirected questions for thought and reflection without giving the client an answer.[558] The licensed mental health professional generally designs the activities to match the goals of the group attending, and appears extremely active in the facilitation of those activities. Facilitation denotes the ability to clearly understand the goals of the group and create activities that will target those goals. Facilitation also suggests that the licensed mental health professional be capable and able to clearly explain an activity, intervene if necessary to maintain the safety of the participants, and facilitate the processing segment either at any point during the activity that processing is deemed necessary, or following the completion of the activity *without controlling the direction that the group takes with any given activity.*[559]

It is important for an EAP licensed mental health professional to be highly aware of the desire that might arise to assume the role of a controlling leader or parent. In 1978 Rick Medrick wrote a paper suggesting that the deeper implications of a Challenge by Choice leadership style is to help counter the potential for instructors (or in this case, licensed mental health professionals) to fall victim to their power and become tempted into a power-over or dominating leadership style, thereby directing the client's choices rather than allowing them the power to choose. He suggested that instead, the instructor should strive towards engaging the participants' adult states and interact with participants on adult terms, respecting their capacity and knowledge with regard to being able to decide the pace of the activity, and draw whatever meaning they choose to from the activities conducted. It is the job of the EAP licensed mental health professional to be attuned to this power dynamic, and work hard to set boundaries that support the client's decision making capabilities.560

As stated above, the EAP licensed mental health professional generally does not engage the client(s) in analysis of their process, or of their reactions or the horses. EAP is not psychoanalytic based psychotherapy and thus does not necessitate clients sharing their past histories or the licensed mental health professional engaging the client in past regressive memory work. EAP licensed mental health professional tend to keep the process focused on the here and now, and recommend that clients remain in the present with both their communications and their thought processes.[561]

In providing EAP, although the licensed mental health professional acts primarily as a facilitator, he or she is also trained, educated, and prepared to move the session into or out of deeper personal reflection or sharing as the needs of the group dictates. The group generally controls the goal setting and the speed at which they move through activities. The licensed mental health professional tends to stay as non-involved in that process as possible, allowing the group to make its own decisions, come to its own conclusions, and engage on whatever level it decides to.

The EAP licensed mental health professional generally works using a team method.[562] In most cases there is a horse specialist who works in concert with the licensed mental health professional and together they will design and implement the activities. The horse specialist should be trained in the method, and understand the ethical and legal ramifications of providing a therapeutic service. The horse specialist may or may not be included in the processing segments of the sessions depending upon the relationship between the mental health professional and the horse specialist. The horse specialist generally provides the group with a comprehensive safety overview prior to each session, and is present during the entirety of the session to provide safety oversight. Other assistants may be used depending upon group size to ensure the safety of all members of the group. The licensed mental health professional usually provides information regarding the goals of the group to the horse specialist so that proper activities could be created that match those goals. The licensed mental health professional may also provide basic information to the assistants so that they can be prepared for the clientele.

The EAP licensed mental health professional is responsible for preparing all members of incoming groups for success to the best of their ability. Each member of the group should be made aware of the provocative and experiential nature of the method. They should all be informed of the inherent danger associated with this method, and be given the right of Challenge by Choice. If participants have been mandated or otherwise forced to attend an EAP session, the EAP licensed mental health professional should still afford them the same right once they have arrived. Clients attending an EAP session should never be forced to participate for any reason.

An EAP licensed mental health professional must function within their scope of practice,[563] and should notify all participants of the therapeutic nature of this method. In many cases when dealing with corporate groups, school groups, or other groups that might desire to do equine teambuilding work, they will not be aware of the potential for this type of work to become immediately and deeply therapeutic, and if the client or group is unprepared or unwilling for that type of interaction, it has the potential to be emotionally damaging. It is the ethical responsibility of the EAP licensed mental health professional to notify all clients that this service *is* a mental health service, and not a coaching, educational or training-based method.

If EAP is being used as an adjunct to traditional group counseling or individual counseling provided by an outside organization or individual licensed mental health professional, the EAP licensed mental health professional is advised to be in contact with the primary licensed mental health professional whose group/client it is to clearly understand the needs of the group/client. Furthermore, it is highly recommended that the primary licensed mental health professional either participate in or observe the EAP process, or obtain a release of information so as to be able to communicate with the facilitator of the EAP experience regarding the groups/client's process.

Client's Experience in Therapy

Ideally, an EAP client would experience the feeling of personal choice from the moment he/she enters the facility until the moment that he/she exits. This feeling may empower the client to make choices and by being given enough information about the method, to make informed decisions.[564] Prior to beginning services, it appears useful for the client to have an understanding of what the method is like, what might be expected of them if they do chose to participate, and be advised as to the inherent risks involved. It is important that clients also receive safety training specific to the method. An atmosphere should be created in which the client feels that it is acceptable to choose not to participate if the risks appear too great and also feels comfortable expressing that the provocative nature of the process is too overwhelming for him/her. This seems to be the case for all clients, but is especially important for those who have been forced or mandated to attend a session.[565]

EAP clients should understand clearly that they are participating in a mental health or therapeutically-based service, not an educational or training-based service. They have the right to request information about the education, licensure, training, and experience of the licensed mental health professional facilitating prior to agreeing to participate in the service.[566] They also should sign a Consent for Treatment form which explains the method.

EAP clients should also understand prior to engaging in the EAP process whether the method is being offered as a short or long term service, and can be given referral sources to an EFC or EFP provider if individual or follow up services are deemed necessary or are recommended or requested.

Practice: Therapeutic Techniques, Processes, and Procedures

Overview

EAP is a method designed to foster cohesion between groups of people. Through the process of gaining cohesion, personal growth and insight generally occur for individual members. EAP utilizes techniques that help create an environment of challenge which promotes teamwork, trust, and communication skills building.

EAP utilizes four core techniques, (1) Group process, (2) Challenge by choice, (3) Experiential activities, and (4) Processing the experience. These core techniques or processes have already been presented in the key concept section of this chapter.

Method Example

This method example was provided by Kim Shook of Bella Terra Equine Adventure in Mattawan, MI.

A client during a group session at Bella Terra Equine Adventure who was newly the director of a local non-profit was working with a horse in the round pen. We placed a jump along the rail and asked the client to name the obstacle based on something she was currently facing in her life. As a new director, she was doing staff performance evaluations for the first time in her career. She was having much difficulty in finding balance in writing these evaluations in terms of providing constructive feedback for improvement. She was very uncomfortable in providing less than positive feedback. She named the jump/obstacle "Performance Evaluations." She tried a few times and was not able to get the horse over the jump. Each time the horse approached the jump, she would create an opening for the horse to avoid the jump.

She became frustrated because she was a horse person and she didn't understand why she couldn't get the horse to jump. We stopped for a moment to discuss what was happening. She shared the distress she was under in writing performance evaluations for the first time. She was not sleeping. She did not know how to deliver constructive feedback; she was in fear of alienating her staff and not being liked. We worked with this client in getting to the present moment and finding her real, authentic feelings. We talked about her self-worth and the value of her opinion in directing her organization to where it needed to be. We talked through options of how feedback could be given in a positive way and that this feedback was an important part of the process to initiate change. We then could see through her body posture that she had become empowered and she said she was ready to get the horse over the jump. She funneled her determination to the hind quarter of the horse and used that energy to push the horse right over the jump. We discussed how the horse accepted her and her boundaries and that the horse did not think less of her because she was assertive. In fact, boundaries and assertiveness were necessary to get the horse to accomplish the goal. We then discussed how she could funnel her energy in the same manner in completing the performance evaluations.

Summary and Evaluation

EAP can be a highly effective method of treatment for groups or families desiring change. EAP is not usually provided as an individual form of treatment, and is generally not considered deep psychotherapy. Licensed mental health professionals providing EAP may collaborate with other facilitators to provide this service, and may utilize other staff members on a regular basis in order to maintain the safety of the activities. EAP does not generally purposely delve into the personal histories or life stories of the clients; rather EAP is present moment focused and relies heavily upon the patterns that emerge through group participation and challenge.

EAP differs from other forms of EFMHS due to the non-relational nature of the horse/human interaction. In EAP the horse is considered a tool and provides an adventure-based experience for groups to build cohesion and gain insight. The horse within the EAP method is not usually encouraged to form deep and long lasting relationships with clients. Instead the horse is generally utilized because of his/her instinctual nature rather than his/her relational nature, and that instinctual nature is played upon by the activities created.

Through personal and group challenge, the EAP clients may move to a higher degree of functionality within their group and as individuals. The EAP licensed mental health professional acts as a facilitator, presenting the activities and then assuming a non-biased, non-judgmental, and non-invasive role which allows the clients to have their own unique experience. The clients decide the goals for the session prior to beginning the session, and the licensed mental health professional designs the activities to target those specific goals or objectives.

EAP may be short term in nature, sometimes providing only one or two sessions to any given group. If EAP is used as a short term treatment method, it is mandatory that the clientele have been screened appropriately to ensure their mental stability and health. If the clients are not appropriate for a short term approach, EAP should be conducted on a longer term basis. Families or more challenged groups should be seen on an ongoing basis and treatment should include goals specific to the deeper issues that they are experiencing. EAP may need to be used in conjunction with another EFMHS method, such as EFC or EFP, dependant upon the issues that arise within the EAP setting. Licensed mental health professionals should understand the limitations of EAP and be prepared to refer out if those limitations impact their client's ability to grow and develop within treatment.

Many professionals currently practicing in the field of EFMH/ES recognize the limitations of this method, and make personal choices to utilize components of the method but facilitate it from a relational orientation. This orientation changes the dynamic between the horses and the humans, fostering relationship and decreasing the likelihood of a flight or fight or fear-based response on the part of the horse. This approach appears safer in all cases reviewed.

CHAPTER FIFTEEN

EQUINE FACILITATED BRIEF INTENSIVES

Introduction

At times during a traditional therapeutic intervention the client may become stuck and may report feeling unable or unwilling to move forward towards change or growth.[567] At this time some clients leave therapy, seek another form of treatment, revert back to old patterns or behaviors, or the primary licensed mental health professional (primary/LMHP)[568] will have to discontinue services due to the unethical ramifications of ineffectual treatment. In many cases the sensation of getting stuck can occur because of a blockage within the client's ability to process, place, or verbalize experiences, thoughts, feelings, or unconscious processes.[569]

Other times, it is the primary/LMHP who feels struck or unsure of the direction in which the client is steering the therapeutic encounter. The primary/LMHP may be questioning the manipulative nature of the client, and may be feeling uncomfortable due to issues of transference or counter-transference as they relate to the therapeutic relationship. The primary/LMHP may feel the desire to witness his or her client in a new setting that has the potential to draw forth a more clearly defined picture of the client's reality and functionality.[570]

In traditional talk therapy the process of gaining personal insight and moving beyond the stories we commonly tell can take a long time.[571] The primary/LMHP generally reflects back, uses appropriate confrontation, and encourages constant self-exploration, but may not have a great deal of other tools to help the process move more quickly.[572] Since it may take years to come to a deeper sense of self-awareness or insight, clients many times are unwilling or unable to spend that much time or money on therapy and so may leave treatment well before they have addressed the fundamental reasons why they sought therapy in the first place.[573]

In therapeutic work with horses, clients are generally given the ability to use non-verbal, and many times unconscious, forms of processing or experiencing their own internal landscape.[574] Through the reflective feedback process or Psychodramatization provided by the horse, the client is able to witness themselves and their own processes in a new and different way, thereby creating different doorways through which insight, growth, and change can occur.[575]

Furthermore, possibly due to the use of reflective feedback and Psychodramatization, within a session or two, clients have a tendency to experience themselves more fully and authentically, seeing the stories that they tell and coming to realizations about their functionality. Once this occurs, the direction of treatment can move from spending time coming to these realizations, to actively engaging in the process of personal change.[576]

For the primary/LMHP, witnessing their client experiencing this dynamic process may lead to new insight and help refocus the therapeutic intervention. The client and the primary/LMHP can utilize the equine experience to guide their future sessions and provide important information for continued therapeutic work.[577]

Equine Facilitated Brief Intensives (EFBI) is a method in which the primary/LMHP and the client alike may be able to reach new levels within both the therapeutic intervention, and their professional relationship. EFBI offers primary/LMHP's who may have little if any understanding of horses or their impact on humans the ability to witness and benefit from the work of EFMHS. EFBI also offers primary/LMHP's the luxury of including an EFMHS services into their practice without having to be specifically trained, educated, and experienced in the field.[578]

EFBI can be successful for a diverse population base, and because EFBI can be utilized in conjunction with any form of traditional mental health service, EFBI has the potential to serve large numbers of people from all walks of life, struggling with all manner of issues or disorders.

EFBI has been used successfully in residential treatment center settings, therapeutic boarding schools, and in conjunction with individual licensed mental health professionals. EFBI is only utilized when the client is already engaged in some sort of formal treatment or therapy, and is intending upon continuing with that treatment. EFBI is not a stand-alone form of treatment, and EFBI/licensed mental health professionals (EFBI/LMHP) will collaborate closely with the client(s) primary/LMHP to ensure that ethical and professional treatment is provided at all times.[579]

Key Concepts

Collaborative Short Term Service

EFBI is utilized as a collaborative short-term service, helping clients to witness their own process in a new and different way. EFBI is facilitated by trained, educated, and experienced LMHP's who work in conjunction with the client(s) primary/LMHP to ensure ethical and professional treatment. The EFBI/LMHP should be considered a part of the client's treatment team, and therefore be allowed to attend any staffings or other meetings in which the client's case is being discussed. Or, if the client is referred to an EFBI session from an independent primary/LMHP, the EFBI/LMHP and the primary/LMHP must both gain signed releases of information from the client so as to be able to freely communicate about the client's case. The EFBI/LMHP should have access to all psychological testing, evaluations, or other written reports generated about the client, and should share all progress notes that document EFBI sessions with the primary/LMHP or treatment team.[580]

In this model EFBI is never provided as a stand alone service and is considered short term in nature. A typical EFBI client would be seen once or twice by the EFBI/LMHP, but would be engaged in on-going treatment with a primary/LMHP. Occasionally EFBI is utilized in a weekend retreat forum, and thus would last up to three consecutive days. In some cases the primary/LMHP may not be on site for the duration of the EFBI treatment, but the EFBI/LMHP will be in direct contact with the primary/LMHP both prior and post to ensure accurate and adequate information is relayed. The EFBI/LMHP should have all documentation regarding the client or clients and should be familiar with the case prior to providing an EFBI service.

EFBI can be used in conjunction with most any traditional therapeutic method and can be used for either group or individual therapy.

Intensity of Treatment ~ Fundamental Shifts within the Psyche
EFBI can be a profound treatment intervention. The EFBI team (which consists of horses, licensed mental health professional(s), and possibly assistants) structures experiences, and activities, and encourages deep reflective processing during the short time that the clients are at the EFBI facility. The energy and focus of the treatment intervention is on creating an environment where insight and awareness is encouraged. Therefore any techniques that further induce that frame of mind may be used. The EFBI team might utilize any of the EFMHS techniques and might include breathwork, music, drumming, or other psycho-spiritual approaches that might be useful in altering the client's experience of self, others, and the natural world.

Upon completion of an EFBI session clients will often report feeling as if they were in an "altered state of consciousness," or that they felt as through they experienced a drastically new approach to the way in which they view life.[581] The intensity of this treatment intervention is such that the client's primary/LMHP is advised to be present or on call immediately after the intervention to help the client process his/her experience and move towards the integration of the experience into their normal treatment setting.

The EFBI/ LMHP is responsible for ensuring the emotional and physical safety of the client during the session, and also for helping the client return safely to the care of their primary/ LMHP. Once the client is out of the immediate supervision of the EFBI/ LMHP, their primary/ LMHP is responsible for ensuring the safety and functionality of the client from there forward.

EFBI clients should be screened to ensure that they are mentally stable enough for this method of intervention. EFBI/ LMHP can also reduce the intensity of the service if the clientele dictates. However a certain level of stability must exist to make EFBI a useful, ethical, or healthful intervention technique. If a client is not appropriate for EFBI, either they should remain in traditional therapy, or be referred to an EFP provider. If EFBI is provided to a group of clients, it is essential that all clients have been screened and have been grouped accordingly so that no one client is over-stimulated by the intervention.

Preparedness for Change

EFBI can be used within the first few weeks of traditional therapy to help prepare clients for the therapeutic process. Preparedness is indicative of the ability to come into present moment awareness and thus gain the perspective necessary to invoke deep personal change. EFBI/ LMHP utilize techniques to help clients prepare for the process of change and growth by facilitating moments of personal reflection, personal observation, and present moment awareness. Learning how to come into the present moment can assist the therapeutic process and move the client into a place where he/she is more observant and more connected to their deeper sense of self. EFBI as an early intervention appears to help people to witness their own stories and encourages personal reflection and observation, therefore allowing the primary/ LMHP to engage the client sooner on a more authentic level.

Once a primary/ LMHP has begun the treatment process with a client or group of clients, he or she generally can tell if EFBI might be a useful treatment intervention to be used near the beginning of treatment. If the primary/ LMHP observes that the client(s) is/are struggling with the process of authentic personal reflection, or are manipulative or stuck within their own stories, it may be useful to utilize one or two EFBI sessions to help focus the direction of treatment from the very onset.

EFBI may not be useful as an early intervention for psychotherapy clients due to the present moment focus of the sessions and the potentially differing initial goals of psychotherapy.[582] However, EFBI used as an early intervention would be ideal for chemical dependency clientele or other addictions issues, individuals diagnosed with eating disorders, youth at-risk, life skills-based counseling clientele, or others seeking a shorter term and solution-focused approach to therapy.

Refocusing of Treatment

EFBI can be used at any point during a therapeutic relationship to help clients move through times when they feel stuck within the treatment process, or need a tangible and tactile understanding of how to implement new concepts into daily functioning. Other times clients come to a place where they cannot perceive their own dysfunctional patterns or behaviors, and therefore struggle to understand the need for change. There are three important components utilized by EFBI/LMHP to help move clients through difficult times, (1) Practicing of new skills learned, (2) Creating corrective experiences, and (3) Understanding the meaning behind actions.

Practicing of New Skills Learned

In traditional therapy clients may come to realize that they need a new skill set in order to deal with presenting issues or problems that they face in their daily lives. With the help of the primary/LMHP they may come to a deeper understanding of what those skills might be and how gaining them would be useful to solve current life problems. However, they are not generally given the opportunity within traditional therapy to practice, with the guidance and support of a primary/LMHP, these new skills. Instead it is suggested that the client practices the new skills on their own. In many cases this proves relatively challenging and sometimes useless as they are unable to remember, recreate, or stick to concepts and ideas discussed within the safety of the therapeutic setting.

If the primary/LMHP is observing that the client is unable to bring about the practical application of such skills into his or her daily life, the primary/LMHP might consider referring the client to an EFBI session. Prior to attending the primary/ LMHP and the EFBI/LMHP will communicate and the EFBI team will be prepared to create activities and experiences that help target the skills that the client has expressed an interest in practicing. The horses provide reflective feedback for the client so that he or she can witness how successful his/her attempts at utilizing the skill has been. Processing then occurs and the client is given the opportunity to try the same skill set again with a new perspective or direction. The client is therefore allowed to practice new skills in a safe, supportive, and non-judgmental environment where he or she can receive immediate feedback about his/her functionality and leave clearer about their strengths and abilities.

Corrective Experiences

Many times clients are not able to conceptualize how their behaviors might be negatively impactful. Therefore therapy may continue to revolve around why the client has constant negative relationships or struggles within the relational world. After a period of time the primary/LMHP may attempt confrontation to help the client see more clearly the reality of their responsibility within the conflicts. This approach may or may not prove useful, and many times the client is stuck within his or her own self-created reality and thus not interested in hearing someone else's thoughts about the issue. If this situation arises within treatment, EFBI can be a highly useful intervention as it will help the client clearly and without question recognize the impact that his or her behaviors have upon others.

With little preparation or activity planning on the part of the EFBI team, clients once in contact with horses will generally witness through the reflective feedback process, their impact upon the horses. Clients who are overly forceful and demand a great deal of attention from those around them may be drawn to or repulsed by a horse with the same characteristics. The horses might avoid the client, and if the client continues to push himself/herself onto them, may even get aggressively abrasive with the client, at which time the EFBI/LMHP will intervene to question why the horses might be acting as they are. The client might be assigned a task to complete with a horse and find himself/herself unable to complete it due to interpersonal struggles resulting from his/her forceful nature. Through any of these examples clients begin to witness how others react and act when in their presence, and they may be able to make connections and come to realizations about their responsibility within relational conflicts. Within this environment it is harder to ignore the responses from the horses, and generally it feels safer to accept their feedback than the feedback of another human being.

Understanding Meaning Behind Action

EFBI can also be helpful to clients who continue to struggle with understanding the meaning behind actions that they engage in repetitively. For instance, women who have been abused may find that they constantly place themselves back into potentially abusive relationships or situations, only to find the same result occurs. Or, an individual may continue to utilize an addictive substance trying over and over again to quit but regardless of treatment, support, or help cannot seem to move beyond the addiction. Many times these repetitive behaviors have deeper meanings stemming from childhood, relational issues with family members, or other deeply buried memories or experiences and it is not until the client has come to a realization about this deeper meaning that change is possible.

In other cases clients engage in actions that are less harmful, but are counter productive to their situations. The client may report that they do not understand why they engage in such actions, and cannot seem to change the behavior. In this situation, many times clients are unaware of subtle motivations that trigger behaviors, and therefore think that they cannot control their actions.

The work of EFBI allows clients a deeper look into their psyches. Through the process of Psychodramatization, the clients are able to witness their own histories complete with current actions and behaviors. The client may then be able to realize complex motivations and understand the origins of deeply held patterns or behaviors. The client may engage in projection and transference as they interact with the horses, and suddenly find themselves witnessing and experiencing their own issues as reflected back to them by the horse.

The Therapeutic Process

Therapeutic Goals

EFBI is purposely focused on helping clients either prepare for successful treatment, or move through challenging or stuck times during traditional therapy. EFBI can help both clients and primary/LMHP by illuminating key issues that have created stagnation within therapy. More specific and individual EFBI therapeutic goals are created by the client and by the primary/LMHP, and facilitated by the EFBI team. The general goals of EFBI are as follows:

- Heightened personal awareness and insight

- Increased present moment focus and awareness

- Ability to recognize the motivations behind problematic behaviors or actions

- Recognition of unsuccessful behavioral patterns

- The ability to practice and hone new skills

Horse's Role, Function, and Relationship to Client

The EFBI horse is versatile, being able to move between the roles of facilitator, co-facilitator, mirror, and occasionally, employee. The horse is asked to connect deeply and rapidly with clients, and is given permission to engage with clients in a reflective feedback or Psychodramatization process. EFBI horses should be clear communicators who are unafraid of expressing their thoughts and feelings loudly when necessary. The short-term nature of the work encourages the EFBI horses to make sure that the clients have truly obtained the information being offered, and sometimes that necessitates more dramatic measures. Essentially the EFBI horse embodies, at one time or another, all aspects of EFMHS. This method is successful due to the immediate and profound reactions of the horses to the clients and visa versa. This method relies upon the horse/human relationship and generally succeeds only when the horses are actively engaged and expressive.

It is the relationship between the client and the horse that is primary, and the relationship with the EFBI/LMHP and the client secondary.

Licensed Mental Health Professional's Role, Function, and Relationship to Client

The EFBI/LMHP's role is to facilitate experiences that bring about a heightened awareness, increase present moment focus, and help clients move to new levels within treatment. They are responsible for understanding the EFBI method completely, and therefore must have a working knowledge of all other forms of EFMHS, as at any given time they may need to utilize one or more of the principles found in the other methods. EFBI is an integration of all EFMHS methods, condensed into one short term approach to be used only in conjunction with on-going traditional therapy. Therefore, the EFBI/LMHP must be prepared to co-facilitate an intensive experience and feel comfortable enough with the primary/LMHP to know that the information within the experience will be utilized ethically and appropriately.

The EFBI/LMHP must be well-trained in many aspects of mental health services, from traditional psychotherapy to expressive arts therapy, and may find useful a background and experience with such methods as holotropic breathwork, shamanic journeying, or the Journey Ride.[583] The EFBI/LMHP is generally expected to be knowledgeable and comfortable with wrap-around care concepts and comfortable working with multiple service providers. He or she should also have a working understanding of common issues relevant to potential clientele, such as chemical dependency, eating disorders, sexual, physical, or emotional abuse, domestic violence, youth at-risk populations, and be prepared to refer if uncomfortable with a specific population.

The EFBI/LMHP's main function is to co-create an environment conducive to this intensive form of treatment. This includes the organization of the facility, the horses chosen to participate in the method, the assistants and/or co-facilitators, and all other forms of equipment or resources that might be needed within any given session. The EFBI/LMHP must be comfortable with the short term nature of the service, and is responsible for ensuring that he or she does not overstep appropriate boundaries with the client or clients. The EFBI/LMHP remains supportive towards the primary/LMHP and should be aware of the potential for the client to engage in "splitting" between the two LMHP's. If for any reason the EFBI/LMHP has reason to believe that the primary/LMHP is inappropriate for the client, or engaging in unethical treatment of the client, the EFBI/LMHP should approach the primary/LMHP or that individual's supervisor to discuss these feelings or thoughts, *not the client.*

The EFBI/LMHP is responsible for the emotional and physical safety of the client while the client is at the EFBI facility. However, upon their departure from the facility the primary/LMHP resumes responsibility. The client should not be given the EFBI/LMHP's contact information, nor should they be encouraged to remain in contact with the EFBI/LMHP. The roles of the two LMHP's should be clearly explained to the client, and it should be made obvious to the client that the EFBI/LMHP is simply there to facilitate the EFBI experience, not as a primary/LMHP for the duration of the client's treatment.

The relationship between the EFBI/LMHP and the client should be more closely related to that of a facilitator to a client. The aim of the EFBI/LMHP is generally to help foster a deep and meaningful relationship between the EFBI client and the horse or horses, not between the client and themselves. Occasionally, depending upon the aim of the session, the EFBI/LMHP may also work to foster a healthful, more trusting, and open relationship between the primary/LMHP and the client. In either case, the EFBI/LMHP should remain as personally removed from the client's process as possible, allowing the client and the horse, or the client and the primary/LMHP to connect as deeply as possible.

Client's Experience in Therapy

The EFBI client should be educated about the treatment intervention and should be comfortable attending such an intervention. He/she is generally made aware of the "challenge by choice" nature of the method, and understands that he/she does not have to participate in any activities that feel too challenging or scary. However, it is also recommended that the client have discussions with the primary/LMHP about the reasons for attending this intervention, and should be prepared for the innate challenge that lies within the work of EFBI.

The client is in agreement that this intensive intervention may be useful for him. It is suggested that he/she demonstrate a level of comfort with alternative treatment methods, and be interested in pursuing a personal experience with such a method.

Prior to the first session, the primary/LMHP will discuss with the client who will be at the facility, what their roles are, and how the first few minutes of the interaction will occur. The primary/LMHP generally explains what his/her role will be during the session (this changes depending upon the unique goals of the treatment team). This could include him/her as observer, as support staff, or as participant. The primary/LMHP can explain where he/she will be physically during the session, and help the client come to a comfort level with the notion that the EFBI/LMHP is in charge for the duration of the EFBI session. He/she could provide the client with details about how the session *might* look - with an opening circle, safety agreements, discussion of goals, meeting the horses, and then into an activity of some sort. The primary/LMHP can also provide the client with information about how the day will end, with debriefing and a closure circle, or whatever the EFBI/LMHP has indicated, and can explain that following the EFBI session he/she and the client will then have their own private time to process the experience. This type of layout for the day is gained through conversation between the EFBI/LMHP and the primary/LMHP, and could change drastically from the model presented above due to specific facilitation styles, goals, and so forth. The primary/LMHP might not even be in attendance during the session, and may meet with the client in her office either after the session or some days later. However, regardless of how it actually looks, the primary/LMHP should be comfortable enough with the service, and have had sufficient conversations with the EFBI/LMHP to be able to prepare the client to some degree for the EFBI experience.

Upon arrival at the EFBI facility, it appears useful if the client has an experience closely related to that which the primary/LMHP has presented. This continuity may help the client gain trust both in his/her primary/LMHP and in the EFBI team. The client will be able to tell that his/her team is in communication and is working for his/her good.

The client and the primary/LMHP should have already discussed potential goals and/or objectives that the client would like to gain from the EFBI experience. Upon arrival at the EFBI facility, the client will generally be asked to openly discuss these goals with the EFBI/LMHP.

The client does not need to feel obliged to give the EFBI/LMHP a complete history during the EFBI session; however he/she will understand that with the release of information that he/she signed, the EFBI/LMHP has had access to his/her complete psychological records, including verbal dialog with his primary/LMHP. The primary/LMHP and the client will have discussed this prior to deciding to utilize EFBI as an intervention, and only clients that are comfortable with this sharing of information should be considered candidates for such an intervention. Since the EFBI/LMHP has an understanding of the client's past history, the client should not be surprised if the EFBI/LMHP refers to areas of his/her life that he/she has not shared verbally with the EFBI/LMHP. For instance, the EFBI/LMHP might say, "Henry, was there anything about that interaction that reminded you of your relationship with your family?"

The client should expect that clear boundaries will be set that help to define the roles of his/her primary/LMHP and his EFBI/LMHP. The client will also understand that he/she might not see the EFBI/LMHP again unless he/she requests the intervention in the future. Furthermore, if the client feels that the EFBI treatment method works better for him/her than his/her traditional treatment method, the client will understand that he/she may be referred to an EFP or EFC service rather than to his/her EFBI/LMHP. This clarification helps stop possible splitting and/or manipulation by the client, an issue that could impede the success of treatment and cause possible unethical relational violations between client and LMHP.

Practice: Therapeutic Techniques, Processes, and Procedures

Overview

The techniques of EFBI are designed to provide the client with an intense, provocative, and profound experience that will help him/her to either prepare for therapy, or refocus the course of their therapeutic experience. In many cases EFBI is used to help clients move through stuck times in treatment. In other cases EFBI can be used to help primary/LMHP's better understand their client's needs, and thus design and guide the therapeutic experience in a more successful direction. EFBI helps clients witness themselves in new and different ways, and the EFBI techniques encourage such realizations and insights.

EFBI can be used in conjunction with any therapeutic method. The primary/LMHP could be client-centered, Jungian, psychodynamic, or utilize a myriad of other approaches, or could focus treatment on chemical dependency, eating disorders, abuse issues, or other specific issues. EFBI can be used as an individual or group intervention.

The EFBI/LMHP is responsible for providing the EFBI service, while the primary/LMHP is responsible for the preparation for the service, and the process that occurs afterwards. The primary/LMHP does not need to be trained or educated in the EFBI intervention, but should be willing to spend enough time speaking with the EFBI/LMHP to understand which clients would be appropriate for the service, and how to explain the service to the clients that are referred.

Screening is a critical component of a successful EFBI intervention. There are clients who are not appropriate for such an intense service, and who should not be accepted by the EFBI team. Such clients are those who are highly mentally and/or emotionally unstable, individuals who are distinctly uncomfortable with alternative interventions, or those who are unsafe in a group environment (if the intervention is group-based). If the intervention is being used outside of a residential setting, the EFBI client should be able to safely handle deep personal insight and provocative cathartic experiences, and should be capable of getting themselves to and from the EFBI facility and remaining safe between visits to the primary/LMHP. Clients who are in a residential treatment setting can present as less stable, as long as their primary/LMHP or another skilled and trained mental health professional accompanies them to and from the EFBI facility and is available to process the experience following the EFBI intervention for as long as the client needs to regain stability.

It is critical to remember that since EFBI is generally only used once or twice with any individual client or group of clients, whatever issues might arise must be processed and worked through by a primary/LMHP in another setting. It is imperative that a system is set up prior to the use of an EFBI intervention that ensures proper processing of the EFBI intervention. It is the responsibility of the EFBI/LMHP to understand the client's support system to ensure that there is an adequate system in place prior to providing the service. If an adequate system is not in place, the EFBI/LMHP should not contract with the organization or individual primary/LMHP.

Integrative Approach

EFBI/LMHP's can utilize any of the EFMHS techniques already discussed within the past chapters. This integrative approach may help to make EFBI the provocative and intensive intervention it appears to be. EFBI/LMHP's should be educated, skilled, and trained in all EFMHS methods, and should understand the techniques associated with each of them. At any given time during an EFBI intervention, one of the various techniques may present as the most useful for that particular individual or group. The EFBI/LMHP should be able to move smoothly between all techniques, still maintaining the basic premise that it is the relationship between the horse and the client that may provide catharsis. Even if the EFBI/LMHP is utilizing an EAP activity, it should be facilitated in a manner that promotes the relationship between client and horse.

Illuminating Reflective Feedback

Probably the most important of all aspects of the EFBI method is the use of reflective feedback from the horse to the client. Regardless of which technique or activity an EFBI/LMHP is utilizing, the response from the horse to the client is generally utilized and capitalized upon above all else. Therefore the EFBI/LMHP must be skilled and trained in the language of Equus, equine behavior, psychology, and physiology. The EFBI method dictates that the EFBI/LMHP should know his/her horse herd well, and work only with his or her own herd. The short term nature of this intervention appears to make working with strange or unknown horses unsafe or ineffective.

Method Example

This method example was provided by Laura Brinkerhoff, of Leap of Faith Equestrian Services. Ms. Brinkerhoff and Leap of Faith provide services for Cottonwood De Tucson, a prestigious treatment center in Tucson, Arizona. Ms. Brinkerhoff is also a student advisor for the Prescott College EFMH/ES Masters program.

Susan was assigned to participate in an Equine Facilitated Brief Intensive session by the treatment team, with the intention of helping her release her defenses and connect emotionally to the underlying grief and fear that was preventing her from making progress in treatment.

She arrived at the barn wearing black clothing, heavy makeup and several piercings. Her diagnosis: alcohol dependence, cocaine dependence and major depression. Susan was 25 at the time of her admission.

She chose to work with Blue, a large blue eyed all black paint/quarter horse. He was led into the round pen and released. Her directions were to enter the round pen with the purpose of exploring what he was there to teach her. She was told to engage with him in whatever way she chose. She went to the middle of the pen and stood. Blue stood with his back to her and his nose towards the gate. Susan looked a bit anxious as she stood in the center, shifting from one foot to the other, when she looked at me and said, "I don't know what to do, he's just standing there, ignoring me." At which point I replied, "And where else in your life do you feel ignored." Susan's eyes welled up with tears and she replied, "Everywhere, I feel invisible all the time." Then she allowed the tears to come. As Susan cried Blue turned on his haunches away from the gate until he was facing her and then took three steps towards her until his face was against her chest. The lesson was clear, when she dropped her persona and allowed her self to be authentic in this safe setting, she was able to receive and be seen. It was as if Blue said, "Oh hi, I hadn't seen you back there, where did you come from." Susan was affirmed in the body, mind and heart that she could be vulnerable and allow people to see her. It was a turning point in Susan's treatment. Emotions are an access point for healing and releasing repressed feeling opens the way to insight and recovery.

Following the use of the EFBI intervention, Susan's primary/LMHP and the rest of the treatment team were able to follow up and capitalize upon her realizations out at the barn. This helped to make the lessons learned from Blue all the more powerful.

Summary and Evaluation

EFBI can provide clients and licensed mental health professionals with new perspectives that help move the therapeutic process forward towards increased personal insight, growth, and change. EFBI appears to be an intense and potentially provocative intervention method and due to its short term nature, requires well-planned and professional coordination of services between the EFBI team and the primary/ LMHP. EFBI/ LMHP's should not engage in a contract with any organization or individual who cannot guarantee an adequate system of follow up, supervision, support, and communication.

EFBI focuses on the relationship between the horse(s) and human(s) and suggests that through such a relationship insight, growth, and change is possible. Therefore, the EFBI/ LMHP's remains as removed from the service as possible, promoting the relationship between horse and client.

EFBI/LMHP demonstrate a clear working understanding of their role in concert with the role of the primary/LMHP, and are highly attuned and aware of the manipulation and/or splitting behaviors of clients. The EFBI/LMHP supports the primary/LMHP at all times in front of the client, and promotes a team support feeling between all members of the therapeutic intervention team. The EFBI/ LMHP communicates directly to the primary/LMHP or contracting agency if any concerns arise during the EFBI session or service, and any conflicts are addressed and worked through without involving the client.

EFBI/LMHP are highly educated, trained, and experienced in all EFMHS methods due to the integrative approach of EFBI and are able to move smoothly between any method as the need arises. It appears essential that EFBI/LMHP's know and understand the language of Equus and have close relationships with their own horse herd.

EFBI/LMHP's should actively engage in screening of all potential EFBI clients, and should educate the primary/LMHP whom they work with or contract with about the service to ensure that the appropriate clients are referred to the service.

CHAPTER SIXTEEN

EQUINE FACILITATED LEARNING

Introduction

Equine Facilitated Learning (EFL) is a service provided by trained, educated, and experienced EFE/L providers that targets special needs populations. EFL focuses on teaching life skills, social skills, communication skills, vocational skills, and work ethics to a therapeutic population who generally do not benefit from insight or cognitive processing-based therapies.[584] EFL is designed to provide all of the benefits of EFC without the deeply probing, personal insight-based nature of the service. EFL is not counseling or psychotherapy, but it does tend to target a population who may struggle from dysfunctions of the brain. Therefore, individuals providing an EFL service should be trained and educated to work with individuals suffering from cognitive disabilities, learning disabilities, other forms of processing issues, and potentially severe mental illness. These are individuals for whom counseling, psychotherapy, or other psychological services have not proven useful, and who are in need of the skills indicated above.

EFL tends to be used in conjunction with; (1) School programs for special needs children to help increase processing abilities, encourage expression, or address learning disabilities, (2) In therapeutic boarding schools to teach respect, work ethic, social skills, life skills, or communication skills, and (3). In concert with services provided for individuals suffering from severe mental illness to promote a greater understanding of cause and effect, and increase normalization, stabilization, socialization, and relational skills.[585]

Individuals providing EFL as a service should be educated, trained, and experienced in working with Individual Education Plans (IEP's),[586] and should be able to work in concert with a team dedicated to assisting with the growth and well-being of the specific client. EFL services may include aspects of the IEP and the instructor should be knowledgeable about how to integrate these components into the EFL session. The EFL instructor should also be capable of creating a learning plan for the client that will demonstrate the inclusion of such goals the team and the client specify.[587]

EFL focuses on teaching clients functional life skills. Within this method, it is assumed that the clients will arrive at the service with an impaired ability to function in daily life. Therefore, the life skills that are taught in an EFL session are fairly simple and functionally oriented. They are designed to help the client achieve a baseline of societal normalcy, not necessarily introduce the client to higher-order thinking or processing skills.[588]

Educational Objectives

Life Skills
Generally individuals participating in an EFL service are ill-equipped to deal with the realities of daily life. Either they were not taught functional living skills, or they were not able to integrate such skills into daily life routines. The United Nations Children's Fund (UNICEF) defines life skills as "A large group of psycho-social and interpersonal skills which can help people make informed decisions, communicate effectively, and develop coping and self-management skills that may help them lead a healthy and productive life. Life skills may be directed toward personal actions and actions toward others, as well as actions to change the surrounding environment to make it conducive to health."[589]

The term life skills will be used in this text both to indicate or include some of the more basic skills such as personal hygiene, cleanliness, nutrition, exercise, and money/money management, and in the broader UNICEF sense.

In the case of EFL, clients tend to gain a deeper and more personal understanding of life skills through their relationship with the horses.[590] Many EFL clients have not been able to witness the tangible meaning behind the vast concept of life skills, nor have they been able to understand how to integrate such living skills into their daily lives, or why such a process is useful. Once they begin to work with horses, they become immersed in a living, breathing, tangible application of such skills. Children with attachment disorders or social dysfunctions that make bonding and connecting to other living beings challenging, or those who struggle for other reasons to create and maintain relationships find themselves connecting with the horses with whom they partner. They may begin to notice cause and effect, and see how their actions can impact others. It is generally the horse who fosters the desire to learn how to take care of such a magnificent creature, one who appears so self-sufficient, but in actuality needs her/his human counterparts to provide daily care. Once this relationship has been formed, the client will generally do anything and everything he or she can to provide for that horse.

The client begins to see how important things like hygiene, nutrition, and exercise really are. Interest is generated by such curious practices as horse shoeing or trimming, the feeding of hay and grain, cleaning stalls, taking care of the equipment that goes along with horses, worming, routine veterinarian calls, and horse exercise procedures. These activities look very differently from those that humans generally engage in, which have been commonly used to teach such clients in the past. With the introduction of EFL, life skills suddenly seem foreign, interesting, and appealing. It is far more intriguing, fun, and challenging to clean out a horse's hoof, learn the food that each horse eats and why, or hold a horse for the vet than it is to be taught now to brush your own teeth, go shopping, plan a menu, or learn why its important to go to the doctor or dentist for regular check-ups. Clients begin participating in the processes that they normally might have avoided. Their parents may report that they refuse to keep their rooms clean, their clothing clean, or assist with house chores. At the barn those same clients might be the ones who are most praised for their stall cleaning abilities, who take the most time grooming their horses so they look shinning and beautiful, or who are always there to help whenever needed. The client builds up a skill set that although based upon the care and well-being of horses and their environment, still has direct and unavoidable connections to the client's daily life. Once that skill set is deeply ingrained within the client and has become routine, the instructor or facilitator can begin the process of transferring the knowledge and skill back to daily life.[591]

Through carefully designed activities, the client may be able to start making connections between the skills learned out at the barn, and the areas of their normal lives where these practices could come into play. Many times this process occurs without a great deal of verbalization or processing. The instructor begins interweaving critical skills that the client needs to understand and be able to demonstrate in daily life into the horse-based curriculum.[592] This could look like the client helping to design his or her horse's diet based upon all the factors he or she learned about proper nutrition and care. During that process the instructor could assign the client the duty of simultaneously designing his/her own diet. When both diets have been presented, the instructor has the opportunity to discuss why the client chose certain foods, if those foods are good for either the horse or the client, and what other options might be better. The client generally becomes engaged in the process since first and foremost it is about the horse, not them.

Social Skills

Although a subset of life skills, social skills denote the ability to function in social settings. Social skills can include the ability to relate to others utilizing both verbal and non-verbal communications, recognizing subtle social cues, understanding the appropriateness of confrontation, understanding appropriate dress and appearance standards, and conceptualizing social structure and acting within that structure.[593] Generally social skills are most needed when interacting with others who are not loved ones or close friends. These skills become particularly necessary when applying for employment, attempting to meet new people, or dealing with the complexities of daily human to human interactions. Many individuals engaging in the EFL process struggle to understand social skills, or put them into practice in their daily lives.

In the process of working with horses clients are able to witness social skills in action both within the herd structure (horse to horse) and within the human structure of the organization (human to human). The client watches closely as a new horse is introduced to the herd, and is able to observe the importance of specific social skills with regard to the situation.[594] Then, later on in the day the client is present when the farrier arrives and the instructor makes small talk, engages the farrier in a minor confrontation regarding the manner in which the horse is being trimmed, or deals with the exchange of funds for service. Although the client might normally not pay attention or care about a human to human exchange such as that, he or she might be more curious and engaged because it directly relates to the animal from whom he/she cares.

Dependant upon the type of client, the instructor might put a specific client in charge of calling the farrier, the vet, or the feed delivery person to make appointments for upcoming visits. If the client has been with horses long enough and is responsible, safe, and knowledgeable, the instructor may assign that client the duty of remaining with the farrier, hay delivery person or vet while the instructor continues teaching a class or session nearby. Through these types of carefully created situations the client begins to put into practice social skills that will be directly useful in daily life.[595]

Occasionally, dependant upon how involved the program or instructor is with the client, the parent, school counselor, or social worker will approach the instructor to help the client prepare for an important social exchange, such as an upcoming job interview. If this occurs, the instructor will generally speak directly with the client about this upcoming event, and structure activities with the horses that help coach and guide the client to a deeper understanding of the event, and teach the necessary skills that apply. Through this process the client may become more comfortable and open discussing socially-related issues and the client and the instructor may be able to tailor sessions to meet specific needs identified by the client.[596]

Communication Skills
Many EFL clients struggle with nuances of communication like non-verbal cues, tone of voice, or choice of words. In many cases the interpersonal relationships between EFL clients and those around them can be damaged or impeded due to these challenges.[597] EFL teaches clients how to recognize non-verbal cues and notice such subtleties as tone of voice. In working with horses, creatures who are physically

large and thoroughly expressive, but who utilize their non-verbal communication skills more than any other form of communication, the clients are able to recognize what non-verbal cues actually are. It is hard to overlook a large horse pinning his ears when another horse approaches the hay pile. The EFL client then observes what happens when the horse ignores the non-verbal communication and continues approaching the hay pile. This interaction helps the client to begin thinking about possible times when he/she has had someone "pin their ears" to convey a message. In many cases the client will assume that he/she was "kicked" without any provocation or warning.[598] These types of communication mishaps may have caused the client to become wary or afraid of trying to engage in a relationship with others. Once the client sees the horse clearly pinning his ears well before kicking out at the other horse, situations from the past take on new meaning. The client may be able to remember a warning sign given to him/her before the "kick" actually came. Once the client can begin to identify non-verbal cues, he/she can start practicing a different sort of awareness when in communications with others. Furthermore, it may help the client stop carrying anger and fear into his/her relationships, and this in and of itself opens new doors for friendships to occur.

The EFL client can also be taught how to adjust tone of voice to become congruent with the message he or she is attempting to convey. In many cases an EFL client will struggle in communications with others because his/her tone of voice does not match the message that is desired. Therefore, confusion occurs between the client and whomever it is that he/she is trying to converse with. This confusion tends to lead back to feelings of frustration, isolation, and loneliness, creating another rift between the client and "normal" society.[599] In working with the horses EFL clients may shout at the horse to calm down, or mumble quietly if they desire the horse to move more quickly. They might sound angry when really they are scared, or aggressive when they want to form a friendship. This sort of incongruence may throw off potential friends, and can create unhealthy confusion between speakers.[600] In an EFL session a client will be taught how to adjust his or her tone of voice to match whatever feeling he/she is attempting to convey. Generally once the client has changed his/her tone of voice, the horse will respond in much the same manner as the client had hoped for, calming down when the tone of voice is soothing, or moving more quickly or responding when the voice is assertive and directive.

As the client forms relationships with both the horses and the EFL staff, conversations can be had about the client's choice of words. For instance, many EFL clients will use harsh language or confusing words to attempt to communicate a thought or point, or they might attempt to snow the instructor with all of the right words, hoping to keep the instructor at arm's length. In many cases an EFL client has had little practice with true friendship, and may feel isolated and alone in the world. EFL clients might be highly manipulative, appearing functional but hiding behind a mask that is only as deep as an image, or they may be unable to create a mask and therefore show all feelings and thoughts without the ability to screen for appropriateness. In either case, these factors tend to make deep and long lasting relationships challenging.[601] Therefore, an EFL client may not have had the experience of someone who cares deeply for them and is not their parent, actually confronting them regarding their use of words, language, or the topics of conversation that they choose. Within the context of relationship, the EFL instructor may have the opportunity to bring to light maladaptive choices without creating anger and distance. If the client has connected deeply with a certain horse, but continues to use communication skills that are harsh, manipulative or not based in reality, the EFL instructor can use the relationship between the client and the horse to begin addressing these malfunctions. The client may be more inclined to listen because the relationship is so important to him/her. Furthermore, if the EFL instructor has also formed a close relationship with the client, hearing hard information can be made much easier. The EFL instructor can use examples based in the here and now of an EFL session, and therefore can help the client actually see how his choice of words, content of conversation or other communication methods impacted another living, breathing creature.

Learning Skills
Many EFL clients are those who struggle with learning challenges. Although the origin of these difficulties may differ between clients, the reality that these challenges do exist remains the same. In many cases these learning differences or difficulties have caused or perpetuated

the other, more obvious, dysfunctional tendencies. Therefore, when attempting to help an individual gain necessary life skills it is essential to understand if a learning difficulty does exist, what is being done to address the situation in the rest of the client's life, and then create a plan for the EFL service that helps address the learning issue. Many programs providing an EFL service go as far as to bring key components of the student's schooling into the barn. For instance, if the student is struggling with mathematical concepts, the teacher may work in conjunction with the EFL instructor to create a lesson plan that addresses these math-related issues. Math will appear in interesting places, all of course related to horses and their general care and well being. Lessons are created that target the missing skill set, and address the learning difficulties.[602]

In order for this to successfully occur, the EFL instructor should be trained, educated, and experienced in learning differences, teaching techniques to help students work through such difficulties, and should be able to convert such traditional knowledge to the work with horses.[603]

Study skills and concentration skills may present issues for the clients within their traditional education setting. If this is the case, the EFL instructor can tailor sessions to include the practice of doing homework, learning new information while at home, or concentrating upon a task for increasing periods of time. Generally, because the client is invested in his/her relationship with the horse and fascinated by anything having to do with horses, the process of studying or learning something new about horses comes easily, and clients tend to engage more fully when the information is something that they are passionate about. The EFL instructor can work with this dynamic, giving the client increasingly more challenging and less directly horse-related topics to research.[604] Over time the client may gain a new-found sense of discipline for the process of studying, and it becomes more habitual for them.

Concentration skills are fundamentally instilled within an EFL session, as without concentration and focus, EFL can be dangerous. Clients learn that their ability to participate fully will be compromised by endangering themselves.[605] They tend to put a great deal of energy and effort into concentration and focus if it becomes clear that this is necessary to get whatever it is that they desire. For instance, if the client is invested in learning to ride independently, and the instructor has created a set of tangible objectives that must be met before that is to occur, and focus/concentration is top on the list of objectives, the client generally finds a way to remain focused and concentrated upon the task at hand. As this becomes a practice, something that one does repeatedly over time, it becomes increasingly easier to achieve a sense of focus and concentration. EFL clients tend to report that through working with horses their ability to focus and concentrate improves drastically, even allowing some of them to discontinue ADD/ADHD medications and retain significantly improved grade point averages.[606]

Work Ethic
Occasionally EFL clients will present with issues involving an inability to maintain employment, such as challenges with consistency, follow through, following directions, or general comprehension regarding the necessity for other such work related skills. These might be individuals who have attempted to obtain and maintain employment in the past, or whose parents feel that obtaining and maintaining a job may be a challenge in the future due to either a lack of functional skills, or a lack of motivation or comprehension.[607]

When relationships form between humans and horses the humans generally come to realize the complexities of caring for horses. It becomes quickly apparent that having horses in one's life is work, although for the average horse lover that work is enjoyable and worth every second. When clients enter into a relationship with a horse, the instructor can begin sharing knowledge and information with the client about how to care for "their" horse. The client tends to feel connection, intimacy, and even love for his/her horse, and thus generally takes an active interest in all things that go on for or with that horse.[608] The instructor can begin the process of teaching work ethic through the introduction of simple chores assigned to the client that directly connect to the well-being of his/her horse. The instructor will be careful to assign initial tasks that provide measurable and obvious success for the client, tasks that he or she can accomplish and feel good about doing. In many cases these tasks only require a short time commitment, although such tasks should be planned to provide a small degree of challenge for the client in regards to concentration and focus. Once the client becomes comfortable with the first task or set of tasks, the instructor can begin incrementally increasing the level of challenge. Finally, once the client has successfully been able to demonstrate over a lengthy period of time that he/she is able to accomplish all tasks set before him/her, the instructor can begin addressing skills that are pointed more clearly towards everyday work-related duties. In this manner the client is guided and assisted towards success at all levels of the process, never feeling as through a task was impossible to complete, or too complex to understand.

Role of the Horse

In an EFL session the horse is generally considered either a co-facilitator or an employee. This indicates that either the horse initiates certain activities or adds different nuances to already existing activities, or cooperates with whatever activity the instructor has created. It is a goal of EFL sessions that the client forms a close and long lasting relationship with the horse of his/her choosing. Therefore, the instructor should support the horse's decision in regards to with whom he/she would like to work.

In EFL a horse should not be forced to work with a client with whom he/she is obviously uncomfortable or dislikes. It is important to remember that this service is not counseling, psychotherapy, or psychological in nature, and thus pairing a client with a horse who does not trust, like, or connect with that client could bring up more deeply psychological issues than are appropriate for the setting.[609] There are many other ways to help an EFL client gain useful information about working through challenging situations and learning life skills without having to trigger possibly deeply emotional issues that stem from a lack of acceptance, love, or other such failures that a client may have experienced.

The EFL horse should be gentle, compassionate, and tolerant. There are many horses for whom the work of EFL is not appropriate. The disposition of the horse, and his or her mental and physical stability should be taken into serious consideration before exposing him/her to an EFL population. In many cases the EFL population is the most challenging for horses, and thus it takes a special type of horse who enjoys the work and can remain healthy. EFL horses may need more time off and a more diverse exercise schedule than other EFMH/ES horses. The barn manager should ensure that these two factors can be provided before supporting the decision to provide an EFL program.[610]

Role of the Instructor

An EFL instructor should be trained, educated, and experienced in a multitude of disciplines. First, he or she should have undergone training and formal schooling as an educator, familiar with the issues of special needs populations. Secondly, he or she should have additional training and education in counseling and psychology, and depending upon the population he or she intends to serve, have an emphasis in either child/adolescent psychology or psychopathology. Thirdly, as with all EFMH/ES professionals, he or she should be well-versed in this specific method and have a solid background with horses. The needs of an EFL instructor indicate that he/she should be able to teach classes in equine nutrition, care, and behavior, as well as technical horse-person skills. Therefore, the EFL instructor must be competent, educated, and practiced in these areas.[611]

Generally volunteers are used within an EFL session, and therefore the instructor needs to be trained and skilled in how to educate, support, and manage a volunteer staff. During an EFL session the instructor generally sets up and facilitates the activities or lessons with the support of the volunteers who assist clients in the application of the material taught. In many cases the EFL instructor moves between clients (if it is a group setting) to observe, provide further instruction, and maintain the general safety of the entire process. Volunteers are paired with clients and are responsible for maintaining the physical safety of that individual client and horse team. Depending upon the severity of the issues of the clientele, multiple volunteers might be used per client. In some cases the instructor would set up a team of one horse, a horse handler and two client support staff. In other cases if the client is high-functioning, the team might only consist of the horse, the client, and one support staff.[612]

The EFL instructor generally uses a strengths-based approach to help the clients experience success without re-traumatization of past failures. The EFL instructor would be cautioned not to set up a situation as a "teachable moment" that re-created a past failure. The instructor usually seeks to create situations that affirm for the client that they are lovable, and that people/creatures can and do care deeply for them. This is why it is important that the client and the horse mutually chose each other. The EFL instructor tends to believe that it is through compassion, caring, respect, and increasing experience with success that clients learn most successfully.[613]

The EFL instructor should clearly understand the difference between the service that he/she provides and a counseling, psychotherapy, or psychological service. They should be adept at the referral process, and understand what type of service is best suited for what populations. If, through the process of EFL, a client gains the ability to move into more insight-based process work, the EFL instructor should refer that client to either an EFP or EFC service or provider.

Practice

Team Approach

EFL is a service that is generally used in conjunction with a wide array of other services. In most cases EFL is not a stand-alone service. Therefore, EFL utilizes a team approach which means that the instructor will need to collaborate with individuals such as volunteers, mental health providers, social workers, parents, school staff, mentors, and any others who work routinely with the client.[614] The EFL instructor should be knowledgeable about all of the other services that the client is receiving outside of the EFL service, gain signed release of information statements, and encourage cooperation and collaboration between all entities. Without such an approach the results of EFL cannot be accurately measured, nor the objectives of the client's plan appropriately adjusted. The majority of the EFL goals revolve around a client becoming more successful in his or her daily life and if the EFL instructor has limited connections to the others involved in the client's life, it is nearly impossible to determine if goals and objectives have been met.

The client should be made aware of this team approach at the onset of the EFL service. Depending upon the functionality of the client, and the legalities surrounding guardianship due to either functionality or age, the client may or may not be given a choice as to whether or not this team approach is acceptable to him or her. In some cases, if the client is more high-functioning, he or she should be made a part of the team. Regardless of the functionality of the client, he or she should be empowered to take part as much as possible in the creation of goals and objectives for the service.[615]

Compliance with IEP's, Treatment Plans, Structured Goals

The EFL instructor should be competent and knowledgeable in regards to Individual Education Plans (IEP's). The instructor should understand the language used in such plans and be able to create lessons with the horses that integrate appropriate goals and objectives that are presented in such a plan. The EFL instructor should feel comfortable sitting in an IEP meeting, and presenting the progress or lack there of made by the client in the EFL service in regards to the IEP goals and objectives.[616]

The EFL instructor should also be able to demonstrate competency in regards to the implementation of a program that deals with specific goals and objectives. EFL clients tend to do well with structured goals, and less well with loosely defined, unclear or intangible goals.[617]

EFL instructors may also need to understand specific components of a therapeutic treatment plan. In many cases EFL will be used in conjunction with a treatment plan to address behavioral or life skills based issues. The EFL instructor must be competent and knowledgeable in regards to the language used in treatment plans, and able to demonstrate a tangible application of that knowledge in the form of specific lesson plans and goals and objectives that target behavioral or life skills issues.

The Learning Plan

The EFL instructor should create and maintain with the help and input of all appropriate parties, a learning plan that details the goals and objectives for each individual client's EFL service. This plan generally includes any of the IEP goals or objectives that are applicable, as well as any life skills goals that are deemed appropriate. This plan should include only tangible, measurable, and accomplishable goals and objectives. This plan should be made available to the client, and with the permission of the client, to parents and other appropriate parties. It is suggested that the EFL instructor facilitate regular monthly meetings during which the progress of the client is discussed with the team, which may or may not include the client, depending upon his/her functionality. The EFL service should be monitored for success, and the instructor should provide the team with tangible results from services rendered.

Method Example

This example comes from the Esperanza Center and is provided by this author.

Susan, an eight-year old female was referred to the Esperanza Center to address her learning disabilities, attachment disorder, and her lack of age appropriate behaviors. Upon arrival at the Esperanza Center it was noted that Susan communicated and acted approximately four to five years behind her biological age. She presented as a timid and shy young lady with limited ability to express her thoughts and feelings. In the home it was reported that Susan had multiple breakdowns where she would scream and physically attack her adoptive parents. She struggled to remember multiple directions and showed difficulty responding to written instructions. The Esperanza Center staff met with her school teachers, her counselor, and her parents to formulate a learning plan for Susan. Once in place, the staff began interweaving Susan's learning goals (following multiple directions, responding to written and verbal directions, and addressing math issues) into her work with horses. In the beginning it was difficult for Susan to follow one directive without constant reminders and assistance. Her sense of self-esteem and self-confidence was low and her verbal and non-verbal skills appeared impaired. After approximately six months of services Susan is now able to follow multiple directions without prompting or assistance. She is able to tack up her horse all by herself and is able to ride without assistance through a pre-memorized obstacle course which might include math problems as a component. She speaks and acts in an age-appropriate manner, and her parents report a significant change in her behaviors and responses at home – she is able to use her language to get her needs met and has shown improvement in mood control and a decrease in manipulative behaviors. All of this was accomplished through teaching Susan how to be with horses in a safe and respectful manner. Almost none of the work with Susan has been through verbal acknowledgment of insights gained. Rather, Susan's changes in behavior while with the horses is transferred (through carefully planned activities) to her home life and her emotional life *without ever having to talk about it.*

Summary

Although EFL may provide services to a therapeutic population, it is not a mental health service. It is important for the EFL instructor to be highly educated, trained, and experienced prior to providing such a service. The instructor must understand the differences between EFL and mental health services, and refer to the appropriate professional if an EFL client appears in need of additional mental health services.

In order for EFL to be successful, the instructor must be able to create lesson plans that work within pre-existing IEP's or treatment plans, and must demonstrate the ability to set and work within structured, measurable, and tangible goals and objectives.

EFL is a success and strength-based method and does not utilize any techniques that might re-create past failures. EFL is focused on the here and now, and encourages the process of new learning regarding life and social skills. It is within the relationship between the client and the horse that life lessons are learned.

The main goal of EFL is to help clients become more functional in daily life. Objectives that might be addressed within an EFL session could include aspects of communication skills, social skills, learning skills or work ethic. EFL clients may or may not be an active part of the team approach depending upon their functionality, but will be included to any degree possible.

Chapter Seventeen

Equine Assisted Education

Introduction

Equine Assisted Education (EAE) is an educational method of EFE/L that is used to enhance already existing educational endeavors. EAE occurs within both alternative and traditional educational institutions and promotes a deeper understanding of the subject matter being taught.

EAE evolved from a course taught by Barbara Rector, Jack Staddacker, and Paul Smith at Prescott College in Prescott, Arizona in 1998. In 2000 Paul Smith and Marie Sonnett co-taught a course in Relational Horsemanship also at Prescott College and in 2002 the concept of working with horses in an educational setting continued to evolve with the introduction of an equine-based Group Process for Adventure Educators course taught by Paul Smith and this author. Prescott College's Adventure Education students learned group facilitation skills through their interaction with horses. From this course Paul Smith, Barbara Rector, Laura Brinkerhoff, Doug Mann, and John Dooley developed Prescott College's Master's Degree in Counseling/ Psychology with an Emphasis in Equine Assisted Mental Health.[618]

EAE is designed specifically to work with a functional population of school students. The students who participate in an EAE service can come from elementary schools, high schools, or colleges. EAE maintains its educational parameters by concentrating on skills and team building initiatives, not on personal reflection from experiencing a therapeutic process. If during an EAE activity a student is triggered into a personal process that could place the instructor in a position to violate his or her scope of practice, the instructor should defuse and stabilize the immediate situation and then refer the student to the appropriate mental health service.

During the process of EAE if it becomes clear to the instructor that a student is unfit or inappropriate for the service, he or she should recommend that the student seek an EFP or EFC service before attempting to complete the course. EAE is not a mental health service, nor should it be facilitated as if it were one. Students who are appropriate for an EAE experience are those who are relatively emotionally stable and who have no current mental health diagnosis that is untreated. In some cases students with a mental health diagnosis, but who are receiving treatment may be successful within an EAE setting. However, the EAE instructor should be aware of the diagnosis and be prepared to help the student stabilize and obtain proper assistance if any of the interactions or activities trigger deeper personal issues.[619]

Educational Objectives

Teamwork and Cooperation Skills Building
Merriam-Webster Dictionary defines teamwork as, "work done by several associates with each doing a part but all subordinating personal prominence to the efficiency of the whole."[620] In many educational institutions, teachers and administrators are beginning to see the value of creating a learning atmosphere that is structured around a team approach. In today's business world the notion of teamwork is highly valued and in many cases it is expected that employees are able to work in a team or in a team-motivated environment. Therefore, it seems logical that team-building should be taught as early as possible, making the transition from school to work smoother and less stressful for the average American. In other cases the concept of teamwork is used to help ease relational struggles between students who spend a great deal of time together, and may engage in negative behaviors towards one another. Teamwork in that context helps students to develop skills such as compassion, empathy, and understanding. Teamwork also promotes listening and communication skills, and allows students to begin learning the art of relational skills.[621]

EAE can be used within a school or educational setting to create an atmosphere that reflects back to students and educators alike how successful the attempts at instilling teamwork are. Then EAE can be used to hone those skills through interactive games and activities. EAE can be highly successful because of the unusual addition of a large, living, breathing, creature- the horse. In many cases students who are struggling with one another may find it easier to bond and connect and reach to achieve a common goal if there is something outside of the group that fosters that sense of connection. The horse not only serves as a distraction but offers kindness and compassion and inspires students to soften. As this process happens the educator may watch as the bully of the class sees the way in which the horse herd treats the bully within the herd. Suddenly it becomes clear that people do not respect bullies but rather move away from them out of fear and dislike. The bully may come to realize that his or her behaviors are impeding the potential success of the group as a whole, and may cease his/her behaviors once the other members of the group point out the subversive nature of his/her actions. In other cases the class may struggle with interpersonal dynamics that are impeding the ability to learn important or necessary information. If this happens it may be useful to expose the class as a group to a series of activities from which they can make both personal and group observations about their functioning, and through these observations change may occur.

The word cooperate is defined by Merriam-Webster Dictionary as, "to act or work with another or others" or "to associate with another or others for mutual benefit."[622] Within the work of EAE students are taught how to work cooperatively with one another to achieve a common goal. This concept can be used in many different settings outside of an educational institution, from meeting work place goals and objectives to creating and maintaining healthful relationships with others. Students who learn cooperation skills-building learn how to successfully negotiate difficult situations with an outcome of a win-win situation for all involved. Cooperation skills also hone communication skills and teach students more effective and healthful ways to present themselves to the world around them. Through work with horses students gain a personal perspective regarding how they impact others in their lives and how challenging life is without cooperation and team building skills.

Cohesion

Merriam-Webster Dictionary defines cohesion as, "the act or state of sticking together tightly."[623] In experientially-based education programs where skills are taught such as rock climbing, white water rafting, or other adventure sports, the concept of cohesion becomes more than a team initiative, it becomes a safety issue. If a group of students is out on an adventure-based trip and has not achieved a state of cohesion, the risk for accidents is higher. Individuals look out for themselves rather than looking out for the good of the group.

The work of EAE offers the horse herd dynamic as a model that students can witness and observe thereby learning what cohesion can look like within a group. EAE also provides provocative activities that can help hone the group's sense of cohesion.

Facilitation, Leadership, or Therapeutic Skills Training

In many fields of study students must learn facilitation, leadership, or therapeutic skills in order to successfully complete their chosen degree. Generally they are taught such skills first in the classroom and are then asked to demonstrate those skills using role plays with other students. Occasionally transference and counter-transference may occur between peers as they attempt to practice such skills with one another. This can lead to unhealthy situations that are counter-productive to the goal of the class. The student's may come out of the experience focused more on the peer interactions that arose due to the dynamics of the role play and less on the actual skill set that they were supposed to be learning. From the classroom the next step is generally an internship or practicum in which the student is expected to utilize the skills learned in the classroom with actual clients (or students depending upon the degree). In many cases the student feels unprepared for such interactions, and may respond with a variety of coping mechanisms which may prove ineffectual with the clientele, leading to a decrease in self-confidence within the student.

With the introduction of EAE, students are able to practice facilitation, leadership, and communication skills, and develop counseling skills such as empathy, authenticity, respect, and confrontation within the safe container of the horse/human relationship. The horses reflect back to the students how successfully they implemented the skill or skill set.

The student can readjust the skill and try again, and if the skill was executed congruently, the horse will respond accordingly. For instance, a business management student may be struggling with leadership styles. In an EAE session that student may be given the assignment of asking his/her horse to move over a series of obstacles. The instructor will suggest that the student choose a leadership or management style that he/she has been struggling with and use that style to attempt to get the horse to move through the obstacles. Either the student will utilize the style in such a way that the horse feels comfortable and confident to move through the obstacles under the direction of the student, or the horse will refuse to do as the student asks. Through this simple exercise the student can begin honing his or her style, and may even choose to learn a new or different approach to leadership or management. The student can practice the skills multiple times over a few months until he or she feels confident and comfortable with the style before ever having to interact with other humans. Once the student feels ready, and the instructor feels he or she is ready, the student can then move into practice with other humans. This approach has two distinct benefits.

First, as already mentioned, when students attempt to practice facilitation, leadership, or therapeutic skills on one another transference and counter-transference can occur, along with the development of unhealthful group or interpersonal dynamics. People will assume roles in an attempt to practice skills that are unhealthy for both themselves and the individual they are trying to work with. Role plays can quickly become personal and lose the original purpose. Personal issues can arise when individuals attempts to practice facilitation, leadership, or therapeutic skills on another, and unethical or unhealthful dynamics can emerge out of this confusion of roles and relationships. EAE removes this entire dynamic, leaving the student to go through a process of trial and error without involving another human being who may become emotionally involved in the role play. Students can witness each others process with the horses, but can remain at a personal distance that helps avoid transference and counter-transference.

Second, when students attempt to practice skills on each other it can be hard to take the scenarios seriously. In many cases students will act unprofessionally because of the discomfort of trying to direct a peer, or will consider the activity to be silly or unimportant, therefore they will not use the actual skills needed to accomplish the desired task. With the introduction of horses, the concepts become real and tangible. The student is asked to perform a task with his/her horse and in order to accomplish this task, must use the skills he or she learned in class. The student tends to become immersed in the seriousness of the activity, such as trying to move a horse to a specific location without using his or her most common leadership style, but rather using one that feels foreign. The feeling of accomplishment or failure becomes real and valuable for the student, and creates the desire to learn more to increase the likelihood for future success.

Students learn concepts such as compassion, empathy, problem solving, time management, and congruent communication skills through their work with horses. Rather than just studying these skills in a book students are able to experience them first hand, and see the benefits of using such concepts. Students learn how to slow down and really listen to those around them, and take the time to ensure that a task is accomplished fully. They also learn the necessity of intention, planning, organization, and rhythm in regards to human interactions, be they group or individual. They realize that without intentionally preparing for the next step clients or students may feel confused and unclear as to what is wanted of them, and may react with anger, frustration, or confusion. Students learn the importance of self-care and listening to intuition and instinct. They learn how to become present in their own bodies and proceed forward from a centered and prepared stance. To learn these skills with horses before ever having to practice them with other humans is invaluable for students and increases the general success that they have when they do begin working with other humans. Using EAE in educational settings to teach these types of skills could provide many with a more positive learning environment, and prepare them more fully for the work that they intend to do upon graduation.

Role of the Horse

Within an EAE service the horse does "assist" the instructor and the student by providing tangible reflective information about a student's style of leadership, facilitation, or therapeutic skills. However, it is generally the instructor who creates the activities thereby insuring that the students are targeting appropriate skill sets. Since the service is educational and is condensed to the length of a class, it is appropriate that the instructor guide and direct the service, not the horse. If the horse were to guide and direct the service, it might become quickly therapeutic or open doors to deeply personal insight and process. The instructor must control the environment closely to ensure that he or she remains within his/her scope of practice, and does not allow the session to descend into deeply personal material. Therefore, the horse should follow the lead of the instructor. However, the horse should feel comfortable reflecting information back to the student within the context of the activity, and should be viewed as a respected and much cared for being whose information is necessary and useful.

The horses assume the role of the client or student and use reflective feedback to demonstrate how the leadership, facilitation, or therapeutic style of the learner is effecting or impacting them.

Role of the Instructor

The instructor within an EAE service could be either an educator who is employed by an educational institution but who is specifically trained and experienced in this method, or an individual who contracts with an educational institution to provide services. Either way, the instructor should be educated, trained, and experienced in providing this method and should work closely with the primary educator or institution to ensure that appropriate goals are being set and met. The instructor should understand such concepts as group facilitation and group dynamics, therapeutic skills, bedside manner, and leadership or management skills. If the instructor is not trained and educated in one of these areas, he or she should not provide an EAE service that suggests the teaching of such skills. The instructor should also be trained and educated in team-building, cooperation, and cohesion skills building, and should be a competent and experienced facilitator.

The EAE instructor should be experienced in creating and maintaining a referral process for students who may become triggered by the work, and be trained in stabilization and de-escalation techniques. The instructor should be able to screen students appropriately for the service, and be comfortable and prepared to refer students when needed. The instructor should work closely with a properly certified and licensed mental health professional to help create the screening and referral process.

Practice

Collaboration with an Educational Institution
Communication and collaboration between the EAE program and the educational institution is necessary for EAE to be successful. If an outside instructor is hired to provide an EAE service, he or she should develop the program based upon the goals and objectives specifically stated by the institution, primary educator, or other school official. In creating contracts with an educational institution to provide an EAE service it is important to have a designated and dedicated contact person who will work closely with the EAE instructor to ensure that goals and objectives are designed to fit the actual needs of the classroom, course, or group of students. It is beneficial if that individual also participates to some degree in the EAE programming so that he or she is able to report upon the progress of goals and objectives and utilize the experience within the classroom or course setting.

Educational Credits for Participation
In most cases educational credit is provided for an EAE service. Either the course becomes a part of a required class, such as in a college setting, or becomes a part of required attendance, such as in an elementary, middle, or high school setting. It is important that the EAE instructor understands such concepts as attendance, grading policies, testing or other evaluation necessities, and written assignment requirements and has come to an agreement with the educational institution as to how such matters will be handled within the EAE program.

It is suggested that the EAE instructor design the program to compliment the curriculum component from which students are obtaining credit. For instance, if the students are gaining science credit for an EAE program, then the EAE instructor could include aspects of environmental science, equine science, or other related subjects. EAE instructors generally create curriculum that includes both a classroom or lecture component and a hands-on component. EAE provides both education and team-building so EAE instructors may have to work with the educational institution to determine how credits are awarded for such activities.

Educational Example (s)

Phoebe Robinson, "Horses in Adventure Education" - Prescott College

What do horses have to do with Adventure Education? How could a class called Group Process for Adventure Educators incorporate horses into a facilitative learning experience? These questions were common in the first few days of January as 12 Prescott College students prepared to spend a month of intensive work with a special group. Suzy, Shawnee, Max, Titan, Skip, Cloud, Excel, Angel, and Scarlet were to be an extension of our group for the course, while at the same time taking on the role of teachers and guides in the art of facilitation. These ten additions added a whole new dimension of learning, one intended to provide our "human" group with the skills necessary to facilitate others.

"Working with this group of horses has given me a new perspective on the different types of people I will be working with in the future," said Maggie O'Brien. Establishing rapport, pacing, leading, framing and re-framing all became meaningful terms as we practiced with the horses.

Over the course a lot of what we learned was about ourselves, how we deal with challenging situations, our leadership styles, and how we come across to others. Ally found that her presence affected the horses, "I feel that I am more aware of my presence (or lack of presence). I need to focus, communicate and then clarify. The process is made very clear and simple, lead a horse - lead a group." Adam said, "I found myself paying attention to my voice tones. I've learned how my intention with the horses needs to be clear and how that relates back to being a leader." Meghan said, "I was put face to face with a lot of my fears of what a group will do, not pay attention, run away, be afraid. I got to witness and practice ways to cope with those situations on a population (horses) that is more forgiving than people."

As the month of working with the group of horses drew to a close, we all agreed the course had been extremely successful. Robyn Bryers summed up a common sentiment by saying, "I think that if horses were incorporated into Experiential and Adventure Education people would gain a more clear perspective of how people work. Instead of having to imagine scenarios or create them you just work with the horses and they give a perfect scenario right in front of you. Working with horses helps in so many ways, no only to build your confidence but to learn valuable lessons that can be applied to everything and everyone." -Phoebe Robinson

Montessori School Program - Provided By Esperanza

Esperanza contracted with a south-central Phoenix, Arizona, Montessori school program that co-existed within a traditional middle school setting. The population was primarily Mexican-American with English spoken as a second language. The EAE program was designed by Esperanza's program director and the school teacher of the class that would be attending the EAE service. The program included three days of experiential education every three months for an entire school year and included aspects of EAE, nature-based services such as kayaking, hiking, basic concepts of rock climbing, and experiential education including "leave no trace" camping, challenge course services, and environmental education. The class population totaled twenty-one students and upon arrival on location, these students were divided into groups of appropriate size dependent upon the activity. For the EAE component one third of the students participated in the EAE activities while the other two-thirds participated in nature-based and environmental science activities at the same location. Therefore we were able to keep the numbers of students interacting with the horses low. Students learned basic horsemanship skills such as meeting and greeting, safely moving around horses, catching, leading, tying, grooming, mounting and dismounting, emergency dismounts, other emergency procedures, and finally basic riding instruction at the walk. Educational games and interactive experiences were created to both educate students about horses, and also to promote teamwork, trust, and communication skills - the personal growth goals of the primary educator. Students were given handouts while at Esperanza that detailed components of the lessons taught, and were given homework assignments to be completed between sessions. These homework assignments were graded by Esperanza staff and returned to the primary teacher. When the students were not at Esperanza the primary teacher used examples from their last session to highlight educational concepts, deal with classroom disturbances, or work with individual student conflicts. Prior to attending a session the primary teacher and the Esperanza staff would meet to discuss any changes or issues that may have arisen between sessions and the staff would prepare activities and group students according to the teacher's needs or recommendations. In this way the learning that occurred while at Esperanza was able to be transferred back into the classroom and the teacher felt supported by Esperanza staff to help address interpersonal and classroom goals. Both the teacher and the students alike found the EAE program to be highly successful and reported noticing a distinct change in the functionality and cohesion of the class over the course of the year.

Summary

EAE appears to be an interesting and potentially viable way of teaching students important skills such as facilitation, teamwork, cohesion, self-awareness, sensitivity, and a myriad of communication skills which support their learning process and may help them to be more successful in future employment endeavors. EAE is rapidly attracting the attention of educational institutions across the United States. From work with horses in nursing and pre-med programs to the introduction of horses in experiential education programs, horses seem to be finding their way into our elementary schools, high schools, and colleges.

CHAPTER EIGHTEEN

EQUINE FACILITATED PROFESSIONAL COACHING

Introduction

Equine Facilitated Professional Coaching (EFPC) is defined as a triad relationship between the coach(s), the specially selected horse(s), and the client(s). It incorporates a mind-body-spirit awareness process that encourages the client to maximize his/her personal and professional potential. EFPC is ideal for corporate or professional clients and teams.[624] EFPC is an adaptation used by professional coaches. In order to understand the EFPC method, it is important to first gain a basic understanding regarding the field of professional coaching. Coaching is defined by the Professional Coaches and Mentors Association as:

> Partnering with clients in a thought-provoking and creative process that inspires them to maximize their personal and professional potential. Coaching is an ongoing relationship which focuses on clients taking action toward the realization of their visions, goals or desires. Coaching uses a process of inquiry and personal discovery to build the client's level of awareness and responsibility and provides the client with structure, support and feedback. The coaching process helps clients both define and achieve professional and personal goals faster and with more ease than would be possible otherwise.[625]

Those within the field of coaching consider professional and life coaching a personal growth method and adamantly feel that it is not a mental health service. It is suggested that professional coaching services focus on an individual's life as it relates to goal setting, outcome creation and personal change management, but does not focus upon or address psychological or pathological reasons that might create such issues. Another distinction that those within the field of coaching make between a coaching service and a mental health service is that coaches do not work with clients who have persisting mental health issues, but rather they engage only with those who are considered "well" or "high-functioning". Furthermore, it appears that if a coach encounters a client whose issues verge into a mental health realm, the client is referred out to a counselor or other mental health professional for services."[626]

According to Zeus and Skiffington authors of *The Complete Guide to Coaching at Work,* coaching is a productive results-oriented dialogue.[627] T.W. Gallway, in *The Inner Game of Work,* describes coaching as an avenue for incorporating a non-judgmental focus and providing appropriate opportunity for natural learning. Those providing a professional or life coaching service view their clients as healthy, functional human beings who are capable of personal awareness, growth, and change.[628]

The field of professional coaching has grown rapidly due to recent corporate adjustments. Down-sizing, restructuring, mergers and other organizational changes have radically altered the workplace milieu making more agile workplaces a necessity. There is organizational unrest as people wrestle with fears around job insecurity and struggle with the pressures of workplace performance. Coaching helps companies to develop inclusive, collaborative work environments which help to achieve strategic business goals. Coaching also helps individuals within corporations make vocational decisions during times of personal challenge and organizational change.[629]

According to Datamation Reporting, the following are professional and personal reasons why coaches are hired: (1) Desire to succeed, (2) Create positive change, (3) Deal with overload, (4) Get rid of what is dragging one down, (5) Acquire new skills and competencies, (6) Find more joy outside of work, (7) Integrate various parts of one's life, (8) Take oneself more seriously, and (9) Set better personal goals.[630]

Currently, the coaching field is undergoing a process similar to the field of EFMH/ES. Coaching is not governed by any state or national certification or licensure board(s) and therefore anyone wishing to provide the service can do so with no educational requirements, state or national licensure or certification. However, as with EFMH/ES, membership organizations and certification organizations have been created to provide support, training, and certification for those interested in pursuing a career in the field.[631]

The International Coach Federation (ICF) is one such membership organization that provides support and resources for coaching. ICF is "The largest worldwide resource for business and personal coaches, and the source for those who are seeking a coach". IFC defines itself as "A nonprofit, individual membership organization formed by professionals worldwide who practice business and personal coaching".[632]

The International Association of Coaching (IAC) is another such organization that provides training and certification. IAC is "An independent, global coach certifying body". IAC's mission is "To inspire the on-going evolution and application of universal coaching standards. Our rigorous certification process evaluates the demonstration of specific proficiencies that are the hallmark of the most effective and distinguished coaches, as well as sets high standards for the coach's ethical, professional, and business behaviors. The purpose of this standard is to provide the clients of coaches a valid measure of assurance that they will receive the best coaching."[633]

IAC trains and tests potential coaches on what they call the "15 Proficiencies" which demonstrate that the coach can: "Engage in provocative conversation, reveal the client to themselves, elicit greatness, enjoys the client immensely, expand the client's best efforts, navigates via curiosity, recognizes perfection in every situation, hones in on what is most important, communicates cleanly, shares what is there, champions the client, enters new territories, relishes truth, designs supportive environments, and respects the client's humanity."[634]

Although there still remains controversy between those in the mental health professions and those engaging in a coaching service as to whether or not the goals and objectives of coaching do merge into territory that once belonged solely to mental health professionals, for the purpose of this text we will assume that EFPC is done as a learning service that focuses on helping people with such goals as leadership and management skills, vocational decisions, and interpersonal skills utilized within the workplace. Within an EFPC format, the horse serves as the unique variable which can elevate the success of the coaching process. Results of the service depend upon the individual or the team's intentions, choices and actions, supported by the coach's efforts, and the horse's presence.

Dr. Ellen Gehrke, Ph.D and Sherri Petro, MBA have isolated four benefits of EFPC which distinguish it from alternative performance improvement processes. First, clients can develop new possibilities for more effective interactions in the workplace by observing the herd dynamics of horses and relating them to their own personal interactions. Second, they can discover their own impact as leaders and learn to develop a climate that is safe, productive and creative. Third, through the interaction with the coach and the horse the client develops a deeper connection to their own ability to be authentic regarding accountability to self and others. This results in an awareness of their personal energy and how they direct their energy. This is a critical and surprising aspect of the EFPC model. Fourth, the uniqueness of the model is that changes can be made in the moment and can result in noticeable changes in behavior after only a few sessions. Clients take ownership of their own destiny to be successful or not.[635]

EFPC appears to take the general objectives from traditional professional or life coaching and add the powerful presence of the horse who may provide a memorable catalyst for sustaining identified behavioral change.

Facilitation Objectives

Professional coaching sessions often focus on developing more effective leadership skills, improving the ability to communicate with others, and building more effective team relationships. The coach initially conducts an assessment of the needs of the client (s) and then designs EFPC sessions to include particular activities that provide opportunities for the clients to achieve their coaching objectives.

Leadership Development

The client(s) who engages in a coaching service may come to develop their leadership skills or learn new approaches to leadership or management. Observing and interacting with horses may allow them to experience the difference between leading with confidence utilizing a partnership model, or leading from fear and domination. The client is afforded the ability to process these insights and experiences within the group or individually with the facilitator, and can determine for themselves more effective ways to lead based on their interactions with the horses. In many cases this approach to teaching leadership has proven to positively affect the client's personal and business relationships.[636]

The coach assists the client in achieving this instructional objective by helping the client to identify and experience the impact their leadership approach had upon the horse. The horse assists in this process by remaining honest and authentic and providing a mirroring reaction to the client. The horse will generally respond to leadership that is authentic, respectful, and confident, but generally will not respond favorably if the client attempts to trick, cajole, manipulate, bribe or plead for the horse to follow or partner with them.[637]

Communication

Dr. Gehrke and Ms. Petro suggest that many EFPC clients have experienced considerable stress in their personal and professional lives. Their organization may be undergoing a merger, reorganization, or other company-wide change. In this time of high stress healthful communication is vital to the individual, the team and organization's future success. In working with horses, EFPC clients begin to learn how to recognize and utilize healthful communication. Dr. Gehrke and Ms. Petro suggest the following communication skills objectives for EFPC. (1) Assist the client in understanding the importance of delivering consistent information so that others experience the client as safe, supportive, clear and responsible for self and others. (2) Support the client in recognizing how the delivery of their communication reflects their ability to relate to others within their personal and professional relationships. (3) Teach the client the importance of clear and concise communication skills.[638]

Horses demand consistency, clarity, and self-responsibility. Through working with horses clients can practice these communication skills and learn how to transfer those skills to their professional lives.[639]

Team Development

Many professionals come to an EFPC session to learn how to create and sustain high performing teams which is an essential component of any organization's success. When teams are aligned, the organization runs more smoothly. With a shared framework, teams communicate more effectively and are more likely to focus on productively meeting their goals. EFPC activities for team-building often include activities that allow the client to recognize characteristics and behaviors that contribute to high performance teams. Dr. Gehrke and Ms. Petro suggest that EFPC: 1) Helps clients to develop more personally authentic approaches to working in team situations, 2) Helps team leaders observe the energetics of their team in regards to how they synchronize the tasks required of them and work in partnership with others outside of their immediate team, 3) Helps individual clients identify areas in which they can make improvements that will benefit the team as a whole, and 4) Helps team leaders and team members collaborate on the creation of a team action plan which will guide the direction of future team-oriented endeavors.[640]

Personal Development

Many people seek EFPC services because they want to discover ways to make lasting changes and gain deeper personal insights regarding what may be blocking or preventing forward movement in their lives. EFPC focuses on personal development which can include issues of stress management, creativity blocks, time management, building personal relationships within the work place that last, and learning how to balance their personal and professional life. Dr. Gehrke and Ms. Petro introduce five ways in which EFPC help clients move towards personal insight and success. (1) EFPC allows the client to learn how to live in the present moment. (2) EFPC helps clients gain an awareness about their own energy sources (draining, uplifting) and make decisions about how they allocate their energy both professionally and personally. (3) EFPC helps the client define their priorities in different areas of their life. (4) EFPC helps clients develop an action plan to manifest this newly experienced balance within both their vocation and their personal life.[641]

To accomplish the learning objectives for personal development, the coach needs to allow the clients to identify for themselves what is going on in their session with the horse. Sometimes deeper issues arise that might require counseling. In this situation, it is appropriate for the coach to refer the client to a counselor.

Role of Horse

In the work of EFPC, the horse is considered a partner. Dr. Gehrke suggests that consideration of the horse should always be first and foremost and the basic assumption about the horse in a coaching session is that the horse does nothing wrong. She believes strongly that all behavior and responses from the horse are natural and energetic, and provide important information for the coach to process with the client. For example, if a horse begins to drift or pull away during a session and the client pulls or tugs on them to make them stand still, this provides information about the client's leadership or management style that the coach can utilize in his or her work with the client. Ms. Gehrke believes that behavior such as this does not indicate the horse was "bad" and/or that the horse should be disciplined for his behavior. Dr. Gehrke reminds us that clients often realize through these interactions with the horse how their timing with other people is not synchronized. The client may recognize that his/her leadership style includes having to correct, pull, tug, and reprimand others to do what he/she wants. This type of realization tends to lead to an awareness about relational and leadership issues that transfers from success with the horse-human relationship to success in human-human relationships.[642]

The horse within an EFPC session appears to both provide reflective feedback and act as an employee, engaging the client in activities that help teach skills such as communication, leadership, and team building. The horses working within an EFPC method are generally allowed the flexibility to choose their human clients, and are encouraged to communicate information and reactions to those clients. EFPC horses are not usually forced into work related situations where the coach chooses the horses for the clients, or allows the client to do hands- on activities with a horse who obviously does not feel safe with that particular client. However, coaches will use interactions between horses and clients as "teachable moments" to help the client or clients see their impact on others around them. This does not necessitate the horse having to actively engage with the client if he or she is uncomfortable around that human being. It can occur from outside of the fence or from observation rather than hands-on experience.[643]

Many EFPC coaches appear to view their horses as partners and treat them accordingly. The horse/human relationship between the coach and his or her horses can help model for the client healthful, respectful leadership methods. Critical to EFPC is the recognition that horses are not tools, that they are living, breathing, feeling beings who have the ability to recognize and respond to the emotional field.[644]

Role of Coach

An EFPC coach should have training and education in a variety of areas. It is important for the coach to have formal academic training, ideally at a Master's level, in areas such as the behavioral sciences: psychology, organizational behavior, human development, or counseling. The coach should associate with a respected organization that oversees the field of coaching, and it is encouraged that they are certified and/or trained as a coach prior to providing a coaching service.[645]

It is critical that EFPC coaches are trained and educated to recognize issues that fall outside of the scope of the service that they provide. Horses may have the ability to elicit emotional responses within the clients who interact with them. This response can occur regardless of how careful the coach is, and how learning-based the service is. Therefore, an EFPC coach would do well to have a referral process strongly embedded in their normal practice and be prepared to refer clients to a mental health service if deeper issues arise. However, that being said, the EFPC coach must also understand how to de-escalate and diffuse emotionally charged situations, especially if they intend to utilize a personal growth approach within their EFPC method.[646] Dr. Ellen Gehrke of Rolling Horse Ranch in Ramona, CA, shares this example:

A client was in the round pen working with one of my horses. The horse chose not to come physically near to the client. This made the client angry. I asked the client what she was experiencing in that moment, expecting the conversation to continue along its previous line about the client's position within the company she was employed by. However, the situation apparently triggered the client. She began talking about her spouse who was having an affair. I recognized that the client was transferring her anger onto the horse. The horse responded by turning his back to her. This precipitated even more anger within the client. I halted the session at that point and removed the horse from the pen. We discussed the experience. Eventually I recommended that she seek professional counseling since the presenting issues were deeper and more complex than was ethically appropriate to address within the context of a coaching session.

In regards to the their horse experience, it is critical, as it is in all areas of EFMH/ES, that the coach have lengthy training, education, and experience in working with horses. Dr. Gehrke suggests that if coaching is practiced in an inappropriate and unethical manner then the work of EFPC may be seriously compromised. She recommends that the EFPC coach have excellent horse handling skills and possess a working knowledge of horse ethology, or "the scientific and objective study of animal behavior especially under natural conditions." She believes that EFPC coaches must be able to understand horse behavior and be able to interpret it accurately in a coaching session.

Dr. Gehrke does not think it necessary for the EFPC coach to personally own the horses who participate in the sessions. However, she feels that it is helpful if the coach knows the horses in advance, prior to engaging in any coaching activities. In her professional practice, she has observed that EFPC coaches can work successfully with other people's horses in different settings, but they must have a strong understanding of equine ethology and have the ability to connect quickly and deeply with horses other than their own. She reminds us that an EFPC coach is primarily responsible for ensuring a safe environment which includes such aspects as the mental, physical, emotional, intellectual and spiritual safety of all their clients. Without such safety measures, the full potential of the coaching session may be compromised. When the environment is not perceived of as safe the results of the session may not be as transformative. Therefore, it is critical that EFPC coaches understand how to keep their clients safe around horses and without a deep understanding of horse behavior, psychology, and physiology it can be difficult to do so.

It is suggested that the EFPC coach take an indirect approach with the client, not telling the client what he or she should or should not be experiencing. The coach merely serves as an interpreter and facilitator of whatever experience the client and the horse have together. The client's are encouraged to take ownership of whatever new insights they might have, and make their own decisions about how to utilize that information in their daily lives.

The coach helps to provide objective assessment and observations that foster the individual's or team members' enhanced self-awareness and awareness of others. Dr. Gehrke and Ms. Petro suggest a number of skills or directives for the EFPC coach: (1) EFPC coaches practice astute listening in order to garner a full understanding of the individual's or team's circumstances. 2) They act as a "sounding board" in support of thoughtful planning and decision making and champion opportunities and potential.(3) They encourage clients to stretch and challenge themselves commensurate with personal strengths and aspirations. (4) Coaches foster shifts in thinking that reveal fresh perspectives and challenge blind spots in order to illuminate new possibilities and support the creation of alternative scenarios. (5) Finally, the coach maintains professional boundaries in the coaching relationship, including confidentiality, and adheres to the coaching profession's code of ethics.

Practice

EFPC is a method designed to increase self-awareness and self-management in one's personal and professional life. EFPC introduces the presence of the horse into traditional coaching methods and that very presence tends to encourage the client to become more aware and more fully present in their bodies, therefore increasing the likelihood of integrated change. The practice of EFPC helps illuminate how perceptive horses can be, and this often leads to deeply moving interactions between humans and horses. Establishing a trusting relationship between the client, coach and horse is paramount to a successful outcome. EFPC can be a powerful alliance that is designed to bring about heightened awareness and encourage deep personal and professional change. EFPC incorporates several practical aspects which support this process.[647]

Personal Interview

The process of EFPC usually begins with a personal interview to assess the individual's current situation. Questions posed include the reason coaching has been identified as a viable option for growth, the preferred scope of the relationship, priorities and specific desired outcomes. The client begins by stating his or her personal and professional goals. Although goals may change over the duration of services provided, it is especially helpful for clients to enter into a coaching relationship with some concept of what they would like to get out of the interaction.

In the work of EFPC clients may begin to recognize the importance of clarity and goal setting through the impact that either their confusion or clarity has upon the horse with whom they are working. The horse reflects back to the client the level of personal engagement with the process, and that information may be useful to both the coach and to the client.

Needs Assessment

An assessment can be integrated if deemed worthwhile. Assessments provide objective information which can enhance the individual's self-awareness as well as awareness of others and their circumstances, provide a benchmark for creating coaching goals and actionable strategies, and offer a method for evaluating progress. One type of assessment that coaches often administer prior to a coaching session is a 360 feedback tool which helps to determine what the client's colleagues observe regarding strengths and weaknesses. The client can use the feedback to determine their own goals and objectives for EFPC.

Preparation

EFPC requires preparation on the part of the client and coach. Clients are encouraged to develop personal and professional goals, identify roadblocks they foresee and determine skills they would like to develop. The coach prepares a semi-structured session that is still flexible enough to allow for changes in direction due to reflective feedback provided by the horse. The session plan may consist of a series of horse exercises, provocative questions and debriefs which shed light on the client's behavior and underlying beliefs.

Dr. Gehrke and Ms. Petro suggest that clients may be asked to challenge themselves both personally and professional during an EFPC session. They believe that it helps both the coach and the client to begin thinking about such areas even during the preparation stage of the EFPC process. They list nine such areas that an EFPC coach may consider introducing to his or her clients. (1) *Focus*—on one's self, the tough questions, the hard truths and one's success. What does the horse indicate to the client when the focus is clear? (2) *Observation*—the behaviors and communications of self and others as they interact with the horse. (3) *Listening*—to one's intuition, assumptions, judgments, and to the way one sounds when one speaks. The horse will let the client know the truth about their listening and intuition skills. (4) *Style*—leveraging personal strengths and overcoming limitations in order to develop a more satisfying balance between life and work. (5) *Decisive actions*—by working with the horses learn to set clear boundaries and take appropriate risks. (6) *Compassion*—for one's self as he or she experiments with new behaviors based on feedback from the horse. (7) *Humor*—committing to not take one's self so seriously, using humor to lighten and brighten any situation. Horses appreciate lightheartedness. (8) *Personal control*—maintaining composure in the face of disappointment and unmet expectations, avoiding emotional reactivity. Applying emotional intelligence skills is an important learning in EFPC coaching. (9) *Courage*—in the work of EFPC, clients learns to challenge themselves in new and different ways and to engage in continual self-examination which may help them to overcome internal and external obstacles.

Approach

Coaching incorporates a strengths-based approach – a simple and profound avenue of unleashing possibility. The coach models constructive communication skills that the individual or team can utilize to enhance personal communication effectiveness. Clients may experience a sense of freedom during an EFPC session due to the non-judgmental nature of the coach in relation to the horse or horses. The client can observe the coach's respectful approach in regards to listening to the horse's feedback regardless of what it might be, and thus may feel safer sharing more personal reflections. The client is encouraged to proactively engage in his or her own process of learning, growth, and change. The coach provides support while continuing to challenge the client to expand his or her own potential. Ann Romberg and Lynn Baskfield of Wisdom Horse Coaching in Minneapolis, Minnesota, agree:

> As coaches, we consider our clients creative, resourceful, and whole, looking to move to another level in life such as creating a business or living with more balance or moving through a transition. They are 'well' people who function fully in life vs. those who are in need of therapy. In coaching, we start in the present and move forward. Emotions are seen as a natural expression of life that contain valuable information that can help the client learn and move forward in life. We most often work with professional adults.[648]

EFPC Activities

EFPC activities can include a multitude of approaches, from team building games played with horses, to individual energetic activities that help foster a deeper understanding of the impact of communication or relational skills on others. EFPC coaches generally utilize such activities as herd dynamic observation, which helps individuals recognize leadership styles, leading activities which foster a deeper understanding of personal leadership styles, and activities that are designed to promote teamwork and communication skills. Each EFPC coach has his or her own unique approach to the activities that they conduct, but it is recommended that all activities are respectful of each horse's unique nature and are designed to allow the client and the horse to form relationship.

EFPC Outcomes

The success of an EFPC session is measured by both internal and external indicators of performance. Since goal-setting is a key component of coaching, outcomes are determined at the beginning of the process and measured by such questions as "What does a successful outcome look like?" Dr. Gehrke and Ms. Petro utilize assessment tools that include self-scoring/self-validating assessments which can be administered initially and at regular intervals in the coaching process, changes in the individual's self-awareness and awareness of others, shifts in thinking which inform more effective actions, and shifts in one's emotional state which inspire confidence. The external indicators are those that can be seen and measured in the environment. Examples may include improved perceptions by management, peers and staff as measured in a 360 feedback tool, a promotion, or more activities accomplished in a set period. Ideally both external and internal metrics are incorporated into an evaluation.

Method Example

This method example was provided by Dr. Ellen Gehrke of Rolling Horse Ranch in Ramona, California.

Some of the most powerful coaching sessions often focus on the client's leadership skills. A president of a large organization came for an initial EFPC session. In the beginning of the session the EFPC coach suggested that the client observe the horse herd who were turned out in a large fenced enclosure. The client was given the directive of isolating one of the horses within the herd whom he felt drawn to. The client entered the pasture and began to move through the horse herd. A tall black mustang began to follow the client as he interacted with the other horses. The client continued to approach and meet the other horses, ignoring the tall black gelding. As the activity was drawing to a close, the client made the comment that he assumed that the black gelding "must do this to everyone." The coach responded, suggesting to the client that in fact, this particular horse generally does not come close to clients during this initial activity. The coach debriefed the client's reaction to the activity, and the client eventually did decide to continue his work that day with the black gelding. The coach presented the next activity, a round pen activity created to observe how the client provided direction for his staff. The coach provided some basic instruction about how to move the horse around the round pen if he should want to do that, and gave him safety guidelines that would keep him safe while engaging with the horse. The client entered into the round pen with the gelding who was waiting attentively in the center of the pen. The client patted the horse and then proceeded to stand in the pen with the horse, not offering him any direction or instruction as to what he wanted to see the horse do. After a few minutes of this, the horse moved away from the client and began nibbling on some grass. The client turned to the coach and asked her what he was supposed to do. The coach provided the client with a reflection, suggesting that it appeared that initially the horse was willing to do whatever the client wanted, and in fact had followed him all around the pasture while he was loose. However, she suggested, once the client entered into the round pen and did not give the horse any direction the horse lost interest and did whatever he wanted to do. The coach asked the client if this might be typical of any patterns he experienced in his current work. The client immediately engaged with the coach, sharing that in fact he expected his staff and the vice presidents of his company to take initiative and "get the job done" without much supervision from him. The coach proceeded to ask if this approach was working for him. The client responded that in fact it was not working. He suggested that he felt irritated and frustrated when the horse wandered away from him in the round pen because it reminded him of how his staff treated him. He shared that he did not feel he could get the horse's attention back once he had lost it, and that this was an ongoing problem at work.

At this point, the coach suggested that the client re-evaluate his intentions and then interact with the horse. The client found that he was still struggling to find his true or "deep" intention, and thus even during the second attempt at the activity the client was unsuccessful at getting the gelding to move around the pen and leave the grass.

Over the following sessions the client struggled to create and maintain a sense of his deeper intentions, both personally and professionally. However, as the sessions continued, the client was able to isolate new ways of interacting and connecting with the gelding, and soon he was able to guide and direct him both in a contained space and also out in a pasture. This shift was observed by his staff over the weeks he worked with the gelding, and soon he had successfully re-integrated as a leader within his company. The staff validated his change by voicing a deeper commitment to the company and to him personally. The big black gelding had done his work.

Summary

EFPC may evoke a powerful relationship between human and horse which can accelerate personal and professional growth in the corporate environment. Leadership and communication skills, as well as team and personal development can be enhanced. By leveraging qualified coaching and horses as partners, clients can set an objective, use insights from the equine experience and allow outcomes to emerge. A successful EFPC process requires safety, flexibility, fluidity, a commitment to living in the moment and a deep respect for client, horse and the energetic relationship between them.

CHAPTER NINETEEN

EQUINE FACILITATED HUMAN DEVELOPMENT

Introduction

Equine Facilitated Human Development (EFHD) is defined by one underlying belief: horses seem to have a place in the evolution of human consciousness. Linda Kohanov says, "It is ironic that for thousands of years these sensitive yet powerful beings [horses] carried our bodies around the world, allowing us to explore terrain we would have struggled to traverse on foot. Yet even as they've been released from their role as beasts of burden, horses have not become obsolete. They stand, beckoning, at the edge of a new wilderness---the landscape of consciousness itself---waiting for us to accept the challenge of living life to its fullest potential."[649] Chris Irwin writes, "I believe that what we can learn from horses is becoming a necessary stage of human evolution."[650] Barbara Rector believes that through working with horses humans find a path towards authentic empowerment. She writes, "Authentically empowered individuals make healthy behavior choices, living comfortably in peace and support of one another and the planet." [651]

An integral part of this book has been the concept that the lessons learned from "walking the way of the horse" may have the potential to bring about significant personal, communal, and global change. As more and more people begin realizing the necessity for long-lasting and impactful change, the work of EFHD becomes increasingly important.

EFHD is a method not easily categorized. It is a melding of therapy, education, and learning. Those providing the services are not necessarily mental health professionals, educators, or coaches. They have eclectic backgrounds combining many skills. Probably the easiest way of categorizing the method is through the individuals it serves.

EFHD is designed to serve fully functional individuals who are seeking to expand their human potential, learn advanced communication and leadership skills, develop their creativity, and engage in meaningful relationships. In order to accomplish such goals, the participants must be at an emotionally and mentally stable point in their development. Clients are screened extensively to ensure that an EFHD service is appropriate for them, and if screening determines differently, they are generally referred to an EFP or EFC service.

Principles of EFHD are used in psychotherapeutic or counseling methods, but since the EFHD provider is not required to be a licensed mental health professional, it is essential that clients who participant in an EFHD service are either free from mental health issues, or that the EFHD provider is a mental health professional or works in conjunction with one.

You may notice that this method is less clearly defined than the others. There are a number of reasons for this. (1) This method should only be facilitated by those who have reached a point in their own human development where they can ethically and appropriately lead others. This includes not only training from specific programs that teach EFHD (see below), but training in counseling, psychology, psychopathology, experiential education, holotropic breathwork, shamanic journeying, creative processes, horse-person-ship, communication skills, energy work, leadership training, and so on. The facilitators of an EFHD experience must have had extensive training from an organization that specializes in the method. Currently Linda Kohanov's Epona Equestrian Services offers a year-long apprenticeship program and then additional advanced training for facilitators. Barbara Rector's Adventures in Awareness program also offers a year-long internship, and the McCormick's Hacienda Tres Aquilas program offers psycho-spiritual analysis training that would be applicable for this method. I want to encourage any who are interested in pursuing EFHD to seek long-term training and personal experience prior to attempting to provide an EFHD service. (2) Since this method is uniquely defined by the professionals who have pioneered it, each of their approaches is different. I have attempted to collect as many commonalities as I could to help accurately represent the method, but I also realize that these pioneers have their own style, terminology, and belief systems that I may not be able to properly display within this edition of the text. (3) Although there are highly recognized pioneers who are providing EFHD services and have been for many years, the method is not yet clearly defined by a majority of the field. In my initial research only a handful of professionals were practicing what I could define as an EFHD method and each facilitated it in their own unique manner. Therefore, in this edition of the text I will aim to present only "the tip of the iceberg", a brief introduction to the method with much more to follow over the next few years.

Facilitation Objectives

Sensitivity, Intuition, and Awareness
Human beings are instinctual animals. We are hard wired to respond and react according to environmental stimuli that we are generally not aware of on a conscious level. The catch is that other animals never have to explain to anyone else why they acted or reacted in the manner that they did. If another animal catches a certain scent in the air, or feels danger near by his/her reaction is completely understandable and accepted. RUN, FIGHT, or HIDE. We humans, however, are not afforded that luxury. Not only are we chastised for immediate reactions to people, places, or situations – considered by many to be "judgmental" at best, but as much of the time these instinctual reactions occur on a unconscious level we cannot even defend our actions. We don't even know why we felt the way that we did or reacted in the manner that we did. Some people struggle more than others with this condition, and for those individuals life can be fraught with personal and interpersonal challenges.

In Riding Between the Worlds, Linda Kohanov shares the research of Elaine N. Aron. Ms. Aron discovered that 15-20 percent of all mammals, including humans, are "highly sensitive" and that an additional 22 percent of humans interviewed are "moderately sensitive". She also found that 42 percent of her study participants felt that they were "not sensitive at all."[652]However, it can be presumed that all humans are instinctual by nature, and therefore all respond consciously or unconsciously to minimal sensory information. We fall onto a continuum. Some of us are more aware of our sensitive and instinctual natures. Others of us find it difficult to connect with that component of human existence. Regardless of where we fall individually, we are all impacted daily. The work of EFHD is especially useful for those who have some understanding and awareness of their instinctual and sensitive natures, but may be searching for a different way to frame their experiences.

EFHD facilitators can help people to interpret minimal sensory information both as they receive it and as they witness others receiving or responding to it. Participants in an EFHD service will gain useful skills that teach them how to manage stimuli and how to successfully communicate to others using language that they can internalize and conceptualize.

Creativity

Creativity could almost be considered the outcome of increased sensitivity, intuition, awareness, and perception. As discussed in Chapter Eight intuition is the obtaining of direct knowledge without the evidence of a "normal" source of information. Once we have learned to open to "non-ordinary" sources of information, new insights, talents, and information arrive to us or move through us. This process could be considered "creative genius", an awakening of the senses that leads us to inventions, creations, and new ways of perceiving concepts. The work of EFHD helps people to discover their own creative genius through teaching them how to utilize their intuition and sensitivity to "non-ordinary" sources of information. Ms. Kohanov provides this about creativity,

> When you've truly made the connection, riding a horse feels like a series of illuminations rewarded by surges of endorphins. Most of these insights, however, are felt and put to use long before the conscious mind can fathom what's taking place. Flashes of clarity mixed with waves of elation flow as a stream of visceral responses. This is the "rider's high" that keeps people coming back for more, despite all the work associated

with these magnificent creatures. It *is* a creative act, a feeling of music in motion, of a sublime and silent improvisation between two souls that can never be accurately described--though artists from Michelaneglo to Kim McElroy have struggled to capture it for millennia.[653]

Relationship Development
Participants in an EFHD service are generally looking for ways to deepen and improve their relationships with self and others. The work of EFHD teaches people how to live congruently and in balance. It teaches people how to own what is theirs and leave what isn't. It targets a level of relationship development that is energetic and non-verbal. EFHD participants learn how to read and respond on an energetic level, and therefore also learn how to meet people where they are, responding and reacting according to all levels of functionality.

Advanced Communication Skills
Communication does not just include verbal or vocal means to convey feelings, thoughts, information, or experiences. Rather, to truly understand the nuances of communication we must learn how to set aside the use of verbalization and focus on our other skills. EFHD facilitators (humans and horses alike) teach participants to recognize and use all forms of communication and help them to recognize which situations are most appropriate for which combination of skills. Horses are ideal teachers from whom to learn non-verbal and energetic communication skills.

Leadership Skills
Teaching or training innovative, passionate, creative, and sensitive leaders is an important component of EFHD. In our world today we need leaders who are in touch with themselves and therefore who have the skills to separate self from other. We need leaders who can be stewards for those who are voiceless – the disadvantaged, children, animals, the earth. The work of EFHD brings people closer to an innate wisdom of self, a place where true strength and passion can be found. It is from here that leaders are born. The Way of the Horse is also a way of leadership, a way of finding balance within the herd without forsaking forward momentum. Through work with horses EFHD participants

experience their own unique leadership styles and learn to hone their skills to become the kind of leader that a herd will follow.

Role of Horse

At the Epona Center in Sonoita, AZ, Ms. Kohanov and her staff provide EFHD to hundreds of clients a year. She strongly believes that the horses who partner with her to provide such services are co-facilitators and teachers in this work and she respects them "as colleagues with certain talents, interests and areas of expertise." She feels that it is important to understand what those specific talents and interests are. She writes,

> We have a number of horses who excel at teaching people about boundaries because they can walk that fine line between keeping people safe while also challenging them to step into their power. We have horses who are masters at supporting people when they feel vulnerable, helping them move into their hearts and access authentic emotions. We have horses with a gift for demonstrating the reality of the energy fields surrounding our bodies, helping people exercise this level of awareness in both reflective and active contexts. We have horses who are generous riding instructors. And we have horses who excel at teaching people how to dance with them and can even trade leadership roles safely with humans. While our horses receive continued training and support in developing their skills in various areas, we also respect those who show a marked dislike for certain activities. To be effective teachers, they must show innate enthusiasm for what we are asking them to teach.[654]

In essence, the EFHD horse is one who has been thoroughly allowed to facilitate, voicing his or her unique message in whatever form or fashion is deemed needed at that time. The horse is generally seen as the catalyst for change, and the relationship between the client and the horse is laden with metaphor and meaning.

Role of Facilitator

First of all, the EFHD professional is someone who has undergone a great deal of training, education, and supervised facilitation experience. This is an individual who has already walked the path that he/she intends to take another down. The work of EFHD is not done lightly, nor done by those who have not experienced it for themselves. EFHD is complex, dynamic, and powerful work that has the potential to radically alter perceptions and life paths. As a facilitator of such work, one must be prepared to walk with the participant through whatever comes. Furthermore, the EFHD facilitator must also have a deep connection to horses and a great deal of knowledge and experience working with horses and humans. Ms. Kohanov suggests that an EFHD facilitator must be able to understand equine training techniques and equine nature well enough to understand how to pair horses and humans successfully. She writes, "Determining what those talents and interests are means that our staff must include experienced human facilitators who not only understand the point of each activity, they are experienced equestrians with a gift for introducing horses to the various activities, assessing who will be most talented at working with humans in each context, and determining what training is needed to help that horse reach his or her potential as a teacher in this context."

In regards to actual facilitation style as it applies to EFHD, Ms. Kohanov offers this,

> This is a complex question, but if I have to sum up our approach in a single phrase, I would have to say that facilitators at Epona learn to "lead by following." This is a taoist phrase, actually, and it sounds paradoxical at first. But basically, it means that we are empowering people, clients as well as facilitators, to develop their own sources of inspiration, intuition, body-mind awareness, etc. as a basis for engaging in authentic relationships with themselves, other people, and the world around them. We are encouraging people to step out of rigid, socially conditioned ways of relating, and exercise their ability to safely, consciously, experiment with new ways of being, perceiving, improvising, and interacting with others.

And so the facilitator must be a master at drawing out a person's innate, authentic wisdom in collaboration with the horses. To do that, the facilitator must be willing to improvise, collaborate, and co-create with the participant and the horse from moment to moment. They must lead their clients into new areas by following and supporting the insights clients and the horses access through the various mind-body-relationship activities.[655]

The EFHD facilitator is also expected to have extensive training and education in the following areas:

- Counseling skills
- Client assessment protocol/tools
- Experiential education – education, training, or experience
- Equine behavior, psychology, and physiology
- General equestrian skills (riding, training, care, etc.)
- Altered states of consciousness
- Expressive arts as healing mediums
- Holotropic breathwork (if the facilitator intends to use that method)
- Meditation or mindfulness practices
- Myth, metaphor, and archetypes
- Relationship training
- Communication styles/skills

Practice

Expressive Arts/Guided Visualizations
As in many other forms of EFMH/ES the expressive arts are found to be useful processing tools for those experiencing EFHD. Drumming and other forms of music are included in many aspects of EFHD.

Ms. Kohanov, who has a degree in music, employs a number of activities involving sound, often collaborating with her husband, internationally-known recording artist Steve Roach. One activity involves teaching total amateurs how to play music together.

> We do this as part of a sequence of equine activities that teach people how to dance with a horse on the ground. Dancing with a horse and playing music with others both require integrating a variety of skills involving assertiveness and sensitivity, improvisation, timing, flow, and authenticity in action. When people make music together, they engage with each other in a powerful, wholly nonverbal, intersubjective interaction that draws on group and individual creativity and experimentation.

> We have a great variety of instruments from around the world, including, drums, rattles, Tibetan singing bowls, crystal bowls, simple flutes, thumb pianos, etc. As Steve records, electronically enhances, and plays along with the participants, they essentially create their own atmospheric sound journey that they then get to meditate or journey to. Some people find this the most powerful experience of the workshop. Others, can hardly bare to attend the music session because of their own performance anxiety, but as they move through their fear and let their own creativity out, they gain confidence in facing a variety of life challenges with a sense of artful adventure.[656]

Another commonly found aspect of the EFHD experience occurs when the facilitator leads the participants through a guided visualization that encourages subtle shifts of consciousness or ways of viewing self, others, or the world. Ms. Kohanov offers an example she calls "Becoming the Horse",

> This is a guided visualization and journey where participants imagine turning into a horse, noticing what color, breed, sex, etc. the horse is, then going into a short journey to see where this horse lives or how he moves, etc., perhaps experiencing a story from this horse's life. Afterward, I invite people to draw their "inner horse," giving them colored pencils or crayons, and both blank paper for those artistically inclined,

and a horse outline that they can color, for those who are less artistically experienced.

If participants have to leave the property, we take a break and then share our inner horses with each other. If people are staying on site, I don't encourage them to share that day, but to "stay in this horse presence" and go outside, move among the herds (over the fence), and immerse themselves in what the world looks, feels, smells like "as a horse." We then share our experience the next day.

I like to do this activity with drumming, leading into a more powerful shamanic oriented piece of recorded music. I prefer Steve's music, most recently a piece called "Artifacts" from his CD *Origins,* but any tribal oriented music around 10 minutes long, with some sense of mystery and some rhythm to replicate a horse running or trotting is effective.[657]

In many cases EFHD facilitators use drawing, painting, spirit horse painting, clay, or collage to help the client experience and utilize forms of non-verbal communication skills to convey feelings, thoughts, or images.

Holotropic Breathwork
Stanislav Grof, M.D. and his wife, Christina Grof, developed Holotropic Breathwork as a powerful and natural technique to alter consciousness in the mid-1970's. This technique originated from modern consciousness research and the Grofs' study of ancient spiritual systems. This method is defined on the Grof webpage,

Holotropic Breathwork is a powerful approach to self-exploration and healing that integrates insights from modern consciousness research, anthropology, various depth psychologies, transpersonal psychology, Eastern spiritual practices, and mystical traditions of the world. The name *Holotropic* means literally "moving toward wholeness". The process itself uses very simple means: it combines accelerated breathing with evocative music in a special set and setting. With the eyes closed and lying on a mat, each person uses their own breath and the music in the room to enter a non-ordinary state of consciousness. This state activates the natural inner healing process of the individual's psyche, bringing him or her a particular set of internal experiences. With the inner healing intelligence guiding the process, the quality and content brought forth is unique to each person and for that particular time and place. While recurring themes are common, no two sessions are ever alike. Additional elements of the process include focused energy release work and mandala drawing. Holotropic Breathwork is usually done in groups, although individual sessions are also possible. Within the groups, people work in pairs and alternate in the roles of experiencer and "sitter". The sitter's role is simply to be available to assist the breather, not to interfere or interrupt the process. The same is true for trained facilitators, who are available as helpers if necessary.[658]

In order to conduct any form of Holotropic Breathwork it is suggested that the professional obtain their Certification in the Grof Transpersonal Training which requires about 600 hours of residential training that takes at least two years to complete.[659]

EFHD professionals may use components of Holotropic Breathwork, generally to a somewhat lessened degree dependant upon set, setting, and desired outcome. The purpose of such an additional intervention is to continue the deep inner process work that altered states of consciousness can provide thereby opening participants up to insights provided during their equine work. If the EFHD professional chooses to use Holotropic Breathwork or any other form of breathwork, he or she should be highly trained and skilled in the method.

Meditation/Mindfulness
Many Eastern traditions can be found within the work of EFHD. Meditation and mindfulness practices are commonly used both by the facilitators of the experience to help them ground and center for the journey that they must lead other on, and by participants, seeking clarity to better take in what is being offered. Once again all EFHD professionals have their own unique approach and methods that they

use to help participants ground, center, and come into their bodies in a meaningful way.

Barbara Rector shares this example of how the work of EFHD can be used,

> The AIA [Adventures in Awareness] process connects mind body and heart in relationship with the energies of an equine. This AIA process engages the sacred while exercising the body, calming the mind, and nurturing the soul. Working with and riding horses may be experienced as "joyful mediation in motion."[660]

Group Process
In many cases EFHD is used in a group setting. The group process can be a valuable resource for all participating, as each individual may gain important skills from practicing the art of relationship with not only horses, but humans as well. The group provides a safe environment for the participants to try out new skills and engage with others who are on a similar path. Within the group, participants may learn how to separate self from other, and hone the skills needed to set and maintain clear energetic and emotional boundaries.

Journey Ride
Barbara Rector first coined the term Journey Ride in 1996 when she started combining Holotropic Breathwork techniques, developmental vaulting positions, and the movement of the horse into one powerful, altering intervention. She explains Journey Ride,

> Horses facilitate an inward journey based on principles of Holotropic (moving into wholeness) consciousness to access non-ordinary states of awareness. Experience the gifts of feelings, information rich emotions, the influence of attention and intention, and the significance of energy principles to expand your awareness, enhance intimacy skills and grow in consciousness. You may expect increased confidence in your intuitive skill and experiential knowledge of multiple realities.[661]

Ms. Rector provides workshops and trainings both to experience the Journey Ride and to learn how to facilitate it. Other EFHD professionals utilize variations of the Journey Ride, or non-mounted experiences that combine the presence of equines with low-grade altered states of consciousness.

Energetic Boundary Awareness
As we begin recognizing that there are many levels of communication, levels which go well beyond the spoken word, we also realize the need to be competent communicators on all of those levels. The research on this topic helps us to better understand our energetic space and how much we can impact people by "the energy we put out." In the work of EFHD participants are taught how to recognize their energy and the energy of others, and learn how to either adjust their energetic boundaries or at least become aware of them. This sensitivity allows participants to make choices about how they impact others or allow themselves to be impacted within relationship.

Intuitive Techniques
As EFHD participants gain a deeper sense of awareness regarding the multiple levels of communication, a sensitivity and respect for their intuition generally develops. EFHD activities may be created to hone the participants' sense of intuition and thereby may help them to become skilled at learning to listen to their intuition.

Intersubjectivity Skills
Ms. Kohanov's interest in exercising "intersubjectivity," a term widely promoted by author, philosopher, and consciousness researcher Christian de Quincey in books like *Radical Knowing*,[662] is closely related to the concept of "minimal sensory information" that is presented in Chapter 6 but expands the idea to include the importance of mutual sensitivity within human-human and human-horse interactions. Ms. Kohanov writes,

> Intersubjective awareness involves paying attention to your own nonverbal experiences/body language cues and those of the people you're interacting with *at the same time*. It's easier said than done. Most adults, in fact, just aren't very good at this because the skills associated with intersubjectivity have

been seriously neglected in our culture. People who are even nominally aware at this level seem to possess an interpersonal gift, a powerful yet vague talent that can't be readily taught. Or can it? Horses are constantly drawing attention to the intersubjective dimension of relationship. They mirror and respond to dynamics that remain largely unconscious in humans. Yet when we become conscious of what we are communicating to others nonverbally, and what they are communicating to us nonverbally, a whole new universe of information is suddenly available to us. This information virtually demands that we develop the ability to improvise as we respond and adapt to these subtle cues on our way to achieving any goal.[663]

Method Example

Epona's "Rasa Dance"[664]

One of Linda Kohanov's core practices involves teaching participants how to dance with horses on the ground, and eventually in the saddle. The following excerpt from her book *Way of the Horse: Equine Archetypes for Self Discovery* outlines the gifts, challenges, history and benefits of this approach integrating equestrian skills, movement, music, relationship skills, creativity, mindfulness, and, expanded states of awareness:

The Gift

Here's where you put all the pieces together, where new concepts and conventional methods fuse and expand, creating unexpected possibilities. Authenticity in action draws on responsiveness, assertiveness, discernment, physical collection, mental and emotional agility, fluidity of consciousness, imagination, nonverbal communication, subtle body awareness, intuition, consensual leadership, and the paradox between boundaries and oneness.

The Challenge

When two beings move in synchrony, a greater consciousness arises, and with it a feeling of ecstasy. Can you stay present and focused during these moments of intense joy? Can you accept the gift of expanded awareness without becoming addicted to it? If the next moment offers frustration, indecision, conflict, performance anxiety, or miscommunication, can you dance with that too?

The Journey

The idea of the Rasa Dance came from an unexpected challenge. Early on, I was surprised to find that some students who accessed greater sensitivity, heart-based awareness, and intuition during a weekend workshop were virtually paralyzed when they returned home. Equestrians seemed to have the hardest time. They not only witnessed horses acting intelligently, these people experienced incidents where their four-legged facilitators taught profound lessons about life, love, and consciousness. Once certain riders and trainers realized that horses could be trusted to guide humans to greater balance and awareness, conventional concepts of riding and training felt like slave-driving. These people weren't just motivated to sample the benefits of "not-doing" they suddenly found themselves stuck there, incapable of asking their mounts to do *anything.*

Horses spend a lot of time milling around in rarefied states of being, but they also connect through movement. They keep to the yin, but they definitely *know* the yang. The Way of the Horse can open our conditioned bodies and minds to a whole new world of sensory and extra-sensory awareness. To make it all worthwhile, however, we must ultimately *live* in this expanded universe, learning to act and feel, assert and respond, all at the same time. Dancing becomes the metaphor for leading without dominating, learning to follow someone else without losing your balance or your boundaries---and, at some point, upping the ante to fluidly *trade* leads in true partnership. Many riding or training techniques previously executed in the spirit of dominance can be resurrected as dance moves, in the same way that one person might teach another the bossa nova. The student has to be willing to defer to her instructor and take some direction. But the teacher has to be clear in his direction, willing to guide his partner without pushing her around.

At the heart of the dance is the art of energy projection and modulation. Some people assume they should be able to move a horse without lifting a finger. And so, I've learned to give them a taste of what a "telepathic" leader feels like: I take the hands of a volunteer, inviting him to dance, and then I stand there, stone faced, "sending," without moving a muscle, the message to take that first step backwards or sideways. No one ever gets it, because I haven't added any initiative to this silent request. My partner mirrors this immobility, waiting, growing increasingly confused and bored---not because he isn't "evolved" enough to engage in mind to mind communication, but because there's no energy, no enthusiasm behind it. If I wait long enough, he may decide to walk away or lead the dance himself. Someone, after all, needs to do *something*, or we might as well be meditating under a tree.

In the same way that I can imagine lifting my arm with absolutely nothing happening, there's some mysterious intermediary force that turns thought into action. That force is what we project outward, big time, to move a thousand-pound being. Yet we must also learn to control it, to dole it out in just the right amount to overcome inertia without over-stimulating our partner, or we may send him careening around the arena in a disorganized frenzy.

Getting the dance started is not about dominance, it's about energy, motivation, and focus. It's also about timing. If I ask the horse to move a certain way, on the ground or in the saddle, I have to make sure I communicate what I want at the exact moment his body is in the position to execute my request, or I'm setting us both up for failure. I have to be patient as we discover what our individual bodies and minds need to collaborate. Even experienced human dancers must practice with new partners to merge in artful synchrony.

A great leader is responsive to her followers. She knows how to motivate without micro-managing. Yet ultimately, there in no formula: Some horses, like people, need more impetus and supervision to follow through than others. An accomplished rider or manager is more like a generator than a dictator; she knows how to turn up or turn down her energy and focus according to the needs of the individual. In jazz, the drummer might be the official leader of an ensemble, yet he has to be willing to let the saxophonist and pianist shine, at times following the tempo of their inspired solos. To keep the beat, he has to be in the groove, and that involves being aware, assertive, yet relaxed. "It don't mean a thing if it ain't got that swing:" If the rhythm section becomes tense and competitive with the horn players, the whole band falls apart.

As much as we've been taught that horses will disrespect us if we neglect to make it clear at every moment that we're alpha, these animals can learn to respectfully trade leads with us, much like musicians trade solos. In working with my mare Rasa, I found it immensely satisfying to follow her ideas now and then. By making it clear that I'd submit to an intriguing impulse, if she didn't step on my toes, we both felt a surge of delight in creating some new moves together. Over time, we began demonstrating this fluid exchange of ideas and leadership roles to others.

Some equestrians are *very* uncomfortable with this notion. And well they should be, not because it's physically dangerous to let a horse lead, as they insist, but because it's immensely more dangerous to realize that such an animal can learn to lead *responsibly.* Just as the abolition of slavery and the rise of women's rights felt incredibly threatening to some people, changing the way we perceive and relate to animals can't help but alter how we justify our very existence. The profound vulnerability we experience moving from owner and exploiter, to caretaker, and finally, collaborator, however, breeds much greater, more creative levels of self-esteem and engagement with life.

When I named my horse Rasa, I was intrigued by its dual meaning. In Latin the phrase *tabula rasa* means "clean slate." In India, *rasa* is an aesthetic term describing the mood, sentiment, or flavor evoked by a work of art. At that time, I had no idea it had an even more appropriate meaning for the journey we would undertake.

After gaining confidence dancing and trading leads with my own mare, I began introducing this concept at clinics around the country. The process involves first teaching people and horses how to set and respect boundaries while walking beside each other on the ground. Then the pair practices some basic "free-longing" techniques: the human directs the horse to move around her at a distance, changing direction and speed off lead, sometimes sending the animal out, sometimes drawing him in to "join up" and walk or trot beside her. Most easily practiced in a round pen at first, these become the rudimentary "dance moves" for subsequent improvisations.

At this point, I add music to the mix, cautioning people to avoid trying to dance to the exact rhythm, or act out what the melody suggests. Instead I encourage them to use the sound to move beyond a task-oriented, left-brained mindset, entering the feeling and *flow* of connection. Instrumental tracks in particular enhance nonverbal communication---and encourage people to dance with whatever comes up.

At its best, music is a language of pure emotion that moves body, mind, and spirit simultaneously, inspiring us to resonate with a surprising array of feeling. People don't shell out fifty bucks for a concert ticket to hear one long, peaceful, happy major chord all evening. They want the full panorama: passion, joy, pathos, jubilation, sadness, longing, rage, ambiguity, gentleness, and triumph. Great musicians and dancers must feel these emotions to convey them, while also remaining present and responsive to the rest of the ensemble. If members dissociate during a particularly exuberant passage, riding the wings of angels in ecstatic rapture, they'll lose their place. If they become uncontrollably tense during a powerful outburst of sound and fury, their fingers and lungs don't work properly. Either way, the performance comes to a crashing halt.

Musicians also learn to move through their own mistakes, feeling out-of-tune or off rhythm with the others at times, yet committing to re-balance without forcing everyone else to stop and start over each time perfection eludes them. Improvisational players actually capitalize on unexpected shifts in tempo or strange twists in melody. What starts out as a glitch often gives birth to new ideas these people never would have glimpsed if they hadn't been committed to "going with the flow."

All of these principles come into play when dancing with a horse on the ground, or even in the saddle. When you're open to letting the horse lead now and then, something even more amazing happens. Horses don't have an extended agenda or the ability to isolate an idea and practice it, methodically working it out over time. They do, however, respond to the overriding *feel* of the moment. When their human partners are willing to sense and follow those impulses, what seems like a mistake in movement or communication turns out to create new dance moves that the human element can remember, rehearse, and reproduce on cue over time. Dancing in this sense involves deferring to the spirit of the moment---even if it's initiated by the horse. Generally, the equine element loses focus, and the human has to follow through. As they're completing this unexpected move, it's also the human's job to come up with another idea and assert it before the team loses momentum. There's a *huge* pot of gold at the end of this rainbow. Seamlessly trading leads sometimes trips a quantum leap in consciousness as horse and human merge into a collective flow that has an intelligence all its own. It feels like a third entity is dancing them both, and the accompanying sense of ecstasy is almost overwhelming.

Dancing with one horse over time increases coordination, familiarity, connection, and trust. Dancing with a variety of horses exercises adaptability and energy modulation.

Each individual requires different levels of assertiveness and sensitivity. Different nonverbal interactions reveal different challenges, creating "mistakes" that lead to new moves---and ultimately, brief yet powerful exchanges with that mystical force connecting us all.

I was actually teaching horse dancing at California's EquuSatori Center when I came across a myth elucidating this profound yet elusive experience. My host Lisa Walters had been to India several years earlier. In her living room, resting on the piano, was a huge, beautifully illustrated book on Krishna. Imagine my surprise when, leafing though the pages, I came to a chapter called "Rasa Dance." The story involved India's version of the cowgirl: the *gopis*, a group of striking yet devoted young women who took care of the herds.

One night, under the light of the moon, the gopis pined for their god Krishna with such fervor that he was compelled to descend into their circle. Each gopi thought she was dancing alone with her sapphire-colored Beloved as he appeared to them simultaneously, aligning with their unique qualities of beauty and grace. As the gopis and Krishna moved together, a blissful musical sound was produced from the tinkling of their bells, ornaments, and bangles. Above this scene, other immortals flew back and forth, trying to catch a glimpse of this spectacle, singing and showering flowers on all the dancers.

A sacred performance is still called a Rasa Dance, signifying a state of grace in which Spirit engages with its many manifestations, expressing different aspects of infinity through the music of connection.

Little did I know that a horse would lead me to a deeper understanding and experience of this soulful cosmic dance.

Summary

Provided by Linda Kohanov

My sense of the mission and potential of Equine Facilitated Human Development is that we are training the leaders and innovators of the future: 21st century Renaissance men and women who by this very definition must be well-rounded. They must rely on their brains *and* hearts, bodies and spirits, reason and intuition, creativity and responsiveness. All of these qualities must be engaged and working in concert. This is a tall order. We're talking about human evolution here, and oddly enough our horses are prepared to help us reach those new heights of awareness, leadership, and co-creativity as they encourage us to move beyond how we've been conditioned to see and relate to the world. Verbal, brain-centered culture *was* an innovation, but we must move beyond these limitations. The survival of our species, and every other species on the planet, depends upon it.

While success in life requires intelligence, the brain isn't the only element, perhaps not even the primary element, involved in developing the true leaders and innovators of the future. It's now commonly recognized that only ten percent of human communication is verbal. And yet in our culture, we've virtually become mesmerized by words as our social and educational systems teach us to dissociate from the body, the environment, and the subtle nuances of nonverbal communication. In his book, *The Other 90%: How to Unlock your Vast Potential for Leadership and Life*, Robert K. Cooper predicts that the "dinosaurs of the future will be those who keep trying to live and work from their heads alone. Much of human brilliance is driven less by the brain in your head than by newly discovered intelligence centers---now called 'brain two and brain three'---in the gut and the heart. The highest reasoning and brightest ingenuity involve all three of those brains working together."

If we're serious about finding solutions to the challenges of this complex technological, now global society we live in, we do in fact need to engage all three of those brains. The true pioneers of the 21st century are those who figure out how to tap the vast resources of nonverbal intelligence. In this respect, horses provide the ultimate shortcut---as they always have. For thousands of years these sensitive yet powerful beings carried our bodies around the world, allowing us to explore terrain we would have struggled to traverse on foot. But there was something much more profound happening in these interspecies associations. Learning to form partnerships with those horses provided the most elusive yet important education a human leader could acquire---that "other 90 percent" exercised at a wholly nonverbal level.

I'm not just talking about balance, will, timing, focus, courage, and assertiveness. I'm talking about *intersubjective* awareness. The fact that few people truly understand what intersubjectivity is explains why we have such a hard time understanding the "mechanics" of relationship, and ultimately, training innovative leaders of all kinds, whether they be CEOs, parents, teachers, or team members.

In our culture, we prize and over-develop objectivity, the ability to stand back and observe without affecting, or being affected by, what we are observing. Subjectivity is considered the artist's prerogative. We appreciate people who communicate their feelings, dreams, and views to us in evocative ways. Yet it's really *intersubjectivity* that we value in a fine work of art, the ability of the artist to depict a truth that we too feel deeply, yet may not have found the right poetry, visual symbol, or music to express. Artists in our culture are worshipped more widely than mystics, because no matter how practical we *think* we are, we're willing to pay good money for songs, films, photographs, books, and paintings that reflect what we crave to understand about deeper layers of nonverbal awareness and experience.

In learning how to sense and set boundaries with a horse, in learning how to motivate, move, communicate nonverbally, and improvise with a thousand-pound being, people see, feel, and know, deep in their bones, what leadership presence really is. In a similar way, business leaders must learn to dance with the changing needs, whims, and perceptions of the market, their clients, their competitors, and their employees. Here we begin to recognize why exceptional leadership is often recognized as an art. The ability to dance with multiple factors and factions to achieve ambitious goals cannot be achieved through purely rational, methodical means. (It's no accident that Donald Trump titled his bestselling autobiography *The Art of the Deal*.)

In engaging the "other 90 percent," we begin to approach our true potential. At that point, work does feel more like an art---and becomes so much more satisfying as a result.

SECTION FIVE

CONCLUSION

Twenty	*Education and Training*
Twenty-One	*National Certification, State Licensure, and Research*
Twenty-Two	*Closing Remarks: A vision for us all*

CHAPTER TWENTY

EDUCATION, TRAINING AND RESEARCH

Introduction

The field of EFMH/ES is complex, dynamic, and filled with possibilities. As the field has grown so has the need to educate people interested in pursuing any of the EFMH/ES methods as a career. Due to safety and ethical considerations, adding an EFMH/ES method to an already existing mental health or educational program should only be done if the professional has had additional education, training, experience, and supervision utilizing the method. Furthermore, with the number of programs available that offer an EFMH/ES method, it has become increasingly important that both clients and professionals who refer clients to an EFMH/ES method, understand the ethical considerations, recognize which method may be most effective with which client, and feel confident that the EFMH/ES professional who is providing the service is educated, trained, and experienced in the method. There are a number of ways in which professionals interested in offering an EFMH/ES method can obtain proper education, training, and experience.

College or University Programs

Prescott College in Prescott, Arizona, offers a Masters degree specifically in EFMH/ES. Prescott College also offers undergraduate courses that target the work of EFMH/ES.[665] Carroll College in Helena, Montana, offers a two-year minor specific to the field of EFMH/ES.[666] Other colleges and universities occasionally offer courses in this work, but do not provide a degree specific to the field.[667] It is the recommendation of this author that any professional interested in providing an EFMH/ES method seek additional formal education and training specific to

435

EFMH/ES from a college or university. Both Prescott College and Carroll College offer additional trainings and programs for those interested in the field who already hold degrees, and other colleges offer courses that community members may be able to take for a fee. To gain validity it is becoming increasingly important that professionals who provide an EFMH/ES method hold a degree specific to the field. As the field grows it is likely that obtaining such a degree will be necessary to practice.

College or university programs are usually designed to provide the student with an all inclusive or well- rounded understanding of the field. This approach allows the student to learn both the positive and negative attributes of a variety of methods or theories. The student is then free to chose which method best suits his or her personality, facilitation style, or belief system. The student can also begin to see which methods might be best for which populations, and where adjustments might need to be made within a method for specific clientele. The student can also seek additional training in any one method that he or she feels the most drawn to, but still has a overall theoretical understanding of the field as a whole. College and university courses are usually designed to broaden the horizons of the students, thereby offering them a multitude of ways to think about any one topic or subject. They are not designed to teach only one method sanctioned by one organization or individual.

"Certification" Programs

Due to the lack of formal educational programs that train individuals in the field of EFMH/ES, "certification" programs have erupted across the country. These programs range from three-day introductory courses to year-long apprenticeship programs with the same general outcome: if you have successfully completed the course, you are "approved" or "certified" to conduct this work.[668] Therefore, an individual who has only gone through a three-day training might consider himself or herself as ready to provide the service as someone who has gone through a year-long course of study. Generally the client is unaware of the differences between the various training programs and may engage in a deeply therapeutic process with someone with limited education, training and experience simply because he or she states that they are "certified."

Unfortunately, the majority of these programs teach participants only their specific model of working with horses and humans. The programs tend not to be inclusive of the various approaches, methods, or theoretical underpinnings related to this vast field, but instead teach a specific practical application of the work designed by an individual or program. Therefore, interested individuals are not usually exposed to the diversity and complexity of the field, and leave such a certification program with a limited understanding of the field as a whole. This limited perspective can lead professionals into unethical territory, providing a service that does not match their clientele, their horse partners, or their educational or professional training.[669] Furthermore, the complexities of this field indicate that individuals wishing to provide an EFMH/ES service should undergo a long-term education, training, and practical application process. Many of the certification programs tend to imply that within a few short days, weeks or months one can become qualified to provide this seemingly provocative, potentially dangerous, and complex service. Wendy Wood of The Red Road in Northern California adds this:

> I believe that it is unethical for associations, organizations, and groups to claim that they 'certify' when they simply are providing 'training' &/or 'certification of attendance.' I can with all confidence state that there is no 'certification process' from these sorts of organizations. Furthermore, I believe that it is unethical for organizations to lead consumers to believe that 'certification' by their organization implies competency… because it truly does not. The longer certification programs are, the more in keeping with the concept that a 'certification' actually could imply competence.

Since these sorts of short term certification programs have become increasingly popular, the rate of accidents per year has increased enough to make many insurance companies either raise their rates for EFMH/ES services, or discontinue the coverage for EFMH/ES services altogether. In a recent conversation with a representative from the Garn Group, the author learned that many of the major insurance companies are reconsidering their decision to offer insurance to EFMH/ES programs due to the lack of formal education and training of the providers, and due to an increase in accidents.[670] If this trend continues, obtaining insurance at a rate that makes this work possible for the average provider may become impossible. Furthermore, the fact that insurance rates have increased due to accidents is not a positive selling point for this field. If we are to move forward in a healthful, ethical, and safe manner, we must begin placing standards and values around the type of training that individuals obtain prior to providing this service.

EFMHA is in the process of creating a long-term all-inclusive certification program that will prepare professionals to sit for the CCEFMHEP exam. Their certification program is slated to include workshops and trainings provided through educational institutions, on-line tests, and supervised practical application of skills learned.

Research

Of the current practitioners in the field of EFMH/ES, many feel strongly that in order to validate the anecdotal evidence that suggests that horses may be psychologically healing for humans, or that work with horses helps individuals learn, grow, and change, we must be able to scientifically prove such concepts. It seems that if we are to gain the support of highly educated and trained professionals we must have a clearer understanding of what is actually happening when horses and humans connect.

We need to further understand the neurological and biochemical implications of working in close proximity to the horse. Investigations into how the energetic fields of both the horse and the human are impacted when they come into contact with each other, and what occurs within the psyche when such connection happens would help us further understand why we "feel better" when in the presence of horses. Efficacy studies that examine the potential benefits of the various EFMH/ES methods would help us understand which methods produce what results, and therefore would allow us to be better able to refer clients to appropriate services for their specific needs. Studies to examine the correlation between already existing research regarding the physiological benefits of being mounted astride a moving horse and how such movement might have psychological ramifications would help us better determine when to use a mounted activity and when to use a ground-based activity.

We also must determine the individual factors that occur when horses and humans come into contact. Thus far we do not know how much of an impact aspects of biophilia and ecopsychology have on the general experience of the horse/human connection. We also do not know how much impact the human facilitator has on the outcome of an EFMHS or EFE/L service. What role does the horse actually play in regard to "healing" the human? These questions and many more have not yet been researched, and this void of "evidence-based" information regarding the field as a whole or specific methods utilized raises questions in many minds.

Those of us providing an EFMH/ES method(s) know in our hearts how powerful this work can be for the clients or students we serve. We see it is working day after day after day. We know something is occurring within our clients, but we generally cannot say exactly why it is working. This can lead to mystifying the work, making it seem magical. The more we know and understand about what may be happening between horses and humans the better we are able to see the components that are logical, understandable, tangible, and it is through that very recognition that we may find renewed excitement about the beauty and perfection of life. Suddenly magical is used to describe something obvious, something wonderfully mundane, a part of the web which we have been removed from for so long. Life in and of itself is magical. Cycles, instincts, nature, all things "tangible, provable, and "evidence-based" still retain their perfection, their beauty, and their magic when we see them in the context of the web of life. Understanding is a wonderful thing, and does not have to replace the mysteries of the universe. Understanding just allows us to go deeper.

Suggestions

Understandably, it will take time for universities and colleges to develop and market degree programs in this field. Until this occurs, those interested in pursuing a career in EFMH/ES should be aware of the differences between programs and seek to find training programs that offer a long term (a year or more), professionally supervised and inclusive education that includes at the least an overview of the entirety of the field, education regarding the theoretical and practical applications of the EFMH/ES methods, specific hands-on training appropriate for the participant's education and background, horse skills training and education specific to this field, and a personal growth and development component that prepares that individual to ethically provide this service.

Individuals or programs interested in providing such training for interested professionals should consider approaching colleges and universities to attempt to develop collaboration projects in which students can be enrolled in a formal Masters program, or obtain college credits while simultaneously undergoing a long-term training program at an EFMH/ES facility that provides an education and training service for professionals. In this manner we can begin stressing the importance of long term and deeply educational training programs for those interested in this field. We can begin setting standards for the types of programs attempting to provide such a service. Through this process we can support the professional growth and development of this field and also foster "best practices" within the field. It is important to understand that the physical and emotional safety of our clients is at risk due to a lack of formal education and training in this field. Through holding ourselves accountable for obtaining lengthy and substantial education and training, we may be able to help keep those interested in pursing treatment utilizing an EFMH/ES method safer.

It is essential that standards are created regarding what comprises a professional EFMH/ES training and education program in which students graduate truly competent to provide an EFMH/ES method or service. It is highly recommended that anyone interested in learning about EFMH/ES or seeking to pursue a career in EFMH/ES spend a great deal of time researching and comparing certification or training programs to ensure that they include a long-term program (at least one year), solid academic content, strong theory base, practical application, supervision, horse skills, and a personal growth and development component. Furthermore, interested parties should examine the credentials, background, and education of those providing the training. The program should be able to clearly define the differences in training and education between a mental health service and an educational service, and should accept only individuals with a background, education, or certification in the appropriate field. In other words, someone with a background and education in coaching, experiential learning, or experiential education should be steered towards a training program that teaches them the EFE/L methods rather than the EFMH methods and, in fact, should not be admitted to a training program that targets EFMHS without obtaining the necessary degree. A counselor or psychotherapist interested in utilizing EFMH/ES methods in clinical practice should be trained and educated in the EFMH methods. However, a counselor or psychotherapist who is interested in ceasing clinical practice and moving into coaching, or experiential learning/education could be admitted to an EFE/L program. Some counselors or psychotherapists may want to become dually trained, and therefore may pursue both training options.

For further information regarding training programs the reader is urged to refer to the Appendix in this text.

CHAPTER TWENTY-ONE

A VISION FOR US ALL

Closing Remarks

Recently, I read Outdoor Magazine's April 2007 "Green Issue." On the front cover is the actor and Governor of California, Arnold Schwarzenegger, surrounded by animals. The magazine highlights "179 solutions for a hot planet," and interviews people like Leonardo DiCaprio, Eddie Vedder, Yvon Chouinard, Will Steger, and many others. Throughout the magazine animals appear, posing with their humans, looking into the camera lens with eyes begging for reason. I was struck by the connection between the hard science of Al Gore's "An Inconvenient Truth" and the unarticulated intermingling of the human/animal bond.

It seems as through our world is starting to awaken to the desperate need for preservation and interconnection. Those who have seen "An Inconvenient Truth," or who follow the scientific data warning us of the impending global ecological catastrophe are recognizing the need for profound change. However, the reality is that in order for us to make the kind of long-lasting lifestyle changes, political changes, and moral reconfigurations that are needed to heal the Earth, something must shift within the very fiber of our beings.

Imagine feeling the Earth beneath our feet, hearing the cry of a bird in the trees above our heads, and smelling the changing of seasons. If we do not have this experience, are we less effective and less passionate about change? If we are connected to the Earth, and in tune with the seasons, with the migration patterns of animals, and changes in smell, air quality, or moisture content, suddenly the concepts of global warming and the other impending environmental disasters encroaching upon us feel very real. Picture a world without connection to nature; a world stripped bare of forests, rivers, grasslands, and all of the creatures who inhabit those environs. Does our disassociation from our physical bodies and disconnection from nature and all that exists within make it more difficult to respond passionately to the environmental crisis that looms in front of us? If we are in our bodies, aware of our present state of being, connected to our surroundings, and in touch with our senses, we can feel change. We can feel the cry of the Earth as it struggles to maintain its equilibrium within the maelstrom of pollutants, climatic shifts, and invasion into its very core. We begin to sense that our mental and physical health is directly linked to the health of our environment, our planet. Is it possible that if we were aware of such an interconnection we might be more prepared to begin actively engaging in the process of long lasting and meaningful change?

Work with horses provides a provocative avenue to explore the realms of our consciousness, as well as bring us more fully into the present, therefore allowing us to feel, listen, and truly hear what is occurring all around us. Through work with horses we learn how to engage in interspecies communications, and therefore develop a new and different sense of what protection and stewardship of our natural world really means. We begin learning and putting into practice new ways of being in the world that are authentic, heart centered, and compassionate. We find patience, understanding and tolerance in a world filled with rush, irritation, and anger. We learn about setting boundaries, becoming congruent, and making choices about not only our own personal direction, but the direction in which we allow ourselves to be led. We learn about politics and leadership, about hierarchy and partnership, and we develop skills that allow us to speak up within our communities, demanding societal and environmental change. The work of EFMH/ES is powerful, sometimes beyond words. I hope that we can learn how to harness that power safely, ethically, and responsibly.

The world is ripe for such change. People are responding, reaching out to help, and calling for reason. They are vocalizing the need for connectedness, recognition of the Divine, belief in the healing power of nature and animals, and most importantly, belief in ourselves as a species *capable of bringing wellbeing and goodness to this earth* rather than illness and destruction.

The horse is waiting, ready to offer gifts that may help us move into a new era of sensitivity, respect, and awareness. I hope that we each can learn to listen to the Earth, and do *whatever it takes* to change ourselves in response to the information we gain from listening. It is up to us. The animals can only warn us and offer us examples of other ways of being. It is we who must change.

Appendices

A Interview Questions for Theoretical Concepts

B. Questionnaire

C. Responses from Survey Question, "Horse as Tool or Horse as Co-Facilitator?

D. Further Resources

APPENDIX A

INTERVIEW QUESTIONS FOR THEORETICAL CONCEPTS

Note: I used these questions for my interviews with Barbara Rector, Linda Kohanov, Laura Brinkerhoff, Ann Alden, Dr. Marilyn Sokolof, Dr. Ellen Gehrke, Molly DePrekal, Tanya Walsh, and Dr. Suz Brooks. I also used selected questions in conversations with Dr. Temple Grandin, Chris Irwin, the Dr.'s McCormick, Dr. Nancy O'Brian, Dr. Stan Maliszewski, and Dr. Anne Perkins. The results from these interviews were used in the creation of this text, especially in regards to the EFMH/ES Methods section.

General Information

Instructions/Explanations:

Method: Please circle which EFMH/ES method you use with clients. If you utilize more than one, please note that as well.

Origination year refers to the year you started this work as a professional.

Education/Training/Degree: Please tell me what your educational background is, what trainings you have gone through to be more prepared to do this work, and what educational degree to you hold.

Accomplishments refer to what you have done to move this field forward, membership organizations you have helped to create, books and articles written, publicity about you and your work, presentations given, conferences spoken at, research, programs you have started, committees you sit on, or anything else notable.

1. **Name:**

2. **Contact Information (email, address, phone):**

3. **Name of program, employer, etc.:**

4. **Education/Training/Degree:**

5. **Method (circle): EFP EAP EFL Other:**

6. **Origination Year:**

7. **Memberships you maintain:**

8. **Accomplishments:**

Background Questions

Instructions/Explanations

Please spend as long as you need to with each question. Use as many pages as you need to answer each question as fully as possible. Simply indicate which question you are answering by using the question number before your answer. I need complete and detailed answers, not short sentences.

Background (how you came to be interested in this work, how you came up with your method, how it all happened – Tell a story of who you are and how this work has changed or transformed you):

Theory Base and Practical Application

Please describe and explain your theory for each of the following – how does each of these methods WORK (some of the below you may not have a theory about) THEORY DOES NOT MEAN DEFINITION – Tell me in your own words how you think each method actually works:

a. **Equine Facilitated Psychotherapy**

b. **Equine Assisted Psychotherapy**

c. **Equine Facilitated Learning**

Please share if there is any other term or name that you call the work you do rather than the above mentioned three. Does it fit into the above categories? Why or why not? What makes it different?

Please explain the application of each of these methods from your own experience with clients.

What are the therapeutic or educational goals set for each of the above methods?

What are your beliefs around safety? What things need to be taken into consideration when providing any of the above methods? Do the safety parameters change with the method?

Ethics of the work – Talk about your beliefs in this area, cite guidelines you utilize.

Discuss your feelings about standardization, training, and education within this field – In your opinion what is occurring and what needs to occur?

The Horse

Please discuss the role of the horse within each of the various methods as you believe it to be from your own experiences.

Do you think it matters how the horses are trained, what breeds, ages, sex, etc.?

In regards to horse care, what observations have you had in regards to how their care impacts their ability to do the work?

What have you noticed about the relationship between the facilitator and the horse? Is the work done more effectively if there is a relationship? Does that matter? How important is the relationship between the horse and the facilitator?

Is the horse more impactful in a session than the facilitator? Explain your feelings about that.

The Facilitator

In your opinion what are your unique contributions or inventions in regards to facilitation of the above methods? How has this changed or evolved over the course of your practice?

Please define in your opinion what the role of the facilitator is in each of the various methods. What types of training and education does the facilitator need to have for the various methods? What sort of participation within the session does the facilitator engage in?

In your opinion does it matter what theoretical background the "therapist" or "educator" comes to the work with? Explain.

What is the role of the psycho-therapeutic method that the therapist utilizes (i.e. Gestalt, Jungian, Behavior Modification, etc.) in an EFMH/ES session if facilitating EFP? Are there some psycho-therapeutic methods that work better than others in EFP sessions? Which do you use if any?

What is the role of the educational model that the educator uses in an EFMH/ES session if facilitating EFL? Are there models that work better than others? Which do you use if any?

Does the work of EFMH/ES have its own psycho-therapeutic or psycho-educational method that is a stand alone from any other? If you believe it does, please explain in detail what that might be.

Or, does the work of EFMH/ES more closely model play therapy or art therapy where people of diverse backgrounds come to the work with different methods? Please explain that model in detail if you believe this to be the case.

Please describe your beliefs about the relationship between the client and the facilitator in the context of an EFMH/ES session. Please share if you note differences between the various methods in regards to client/facilitator relationship.

What are your beliefs around the facilitator being or not being a horse person? Do you believe in the model of the horse professional and the therapist? Do you think that this model works? Why or why not?

What would you like to see in a facilitator in regards to horsemanship skills?

Clientele

What populations do you feel this work works for? Are there populations who benefit from a specific method vs. a different one? How do you make assessments as to who is right for this and what type of service they should receive?

Describe your typical client:

What are the contraindications for the various methods? Who should not be doing which method and why?

Please provide a "case study" that helps readers visualize the work you do with clients. Take readers through the actual process that the client goes through from the beginning of the session to the end. Demonstrate your methodology and how it is used in practice with a real client.

Assessment

How do you measure "success" or change in a client or in a session?

Please share your observations about the longevity of the "success" or change that occurs. Is it short term (change only occurs while with the horses), or long term (change lasts for years)?

What occurs within a session to make it "successful" in the long term vs. the short term? What factors need to be in place for long lasting change to happen?

Do you believe that good is derived from short term or even "crisis management" treatment? Please discuss your thoughts about this.

In your experience, has there been adequate documentation about the "failures" of EFMH/ES? What do you think are those failures and how are they manifested in your own work?

What research have you conducted to help provide validity to the work that you do? If you have not done any, what research do you use that helps provide validity? Please share these sources and how to obtain them. Talk about the results of such research and how that impacted your approach to treatment or education.

What research would you like to either conduct or see conducted? What is holding you back from doing that research (if anything) and what resources would you need to make that research possible?

Administration

Please discuss critical components of administration that readers need to be aware of. Talk about the types of forms you use, the insurance, the facility, staff, staff training and burnout, management, roles within the company, what you would do differently if you could do it all over again, and anything else newcomers to the field should know before embarking upon this career path.

Horses and Healing

A. What is healing? Give your definition.

B. Do you believe that "healing" is what is occurring between humans and horses? What other words do you use to describe what occurs between horses and humans in or after a session?

C. What is occurring physiologically within the human that leads to a sense of psychological well-being when in the presence of horses?

D. What makes EFMH/ES work? How much of it is the intervention between therapist or educator and client, and how much of it is between the horse and the client?

E. Could that answer be found in the ways people facilitate the work, explain?

F. How much of the benefit is derived from ecopsychology concepts vs. the horse? This means is it the horse at all, or simply that humans deeply crave interconnection with nature, and being at an EFMH/ES session fulfills that for them.

G. How do you separate those two concepts to come up with an answer for that question? Is it possible? How would you defend the notion that horses bring something beyond connection with nature to those who might question that concept?

H. How much of it is that the human facilitators who are brought to this work are different, more aware, etc. and therefore it's the "therapeutic presence" of the human person that makes such a sizable impact?

I. Could the horse be channeling something we have no real idea about at all? Something that is far beyond our current ability to understand, and that it is simply the horses who truly do all of the work, except the safety container and the interpretation of the work which is created/done by the human facilitator?

J. Does the client go into an "altered state of consciousness" when in the presence of the horse? How can you tell, what factors do you assess to determine whether or not they are in an "altered state of consciousness"?

K. If you believe that the client enters into an altered state, how does that impact the effectiveness of the service? Is it because they go into an altered state that "healing" occurs?

L. Do you think that an "altered state" is necessary for healing to occur?

M. How do you think the horse impacts consciousness? What makes the client enter into a non-ordinary state?

N. Why does EFMH/ES succeed where other therapeutic methods have failed?

O. Or does it?

Appendix B

Questionnaire

Note: This questionnaire was sent out to approximately five hundred individuals currently practicing in the field of Equine Facilitated Mental Health/Educational Services. The results were used in various parts of the text, as well as in the conceptual process of designing the layout for the book.

Questionnaire

General Information

Name: _____

Organization:_____

Location:_____

Email:_____

Year you started this work:_____

Method (Circle what you do): EFP EAP EEL
Other:_____

Who did you learn from?_____

What organizations (NARHA, EFMHA, EAGALA, EGEA, etc) are you associated with?

What trainings, workshops, or certifications have you done/do you have (this includes education: traditional, equine, and method specific)?

Questions

Please answer these questions with as much clarity and depth as possible. Use as much space as you need to.

1. Please write your definition of the EFMH/ES method(s) that you utilize:

2. Please write your theory about how the method you use WORKS, what makes it helpful, healing, etc. for your clients:

3. Please record ethical considerations that others should be aware of:

4. What populations do you find this method effective with?

5. Role of the Horse ~ Please record your view in regards to the role of the horse in your work.

6. Horse Care ~ Please tell me about any horse care practices you have found effective that are specific to EAMH/ES horses (living arrangements/conditions, herd dynamics, feeding, exercise, type of horses, amount of horses in your herd, breeds, etc.)

7. What education do you feel is required to provide the method that you provide?

8. Please share some of your favorite activities including the below information:

   - Activity Name
   - Intended Population (s)
   - Description of how to facilitate the activity
   - Number of horses, volunteers, clients
   - Equipment needs
   - Facility needs (arena, round pen, field, whatever)
   - Amount of time needed
   - Safety concerns

- Set up/Debrief questions
- Modality the activity is used for (EEL, EFP, EAL, other) and adaptations to be able to use it for another modality.

9. If you would like, share a touching, important, descriptive, story about an experience you had facilitating this work…. Showing how it works, why it's important, something beautiful, poignant, etc. (obviously not sharing the client's real name!)

10. Share any photographs you feel would highlight your story.

APPENDIX C

RESPONSES TO TERMINOLOGY QUESTION: HORSE AS TOOL OR HORSE AS CO-FACILITATOR?

Note: This is a sampling taken from the responses to this question that the author received from professionals practicing an EFMH/ES method. Although these responses do not represent the opinions of everyone working in the field, they do demonstrate a pattern in thinking. Out of the 35 professionals questioned, one responded suggesting that she believed that the term "tool" was an appropriate description of the horse in an EFMH/ES method and six suggested although they were more inclined to use the term "co-facilitator," they were not directly opposed to the use of the term "tool." The remaining 28 felt strongly that the term "tool" was an inappropriate description of the horse within an EFMH/ES method. These quotes are taken verbatim from email correspondence and not altered or edited in any fashion.

"What an insightful question. I have been grappling with this distinction myself of late. If I had to choose one, I would choose co-facilitator but I believe the horse is a powerful tool, too. The distinction that I see is that the horse is a therapeutic tool in that his presence in the session adds so much that would never be present in an office visit. But the instant and honest feedback he gives the client really makes the client dig deep inside for the answer or solution. Also, since the horse is a living thinking, feeling creature, I believe he should be thought of a a co-facilitator and not just a tool." - Sue Hahn, Executive Director, Green Gate Farm

"I do EAL only and do not deal with mental health issues. I work with youth on leadership, communication, problem solving etc. I view the horse as a team member because activities I plan require all team members to work together in order to come up with a solution or complete a task. It allows us to work on getting everyone to participate and contribute equally. It brings up great discussion." ~ Jeanne Castillo

"Although we refer to our horses as the 'tools of our trade,' we always consider them co-facilitators. Specifically, we consider them 'team members,' whereas a tool would be for our 'use,' team members are active participants in the therapeutic process." ~ Janet Cederlund, Executive Director, Light Center Foundation

"To me a tool would be inanimate. A horse is animate with his own feelings and personality so there is a definite relationship/connection made between the horse and the client." ~ Janet LeBlanc

"That's easy Leif, A tool is an object. A horse is a sentient being. A horse co-facilitates by BEING A HORSE. An object just does what it is supposed to do." ~ Harriet Power ~ Fullpower Equine Assisted Psychotherapy

"A horse is a co-facilitator. Horses mirror back feelings and things we as humans may miss. A tool is inanimate." ~ Honey Cowan

"I see the horse as a co-facilitator because it responds to the client. A tool, to me, is something more concrete that is constant in it's use without any variables. The horse has many variables including how it was created, it's own background, it's own personality, it's present circumstance and it's response to the client's variables." ~ Roxanne

"At Kaleidoscope Learning Circle we refer to horses as 'four-legged facilitators' and definitely view them as partners in the work. I believe that how the human facilitator relates to the horse has a fundamental impact on the entire EAP/EAL/EFP/EFL experience. That is not to say that there is a distinct line between these two belief systems, but rather a continuum upon which all facilitators appear. The primary reasons that I believe horses are our partners relates to my definitions of facilitator and tool. First of all, similar to competent human facilitators, they are objective, skilled at reading the dynamics of the individual or group, adapt to different situations, and evoke participation and creativity. (reference: Magic of the Facilitator, Brian Stanfield, http://www.iaf-world.org/i4a/pages/Index.cfm?pageid=3294). Secondly, if one considers a horse a 'tool' then that relegates the horse to the same thing as an inanimate object or similar learning resource. It is our belief that it is because they are horses they facilitate learning opportunities for humans." Dr. Tracy Weber

"It is hard to see a horse as a tool since they are so interactive in the session. For example I did a family session this summer in which the mother started out shouting commands and directions at her children. I had six horses in the arena with the family, 4 of which were pregnant mares. Three of the pregnant mares came over and surrounded the mother and backed her up against the fence--not only was she unable to shout at her children the mares effectively blocked her view of them. This incident created so much more dynamics to process than any activity we could have created. The horses act differently toward each and every client and change how they interact as the client changes. I use tools in therapy, such as confrontation or structure behavioral techniques. The horses provide interactions that the client can practice their coping skills to deal with." ~ Kay Kelly Anderson, M.Ed

"I'd like to address the question. It's a good one. I personally view the horse as a co-facilitator rather than a 'tool.' I view a 'tool' as an instrument, implement, utensil. I'm not very familiar with ropes courses, but I see the ropes course as a 'tool.' The horse is not only reactive but is a proactive member of the team. I work with adolescents who are chemically dependent and I've seen the kids drop their defenses and open up based on their relationships with the horses. The kids come to care for and care about the horses and the horses get to know the kids and treat each of them differently. In return, the kids treat each of the horses differently based on the horse's distinct personality. We have a yearling in our barn that I've owned since he was 3 1/2 months old. The teens in my recovery group taught him to lead, they've had a big part in socializing him. In return, the yearling has taught my clients by example how horses form relationships and about the hierarchy of the equine herd and how that pertains to human relationships. We did a whole series of exercises on 'Healthy Relationships' based on the

relationships that the horses have with each other. Does that sound like a tool or a co-facilitator to you?"
~ Linda Myers

"In response to your questions, I do not think of the horse as a tool. The horse is a sensate, feeling, alive being with its own intelligence and responsiveness. Co-facilitator comes closer in that it conveys relationship. However facilitator is a human concept and role so that does not fit either. I think of the horses in my work as being a partner working in relationship with me and my client from our human self and the horse from its horse self. There is a unique relationship of empathy and communication that develops and can be drawn upon in support of the client." ~ Jackie Lowe Stevenson

"Like the psychotherapist him/herself, the horse 'co-facilitates' EAP sessions by the process of the relationship formed between the clients and the horses, who cue off/respond to each other. Horses are metaphors for other relationships/situations in the clients' lives; and through the interaction with the horse, a client can shift cognitively and emotionally." ~ Sherry Simon-Heldt MS, LISAC, CSAT

"I think of my horses as co-facilitators. I think of a tool as an inanimate object used to help with a process. A co-facilitator engages in the process and has the power to direct the process in a different direction. For instance, in experiential therapy utilizing ropes courses, the rope is a tool. There is the possibility that a rope could break, and change the direction of the activity (and the insurance costs!), but it doesn't provide input as to a reason for changed direction. A horse, on the other hand, can direct us in a completely different direction than our original game plan! If a horse doesn't want to cooperate, that gives us information, and we can proceed - but not how we planned. Any response at any time by the horse can change our therapeutic experience. In this sense they co-facilitate." ~ Cindy Wright-Jones, Moriah Mounts, LLC

"To me, tool should not even be considered as an option for comparison. A tool has no feelings, expressions, emotions, and a tool is manufactured to meet the need of the consumer. To use a tool, one must have control, and knowledge, to accomplish the task at hand. Follow me? The horse is full of life, and even surprises.........depending upon the situation. The non-verbal communication between the horse and human is profound, and always present........you just can't lay it down and turn it off." ~ Daniel L. Stegman, Equine Specialist, Gaits of Growth Bison, KS

"I consider our horses the therapists. We are the facilitators. We bring the client and the horse together." ~ MaryAnn Brewer, Equine Specialist

"The horse is definitely a co-facilitator.. A tool is used...without a response from the tool. A horse does respond to the actions of the client...a horse gives instant feedback - has likes and dislikes - has to have education to do the job and continuing education (a tool does not). However, a horse is not a human with the same reasoning powers of a human. This is an advantage, as a horse does not come to a session with any pre-conceived opinions of the client. No matter how much humans try.... humans are still often judgmental." ~ Sue Rosen, The Adaptive Riding Institute

"For me, the horse is co-facilitator and at times leads the session while I interpret or ask questions. The horse is a living being with a mind of its own and a heart of its own....its not a hammer or screwdriver." ~ Pam Roberts, Equine Partners

"There is a BIG difference between a co-facilitator and a tool. I believe that the horse is a co-facilitator. This means that the horse is treated with respect and that emotional and physical needs are taken into account. Tools are used and often abused. Tools are used to get a job done no matter what the cost. Tools can be replaced. Tools can be duplicated. No two horses are the same. They cannot be duplicated. Horses can be exposed to stress during EAP sessions, and the human part of the teams evaluate whether the horse is managing the stress in a healthy way. If there is any doubt as to the mental health of the horse, then we must not ask the horse to do more than what he/she is capable of. The human facilitators are also exposed to stress, and we debrief, and manage the stress in a healthy way. I cringe when someone refers to a living being as 'a tool'." ~ Barb Bielak

"The horse is emphatically not a tool, but a co-facilitator. My philosophy is based on the horse as a thinking, feeling, responsive participant, whose feedback, personality, and reactions offer the client valuable information and experiences. The problem with the idea of the horse as "tool" is that it depersonalizes the relationship, allows for detachment, and can manifest as emotionally abusive--all areas that we are trying to help our clients move away from." ~ Marilyn Sokolof

FURTHER RESOURCES

**EFMH/ES Programs Mentioned in this Text
(With and Without Training Programs)**

Membership or Informational Organizations
   Equine Related
   Other Animals
   Mental Health Related
   Educationally Related
   Coaching Related

Research Organizations

University or College Programs in Human/Animal Bonding or Equine Specific Courses of Study

Forms
   Liability Release Form
   Release for Medical Treatment Form
   Release of Information Form
   Consent to Treatment Form

EFMH/ES Programs Mentioned in this Text

* = Programs that offer education and training for professionals interested in learning about EFMH/ES

* Adventures in Awareness
Tucson, Arizona
Barbara Rector
www.adventuresinawareness.net

Betty Ford Clinic
Rancho Mirage, California
Nancy O'Brian
www.bettyfordcenter.org

Bella Terra, Inc.
Mattawan, MI
Kim Shook
www.bellaterrainc.org

* Centaur Leadership Services
Prescott, Arizona
Paul Smith
www.prescott.edu

Cottonwood De Tucson
Tucson, AZ
Laura Brinkerhoff
www.cottonwooddetucson.com

* Carroll College
Helena, MT
Dr. Anne Perkins/Leif Hallberg
www.carroll.edu

* Epona Equestrian Services
Sonoita, Arizona
Linda Kohanov
www.taoofequus.com

Equinection
Asheville, NC
Karen Head
klillian@BellSouth.net

Equine Partners, LLC
Florissant, Colorado
Pam Roberts
equinepart@aol.com

* Esperanza
Bozeman, MT
Leif Hallberg
www.esperanzainformation.com
esperanza_eelc@hotmail.com

Green Chimneys
Dr. Suz Brooks and Michael Kauffmann
www.greenchimneys.com

* Hacienda Tres Aquilas, LTD.
Three Eagles Ranch
The McCormicks
www.therapyhorsesandhealing.com

Harvest of Hope Family Services Inc- Gaits of Growth
Bison, Kansas
Gayle Edwards-Stegman
hhfs@rualtel.net

Healing With Horses
Tucson, Arizona
Sherry Simon-Heldt
www.healingwithhorseseap.com

* Horse Power
Temple, New Hampshire
Boo McDaniel
www.horse-power.org

* Horsepower Productions
Chris Irwin
www.chrisirwin.com

Horse Sense of the Carolina's Inc
Marshall, NC
Laura Anthony
laura@horsesenseotc.com

HorseTime
Covington, Georgia
Maureen Vidrine
www.horsetime.org

Kaleidoscope Learning Circle
Birch Run, MI
Tracy Weber

L Lazy E Ranch
Tucson, Arizona
Ann Alden
www.llazyeranch.com

Marilyn Sokolof

Minnesota Linking Individuals, Nature, and Critters
Molly DePrekal and Tanya Walsh
www.mnlinc.com

Miraval Life In Balance
Tucson, Arizona
Wyatt Webb
www.miravalresorts.com

Moriah Mounts, LLC
LaPorte, Colorado
Cindy Wright-Jones
moriahmounts@frii.com

* OK Corral Series
Greg Kersten
www.okcorralseries.com

The Red Road
Northern California
Wendy Wood
wendy@theredroad.net

Remuda Ranch
Wickenburg, Arizona
Cheryl E. Musick
cheryl.musick@remudaranch.com

Rolling Horse Ranch
Ramona, CA
Dr. Ellen Gehrke
www.rollinghorseranch.com

Susan Taylor
www.equinepsychotherapy.org

Wisdom Horse Coaching, LLC
Minneapolis, Minnesota
Ann Romberg and Lynn Baskfield
www.WisdomHorseCoaching.com

Membership or Informational Organizations

This section is designed to provide the reader with additional information and resources that may be of use to those interested in pursuing the field of EFMH/ES further.

Equine Related
North American Riding for the Handicapped Association (NARHA)
PO Box 33150 Denver, CO 80233
voice: 800-369-7433 or (303) 452-1212
fax: (303) 252-4610
www.narha.org

Equine Facilitated Mental Health Association (EFMHA)
PO Box 33150 Denver, CO 80233
voice: 800-369-7433 or (303) 452-1212
fax: (303) 252-4610
www.narha.org

American Hippotherapy Association (AHA)
136 Bush Road Damascus, PA. 18415
(888) 851-4592 \ Fax: (570) 224-4462
www.americanhippotherapyassociation.com

Equine Assisted Growth and Learning Association (EAGALA)
PO Box 993 Santaquin, UT 84655
Toll Free (in U.S.): (877) 858-4600 Phone: (801) 754-0400 Fax: (801) 754-0401
www.eagala.org

Equine Guided Education Association (EGEA)
P.O. Box 337 Valley Ford, California 94972
707-876-1908 Phone 707-876-1908 Fax Email: Info@ equineguidededucation.org
www.equineguidededucation.org

United States Pony Club (USPC)
4041 Iron Works Parkway Lexington, KY 40511
859-254-7669 Fax: 859-233-4652
www.ponyclub.org

American Riding Instructors Association (ARIA)
28801 Trenton Court Bonita Springs, FL 34134-3337
Phone: 239-948-3232 Fax: 239-948-5053 E-mail: aria@riding-instructor.
com
www.riding-instructor.com

Certified Horsemanship Association (CHA)
5318 Old Bullard Rd. Tyler, TX 75703
800-399-0138 or 903-509-AHSE Fax: 903-509-2474 E-mail: horsesafty@
aol.com
www.cha-ahse.org

American Association for Horsemanship Safety (AAHS)
Drawer 39 Fentress, TX 78622
512-488-2220 Fax- 512-488-2319 E-mail: mail@horsemanshipsafety.com
www.horsemanshipsafety.com

American Camp Association (ACA)
5000 State Road 67 North Martinsville, IN 46151-7902
Phone: 765-342-8456 Fax: 765-342-2065
www.ACAcamps.org

Horsemanship Safety Association (HSA)
120 Ohio Avenue Madison, WI 53704
800-798-8106

Other Animals

Delta Society
875 124th Ave. NE, Ste. 101 Bellevue, WA 89005-2531
(425) 679-5500 email: info@deltasociety.org
www.deltasociety.org

People, Animals, Nature (PAN)
1820 Princeton Circle Naperville, IL 60565
e-mail address is: pan@pan-inc.org
www.pan-inc.org

International Association of Human-Animal Interaction Organizations (IAHAIO)
www.iahaio.org

Mental Health Related

American Psychological Association (APA)
750 First Street, NE, Washington, DC 20002-4242
Telephone: (800) 374-2721 or (202) 336-5500
www.apa.org

American Counseling Association (ACA)
5999 Stevenson Ave. Alexandria, VA 22304
Fax Number: (703) 823-0252 Phone: (800) 347-6647
www.counseling.org

National Board of Certified Counselors (NBCC)
3 Terrace Way Greensboro, North Carolina 27403-3660
Phone: 336.547.0607 Fax: 336.547.0017
www.nbcc.org

American Psychotherapy Association (APA)
2750 E. Sunshine St. Springfield, MO 65804
(800) 205-9165 phone (417) 823-9959 fax
www.americanpsychotherapy.com

National Association of Social Workers (NASW)
750 First Street, NE • Suite 700 • Washington, DC 20002-4241
www.naswdc.org

American Art Therapy Association (AATA)
5999 Stevenson Ave. Alexandria, VA 22304
1-888-290-0878/703-212-2238 E-mail: info@arttherapy.org
www.arttherapy.org

Association for Play Therapy (APT)
2060 N. Winery Avenue, #102 · Fresno, CA 93703 USA
Tel: 559·252·2278 / Fax: 559·252·2297 / E·mail: info@a4pt.org
www.a4tp.org

The American Society of Group Psychotherapy and Psychodrama (ASGPP)
301 N Harrison St. Suite 508 Princeton, NJ 08540
Telephone 609-452-1339 E-mail: asgpp@asgpp.org, Fax: 732-605-7033
www.asgpp.com

The American Psychoanalytic Association (APSAA)
309 East 49th Street New York, New York 10017-1601
Phone: (212) 752-0450 Fax: (212) 593-0571 Email: info@apsa.org
www.apsa.org

International Psychoanalytic Association (IPA)
Broomhills, Woodside Lane, London N12 8UD,United Kingdom
Phone: **+44 20 8446 8324** Fax: **+44 20 8445 4729** Email: ipa@ipa.org.uk
www.ipa.org

The Society for Gestalt Theory and its Applications (GTA)
c/o Dipl.Psych. Michael Ruh Steinweg 11, D-35066 Frankenberg, Germany
Phone: (+49) 6451-716700 / Fax: (+49) 6451-718556
www.gestalttheory.net

World Association for Person-Centered and Experiential Psychotherapy and Counseling (WAPCEPC)
PO Box 142, Ross-on-Wye, HR9 9AG, United Kingdom
www.pce-world.org

Association for Humanistic Psychology (AHP)
1516 Oak St, #320A Alameda, CA 94501-2947
Phone: 510/769-6495 ahpoffice@aol.com
www.aphweb.org

The International Community for Ecopsychology (ICE)
www.ecopsychology.org

The Ecopsychology Institute
www.ecopsychology.athabascau.ca.

Project NatureConnect
www.ecopsych.com

The National Association of Alcohol and Drug Abuse Counselors (NAADAC)
901 N. Washington St. Suite 600 Alexandria, VA 22314
703-741-7686/ 800-548-0497phone 703-741-7698/800-377-1136 fax
E-mail naadac@naadac.org
www.naadac.org

National Association of Addiction Treatment Providers (NAATP)
313 W. Liberty Street, Suite 129, Lancaster, PA 17603-2748 - Phone: 717
392-8480 - Fax: 717 392-8481 - rhunsicker@naatp.org
www.naatp.org

Alcoholics Anonymous (AA)
P.O. Box 459, New York, NY 10163
(212) 870-3400
www.alcoholics-anonymous.org

Narcotics Anonymous (NA)
PO Box 9999 Van Nuys, California 91409 USA
Telephone (818) 773-9999 Fax (818) 700-0700
www.na.org

Al-Anon
1600 Corporate Landing Parkway Virginia Beach, VA 23454-5617
Tel: (757) 563-1600 Fax: (757) 563-1655 email us: wso@al-anon.org
www.al-anon.alateen.org

Educationally-Related

The Association for Experiential Educators (AEE)
3775 Iris Avenue, Suite #4
Boulder, CO 80301-2043 USA
Phone: (+1) 303-440-8844 **Toll Free:** 866-522-8337 **Fax:** (+1) 303-440-9581
www.aee.org

National Society for Experiential Education (NCEE)
c/o TALLEY MANAGEMENT GROUP, INC.
19 Mantua Road Mt. Royal, NJ 08061
(856) 423-3427 (856) 423-3420 (fax) Email: nsee@talley.com
www.nsee.org
The National Association of Therapeutic Schools and Programs (NATSAP)
126 North Marina, Prescott, Arizona 86301
928.443.9505
www.natsap.org

Independent Educational Consultants Association (IECA)
3251 Old Lee Highway, Suite 510 Fairfax, Virginia 22030-1504
Phone: 703-591-4850 Fax: 703-591-4860 info@IECAonline.com
www.educationalconsulting.org

Coaching Related

The International Association of Coaching (IAC)
www.certifiedcoach.org

The International Coaching Federation (ICF)
2365 Harrodsburg Rd, Suite A325
Lexington, KY 40504 Phone: 888.423.3131 (toll-free) +1.859.219.3580
Fax: +1.859.226.4411
Email: icfheadquarters@coachfederation.org
www.coachfederation.org

The Professional Coaches and Mentors Association (PCMA)
Tel: 800-768-6017
www.pcmaonline.com

Research
Network for Research on Experiential Psychotherapies
Robert Elliott, Ph.D. Department of Psychology, University of Toledo,
Toledo, OH 43606 USA
telephone: 419-530-2715 (office/voicemail); 419-530-8479 (fax)
e-mail: relliot@uoft02.utoledo.edu
www.experiential-researchers.org

Horses and Humans Foundation
P.O. Box 480, Chagrin Falls, Ohio 44022
440-543-8306 • info@horsesandhumans.org
www.horsesandhumans.org

Companion Animal Information and Research Center
http://www.cairc.org/

Ethologia
http://users.skynet.be/ethologia/
Description: Encourages and initiates studies on human-pet relations, and examines the role and the place of pets in our society.

EFMH/ES College or University Programs

Institution: Prescott College, Prescott, AZ
Degree: Masters Degree in Counseling/Psychology with an Emphasis in Equine Assisted Mental Health Services.
EFMH/ES Course Specific Examples: Foundations of EAMH, EAMH Program Evaluation, Equine Facility Management, Building Self-esteemThrough Equine Therapy, EAGALA Level One Training.
Instructor: Paul Smith, M.A., psmith@prescott.eedu
Summary: This concentration allows students seeking licensure or certification as a psychotherapist or in counseling psychology to develop competence in the rapidly evolving area of EAMH. In addition to the established core requirements designed for professional licensure, this course work explores the theoretical understanding, ethical issues, facilitation skills, and relational horsemanship skills crucial for mastery in this area of counseling.

Institution: Carroll College, Helena, MT
Degree: Minor/Major in Human/Animal Bonding with an Emphasis in Equine Facilitated Mental Health/Educational Services.
EFMH/ES Course Examples: Foundations of EFMH/ES, Introduction to Equine Psychology, Physiology, and Behavior, Introduction to Equine Safety, Introduction to EFMH/ES Facilitation Skills, EFE/L or EFMHS Concentration Courses, Research Methods and Design.
Instructor: Leif Hallberg, M.A., lhallberg1@hotmail.com
Summary: Carroll College's EFMH/ES educational program was designed by Leif Hallberg in conjunction with Dr. Anne Perkins, head of the Human/Animal Bonding Program. The EFMH/ES courses provide students with an introduction to the theoretical and practical applications of EFMH/ES methods, teach students the ethical and legal considerations applicable to the field, and prepare students for enrollment in a Masters program specific to their area of interest (EFE/L or EFMHS).

Animal Assisted College/University Programs

Institution: Animal Behavior Institute, Inc. Furlong, PA 18925
Course Title: Animal Assisted Therapy (ABI 211)
Instructor: Janis G. Hammer, VMD, hammerj@animaledu.com ,
866-755-0448
Summary: This is an online course. There is a rapidly growing
movement to incorporate animals as part of the therapeutic setting.
Students learn about the difference between animal assisted activities,
therapy and education (AAA/T/E), working animals and assistance
animals. The course covers working with animals and children,
adults, the elderly, and the disabled in various settings including
hospitals, nursing homes, schools and prisons. We will also review
what is required to start and run a safe and effective program.

Institution: Animal Behavior Institute, Inc. Furlong, PA 18925
Course Title: The Human-Animal Bond (ABI 232)
Instructor: Janis G. Hammer, VMD, hammerj@animaledu.com ,
866-755-0448
Summary: This course explores the history and psychology of
human relationships with animals and nature and will be run
completely online. The student will learn about the relationship
between people and animals by discussing domestication,
socialization, religion, culture, farming, research, and pets. Other
topics include pet overpopulation, relinquishment, bonding,
and health benefits from the bond (for people and animals). The
principal objective is to gain an understanding of the various roles
animals play in our lives.
Course offering information: This course will be taught for the first
time beginning in January 2006.

Institution: Camden County College, Blackwood, NJ 08012
Course Title: Survey Course in Animal-Assisted Therapy and
Animal-Assisted Activities
Instructor: Phil Arkow, Animal Technology Program, arkowpets@
snip.net
Coordinator: Kathy Forsythe, Continuing Education Office, 856-
374-4955, kforsythe@camdencc.edu

Summary: A 12-week Continuing Education Certificate program course offered in the Spring and Fall semesters to introduce students to the human-companion animal bond and its therapeutic applications in a variety of healing environments. Designed for professionals in the animal care and human health fields as well as individuals seeking vocational and volunteer opportunities. Curriculum includes renowned guest lecturers and field trips to explore such topics as AAT in hospitals, nursing homes, and children's institutions; therapeutic riding; animal welfare issues; the human-companion animal bond in different cultures; service animals; pet loss; animal behavior; and the link between animal abuse and interpersonal violence. For students who are unable to attend locally, a Distance Learning version is available through Harcum College in Bryn Mawr, PA.

Institution: Delaware Valley College, Doylestown, PA 18901-2697
Course Title: People and Animals
Instructor: Janis G. Hammer, VMD, hammerj@devalcol.edu
Summary: The course covers many topics regarding the positive aspects of our relationship with animals as well as the much less common but negative aspects. The topics discussed include but are not limited to; animals in religion, domestication, service and working animals, the changing role of animals in society over time (e.g. ownership vs. guardian, pet insurance), the role of animals in different cultures, animal abuse, inappropriate bonding, and the health benefits of the bond for both man and animals. This course is a prerequisite for the spring course; Animal Assisted Activities and Therapy; Programs, Procedures, nad Responsibilities.

Institution: Harcum College, Bryn Mawr, PA 19010
Course Title: Introduction to Animal-Assisted Therapy and Animal-Assisted Activities--Distance Learning Certificate course for **Fall 2006** (AAT 101-IN)
Instructor: Phil Arkow, (856) 627-5118, arkowpets@snip.net
Coordinator: To register, contact Kelly Wilson, Continuing Studies, (610) 526-6083, kwilson@harcum.edu
Summary: This new, comprehensive Introduction to Animal-Assisted Therapy & Activities is taught by internationally renowned

human-animal bond and AAT author Phil Arkow. The course offers a Certificate of Completion: this Certificate may be eligible for employer reimbursement and Continuing Education Units depending upon the requirements of the student's employer and/or professional association. This course covers the human-animal bond and its therapeutic applications. It is designed both for professionals from a wide range of disciplines, and for volunteers, students and newcomers who wish to further their knowledge and explore career opportunities in this emerging, multi-disciplinary field. International students are particularly welcomed. Students will examine how contact with animals can enhance human well-being when incorporated into health care, social services, psychology, psychiatry, education, allied health, therapy, and many more fields. Students may already be trained in these or similar fields, or may be seeking to enter the field. The course explores conceptual frameworks, research, and practical techniques that will empower you to introduce animals in a variety of milieus. It enhances students' personal growth and professional development. Through extensive reading, on-line research, site visits to local facilities, and networking in on-line discussion groups, students will obtain both an overview of the human-companion animal bond (HCAB) and Animal-Assisted Therapy & Activities (AAT/AAA), and opportunities to concentrate on specific programs or applications of particular personal and/or professional interest.

Institution: Mercy College, New York
Course Title: Animal Assisted Therapy (Course as part of Certificate Program)
Instructor: Suz Brooks, Psy.D., Adjunct Professor at Mercy College in the Veterinary Technology Department, and Psychologist at the Green Chimneys Farm, sbrooks@greenchimneys.org
Other Contact: Kelly, Mercy College, 914-674-7560
Summary: This year long certificate program has been in existence as a single course since 1991, and has existed as a certificate program since 1996 encompassing 6 classes and a 150 hour internship. The certificate combines both hands-on training in animal behavior as well as training in learning to build a relationship to work within the human - animal bond. Currently the courses in this certificate

include: An Overview into AAT, Applied Animal Behavior, Animal Behavior, Learning Disabilities, Working with the Elderly, and Abnormal Psychology. Each course is 8 weeks long, and 5 or 6 hours per course, depending on the course. Class size has ranged from 7-15 students, most who are already licensed in a field and are learning how to bring animals into their practices. The basic format of hands-on learning is integrated throughout all classes with theory, principles, and issues.

Institution: People, Animals, Nature, Inc.--PAN, 1807 South Washington Street, Suite 110, Naperville, IL 60565-2050
Course Title: Animals and Nature in Healing Environments: Certificate Course in Animal-Assisted Therapy and Education
Contact: Bill Samuels at wesamuels@gmail.com or Debbie Coultis, President and CEO, at coultis@gmail.com
Summary: Animals and Nature in Healing Environments (Animal-Assisted Intervention) is offered to professionals who are interested in learning how to incorporate animals and nature into the work they are already trained to do. The course is designed for health care practitioners, educators, veterinarians, researchers and other human service providers. For more information about this program, see http://snl.depaul.edu/ and http://www.pan-inc.org/certfprogm.php .

Institution: University of Denver, Denver, Colorodo
Course Title: Integration of Animals into Therapeutic Settings
Instructors: Philip Tedeschi, MSSW, LCSW, Graduate School of Social Work and Jennifer Fitchett, MSW, 303-871-3833, jfitchet@du.edu; ptedesch@du.edu
Summary: This course is the prerequisite course required for the Animal-Assisted Social Work Certificate offered at the University of Denver. It is also a second year elective and will expose all participants to the use of animals as an adjunct to Social Work practice. The course explores the human-animal bond and potential for therapeutic intervention with the animal as teacher, therapist, facilitator, and companion in a number of therapeutic settings. It focuses on core skills for social workers seeking to integrate this clinical approach into their practice.

Website: See www.du.edu/gssw/professionalDev/
animalsHumanHealth/ for more information.

Institution: University of Denver, Denver, Colorodo
Course Title: Animal Assisted Application to Social Work Practice
Instructors: Philip Tedeschi, MSSW, LCSW, Graduate School of
Social Work
Summary: This course is the second, more in-depth application
course required for the Animal-Assisted Social Work Certificate
offered at the University of Denver. It is also a second year elective
and will expose all participants to the use of animals as an adjunct to
Social Work practice. Social Work Practice provides a comprehensive
examination of approaches to Animal-Assisted Social Work (AASW)
and emphasizes clinical application skills utilized with a broad
array of persons and in a number of therapeutic settings. Students
will learn to design, implement, and analyze the efficacy of AASW
approaches within their chosen area of specialization, providing an
opportunity to practice these approaches at their field internships.
Students will learn to clearly articulate, assess and intervene in "link"
violence as it relates to social work pratice and AASW implications.
Website: See http://www.du.edu/gssw/certificate/animalAssisted.htm
for more information.

Institution: University of Denver, Denver, Colorodo
Course Title: Animals and Human Health
Instructor: Sue Teumer, steumer@du.edu
Summary: Animals and Human Health course seeks to understand
the remarkable human-animal bond and potential for therapeutic
intervention with the animal as teacher, therapist, facilitator and
companion in a number of therapeutic settings. Focus is placed on
developing knowledge, ethics, values and the skills for individuals
seeking to integrate these clinical approaches into a wide range of
settings. Students will also be expected to examine the link between
animal abuse and other forms of violence. This course is designed to
provide students a foundation in understanding human and animal
connection. Animals can be introduced into a number of therapeutic
settings, with diverse populations. The application of Animal-

Assisted Therapy/Activities/Leaning (AAT/AAA/AAL) can be used with individuals, groups and families in varied settings.

Institution: University of North Texas, Denton, Texas 76203
Course Title: Animal Assisted Therapy (COUN 5530)
Instructor: Cynthia Chandler, Ed.D., LPC, LMFT, BCIA-C & EEG, Professor of Counseling, chandler@coe.unt.edu , 940-565-2910
Summary: This course is graduate level, but undergraduates may also take it as a special problems course. The course covers research and methods for the application of animal assisted therapy in the field of mental health counseling and closely related fields. The course emphasizes how a professional counselor may utilize the special relationship she/he has with his/her pet to provide services for persons in need. The safety and welfare of the therapy pet are also emphasized.
Website: www.coe.unt.edu/CDHE/AAT/

Institution: West Chester University, West Chester, PA 19383-2515
Course Title: Special Topics: Animals in Health and Human Service
Instructor: Lynn Carson, Ph.D., CHES, lcarson@wcupa.edu
Summary: To validate the significant purpose that animals serve in people's health and well being, this course will provide students with a thorough understanding of the role of service and therapy animals in improving the quality of life for disabled individuals and others in need. Course content is specifically designed for health and human service professionals who are considering introducing animal service and animal therapy into their work environments. Students will be introduced to the various types of service animals and a major emphasis will be placed on the types of services these animals perform for physically disabled, hearing impaired, and sight impaired individuals. An overview of the role of service/therapy animals and practice settings (homes, employment sites, nursing homes, hospitals, schools, and prisons) will be presented to demonstrate the wide diversity of service opportunities for animals. The use of animals as therapeutic agents will be highlighted with a focus on the roles of dogs and horses in practice settings (i.e. physical therapy, speech therapy, occupational therapy and psychotherapy). Other service

roles (search and rescue and criminal justice) will be included. Guest speakers, visits to training facilities and discussions with trainers, owners, volunteers will help students understand how service/therapy animals are versatile reliable assistants serving an important role in supportive and therapeutic care.

Human-Animal Bond University Centers

Purdue University http://www.vet.purdue.edu/chab/links.htm

University of Pennsylvania
http://www.vet.upenn.edu/research/centers/CIAS/

University of California, Davis
http://www.vetmed.ucdavis.edu/CCAB/paws.htm

Washington State University
http://www.vetmed.wsu.edu/depts-pppp/

Washington State University, People-Pet Partnership
http://www.vetmed.wsu.edu/deptspppp/research.asp

University of Minnesota http://www.censhare.umn.edu/

Colorado State University http://www.argusinstitute.colostate.edu/

Washington State University
http://www.vetmed.wsu.edu/depts-CSAW/index.html

Tuskegee University
http://hometown.aol.com/sebi2i/myhomepageindex.html

Human-Animal Bond in Tennessee
http://web.utk.edu/~vetmed/habit/index.html

Human-Animal Bond Initiative, College of Nursing, Michigan State
University   http://nursing.msu.edu/habi/index.html

Description: The College of Nursing, in collaboration with
veterinarians and animal behaviorists, announces the development of
Human-Animal Bond Initiative. Our goal is to better understand the
interactions between humans and animals and to better assess how
animals enrich our lives.

Forms

SAMPLE FORM

Liability Release
Agreement and Liability Release
Read Carefully Before Signing

For valuable consideration the receipt and legal sufficiency of which is acknowledged, I agree with_____ (referred to herein as "_____") as a condition for its allowing me, and the other persons identified below to enter the property of the _____, and or/ride or be near horses on, near, or of _____or its staff or volunteers.

NAME OF CONTRACTING PARTY:

_____

ADDRESS:

_____

PHONE: (HOME)_____
(BUSINESS)_____

All parts of this agreement shall apply to me, and the children/legal wards listed above. (We will collectively call ourselves "I", "me", or "my" throughout this agreement.) This agreement is binding whenever _____, now or in the future, permits me to enter the property of _____, be near horses, and/or ride horses on, near, or off of _____property.

IT IS HEREBY AGREED AS FOLLOWS:

1. I have requested to enter the premises and/or ride horses on, near, or off _____ property.

2. I understand that anyone riding or being near to horses (equines) can suffer bodily harm and other injuries and that there are inherent risks in equine activities, which include but are not limited to the following:

   a. the propensity of a horse to behave in ways that may result in injury, harm, or death to persons on or around it;

   b. the unpredictability of a horse's sudden reactions to such things as sounds, sudden movement, unfamiliar objects, people, or subsurface conditions, collisions with other equines or objects, people, or other animals;

   c. hazards such as surface or subsurface conditions, collisions with other equine or objects, and many others.

Horses are known to kick, buck, rear, bite, run, or spook. I know that any horse can do these things without warning. I understand these and other inherent risks and dangers, and I voluntarily agree to assume them.

3. I am fully responsibly for my own safety while on, near, or off of _____property. I understand That_____ has advised me to wear properly fitted and secured ASTM-certified/SEI-approved protective equestrian headgear when riding or near horses in order to prevent or reduce the severity of some head injuries as a result of a fall of other occurrences.

4. I hereby state that I am physically able to undertake all riding/horse orientated activities and I have presented_____ with a medical statement indicating physicians approval if any medical condition(s) do exist. I also state that I will participant in these activities at my own risk.

Leif Hallberg

LIABILITY RELEASE:

I assume full responsibility for any and all bodily injuries or damages which I may sustain when on, near, or off of _____property as well as when riding horses, on, hear, or off of _____property. By the term, 'damages', I mean, for example, medical expenses, expenses incurred because of bodily injury or property damages, and/or personal property damages. I, or my heirs, administrators, personal representatives, or assigns release and discharge_____ ____, and its respective members, owners, agents, officers, directors, partners, employees, managers, volunteers, trainers, instructors, heirs, representatives, assistants, insurers, assigns, and others acting on their behalf of and from all claims, demands, actions, omissions, rights of action, or causes of action (present and future), whether the sums be known or unknown, anticipated or unanticipated, resulting from or arising out of me or my guest's bodily injury or damage that may be sustained or property damage which may occur as a result of my being on, near, or off of the premises of _____ (unless _____caused the injury, damage or loss intentionally or in reckless disregard for my safety).

INDEMNIFICATION:

I also hereby agree to indemnify and hold harmless_____ _, and its respective members, owners, agents, officers, directors, partners, employees, managers, volunteers, trainers, instructors, heirs, representatives, assistants, insurers, assigns, and others acting on their behalf against all damages sustained or suffered by any third person(s) (people who are not parties to this agreement, including, but not limited to, my relatives, guests, etc.) including any and all injuries or damages whatsoever that I may cause while being on the premises of _____, riding or near horses around _____property, and /or riding horses off of _____property. This indemnification shall also include reasonable attorney fees and costs. I have read this agreement, and had an opportunity to seek independent legal advice prior to signing this agreement and liability release.

I represent that I am and will be at all times while on or near _____property, covered by accident, and/or medical insurance or I have sufficient funds to cover my medical expenses.

My insurance company is: _____

Policy Number: _____.

(State of Operation) law shall govern this agreement. Should any clause conflict with state law, that clause will be null and void and the remainder of the Agreement and Liability Release shall remain in effect.

_____

Signature of Contracting Party

_____

Date of Signature

_____

Signature of Representative

_____

Date of Signature

SAMPLE FORM

Rider's Authorization for Emergency Medical Treatment Form

In the event emergency medical aid/treatment is required due to illness or injury during the process of receiving services or while being on the property of the agency, I authorize _____ to:

1) Secure and retain medical treatment and transportation if needed.
2) Release client records upon request to authorized individual or agency in the medical emergency treatment.

Consent Plan

Client's Name: _____
Phone: _____

Address: _____
City: _____ State: _____ Zip:_____

In the event that I cannot be reached:

Contact: _____ Phone:_____

Contact: _____ Phone: _____

Physician's name: _____

Preferred Medical Facility: _____

Health Insurance: _____

Policy #: _____

Consent Plan

This authorization includes x-rays, surgery, hospitalization, medication, and any treatment procedure deemed "life-saving" by physician. This provision will only be invoked if the person below is unable to be reached.

Date: _____

Consent Signature: _____
                              Client, Parent or Guardian

Non-Consent Plan

I do not give my consent for emergency medical treatment/aid in the case of illness or injury during the process of receiving services or while being on the property of the agency. In the event emergency treatment/aid is required I wish the following procedures to take place:

Date: _____

Non-Consent Signature: _____
                                   Client. Parent or Guardian

SAMPLE FORM

Consent for Release of Information

To: _____

Address: _____

Phone:_____Fax:_____
Email:_____

I, _____ hereby give
permission to the therapeutic staff of _____
in connection with my treatment to disclose the following:

_____ Medical Records (please describe physical limitations
      or any medical condition that exists)

_____ My mental health record in its entirety; or

_____ My substance abuse record in its entirety; or

_____ Only the following checked information:

_____ Mental Health Evaluation

_____ Diagnosis Assessment

_____ Substance Abuse Evaluation

_____ Treatment Plan

_____ Treatment Recommendations

_____ Progress Report on my Treatment

_____ Attendance Records Only

_____ Other_____

Please provide this information as follows:
_____ Verbally _____ Written _____Other_____

The purpose for such disclosure is:

_____ To permit continuity of care

_____ To permit Case Management (including reimbursement determinations and processing benefit claims)

_____ To enable my employer to make a determination of my employment status

_____ Other_____

I may revoke this consent at any time except to the extent that action has been taken in reliance upon it. If I do not revoke it, consent will expire one year after I have terminated treatment with the therapeutic staff of _____.

_____   _____
Client/Student   Parent/Guardian

_____   _____
Witness   Date

SAMPLE FORM

Informed Consent Form

Note: This form is very specific to Esperanza's services and program. However, it may help as a model for what such forms might include. This form is only given to those participating in a mental health service. Those who engage in a learning or education service receive a different informational packet that does include aspects of this contract but tailored to the work that they will be doing at Esperanza.

OUTPATIENT SERVICES CONTRACT

Welcome to the Esperanza Center. This document contains important information about the Center's professional services and business policies. Please read it carefully. When you sign this document, it will constitute an agreement between you as the "client" and Esperanza as the "service provider."

PSYCHOLOGICAL SERVICES

At Esperanza we provide Equine Facilitated Mental Health Services. These services are designed to address psychological, relationship, and communication skills issues, self confidence and self esteem issues, attention and focus issues, family issues, and to help promote the health and wellness of the whole person. Equine Facilitated Mental Health Services include horses as co-facilitators of the therapeutic experience. Due to this inclusion, your treatment will look different from a more traditional therapeutic service.

First, you will be in close proximity to the horses. You will be engaging with the horses in a number of ways that could include observation, touching, grooming, leading, free-form interactions, and even riding. Therefore, it is essential that you understand the inherent risk factor that comes with the horse/human relationship. Horses are large and potentially dangerous and may act or re-act suddenly without noticeable warning. The Esperanza Center staff will provide you with important safety information prior to coming into close proximity with horses, and will utilize any and all safety precautions needed to help keep you safe. However, it is still important that you understand the inherent risks and dangers associated with this form of treatment, and that you voluntarily agree to assume them. You will be asked to read and sign a Liability Release that further demonstrates your agreement to assume these risks.

Second, in our practice, psychotherapeutic work with horses appears to deeply impact some clients. You may experience intense emotional states when in the presence of horses. You may also experience sudden change, personal realizations, or make new decisions about old situations.

Furthermore, the horses tend to require that we are honest and authentic about ourselves and our situations. Therefore, during treatment you may experience uncomfortable feelings like sadness, guilt, anger, frustration, loneliness, and helplessness. At the closure of a session you may feel particularly raw and emotionally exposed. We recommend that you do not drive immediately following a session, but rather take some time to come back into your body, refocus, and prepare for departure back to your "normal" life. We also recommend that you drink plenty of water and have a snack available in your car for your drive following the session.

Third, counseling and psychotherapeutic services call for a very active effort on your part. In order for the therapy to be most successful, you will have to work on the things we address both during our sessions and at home. Since the horses ask us to be authentic, congruent, and honest with ourselves, you may find that our services are more confrontational than traditional psychotherapeutic services. It is important that you are aware of and agree to a psychotherapeutic service that may induce more rapid change due to the intensity, confrontation, and focus of the service.

Forth, your services will generally be conducted outside, sometimes regardless of the elements, and will be with or around horses. You will need to be prepared for varying weather conditions and/or environmental conditions and dress accordingly. This means wearing close toed shoes, pants, and being prepared with layers appropriate for the weather conditions. In the summertime that would look like wearing a sun hat, sun screen, and light weight clothes. In the fall or winter that would look like wearing a warm hat, gloves, warm boots, jacket, and bringing plenty of layers. Water is important year around, so make sure to bring a water bottle regardless of the season.

Fifth, in many cases we utilize art activities that help illuminate presenting issues. We may also use nature-based approaches, guided imagery, and meditative exercises.

Sixth, we believe in a wrap-around approach to treatment. This means that during your treatment at Esperanza we may ask to speak with any and all other services providers who you see. We will probably want to see any past psychological testing results, or other applicable supplementary documentation of prior treatment. We will request that you sign a Release of Information which will allow us to speak with any of your other treatment providers. In order for them to speak with us, they will probably also request that you sign a Release of Information as well. We may also suggest a marriage/family counseling approach be taken dependant upon your situation, and therefore may suggest inviting other members of your family or your significant other to join us. During treatment at Esperanza we may recommend additional services to you. This could look like getting a massage, seeing a different type of doctor (psychiatrist, naturopath, etc.), seeing a nutritionalist, or obtaining further testing or evaluation.

Our first few sessions will involve an evaluation of your needs. By the end of the evaluation, we will be able to offer you some first impressions of what our work may include and a treatment plan to follow, if you decide to continue with therapy. You should evaluate this information along with your own opinions of whether you feel comfortable working with us and within this specific treatment method. Therapy involves a large commitment of time, money, and energy, so you should be very careful about the service you select. If you have questions about our procedures, we should discuss them whenever they arise. If your doubts persist, we will be happy to help you set up a meeting with another mental health professional for a second opinion.

MEETINGS
We normally conduct an evaluation that will last from 2 to 4 sessions. During this time, we can both decide if this service is right for you and if we can meet your treatment goals. If services are to continue, we will usually schedule one 1 hr. 15 min session per week at a time we agree on, although some sessions may be longer or more frequent. Once an appointment hour is scheduled, you will be expected to pay for it unless you provide 24 hour advance notice of cancellation [unless we both agree that you were unable to attend due to circumstances beyond your control. If it is possible, we will try to find another time to reschedule the appointment.] Due to the nature of our work, sometimes we have to cancel due to weather. We ask that on the day of services we have a way to contact you in case weather does not allow us to provide the service. If this is the case, there is no charge for services and we will re-schedule as soon as possible.

PROFESSIONAL FEES
Esperanza's hourly fee is _____ for individual sessions. This fee may differ for groups, or be increased if multiple facilitators are recommended or required. In addition to weekly appointments, we charge this amount for other professional services you may need, though we will break down the hourly cost if we work for periods of less than one hour. Other services include report writing, telephone conversations lasting longer than 15 minutes, attendance at meetings with other professionals you have authorized, preparation of records or treatment summaries, and the time spent performing any other service you may request of us. If you become involved in legal proceedings that require our participation, you will be expected to pay for our professional time even if we are called to testify by another party.

BILLING AND PAYMENTS
We invoice clients on a monthly basis. We expect to receive payment for services within ten (10) business days. Payment schedules for other professional services will be agreed upon when they are requested. In circumstances of unusual financial hardship, Esperanza offers a sliding scale payment plan. If such need exists, the Esperanza staff will give you an application to fill out to help us assess need and we will co-create a sustainable payment arrangement.

If your account has not been paid for more than 60 days and arrangements for payment have not been agreed upon, we have the option of using legal means to secure the payment. This may involve hiring a collection agency or going through small claims court. [If such legal action is necessary, its costs will be included in the claim.] In most collection situations, the only information we release regarding a patient's treatment is his/her name, the nature of services provided, and the amount due.

INSURANCE REIMBURSEMENT
At this time we do not accept insurance for our services.

CONTACTING US
We are often not immediately available by telephone. While we are usually on the farm between 9 AM and 5 PM, we will not answer the phone when with a client. We will make every effort to return your call on the same day you make it or the next day, with the exception of weekends and holidays. If you are difficult to reach, please inform us of some times when you will be available. If you are unable to reach us and feel that you can't wait for us to return your call, contact your family physician or the nearest emergency room and ask for the psychologist or psychiatrist on call.

PROFESSIONAL RECORDS
The laws and standards of our profession require that we keep treatment records. Clients may have access to their own health records, unless we feel that such access is detrimental to the health and welfare of the client. Only the material that is so determined to be detrimental may be withheld. If a client requests review of their records, we shall try to be present to provide explanation. We cannot withhold access if the client refuses to meet with the provider unless such access is determined to be detrimental to the health and welfare of the client.

MINORS
If you are under eighteen years of age, please be aware that the law may provide your parents the right to examine your treatment records or request information regarding your treatment from us without prior notification or permission from you. In general, it is our policy to speak with you prior to speaking with or providing information to

your parents or other individuals whom your parents may have given us permission to speak with. We will talk with you about our intentions before speaking with them, and give you a brief synopsis of what we intend to talk about. But, if we feel that it would be detrimental to your treatment if we spoke with you first, we may speak with your parents or other involved individuals without prior notification.

CONFIDENTIALITY – Limits and Exceptions

In general, the privacy of all communications between a client and a counselor is protected by law, and we can only release information about our work to others with your written permission. But there are a few exceptions.

In most legal proceedings, you have the right to prevent us from providing any information about your treatment. In some proceedings involving child custody and those in which your emotional condition is an important issue, a judge may order our testimony if he/she determines that the issues demand it.

There are some situations in which we are legally obligated to take action to protect others from harm, even if we have to reveal some information about a patient's treatment. For example, if we believe that a child, elderly person, or disabled person is being abused, we must file a report with the appropriate state agency.

If we believe that a client is threatening serious bodily harm to another, we are required to take protective actions. These actions may include notifying the potential victim, contacting the police, or seeking hospitalization for the client. If the client threatens to harm himself/herself, we may be obligated to seek hospitalization for him/her or to contact family members or others who can help provide protection. Should any of these situations arise, we will make every effort to fully discuss it with you before taking any action.

We may occasionally find it helpful to consult other professionals about a case. During a consultation, we make every effort to avoid revealing the identity of the client. The consultant is also legally bound to keep the information confidential. If you don't object, we will not tell you about these consultations unless we feel that it is important to our work together. Furthermore, Esperanza's staff engage in on-site supervision meetings each week during which we discuss our cases and obtain insight and assistance from each other. These meetings occur between Esperanza staff only and are confidential. If we feel the need to speak with other treatment providers (discussed earlier – wrap around care approach), we will obtain a release of information from you which allows us to speak with the other treatment providers.

At Esperanza, due to the barn milieu, individuals who are not Esperanza staff may come unexpectedly onto the premises without prior notice or warning. Therefore, any client of Esperanza's may be seen by other people who are not directly connected to the program. If this occurs during a session, the Esperanza staff facilitating the experience will generally cease conversation or the activity, if possible, until the individual has left the premises. However, Esperanza cannot guarantee what such individuals may see or hear while on site, and therefore cannot guarantee that the same level of confidentiality that exists within a private office therapeutic setting will exist within the barn milieu. All clients should be aware of this difference prior to starting services and are encouraged to discuss this aspect with us if they feel uncomfortable with such an arrangement.

In some cases we employ the help of trained volunteers or other staff members to act as safety support during your treatment. We will always obtain your permission before introducing a safety support person into the team, but it is important to be aware that such a request may occur during your treatment.

Ian McNairy, Leif Hallberg, Nancy Hallberg, and John Hallberg live on-site at Esperanza and during your treatment at Esperanza you will probably see and meet all of them. Leif Hallberg, Nancy Hallberg, our office manager, and other assorted volunteers or staff members are employees of Esperanza and therefore are bound by the same laws regarding confidentiality. Ian McNairy and John Hallberg also understand the laws regarding confidentiality and will not share any information regarding anyone who is on-premises.

MULTIPLE RELATIONSHIPS
Bozeman is a small town. We are extremely involved in the community and have connections within the local school systems, probation department, social service organizations, and with other mental health providers. We also have connections with a variety of horse-related services – vets, shoers, trainers, boarding facilities, etc. We frequent the businesses that you do, or even businesses that you work for. We eat at the same restaurants, and may be at the same social gatherings. It is inevitable that our paths will cross those of our clients in both social and business circles. In many cases our clients may be already known to us and then seek us out for services *because* of that relationship. In other cases our clients transition between receiving therapeutic services, taking riding lessons, and possibility even eventually volunteering with other clients.

We feel we have an obligation to inform all our clients that there is a strong possibility (almost a certainty) that we may have or will have multiple relationships. You should not work with us as a client if this concept feels unsafe to you.

Our approach is personal. You will see us in relationship with other people who we care deeply about. You will see us in relationship with the horses who we care deeply about. You will see us dealing with challenges and successes. Receiving services at Esperanza may be a very different experience for you because of this unique approach to therapy. If you do not feel comfortable within this context, please speak with us and we can help to find you a more appropriate treatment option.

While this written summary of exceptions to confidentiality should prove helpful in informing you about potential problems, it is important that we discuss any questions or concerns that you may have at our next meeting.

STAFF
At Esperanza all services are provided by mental health professionals with additional education, training, and experience in Equine Facilitated Mental Health Services. Some of our mental health professionals are licensed within the state of Montana, others provide services under the supervision of a licensed mental health professional, and others

act as life coaches, but all have their Master's degree in counseling/
psychology and are dually trained professionals (equine skills and
mental health) who have been trained and educated to provide this
specific therapeutic intervention.

STATEMENT OF UNDERSTANDING AND AGREEMENT

Your signature below indicates that you have read the information in
this document and agree to abide by its terms during our professional
relationship.

_____   _____

Client Signature   Date

_____   _____

Esperanza Staff Signature   Date

Chapter Notes

Introduction Notes

[1] Kanner, A.D., Roszak, T., & Gomes, M.E., *Ecopsychology: Restoring the earth, healing the mind.* (New York: Random House, 1995); Wilson, E.O., & Kellert, S.R., *The Biophilia Hypothesis.* (Washington, D.C: Island Press, 1993); Cohen, M., *Reconnecting With Nature: Finding Wellness Through Restoring Your Bond With the Earth.* (Ecopress, 1997); Metzner, R., *Green Psychology: Transforming our Relationship to the Earth* (Vermont: Park Street Press, 1999); Glendinning, C., *My Name is Chellis and I'm in Recovery from Western Civilization.* (Boston, MA: Shambhala Publications, 1994) Schoen, A., *Kindred Spirits: How the Remarkable Bond Between Humans and Animals Can Change the Way we Live.* (New York: Random House, 2001); Sheldrake, R., *The Presence of the Past: Morphic Resonance and the Habits of Nature.* (Vermont: Park Stress Press, 1995); Sheldrake, R., *Dogs That Know When Their Owners Are Coming Home: And Other Unexplained Powers of Animals.* (New York: Three Rivers Press, 1999).

[2] Sierra Tucson, a world renowned addictions and recovery treatment center located in Tucson, Arizona. Sierra Tucson also provides treatment services for other mental health-related issues such as depression, anxiety, abuse, bi-polar, and obsessive-compulsive disorder. Further information about Sierra Tucson can be obtained via their web page: www.sierratucson.com

[3] *"One can now obtain both an undergraduate degree and a master's degree in the field of Equine Facilitated Mental Health/Educational Services."* Prescott College in Prescott, Arizona, offers both a masters and undergraduate degree in aspects of EFMH/ES. Further information about Prescott College can be obtained via their web page: www.prescott.edu . Carroll College in Helena, Montana, also offers a minor called Human-Animal Bonding which includes the work of EFMH/ES. They can be reached

via their web page: www.cc.edu. Other educational institutions that offer related degrees can be found in the Further Resource section of this text.

⁴ Merriam-Webster's On-Line Dictionary is used for the following definitions; "facilitated," "assisted", "healing": www.merriam-webster.com.

⁵ *"Out of thirty-one (31) professionals questioned, only one disagreed with the notion that horses can and generally do, "facilitate" an experience for the client or student."* This information came from a survey done by the author in November, 2006 to determine word use for the text. The survey was sent out to approximately fifty (50) provides of an EFMH/ES service. Thirty-one (31) providers responded as indicated above. The results of the survey are unpublished and have only been utilized for this text to date. See Appendix A.

⁶ *"Equine Facilitated Mental Health/Educational Services (EFMH/ES) as it is defined, 'An umbrella term used to describe both educational and therapeutic services in which humans work in partnership with horses to learn, grow, and change.'"* This definition was created by the author in 2005 and has been used in a variety of promotional material by Esperanza, An Experiential Healing Center.

⁷ *"At the time of publication, under this umbrella term four (4) methods for providing mental health services in partnership with horses and three (3) methods for providing an educational or learning service in partnership with horses have been defined."* These methods are defined within the body of this text by the author, but have not been defined as such in any other text or written material to date.

⁸ McCormick, A., & McCormick, M., *Horse Sense and the Human Heart.* (Deerfield Beach, FL.: Health Communications, 1997); McCormick, A.R., McCormick, M.D., & McCormick, T.E., *Horses and the Mystical Path.* (Novato, CA.: New World Library, 2004); Kohonov, L., *The Tao of Equus.* (Novato, CA: New

World Library, 2001); Kohonov, L., *Riding Between the Worlds.* (Novato, CA: New World Library, 2003); Rector, B., *Adventures in Awareness.* (Bloomington, IN.: Authorhouse, 2005).

9 Merriam-Webster's On-Line Dictionary is used for the following definitions; "healing", "health": www.merriam-webster.com.

10 Stempsey, W.E.,"Plato and Holistic Medicine," *Medicine, Health Care, and Philosophy* 201-209, no.2 (May, 2001).

11 Roberts, M., *The Man Who Listens to Horses.* (New York: Random House, 1996).

12 Hill, C., *How to Think Like a Horse.* (Story Publishing, 2006); Ainslie, T., & Ledbetter, B., *The Body Language of Horses.* (New York: William Morrow and Company, 1980).

13 Merriam-Webster's On-Line Dictionary is used for the following definition; "anthropomorphism": www.merriam-webster.com.

14 Witter, R.F., *Living with HorsePower.* (Vermont: Trafalgar Square Publishing, 1998).

Chapter One Notes

15 Budiansky, S., *The Nature of Horses.* (New York: The Free Press, 1997); Scalen, L., *Wild about Horses.* (New York: HarperCollins Publishing, 1998); and Chamberlin, J.E., *Horse: How the horse has shaped civilizations.* (New York: Bluebridge, 2006).

16 Scalen, L., *Wild about Horses.* (New York: HarperCollins Publishing, 1998).

17 This information was gained from a variety of sources as follows, Budiansky, S., *The Nature of Horses.* (New York: The Free Press, 1997); Scalen, L., *Wild about Horses.* (New York: HarperCollins Publishing, 1998); and Chamberlin, J.E., *Horse: How the horse has shaped civilizations.* (New York: Bluebridge, 2006) and

Hidinger, E., *Warriors of the Steppe.* Cambridge, MASS.: DA CAPO Press, 1997).

[18] The majority of information used in this chapter came from the following sources: David Anthony, Dimitri Telegin, Dorcas Brown, and Natalya Belan-Timchenko, "The Origin of Horseback Riding," *SCIENTIFIC AMERICAN, (December 1991)*; David Anthony "Horseback Riding, Warfare, and Social Differentiation in the Eneolithic," Dimitri Telegin, "Dereivka, a settlement and cemetery of Copper Age horse keepers on the Middle Dnieper," Vol. 287, *BAR International Series*; David W. Anthony, Peter Bogucki, Eugen Comsa, Marija Gimbutas, Borislav Jovanovic, J. P. Mallory, Sarunas Milisaukas "The 'Kurgan Culture,' Indo-European Origins, and the Domestication of the Horse: A Reconsideration" *Current Anthropology*, Vol. 27, No. 4 (Aug. - Oct., 1986), pp. 291-313; Brown, D. R., and D. W. Anthony, "Bit wear, horseback riding, and the Botai site in Kazakstan." *Journal of Archaeological Science* 25:331-347 (1998); Anthony, D. W., and D. Brown, "Eneolithic horse exploitation in the Eurasian steppes: diet, ritual, and riding." *Antiquity* 74:75-86. (2000). Further information came from The Institute of Ancient Equestrian Studies web site at http://users.hartwick.edu

[19] Levine, M., "Botai and the origins of horse domestication." *Journal of Anthropological Archaeology* 18:29-78. (1999); Levine, M., and A. M. Kislenko, "New Eneolithic and Early Bronze Age radiocarbon dates for northern Kazakhstan and south Siberia." *Cambridge Archaeological Journal* 7(2):297-300. (1997); Levine, M., "Domestication, Breed Diversification, and Early History of the Horse." *McDonald Institute for Archaeological Research* (www3.vet.upenn.edu).

[20] Olsen, S., "New Evidence of Early Horse Domestication." *The Geological Society of America, GSA* Release No. 06-49. (October 2006); Olsen, S., "Horses in Prehistory." *Section of Anthropology - Carnegie Museum of Natural History* (www.carnegiemnh.org);

Larry O'Hanlon, "Ancient Corral Shows Horse Domestication." *Discovery News*; Richard A. Lovett, "Ancient Manure May Be Earliest Proof of Horse Domestication." *National Geographic News,* (October, 2006); Weed, W.S., "First to Ride." *Discover,* Vol. 23 No. 03 (March, 2002).

[21] See 5-6

[22] See 5-6

[23] See 5-6

[24] Budiansky, S., *The Nature of Horses.* (New York: The Free Press, 1997).

[25] A fictional account written by the author with no intentions to provide scientific data to prove that such an encounter ever occurred.

[26] Hidinger, E., *Warriors of the Steppe.* Cambridge, MASS.: DA CAPO Press, 1997).

[27] *"Scholars believe that it was due to the domestication of the horse that our modern languages came into existence as they did."* David Bank, "The Nominees for Best Invention of the Last Two Millennia Are..." *The Wall Street Journal* (January, 1999) quotes Stephan Budiansky stating, "I would argue that the single invention that has changed human life more than any other is the horse — by which I mean the domestication of the horse as a mount." Other sources are Budiansky, S., *The Nature of Horses.* (New York: The Free Press, 1997); Scalen, L., *Wild about Horses.* (New York: HarperCollins Publishing, 1998); and Chamberlin, J.E., *Horse: How the horse has shaped civilizations.* (New York: Bluebridge, 2006) and Hidinger, E., *Warriors of the Steppe.* Cambridge, MASS.: DA CAPO Press, 1997).

[28] Budiansky, S., *The Nature of Horses*. (New York: The Free Press, 1997); Scalen, L., *Wild about Horses*. (New York: HarperCollins Publishing, 1998).

Chapter Two Notes

[29] Howey, M.O., *The horse in Magic and Myth*. (New York: Dover Publications, 2002).

[30] Montana State University's Museum of the Rockies.

[31] Sheldrake, R., *Dogs That Know When Their Owners Are Coming Home: And Other Unexplained Powers of Animals*. (New York: Three Rivers Press, 1999). Pg.245-263

[32] Scientists believe that by studying the sun and its unique behaviors, we will understand what exists outside of our solar system, and be prepared to evolve as a species well before our sun meets its end.

[33] Dossey, L., *Recovering the Soul*. (New York: Bantam Books, 1989).

[34] Jung, C., *Memories, Dreams, Reflections*. (New York: Vintage Press, 1968); Dossey, L. *Recovering the Soul*. (New York: Bantam Books, 1989); Watson, L., *Gifts of Unknown Things*. (New York: Simon & Schuster, 1996); Watson, L. "Natural Harmony: The biology of being appropriate," *The Isthmus Institute, Dallas, Texas* (April 1989); Sheldrake, R., Sheldrake, R., *The Presence of the Past: Morphic Resonance and the Habits of Nature*. (Vermont: Park Stress Press, 1995); Pert, C., Molecules of Emotion. (New York: Touchstone, 1997); Einstein, A., quoted in Dossey, L., *Recovering the Soul*. (New York: Bantam Books, 1989).

[35] McCormick, A.R., McCormick, M.D., & McCormick, T.E., Horses and the Mystical Path. (Novato, CA.: New World Library, 2004). Pg. xiii-xv.

36 Kohonov, L., *Riding Between the Worlds*. (Novato, CA: New World Library, 2003).

37 Howey, M.O., *The horse in Magic and Myth*. (New York: Dover Publications, 2002). Pg. 29

38 Howey, M.O., *The horse in Magic and Myth*. (New York: Dover Publications, 2002). Pg. 30

39 Howey, M.O., *The horse in Magic and Myth*. (New York: Dover Publications, 2002). Pg. 133

40 Howey, M.O., *The Horse in Magic and Myth*. (New York: Dover Publications, 2002). Pg. 226.

41 Howey, M.O., *The Horse in Magic and Myth*. (New York: Dover Publications, 2002). Pg. 19

42 McCormick, A., & McCormick, M., *Horse Sense and the Human Heart*. (Deerfield Beach, FL.: Health Communications, 1997); McCormick, A.R., McCormick, M.D., & McCormick, T.E., *Horses and the Mystical Path*. (Novato, CA.: New World Library, 2004); Grof, S., *The Holotropic Mind*. (New York: HarperCollins, 1993).

43 Grof, S., *The Holotropic Mind*. (New York: HarperCollins, 1993). Pg. 120

44 McCormick, A.R., McCormick, M.D., & McCormick, T.E., *Horses and the Mystical Path*. (Novato, CA.: New World Library, 2004).

45 Grof, S., *The Holotropic Mind*. (New York: HarperCollins, 1993); McCormick, A.R., McCormick, M.D., & McCormick, T.E., *Horses and the Mystical Path*. (Novato, CA.: New World Library, 2004).

[46] Friedmann, E., Katcher, A.H., Lynch, J, and Thomas, S., "Animal companions and one year survival of patients following discharge from a coronary care unit." *Public Health Reports* 95 (4) 307-312. (1980).

[47] Seeman, T.E., Dubin, L.F., & Seeman, M., "Religiosity/ Spirituality and Health: A Critical Review of the Evidence for Biological Pathways" University of California, Los Angeles, American Psychologist (January 2003); Wachholtz, A.B., and Pargament, K.I., "Is Spirituality a Critical Ingredient of Meditation? Comparing the Effects of Spiritual Meditation, Secular Meditation, and Relaxation on Spiritual, Psychological, Cardiac, and Pain Outcomes" Bowling Green State University, *Journal of Behavioral Medicine* Volume 28, Number 4. (August, 2005); Tartaro, J., Luecken, L.J., Gunn, H. E., "Exploring Heart and Soul: Effects of Religiosity/Spirituality and Gender on Blood Pressure and Cortisol Stress Responses." Journal of Health Psychology, Vol. 10, No. 6, 753-766 (2005); The Institute of HeartMath also includes research regarding the effects of spirituality and stress. This information can be found on their web page: www.heartmath.org.

[48] McCormick, A.R., McCormick, M.D., & McCormick, T.E., *Horses and the Mystical Path.* (Novato, CA.: New World Library, 2004). Pg. 53

[49] This information comes from years of observation of horse herds by the author and discussion with other horse people regarding the topic. Such information has been supported by the work of Hill, C., *How to Think Like a Horse.* (Story Publishing, 2006); Roberts, M., *The Man Who Listens to Horses.* (New York: Random House, 1996).

[50] National Association of Therapeutic Schools and Programs (NATSAP): www.natsap.org; San Cristobal Ranch Academy: www.sancristobalranchacademy.com.

[51] "How we can win the war on poverty." *Fortune* (Apr 10 1989): p127

[52] Wald, M., & Martinez, T., "Connected by 25: Improving the Life Chances of the Country's Most Vulnerable 14-24 Year Olds." *Stanford University*. Pg. 2

[53] Kathrens, G., *Cloud: Wild Stallion of the Rockies*. (BowTie Press, 2001).

[54] Dossey, L. *Recovering the Soul*. (New York: Bantam Books, 1989). Pg. 44

[55] Eckhart Tolle, E. *The Power of Now*. (Novato, CA.: New World Library, 1999).

[56] Dossey, L. *Recovering the Soul*. (New York: Bantam Books, 1989). Pg. 67

[57] Boyer, B. & Nissenbaum, S., *Salem Possessed: The Social Origins of Witchcraft*. (Harvard University Press, 1974); Briggs, R. *Witches and Neighbors: The Social and Cultural Context of European Witchcraft*. (Viking, 1996); Henningsen, G., *The Witches' Advocate: Basque Witchcraft and the Spanish Inquisition* (University of Nevada Press, 1980); Hutton, R. *The Triumph of the Moon: A History of Modern Pagan Witchcraft* (Oxford University Press, 1999); Midelfort, H.C., *Witch Hunting in Southwestern Germany 1562-1684: The Social and Intellectual Foundations* (Stanford University Press, 1972); Sharpe, J. *Instruments of Darkness: Witchcraft in Early Modern England* (University of Pennsylvania Press, 1996); Starhawk, *Dreaming the Dark: Magic, Sex and Politics* (Beacon, 1988); Green, R.J., "How many witches?", www.holocaust-history.org/~rjg/witches.shtml.

[58] Howey, M.O., *The Horse in Magic and Myth*. (New York: Dover Publications, 2002). Pg. 172.

[59] North American Riding for the Handicapped Association, *NARHA Guide*. (Denver, CO: North American Riding for the Handicapped Association, 1996). www.narha.org.

Chapter Three Notes

[60] McCormick, A., & McCormick, M., *Horse Sense and the Human Heart*. (Deerfield Beach, FL.: Health Communications, 1997); McCormick, A.R., McCormick, M.D., & McCormick, T.E., *Horses and the Mystical Path*. (Novato, CA.: New World Library, 2004); Kohonov, L., *The Tao of Equus*. (Novato, CA: New World Library, 2001); Kohonov, L., *Riding Between the Worlds*. (Novato, CA: New World Library, 2003); Howey, M.O., *The Horse in Magic and Myth*. (New York: Dover Publications, 2002); Scalen, L., *Wild about Horses*. (New York: HarperCollins Publishing, 1998); and Chamberlin, J.E., *Horse: How the horse has shaped civilizations*. (New York: Bluebridge, 2006).

[61] Therapeutic Riding is defined by the North American Riding for the Handicapped Association (NARHA) as, "Mounted activities including traditional riding disciplines or adaptive riding activities conducted by a NARHA certified instructor." www.narha.org; Hippotherapy is defined by the American Hippotherapy Association (AHA) as, "A physical, occupational and speech therapy treatment strategy that utilizes equine movement. Hippotherapy is utilized as part of an integrated treatment program to achieve functional outcomes." www.americanhippotherapyassociation.org.

[62] North American Riding for the Handicapped Association, NARHA Guide. (Denver, CO: North American Riding for the Handicapped Association, 1996).

[63] North American Riding for the Handicapped Association: www.narha.org.

64 Rennie, A., "The therapeutic relationship between animals and humans." *SCAS Journal* IX, 1-4 (1997); Bustad, L., "The role of pets in therapeutic programmes, historic perspectives." in Robinson, I., *The Waltham Book of Human-Animal Interaction: Benefits and Responsibility of Pet Ownership.* (Oxford: Pergamon Press, 1995). pp 55-57.

65 Tuke, S. *Description of The Retreat, an Institution near York for Insane Persons, 1st edition.* (York: Process Press, 1813).

66 Nightingale, F., *Notes on Nursing.* (1860) (London: Harrison and Sons, Reprinted 1946). In: Ormerod, E. J., Edney, A. T. B., Foster, S. J., & Whyham, M. C., "Therapeutic applications of the human-companion animal bond." *The Veterinary Record,* (November 26, 2005).

67 Lorenz, K., *Man Meets Dog.* (Methuen & Co, Ltd., 1954).

68 Levinson, B. *Pets and Human Development.* (Springfield, Ill.: Charles C. Thomas, 1972); Levinson, B., & Mallon, G.P., *Pet Oriented Child Psychotherapy.* (Springfield, Ill.: Charles C. Thomas, 1997).

69 The Delta Society: www.deltasociety.org

70 The Society for Companion Animals (SCAS): www.scas.org

71 International Association of Human-Animal Interaction Organizations (IAHAIO): www.iahaio.org

72 The World Health Organizations (WHO): www.who.int/en/

73 See **Animal Assisted Therapy** in this chapter.

74 North American Riding for the Handicapped Association: www.narha.org; The Delta Society: www.deltasociety.org

[75] DePauw, K. "Therapeutic horseback riding in Europe and America." In: Anderson, R.K., & Hart, B.L., The Pet Connection: Its influence on our health and daily life. (Minneapolis: Center to Study Human-Animal Relationships and Environments, 1984). Pg.141-153.

[76] North American Riding for the Handicapped Association: www.narha.org

[77] American Hippotherapy Association: www.aha.org.

[78] Tissot, J.C., *Medicinal and Surgical Gymnastics or Essay on the usefulness of Movement, or different Exercises of the body, and of rest, in the treatment of Diseases*, (Paris, Bastian, 1780).

[79] Evens, J.W., "A Review of Relevant Literature." In: "Cerebral Palsy and Therapeutic Riding." *NARHA Strides Magazine*, Vol. 1 No. 1 (October, 1995).

[80] Satter, L., "Horseback Riding Therapy for Children with Movement Malfunction Considering Especially Cerebral Palsy Patients," *Pediatric and Padologie*, Vol. 13. (1977). Pg. 333-337.

[81] Tauffkirchen, E., "Hippotherapy – A Supplementary Treatment for Motion Disturbances Caused by Cerebral Palsy." *Pediatric and Padologie*, Vol. 13 (4), (1978), pg. 405- 411.

[82] Bertoti, D.B., "Effect of Therapeutic Horseback Riding on Posture in Children with Cerebral Palsy," Journal of Physical Therapy, Vol. 8 (10) (1988). Pg. 1505-1512.

[83] Brock, B.J., "Effect of Therapeutic Horseback Riding on Physically Disabled Adults," *Therapeutic Recreation Journal*. Vol. 22 (1988). Pg. 34-42.

[84] Benda, W., McGibbon, N.H., & Grant, K.L., "Improvements in Muscle Symmetry in Children with Cerebral Palsy after Equine-

Assisted Therapy (Hippotherapy)," *Journal of Alternative and Complementary Medicine*, Vol. 9, No. 6 (December, 2003). Pg. 817-825.

85 Aetna, "Hippotherapy for Cerebral Palsy and Other Motor Dysfunction," *Clinical Policy Bulletins*, No. 0151. (March 24, 2006); Hammer, A., Nilsagard, Y., Forsberg, A., et al., "Evaluation of Therapeutic Riding (Sweden)/ Hippotherapy (United States). A single-subject experimental design study replicated in eleven patients with multiple sclerosis." *Physiotherapy Theory Practitioner. Vol.* 21, No. 1 (2005). Pg. 51-77.

86 Aetna, "Hippotherapy for Cerebral Palsy and Other Motor Dysfunction," Clinical Policy Bulletins, No. 0151. (March 24, 2006).

87 Splinter-Watkins, K. "Research: Past to Future, How far have we come? How far have we to go?" NARHA Strides (North American Riding for the Handicapped Association), Vol. 8, No. 4, (Winter 2002/2003). Pgs. 22-25.

88 Delta Society: www.deltasociety.org.

89 International Association of Human-Animal Interaction Organizations (IAHAIO): www.iahaio.org.

90 People, Animals, Nature (P.A.N.): www.pan-inc.org.

91 Odendaal, J.S.J., "The Human-Animal Interaction Movement in South Africa (1981-2004)," *National Clinicians' Group Newsletter.* (November, 2004). Pg. 5-7.

92 Levinson, B., "The Dog as Co-Therapist," Mental Hygiene, Vol. 46 (1962). Pg. 59-65.

93 Barker, S. B., "Therapeutic Aspects of the Human-Companion Animal Interaction," Psychiatric Times, Vol. XVI, Issue 2. (February, 1999).

[94] Campbell, C., & Katcher, A., "Animal Assisted Therapy Dogs for Autistic Children: Quantitative and qualitative results," Presented at the Sixth International Conference on Human-Animal Interactions, Montreal. In: Barker, S. B., "Therapeutic Aspects of the Human-Companion Animal Interaction," Psychiatric Times, Vol. XVI, Issue 2. (February, 1999).

[95] Study conducted by the Rehabilitation Services of Roanoke, Virginia found in: Sepsas, N., & Montgomery, A., "The Physiological and Psychological Effects of Animal Therapy: Examining the Healing Power of Animals," The Journal of the American Nutraceutical Association, Vol. 9, No. 1. (2006). Pg. 7-12.

[96] Odendaal, J.S.J., "The Human-Animal Interaction Movement in South Africa (1981-2004)," *National Clinicians' Group Newsletter.* (November, 2004). Pg. 5-7; Odendaal, J. S. J., "Animal-assisted therapy: Magic or medicine?" *Journal of Psychosomatic Research,* (October, 2000). 49 (4): 275-280; Lategan, A., Odendaal J.S.J., du Plooy, W.J., & Modipane, A., "The therapeutic value of positive human-animal interaction: the role of b- phenylethylamine." *South African Journal of Sciences,* (94): Suppl. 1 (1998); Yeates, S.V. & Odendaal, J.S.J., "Human-dog interaction: an interspecies evaluation of blood pressure changes as possible indicators of neurochemical changes." *Physiological Medicine* (June, 1998) pg. 5.; Odendaal, J.S.J., & Lehmann, S.M.C., "The role of phenylethylamine during human-dog interaction." *Acta Veterinaria BRNO* (2000), 69(3). Pg. 87-92.; Johnson, RA: Odendaal, J.S.J., & Meadows, R., "Animal-Assisted Interventions of Nursing Research: Issues and Answers." *Western Journal of Nursing Research,* (2002), 24 (4). Pg. 422-440.; Swanepoel, H.C. & Odendaal, J.S.J., "Elephant-facilitated psychotherapy – a clinical evaluation." *Pakistan Journal for Social Sciences,* (2005) 3 (1). Pg. 205 – 209.; Odendaal, J.S.J., "Animals as therapeutic facilitators – theory and neurophysiology." *Journal of the South African Board for Companion Animal Professionals* (2006), 1(2). Pg.12-14.

[97] Odendaal, J.S.J., "The Human-Animal Interaction Movement in South Africa (1981-2004)," *National Clinicians' Group Newsletter.* (November, 2004). Pg. 5-7.

[98] Benda, W., & Lightmark, R., "People Whisperers." *IONS Noetic Sciences Review- Shift,* Issue 3, (June, 2004).

[99] Barker, S.B., & Barker, R.T., "The Human-Canine Bond: Closer than family ties?" *The Journal of Mental Health Counseling,* Vol. 10 No.1 (January, 1988). Pg. 46-56.

[100] See following research.

[101] Friedman, E., Katcher, A.H., & Thomas, S.A., "Social interaction and blood pressure: Influence of companion animals." *The Journal of Nervous and Mental Disease,* (1983) 171 (8). Pg. 461-465

[102] Friedmann, E., Katcher, A.H., Lynch, J, & Thomas, S., "Animal companions and one year survival of patients following discharge from a coronary care unit." *Public Health Reports,* (1980) 95 (4). Pg. 307-312.

[103] Allen, K.M., Blascovitch, J., Tomaka, J., & Kelsey, R.M., "Presence of human friends and pet dogs as moderators of autonomic responses to stress in women," *The Journal of Personality and Social Psychological,* (1991) 61(4). Pg. 582-589.

[104] Headey, B.W., "Health Benefits of Pets: Results from the Australian People & Pets Survey," *Petcare Information and Advisory Service.* (Melbourne, 1995); Headey, B.W., & Anderson, W., "Health Cost Savings. The impact of pets on the Australian health budget." *Anthrozoology,* Baker Medical Research Institute, The Centre for Public Policy, The University of Melbourne, (November 1995).

[105] American Heart Association Annual Meeting, November 11, 2005, Dallas, Texas. http://www.americanheart.org/prg/presenter. jhtml?identifier=3035327.

[106] Prothmann, A., Albrecht, K., Dietrich, S., Hornfeck, And, Stieber, S., Ettrich, C., "Interaction of psychologically disturbed children with a therapy dog," In: *People and Animals: A timeless Relationship.* (The Blue CROSS, Burford, 2004).

[107] Suthers-McCabe, H.M., Van Voorhees, E.E., & Fournier, A.K., "Psychological impact of a service dog training program on inmate trainers," Center for Animal-Human Relationships, Viginia-Maryland Regional College of Veterinary Medicine, and Department of Psychology, Virginia Tech, Blacksburg, Virginia 24061, United States. Presentation from the 10th International Conference on Human-Animal Interactions, People and Animals: A timeless Relationship, Glasgow, Scotland, October 6-9, 2004.

[108] References to the development of NARHA come from personal conversations with Marge Kittridge (1997) and Barbara Rector.

[109] Personal communication and interview with Barbara Rector, October, 2006.

[110] Hallberg, L., "Emergence of Equine Facilitated Psychotherapy programs in therapeutic riding facilities across the United States: Efficacy and Program Design." *Animal Therapy Association of Arizona,* 1997.

[111] All references to Ms. Rector's personal story come from personal interviews conducted by this author with Ms. Rector.

[112] All references to the development of EFMHA come from the following sources; Ann Alden, 2005-2007 EFMHA President, personal interviews; Barbara Rector, 1996-1998 EFMHA President, personal interviews; Molly DePrekel, EFMHA board member, personal interview; Marilyn Sokolof, EFMHA board

member, personal interview; A document entitled, "Equine-Facilitated Mental Health Association (A proposed section of NARHA)" created at the first official EFMHA meeting held on February 13, 1996 at Pony Farm in Temple, New Hampshire; The first EFMHA Newsletter, Vol.1, Issue 1, dated March 1997; A document entitled, "Equine Facilitated Mental Health Association (EFMHA), A Section of NARHA, A Full Board Meeting" dated August 13-15, 1999.

[113] All references to the current state of EFMHA come from the following sources; Ann Alden, 2005-2007 EFMHA President, personal interviews; Barbara Rector, 1996-1998 EFMHA President, personal interviews; North American Riding for the Handicapped Association 2006 National Conference and Annual Meeting, November 8-11, 2006, Indianapolis, IN.

[114] References to Greg Kersten and Lynn Thomas come from the following source; Hallberg, L. & Brinkerhoff, L., "Defining the Theory and Practice of Equine Facilitated or Assisted Psychotherapy." (Unpublished, 2001).

[115] Personal communication with Lynn Thomas, Co-Founder and Executive Director of EAGALA; EAGALA's web page, www.eagala.org; Hallberg, L., "Project Textbook: Defining our past, present, and future." (Unpublished, 2006).

[116] Hallberg, L., "Terminology Survey: Facilitated vs. Assisted?" (Unpublished, 2006).

[117] Personal communications with 2005-2007 EFMHA President, Ann Alden.

[118] Greg Kersten's "O.K. Corral Series" web page, www.okcorralseries.com

[119] All references to Green Chimneys, Suz Brooks, or Michael Kaufmann come from the following sources; the Green

Chimney's web page, www.greenchimneys.org; Suz Brooks, personal correspondence.

[120] All references to Miraval Resort, Life in Balance and Wyatt Webb come from the following sources; Miraval Resort's web page, www.miravalresort.com; Webb, W. *It's Not About the Horse,* (Carlsbad, CA, 2002); Barbara Rector, personal correspondence.

[121] All references to Monty Roberts come from the following sources; Roberts, M., *The Man Who Listens to Horses.* (New York: Ballentine Publishing Group, 1996); Roberts, M., *Horse Sense for People.* (New York: Penguin Books, 2000).

[122] All references to Adele von Rust McCormick and Marlena Deborah McCormick come from the following sources; McCormick, A.R., & McCormick, M.D., *Horse Sense and the Human Heart.* (Deerfield Beach, FL.: Health Communications, 1997); McCormick, A.R., McCormick, M.D., & McCormick, T.E., *Horses and the Mystical Path.* (Novato, CA: New World Library, 2004).

[123] All references to Sharon Janus and Rebekah Ferran Witter come from the following sources; Janus, S., *The Magic of Horses.* (SunShine Press Publications, 1997); Witter, R.F., *Living with HorsePower.* (Vermont: Trafalgar Square Publishing, 1998).

[124] All references to Chris Irwin come from the following sources; Irwin, C., *Horses Don't Lie.* (New York: Marlowe and Company, 1998); Irwin, C., *Dancing With Your Dark Horse.* (New York: Marlowe and Company, 2005); Irwin, C., personal correspondence.

[125] All references to Linda Kohanov come from the following sources; Kohonov, L., *The Tao of Equus.* (Novato, CA: New World Library, 2001); Kohonov, L., *Riding Between the Worlds.*

(Novato, CA: New World Library, 2003); Kohonov, L., personal correspondence and interviews with the author.

[126] Kohonov, L., *The Tao of Equus.* (Novato, CA: New World Library, 2001). Pg. 213.

[127] Burgon, H., "Case studies of adults receiving horse-riding therapy," *Anthrozoos,* Vol. 13, (2003). Pg. 262-76.

[128] Bizub, A., Joy, A., & Davidson, L., "It's like being in another world." Psychiatric Rehabilitation Journal, Vol. 26, No. 4, (2003). Pg. 377-384.

[129] Kaiser, L., Spence, L.J., Lavergne, A.G., & Vanden Bosch, K.L., "Can a week of therapeutic riding make a difference? A pilot study" *Anthrozoos,* Vol. 17, No. 1. (2004). Pg. 63.

[130] Roberts, F., Bradberry, J., & Williams, C.

[131] Gatty, C.M., "Psychosocial impact of therapeutic riding: A pilot study." NARHA, www.narha.org/PDFfiles/Psychosocial_Impact.pdf

[132] All information regarding Dr. Gehrke's pilot study and reflects from Ms. Gehrke come from the following sources; Gehrke, E.K., "Horses and Humans Energetics: The study of Heart Rate Variability (HRV) between horses and Humans." (Self Published, 2006); HeartMath: www.heartmath.org; Personal interview and correspondence.

[133] Horses and Humans Foundation: www.horsesandhumans.org

[134] References to Ann Alden and Marilyn Sokolof are the result of personal interviews with both individuals.

Chapter Four Notes

[135] "Sentient" is defined by Merriam-Webster's On-Line Dictionary as, "responsive to or conscious of sense impressions," or "finely

sensitive in perception or feeling." Many professionals in the field including Barbara Rector, Linda Kohanov, and EFMHA as an entire organization, believe the horse to be "sentient", and feel strongly that the work of EFMH/ES should be done from this orientation.

[136] Hill, C., *How to Think Like a Horse.* (Story Publishing, 2006). Pg. 108.

[137] Hill, C., *How to Think Like a Horse.* (Story Publishing, 2006).

[138] "Equine Facilitated Learning" and "Equine Facilitated Psychotherapy," see Section Four, chapters 12 and 16 in this text.

[139] All statements about the role of the horse within EFMH/ES are based upon this authors personal experience and beliefs, and also information gained from the following sources; Hallberg, L., "Emergence of Equine Facilitated Psychotherapy programs in therapeutic riding facilities across the United States: Efficacy and Program Design. *Animal Therapy Association of Arizona,* 1997; personal interviews with Barbara Rector, Ann Alden, and Laura Brinkerhoff.

[140] References to early saddles come from the following sources; Hidinger, E., *Warriors of the Steppe.* (Cambridge, MASS.: DA CAPO Press, 1997); Lawrence, E.A., *Hoofbeats and Society.* (Bloomington, IN.: Indiana University Press, 1985); Hyland, A., *The Horse in the Ancient World.* (Praeger Publishers, 2003).

[141] Xenophon, *The Art of Horsemanship.* (J.A. Allen & Company, Limited, 1987).

[142] McCormick, A.R., McCormick, M.D., & McCormick, T.E., *Horses and the Mystical Path.* (Novato, CA.: New World Library, 2004). Pg. 23-24.

[143] References to the history of Western riding came from the following sources; Lawrence, E.A., *Hoofbeats and Society.* (Bloomington, IN.: Indiana University Press, 1985); Encyclopedia of American History, Edwards, E. H., *The Encyclopedia of the Horse.* (London and New York: Dorling Kindersley, 1994); Ward, K. R., *The American Horse: From Conquistadors to the 21st Century.* (Belleville, Mich.: Maple Yard Publications, 1991.); J. Clutton-Brock, *Horse Power* (Harvard University Press, 1992); equestrianmag.com: www. equestrianmag.com; Wikipedia: http://en.wikipedia.org/wiki/ Equestrianism#.22Western.22_riding

[144] "Horseback Riding: A History of Style," *equestrianmag.com*, (www.equestrianmag.com/article/riding-styles.html).

[145] Xenophon, *The Art of Horsemanship.* (J.A. Allen & Company, Limited, 1987).

[146] Scanlan, L., *Wild about Horses.* (New York: HarperCollins, 1998). Pg. 90.

[147] Dorrance, T., *True Unity: Willing Communication between Horse and Human.* (Word Dancer Press, 1994); Roberts, M., *The Man Who Listens to Horses.* (New York: Ballantine Publishing Group, 1996).

[148] Barbara Rector, personal communication.

[149] See "Inherent Risk" in Section Four, Chapter 14.

[150] EFMHA, Psycho-Social Guidelines, *EFMHA Standards Manual,* Section J, Pg. 9.

[151] All statements about the care and lifestyle of an EFMH/ES horse are by this author. They are supported, although not necessarily in their entirety, by the following sources; Hallberg, L., "Emergence of Equine Facilitated Psychotherapy programs in

therapeutic riding facilities across the United States: Efficacy and Program Design. *Animal Therapy Association of Arizona,* 1997; Hallberg, L., "Project Textbook: Defining our past, present, and future." (Unpublished, 2006); Hallberg, L., "Terminology Survey: Horse as 'tool' vs. Horse as 'facilitator'?" (Unpublished, 2006); personal interviews with Barbara Rector, Ann Alden, and Laura Brinkerhoff.

[152] Assistance Dogs International (ADI): www.adionline.org; Delta Society: www.delta.org ; Therapet: www.therapet.com; Therapy Dogs International (TDI): www.tdi-dogs.org.

[153] Ann Alden, personal communication.

Chapter Five Notes

[154] References made to horse nature as healing come from the following sources; Roberts, M., *The Man Who Listens to Horses.* (New York: Ballantine Publishing Group, 1996); Roberts, M., *Horse Sense for People.* (New York: Penguin Books, 2002); Irwin, C., *Horses Don't Lie.* (New York: Marlowe and Company, 1998); Irwin, C., *Dancing With Your Dark Horse.* (New York: Marlowe and Company, 2005); McCormick, A., & McCormick, M., *Horse Sense and the Human Heart.* (Deerfield Beach, FL.: Health Communications, 1997); McCormick, A.R., McCormick, M.D., & McCormick, T.E., *Horses and the Mystical Path.* (Novato, CA.: New World Library, 200); Kohonov, L., *The Tao of Equus.* (Novato, CA: New World Library, 2001); Kohonov, L., *Riding Between the Worlds.* (Novato, CA: New World Library, 2003); Rector, B., *Adventures in Awareness.* (Bloomington, IN.: Authorhouse, 2005); Midkiff, M., *She Flies Without Wings.* (New York: Dell Publishing, 2001); Soren, I., *The Zen of Horses.* (Little, Brown, and Company, 2002); Witter, R.F., *Living with HorsePower.* (Vermont: Trafalgar Square Publishing, 1998); Brinkerhoff, L., "Catharsis in Equine Facilitated Mental Health Work." (Self Published, 2003); Taylor, S., *Equine Facilitated Psychotherapy: An Emerging Field.* (Self Published, 2001); Kuhn, M.G., *Toward an Integral Model of Equine-Assisted Psychotherapy.*

(Self Published, 2006); Hallberg, L. *Horses as Healers: Exploring the Psychological Implications of the Horse/Human Relationship.* (Self Published, 2003).

155 References made to horse behavior and nature come from the following sources; Scanlan, L., *Wild about Horses.* (New York: HarperCollins, 1998); Hill, C., *How to Think Like a Horse.* (Story Publishing, 2006); Budiansky, S., *The Nature of Horses.* (New York: The Free Press, 1997); Hempfling, K.F., *Dancing with Horses.* (Vermont: Trafalgar Square Publishing, 2001); Hempfling, K.F., *What Horses Reveal.* (Vermont: Trafalgar Square Publishing, 2004); Rashid, M., *Considering the Horse.* (Spring Creek Press, 1993); Rashid, M., *Horses Never Lie.* (Bolder, CO.: Johnson Publishing Company, 2000); Rashid, M., *Life Lessons from a Ranch Horse.* (David and Charles Publishing, 2004); Rashid, M., *Horsemanship Through Life.* (Spring Creek Press, 2005) Ainslie, T., & Ledbetter, B., *The Body Language of Horses.* (New York: William Morrow and Company, 1980); Roberts, M., *The Man Who Listens to Horses.* (New York: Ballantine Publishing Group, 1996); Roberts, M., *Horse Sense for People.* (New York: Penguin Books, 2002).

156 Burgon, H., "Case studies of adults receiving horse-riding therapy," *Anthrozoos,* Vol. 13, (2003). Pg. 262-76; Bizub, A., Joy, A., & Davidson, L., "It's like being in another world." Psychiatric Rehabilitation Journal, Vol. 26, No. 4, (2003). Pg. 377-384; Kaiser, L., Spence, L.J., Lavergne, A.G., & Vanden Bosch, K.L., "Can a week of therapeutic riding make a difference? A pilot study" *Anthrozoos,* Vol. 17, No. 1. (2004). Pg. 63; Gatty, C.M., "Psychosocial impact of therapeutic riding: A pilot study." NARHA, www.narha.org/PDFfiles/Psychosocial_Impact.pdf.

157 Hallberg, L., "Emergence of Equine Facilitated Psychotherapy programs in therapeutic riding facilities across the United States: Efficacy and Program Design. *Animal Therapy Association of Arizona,* 1997; Hallberg, L. & Brinkerhoff, L., "Defining the Theory and Practice of Equine Facilitated or Assisted

Psychotherapy." (Unpublished, 2001); Hallberg, L., "Horses as Healers." *EFMHA News*, Vol. 7, Issue 2, Summer, 2003; Hallberg, L., "Horses as Healers: Exploring the psychological implications of the horse/human relationship." (Self Published Thesis, 2003); Hallberg, L., "Project Textbook: Defining our past, present, and future." (Unpublished, 2006).

[158] Merriam-Webster Dictionary on-line version can be found at www.merriam-webster.com. Within this section Merriam-Webster's on-line dictionary is used for the following definitions; "herd" and "gregarious".

[159] Hill, C., *How to Think Like a Horse*. (Story Publishing, 2006). Pg. 63.

[160] Hill, C., *How to Think Like a Horse*. (Story Publishing, 2006). Pg. 9.

[161] Budiansky, S., *The Nature of Horses*. (New York: The Free Press, 1997). Pg. 156.

[162] Watson, L., *Jacobson's Organ*. (New York: Penguin Books, 1999).

[163] Hill, C., *How to Think Like a Horse*. (Story Publishing, 2006). Pg. 30.

Chapter Six Notes

[164] Merriam-Webster On-Line Dictionary is used for the following definition; "communication". www.merriam-webster.com.

[165] The four levels of equine communication are the creation of this author although supported by the work of many equine communication experts such as; Budiansky, S., *The Nature of Horses*. (New York: The Free Press, 1997); Hill, C., *How to Think Like a Horse*. (Story Publishing, 2006); Ainslie, T., & Ledbetter, B., *The Body Language of Horses*. (New York: William Morrow

and Company, 1980); Roberts, M., *Horse Sense for People.* (New York: Penguin Books, 2000); and many others.

[166] References in this chapter to the vocal communications of horses come from the following sources; Budiansky, S., *The Nature of Horses.* (New York: The Free Press, 1997); Hill, C., *How to Think Like a Horse.* (Story Publishing, 2006).

[167] Beck, A., & Katcher, A., *Between Pets and People.* (Purdue, 1996

[168] Merriam-Webster On-Line Dictionary is used for the following definition; "intention."www.merriam-webster.com

[169] Grandin, T., *Thinking in Pictures.* (New York: First Vintage Books, 1995).

[170] Grandin, T., "Thinking the Way Animals Do," Western Horseman, (1997). Pg.140-145.

[171] Willis and Sharon Lamm of KBR Horse Training: www.kbrhorse.net/pag/train.html.

[172] Roberts, M., *The Man Who Listens to Horses.* (New York: Ballentine Publishing Group, 1996); Roberts, M., *Horse Sense for People.* (New York: Penguin Books, 2002); Brannaman, B., *The Faraway Horses and the Story of the Real Horse Whisperer.* (David and Childs Publishing, 2004); Brannaman, B., *Believe.* (The Lions Press, 2006).

[173] Roberts, M., *Horse Sense for People.* (New York: Penguin Books, 2002).

[174] Personal observation of Ms. Rector's work and communications and interviews with Ms. Rector.

[175] Esperanza, An Experiential Healing Center: www.esperanzainformation.com.

[176] Perkins, A., Personal Cooraspondance.

[177] Budiansky, S., *The Nature of Horses*. (New York: The Free Press, 1997). Pg. 165-167; Johnson, W., *The Rose-Tinted Menagerie*. (Heretic Books, Ltd., 1990); *Pfungst, O. Clever Hans (The Horse of Mr. von Osten)*. (Thoemmes Continuum; English E. 1911 edition, 2000); Thomas A. Sebeok, T.A., & Rosenthal, R., "Clever Hans Phenomenon: Communication With Horses, Whales, and People," *New York Academy of Sciences*. (December, 1970).

[178] Watson, L., *Dreams of Dragons*. (Destiny Books, 1987). Pg. 11-19.

[179] Wilson, E.O., & Kellert, S.R., *The Biophilia Hypothesis*.

[180] Budiansky, S., *The Nature of Horses*. (New York: The Free Press, 1997). Pg. 89.

[181] Budiansky, S., *The Nature of Horses*. (New York: The Free Press, 1997). Pg. 91.

[182] References in this chapter to the body language or behavior of horses came from the following sources; Budiansky, S., *The Nature of Horses*. (New York: The Free Press, 1997); Hill, C., *How to Think Like a Horse*. (Story Publishing, 2006); Roberts, M., *Horse Sense for People*. (New York: Penguin Books, 2000); the author's personal experience and observation of horses.

[183] Budiansky, S., *The Nature of Horses*. (New York: The Free Press, 1997).

[184] Merriam-Webster On-Line Dictionary is used for the following definition; "violent". www.merriam-webster.com.

[185] Merriam-Webster On-Line Dictionary is used for the following definitions; "instinct", "instinctual". www.merriam-webster.com.

186 Albert Einstein. In: Dossey, L., *Recovering the Soul.* (New York: Bantam Books, 1989). Pg. 33. From: Weisburd, "The Spark: Personal Testimonies of Creativity," *Science News,* 132, Nov. 7, 1987, pg. 289.

187 Arthur Koestler. In: In: Dossey, L., *Recovering the Soul.* (New York: Bantam Books, 1989). Pg. 33. From: Koestler, A., *The Act of Creation.* (New York: Dell, 1964). Pg. 177.

188 Personal communication with Barbara Rector.

189 Barbara Rector. In: Hallberg, L., *Horses as Healers: Exploring the psychological implications of the horse/human relationship.* (Self Published, 2003). Pg. 36. From: Rector, B.K., personal communication, February, 2003.

190 Sheldrake, R., *Dogs That Know When Their Owners Are Coming Home: And Other Unexplained Powers of Animals.* (New York: Three Rivers Press, 1999).

191 Sheldrake, R., *The Presence of the Past: Morphic Resonance and the Habits of Nature.* (Vermont: Park Stress Press, 1995). xviii-xix.

192 Sheldrake, R., *The Presence of the Past: Morphic Resonance and the Habits of Nature.* (Vermont: Park Stress Press, 1995). xviii.

193 Albert Einstein. In: Dossey, L., *Recovering the Soul.* (New York: Bantam Books, 1989). Pg. 33. From: Weisburd, "The Spark: Personal Testimonies of Creativity," *Science News,* 132, Nov. 7, 1987, pg. 289; Arthur Koestler. In: In: Dossey, L., *Recovering the Soul.* (New York: Bantam Books, 1989). Pg. 33. From: Koestler, A., *The Act of Creation.* (New York: Dell, 1964). Pg. 177.

194 Merriam-Webster On-Line Dictionary is used for the following definitions; "intention," "intent". www.merriam-webster.com.

[195] Sheldrake, R., *The Presence of the Past: Morphic Resonance and the Habits of Nature.* (Vermont: Park Stress Press, 1995); Sheldrake, R., *Dogs That Know When Their Owners Are Coming Home: And Other Unexplained Powers of Animals.* (New York: Three Rivers Press, 1999); Dossey, L., *Time, Space, and Medicine.* (Shambhala Publications, 1982); Dossey, L. *Recovering the Soul.* (New York: Bantam Books, 1989); Dossey, L., *Be Careful What You Pray For... You Just Might Get It.* (New York: HarperCollins, 1997); Dossey, L., *Meaning and Medicine.* (New York: Bantam Books, 1992); Dossey, L., *Healing Words.* (New York: HarperCollins, 1993); Dossey, L., *Reinventing Medicine.* (New York: HarperCollins, 1999); Dossey, L., *Healing Beyond the Body.* (Shambhala Publications, 2001); Watson, L., *Super Nature.* (Anchor Press of Doubleday, 1973); Watson, L., *The Romeo Error.* (Anchor Press, 1975); Watson, L., *Life Tide.* (New York: Bantam Books, 1980); Watson, L., *Beyond Supernature.* (New York: Bantam Books, 1987); Watson, L., *Dreams of Dragons.* (Destiny Books, 1987); Watson, L., *Dark Nature.* (Harper Perennial, 1997); Watson, L., Gifts *of Unknown Things.* (Destiny Books, 1991); Watson, L., *Jacobson's Organ.* (New York: Penguin Books, 2001); Watson, L., *Elephantoms.* (W.W. Norton and Company, 2002).

[196] Dossey, L., *Recovering the Soul.* (New York: Bantam Books, 1989); Jung, C.G., *Psychology and the East.* (Routledge, 1987).

[197] Henry Margenau. In: Dossey, L., *Recovering the Soul.* (New York: Bantam Books, 1989). Pg. 161. From: Margenau, H., *The Miracle of Existence.* (Woodbridge, CT: Ox Bow Press, 1984).

[198] Dossey, L., *Healing Words.* (New York: HarperCollins, 1993).

[199] Dossey, L., *Recovering the Soul.* (New York: Bantam Books, 1989). Pg. 120.

[200] Sheldrake, R., *The Presence of the Past: Morphic Resonance and the Habits of Nature.* (Vermont: Park Stress Press, 1995). Pg. xix.

201 Sheldrake, R., *Dogs That Know When Their Owners Are Coming Home: And Other Unexplained Powers of Animals.* (New York: Three Rivers Press, 1999). Pg. 87-88.

202 Watson, L., *Dreams of Dragons.* (Destiny Books, 1987). Pg. 33-37.

203 Watson, L., *Dreams of Dragons.* (Destiny Books, 1987). Pg. 44-45.

204 Robinson, P., "The Equine Experience: The role of horses in adventure education," *Transitions,* Winter/Spring, 2003, pg. 18.

205 Merriam-Webster On-Line Dictionary is used for the following definition, "assertion." www.merriam-webster.com.

206 Budiansky, S., *The Nature of Horses.* (New York: The Free Press, 1997). Pg. 91-93.

207 Irwin, C., *Horses Don't Lie.* (New York: Marlowe and Company, 1998). Pg. 63.

208 Irwin, C., Horses Don't Lie. (New York: Marlowe and Company, 1998). Pg 63.

209 Tolle, E., *The Power of Now.* (Novato, CA: New World Library, 1999). Pg. 17.

210 Tolle, E., *The Power of Now.* (Novato, CA: New World Library, 1999). Pg. 79.

211 Merriam-Webster On-Line Dictionary is used for the following definitions; "congruence", "congruous". www.merriam-webster.com.

212 EFMH/ES definition of "congruence" as proposed by this author.

213 Irwin, C., *Horses Don't Lie.* (New York: Marlowe and Company, 1998).

[214] Roberts, M., *The Man Who Listens to Horses*. (New York: Ballentine Publishing Group, 1996); Roberts, M., *Horse Sense for People*. (New York: Penguin Books, 2000); Rees, L., *The Horse's Mind*. (Arco, 1985); Witter, R.F., *Living with HorsePower*. (Vermont: Trafalgar Square Publishing, 1998); and Irwin, C., *Horses Don't Lie*. (New York: Marlowe and Company, 1998).

[215] Roberts, M., *The Man Who Listens to Horses*. (New York: Ballentine Publishing Group, 1996); Roberts, M., *Horse Sense for People*. (New York: Penguin Books, 2000); Rees, L., *The Horse's Mind*. (Arco, 1985); Budiansky, S., *The Nature of Horses*. (New York: The Free Press, 1997); Scanlan, L., *Wild about Horses*. (New York: HarperCollins, 1998).

[216] See the Introduction to this text for a definition and clarification. Also see Roberts, M., *The Man Who Listens to Horses*. (New York: Ballentine Publishing Group, 1996); Roberts, M., *Horse Sense for People*. (New York: Penguin Books, 2000); Kohonov, L., *The Tao of Equus*. (Novato, CA: New World Library, 2001).

[217] Barbara Rector, personal communication and the personal experience of the author while working with Ms. Rector.

[218] Irwin, C., *Horses Don't Lie*. (New York: Marlowe and Company, 1998); Roberts, M., *The Man Who Listens to Horses*. (New York: Ballentine Publishing Group, 1996); Roberts, M., *Horse Sense for People*. (New York: Penguin Books, 2000); Rees, L., *The Horse's Mind*. (Arco, 1985).

[219] Roberts, M., *Horse Sense for People*. (New York: Penguin Books, 2000).

[220] Irwin, C., Horses Don't Lie. (New York: Marlowe and Company, 1998). Pg. 3.

[221] Irwin, C., Horses Don't Lie. (New York: Marlowe and Company, 1998). Pg.

²²² McCormick, A., & McCormick, M., *Horse Sense and the Human Heart*. (Deerfield Beach, FL.: Health Communications, 1997). Pg. 23.

²²³ Sheldrake, R., *The Presence of the Past: Morphic Resonance and the Habits of Nature*. (Vermont: Park Stress Press, 1995).

²²⁴ "The Interpreter", 20005. Directed by Sydney Pollack. Produced by Eric Fellner, Kevin Misher, Tim Bevan. Written by Charles Randolph, Scott Frank, Steven Zaillian.

Chapter Seven Notes

²²⁵ Schoen, A., *Kindred Spirits*. (New York: Broadway Books, 2001). Pg. 176.

²²⁶ Wilson, E.O., & Kellert, S.R., *The Biophilia Hypothesis*. (Washington, D.C: Island Press, 1993).

²²⁷ Bernstein, J., *Living in the Borderland*. (New York: Routledge, 2005). Pg. 33-34.

²²⁸ Carl Jung. In: Bernstein, J., *Living in the Borderland*. (New York: Routledge, 2005). Pg. 72. From: Jung, C.G., *Man and His Symbols*. (New York: Doubleday, 1964).

²²⁹ References to the need for connection to nature and its benefits come from the following sources; Kanner, A.D., Roszak, T., & Gomes, M.E., *Ecopsychology: Restoring the earth, healing the mind*. (New York: Random House, 1995); Wilson, E.O., & Kellert, S.R., *The Biophilia Hypothesis*. (Washington, D.C: Island Press, 1993); Cohen, M., *Reconnecting With Nature: Finding Wellness Through Restoring Your Bond With the Earth*. (Ecopress, 1997); Metzner, R., *Green Psychology: Transforming our Relationship to the Earth* (Vermont: Park Street Press, 1999); Glendinning, C., *My Name is Chellis and I'm in Recovery from Western Civilization*. (Boston, MA.: Shambhala Publications, 1994)

230 Bioneers: www.bioneers.org; Wilson, E.O., & Kellert, S.R., *The Biophilia Hypothesis.* (Washington, D.C: Island Press, 1993); Wilson, E.O., *The Creation.* (W.W. Norton, 2006); Wilson, E.O., *Sociobiology.* (Belknap Press, 25th Anniversary edition, 2000); Wilson, E.O., *The Diversity of Life.* (New York: Penguin Books, Ltd. New Ed edition, 2001).

231 Personal experience of the author while working with Native American youth at the Salt River Pima-Maricopa Indian Community Juvenile Correctional Department.

232 Schoen, A., *Kindred Spirits.* (New York: Broadway Books, 2001); Sheldrake, R., *Dogs That Know When Their Owners Are Coming Home: And Other Unexplained Powers of Animals.* (New York: Three Rivers Press, 1999).

233 Rogers, C., *On Being a Person.* (New York: Houghton Mifflin, 1961).

234 Yalom, I.D., *The Gift of Therapy.* (New York: HarperCollins, 2002). 23-25.

235 McCormick, A.R., McCormick, M.D., & McCormick, T.E., *Horses and the Mystical Path.* (Novato, CA.: New World Library, 2004). Pg. 98.

236 Roberts, M., *The Man Who Listens to Horses.* (New York: Ballantine Publishing Group, 1996); Roberts, M., *Horse Sense for People.* (New York: Penguin Books, 2000); Irwin, C., *Horses Don't Lie.* (New York: Marlowe and Company, 1998); Budiansky, S., *The Nature of Horses.* (New York: The Free Press, 1997).

237 Susan Boucher. In: Midkiff, M., *She Flies Without Wings.* (New York: Dell Publishing, 2001). Pg. 147. From: Boucher, S. "Partnering Pegasus." In: Hogan. L., *Intimate Nature: The bond between women and animals.* (New York: Ballantine Books, 1998).

[238] References to herd nature come from the following sources; Roberts, M., *The Man Who Listens to Horses.* (New York: Ballantine Publishing Group, 1996); Budiansky, S., *The Nature of Horses.* (New York: The Free Press, 1997); Hill, C., *How to Think Like a Horse.* (Story Publishing, 2006); Ryden, H., *Wild Horses I have Known. (*New York: Clarion Books, 1999); Anecdotal accounts from horse people; and the authors personal experience and observation of horse herds.

[239] Rashid, M., *Horses Never Lie.* (Boulder, CO.: Johnson Publishing Company, 2000).

[240] Irwin, C., *Horses Don't Lie.* (New York: Marlowe and Company, 1998). Pg. 63.

[241] Irwin, C., *Horses Don't Lie.* (New York: Marlowe and Company, 1998).

[242] Marianne Williamson, M., *A Return To Love: Reflections on the Principles of A Course in Miracles.* (New York: HarperCollins, 1994).

[243] Rector, B.K., personal communication.

[244] Exley, H., Horse Quotations. (Exley Giftbooks, 1992). Pg. 11.

[245] Scanlan, L., *Wild about Horses.* (New York: HarperCollins, 1998).

[246] Miller, R., *Revolution in Horsemanship.* (Lyons Press, 2005).

[247] References to the power of horses in our lives come from the following sources; Scanlan, L., *Wild about Horses.* (New York: HarperCollins, 1998); Decaire, C., & Watkins, M., Girls and Their Horses. (American Girl, 2006); Eastman, M., Horses. (Knopf, 2003); Canfield., J., Hansen, M.,V., Becker, M., Seidler, G., Peluso, T., & Vegso, P. *Chicken Soup for the Horselover's Soul.* (Health Communications, Inc., 2003); Richards, S., *Chosen*

By a Horse. (New York, Soho Press, 2006); Goble, P., *The Girl Who Loved Wild Horses.* (New York; Simon & Schuster, 1978); GaWaNi Pony Boy. *Of Women and Horses.* (BowTie Press, 2000); Johns, C., *Horses: History, Myth, and Art.* (Harvard University Press, 2007); Kohanov, L., & Stromberg, T., *Spirit Horses.* (Novato, CA: New World Library, 2005); Korda, M., *Horse People: Scenes from the Riding Life.* (New York: Harper Perennial, 2004); Rappaport, J., Wilkinson, W., & Soloman, L., *People We Know, Horses They Love.* (Rodale Books, 2004); Hale, C., *A Passion for Horses: My Conversations with Horse Lovers.* (BowTie Press, 2004); Nusser, S., *In Service to the Horse: Chronicles of a Labor of Love.* (New York: Little, Brown, and Company, 2004); Gouraud, J.L., & Bertrand, Y.A., *Horses.* (Artisan, 2004); Sovey-Nelson, M., & Barrett, M.J., *If I Had a Horse: How Different Life Would Be.* (Willow Creek Press, 2004); Sovey, M. Horse Women: Strength, Beauty, Passion. (Willow Creek Press, 2005); Hyde, D.O., Summers, R., & Summers, C.G., *All the Wild Horses: Preserving the Spirit and Beauty of Worlds Wild Horses.* (Voyageur Press, 2006); Boiselle, G. *Horses.* (White Star, 2004); Antidotal accounts, and the author's observations.

[248] See 23.

[249] See 23.

[250] See 23.

[251] References to intimacy come from the following sources; Kohanov, L., *The Tao of Equus.* (Novato, CA: New World Library, 2001); Johnson, D.H., Body: *Recovering Our Sensual Wisdom.* (Berkeley, CA: North Atlantic Books, 1992); Kelly, M., *The Seven Levels of Intimacy: The Art of Loving and the Joy of Being Loved.* (New York: Fireside, 2005).

[252] Kohanov, L., *The Tao of Equus.* (Novato, CA: New World Library, 2001). Pg. 209.

253 References to entrainment, coherence, and connection and quotes from HeartMath come from the following source; HeartMath: www.heartmath.org

254 References to entrainment, coherence, and connection and quotes from HeartMath come from the following source; HeartMath: www.heartmath.org

255 References to entrainment, coherence, and connection and quotes from HeartMath come from the following source; HeartMath: www.heartmath.org

256 References to entrainment, coherence, and connection and quotes from HeartMath come from the following source; HeartMath: www.heartmath.org

257 References to entrainment, coherence, and connection and quotes from HeartMath come from the following source; HeartMath: www.heartmath.org

258 Wikipedia, an on-line dictionary can be found at www.wikipedia. org. Within this chapter Wikipedia's on-line dictionary is used for the following definitions; "entrainment"

259 Reference to "*Christiaan Huygens.*" Retrieved: http://nl.wikipedia. org/wiki/Christiaan_Huygens

260 All references to Ellen K. Gehrke or her research comes from the following sources; Gehrke, E.K., "Horses and Humans Energetics: The study of Heart Rate Variability (HRV) between horses and Humans." (Self Published, 2006); Personal interview and correspondence.

261 McCormick, A., & McCormick, M., *Horse Sense and the Human Heart.* (Deerfield Beach, FL.: Health Communications, 1997). Pg. 23.

[262] See 36.

[263] This statement was made by an Esperanza client in reference to learning how to nurture and care for herself.

[264] References to the state of employment, wages, and health insurance in America come from the following sources; Mishel, L., Bernstein, J.,& Boushey, H., *The State of Working America 2003-04.* (Cornell University Press, 2003); Mishel, L., Bernstein, J., & Allegretto, S., *The State of Working America 2006-07.* (Cornell University Press, 2006); Bernstein, J., "Economic Opportunity and Poverty in America,": This testimony was given before the subcommittee on income security and family support of the Committee On Ways and Means of the U.S. House of Representatives, February 13, 2007. Retrievable: www.epi.org/content.cfm?id=2638 ; Democratic Staff of the Committee on Health, Education, Labor and Pensions Committee, United States Senate, "The Decline in the Minimum Wage for America's Workers," July 1, 2004: Retrievable: www.policyalmanac.org/economic/archive/minimum_wage02.shtml; United Food and Commercial Workers (UFCW): www.ufcw.org; State of the Economy Address, President George Bush, January, 2007: http://www.whitehouse.gov/infocus/economy/state_economy2007.pdf.

[265] Midkiff, M., *She Flies Without Wings.* (New York: Dell Publishing, 2001). Pg. 132.

[266] Self report from Esperanza clients.

[267] Laura Brinkerhoff, personal communication.

[268] Personal observation of the author; personal communications with other EFMH/ES professionals.

[269] American Heritage Dictionary on-line version is used to define "presence": education.yahoo.com/reference/dictionary/entry/presence.

270 Rogers, C., *On Being a Person.* (New York: Houghton Mifflin, 1961); Yalom, I.D., *The Gift of Therapy.* (New York: HarperCollins, 2002).

271 Paterson, J.G., & Zderad, L.T. *Humanistic Nursing.* (New York: John Wiley &
Sons, 1976). In: MacDonald du Mont, P., "The Concept of Therapeutic Presence in Nursing," The University of Tennessee. Pg. 5. Retrievable: www.temple.edu/ispr/prev_conferences/ proceedings/2002/Final%20papers/du%20Mont.pdf.

272 Scurlock-Durana, S., "Developing Therapeutic Presence." In: Carlson, J., *Complementary Therapies and Wellness Practice Essentials for Holistic Health Care.* (Prentice Hall, 2003). Chapter Seven.

273 Goode, V., & Anselmo, J., "Connection to Purpose, Law in the Service of Human Law in the Service of Human Needs: Social Justice and Contemplative Practice." Retrievable: www.aals.org/ am2006/program/balance/JeannePresentation.pdf.

274 Watson, J., *Nursing: Human Science and Human Care.* (Jones & Bartlett Publishers, 1999).

275 *The New Testament,* Matthew 18:20.

276 Dossey, L., *Recovering the Soul.* (New York: Bantam Books, 1989); Sheldrake, R., *The Presence of the Past: Morphic Resonance and the Habits of Nature.* (Vermont: Park Stress Press, 1995).

277 Capra, F., *The Tao of Physics.* (Berkeley: Shambhala Publications, Inc., 1975); Gribbin, J., *In Search of Schrodinger's Cat: Quantum Physics and Reality.* (New York: Bantam Books, Inc. 1984); Murchie, G., *Music of the Spheres - Volume II. The Microcosm: Matter, Atoms, Waves, Radiation, and Relativity.* (New York: Dover Publications, Inc., 1967); Pert, C., *Molecules of Emotion: Why you feel the way you feel.* (New York: Simon and Schuster, Inc., 1997);

Zukav, G., *The Dancing Wu Li Masters: An overview of the new physics.* (New York: William Morrow & Company, Inc., 1979).

[278] HeartMath: www.hearthmath.org.

[279] Andrew Weil. In: Rector, B., *Adventures in Awareness.* (Bloomington, IN.: Authorhouse, 2005). Pg. 12.

[280] Encarta On-Line Dictionary is used for the following definitions; "mirror" and "reflective". Http://encarta.msn.com.

[281] McCormick, A., & McCormick, M., *Horse Sense and the Human Heart.* (Deerfield Beach, FL.: Health Communications, 1997). Pg. xxix.

[282] Soren, I., *Zen and Horses.* (Rondale, Inc., 2002). Pg. 44.

[283] Budiansky, S., *The Nature of Horses.* (New York: The Free Press, 1997). Pg. 93.

[284] Kohanov, L., *Riding Between the Worlds.* (Novato, CA: New World Library, 2003).

[285] Larry Dossey. In: McCormick, A., & McCormick, M., *Horse Sense and the Human Heart.* (Deerfield Beach, FL: Health Communications, 1997). Pg. xx.

[286] Rector, B., *Adventures in Awareness.* (Bloomington, IN.: Authorhouse, 2005). Pg. 51.

[287] Rector, B., *Adventures in Awareness.* (Bloomington, IN.: Authorhouse, 2005). Pg. 15.

[288] Watson, L., *Jacobson's Organ.* (New York: Penguin Books, 1999).

[289] McCormick, A., & McCormick, M., *Horse Sense and the Human Heart.* (Deerfield Beach, FL.: Health Communications, 1997). Pg. 23.

[290] Barbara Rector states, "The horses who volunteer to participant in the intensity of this work mirror the deep inner psychic processes of the participant. Sometimes this immense energy is frightening to those not familiar with unconscious emotions cathartically expressed." In: Rector, B.K., Rector, B., *Adventures in Awareness.* (Bloomington, IN.: Authorhouse, 2005). Pg. 78. Such instances of deeply personal reveal have been witnessed by this author and have been anecdotally reported evidence by other professionals within the field of EFMH/ES.

[291] References to anecdotal evidence regarding reflective feedback come from the following sources; Rector, B., *Adventures in Awareness.* (Bloomington, IN.: Authorhouse, 2005); Hallberg, L. "Horses as Healers: Exploring the Psychological Implications of the horse/human relationship." (Self Published Thesis, 2003); McCormick, A., & McCormick, M., *Horse Sense and the Human Heart.* (Deerfield Beach, FL.: Health Communications, 1997); McCormick, A.R., McCormick, M.D., & McCormick, T.E., *Horses and the Mystical Path.* (Novato, CA.: New World Library, 2004); Kohonov, L., *The Tao of Equus.* (Novato, CA: New World Library, 2001); Kohanov, L., *Riding Between the Worlds.* (Novato, CA: New World Library, 2003); Personal communications and interview with Barbara Rector, Laura Brinkerhoff, and many other EFMH/ES professionals.

[292] Barbara Rector, personal observation of Ms. Rector's use of "round pen reasoning."

[293] Roberts, M., *Horse Sense for People.* (New York: Penguin Books, 2000); Roberts, M., *The Man Who Listens to Horses.* (New York: Ballantine Publishing Group, 1996).

[294] Freud, S., *An Outline of Psychoanalysis.* (New York: Norton, 1949); Elliot, A., *Psychoanalytic Theory: An Introduction.* (Oxford UK & Cambridge, USA: Blackwell, 1994); Faber, M.D., *Synchronicity: C. G. Jung, Psychoanalysis, and Religion.* (Praeger Publishers, 1998); Jung, C.G., Adler, G., & Hull, R.F.C., *Freud and Psychoanalysis.* (Princeton University Press, 1961); Jung, C.G., *Analytical Psychology.* (Routledge; 1 edition, 1986).

[295] Grant, J.,& Crawley, J., *Transference and Projection: Mirrors to the Self.* (Open University Press, 2002); Franz, M.L., *Projection and Re-Collection in Jungian Psychology: Reflections of the Soul.* (Open Court Publishing Company, 1987); Goldstein, W., *Using the Transference in Psychotherapy.* (Jason Aronson, 2006).

[296] Linda Kohanov. Personal communication and interview.

[297] Encarta On-Line Dictionary is used for the following definition, "boundary." Http://encarta.msn.com.

[298] Irwin, C., *Horses Don't Lie.* (New York: Marlowe and Company, 1998); Hill, C., *How to Think Like a Horse.* (Story Publishing, 2006); Budiansky, S., *The Nature of Horses.* (New York: The Free Press, 1997); Hempfling, K.F., *Dancing with Horses.* (Vermont: Trafalgar Square Publishing, 2001); Hempfling, K.F., *What Horses Reveal.* (Vermont: Trafalgar Square Publishing, 2004); Rashid, M., *Considering the Horse.* (Spring Creek Press, 1993); Rashid, M., *Horses Never Lie.* (Boulder, CO.: Johnson Publishing Company, 2000); Rashid, M., *Life Lessons from a Ranch Horse.* (David and Charles Publishing, 2004); Rashid, M., *Horsemanship Through Life.* (Spring Creek Press, 2005) Ainslie, T., & Ledbetter, B., *The Body Language of Horses.* (New York: William Morrow and Company, 1980); Roberts, M., *The Man Who Listens to Horses.* (New York: Ballantine Publishing Group, 1996); Roberts, M., *Horse Sense for People.* (New York: Penguin Books, 2002).

[299] Jung, C.G., *Psychology and the East.* (Routledge, 1987).

[300] Dossey, L., *Recovering the Soul.* (New York: Bantam Books, 1989).

[301] Bernstein, J., *Living in the Borderland.* (New York: Routledge, 2005).

[302] References to depression come from the following sources; "Largest Survey On Depression Suggests Higher Prevalence In U.S," *Columbia University's Mailman School of Public Health,* October 27, 2005. Retrievable: www.mailman.hs.columbia.edu/ news/hasin-mdd-study.html; Bernard L. Harlow, B.L., Cohen, L.S., Otto, M.W., Spiegelman, D.,& Cramer, D.W., "Prevalence and Predictors of Depressive Symptoms in Older Premenopausal Women: The Harvard Study of Moods and Cycles," *Arch Gen Psychiatry.* 1999; 56: 418-424; Bernstein, J., *Living in the Borderland.* (New York: Routledge, 2005).

[303] "Learned helplessness" is a psychological condition in which a human or animal has learned to believe that it is helpless. It thinks that it has no control over its situation and that whatever it does is futile. As a result it will stay passive when the situation is unpleasant or harmful and damaging. It is the view that depression results from the perception of a lack of control over the reinforcements in one's life that may result from exposure to uncontrollable negative events. Wikipedia: www.wikipedia. org/wiki/Learned_helplessness; Peterson, C. *Learned Helplessness : A theory for the age of personal control. (*New York : Oxford University Press, 1993.) Pg. xi; Mikulincer, M., *Human Learned Helplessness.* (The Springer Series in Social/Clinical Psychology, 1994.).

Chapter Eight Notes

[304] Rogers, C., *On Becoming a Person.* (New York: Houghton Mifflin, 1961).

[305] Tart, C., *Waking Up.* (Shambhala Publication, 1986). Pg. 171.

[306] This statement is based upon anecdotal accounts from EFMH/ES professionals, and from the personal observation of this author over a ten-year span providing EFMH/ES to a diverse clientele.

[307] Soren, I., *Zen and Horses.* (Rondale, Inc., 2002). Pg. 67.

[308] Tolle, E., *The Power of Now.* (Novato, CA: New World Library, 1999). Duncan, S., *Present Moment Awareness.* (Novato, CA.: New World Library, 2004); Jacobson, L., *Embracing the Present: Living an Awakened Life.* (Conscious Living Publications, 1997); Keating, T., *Invitation to Love: The Way of Christian Contemplation.* (Continuum International Publishing Group; New Ed edition, 1994); McGaa, E., *Mother Earth Spirituality: Native American Paths to Healing Ourselves and Our World.* (New York: HarperCollins, 1989).

[309] Tolle, E., *The Power of Now.* (Novato, CA: New World Library, 1999). Pg. 43.

[310] Bizub, A., Joy, A., & Davidson, L., "It's like being in another world." *Psychiatric Rehabilitation Journal,* Vol. 26, No. 4, (2003); Anecdotal evidence provided by EFMH/ES professionals.

[311] Roberts, M., *Horse Sense for People.* (New York: Penguin Books, 2002); Irwin, C., *Horses Don't Lie.* (New York: Marlowe and Company, 1998).

[312] Witter, R.F., *Living with HorsePower.* (Vermont: Trafalgar Square Publishing, 1998).

[313] Tolle, E., *The Power of Now.* (Novato, CA: New World Library, 1999). Pg. 41.

[314] Sundberg, N.D., Latkin, C.A., Farmer, R.F., & Saoud, J., "Boredom in Young Adults," *Journal of Cross-Cultural Psychology,* Vol. 22, No. 2, 209-223 (1991); Ferrell, J., Boredom, Crime,

and Criminology," *Theoretical Criminology*, Vol. 8, No. 3, 287-302 (2004).

315 Stern, D.N., *The Present Moment in Psychotherapy and in Everyday Life.* (New York: W.W. Norton and Company, 2004).

316 Burgon, H., "Case studies of adults receiving horse-riding therapy," *Anthrozoos*, Vol. 13, (2003). Pg. 262-76; Polster, E., & Polster, M., *Gestalt Therapy Integrated: Contours of theory and practice.* (New York: Brunner/Mazel, 1973).

317 Irwin, C., *Horses Don't Lie.* (New York: Marlowe and Company, 1998). Pg. 47.

318 Irwin, C., *Horses Don't Lie.* (New York: Marlowe and Company, 1998). Pg. 48.

319 This statement is based off of the author's personal experience.

320 Rogers, C., *On Becoming a Person.* (New York: Houghton Mifflin, 1961).

321 Rector, B., *Adventures in Awareness.* (Bloomington, IN.: Authorhouse, 2005).

322 World Health Organization, "World Report on Violence and Health," *World Health Organization*, Geneva. (2002). Retrievable: www.who.int/violence_injury_prevention/violence/world_report/en/full_en.pdf.

323 Strimple, E.O., "A History of Prison Inmate-Animal Interaction Programs," *American Behavioral Scientist*, Vol. 47, No. 1, 70-78 (2003); Deaton, C "Humanizing Prisons with Animals: A Closer Look at "Cell Dogs" and Horse Programs in Correctional Institutions," *Journal of Correctional Education,* March, 2005.

324 Canon City Program: www.csc-scc.gc.ca/text/prgrm/fsw/pet-38_e.shtml

325 Warm Springs Program: http://www.doc.nv.gov/wscc/ ; http://www.mustangs4us.com/prisonhorses.htm#_HANK_CURRY; www.nv.blm.gov/news_releases/Press_Releases/fy2003/PR_03_62.htm

326 Marion County Correctional Institute: www.thoroughbredadoption.com/FL%20Kat.htm; www.dc.state.fl.us/pub/compass/0212/10.html.

327 Osho, *Awareness: The Key to Living in Balance.* (St. Martin's Griffin, 2001); Parloff, M.B., Kelman, H.C., & Frank, J.D., "Comfort, Effectiveness, And Self-Awareness As Criteria Of Improvement In Psychotherapy," *American Journal of Psychiatry*, 111:343-352, November, 1954.

328 Personal experience of the author while providing EFMH/ES to inmates from the Salt River Pima-Maricopa Indian Community.

329 De Mause, L., *Emotional Life of Nations.* (New York: Other Press, 2002). De Mause, L., "Restaging Fetal Traumas in War and Social Violence." *Journal of Psychohistory.* Vol. 10(4) (Summer) & Vol 23(4) (Spring).

330 Sogn, H., Lorentzen, J., & Gullvåg Holter, Ø., "Research on Violence in Norway," *Norwegian Information and Documentation Centre for Women's Studies and Gender Research,* Oslo, (2006).

331 Pert, C., Molecules of Emotion. (New York: Touchstone, 1997).

332 Keen, S., *Fire in the Belly.* (New York: Bantam Books, Reissue edition, 1992); Bly, R., *Iron John.* (New York: Random House, 1990); Moore, R., & Gillette, D., *King, Warrior, Magician, Lover: Rediscovering the Archetypes of the Mature Masculine.* (HarperSanFrancisco; Reprint edition, 1991).

[333] Rodewalt, F. & Tragakis, M. W. "Self-esteem and self-regulation: Toward optimal studies of self-esteem," *Psychological Inquiry,* 14(1), 66–70. (2003); Sedikides, C., & Gregg. A. P. "Portraits of the self." In M. A. Hogg & J. Cooper (Eds.), *Sage handbook of social psychology* (London: Sage Publications, 2003). Pg. 110-138; Baumeister, R., Smart, L. & Boden, J. "Relation of threatened egotism to violence and aggression: The dark side of self-esteem." *Psychological Review,* 103, 5–33. (1996).

[334] Wikipedia: www.wikipedia.org

[335] James, W. *The principles of psychology.* (Cambridge, MA: Harvard University Press, 1983). Branden, N. *The psychology of self-esteem.* (New York: Bantam, 1969).

[336] Sedikides, C., & Gregg. A. P. "Portraits of the self." In M. A. Hogg & J. Cooper (Eds.), *Sage handbook of social psychology* (London: Sage Publications, 2003). Pg.110-138.

[337] Carlson, E., "The effects of a program of therapeutic horsemanship on the self-concept and locus of control orientation of the learning disabled," (Doctoral dissertation, United States International University,1983); Dismuke, R. P., "Rehabilitative horseback riding for children with language disorders," In: Anderson, R. H., Hart, B. L. &. Hart, L. A., *The pet connection.* (Minneapolis: University of Minnesota, 1984). Pg. 131-140; Brock, B.J., Effect of therapeutic horseback riding on posture in children with cerebral palsy." *Physical Therapy,* 68. Pg. 1505-1512; Mason, M. J., "Effects of a therapeutic riding program on self concept in adults with cerebral palsy," Unpublished doctoral dissertation, New York University, New York (1988); Stuler, L. R. "The impact of therapeutic horseback riding on the self-concept and riding performance of children and adolescents with disabilities." Unpublished master's thesis, Pennsylvania State University, Pennsylvania (1993); Crawley, R., Crawley, D., & Retter, K., "Therapeutic horseback riding and self-concept in adolescents with special educational needs."

Anthrozoos, 7, 129-134. (1994); Gatty, C.M., "Psychosocial impact of therapeutic riding: A pilot study." NARHA, www.narha.org/PDFfiles/Psychosocial_Impact.pdf; Bizub, A., Joy, A., & Davidson, L., "It's like being in another world." Psychiatric Rehabilitation Journal, Vol. 26, No. 4, (2003). Pg. 377-384; Cody, P., "Therapeutic horseback riding and children adopted from foster care," NARHA Annual Conference, November, 2006; Meinersmann, K., Roberts, F., Bradberry, J., "Lived experience of equine facilitated psychotherapy among adult survivors of abuse," NARHA Annual Conference, November, 2006.

[338] McCormick, A., & McCormick, M., *Horse Sense and the Human Heart.* (Deerfield Beach, FL.: Health Communications, 1997); McCormick, A.R., McCormick, M.D., & McCormick, T.E., *Horses and the Mystical Path.* (Novato, CA.: New World Library, 2004); Kohonov, L., *The Tao of Equus.* (Novato, CA: New World Library, 2001); Kohonov, L., *Riding Between the Worlds.* (Novato, CA: New World Library, 2003); Rector, B., *Adventures in Awareness.* (Bloomington, IN.: Authorhouse, 2005); Midkiff, M., *She Flies Without Wings.* (New York: Dell Publishing, 2001); Soren, I., Zen and Horses. (Rondale, 2002); Witter, R.F., *Living with HorsePower.* (Vermont: Trafalgar Square Publishing, 1998); Roberts, M., *Horse Sense for People.* (New York: Penguin Books, 2002); Irwin, C., *Horses Don't Lie.* (New York: Marlowe and Company, 1998); Hallberg, L., "Horses as Healers: Exploring the psychological implications of the horse/human relationship," (Self Published Thesis, 2003); anecdotal evidence resulting from surveys, questionnaires, and interviews conducted by this author.

[339] Linda Kohanov. Personal interview, 2006.

[340] Ann Alden. Personal interview, 2006.

[341] Merriam-Webster's On-Line Dictionary is used for the following definition, "intuition": www.merriam-webster.com.

342 Merriam-Webster's Unabridged Dictionary is used for the following definition, "intuition."

343 Fuller, B., Critical Path. (St. Martin's Griffin, 1982); Fuller, B., Intuition. (DoubleDay, 1973).

344 Dossey, L., *Recovering the Soul.* (New York: Bantam Books, 1989); Sheldrake, R., *The Presence of the Past: Morphic Resonance and the Habits of Nature.* (Vermont: Park Stress Press, 1995). Jung, C.G., *Psychology and the East.* (Princeton: Princeton University Press, 1978).

345 Kuczmarski RJ., "Prevalence of overweight and weight gain in the United States," *American Journal of Clinical Nutrition,* 55 (2 Suppl): Pg.495S-502S. (February, 1992); Hedley, A.A., Ogden, C.L., Johnson,C.L., Carroll, M.D.,Curtin, L.R., Flegal, K.M., "Prevalence of Overweight and Obesity Among US Children, Adolescents, and Adults, 1999-2002," *Journal of the American Medical Association,* 291:2847-2850. (2004); Allison, D.B., Fontaine, K.R., Manson, J.E., Stevens, J., VanItallie, T.B., *"Annual Deaths Attributable to Obesity in the United States,"* *Journal of the American Medical Association,* 282:1530-1538. (1999); Lucas J.W., Schiller J.S., Benson V., "Summary health statistics for U.S. adults: National Health Interview Survey, *Vital and Health Statistics.* Series 10, Data from the National Health Survey, (2001).

346 References to instinct and intuition come from the following sources; Runciman, W.G., The Social Animal. (University of Michigan Press, 2000); Trotter, W., Instincts of the Herd in Peace and in War. (Cosimo Classics, 2005); Cappon, D., *"Intuition from Instinct," R&D Innovator,* Volume 2, Number 2. (February 1993), Retrievable: www.winstonbrill.com/bril001/html/article_index/articles/1-50/article26_body.html; Robbie E., Davis-Floyd, P., & Arvidson, S., *Intuition: The Inside Story.* (New York: Routledge, 1997).

[347] References to the Divine and horses come from the following sources; McCormick, A., & McCormick, M., *Horse Sense and the Human Heart.* (Deerfield Beach, FL.: Health Communications, 1997); McCormick, A.R., McCormick, M.D., & McCormick, T.E., *Horses and the Mystical Path.* (Novato, CA.: New World Library, 2004); Kohonov, L., *The Tao of Equus.* (Novato, CA: New World Library, 2001); Kohonov, L., *Riding Between the Worlds.* (Novato, CA: New World Library, 2003); Scanlan, L., *Wild about Horses.* (New York: HarperPerennial, 1998); Chamberlin, J.E., *Horse: How the horse has shaped civilizations.* (BlueBridge, 2006); Janus, S. *The Magic of Horses.* (SunShine Press Publications, 1997); Hildinger, E., *Warriors of the Steppe.* Da Capo Press, 2001); Howey, M.O., *The Horse in Magic and Myth.* (New York: Dover Publications, 2002, reprint from 1923); Midkiff, M., *She Flies Without Wings.* (New York: Dell Publishing, 2001); Hallberg, L., "Horses as Healers: Exploring the psychological implications of the horse/human relationship," (Self Published Thesis, 2003); and information gained from numerous surveys, questionnaires, and interviews conducted by this author. NOTE: These references only represent a miniscule number of the references that suggest a connection between horses and the Divine. Please see the bibliographies in the back of Howey's book and the McCormick's books to better understand the scope of this notion. This reference does not include religious publications such as the Bible and the Koran which speak at length about the connection between horses and the Divine, nor does it include mythology sources that speak to the same concept.

[348] Wald, M., & Martinez, T., "Connected by 25: Improving the Life Chances of the Country's Most Vulnerable 14-24 Year Olds," *Stanford University,* William and Flora Hewlett Foundation Working Paper, (November, 2003). Retrievable: www.billwilsoncenter.org/Downloads/pdfs/ FinalVersionofDisconnectedYouthPaper.pdf; Skyes, C.J., *The Dumbing Down of Our Kids.* (St. Martins Press, 1996); Washburn, K., Thornton, J.F., & Simon, J.I., *Dumbing Down:*

Essays on the Strip Mining of American Culture. (W. W. Norton & Company, 1996); Gross, M.L., *The Conspiracy of Ignorance: The Failure of American Public Schools.* (New York: HarperCollins, 1999); "How we can win the war on poverty" Fortune (Apr 10 1989): p127.

[349] Livergood, N.D., "The Destruction of American Education." Retrievable: www.hermes-press.com/education_index.htm.

[350] Livergood, N.D., "The Destruction of American Education." Retrievable: www.hermes-press.com/education_index.htm.

[351] Kutner, M., Greenberg, E., Jin, Y., & Paulsen, C., "The Health Literacy of America's Adults: Results from the 2003 National Assessment of Adult Literacy" *National Center for Educational Statistics,* (2006). Retrievable: http://nces.ed.gov/pubs2006/2006483.pdf.

[352] Peterson, C. *Learned Helplessness : A theory for the age of personal control.* (New York : Oxford University Press, 1993.) Pg. xi; Mikulincer, M., *Human Learned Helplessness.* (The Springer Series in Social/Clinical Psychology, 1994.).

[353] Observation from the author based upon Esperanza's client services.

[354] References to the state of youth today comes from the following sources; Cousin Sam, *Youth Quake.* (Trafford Publishing, 2001); Beale, S., *Millennial Manifesto.* (Instant Publisher, 2003); Gruber, J., *Risky Behavior among Youths: An Economic Analysis.* (Chicago, University of Chicago Press, 2001); Barna, G., *Generation Next: What You Need to Know About Today's Youth.* (Regal Books, 1996); United Nations, *World Youth Report 2005: Young People Today, and in 2015.* (United Nations Publication, 2005); Giroux, H.A., *Channel Surfing: Race Talk and the Destruction of Today's Youth.* (St. Martins Press, 1998).

[355] Observation from the author based upon self reporting from Esperanza clients.

Chapter Nine Notes

[356] Boeree, C.G., *The History of Psychology*. E-Text Source: http://www.ship.edu/%7Ecgboeree/historyofpsych.html; Fancher, R. E., *Pioneers of Psychology*. (New York: W. W. Norton & Company, 1979); "Descartes and Kant: Philosophical Origins of Psychology." Retrievable: http://www.psychology.sbc.edu/Descartes%20and%20Kant.htm.

[357] Roger, P.R., & Stone, G., "Counseling vs. Clinical: What is the difference between a clinical psychologist and a counseling psychologist?" Retrievable: http://www.div17.org/students_differences.html

[358] Corey, G., *Theory and Practice of Counseling and Psychotherapy 6th Edition*. (Brooks/Cole, 2001); Freud, S., *An Outline of Psychoanalysis*. (New York: Norton, 1949); Elliot, A., *Psychoanalytic Theory: An Introduction*. (Oxford UK & Cambridge, USA: Blackwell, 1994).

[359] American Psychology Association (APA): www.apa.org.

[360] National Board for Certified Counselors (NBCC): http://www.nbcc.org/extras/pdfs/exam/licensurechart.pdf; see Appendix for chart.

[361] American Counseling Association (ACA): www.counseling.org.

[362] American Counseling Association: www.counseling.org/Files/FD.ashx?guid=ab7c1272-71c4-46cf-848c-f98489937dda - ; National Board for Certified Counselors: www.nbcc.org/ethics2

[363] National Association of Addiction Treatment Providers (NAATP): www.naatp.org; Nation Association for Addictions Professional (NAADAC): www.naadac.org; American Mental Health

Counselors Association; www.amhca.org; State Licensing Boards
Contact Information: www.stopbadtherapy.com; Each state
has their own licensing requirements which include training,
education, and supervision requirements. If the reader is
interested in the licensure requirements within his/her own state,
please visit these websites for further information.

[364] Association for Social Work Boards: www.aswb.org.

[365] The information used in the creation of these EFMHS
methods came from the following sources and is subject to
the interpretation of this author. This information does not
necessarily represent in its entirety, the feelings, thoughts, or
ideals of any of the individuals mentioned hereafter; Hallberg,
L., "Emergence of Equine Facilitated Psychotherapy programs
in therapeutic riding facilities across the United States: Efficacy
and Program Design. *Animal Therapy Association of Arizona,*
1997; Hallberg, L. & Brinkerhoff, L., "Defining the Theory
and Practice of Equine Facilitated or Assisted Psychotherapy."
(Unpublished, 2001); Hallberg, L., "Horses as Healers." *EFMHA
News*, Vol. 7, Issue 2, Summer, 2003; Hallberg, L., "Horses as
Healers: Exploring the psychological implications of the horse/
human relationship." (Self Published Thesis, 2003); Hallberg,
L., "Project Textbook: Defining our past, present, and future."
(Unpublished, 2006); Hallberg, L., "Terminology Survey:
Facilitated vs. Assisted?" (Unpublished, 2006); Hallberg, L.,
"Terminology Survey: Horse as 'tool' vs. Horse as 'facilitator'?"
(Unpublished, 2006); interviews with Linda Kohanov, Temple
Grandin, Barbara Rector, Laura Brinkerhoff, Ann Alden,
Marilyn Sokolof, Molly DePrekel, Tanya Walsh, Ellen Gekrhe;
personal correspondence with Adele von Rust McCormick and
Marlena D. McCormick, Chris Irwin, Dr. Ann Perkins, Dr. Stan
Maliszewski, Maureen Vidrine, Nancy O'Brian, Dr. Suz Brooks;
personal observations and experience within the field of EFMH/
ES since 1996.

[366] A "brief" *intervention* is defined by this author as a one to three day workshop commonly seen within the field of EFMH/ES. This intervention does not include assessment, initial interviews, goal setting, treatment planning, or follow up. Rather, individuals within the field utilizing this technique see their "clients" for only the period of the workshop. This term does not relate to methods of "brief psychotherapy" as defined by Garfield, S.L, *The Practice of Brief Psychotherapy, Second Edition.* (Wiley, 1998). Pietro Castelnuovo-Tedesco's article, Brief Psychotherapy: Current Status" helps clarify the differences between a brief approach and a long term treatment, *"Brief psychotherapy aims at relief of the patient's major current conflicts rather than at change of his personality structure, which generally requires long-term treatment."* See chapter ** for a definition of "equine facilitated brief intensives."

[367] Observations of EFMH/ES professionals opinions regarding the use or mis-use of the term "psychotherapy" as applied to EFMH/ES come from surveys, questionnaires, and interviews conducted by this author. Due to the apparently heated nature of this topic, the majority of individuals commenting asked for their names not to be specifically utilized in this section.

[368] American Counseling Association: www.counseling.org/Files/FD.ashx?guid=ab7c1272-71c4-46cf-848c-f98489937dda - ; National Board for Certified Counselors: www.nbcc.org/ethics2

[369] Merriam-Webster's On-Line Dictionary is used for the following definitions, "psychotherapy" and "counseling": www.merriam-webster.com.

[370] Pulliam, J.D., & Patten, J.J., *History of Education in America, Ninth Edition.* (Prentice Hall, 2006).

[371] Beard, C., & Wilson, J.P., *Experiential Learning: A Handbook of Best Practices for Educators and Trainers.* (Kogan Page Ltd., 2006); Schoel, J.,& Maizell, R., *Exploring Islands of Healing:*

New Perspectives on Adventure Based Counseling. (Kendall Hunt Publishing Company, 2002); Personal observation of this author who attended both an "alternative" high school and college.

[372] Dr. Anne Perkins, personal communication, February, 2007

[373] Freud, S., *An Outline of Psychoanalysis.* (New York: Norton, 1949); Jung, C.G., *The Undiscovered Self.* (Signet; Reissue edition, 2006); Adler, A., *What Life Should Mean to You.* (New York: Capricorn, 1958).

[374] Dr. Anne Perkins, personal communication, February, 2007.

[375] Van de Creek, L., & Allen, J.B., *Innovations in Clinical Practice: Focus on Health & Wellness.* (Professional Resource Press, 2005); Dacher, E.S., *Integral Health: The Path to Human Flourishing.* (Basic Health Publications, 2006).

[376] Utesch, W.E., "From a glass half empty to a glass half full: A review of the Transition from Deficit to Strength-Based approaches." Retrievable: www.foellinger.org/ResourcesLinks/ UteschArticle.pdf.

[377] Dr. Stan Maliszewski, personal communication, February, 2007.

[378] Dr. Stan Maliszewski, personal communication, February, 2007.

[379] Utesch, W.E., "From a glass half empty to a glass half full: A review of the Transition from Deficit to Strength-Based approaches." Retrievable: www.foellinger.org/ResourcesLinks/ UteschArticle.pdf.

[380] Davis, J., & Berman, D.S., "The wilderness therapy program: An empirical study of its effects with adolescents in an outpatient setting," *Journal of Contemporary Psychotherapy,* Volume 19, Number 4, (December, 1989). Pg. 271-281; Russell, K.C., "Exploring How the Wilderness Therapy Process Relates

to Outcomes," *Journal of Experiential Education,* Vol. 23, No. 3 (Winter, 2000). Pg. 170-76; McKenzie, M.D., "How are Adventure Education Program Outcomes Achieved?: A review of the literature." Retrievable: wilderdom.com/pdf/ McKenzie2000AJOEVol5No1.pdf.

[381] Association for Adventure Educators, *Standards: 2.02. Retrievable: www.aee.org/skin1/pages/US/pdf/Accreditation_PDF_Forms/ Standards_Sample.pdf;* National Board for Certified Counselors, *Code of Ethics*: 7. Retrievable: www.nbcc.org/extras/pdfs/ethics/ nbcc-codeofethics.pdf; American Psychological Association, *Ethical Principles for Psychologists and Code of Conduct,* 2.01. Retrievable: www.apa.org/ethics/code2002.html#2_01; American Counseling Association, *Code of Ethics,* C.2.,a, C.2.b. Retrievable: www.counseling.org/Resources/CodeOfEthics/TP/ Home/CT2.aspx; Equine Facilitated Mental Health Association, *Code of Ethics,* 2.2. Retrievable: www.narha.org/PDFfiles/ EFMHACodeofethicsapproved.pdf.

[382] See sample forms in the Appendix of this text.

[383] "Informed Consent" American Psychological Association, *Ethical Principles for Psychologists and Code of Conduct,* 10.01. Retrievable: www.apa.org/ethics/code2002.html#10_01; American Counseling Association, *Code of Ethics,* A.2. Retrievable: www.counseling.org/Resources/CodeOfEthics/TP/ Home/CT2.aspx.

[384] See ethics information provided above

[385] See 26.

[386] These definitions are created solely by this author and are intended to be of use for readers during the upcoming section of this text. They are written with the support of Merriam-Webster's On-Line Dictionary, American Heritage On-Line Dictionary, information from Dr. Stan Maliszewski and Dr. Anne Perkins,

and information from Pulliam, J.D., & Patten, J.J., *History of Education in America, Ninth Edition.* (Prentice Hall, 2006).

387 See **Chapter Nine: Relational Skills,** Mirroring or Reflective Feedback.

388 Hallberg, L., "Emergence of Equine Facilitated Psychotherapy programs in therapeutic riding facilities across the United States: Efficacy and Program Design. *Animal Therapy Association of Arizona,* 1997; Hallberg, L., "Project Textbook: Defining our past, present, and future." (Unpublished, 2006); personal observation of this author.

389 All references to The Association for Experiential Education (AEE) or quotes from the AEE come directly from their web page: www.aee.org; www.aee.org/skin1/pages/US/pdf/ Accreditation_PDF_Forms/Standards_Sample.pdf

390 Greenberg, L.S., Watson, G.C., & Lietaer, G.O., *Handbook of Experiential Psychotherapy.* (The Guilford Press, 1998); Schoel, J.,& Maizell, R., *Exploring Islands of Healing: New Perspectives on Adventure Based Counseling.* (Kendall Hunt Publishing Company, 2002).

391 The Association for Experiential Education (AEE): www.aee.org.

392 Corey, G., *Theory and Practice of Counseling and Psychotherapy 6th Edition.* (Brooks/Cole, 2001).

393 The Association for Experiential Education (AEE): www.aee.org

394 See **Overview and Introduction of Education and Learning**

395 Luckner, J.L., & Nadler, R.S., *Processing the Experience: Enhancing and Generalizing Learning Second Edition.* (Kendall/ Hunt Publishing Company, 1997); Beard, C., & Wilson, J.P.,

Experiential Learning: A Handbook of Best Practices for Educators and Trainers. (Kogan Page Ltd., 2006).

[396] The majority of "wilderness therapy" programs across the United States are currently being facilitated on a daily basis by those with undergraduate degrees in fields like experiential education. The clients of these programs are generally seen by a licensed mental health professional once or twice a week when that individual hikes in to meet the group. The rest of the time (24 hours a day) the group process is facilitated by unlicensed individuals who generally appear savvy in the art of group facilitation and process. (Ascent: www.Ascent4Teens.com; SageWalk: www.sagewalk.com; Adirondack Leadership Expeditions: www.AdirondackLeadership.com; Aspen Achievement Academy: www.AspenAcademy.com; Passages to Recovery: www.PassagesToRecovery.com; Catherine Freer: www.CFreer.com; Second Nature: www.SNWP.com; for more information see: www.wilderness-programs.org/Programs.html) References to the success of such programs comes from the following sources; Davis-Berman, J., & Berman, D.S., "The wilderness therapy program: An empirical study of its effects with adolescents in an outpatient setting," *Journal of Contemporary Psychotherapy,* Volume 19, Number 4, (December, 1989). Pg. 271-281; Davis-Berman, J., & Berman, D.S., "Research Update: Two-Year Follow-up Report for the Wilderness Therapy Program," *Journal of Experiential Education,* Vol. 17 No. 1, (May, 1994). Pg. 48-50; Bandoroff, S., & Scherer, D.G., "Wilderness family therapy: An innovative treatment approach for problem youth," Journal of Child and Family Studies, Volume 3, Number 2, (June, 1994). Pg. 175-191.

[397] This information was gained from the personal observation of the author and conversations had with professionals providing an EFE/L service.

[398] All references to Barbara Rector's role in the development of the field come directly from personal correspondence and interviews.

Chapter Ten Notes

[399] Statements regarding competency came from the following sources; Hallberg, L., "Emergence of Equine Facilitated Psychotherapy programs in therapeutic riding facilities across the United States: Efficacy and Program Design. *Animal Therapy Association of Arizona,* 1997; Hallberg, L. & Brinkerhoff, L., "Defining the Theory and Practice of Equine Facilitated or Assisted Psychotherapy." Unpublished, 2001; Hallberg, L., Horses as Healers." *EFMHA News,* Vol. 7, Issue 2, Summer, 2003; Hallberg, L., Project Textbook: Defining our past, present, and future." Unpublished, 2006; Hallberg, L., Terminology Survey: Facilitated vs. Assisted? Unpublished, 2006; Hallberg, L., Terminology Survey: Horse as "tool" vs. Horse as "facilitator? Unpublished, 2006; interviews with Linda Kohanov, Temple Grandin, Barbara Rector, Laura Brinkerhoff, Ann Alden, Marilyn Sokolof, Molly DePrekel, Tanya Walsh, Ellen Gehrke; personal correspondence with Adele von Rust McCormick and Marlena D. McCormick, Chris Irwin, Dr. Ann Perkins, Dr. Stan Maliszewski, Maureen Vidrine, Nancy O'Brian, Dr. Suz Brooks; personal observations and experience within the field of EFMH/ES since 1996.

[400] www.equinefacilitatedprofessional.org

[401] www.equinefacilitatedprofessionals.org; Further information regarding the CCEFMHP exam and organization comes from the personal experience of the author as a "subject matter expert" assisting in the creation of the exam, and from personal conversations with CCEFMHP board members.

[402] National Board for Certified Counselors: www.nbcc.org.

[403] The Art Therapy Association: www.arttherapy.org

[404] The Association for Challenge Course Technology: www.acctinfo.org; Project Adventure: www.pa.org; Adventure Experiences, Inc.: www.advexp.com; Adventure-Based Experiential Educators, Inc.:

www.abeeinc.com; Association for Experiential Education: www. aee.org.

[405] All references to the National Board for Certified Counselors (NBCC) or quotes from the NBCC come directly from their web page: www.nbcc.org; www.nbcc.org/ethics2.

[406] All references to the American Psychological Association (APA) or quotes from the APA come directly from their web page: www. apa.org; or www.apa.org/ethics/code2002.html#2_01.

[407] All references to the American Counseling Association (ACA) or quotes from the ACA come directly from their web page: www. counseling.org; www.counseling.org/Resources/CodeOfEthics/ TP/Home/CT2.aspx.

[408] All references to the National Board for Certified Counselors (NBCC) or quotes from the NBCC come directly from their web page: www.nbcc.org; www.nbcc.org/ethics2.

[409] The Equine Facilitated Mental Health Association (EFMHA): www.narha.org.

[410] The Equine Assisted Growth and Learning Association (EAGALA): www.eagala.org.

[411] All references to The Association for Experiential Education (AEE) or quotes from the AEE come directly from their web page: www.aee.org; www.aee.org/skin1/pages/US/pdf/ Accreditation_PDF_Forms/Standards_Sample.pdf.

[412] See Appendix D.

[413] Statement made based upon the results from surveys questionnaires, and interviews conducted by the author.

414 Taylor, S., "Equine Facilitated Psychotherapy: An emerging field." (Self Published Thesis, 2001). Pg. 40.

415 Allen, M..A.,"The human-animal abuse connection." *The Latham Letter 19*(2), (1998). 9-15.; Arkow, P., "The relationships between animal abuse and other forms of family violence," *Family Violence & Sexual Assault Bulletin 12*(1-2), (1996). Pg.29-34; Kanner, A.D., Roszak, T., & Gomes, M.E., *Ecopsychology: Restoring the earth, healing the mind.* (New York: Random House, 1995); Marcus, C.C., *House as Mirror of Self.* (Conari Press, 1995); Gallagher, W., *The Power of Place: How Our Surroundings Shape Our Thoughts, Emotions, and Actions.* (Harper Perennial, 2007).

Chapter Eleven Notes

Note: The section regarding cross-training for mental health professionals and educators is primarily the creation of the author, however, references from the following sources were used in its creation; Kohanov, L., personal interview; Rector, B., personal interview; Alden, A., personal interview; Gehrke, E.K., personal interview; and other professionals within the field of EFMH/ES.

416 The National Board for Certified Counselors (NBCC): www.nbcc.org/ethics2; The Association for Experiential Education (AEE): www.org/skin1/pages/us/pdf/accreditation_PFF_forms/standards_sample.pdf; The American Psychological Association (APA): www.apa.org;orwww.apa.org/ethics/code2002.html#2_01; American Counseling Association (ACA): www.counseling.org/Resources/CodeOfEthics/TP/Home/CT2.aspx; Equine Facilitated Mental Health Association (EFMHA): www.narha.org/PDFfiles/EFMHACodeofethicsapproved.pdf; Equine Assisted Growth and Learning Association (EAGALA): www.eagala.org/Ethics.htm.

417 The Experiential Education Association: www.aee.org/customer/pages.php?pageid=47.

418 The NBCC: : www.nbcc.org; www.nbcc.org/ethics2 ; the ACA: www.counseling.org;www.counseling.org/Resources/ CodeOfEthics/TP/Home/CT2.aspx; EFMHA: www.narha.org/ PDFfiles/EFMHACodeofethicsapproved.pdf ; EAGALA: www. eagala.org/Ethics.htm.

419 See **Chapter** 3.

420 See Appendix D.

421 Rector, B.K., *Adventures in Awareness: Learning with the Help of Horses.* ((Bloomington, IN.: Authorhouse, 2005).

422 Hallberg, L., "Project Textbook: Defining our past, present, and future." (Unpublished, 2006); personal interviews with many professionals in the field.

Chapter Twelve Notes

423 References to those who were providing a "psychotherapeutic" method of EFMH/ES early in the field's development; Barbara Rector, the McCormicks, Maureen Vidrine, Marilyn Sokolof, and Suz Brooks. Please note that this list represents only a handful of those providing a psychotherapeutic approach.

424 At that time Arizona did not have state licensure for those providing mental health services, and Ms. Rector's Masters degree in Spiritual Psychology afforded her the ability to practice "psychotherapy" legally.

425 EFMHA's EFP definition. Retrievable: www.narha.org/ SecEFMHA/WhatIsEFMHA.asp.

426 Hallberg, L. & Brinkerhoff, L., "Defining the Theory and Practice of Equine Facilitated or Assisted Psychotherapy." Unpublished, 2001; Hallberg, L., Horses as Healers." *EFMHA News*, Vol. 7, Issue 2, Summer, 2003; Hallberg, L., Project Textbook: Defining our past, present, and future." Unpublished, 2006; Hallberg, L.,

Terminology Survey: Facilitated vs. Assisted? Unpublished, 2006; Hallberg, L., Terminology Survey: Horse as "tool" vs. Horse as "facilitator? Unpublished, 2006; interviews with Linda Kohanov, Temple Grandin, Barbara Rector, Laura Brinkerhoff, Ann Alden, Marilyn Sokolof, Molly DePrekel, Tanya Walsh, Ellen Gekrhe; personal correspondence with Adele von Rust McCormick and Marlena D. McCormick, Chris Irwin, Dr. Ann Perkins, Dr. Stan Maliszewski, Maureen Vidrine, Nancy O'Brian, Dr. Suz Brooks; personal observations and experience within the field of EFMH/ES since 1996.

[427] The American Heritage® Stedman's Medical Dictionary, 2nd Edition Copyright. (Houghton Mifflin Company, 2004).

[428] Reflective Feedback: See Chapter 7

[429] Internal Locus of Control: See Chapter 8

[430] Moreno, J., *Who Shall Survive: Foundations of Sociometry, Group Psychotherapy and Sociodrama.* (Mental Health Resources, 1993, originally printed in 1977); Moreno, *Psychodrama & Group Psychotherapy Forth Edition.* (Mental Health Resources, 1994); Holmes, P., *Psychodrama Since Moreno: Innovations in Theory and Practice.* (Routledge, 1994).

[431] Merriam-Webster's On-Line Dictionary is used for the following definition, "psychodrama." www.merriam-webster.com.

[432] Wikipedia's On-Line Dictionary is used for the following definition, "psychodrama." www.wikipedia.org.

[433] Corey, G., *Theory and Practice of Counseling and Psychotherapy 6th Edition.* (Brooks/Cole, 2001); Freud, S., *An Outline of Psychoanalysis.* (New York: Norton, 1949).

[434] Conger, J.P., *The Body in Recovery: Somatic Psychotherapy and the Self.* (Frog Ltd., 1994); Aposhyan, S., *Body-Mind Psychotherapy:*

Principles, Techniques, and Practical Applications. (W. W. Norton & Company, 2004).

[435] Watson, L., *Jacobson's Organ.* (New York: Penguin Books, 1999).

[436] Kellert, S.R., *The Value of Life: Biological Diversity And Human Society.* (Island Press, 1996).

[437] Kanner, A.D., Roszak, T., & Gomes, M.E., *Ecopsychology: Restoring the earth, healing the mind.* (New York: Random House, 1995); Wilson, E.O., & Kellert, S.R., *The Biophilia Hypothesis.* (Washington, D.C: Island Press, 1993); Cohen, M., *Reconnecting With Nature: Finding Wellness Through Restoring Your Bond With the Earth.* (Ecopress, 1997); Metzner, R., *Green Psychology: Transforming our Relationship to the Earth* (Vermont: Park Street Press, 1999); Glendinning, C., *My Name is Chellis and I'm in Recovery from Western Civilization.* (Boston, MASS: Shambhala Publications, 1994) Schoen, A., *Kindred Spirits: How the Remarkable Bond Between Humans and Animals Can Change the Way we Live.* (New York: Random House, 2001).

[438] See Section Two

[439] Rotter, J. B., "Generalized expectancies for internal versus external control of reinforcement." *Psychological Monographs, 80.* (Whole No. 609, 1966).

[440] Personal interview with Marilyn Sokolof.

[441] Tissot, J.C., *Medicinal and Surgical Gymnastics or Essay on the usefulness of Movement, or different Exercises of the body, and of rest, in the treatment of Diseases,* (Paris, Bastian, 1780); Evens, J.W., "A Review of Relevant Literature." In: "Cerebral Palsy and Therapeutic Riding." *NARHA Strides Magazine,* Vol. 1 No. 1 (October, 1995); Satter, L., "Horseback Riding Therapy for Children with Movement Malfunction Considering Especially Cerebral Palsy Patients," *Pediatric and Padologie,* Vol. 13.

(1977). Pg. 333-337; Tauffkirchen, E., "Hippotherapy – A Supplementary Treatment for Motion Disturbances Caused by Cerebral Palsy." *Pediatric and Padologie,* Vol. 13 (4), (1978), pg. 405- 411; Bertoti, D.B., "Effect of Therapeutic Horseback Riding on Posture in Children with Cerebral Palsy," Journal of Physical Therapy, Vol. 8 (10) (1988). Pg. 1505-1512; Brock, B.J., Effect of Therapeutic Horseback Riding on Phsyically Disabled Adults," *Therapeutic Recreation Journal.* Vol. 22 (1988). Pg. 34-42; Benda, W., McGibbon, N.H., & Grant, K.L., "Improvements in Muscle Symmetry in Children with Cerebral Palsy after Equine-Assisted Therapy (Hippotherapy)," *Journal of Alternative and Complementary Medicine*, Vol. 9, No. 6 (December, 2003). Pg. 817-825; Aetna, "Hippotherapy for Cerebral Palsy and Other Motor Dysfunction," *Clinical Policy Bulletins,* No. 0151. (March 24, 2006); Hammer, A., Nilsagard, Y., Forsberg, A., et al., "Evaluation of Therapeutic Riding (Sweden)/ Hippotherapy (United States). A single-subject experimental design study replicated in eleven patients with multiple sclerosis." *Physiotherapy Theory Practitioner. Vol.* 21, No. 1 (2005). Pg. 51-77.

[442] Benda, W., Lightmark, R., "People Whisperers," *Shift,* Issue 3, (June, 2004).

[443] Taylor, S., "Equine Facilitated Psychotherapy: An emerging field." (Self Published Thesis, 2001). Pg.18.

[444] Hallberg, L. Horses as Healers: Exploring the psychological implications of the horse/human relationship." (Self Published Thesis, 2003). Pg. 40-41.

[445] As documented by the extensive historical literature review reported in Section One of this text.

[446] This is a goal commonly associated with insight-based or psychoanalytical psychotherapy. Corey, G., *Theory and Practice of Counseling and Psychotherapy 6th Edition.* (Brooks/Cole, 2001);

Freud, S., *An Outline of Psychoanalysis.* (New York: Norton, 1949); Elliot, A., *Psychoanalytic Theory: An Introduction.* (Oxford UK & Cambridge, USA: Blackwell, 1994); Taylor, S.

[447] Goals are the creation of this author with the suggestion and support of the following sources; Corey, G., *Theory and Practice of Counseling and Psychotherapy 6th Edition.* (Brooks/Cole, 2001); Freud, S., *An Outline of Psychoanalysis.* (New York: Norton, 1949); Elliot, A., *Psychoanalytic Theory: An Introduction.* (Oxford UK & Cambridge, USA: Blackwell, 1994); Aposhyan, S., *Body-Mind Psychotherapy: Principles, Techniques, and Practical Applications.* (W. W. Norton & Company, 2004); The responses from the interviewees and those who responded to surveys or questionnaires.

[448] Corey, G., *Theory and Practice of Counseling and Psychotherapy 6th Edition.* (Brooks/Cole, 2001); Freud, S., *An Outline of Psychoanalysis.* (New York: Norton, 1949); Taylor, S., Equine Facilitated Psychotherapy: An emerging field." (Self Published thesis, 2001).

[449] Grant, J.,& Crawley, J., *Transference and Projection: Mirrors to the Self.* (Open University Press, 2002); Franz, M.L., *Projection and Re-Collection in Jungian Psychology: Reflections of the Soul.* (Open Court Publishing Company, 1987); Goldstein, W., *Using the Transference in Psychotherapy.* (Jason Aronson, 2006).

[450] Unconditional positive regard; Wilkins, P., "Unconditional positive regard reconsidered," *British Journal of Guidance and Counselling,* Volume 28, Number 1/February 1, 2000, (February, 2004). Pg. 23-36; Kirschenbaum, H., & Henderson, V. (Eds.), *The Carl Rogers Reader* (Boston: Houghton Mifflin, 1989); Corey, G., *Theory and Practice of Counseling and Psychotherapy 6th Edition.* (Brooks/Cole, 2001); Taylor, S., "Equine Facilitated Psychotherapy: An emerging field." (Self Published Thesis, 2001). Pg. 38; O'Neill, J.V., "Therapy technique may not matter much," National Association of Social Work, (March,

2002). Pg. 3. In: Hallberg, L., "Horses as Healers: Exploring the psychological implications of the horse/human relationship." (Self Published Thesis, 2003). Pg. 81.

451 Jordan, J.V., Kaplan, A.G., Baker, J.B., Stiver, I.P., & Surrey, J.L., *Women's Growth and Connection: Writings from the Stone Center, The Complexity of Connection.*(The Guilford Press, 1991) Jordan, J.V., Walker., M., Hartling, L.M., *The Complexity of Connection.* (Guildford Press, 2004).

452 Corey, G., *Theory and Practice of Counseling and Psychotherapy 6th Edition.* (Brooks/Cole, 2001).

453 This suggested role is the product of consensus of those responding to surveys, questionnaires, and interviews.

454 Taylor, S., "Equine Facilitated Psychotherapy: An emerging field." (Self Published Thesis, 2001). Pg. 38-40.

455 Taylor, S., "Equine Facilitated Psychotherapy: An emerging field." (Self Published Thesis, 2001). Pg. 22.

456 The NBCC: : www.nbcc.org; www.nbcc.org/ethics2 ; the ACA: www.counseling.org;www.counseling.org/Resources/ CodeOfEthics/TP/Home/CT2.aspx; EFMHA: www.narha.org/ PDFfiles/EFMHACodeofethicsapproved.pdf ; EAGALA: www. eagala.org/Ethics.htm.

457 Kuhn, M.G., "Toward an Integral Model of Equine-Assisted Psychotherapy." (Self Published Thesis, 2006).

458 Corey, G., *Theory and Practice of Counseling and Psychotherapy 6th Edition.* (Brooks/Cole, 2001).

459 Taylor, S., "Equine Facilitated Psychotherapy: An emerging field." (Self Published Thesis, 2001); Marilyn Sokolof; EFMHA:

www.narha.org/PDFfiles/EFMHACodeofethicsapproved.pdf ;
EAGALA: www.eagala.org/Ethics.htm.

[460] See the Equine Facilitated Counseling chapter in this text. It helps
clarify key differences that would make referral useful.

[461] Corey, G., *Theory and Practice of Counseling and Psychotherapy 6th
Edition.* (Brooks/Cole, 2001).

[462] Personal communication and interviews with the following
individuals; Marilyn Sokolof, Barbara Rector, Nancy O'Brien.

[463] These five techniques emerged from the surveys, questionnaires,
and interviews conducted by this author and are subject to the
interpretation of the author.

[464] Bakal, D.A., *Minding the Body: Clinical Uses of Somatic Awareness.*
(The Guilford Press, 2001); Bloom, K., *Moves: A Sourcebook of
Ideas for Body Awareness and Creative Movement.* (Routledge,
1998); McHose, C., Frank, K., *How Life Moves: Explorations
in Meaning and Body Awareness.* (North Atlantic Books, 2006);
Hartley, L., *Somatic Psychology: Body, Mind and Meaning.* (Wiley,
2005).

[465] Personal observation by the author of Esperanza's clients.

[466] Fried, R., *The Breath Connection: How to Reduce Psychosomatic
and Stress Related Disorders With Easy-To-Do Breathing Exercises.*
(Plenum Medical Book Company, 1990); Lewis, D., *Free Your
Breath, Free Your Life: How Conscious Breathing Can Relieve Stress,
Increase Vitality, and Help You Live More Fully.* (Shambhala,
2004); Starhawk, *The Earth Path: Grounding Your Spirit in the
Rhythms of Nature.* (HarperSanFrancisco, 2004); Poole, J., *The
Little Grounding Book.* (Pooled Resources, 1993); Rossman,
M.L., *Guided Imagery for Self-Healing Second Edition.* (New
World Library, 2000); Schwartz, A.E., *Guided Imagery for Groups:*

Fifty Visualizations That Promote Relaxation, Problem-Solving, Creativity, and Well-Being. (Whole Person Associates,1995).

[467] Bakal, D.A., *Minding the Body: Clinical Uses of Somatic Awareness.* (The Guilford Press, 2001); Hartley, L., *Somatic Psychology: Body, Mind and Meaning.* (Wiley, 2005); Conger, J.P., *The Body in Recovery: Somatic Psychotherapy and the Self.* (Frog Ltd., 1994); Aposhyan, S., *Body-Mind Psychotherapy: Principles, Techniques, and Practical Applications.* (W. W. Norton & Company, 2004).

[468] See definition of "psychodrama" in the Psychodramatization and Reflective Feedback section of this chapter, notes 8,9,10.

[469] Taylor, S., "Equine Facilitated Psychotherapy: An emerging field." (Self Published Thesis, 2001). Pg. 34.

[470] Taylor, S., "Equine Facilitated Psychotherapy: An emerging field." (Self Published Thesis, 2001); Grant, J.,& Crawley, J., *Transference and Projection: Mirrors to the Self.* (Open University Press, 2002); Franz, M.L., *Projection and Re-Collection in Jungian Psychology: Reflections of the Soul.* (Open Court Publishing Company, 1987).

[471] References made to reflective feedback or "mirroring" come from the following sources; Rector, B., *Adventures in Awareness.* (Bloomington, IN.: Authorhouse, 2005); McCormick, A., & McCormick, M., *Horse Sense and the Human Heart.* (Deerfield Beach, FL.: Health Communications, 1997); McCormick, A.R., McCormick, M.D., & McCormick, T.E., *Horses and the Mystical Path.* (Novato, CA.: New World Library, 2004); Kohonov, L., *The Tao of Equus.* (Novato, CA: New World Library, 2001); Kohonov, L., *Riding Between the Worlds.* (Novato, CA: New World Library, 2003); Kuhn, M.G., "Toward an Integral Model of Equine-Assisted Psychotherapy." (Self Published Thesis, 2006); Taylor, S., "Equine Facilitated Psychotherapy: An emerging field." (Self Published Thesis, 2001); Hallberg, L., "Horses as Healers: Exploring the psychological implications of the

horse/human relationship." (Self Published Thesis, 2003). The information regarding how to utilize the concepts of reflective feedback or "mirroring" are creations of this author and are not necessarily indicative of the works of any of the above sources.

[472] Levine, S.K., & Levine, E.G., *Foundations of Expressive Arts Therapy: Theoretical and Clinical Perspective.* (Jessica Kingsley Publishers, 1999); Atkins, S. S., *Expressive Arts Therapy: Creative Process in Art and Life.* (Parkway Publishers, 2002); Malchiodi, K.A., *Expressive Therapies.* (The Guilford Press, 2006).

[473] Hallberg, L., "Horses as Healers: Exploring the psychological implications of the horse/human relationship." (Self Published Thesis, 2003). Pg. 39-41.

[474] Free association. Bollas, C., *Free Association in Psychoanalysis.* (Totem Books, 2002).

[475] Friedman, R.L., *The Healing Power of the Drum.* (White Cliffs Media, 2000).

[476] Peck, A.S., *Discovering Ourselves Through Acts of Creation: The Healing Tools of Journaling.* (Andrea S. Peck, 2003).

[477] Spirit Horse Painting: Barbara Rector introduced spirit horse painting in 1997. It is a technique used by many EFMH/ ES professionals and each have their own unique manner of facilitation. The facilitation method specified in this section refers to the author's own use of the technique.

Chapter Thirteen Notes

[478] Merriam-Webster's On-Line Dictionary is used for the following definition, "integrate." www.merriam-webster.com.

[479] Furman, R., & Jackson, R., "Wrap-around services: An analysis of community-based mental health services for children." *Journal of Child and Adolescent Psychiatric Nursing,* (Jul-Sep

2002). Retrievable: www.findarticles.com/p/articles/mi_qa3892/
is_200207/ai_n9088511; VanDenBerg, J.E. "What is the
wraparound process?" (2000). Retrievable: http://cecp.air/.ora/
wraparound/intro.html; VanDenBerg, I.E., "History of the
wraparound process." (2000). Retrievable: http://cecp.air.org/
wraparound/ history/html.

480 See Section Two, Chapter 8 "The Now: Grounding, Focus,
Awareness, and Presence

481 Fried, R., *The Breath Connection: How to Reduce Psychosomatic
and Stress Related Disorders With Easy-To-Do Breathing Exercises.*
(Plenum Medical Book Company, 1990); Lewis, D., *Free Your
Breath, Free Your Life: How Conscious Breathing Can Relieve Stress,
Increase Vitality, and Help You Live More Fully.* (Shambhala,
2004); Starhawk, *The Earth Path: Grounding Your Spirit in the
Rhythms of Nature.* (HarperSanFrancisco, 2004); Poole, J., *The
Little Grounding Book.* (Pooled Resources, 1993); Rossman,
M.L., *Guided Imagery for Self-Healing Second Edition.* (New
World Library, 2000); Schwartz, A.E., *Guided Imagery for Groups:
Fifty Visualizations That Promote Relaxation, Problem-Solving,
Creativity, and Well-Being.* (Whole Person Associates, 1995).

482 Trent, J., Life Mapping. (WaterBrook Press, 1998); Cohen, B.,
*Life Mapping: A Unique Approach To Finding Your Vision And
Reaching Your Potential.* (Harper Perennial, 1998).

483 Mind Tools. (Wimbledon, London, UK: Mind Tools,
Ltd.). Retrievable: www.mindtools.com/cgi-bin/sgx2/shop.
cgi?page=orderform_mindtools.htm

484 Glasser, W., *Counseling with Choice Theory.* (Harper Paperbacks;
New Ed edition, 2001); Corey, G., *Theory and Practice of
Counseling and Psychotherapy 6th Edition.* (Brooks/Cole, 2001).

485 Schinke, S., & Gilchrist, L., *Life Skills Counseling With Adolescents.*
(Professional Education Publications, 1983); Oliver, J., Ryan, M.,

The ABCs of Life : Lesson One: The Skills We All Need but Were Never Taught. (Fireside, 2003).

486 See **Chapter Six: Communication**

487 See **Chapter Seven: Relational Skills.**

488 Rogers, C., *Client Centered Therapy.* (Houghton Mifflin, 1951); Corey, G., *Theory and Practice of Counseling and Psychotherapy 6th Edition.* (Brooks/Cole, 2001).

489 Rodewalt, F. & Tragakis, M. W. "Self-esteem and self-regulation: Toward optimal studies of self-esteem," *Psychological Inquiry,* 14(1), 66–70. (2003); Sedikides, C., & Gregg. A. P. "Portraits of the self." In M. A. Hogg & J. Cooper (Eds.), *Sage handbook of social psychology* (London: Sage Publications, 2003). Pg. 110-138.

490 See **Chapter Eight: Development of Self through Horse-Person-Ship,** sub section Self-esteem and Self Confidence.

491 Frankl, V., *The Will to Meaning: Foundations and applications of logotherapy.* (New York: New American Library, 1969); Krankl, V., *Man's Search for Meaning.* (Beacon, 1963); Corey, G., *Theory and Practice of Counseling and Psychotherapy 6th Edition.* (Brooks/Cole, 2001).

492 Polster, E., Polster, M., *Gestalt Therapy Integrated: Contours of theory and practice.* (New York: Brenner/Mazel, 1973).

493 Statement based upon the personal observation of the author and personal communications with other professionals within the field.

494 Greenberg, L.S., Watson, G.C., & Lietaer, G.O., *Handbook of Experiential Psychotherapy.* (The Guilford Press, 1998); Schoel, J.,& Maizell, R., *Exploring Islands of Healing: New Perspectives on Adventure Based Counseling.* (Kendall Hunt Publishing Company,

2002); Cole, E., Erdman, E., & Rothblum, E.D., *Wilderness Therapy for Women: The Power of Adventure.* (Haworth Press, 1994).

495 Summers, N., *Fundamentals of Case Management Practice: Skills for the Human Services, Second Edition.* (Wadsworth Publishing, 2005).

496 Hecker, L.L., & Wetchler, J.L., *An Introduction to Marriage and Family Therapy.* (Haworth Clinical Practice Press, 2003).

497 The practice of EFC attempts to keep the client in the present moment and therefore the counselor's facilitation and processing should mirror that notion. Furthermore, if the counselor keeps the client's focus on life skills, relational skills, or communication skills, the client may be more apt to stay solution oriented. Guterman, J.T., *Mastering the Art of Solution-Focused Counseling.* (American Counseling Association, 2006); Polster, E., & Polster, M., *Gestalt Therapy Integrated: Contours of theory and practice.* (New York: Brunner/Mazel, 1973); Frankl, V., *The Will to Meaning: Foundations and applications of logotherapy.* (New York: New American Library, 1969).

498 See 21.

499 Corey, G., *Theory and Practice of Counseling and Psychotherapy 6th Edition.* (Brooks/Cole, 2001); Rogers, C., *Client Centered Therapy.* (Houghton Mifflin, 1951).

500 Beard, C., Wilson, J.P., *Experiential Learning: A Handbook of Best Practices for Educators and Trainers Second Edition.* (Kogan Page, 2006); Nadler, R.S., & Luckner, J.L., *Processing the Adventure Experience: Theory and Practice.* (Kendall/Hunt Publishing Company, 1991).

501 Guterman, J.T., *Mastering the Art of Solution-Focused Counseling.* (American Counseling Association, 2006); Bertolino, B., &

O'Hanlon, B., *Collaborative, Competency-Based Counseling and Therapy.* (Allyn & Bacon, 2002).

[502] Frankl, V., *The Will to Meaning: Foundations and applications of logotherapy.* (New York: New American Library, 1969).

[503] *"Populations best served by EFIC are those without serious psychological issues."* This statement is based upon the suggestions of professionals within the field taken from surveys, questionnaires, and interviews conducted by this author.

[504] These techniques are based upon the suggestions of professionals within the field taken from surveys, questionnaires, and interviews conducted by this author.

[505] Greenberg, L.S., Watson, G.C., & Lietaer, G.O., *Handbook of Experiential Psychotherapy.* (The Guilford Press, 1998); Schoel, J.,& Maizell, R., *Exploring Islands of Healing: New Perspectives on Adventure Based Counseling.* (Kendall Hunt Publishing Company, 2002); Cole, E., Erdman, E., & Rothblum, E.D., *Wilderness Therapy for Women: The Power of Adventure.* (Haworth Press, 1994).

[506] Jordan, J.V., Kaplan, A.G., Baker, J.B., Stiver, I.P., & Surrey, J.L., *Women's Growth and Connection: Writings from the Stone Center, The Complexity of Connection.*(The Guilford Press, 1991) Jordan, J.V., Walker., M., Hartling, L.M., *The Complexity of Connection.* (Guildford Press, 2004).

[507] These concepts are based upon the suggestions of professionals within the field taken from surveys, questionnaires, and interviews conducted by this author, as well as based upon the authors personal experience and professional practice.

[508] This notion is controversial within the field of EFMH/ES. Many professionals believe that including riding as a component to therapy is too dangerous, others feel that it is a useful and even

powerful activity that should be included in an EFMHS session.
A number of different research projects appear to substantiate
the concept that riding can be a viable and helpful technique
or activity; Burgon, H., "Case studies of adults receiving horse-
riding therapy," *Anthrozoos,* Vol. 13, (2003). Pg. 262-76; Bizub,
A., Joy, A., & Davidson, L., "It's like being in another world."
Psychiatric Rehabilitation Journal, Vol. 26, No. 4, (2003).
Pg. 377-384; Kaiser, L., Spence, L.J., Lavergne, A.G., &
Vanden Bosch, K.L., "Can a week of therapeutic riding make a
difference? A pilot study" *Anthrozoos,* Vol. 17, No. 1. (2004). Pg.
63; Gatty, C.M., "Psychosocial impact of therapeutic riding: A
pilot study." NARHA, www.narha.org/PDFfiles/Psychosocial_
Impact.pdf; Gehrke, E.K., "Horses and Humans Energetics:
The study of Heart Rate Variability (HRV) between horses
and Humans." (Self Published, 2006); Personal interview and
correspondence; HeartMath: www.heartmath.org; Rothe, E.Q.,
Vega, B.J., Torres, R.M., Soler, S.M.C., & Pazos, R.M.M., "From
Kids and Horses: Equine facilitated psychotherapy for children."
International Journal of Clinical and Health Psychology, Vol.5, No.
002, (May, 2005).

[509] Lane, R.D., & Schwartz, G.E., "Levels of emotional awareness:
a cognitive-developmental theory and its application to
psychopathology," *American Journal of Psychiatry,* Vol. 144,
(April, 1987). Pg. 133-143.

[510] Lane, R.D., & Schwartz, G.E., "Levels of emotional awareness:
a cognitive-developmental theory and its application to
psychopathology," *American Journal of Psychiatry,* Vol. 144,
(April, 1987). Pg. 133-143; see Present Moment Focused in this
chapter, 4 & 5.

[511] Rothe, E.Q., Vega, B.J., Torres, R.M., Soler, S.M.C., &
Pazos, R.M.M., "From Kids and Horses: Equine facilitated
psychotherapy for children." *International Journal of Clinical
and Health Psychology,* Vol.5, No. 002, (May, 2005); Rector,
B., *Adventures in Awareness.* (Bloomington, IN.: Authorhouse,

2005); Soren, I., *Zen and Horses.* (Rodale, 2002); Witter, R.F.,
Living with HorsePower. (Trafalgar Square, 1998); Taylor, S.,
"Equine Facilitated Psychotherapy: An emerging field." (Self
Published Thesis, 2001); Irwin, C., *Horses Don't Lie.* (New York:
Marlowe and Company, 1998); Roberts, M., *Horse Sense for
People.* (New York: Penguin Books, 2002).

[512] See **Chapter Seven: Relational Skills**, Boundary Setting; Gehrke,
E.K., "Horses and Humans Energetics: The study of Heart Rate
Variability (HRV) between horses and Humans." (Self Published,
2006); Personal interview and correspondence; HeartMath: www.
heartmath.org.

[513] See **Chapter Eight: Development of Self through Horse-
Person-Ship,** The Now: Grounding, Focus, Awareness, and
Presence; Tolle, E., *The Power of Now.* (Novato, CA: New World
Library, 1999).

[514] References to story telling and use of metaphor come from the
following sources; Whitaker, L.L., "Healing the mother/daughter
relationship through the therapeutic use of fairy tales, poetry,
and stories," *The Journal of Poetry Therapy*, Volume 6, Number
1 (September, 1992); Campbell, J., *The Hero With a Thousand
Faces.* (New York: MJF Books, 1949); McAdams, D. P., *The
Stories We Live By: Personal Myths and the Making of Self.* (New
York: The Guilford Press, 1993); Parry, A., & Doan, R.E., *Story
re-visions: Narrative therapy in the postmodern world.* (New York:
Guilford, 1994); Witztum, E., & van der Hart, O., & Friedman,
B., "The use of metaphors in psychotherapy," *Journal of
Contemporary Psychotherapy*, Volume 18, Number 4, (December,
1988); The author's own use of story, myth, and metaphor
within EFMH/ES sessions.

[515] Trent, J., Life Mapping. (WaterBrook Press, 1998); Cohen, B.,
*Life Mapping: A Unique Approach To Finding Your Vision And
Reaching Your Potential.* (Harper Perennial, 1998).

516 Rothe, E.Q., Vega, B.J., Torres, R.M., Soler, S.M.C., & Pazos, R.M.M., "From Kids and Horses: Equine facilitated psychotherapy for children." *International Journal of Clinical and Health Psychology,* Vol.5, No. 002, (May, 2005); Rector, B., *Adventures in Awareness.* (Bloomington, IN.: Authorhouse, 2005); Taylor, S., "Equine Facilitated Psychotherapy: An emerging field." (Self Published Thesis, 2001); Witter, R.F., *Living with HorsePower.* (Trafalgar Square, 1998); McCormick, A., & McCormick, M., *Horse Sense and the Human Heart.* (Deerfield Beach, FL.: Health Communications, 1997).

Chapter Fourteen Notes

517 Greenberg, L.S., Watson, G.C., & Lietaer, G.O., *Handbook of Experiential Psychotherapy.* (The Guilford Press, 1998); Schoel, J.,& Maizell, R., *Exploring Islands of Healing: New Perspectives on Adventure Based Counseling.* (Kendall Hunt Publishing Company, 2002); Cole, E., Erdman, E., & Rothblum, E.D., *Wilderness Therapy for Women: The Power of Adventure.* (Haworth Press, 1994); Gass, M. A., *Adventure therapy: Therapeutic applications of adventure programming.* (Dubuque, IA: Kendall/Hunt, 1993); Beard, C., & Wilson, J.P., *Experiential Learning: A Handbook of Best Practices for Educators and Trainers.* (Kogan Page Ltd., 2006); Association for Adventure Education: www.aee.org.

518 Rohnke, K.E., *Silver Bullets: A Guide to Initiative Problems, Adventure Games and Trust Activities.* (Kendall/Hunt Publishing Company, 1989); Rohnke, K.E., *Cowstails and Cobras II : A Guide to Games, Initiatives, Ropes Courses & Adventure Curriculum.* (Kendall/Hunt Publishing Company, 2003); The Association for Challenge Course Technology: www.acctinfo.org; Project Adventure: www.pa.org; Equine Assisted Growth and Learning Association: www.eagala.org.

519 See above.

520 See adventure or experiential education, challenge course activities, or other adventure-based activities.

[521] This comment is made soley on the professional observation and practice of the author and is not based upon research or evidence that would suggest it to be empirically valid. However, others in the field of EFMH/ES have supported this belief based upon their own opinions and personal practices.

[522] Kersten, G., & Thomas, L., *Equine-assisted psychotherapy and learning un-training manual: Level One.* (Santaquin, UT: Equine Assisted Growth and Learning Association, 2004); Equine Assisted Growth and Learning Association Level One Certification program, (2001).

[523] Newes, S.L., "Adventure-Based Therapy: Theory, Characteristics, Ethics, and Research," (Self Published Doctoral Paper). Retrievable: http//wilderdom.com/html/ NewesAT3comps.htm; Hans, T.A., "A Meta-Analysis of the Effects of Adventure Programming on Locus of Control," *Journal of Contemporary Psychotherapy,* Vol. 30(1), (May, 200). Pg. 33-60. Retrievable: http://wilderdom.com/pdf/ Hans2000AdventureTherapyLOCMetaanalysis.pdf; Paxton, T., & McAvoy, L., "Social Psychological Benefits of a Wilderness Adventure Program," *USDA Forest Service Proceedings,* 2000. Retrievable: www.fs.fed.us/rm/pubs/rmrs_p015_3/rmrs_ p015_3_202_206.pdf.

[524] References made to challenge course operations, safety, training, or facilitation come from the following sources; The Association for Challenge Course Technology: www.acctinfo.org; Project Adventure: www.pa.org; Adventure Experiences, Inc.: www. advexp.com; Adventure-Based Experiential Educators, Inc.: www. abeeinc.com; Association for Experiential Education: www.aee. org.

[525] NARHA site accreditation: www.narha.org.

[526] EFMHA: www.narha.org; EAGALA: www.eagala.org.

[527] See the state licensing requirements specific to your state of residence; American Counseling Association: www.counseling.org; American Psychological Association: www.apa.org; National Board for Certified Counselors: www.nbcc.org; Association for Social Work Boards: www.aswb.org; Nation Association for Addictions Professional (NAADAC): www.naadac.org; American Mental Health Counselors Association; www.amhca.org.

[528] EAGALA Level One Training, 2001; personal communications with Level One EAGALA certified professionals; personal observations of EAGALA Level One certified professionals.

[529] Greenberg, L.S., Watson, G.C., & Lietaer, G.O., *Handbook of Experiential Psychotherapy.* (The Guilford Press, 1998); Schoel, J.,& Maizell, R., *Exploring Islands of Healing: New Perspectives on Adventure Based Counseling.* (Kendall Hunt Publishing Company, 2002); Cole, E., Erdman, E., & Rothblum, E.D., *Wilderness Therapy for Women: The Power of Adventure.* (Haworth Press, 1994); Gass, M. A., *Adventure therapy: Therapeutic applications of adventure programming.* (Dubuque, IA: Kendall/Hunt, 1993).); Beard, C., & Wilson, J.P., *Experiential Learning: A Handbook of Best Practices for Educators and Trainers.* (Kogan Page Ltd., 2006).

[530] Kersten, G., & Thomas, L., *Equine-assisted psychotherapy and learning un-training manual: Level One.* (Santaquin, UT: Equine Assisted Growth and Learning Association, 2004); Equine Assisted Growth and Learning Association Level One Certification program, (2001; EAGALA Level One Training, 2001; personal communications with Level One EAGALA certified professionals; personal observations of EAGALA Level One certified professionals; Rohnke, K.E., *Silver Bullets: A Guide to Initiative Problems, Adventure Games and Trust Activities.* (Kendall/Hunt Publishing Company, 1989); Rohnke, K.E., *Cowstails and Cobras II : A Guide to Games, Initiatives, Ropes Courses & Adventure Curriculum.* (Kendall/Hunt Publishing Company, 2003).

[531] The Association for Challenge Course Technology: www.acctinfo. org; Project Adventure: www.pa.org; Adventure Experiences, Inc.: www.advexp.com; Adventure-Based Experiential Educators, Inc.: www.abeeinc.com; Association for Experiential Education: www. aee.org.

[532] See "Check List for Consumers and Providers" in the appendix of this book as well as the "Ethics" section of this text.

[533] References to "Challenge by Choice" come from the following sources; Itin, C., "Challenge by choice as professional enabling," *Rocky: Newsletter of the Rocky Mountain Region of the Association for Experiential Education*, 6(2), 2. (1996); Itin, C. "The impelling principle in challenge by choice," *Rocky: Newsletter of the Rocky Mountain Region of the Association for Experiential Education*, 7(1). (1997); Rohnke, K., Kurt Hahn address - 2000 AEE International Conference. *Journal of Experiential Education, 23*, 166-169' Schoel, J., & Maizell, R. *Exploring islands of healing: New perspectives on adventure based counseling.* (Beverly, MA: Project Adventure, 2002); Schoel, J., Prouty, D., & Radcliffe, P. *Islands of healing: A guide to adventure based counseling.* (Hamilton, MA: Project Adventure, 1988); Project Adventure: www.pa.org.

[534] Rohnke, K.E., *Silver Bullets: A Guide to Initiative Problems, Adventure Games and Trust Activities.* (Kendall/Hunt Publishing Company, 1989); Rohnke, K.E., *Cowstails and Cobras II : A Guide to Games, Initiatives, Ropes Courses & Adventure Curriculum.* (Kendall/Hunt Publishing Company, 2003).

[535] References to personal choice come from the following sources; San Cristobal Ranch Academy: www.sancristobalranchacademy. org; Aspen Education Group: www.aspeneducation.com; Passages to Recovery: www.passagestorecovery.com.

[536] Nihart, T., Lersch, K.M., Sellers, C.S., & Mieczkowski, T., "Kids, Cops, Parents and Teachers: Exploring Juvenile Attitudes Toward

Authority Figures," *Western Criminology Review* 6(1), 79-88 (2005); Drury, J., "Adolescent Communication With Adults In Authority," *Journal of Language and Social Psychology,* Vol. 22, No. 1, 66-73 (2003); The EFFECTIVE NATIONAL DRUG CONTROL STRATEGY 1999, Rational #2: Retrievable: www. csdp.org/edcs/page10.htm.

537 See 18.

538 The concept of the horse having the right to choose whether or not to participate is supported by the work of Barbara Rector, Linda Kohanov, and this author, along with the work of many others within the field.

539 Greenberg, L.S., Watson, G.C., & Lietaer, G.O., *Handbook of Experiential Psychotherapy.* (The Guilford Press, 1998); Schoel, J.,& Maizell, R., *Exploring Islands of Healing: New Perspectives on Adventure Based Counseling.* (Kendall Hunt Publishing Company, 2002); Cole, E., Erdman, E., & Rothblum, E.D., *Wilderness Therapy for Women: The Power of Adventure.* (Haworth Press, 1994); Gass, M. A., *Adventure therapy: Therapeutic applications of adventure programming.* (Dubuque, IA: Kendall/Hunt, 1993). *Adventure therapy: Therapeutic applications of adventure programming.* (Dubuque, IA: Kendall/Hunt);); Beard, C., & Wilson, J.P., *Experiential Learning: A Handbook of Best Practices for Educators and Trainers.* (Kogan Page Ltd., 2006).

540 "Ice breakers"; Rohnke, K.E., *Silver Bullets: A Guide to Initiative Problems, Adventure Games and Trust Activities.* (Kendall/Hunt Publishing Company, 1989); Rohnke, K.E., *Cowstails and Cobras II : A Guide to Games, Initiatives, Ropes Courses & Adventure Curriculum.* (Kendall/Hunt Publishing Company, 2003).

541 Kersten, G., & Thomas, L., *Equine-assisted psychotherapy and learning un-training manual: Level One.* (Santaquin, UT: Equine Assisted Growth and Learning Association, 2004); Equine Assisted Growth and Learning Association Level One

Certification program, (2001; EAGALA Level One Training, 2001.

542 Results from survey, questionnaire, and interview questions conducted by this author as well as the personal observation of EAP programs by this author.

543 This statement is based upon the comments of those responding to questionnaires and interviews conducted by this author. These individuals felt that EAEC activities may be re-traumatizing to the survivors of abuse due to the prevalence in such activities of chasing horses, cornering horses, or otherwise controlling horses. They also felt that such activities might not be useful for perpetrators of such abuses as they might appear to closely linked to the manner in which such individuals have treated others in their lives. It is important to remember that these observations are based upon the manner in which both this author and those responding have personally observed EAP being conducted and it is not to say that there are other ways of providing the service that would be conducive to work with such populations.

544 Luckner, J.L., & Nadler, R.S., *Processing the Experience: Enhancing and Generalizing Learning Second Edition.* (Kendall/Hunt Publishing Company, 1997); Greenberg, L.S., Watson, G.C., & Lietaer, G.O., *Handbook of Experiential Psychotherapy.* (The Guilford Press, 1998); Schoel, J.,& Maizell, R., *Exploring Islands of Healing: New Perspectives on Adventure Based Counseling.* (Kendall Hunt Publishing Company, 2002).

545 Yalom, I.D., & Leszcz, M., *The Theory and Practice Of Group Psychotherapy Fifth Edition.* (Basic Books, 2005); Rogers, C., *Carl Rogers on Encounter Groups.* (Harper and Row, 1970).

546 Kersten, G., & Thomas, L., *Equine-assisted psychotherapy and learning un-training manual: Level One.* (Santaquin, UT: Equine Assisted Growth and Learning Association, 2004); Equine Assisted Growth and Learning Association Level One

Certification program, (2001; EAGALA Level One Training, 2001.

[547] This is an observation made by this author with support from comments made by others practicing EAP. This observation is based primary upon the activities as they are suggested by EAGALA's training manual and Level One training program. The majority of the activities taught by EAGALA are designed to work for multiple people, and would not successfully work with only one individual. There may be ways in which EAP could work for only one person, but such methods were not presented as a consensus during the survey, questionnaire, and interview process.

[548] Rogers, C., *Carl Rogers on Encounter Groups.* (Harper and Row, 1970); Yalom, I.D., & Leszcz, M., *The Theory and Practice Of Group Psychotherapy Fifth Edition.* (Basic Books, 2005).

[549] This statement comes from the observations of this author regarding the facilitation styles of professionals practicing EAP. There are many different ways to provide the service, and each professional may adjust or adapt their style of facilitation based upon the client or group who they are working with.

[550] Egolf, D.B., *Forming Storming Norming Performing: Successful Communication in Groups and Teams.* (Writers Club Press, 2001); Ringer, M.T., *Group Action: The Dynamics of Groups in Therapeutic, Educational and Corporate Settings.* (Jessica Kingsley Publishers, 2002).

[551] Yalom, I.D., & Leszcz, M., *The Theory and Practice Of Group Psychotherapy Fifth Edition.* (Basic Books, 2005).

[552] Schoel, J.,& Maizell, R., *Exploring Islands of Healing: New Perspectives on Adventure Based Counseling.* (Kendall Hunt Publishing Company, 2002).

[553] The references to goals for EAP as they are presented here come from the responses of those participating in surveys, questionnaires, and interviews conducted by this author, but are subject to the interpretation of the author.

[554] Kersten, G., & Thomas, L., *Equine-assisted psychotherapy and learning un-training manual: Level One.* (Santaquin, UT: Equine Assisted Growth and Learning Association, 2004); Equine Assisted Growth and Learning Association Level One Certification program, (2001); EAGALA Level One Training, 2001; EAGALA: www.eagala.org.

[555] References to the behavior of the horse in an EAP session is based upon this author's personal experience observing and participating in EAP sessions and from EAGALA's Level One Training, 2001. There are many other ways in which people view the role of the horse within an EAP session and facilitate the experience.

[556] EAGALA's Level One Training, 2001; Personal communications with Lynn Thomas regarding the role of the horse; Webb, W., *It's Not About The Horse.* (Hay House, 2003).

[557] From the observations of this author, some professionals providing an EAP service do not have their own horse herd, rather they team up with a "horse professional" who has horses. Some of the other examples involve licensed mental health professionals who travel to provide workshops, clinics, or group services and therefore work with horses on location who they do not have a prior relationship with. Since EAP appears to be provided in many cases in a workshop, weekend, or other short term approach, and since the method is primarily activity based, the clients tend to have limited time to just spend getting to know the horses and forming relationships with them.

[558] Luckner, J.L., & Nadler, R.S., *Processing the Experience: Enhancing and Generalizing Learning Second Edition.* (Kendall/

Hunt Publishing Company, 1997); Beard, C., & Wilson, J.P., *Experiential Learning: A Handbook of Best Practices for Educators and Trainers.* (Kogan Page Ltd., 2006).

[559] Justice, T., & Jamieson, D., *The Complete Guide to Facilitation: Enabling Groups to Succeed.* (HRD Press, 1998); Corey, M.S., & Corey, G., *Groups: Process and Practice Seventh Edition.* Thomson Brooks/Cole, 2006); Barker, L.L., Wahlers, K.J., & Watson, K.W., *Groups in Process: An Introduction to Small Group Communication Sixth Edition.* (Allyn & Bacon, 2000).

[560] Medrick, F. W., "Confronting passive behavior through outdoor experience." (Denver, CO: Outdoor Leadership Training Seminars, 1978).

[561] EAGALA's Level One Training, 2001.

[562] The references to the team approach in EAP and to the role of the horse professional are based upon the results of surveys, questionnaires, and interview conducted by this author, as well as upon the personal observations of the author. EAGALA also trains their participants to this model.

[563] The NBCC: : www.nbcc.org; www.nbcc.org/ethics2 ; the ACA: www.counseling.org;www.counseling.org/Resources/CodeOfEthics/TP/Home/CT2.aspx; EFMHA: www.narha.org/PDFfiles/EFMHACodeofethicsapproved.pdf ; EAGALA: www.eagala.org/Ethics.htm.

[564] Cole, E., Erdman, E., & Rothblum, E.D., *Wilderness Therapy for Women: The Power of Adventure.* (Haworth Press, 1994).

[565] Personal experience of the author working with "disempowered" youth and adults within the Department of Corrections system.

[566] See "Check List for Consumers and Providers" in the appendix of this book.

Chapter Fifteen Notes

The references for this entire chapter come primary from the following sources; Personal conversations and interview with Laura Brinkerhoff, Program Director of Cottonwood De Tucson's Equine Program; the personal experience of this author providing EFBI services to clients referred from organizations such as Child Protective Services, Empact, Value Options, Jewish Youth and Family Services, and other such state and national service providers; the works of Dryden, W., & Neenan, M., *Rational Emotive Behaviour Group Therapy.* (Wiley, 2005); Ellis, A. & Grieger, R., *Handbook of Rational-Emotive Therapy.* (New York: Spring, 1977); Gustafson, J.P., *Very Brief Psychotherapy.* (Routledge, 2005); Budman, S.H., & Gurman, A.S., *Theory and Practice of Brief Therapy.* (The Guilford Press, 2002); The National Board for Certified Counselors, *Code of Ethics*: Retrievable: www.nbcc.org/extras/pdfs/ethics/nbcc-codeofethics.pdf; The American Counseling Association American Psychological Association, *Ethical Principles for Psychologists and Code of Conduct*, Retrievable: www.apa.org/ethics/code2002.html#2_01; American Counseling Association, *Code of Ethics,* Retrievable:www.counseling.org/Resources/CodeOfEthics/TP/Home/CT2.aspx; Equine Facilitated Mental Health Association, *Code of Ethics*, Retrievable: www.narha.org/PDFfiles/EFMHACodeofethicsapproved.pdf. and information already presented within various chapters and sections of this text.

For the duration of these notes the author will only insert references if they diverge from the above mentioned sources.

The method of EFBI, although it appears to be utilized in many different treatment centers, and by many independent EFMHS facilities across the country, lacks the written structure or organization that the other methods already presented in this text have. Furthermore, EFBI relies heavily upon the knowledge of all other EFMHS methods already presented in prior chapters.

EFBI as it is presented here is solely based upon the options and beliefs of a few individuals practicing this method in the field. Inevitability there are many other ways in which to practice this method, however, both Ms. Brinkerhoff and this author feel strongly that the manner in which this method is presented here reflects an ethical and safe approach to utilizing the method.

[567] Curtis, C., The Art of Letting Go," Retrievable: www. achangeinthinking.com/releasetechnique.html.

[568] Primary/LMHP will be used to describe the licensed mental health professional who works on a regular basis with the client outside of the EFBI service and is generally not employed by the EFBI program. EFBI/LMHP will be used to describe the EFBI trained mental health professional who facilitates the equine experience.

[569] Otani, A., "Resistance management techniques of Milton H. Erickson, M.D.: An application to nonhypnotic mental health counseling." *Journal of Mental Health Counseling,* 11(4), 325-334. (1989). Mitchell, C., "Resistant Clients: We've All Had Them; Here's How to Help Them," *Psychotherapy.net.*

[570] Felton, A., "Resistance in Psychotherapy." University of Missouri-Columbia School of Medicine; Patterson, C.H., *Counseling and Psychotherapy: Theory and Practice.* (New York: Harper and Row, 1959); Yalom, I.D., *The Gift of Therapy.* (New York: HarperColllins, 2002).

[571] Freud, S., *An Outline of Psychoanalysis.* (New York: Norton, 1949); Corey, G., *Theory and Practice of Counseling and Psychotherapy 6th Edition.* (Brooks/Cole, 2001); Jung, C.G., *The Undiscovered Self.* (Signet; Reissue edition, 2006).

[572] Martin, D.G., *Counseling and Therapy Skills, Second Edition.* (Waveland Press, 1999).

[573] Brief Psychotherapy, as an intervention was introduced primarily in response to insurance companies' resistance to pay for long term therapy. Therefore, clients who might otherwise engage in a longer term treatment approach may find themselves mandated

by their insurance policy to seek a short term treatment. If their insurance policy only covers four to six sessions, they may discontinue services due to financial inability to pay for continued services out of pocket. In some cases this means that clients leave therapy before attending to the core issues that caused dysfunction or dis-health in the first place.

[574] See **Chapter Seven: Communication**

[575] See **Chapter Eight: Relational Skills,** Reflective Feedback or Mirroring and **Chapter Twelve: Equine Facilitated Psychotherapy:** Psychodramatization and Reflective Feedback.

[576] Karol, J., "Applying a Traditional Individual Psychotherapy Model to Equine-facilitated Psychotherapy (EFP): Theory and Method," *Clinical Child Psychology and Psychiatry,* Vol. 12, No. 1, 77-90 (2007); Vidrine, M., Owen-Smith P., & Faulkner P., "Equine-facilitated group psychotherapy: applications for therapeutic vaulting," Issues in Mental Health Nursing, Vol. 23(6):587-603. (September, 2002); Malek, M.J., "Combination of Lifelong Passion and Innovation Fuels New Psychologist's Practice OPA Member Champions an Equine-Assisted Approach While Serving the Underserved" Retrievable: www.apadiv31.org/Coop/ EquineAssistedTherapy.pdf .

[577] Personal conversations and interview with Laura Brinkerhoff, Program Director of Cottonwood De Tucson's Equine Program.

[578] Personal conversations and interview with Laura Brinkerhoff; Cottonwood De Tucson: www.cottonwooddetucson. com; Remuda Ranch: www.remuda-ranch.com; Betty Ford Clinic: www.bettyfordcenter.org; Carolina House: www. carolinaeatingdisorders.com; Many other programs utilize a EFBI approach where a licensed mental health professional refers clients to a EFMHS program and may even attend sessions to observe their client.

[579] Personal conversations and interview with Laura Brinkerhoff, Program Director of Cottonwood De Tucson's Equine Program.

[580] The majority of recommendations regarding the ethical and legal ramifications of providing an EFBI service come from personal conversations and interviews with Laura Brinkerhoff, the personal experience of this author providing EFBI services to clients referred from organizations such as Child Protective Services, Empact, Value Options, Jewish Youth and Family Services, and other such state and national service providers, and HIPPA guidelines for client confidentiality.

[581] Anecdotal responses taken from clients participating in EFBI services.

[582] This statement makes an assumption that in some cases "psychotherapy" indicates a process of deep personal reflection based upon a retrieving of the past history of the client. As is indicated in **Chapter Nine: Overview of Theoretical Perspectives,** psychotherapy can be interpreted or defined in a number of different ways.

[583] See Barbara Rector's Adventures in Awareness model: www.adventuresinawareness.net.

Chapter Sixteen Notes

[584] Ewing, C.A., MacDonald, P.M., Taylor, M., & Bowers, M.J., "Equine-Facilitated Learning for Youths with Severe Emotional Disorders: A Quantitative and Qualitative Study," *Child and Youth Care Forum,* Volume 36, Number 1. (February, 2007). Pg. 59-72; McDaniel, B., What Exactly Is "Equine Facilitated Mental Health & Equine Facilitated Learning?" NARHA *Strides magazine,* Vol. 4, No. 1 (Winter 1998); Strides to Success: www.stridestosuccess.org; Great Strides: www.greatstrides.org.

[585] Strides to Success: www.stridestosuccess.org; Equibest Equestrian Center: www.equibest.com; Horse Power: www.horse-power.org;

San Cristobal Ranch Academy: www.sancristobalranchacademy.
org; Aspen Education Group: www.aspeneducation.com; In
Balance Ranch Academy: www.inbalranch.com; Esperanza, An
Experiential Healing Center: www.esperanzainformation.com.

[586] U.S. Department of Education, "A Guide to the Individualized
Education Program." Retrievable: www.ed.gov/parents/needs/
speced/iepguide/index.html; Cornwall, J., & Robertson, C.,
*Physical Disabilities And Medical Conditions: Individual Education
Plans.* (David Fulton Publishers, 2004).

[587] A "learning plan" may resemble a "treatment plan" in that it
lays out goals specific to the student's participation in an EFL
program.

[588] Ewing, C.A., MacDonald, P.M., Taylor, M., & Bowers, M.J.,
"Equine-Facilitated Learning for Youths with Severe Emotional
Disorders: A Quantitative and Qualitative Study," *Child and
Youth Care Forum,* Volume 36, Number 1. (February, 2007);
Bizub, A., Joy, A., & Davidson, L., "It's like being in another
world." Psychiatric Rehabilitation Journal, Vol. 26, No. 4,
(2003). Pg. 377-384.

[589] The United Nations Children's Fund (UNICEF), life skills.
Retrievable: www.unicef.org/lifeskills/index_7308.html.

[590] Ewing, C.A., MacDonald, P.M., Taylor, M., & Bowers, M.J.,
"Equine-Facilitated Learning for Youths with Severe Emotional
Disorders: A Quantitative and Qualitative Study," *Child and
Youth Care Forum,* Volume 36, Number 1. (February, 2007);
Bizub, A., Joy, A., & Davidson, L., "It's like being in another
world." Psychiatric Rehabilitation Journal, Vol. 26, No. 4,
(2003). Pg. 377-384. Rector, B.K., Adventures in Awareness:
Learning with the Help of Horses. (AuthorHouse, 2005); Alston,
A.J., & Miller, J.H., "Therapeutic Riding: An Educational Tool
for Children with Disabilities as Viewed by Parents." Retrievable:
http://pubs.aged.tamu.edu/jsaer/pdf/Vol54/54-01-113.pdf.

591 These statements are based upon this author's experience of student and parent self reporting and upon personal observation of EFL students and their parents.

592 Strides to Success: www.stridestosuccess.org; Esperanza, An Experiential Healing Center: www.esperanzainformation. com; Alston, A.J., & Miller, J.H., "Therapeutic Riding: An Educational Tool for Children with Disabilities as Viewed by Parents." Retrievable: http://pubs.aged.tamu.edu/jsaer/pdf/ Vol54/54-01-113.pdf.

593 Grandin, T., & Barron, S., *The Unwritten Rules of Social Relationships*. (Future Horizons, 2005); Dowd, T., & Tierney, J., *Teaching Social Skills to Youth, Second Edition*. (Boys Town Press, 2005); Duke, M., Nowicki, S., & Martin, E.A., *Teaching Your Child the Language of Social Success*. (Peachtree Publishers, 1996).

594 Budiansky, S., *The Nature of Horses*. (New York: The Free Press, 1997); Hill, C., *How to Think Like a Horse*. (Story Publishing, 2006); Roberts, M., *The Man Who Listens to Horses*. (New York: Ballentine Publishing Group, 1996).

595 This author's professional experience, especially related to the San Cristobal Ranch Academy EFL program.

596 This author's professional experience relating to San Cristobal Ranch Academy, contracts with Child Protective Services, Empact, and Chicano's Por La Causa.

597 Non-Verbal Learning Disorders Association: www.nlda.org; Thompson, S., *The Source for Nonverbal Learning Disorders*. (LinguiSystems, 1997); Molenaar-Klumper, M., *Non-verbal Learning Disabilities: Diagnosis and Treatment within an Educational Setting*. (Jessica Kingsley Publishers, 2002).

598 See **Chapter Six: Communication.**

[599] See 10 and 14.

[600] See **Chapter Six: Communication,** Congruent Message Sending.

[601] Nowicki, S., Duke, M.P., *Helping the Child Who Doesn't Fit in.* (Peachtree Publishers, 1992); Molenaar-Klumper, M., *Nonverbal Learning Disabilities: Diagnosis and Treatment within an Educational Setting.* (Jessica Kingsley Publishers, 2002).

[602] Alston, A.J., & Miller, J.H., "Therapeutic Riding: An Educational Tool for Children with Disabilities as Viewed by Parents." Retrievable: http://pubs.aged.tamu.edu/jsaer/pdf/Vol54/54-01-113.pdf; Rothe, E.Q., Vega, B.J., Torres, R.M., Soler, S.M.C., & Pazos, R.M.M., "From Kids and Horses: Equine facilitated psychotherapy for children." *International Journal of Clinical and Health Psychology,* Vol.5, No. 002, (May, 2005); TherAplay: www.childrenstherapy.org.

[603] Lerner, J.W., & Kline, F., *Learning Disabilities and Related Disorders: Characteristics and Teaching Strategies, Tenth Edition.* (Houghton Mifflin Company, 2005); Harwell, J.M., *Complete Learning Disabilities Handbook: Ready-to-Use Strategies & Activities for Teaching Students with Learning Disabilities, Second Edition.* (Jossey-Bass, 2001).

[604] Alston, A.J., & Miller, J.H., "Therapeutic Riding: An Educational Tool for Children with Disabilities as Viewed by Parents." Retrievable: http://pubs.aged.tamu.edu/jsaer/pdf/Vol54/54-01-113.pdf.

[605] See **Chapter Eight: Development of Self through Horse-Person-Ship,** The Now: Grounding, Focus, Awareness, and Presence.

[606] This statement is the outcome of four years of personal observation and professional practice by this author at the San Cristobal Ranch Academy. The San Cristobal Ranch Academy

utilized EFL as a tool to help young men with ADD/ADHD become medication free. Anecdotal evidence that demonstrated a decrease in medication usage and an increase in grade point averages at the University of New Mexico-Taos was collected on over sixty (60) participants. The students indicated that they felt this change was due to the EFL program, however, although interesting, too many other treatment variables existed during each individual student's participation in the equine program to discern if EFL was the leading cause of change.

[607] Bizub, A., Joy, A., & Davidson, L., "It's like being in another world." Psychiatric Rehabilitation Journal, Vol. 26, No. 4, (2003). Pg. 377-384.

[608] Rothe, E.Q., Vega, B.J., Torres, R.M., Soler, S.M.C., & Pazos, R.M.M., "From Kids and Horses: Equine facilitated psychotherapy for children." *International Journal of Clinical and Health Psychology,* Vol.5, No. 002, (May, 2005).

[609] This statement is based upon this author's professional experience in which clients who experience feelings of rejection, dislike, or a lack of trust may transgress more easily into a dissociative state. If this occurs, generally a therapeutic technique may be needed to help them process or move through such a state. This is not to suggest that there are not many other ways to facilitate an EFL session in which a client works with a horse who is unwilling or uninterested in participating that can be educational and not therapeutic for the client.

[610] Hallberg, L., "Emergence of Equine Facilitated Psychotherapy programs in therapeutic riding facilities across the United States: Efficacy and Program Design. *Animal Therapy Association of Arizona,* 1997; personal observations of this author following this study of horses working in EFL programs.

[611] Hallberg, L., Project Textbook: Defining our past, present, and future." Unpublished, 2006; Personal communications and interview with Ann Alden, professional experience of this author.

[612] Strides to Success: www.stridestosuccess.org; Equibest Equestrian Center: www.equibest.com; Horse Power: www.horse-power.org; Ewing, C.A., MacDonald, P.M., Taylor, M., & Bowers, M.J., "Equine-Facilitated Learning for Youths with Severe Emotional Disorders: A Quantitative and Qualitative Study," *Child and Youth Care Forum,* Volume 36, Number 1. (February, 2007).

[613] Bozarth, J., & Wilkins , P., *Rogers Therapeutic Conditions Evolution Theory & Practice: Unconditional Positive Regard.* (PCCS Books, 2001); Merritt, J., & Bloch, D., *The Power of Positive Talk: Words to Help Every Child Succeed : A Guide for Parents, Teachers, and Other Caring Adults.* (Free Spirit Publishing, 2003).

[614] See "Wrap Around Services," **Chapter 13: Equine Facilitated Counseling.**

[615] American Counseling Association, Code of Ethics, A.2.d. Retrievable: www.counseling.org/Resources/CodeOfEthics/TP/Home/CT2.aspx.

[616] See 3 (IEP's).

[617] Statement based upon this author's professional experience and the following references; Molenaar-Klumper, M., *Non-verbal Learning Disabilities: Diagnosis and Treatment within an Educational Setting.* (Jessica Kingsley Publishers, 2002); Lerner, J.W., & Kline, F., *Learning Disabilities and Related Disorders: Characteristics and Teaching Strategies, Tenth Edition.* (Houghton Mifflin Company, 2005); Harwell, J.M., *Complete Learning Disabilities Handbook: Ready-to-Use Strategies & Activities for Teaching Students with Learning Disabilities, Second Edition.* (Jossey-Bass, 2001).

Chapter Seventeen Notes

[618] Carey, M., "Horses Leap Straight into the Heart of Prescott College," *Transitions,* Vol. 26, No. 2, (Fall, 2005). Pg. 2-4; Robinson, P., "The equine experience: the role of horses in adventure education," *Transitions,* Vol. 3. (Winter/Spring, 2003). Pg. 16-19; the personal experience and involvement of this author, and personal communications with Paul Smith.

[619] The majority of this chapter is written from the professional experience of this author, personal observations from working with Paul Smith, and utilizes personal involvement with this method as an experiential learning concept. There is little written to support the theoretical underpinnings of such a method specific to horses, but the author feels that over time this method will be more clearly defined and honed as a potentially useful experiential education method. The references regarding experiential education approaches come from the following sources; Beard, C., & Wilson, J.P., *Experiential Learning: A Handbook of Best Practices for Educators and Trainers.* (Kogan Page Ltd., 2006); Association for Adventure Education: www. aee.org; and Chapter Thirteen: Equine Assisted Experiential Therapy. References to the use of EAE come from; Robinson, P., "The equine experience: the role of horses in adventure education," Transitions, Winter-Spring, Vol. 3. Pg. 16-19; Carey, M., "Horses Leap Straight into the Heart of Prescott College," *Transitions,* Vol. 26, No. 2, (Fall, 2005). Pg. 2-4; Centaur Leadership Services: www.prescott.edu/cls/index.html; Prescott College: www.prescott.edu; personal conversations with Dr. Ellen Gehrke of Alliant International University; and this author's professional experience providing the service to a number of school programs in the Phoenix, Arizona area between 1999-2003. The author will only cite references or sources that differ from the above statement.

[620] Merriam-Webster's On-Line Dictionary is used for the following definition, "teamwork". www.merriam-webster.com.

[621] Thompson, R., *Nurturing Future Generations: Promoting Resilience in Children and Adolescents Through Social, Emotional, and Cognitive Skills, Second Edition.* (Brunner-Routledge, 2006).

[622] Merriam-Webster's On-Line Dictionary is used for the following definition, "cooperation". www.merriam-webster.com.

[623] Merriam-Webster's On-Line Dictionary is used for the following definition, "cohesion." www.merriam-webster.com.

Chapter Eighteen Notes

[624] This definition and the majority of the information used in this chapter comes from the professional work of Dr. Ellen Gehrke of Rolling Horse Ranch; Gehrke, E. K., "Analyzing and Sustaining Positive Energetic Environments in Organizations." American *Association of Business and Behavioral Sciences Conference Proceedings.* Las Vegas, NV. (2007); Gehrke, E.K., "Creating and Sustaining leadership in Partnership with Horses." *Proceedings from the Southwest Academy of Management Annual Meeting,* San Diego, CA. (2007); Gehrke, E. K., "Developing Coherent Leaders in Partnership with Horses." Unpublished coaching manual, 2006); and the work of Sherri Petro, MBA; Petro, S. B. "An Introduction by Coaching" Article published with Intuit Proconnection, 2004; Petro, S. B., "Beyond Words, Creating An Authentic Organization" (Unpublished manuscript, 2007); Petro, S. B. "Coaching for Managers Presentation." *Nonprofit Management Solutions,* San Diego CA, 2007. Permission to utilize this material has been granted by both Dr. Gehrke and Ms. Petro.

[625] Professional Coaches and Mentors Association: www.pcmaonline.com.

[626] Personal conversations with Joe Esparza and Ris Higgins of Leadership Outfitters and conversations with Dr. Ellen Gehrke.

627 Zeus, P., & Skiffington, S., *The Complete Guide to Coaching at Work.* (McGraw Hill: Australia, 2001).

628 Gallway, T., W., *The Inner Game of Work.* (Random House, 2000).

629 This statement is according to Dr. Ellen Gehrke and Ms. Petro.

630 Williams, A.R., "Coached to Success," *Datamation.* Retrievable: http://itmanagement.earthweb.com/career/article.php/618981#a_top10.

631 Statement based upon the author's research into the field of coaching.

632 International Coach Federation: www.coachfederation.org.

633 International Association of Coaching: www.certifiedcoach.org.

634 International Association of Coaching, 15 Proficiencies. Retrievable: www.certifiedcoach.org/learningguide/proficiencies.html.

635 Dr. Ellen Gehrke and Ms. Petro, personal communication and written correspondence.

636 Statement based from the work of Dr. Ellen Gehrke, Joe Esparza and Ris Higgins.

637 Roberts, M., *Horse Sense for People.* (New York: Penguin Books, 2002); Irwin, C., *Horses Don't Lie.* (New York: Marlowe and Company, 1998); Rashid, M., *Horses never lie: The art of passive leadership.* (Johnston Publishing Company, 2000).

638 Dr. Ellen Gehrke and Ms. Petro, personal communication and written correspondence.

[639] Roberts, M., *Horse Sense for People*. (New York: Penguin Books, 2002); Irwin, C., *Horses Don't Lie*. (New York: Marlowe and Company, 1998); Rashid, M., *Horses never lie: The art of passive leadership*. (Johnston Publishing Company, 2000).

[640] Dr. Ellen Gehrke and Ms. Petro, personal communication and written correspondence.

[641] Dr. Ellen Gehrke and Ms. Petro, personal communication and written correspondence.

[642] Dr. Ellen Gehrke, personal communication and written correspondence.

[643] Dr. Ellen Gehrke, personal communication and written correspondence; Joe Esparza and Ris Higgins of Leadership Outfitters, personal communications.

[644] This is the personal belief of Dr. Ellen Gehrke based upon her new research findings (Gehrke, E.K., "Horses and Humans Energetics: The study of Heart Rate Variability (HRV) between horses and Humans." (Unpublished pilot study, 2006); and is can be assumed that not all those providing an EFC service feel the same way. However, the statement is included here because of the author's similar feelings regarding the role of the horse.

[645] All statements regarding the role of the coach in an EFCS session are based upon personal communication and written correspondence from Dr. Ellen Gehrke and Ms. Petro. These are only the recommendations of two individuals providing an EFC service, but they appear to represent an ethically stable and educationally-based method for facilitating such a service. It is assumed that there are other diversely different ways of facilitating EFCS that are equally ethical.

[646] See **Chapter Seven: Relational Skills,** Mirroring or Reflective Feedback

[647] All of the practical applications of EFCS were provided by Dr. Ellen Gehrke and Ms. Petro. They utilized the following sources; Gehrke, E. K., "Analyzing and Sustaining Positive Energetic Environments in Organizations." American *Association of Business and Behavioral Sciences Conference Proceedings.* Las Vegas, NV. (2007); Gehrke, E.K., "Creating and Sustaining leadership in Partnership with Horses." *Proceedings from the Southwest Academy of Management Annual Meeting,* San Diego, CA. (2007); Gehrke, E. K., "Developing Coherent Leaders in Partnership with Horses." Unpublished coaching manual, 2006); and the work of Sherri Petro, MBA; Petro, S. B. "An Introduction by Coaching" Article published with Intuit Proconnection, 2004; Petro, S. B., "Beyond Words, Creating An Authentic Organization" (Unpublished manuscript, 2007); Petro, S. B. "Coaching for Managers Presentation." *Nonprofit Management Solutions,* San Diego CA, 2007; Roberts, M., *Horse Sense for People.* (New York: Penguin Books, 2002); Irwin, C., *Horses Don't Lie.* (New York: Marlowe and Company, 1998); Rashid, M., *Horses never lie: The art of passive leadership.* (Johnston Publishing Company, 2000); Zeus, P., & Skiffington, S., *The Complete Guide to Coaching at Work.* (McGraw Hill: Australia, 2001); Gallway, T., W., *The Inner Game of Work.* (Random House, 2000). This section was edited and revised by this author. The comments made in this section represent the beliefs of Dr. Gehrke, Ms. Petro, and this author but are not necessarily representative of the rest of the field.

[648] Personal response to questionnaire conducted by author.

Chapter Nineteen Notes

This chapter was written in collaboration with Linda Kohanov, author and founder of Epona Equestrian Services. EFHD as it is presented here is solely based upon the options and beliefs of a few individuals practicing this method in the field, and especially upon the written and practical applications provided by Linda Kohanov. Inevitability there are many other ways in which to practice this method, however, both Ms. Kohanov and this author feel strongly that the manner in which this method is presented here reflects an ethical and safe approach to utilizing the method.

References for this entire chapter come primary from the following sources; Personal conversations and written collaboration with Linda Kohanov; the personal experience of this author providing EFHD service and working with Barbara Rector learning her unique approach to EFHD, and the works of; Kohonov, L., *The Tao of Equus.* (Novato, CA: New World Library, 2001); Kohanov, L., *Riding Between the Worlds.* (Novato, CA: New World Library, 2003); McCormick, A., & McCormick, M., *Horse Sense and the Human Heart.* (Deerfield Beach, FL.: Health Communications, 1997); McCormick, A.R., McCormick, M.D., & McCormick, T.E., *Horses and the Mystical Path.* (Novato, CA.: New World Library, 2004); Rector, B.K. *Adventures in Awareness: Learning with the help of horses.* (Bloomington, IN: Authorhouse, 2005); Irwin, C. *Horses Don't Lie.* (New York: Marlowe & Company, 2001); Irwin, C., *Dancing With Your Dark Horse.* (New York: Marlowe and Company, 2005).

For the duration of these notes the author will only insert references if they diverge from the above mentioned sources or are specific quotes.

[649] Personal correspondence with Linda Kohanov.

[650] Irwin, C. *Horses Don't Lie.* (New York: Marlowe & Company, 2001). Pg. 5

[651] Rector, B.K. *Adventures in Awareness: Learning with the help of horses.* (Bloomington, IN: Authorhouse, 2005). Pg. xvi

[652] Kohanov, L., *Riding Between the Worlds.* (Novato, CA: New World Library, 2003). Pg. 56.

[653] Kohanov, L. *The Way of the Horse.* (Novato, CA: New World Library, 2007).

654 Personal written correspondence with Linda Kohanov. This quote came from a handout that Ms. Kohanov shares as a part of her apprenticeship program.

655 Personal correspondence with Linda Kohanov. This quote was a result of Ms. Kohanov and this author's collaboration to define EFHD.

656 Personal correspondence with Linda Kohanov. This quote was a result of Ms. Kohanov and this author's collaboration to define EFHD.

657 Personal written correspondence with Linda Kohanov. This quote came from a handout that Ms. Kohanov shares as a part of her apprenticeship program.

658 Retrieved from: www.holotropic.com.

659 Retrieved from: www.holotropic.com.

660 Retrieved from: www.adventuresinawareness.net.

661 Retrieved from: www.adventuresinawareness.net.

662 De Quincey, C. *Radical Knowing*. (Rochester, Vermount: Park Street Press, 2005).

663 Personal correspondence with Linda Kohanov. This quote was a result of Ms. Kohanov and this author's collaboration to define EFHD.

664 Permission was granted by Linda Kohanov to use this excerpt from *The Way of the Horse*.

Chapter Twenty Notes

665 Prescott College: www.prescott.edu.

⁶⁶⁶ Carroll College: www.carol.edu.

⁶⁶⁷ See Appendix, EFMH/ES College and University Programs.

⁶⁶⁸ See Appendix, EFMH/ES College and University Programs.

⁶⁶⁹ This statement is made based upon the personal observations and experiences of this author.

⁶⁷⁰ Personal correspondence with a representative from the Garn Group, New York, NY.

Leif Hallberg, an expert in Equine Facilitated Mental Health and Educational Services, studies the psychological implications of the horse-human relationship. A former horse trainer turned mental health professional; she is the founder and director of The Esperanza Center, a nonprofit organization that provides equine facilitated services, and an adjunct professor for Carroll College's Human-Animal Bond Program. She lives in Bozeman, MT with her two and four legged family. For more information, her website is: www.walkingthewayofthehorse.com.

Index

A

"An Inconvenient Truth" (Gore) 443
AAE 248
acting outside of self 19
Adventures in Awareness 47, 103, 164, 168, 410, 420, 468
Adventures in Awareness: Learning with the Help of Horses xxxiv
Aetna 33
Ainslie, T & Ledbetter, B. 89
Allen, K.M. 40
American Counseling Assciation (ACA) 223, 246, 261, 474
  ACA 227, 247, 305, 473
American Heart Association 40, 41
American Hippotherapy Association (AHA) 31, 472
American Psychological Association 246, 261, 474
ancestors. *See* Communication With
animal assisted activities 29, 30, 43
animal assisted activities/therapy 57
animal assisted therapy 4, 34, 81, 480, 482, 485
Anthony, David 3, 5, 11, 12
Anthony, Laura 325, 470
anthropomorphism xxxv, xxxvi
Anthrozoos 35, 42, 63, 66
archetypal 4, 13, 26, 87, 210
archetype xxiii, 17
art therapy; as the field relates to EFMH/ES 69, 245, 246, 249, 296, 452
Aspen Ranch 49
assertiveness 122, 345, 417, 422, 428, 430
assist v, xxviii, xxxii, 127, 162, 256, 264, 273, 281, 288, 307, 310, 313, 351, 367, 375, 387, 419
assisted v, xviii, xx, xxiii, xxix, xxxii, 29, 30, 34, 36, 40, 43, 45, 47, 48, 50, 52, 53, 57, 69, 228, 243, 274, 374, 480, 485, 506
Association for Adventure Educators 248
Australian Department of Human Services; research 40
awareness, self- 61, 62, 65, 181, 183, 191, 192, 195, 196, 206, 214, 230, 249, 281, 289, 311, 312, 314, 320, 337, 347, 391, 402, 403, 406

B

Backster, Cleve 119
Barker, S.B. & Barker, R.T.; research 38
barn milieu 57, 59

Baskfield, Lynn 229, 236, 243, 405, 471

Beck, A. 100

Belan-Timchenko, Natalya 5

Bella Terra; program 249, 344, 468

Benda, McGibbon, & Grant; research 32

Benda, W. & Lightmark, R.; research 38

Bernstein, Jerome 134

Bertoti, D.B.; research 32, 33

Between Pets and People (Beck & Katcher) 100

bible; teachings 17

bioneers 135

biophilia 57, 133, 439

Bizub, Joy, & Davidson; research 64

bluffing 108, 113, 122

body awareness 158, 186, 204, 290, 291, 302, 422

body language; in horses xvi, xvii, xix, xxiii, 73, 99, 121, 126, 127, 172, 295, 326, 421

bonding; horse-horse, horse-human 43, 92, 95, 200, 367, 480, 481

borderland 134

borderlanders 180

Botai 6, 7, 8

boundaries; horses, the human struggle, levels, learned helplessness; energetic 177–180

Brannaman, Buck 103

breathwork. *See* Grof, Stanislav

Brock, B.; research 32

Brown, Dorcus 6

Budiansky, Stephan 89, 96, 99, 122, 166

Burgon, Hannah; research 63

burning times 24

C

C.A.R.D. 27

Celtic xxxiv, 18, 19, 55

Celts 14, 15

certification programs 83, 437

challenge by choice 334–337, 341, 342

challenge course(s) 243, 245, 257, 329, 331–333, 390

Chamberlin, Edward 3

Chiron 16. *See also* healer, wounded

City University of New York, School of Law 162

Clever Hans 104

Clinic of Child Adolescent Psychiatry and Psychotherapy; Prothmann, A.; research 41

Cloudy; the horse vii, 207, 299–301
co-evolution 8, 11, 12
coaching, professional xxv, 393, 394
Cohen, Michael xxix
coherence 154–157
collaboration; with educational institutions, with mental health professionals 67,
    376, 388, 416, 440, 487
collective unconscious 44, 118, 179, 202, 205
Commission for Certified Equine Facilitated Mental Health and Education Profes-
    sionals (CCEFMHEP) 241
communication; horse-human, horse-horse, interspecies, advanced communication
    skills xix, xxxiii, 12, 18, 28, 36, 49, 50, 54, 55, 58–60, 74–76, 80, 89, 94,
    99–102, 104–108, 110–112, 116, 117, 119, 121–123, 127–131, 136, 154,
    166, 169–172, 186, 192, 203, 234, 244, 276, 278, 293, 305, 306, 309,
    310, 312, 327, 337, 339, 344, 358, 363, 365, 370–372, 380, 382–384,
    386, 391, 397, 399, 405, 408, 410, 413, 418, 421–423, 424, 426, 427,
    429, 462, 464, 496
communication with ancestors 18
compassion 72, 128, 130, 137, 140, 141, 143, 170, 195, 214, 289, 376, 382, 386
competence 65, 149, 198, 241, 246–248, 437, 479
Complementary Therapies and Wellness (Scurlock-Durana) 161
Complete Guide to Coaching at Work, The (Zeus & Skiffington) 394
Complexity of Connection, The (Jordan) 285
confidentiality 249–251, 256, 288, 302, 317, 402, 502, 503
congruent; definition; congruent communication; congruent message sending ; im-
    plications for 104, 113, 117, 121, 126–132, 165, 172, 370, 386, 444, 497
consent, informed 233, 249, 251, 256
consent to treatment 233, 467
corrective experiences 352
Cottonwood De Tucson; equine program xxv, 361, 468
counseling; definition 227
creativity 114, 183, 398, 410, 412, 417, 422, 429, 463
cross-training for professionals 255
cultural evolution; and the horse 11
Cult Stallion of Dereivka, The 3

D

Dancing with Your Dark Horse (Irwin) 56
Datamation Reporting 394
de-mystifying; the process 439
Delta Society 29, 34, 42, 473
Depauw, K. 30
DePrekel, Molly 44
Dereivka 3, 208

Descartes 221

development of self; becoming yourself, the Now, forward movement, self awareness and self image, self esteem and self confidence, intuition, power,
responsibility, integrity, commitment, normalization 183

Divine xxix, xxxi, xxxv, 13, 16–19, 24–26, 27, 87, 118, 152, 205, 259, 444

domestication 8–10, 12, 13, 480, 481

Dooley, John 381

Dorrance, Tom 77, 79

Dossey, Larry 14, 23, 117, 163, 167, 179, 202

Dreams of Dragons (Watson) 105, 119

Druids 14, 15

E

Ecopsychology 57, 262, 475, 505

education; education services; educator; professional education v, xvii, xviii, xxii,
xxxiii, xxxvii, 35, 50, 51, 52, 63, 69, 83, 88, 99, 113, 121, 148, 149, 150,
162, 171, 174, 177, 180, 182, 183, 187, 189, 195, 201, 202, 206, 209,
223–227, 229–234, 236–239, 241–248, 253, 254, 255–261, 264–266,
268, 273, 274, 292, 311, 315, 320, 331–334, 344, 372, 375, 384, 389,
390, 391, 400, 401, 409, 410, 415, 416, 430, 435–437, 440–442, 451,
452, 454, 458, 465, 468, 480, 482, 496, 503

Einstein, Albert; language xx, 114, 116

empathy xx, xxi, 137, 138, 141–143, 255, 382, 385, 386, 464

Epona (horse goddess) 414, 422

Epona Equestrian Services 410, 468

Equinection 249, 294, 469

Equine Assisted Education (EAE) 269

Equine Assisted Growth and Learning Association (EAGALA); definition, history,
overview 50, 247, 332, 472

Equine Assisted Psychotherapy (EFP) 49, 52, 225, 231, 269, 274, 329, 450, 462

equine communication: vocal communication, levels of communication, instinctual, assertive , non verbal, congruent 94, 99–101, 108, 110–112, 128,
171, 293

Equine Facilitated Brief Intensives (EFBI) 269, 347, 348

Equine Facilitated Counseling (EFC) xxviii, 269, 274, 289, 305, 316

Equine Facilitated Education/Learning Services (EFE/L) xxxvii, 253, 273, 274,
365, 381, 439, 441, 479

Equine Facilitated Human Development (EFHD) 269, 274, 409, 429

Equine Facilitated Learning 74, 269, 274, 365, 450, 524

Equine Facilitated Mental Health and Education Services (EFMH/ES) vi, xxxii,
xxxiii, xxxvii, 1, 4, 15, 26, 27, 30, 34, 43, 44, 47, 48–54, 56, 59, 60–63,
68–70, 78, 79–82, 87, 88, 96, 98, 100, 101, 108, 110, 112, 116, 126, 132,
136, 149, 159, 165, 166, 171, 172, 174, 175, 181, 186, 188, 189, 192,
193, 195–203, 206, 207, 211–214, 217, 219, 225–229, 231–234, 236,

238, 239, 241–244, 245, 247, 248, 250–254, 271–274, 275, 281, 282, 293, 332, 346, 361, 375, 394, 401, 416, 435–441, 444, 449, 452–455, 458, 461, 467, 468, 472, 479, 505, 506

Equine Facilitated Mental Health Association (EFMHA) vi, 44–52, 69, 81–83, 200, 247, 256, 261, 275, 282, 332, 438, 457, 472

Equine Facilitated Mental Health Services (EFMHS) 228, 249–253, 272–274, 275, 288, 317, 329, 330, 340, 346, 348, 350, 355, 361, 363, 439, 441, 479

Equine Facilitated Professional Coaching (EFPC) 274, 393, 396–407, 408

Equine Facilitated Psychotherapy (EFP) 225, 226, 274, 275–277, 280–291, 293–296, 302, 303, 308, 313, 316, 317, 328, 344, 346, 351, 359, 376, 382, 410, 450, 452, 457, 459, 462

Equine Partners 280, 287, 465, 469

Esperanza Center, The 60, 251, 378, 496

ethics; of EFMH/ES xxi, xxiii, 27, 47, 50, 236, 247, 255, 261, 273, 365, 402, 484

evolution; definition & use, other xxii, xxix, xxxvi, 1, 3, 4, 7, 8, 11–13, 14, 43, 87, 105, 106, 116, 129, 202, 395, 409, 429

evolve; definition & use, other xxii, xxiv, xxxi, xxxvi, 12, 14, 75, 106, 107, 115, 133, 136, 381

Excell; the horse vii, 138, 207, 208

experiential education 236, 257, 476

experiential learning 232, 237, 238, 245, 257, 441

expressive arts; in EFMH/ES 290, 302, 356, 416

F

facilitate xxxii, 35, 47, 67, 115, 183, 184, 202, 207, 235, 237, 238, 245, 252, 258, 262, 264, 265, 272, 273, 275, 288, 289, 296, 300, 302, 313–316, 318–320, 322, 325, 328, 333, 335, 341, 346, 355, 357, 378, 389, 414, 420, 454, 458, 463, 465, 506

facilitated v, xxxi–xxxiii, xxxvii, 1, 27, 46, 52, 62, 74, 170, 173, 200, 217, 220, 225, 228, 241, 243, 247, 269, 272, 273, 274, 275, 276, 289, 305, 316, 332, 347, 348, 362, 365, 393, 409, 429, 450, 457, 472, 479, 496, 503, 505, 506

facilitation skills 188, 201, 236, 238, 245, 336, 381, 479

facilitator xxxvii, 51, 80, 82, 83, 101, 108, 110, 123, 162, 171, 172, 174–176, 188, 189, 200–202, 229, 232, 233, 236, 243, 249, 255, 256, 259, 260, 261, 265, 267, 273, 275, 285, 313, 314, 328, 333, 335, 341, 343, 346, 355, 357, 368, 374, 387, 397, 402, 415–418, 439, 451–453, 455, 461–465, 483, 484

fight, flight, freeze 244

focus xvi, xviii, xx, xxiii, 30, 39, 42, 43, 51, 53, 56, 61, 117, 123, 127, 160, 161, 177, 185, 186, 193, 220, 234, 294, 306, 307, 311, 315, 316, 319, 320, 327, 329, 336, 338, 340, 350, 351, 355, 360, 372, 373, 389, 393, 394, 396, 398, 404, 406, 413, 424, 427, 430, 485, 496, 497

forward movement 189, 325, 398

Four Mile Correctional Center 192
Fredrickson-MacNamara, Maureen 44, 46
Freud, Sigmund 172, 221
Friedmann, E.; research 39
Friedmann, Katcher, Lynch, Thomas; research 19

G

"greatest self" 137
gangs; equine facilitated interventions 139, 140
Gatty, C.M.; research 66, 198
Gehrke, E.; research, HeartMath, coaching ix, 67, 396, 400, 406, 449, 471
Generation Farms 253, 260
Glendinning, Chellis xxix
Goode, Victor & Anselmo, Jeanne 162, 163
Grandin, T. ix, 102, 449
Greeks, ancient 16
Grof, Stanislav 18, 45, 418, 419
grounding 124, 186, 204, 242, 290, 291, 299, 302, 308
group process 238, 258, 333, 336, 337, 339, 420

H

Hartel, Liz 25, 27
Head, Karen 249, 294, 469
healer, wounded 17
healing xviii, xxi, xxviii, xxix, xxxi, xxxiv, 1, 3, 4, 13, 17, 25, 27–31, 34–38, 40, 44, 55, 57, 59, 73, 74, 82, 83, 88, 112, 116, 123, 128, 141, 142, 161, 163–165, 188, 206, 241, 243, 271, 283, 306, 362, 416, 418, 438, 439, 444, 454, 455, 458, 481, 505–506
healing nature of horses 85
HeartMath Institute, The; Dr. Gehrke; coherence, entrainment; heart rate variability 67
Hempfling, K.F. 89
herd; herd dynamics, herd nature 91, 144
hierarchical xxx, 4, 11, 144, 148, 324
hierarchy 20, 91, 144, 324, 444, 463
higher power xxxv, 205
Hill, Cherry 72, 89, 93
Hindu mythology 16
hippotherapy 4, 27, 30–33, 43, 57, 64, 82
holotropic breathwork 18, 45, 418–420
Holotropic Mind, The (Grof) 18
horse-person-ship 54, 71, 89, 121, 148, 183, 199, 261, 320, 321, 410
horse; care 48, 74, 75, 78–81, 83, 451, 458
horse; physiology: smell, hearing, vision, touch xxii, 39, 51, 69, 91, 98, 154, 243,

245, 260, 320, 361, 402, 416
horse; the EFMH/ES horse 4, 72–76, 79, 81
horse; training, EFMH/ES 440
Horses and Humans Foundation 69, 477
Horses Don't Lie (Irwin) 56, 123
Horses Never Lie (Rashid) 145
HorseTime 275, 470
Horse (Chamberlin) 3
horse nature: curiosity, stability and adaptability, communicative, mutual grooming,
    play, learners 55, 89, 94, 137, 167
Horse Sense and the Human Heart (McCormick and McCormick) xxxiv, 54, 129,
    157, 167, 506
Horse Sense for People (Roberts) 54, 103
Horse Sense of the Carolina's 325, 470
Howey, M.O. 25
How to Think Like a Horse (Hill) 72
Hunt, Ray 77
Huygens, Christian 155

I

image; self 196, 197, 199
informed consent. *See* consent for treatment
inherent risk 333, 335
Inner Game of Work, The (Gallway) 394
instinct; definition 20, 113–116, 144, 159, 204, 205, 206, 208, 311, 386
instinctual communication 203
instinct and evolution 115
instinct and present moment awareness 116
instinct and safety 114
instinct and the spoken language 114
integrative approach 282, 361
integrative medicine xxix
intensity of treatment 350
intention; definition 101
intentional communication; one mind/collective unconscious, morphic fields, other
    species, horses 117–122
International Association of Coaching (IAC) 395, 477
International Association of Human-Animal Interaction Organizations (IAHAIO)
    35, 474
International Coach Federation (ICF) 395
interspecies communication 58, 105, 107, 136
intersubjectivity 421, 430
intimacy 130, 131, 151–157, 164, 373, 420
intuition; definition, finding our bodies, listening to our bodies, modeling, connec-

tion to non-ordinary source, implications 202–206, 411

Irwin, Chris ix, xxiv, 55, 88, 123, 126, 129, 144, 147, 179, 189, 409, 449, 470

It's Not About the Horse (Webb) 54

J

Jacobson's Organ (Watson) 96, 169

Janus, Sharon 55

Jesus Christ 3, 163

Jordan, Judith 285

journey ride 356, 420

Jung, Carl 15, 118, 135, 172, 179, 202, 205, 221

K

Kaiser, Spence, Lavergne, and Bosch; research 65

Kaleidoscope Learning Circle 252, 266, 333, 462, 470

Katcher, A. 100

Kaufmann, Michael, Suz Brooks, and Green Chimneys 52

Kersten, Greg 49, 50, 471

Kindred Spirits (Schoen) 133

Koestler, Arthur 114, 116

Kohanov, Linda v, ix, xxx, 15, 56, 88, 153, 167, 175, 199, 200, 271, 409–411, 422, 429, 449, 468

Kuhn, M.G. 88

L

"loneliness epidemic" 158

Lamm, Willis and Sharon 102

language of Equus, human xxxv, 72, 103, 127, 132, 167, 171, 201, 286, 321, 323, 361, 363

leadership skills 339, 396, 406, 410

leadership training 67, 410

Leap of Faith Equestrian Services 159, 361

learning xvi, xviii, xxv, xxviii, xxxii, xxxiv, 18, 23, 45, 46, 49, 51–53, 58, 59, 66, 78, 83, 87, 88, 93, 96, 99, 104, 126, 127, 128, 131, 132, 136, 140, 147, 148, 150, 151, 154, 161, 163, 171, 172, 175, 178, 180, 183, 186, 190, 198, 202–204, 207, 211, 220, 229–239, 241, 245, 257, 258, 271–274, 284, 286, 306, 308, 315, 316, 319–321, 325, 365, 371, 372, 374, 378–380, 382, 384, 386, 389, 391, 394, 398, 400, 404, 405, 409, 421, 423, 430, 440, 441, 444, 463, 468, 482, 483, 496

learning services xxxiii, 233, 256

Levine, Marsha 3, 7, 12

Levinson, Barker, Campbell, & Katcher; research 36

Levinson, Boris 28, 36

Licensed Drug and Alcohol Counselors 224
Licensed Mental Health Professionals; definitions 82, 226, 231, 248, 249–251, 253, 264, 265, 330, 333, 336, 341, 349, 363
Licensed Social Workers 225, 376, 474, 483
life skills 64, 224, 227, 234, 235, 252, 305, 308–310, 312–314, 317, 352, 365–368, 372, 374, 377
Livergood, Norman 209
Living in the Borderland (Bernstein) 134
Living with HorsePower (Witter) xxxvi, 55
Lorenz, Konrad 28

M

MacDonald du Mont, Phyllis 161
Magic of Horses, The (Janus) 55
Maliszewski, Stan v, ix, 231, 449
Mann, Doug 381
Man and His Symbols (Jung) 535
Man Who Listens to Horses, The (Roberts) xxxv, 54
Margenau, H. 118
Marion Country Correctional Institute 192
Marshall, Deb 253, 260
Mary; the story of 298–301
Mause de, Lloyd 195
McCormick, Adele von Rust and Marlena Deborah xxxiv, 19, 54
McCulloch, Michael 34
McDaniel, Isabella "Boo" ix, 44, 46, 469
McDonald Institute for Archaeological Research 7
McGibbon, Nancy 32, 45
Medical and Surgical Gymnastics (Tissot) 31
men; and horses 22, 76, 138–142, 192, 197, 209, 285, 429
mental health v, xvii, xviii, xxii, xxxii, xxxiii, xxxvii, 28, 47, 48, 49, 51, 53, 60–64, 81–83, 134, 160, 161–163, 169, 173, 175, 187, 188, 191, 200, 201, 206, 223–233, 236–239, 241–244, 246–254, 255–259, 261–266, 272, 273, 276, 277, 278, 280, 282, 284, 286–293, 295–297, 302, 303, 305, 306, 317, 329, 330, 332–343, 345, 346, 347, 349, 350, 356, 360, 363, 376, 379, 382, 388, 393, 395, 400, 410, 435, 441, 462, 466, 485, 494, 496, 498, 503, 504
mental health services xxxiii, xxxvii, 48, 53, 83, 187, 223, 225, 229, 231–233, 238, 244, 259, 272, 356, 379
metaphor, metaphoric xvii, xxx, 182, 189, 190, 259, 283, 286, 287, 307, 309–311, 318–320, 323, 325, 414, 416, 423
Metzner, Ralph xxix
Midkiff, Mary 88, 144, 159, 199
minimal sensory information 100, 104–106, 171, 278, 412, 421

Miraval Resort 53
Mirroring 165, 559, 590, 600
   Integrity xxii–xxiii, 212–214, 243, 612
   Intersubjective Awareness/Skills 421
Moreau, Leslie 44
Moriah Mounts 265, 465, 470
movement xviii, xxi, 10, 25, 27, 30–32, 37, 61, 62, 73, 76, 91, 107, 130, 135,
      144, 170, 185, 189, 207, 282, 283, 291, 300, 321, 323, 325, 398, 420,
      422, 423, 427, 439, 480, 489
moving forward 190
Musick, Cheryl 471
myth xxxi, 4, 13, 16, 17, 259, 416, 428

N

National Assessment of Adult Literacy (NAAL) 209
National Board for Certified Counselors 231, 242, 246, 247, 261, 474
National Center for Education Statistics 210
natural horsemanship xxi, 79, 166
Nature of Horses, The (Budiansky) 3, 166
Nightingale, Florence 28
non-local mind 15, 163, 179
non-verbal communication 107, 116, 370, 418, 422, 426, 429, 465
normalization 214, 365
North American Riding for the Handicapped Association (NARHA) vi, 28, 30,
      31, 34, 43, 46–48, 50, 81, 332, 457, 472
Norwegian Information and Documentation Centre for Women's Studies and Gen-
      der Research - KILDEN 196
Nursing: Human Science and Human Care (Watson) 163
nurturing 39, 138, 150, 158–160, 161, 180, 420

O

Odendaal, J.; research 37, 38
OK Corral Series 471
Olsen, Sandra 6, 12
On Becoming a Person (Rogers) 183

P

pagan; paganism 24, 25
parenting 195, 209, 213
pecking order 20, 80, 91, 92, 95, 108, 112, 144, 179
Pegasus 536
People, Animals, Nature, Inc (PAN) 35, 473
Persian; teachings, myths 12, 16

personal growth xviii, xxviii, 149, 174, 206, 224, 249, 266, 305, 317, 344, 391, 393, 400, 440, 482

Pert, Candace 15

Petro, Sherri 396

pioneers; in the field of EFMH/ES v, xxvii, xxxii, 56, 79, 272, 411, 429

Plato xxxiv, 221

play therapy; as the field relates to EFMH/ES 69, 245, 249, 452

potential; expanding human potential xv, xviii, xix, xxviii, xxx, xxxiv, xxxvi, 1, 19, 30, 31, 51, 60, 82, 111, 115, 157, 164, 170, 180, 183, 184, 188, 199, 201, 202, 206, 209, 213, 215, 231, 236, 263–265, 271, 273, 289, 293, 296, 306, 308, 311, 314, 317, 319, 325, 327, 330, 341, 343, 347, 349, 356, 358, 363, 370, 383, 393, 395, 402, 405, 409, 415, 429, 431, 438, 483, 484, 501, 503

power viii, xx, xxix, xxxv, 4, 9, 10, 15, 16, 18, 19, 27, 34–38, 49, 54, 57, 59, 60, 75, 103, 106, 108, 116–118, 120, 123, 128, 131, 134, 141, 142, 146, 149–151, 177, 180, 190, 202, 208–215, 232, 259, 281–284, 308, 310, 324, 330, 333–335, 341, 414, 444, 464, 469

Power of Now, The (Tolle) 23, 124, 185

Prescott College xxvi, 121, 361, 381, 389, 435, 479

presence xxxiv, 10, 15, 17–19, 23, 28, 39, 41, 43, 55, 67, 107, 115, 116, 121, 123–125, 136, 137, 151, 156, 157, 159–165, 170, 179, 186, 188, 196, 197, 199–201, 204–207, 213, 252, 259, 283, 285, 288, 321, 324, 353, 389, 396, 402, 418, 421, 430, 438, 454, 455, 461, 497

Presence of the Past, The (Sheldrake) 118

Professional Coaches and Mentors Association 393, 477

Project Adventure 334

Prussian Academy of Science 104, 107

psychodrama; with horses 277, 280, 290–292, 475

psychology; definition 57, 69, 98, 221–223

psychotherapy 41, 221, 225–228

R

Rasa Dance 422, 428

Rashid, Mark 89, 145

Recovering the Soul (Dossey) 510, 513, 530–532, 541, 545, 551

Rector, Barbara viii, xxxiv, 44, 46, 88, 103, 114, 115, 127, 150, 164, 168, 171, 199, 238, 265, 271, 275, 381, 409, 410, 420, 449, 468

Red Road, The 257, 437, 471

Rees, L. 126, 128

reflective feedback ; souls bared clean; reality, reflective feedback in an educational or learning environment; reflective feedback in a therapeutic environment ; potential dangers 165, 169–172, 174, 176, 207, 236, 255, 265, 277–281, 283–285, 290, 293, 294, 315, 340, 352, 353, 355, 361, 387, 399, 404

relationship with horses; empathy and compassion, respect, companionship, coher-

ence, bonding, nurturing, therapeutic presence, mirroring, reflective feedback, boundaries xxxi, 13, 38, 39, 41, 91, 93, 137, 141, 143, 150, 161–
167, 168–172, 174, 176, 207, 214, 236, 255, 265, 277–281, 283–285,
290, 293, 294, 300, 315, 340, 352, 353, 355, 361, 387, 397, 399, 404, 455
Remuda Ranch 471
research; projects, suggestions, organizations v, xxvi, xxvii, xxviii, xxxiii, 3, 7, 11,
14, 28–30, 32–39, 43, 48, 59, 61–66, 68, 69, 82, 89, 105, 106, 118, 137,
154–158, 163, 165, 193, 196, 198, 202, 209, 222, 246, 262, 272, 282,
332, 372, 411, 418, 421, 433, 438, 439, 449, 453, 454, 467, 477–480,
482, 485, 487
resonance 118, 119
respect; herd dynamics, leadership, earning it, equality and partnership 144–150
responsibility iv, xx, 81, 82, 181, 184, 192, 195, 212–214, 219, 224, 232, 233,
236, 237, 239, 242, 261, 284, 286, 287, 310, 329, 336, 343, 353, 357,
360, 393, 398
Restaging Fetal Traumas in War and Social Violence (Mause) 195
riding; therapeutic use of 4, 25, 27, 30–33, 43, 46, 47, 57, 61, 65–67, 82, 282,
481
Riding Between the Worlds (Kohanov) xxx, 411
Roberts, Bradberry, & Williams; research 66
Roberts, Monty xxxv, 54, 72, 77, 79, 88, 103, 128, 144, 179
Roberts, Pam 280, 287, 465, 469
Robinson, Phoebe 121, 389, 390
Rogers, Carl 60, 142, 183, 191, 214
Rohnke, Karl 334
Romberg, Ann 229, 236, 243, 405, 471
Rosenberg, Maurice 198
Roszak, Theodore xxix
round pen reasoning 127, 128, 171

S

saddles; english vs. western 75, 76
safety agreements 358
Salt River Pima Maricopa Indian Community (SRP-MIC) Juvenile Correctional
Facility ix, 138, 141, 142
San Cristobal Ranch Academy, The vii, 209, 324
satori 124, 125
Scalen, Lawrence 3
Schoen, Allen xxix, 133
scope of practice 35, 177, 223–226, 232, 241, 273, 342, 381, 387
Scurlock-Durana, Suzanne 161
self-esteem; definition, EFMH/ES research (Carlson, Dismuke, Brock, Mason,
Stuler, Crawley, Crawley , & Retter, Gatty, Meinersmann, Roberts, Bradber-
ry, and Cody) , reality check 32, 42, 61, 62–66, 157, 191, 192, 197–200,

202, 281, 311, 312, 314, 317, 320, 337, 339, 378, 425
Self-Esteem and Self-Regulation: Toward Optimal Studies of Self-Esteem (Rode-
    walt, F. & Tragakis, M.W.) 197
Sheldrake, Rupert; morphic fields xxix, 15, 115, 117, 118, 130, 163, 202
She Flies Without Wings (Midkiff) 159
Shook, Kim 249, 344, 468
shut down, horse 72, 74, 80, 148
Sierra Tucson; equine facilitated psychotherapy program; Barbara Rector xxv, 45,
    47, 54, 275
Smith, Paul ix, 381, 468, 479
social skills 365, 368, 369, 379
Society for Companion Animal Studies (SCAS) 29
Sokolof, Marilyn ix, 44, 69, 275, 282, 449, 466, 470
Soren, Ingrid 88, 165, 185
species-centric 3
spirit horse painting 296, 418
Splinter-Watkins, K.; research 34
Sredni-Stog 5, 6, 10
stallion 3, 5, 6, 9, 10, 20, 22, 23, 91, 108, 144, 145, 147, 208, 324
Story of "T", The 193
Strandloopers 105, 106
Sunny; the horse vii, 138, 193–196, 207, 208
Suzy Q; the horse vii, 103, 138
Swift, Sally 77
symbol; horse as 4, 430

T

Taja, the story of 138–141
Tart, Charles 184
Tauffkirchen, E.; research 32
Taylor, Susan 88, 471
teamwork 337, 339, 344, 382, 391, 405
Telegin, Dimitri 5
Tellington-Jones, Linda 77
therapeutic presence 160–165, 455
therapeutic riding; definition, history, research 4, 25, 27, 30–33, 43, 46, 47, 57,
    61, 65–67, 82, 282, 481
Therapeutic Riding of Tucson (TROT) 45, 47
Therapeutic Use of Riding 57, 61. *See also* riding, therapeutic use
therapist 31, 45, 61, 142, 161, 223, 231, 245–247, 308, 327, 452, 454, 483, 484
therapy 30, 34–37, 40–43, 44, 53, 57, 63, 69, 81, 83, 112, 141, 161, 226, 230,
    231, 237, 239, 245, 246, 249, 252, 258, 265, 277, 282, 283, 295, 296,
    302, 308, 329, 347–352, 354, 356, 359, 405, 409, 452, 463, 464, 480,
    482, 485, 486, 497, 498, 503

the now; grounding, focus, awareness, presence 185
The Tao of Equus xxx, xxxiv, 56, 61, 153, 271
Thinking in Pictures (Grandin) 102
Thomas, Lynn 49, 52
Thoroughbred Retirement Foundation 192
Tissot, Chassaine, and Satter; research 31
Titan, the story of vii, 173, 174, 389
Tolle, Eckhart 23, 124, 185, 186
touch; ethics and appropriateness 250–252
trauma survivors 23, 54, 73, 170, 177, 215, 290

V

Vidrine, Maureen viii, ix, 44, 275, 470
violence; equine: the scream 13, 23, 61, 72, 92, 94, 108, 112, 138, 140–142, 145, 148, 168, 174, 191, 192, 195, 209, 212, 249, 327, 337, 356, 481, 484
Virginia-Maryland Regional College of Veterinary Medicine; research 42
Von Osten, Wilhelm 104

W

Waking Up (Tart) 184
Wald, M. & Martinez, T.; research 22
Warm Springs Correctional Facilities 192
Watson, J. 163
Watson, Lyall 15, 96, 105, 119, 169
wear marks, teeth 6
Webb, Wyatt 53, 54, 470
Weber, Tracy, Dr. 252, 266, 333, 463, 470
Weil, Andrew 164
Wellington, Robin ix
Why Dogs Know When Their Owners Are Coming Home (Sheldrake) 119
Why Horses? 166
Wild About Horses (Scalen) 3, 78
Williamson, Marianne 149
Wilson, Edward O. xxix, 106
Wisdom Horse Coaching 229, 236, 243, 405, 471
Witter, Rebekah F. xxxvi, 55, 88, 126
Women's Growth and Connection: Writings from the Stone Center (Jordan) 285
Wood, Wendy 257, 437, 471
work ethic 212, 365, 373, 380
World Health Organization (W.H.O.) 29, 191
World Report on Violence and Health 191
wounded healer. See healer, wounded
wrap around services 175, 316
Wright-Jones, Cindy 265, 465, 470

X

Xenophon 76–78

Y

Yalom, I. 142, 160, 339
York Retreat, The 28
youth, state of 21, 22, 45, 49, 103, 141, 197, 213, 318, 334, 337, 352, 356, 462

Z

Zen and Horses (Soren) 165

Made in the USA
Lexington, KY
30 March 2010